For Eirene

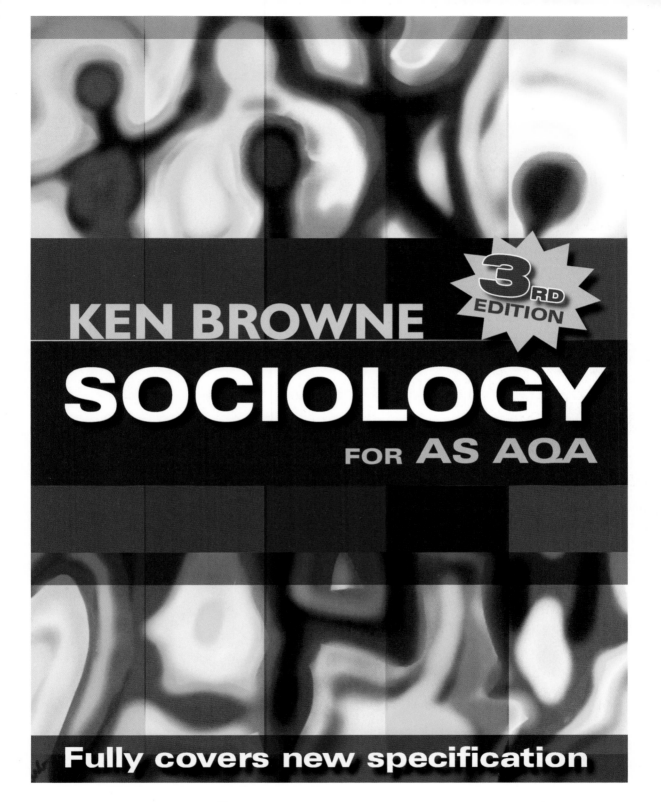

KEN BROWNE

3RD EDITION

SOCIOLOGY

FOR **AS AQA**

Fully covers new specification

polity

Ken Browne · Sociology for AS AQA

3RD EDITION

Dear Teachers and Students

Over the past few months, I've been working hard to revise my AS book to make sure it's in line with the new AQA exam specification. You'll find lots of exciting innovations in the book, which will be published in Spring 2008. For the first time the book will be in full colour, so I've had a great time choosing lots of thought-provoking photos and other colour illustrations. If you click on the book cover to the right, you can see a sample chapter. This hasn't been finalised yet, so don't worry if you spot a few typos!

I am also developing a free website to help you get the most out of the book, which will be available here in about March 2008 – watch this space! The site will include separate sections for students and teachers. There will be a range of extra activities, including:

For students:
- Multiple choice quizzes
- Extra Internet links
- Worksheets
- A searchable glossary
- Extra exercises

For teachers:
- Sample lesson plans
- Answers to all the activities
- Graphs, tables and diagrams from the book

I am currently working on an A2 version of the book with some colleagues, which is also being written to meet the new exam specification. If you have any ideas about what you'd like to see included in the A2 book, or on this website, please do let me know. You can contact me at: ken.browne@polity.co.uk.

All the best,
Ken Browne

KEN BROWNE
SOCIOLOGY
FOR AS AQA

Fully covers new specification

Click here for a sample chapter

e-alerts · privacy policy · contact webmaster

This feature-packed website includes:

For students	For teachers
• Multiple choice quizzes for every chapter	• Sample lesson plans
• Extra internet links	• Answers to all the activities
• Worksheets	• Graphs, tables and diagrams from the book for use in your own slides.
• A searchable glossary ideal for revision	
• Extra exercises	

First published in 2008 by Polity Press

Polity Press
65 Bridge Street
Cambridge CB2 1UR, UK

Polity Press
350 Main Street
Malden, MA 02148, USA

ISBN-13: 978-0-7456-4177-5
ISBN-13: 978-0-7456-4178-2 (pb)

A catalogue record for this book is available from the British Library.

Typeset in 9.5pt on 13pt Utopia
by Servis Filmsetting Ltd, Manchester
Printed and bound in Slovenia by 1010 Printing International Ltd

The publisher has used its best endeavours to ensure that the URLs for external websites referred to in this book are correct and active at the time of going to press. However, the publisher has no responsibility for the websites and can make no guarantee that a site will remain live or that the content is or will remain appropriate.

Every effort has been made to trace all copyright holders, but if any have been inadvertently overlooked the publishers will be pleased to include any necessary credits in any subsequent reprint or edition.

For further information on Polity, visit our website: www.polity.co.uk

Contents

Detailed Chapter Contents   *viii*
Acknowledgements   *xvi*
Illustration credits   *xvii*
AS Sociology   *xx*

1   Introducing Sociology   *1*
2   Culture and Identity   *29*
3   Families and Households   *113*
4   Wealth, Poverty and Welfare   *205*
5   Sociological Methods   *261*
6   Education   *325*
7   Health   *417*

Glossary   *497*
Bibliography   *513*
Index   *520*

Detailed Chapter Contents

Acknowledgements   *xvi*
     Illustration Credits   xvii

AS Sociology   *xx*

The AS Specification   *xxi*
     Assessment   xxii
     Two themes   xxiii
How to use this book   *xxiii*
Websites   *xxiv*

1 Introducing Sociology

Key issues   *3*
What is sociology?   *3*
Sociology and common sense   *4*
Sociology and naturalistic explanations   *5*
Some key introductory ideas   *6*
     Socialization, culture and identity   6
     Roles, role models and role conflict   6
     Values and norms   7
     Social control   9
     Social class, social mobility and status   10
Sociological perspectives   *13*
     Structuralism   14
     Social action or interpretivist theories   19
     Structuration: a middle way between structure and action   21
     Feminist perspectives   23
     New Right perspectives   24
     Postmodernism   24
Sociological problems, social problems and social policy   *26*
     Accidents as a social and a sociological problem   27
Chapter summary   *28*
Key terms   *28*

2 Culture and Identity

Key issues   *31*
The meaning and importance of culture   *31*
     Dominant culture   31

Subculture   32
Folk culture   32
High culture   32
Mass, popular or low culture   33
The changing distinction between high culture and mass culture   35
Global culture   36

The concept of identity   *38*
Different types of identity   41

The socialization process   *43*
Primary socialization   44
Secondary socialization   44

Socialization and the social construction of self and identity   *46*

Theoretical approaches to the role of socialization in the formation of culture
    and identity   *46*
Structural approaches   47
Social action approaches   47
A third way: structuration   50

Social class and identity   *50*
Social class   50
Life chances   51
Objective and subjective dimensions of class   52
Social class cultures   53
Is social class of declining importance in forming identities?   59
The continuing importance of social class   60

Gender and identity   *61*
Sex and gender   61
Gender and biology   62
The significance of gender as a source of identity   63
Gender stereotypes and hegemonic gender identities in Britain   63
*The social construction of hegemonic gender identities through
    socialization   65*
Changing gender identities   70
Is there a crisis of masculinity?   74
Is gender still an important source of identity?   74

Sexuality and identity   *76*
Gender, sexuality and 'normal' sex   76
Changing sexual identities   76
Stigmatized or spoiled sexual identities   77
Gay and lesbian identities   77
A note of caution   78

Ethnicity and identity   *79*
What is meant by an ethnic identity?   79
Diaspora and globalization   80
Changing ethnic identities: new ethnicities and hybrid ethnic identities   81
Ethnicity as resistance   82
Ethnic identities in Britain   82

Nationality and identity   *87*
What is nationality?   87
Nationality as a source of identity   88

What is meant by a British identity?   88
Globalization and declining national identities   91
A British identity crisis?   92
Disability and identity   93
The social construction of disability   93
Disability, socialization and stereotyping   94
Disability as a 'master identity'   95
Disability – a stigmatized or spoiled identity: an identity of exclusion   95
Age and identity   96
The social construction of age   96
Age groups and identity   97
Leisure, consumption and identity   100
Postmodernism and identity   100
The creation of identity in a media-saturated society   101
How much free choice is there in choosing identities and lifestyle?   103
Conclusion on leisure, consumption and identity   109
Chapter summary   110
Key terms   111
Exam question   112

3 Families and Households

Key issues   115
What is the family?   115
What is a household?   115
Different forms of the family and marriage   116
Is the nuclear family a universal institution?   116
The Nayar   116
Communes   116
The kibbutz   119
Lone parent families   119
Gay and lesbian families   119
Foster care and children's homes   120
Sociological perspectives on the family   121
The functionalist perspective   121
The traditional Marxist perspective   123
Marxist feminist and radical feminist perspectives   124
Demographic change and the family   129
The decline in the death rate and infant mortality rate   129
The ageing population   132
The decline in the birth rate, fertility rate and average family size   135
Other major changes in the family   139
Family change 1: has the family lost its functions?   139
Family change 2: the decline of the classic extended family and the emergence of the privatized nuclear family?   142
Family change 3: the emergence of the symmetrical family?   147
Family change 4: the changing position of children   160
Family change 5: the rising divorce rate   169

Family change 6: remarriage and the growth of the reconstituted family   176
Family change 7: the growth of the lone parent family   177
Family change 8: the decline in marriage and the growing incidence and acceptance of cohabitation   180
Family change 9: the growth in 'singlehood' – living alone   181
Family change 10: more births outside marriage   182
Family diversity and the myth of the 'cereal packet' family   *182*
Why is the 'cereal packet' stereotype misleading?   183
The 'darker side' of family life   *189*
The abuse of children   190
Domestic violence   191
Family ideology   *194*
Politics, social policy and the family   *195*
Laws and social policies affecting the family and households   197
Postmodernism and the family   *198*
Is the family a declining social institution?   *199*
Chapter summary   *201*
Key terms   *202*
Exam question   *204*

4 Wealth, Poverty and Welfare

Key issues   *207*
Introduction   *207*
Wealth and income   *208*
The distribution of wealth and income   *208*
Who are the rich?   209
Attempts to redistribute wealth and income   211
Explaining the distribution of wealth and income   212
The welfare state   *215*
What is the welfare state?   215
Who provides welfare?   217
Theoretical approaches to welfare   *220*
The social democratic approach (the welfare model)   220
The New Right or market liberal approach   221
Marxist approaches   221
Feminist approaches   222
The welfare state and social inequality   *223*
The inverse care law   224
Inequalities between ethnic groups   225
Gender inequality   225
The welfare state and poverty   *226*
The Labour government of 1997   226
Poverty   *227*
Changing views of poverty   227
Defining poverty (1): absolute or subsistence poverty   228
Defining poverty (2): relative poverty   230

Who are the poor in the United Kingdom?   240
Explaining poverty: cultural explanations   243
Explaining poverty: material explanations   246
Poverty and value judgements   255

Chapter summary   257
Key terms   258
Exam question   259

5 Sociological Methods

Key issues   263
Influences on the choice of research method   264
Positivism and research methods   265
Interpretivism and research methods   265
Other influences on the choice of research method   269
Key issues in social research   269
Reliability   271
Validity   271
Ethics   271
Primary and secondary data   272
Qualitative secondary sources   272
The advantages and uses of qualitative secondary sources   272
The disadvantages and limitations of qualitative secondary sources   273
Content analysis   274
Quantitative secondary sources   275
The advantages and uses of official statistics   276
The problems and limitations of official statistics   276
The experimental (laboratory) method of research   281
Problems of using the experimental method in sociology   281
Field experiments   283
The comparative method   283
Surveys and sampling methods   285
Who uses the survey method?   285
Representativeness and sampling   285
The stages of a survey   291
Problems of the social survey   293
Questionnaires   294
The nature and use of questionnaires   294
Questionnaire design: some principles and problems   295
Types of questionnaire   297
The validity of questionnaire research   298
Interviews   301
Structured or formal interviews   301
Unstructured or informal (in-depth) interviews   303
General problems of interviews   306
Concluding remarks on interviews   308
Participant observation   309
The theoretical context of participant observation   309
The stages of participant observation and related problems   310

The strengths and weaknesses of participant observation   313
Reliability and validity in participant observation   315
Non-participant observation   *316*
Longitudinal studies   *318*
Case studies and life histories   *319*
Methodological pluralism and triangulation   *321*
Chapter summary   *323*
Key terms   *324*

6 Education

Key issues   *327*
Education in Britain before the 1970s   *327*
Comprehensive schools and selection   *328*
The case against selection: the advantages of comprehensive education   *329*
The case for selection: criticisms of comprehensive education   *331*
Education from 1988 onwards: the free market in education   *332*
The marketization of education   *332*
The key aims of educational change   *335*
Vocational education   *335*
Raising standards   *336*
*Equality of educational opportunity and helping the most disadvantaged
groups*   *339*
Criticisms of the free market in education, vocational education and other
recent changes   *340*
The middle class has gained the most   *340*
Student needs at risk and social divisions increased   *340*
Specialist schools and selection by ability   *341*
The unfairness of league tables   *341*
Difficulties in improving schools and colleges   *342*
'Dumbing down'   *342*
Problems with the National Curriculum and testing   *342*
Inadequate vocational education   *343*
Sociological perspectives on education   *344*
The functionalist perspective on education   *344*
Marxist perspectives on education   *348*
A comparison of functionalist and Marxist perspectives on education   *353*
Interactionist perspectives on education   *355*
Is contemporary Britain a meritocracy?   *355*
Natural Intelligence or IQ   *356*
Social class differences in educational achievement   *357*
Explaining social class differences in educational achievement   *359*
Gender differences in educational achievement: the underachievement of
boys   *381*
Problems remaining for girls   *383*
Explaining gender differences in education   *383*
Some concluding comments on gender and underachievement   *390*

Ethnicity and educational achievement   *393*
    Explanations for ethnic group differences in education   *394*
    Some words of caution   *399*
Private education: the independent schools   *401*
    The case for independent schools   *402*
    The case against independent schools   *403*
    Elite education and elite jobs   *403*
Researching education   *406*
    Collecting information on education   *406*
    Examples of research   *409*
Chapter summary   *413*
Key terms   *413*
Exam question   *414*

7 Health

Key issues   *419*
The social construction of the body, health, illness and disease   *420*
    The social construction of the body   *420*
    The social construction of health, illness and disease   *422*
Disability   *423*
The medical and social models of health   *424*
    The medical (biomedical) model of health   *424*
    The social model of health   *429*
Marxist approaches to health and medicine   *431*
How society influences health   *431*
    Improvements in health in the nineteenth and early twentieth
        centuries   *432*
The new disease burden   *433*
    What are the causes of these new diseases?   *434*
Becoming a health statistic   *436*
Medicine and social control: the sick role   *438*
    Features of the sick role   *438*
    Criticisms of Parsons and the sick role   *440*
The power of the medical profession   *440*
    Protecting the patient?   *441*
    Criticisms of the medical profession   *442*
The erosion of medical power and other contemporary changes in health and
    health care   *443*
    The erosion of medical power in favour of the patient?   *443*
    A shift from the medical to social model of health?   *444*
    Consumer choice   *444*
Inequalities in health   *446*
    Social class inequalities in health   *446*
    Gender differences in health   *461*
    Ethnic inequalities in health   *466*
Other inequalities in health   *467*
    Access to health care   *467*
    Regional and international inequalities in health   *471*

Mental illness   *477*
    What is mental illness?   478
    Care in the community   478
    The biomedical approach to mental illness   478
    The social construction of mental illness   480
Researching Health   *486*
    Collecting information on health   487
    Examples of research   490
Chapter summary   *494*
Key terms   *494*
Exam question   *495*

Glossary   497
Bibliography   513
Index   520

Acknowledgements

I'd like to thank the anonymous readers approached by Polity, who provided me with some very constructively critical and supportive comments, many of which I have incorporated into the finished text, and Eirene Mitsos for some useful help and ideas, and for reading various drafts.

Ken Pyne has drawn some new cartoons to illustrate ideas in the text, and he has once again shown himself to be excellent at interpreting my vague suggestions, and I thank him for being so responsive.

I would like to thank all the staff at Polity, particularly Emma Longstaff, who has been a brilliant editor, and also Neil de Cort, Breffni O'Connor and Jonathan Skerrett. Thanks too to Sarah Dancy for copy-editing.

I am grateful to Penguin Books, Tom Shakespeare, the Joseph Rowntree Foundation, the Mayor's Office (Greater London Authority) and Warwickshire County Council for permission to reproduce copyright material. The source of copyright material is acknowledged in the text. Should any copyright-holder have been inadvertently overlooked, the author and publishers will be glad to make suitable arrangements at the first possible opportunity.

Illustration credits

The publisher and the author would like to thank the following for permission to reproduce copyright material:

Photos	*Pages*
Franziska Richter	*9*
Nuno Silva	*21, 173*
Slobo Mitic	*34, 126*
Amanda Rohde	*40, 136, 138, 165*
Alex Nikada	*42*
Serdar Yagci	*54*
Joseph Luoman	*54*
Steve Geer	*54, 405*
Angel Herrero de Frutos	*56, 273*
Tomas Bercic	*58*

Photos	*Pages*
Pavel Losevsky	*59*
Michael Blackburn	*62*
Ted Foy	*64, 70*
Franky De Meyer	*66*
Suzanne Tucker	*66*
Cliff Parnell	*75*
Joe Augustine	*78*
Jakub Niezabitowski	*78*
Helle Bro Clemmensen	*81*
Miroslav Ferkuniak	*84*
Chris Meadows	*85*
Lise Gagne	*85*
Duncan Walker	*85*
Alanna Jurden	*85*
Vasko Miokovic	*85*
Steven Allan	*85*
Ufuk Zivana	*89*
Andres Balcazar	*96*
Oktay Ortakcioglu	*96*
Max Blain	*96*
Karina Tischlinger	*98*
Roberta Osborne	*98*
Joseph Jean Rolland Dubé	*99*
Phil Berry	*101*
Gautier Willaume	*104*
Tomaz Levstek	*104*
Sean Locke	*108, 166, 333*
Mark Evans	*132, 289*
Hermann Danzmayr	*136*
Gregory Lang	*137*
Glenda Powers	*138*
Sharon Dominick	*151, 471*
Slawomir Faje	*160*
Heiko Bennewitz	*160*
Jelani Memory	*160*
Maartje van Caspe	*160*
Skip O'Donnell	*174*
Justin Horrocks	*180, 363*
Marcel Pelletier	*192*
Mark Skinner	*211*
Andrew Gentry	*218*
Vasiliki Varvaki	*233*

Photos	Pages
David Freund	250
Ugur Evirgen	264
Nicholas Sutcliffe	266
Mikael Damkier	279
Laurence Gough	282
Richard Hobson	286
Stefan Klein	295, 315
Lisa F. Young	320, 447
Alexander Hafemann	336
Lisa Klumpp	343
Monika Adamczyk	358
Carmen Martínez Banús	369
Kurt Gordon	374
Monika Wisniewska	387
Yvonne Chamberlain	387
Maciej Gozdzielewski	402
Jacom Stephens	405
Leigh Schindler	405
Scott Dunlap	410
Eliza Snow x 2	421
Mike Tolstoy	421
Drazen Vukelic	421
Jaimie Duplass	421
Christine Villarin-Jarina	425
Marcelo Wain	427
Levent Ince	427
Joe Gough	435
Greg Nicholas	435
Maria Bibikova	435
Chris Schmidt	441
Kent Rosengaard	447
Anna Pustovaya	454
Kelvin Wakefield	454
Kathleen and Scott Snowden	468
Sean Warren x 2	473
Diane Deiderich	479

Every effort has been made to trace copyright holders and to obtain their permission for the use of copyright material. The publisher apologizes for any errors or omissions in the above list and would be grateful if notified of any corrections that should be incorporated in future reprints or editions of this book.

The publisher recognizes that the trademarks referred to in the text or featured in the photographs on page 38 are registered trademarks, and stresses that they are being used solely for academic and educational purposes.

AS Sociology

This book is based on four main assumptions:

1 That many students find sociology A-level courses very difficult and confusing compared to GCSE, particularly in the first year.
2 That many students find the wealth of theories, research and data in A-level sociology confusing, often finding it difficult to see their way through this intellectual maze, and easily getting lost in a range of detail which obscures rather than enhances understanding. These problems are likely to be more pronounced on a one-year AS-level course.
3 That, with AS level, students will need a straightforward textbook which will bring them from GCSE to AS level within one year.
4 That many students don't read nearly as much as teachers think they should.

This book therefore takes a straightforward and instrumental approach. It provides comprehensive coverage for AS Sociology, and is primarily a student book. It aims to give students the knowledge and understanding necessary to successfully achieve an AS qualification in sociology. It aims to help in the development of the skills of identification, analysis, interpretation and evaluation, though these skills are often best developed in the classroom, through discussion and individual or group activities. There is a range of activities to develop these skills in the main chapters covering the various subject areas. This book aims to achieve a simple, concise and readable approach to subject content, while still maintaining the integrity of the subject and recognizing some of its complexities.

The book is based mainly on the AQA specification, but much of the material can also be used for the OCR specification, particularly the chapters on the family, culture and identity, sociological methods and health.

The AS specification

The AQA AS specification involves the following units:

Unit 1

Any *one* from these:

- Culture and Identity
- Families and Housholds
- Wealth, Poverty and Welfare

Answer all parts of one stimulus response/structured question, chosen from *one* of the three topics. Each question in five parts – three short questions together worth 12 marks + two short essays each worth 24 marks. Total marks = 60. 40 per cent of AS-level marks and 20 per cent of the total A-level marks. Exam is 1 hour.

Unit 2

Either

- Education

or

- Health

and

- Sociological Methods

Answer *three* questions chosen from *one* of the two sections provided on Education and Health.

- One stimulus response/structured question on the chosen topic, each consisting of four parts – two short questions together worth up to 8 marks + two short essays, one worth 12 marks and the other worth 20 marks. *And*
- One stimulus response question on sociological research methods in the context of the chosen topic. Question has one part essay answer, with an either/or option, worth 20 marks. *And*
- One four-part question on free-standing sociological research methods. Three short questions together worth up to 10 marks + one short essay, worth 20 marks.

Total marks = 90. 60 per cent of the total AS-level marks and 30 per cent of the total A-level marks. Exam is 2 hours.

This book covers all the subject requirements for the AS exam, but students only have to study a minimum of one subject area for each unit, plus sociological methods in Unit 2. This gives students a complete choice of areas on each paper.

Assessment

At AS Sociology, students are assessed on two main objectives:

1 Knowledge and understanding

This involves sociological theories, concepts and research, and an understanding of how sociologists use a range of methods and sources of information, and the practical, ethical and theoretical issues arising in sociological research.

> *Knowledge and understanding* is likely to be tested in *questions* by the use of words like:

Outline	Explain
Examine	Describe
Discuss	Give reasons for

2 The application of the skills of application, interpretation, analysis and evaluation

This involves things like being able to recognize and criticize sociologically significant information, to 'make sense of' data, and recognize the strengths and weaknesses of sociological theories and evidence, and reach conclusions based on the evidence and arguments presented.

> The skills of *application* and *interpretation* are likely to be tested in *questions* by the use of words like:

Identify	Illustrate
Give an example	Suggest
How might . . . ?	In what ways . . . ?
With reference to item A	

> The skills of *analysis* and *evaluation* are likely to be tested in *questions* by the use of words like:

Assess	Evaluate
To what extent . . . ?	How useful . . . ?
Critically discuss	Compare and contrast
. . . for and against the view . . .	

To show the examiner that you are using the skill of *analysis* you might consider using the following words and phrases:

the relevance of this is	this indicates
this is similar to/different from	so
therefore	this means/does not mean
hence	a consequence of
the implication of	the contrast between
put simply	

For *evaluation skills*, you might use the following words and phrases:

a strength/weakness of this	an argument for/against
an advantage/disadvantage of	the importance of
this is important because	this does not take account of
however	alternatively
a criticism of this is	others argue that
a different interpretation is	on the other hand
provided by . . .	this does not explain why . . .
the problem with this is	this argument/evidence suggests
to conclude	

Two themes

There are two themes or threads that run through the whole AS- (and A-level) course:

- socialization, culture and identity
- social differentiation, power and stratification

These are not expected to be taught as specific subjects, but rather as themes that should be referred to throughout the course. For example, in the family unit you might consider the socialization of children, or inequalities of power and status between men and women. In the poverty unit you might consider issues such as the way children are socialized into the 'culture of poverty' or a dependency culture, or the way that the poor lack the power and resources to challenge and change their position. In education, you might consider the role of the hidden curriculum or the labelling process in forming student identities, or how the education system contributes to reproducing an unequal society. If you study the culture and identity topic in chapter 2, you will obviously cover socialization, culture and identity very thoroughly.

How to use this book

Each chapter of this book is designed to be more or less self-contained, and to cover the knowledge and skills required to achieve success at AS-level

Sociology. *All students should read chapter 1*, as it lays out some important introductory ideas which are developed and referred to in later chapters.

Important terms are highlighted in colour when they first appear in the text, and in **bold type** in the page margins. These are normally explained in the text, and listed at the end of the chapter. They are also included in a comprehensive glossary at the end of the book. Unfamiliar terms should be checked in the glossary or index for further explanation or clarification. The contents pages or the index should be used to find particular themes or references. The bibliography consists of all research referred to in the book, in case you should wish to explore further any of the topics. There are activity-based sections on research at the end of chapters 6 and 7 on education and health. These should help to prepare you for that part of the examination question in Unit 2 which asks you to apply your knowledge of research methods to particular issues in education or health.

Chapter summaries outline the key points that should have been learnt after reading each chapter. These should be used as checklists for revision – if you cannot do what is asked, then refer back to the chapter to refresh your memory. The glossary at the end of the book also provides both a valuable reference source and a revision aid, as you can check the meaning of terms. A typical examination question is included at the end of every chapter, except for chapters 1 and 5. Students should attempt these under timed conditions, both as practice and to gauge how ready they are for the examination in that unit.

Websites

The internet is a valuable source of information for sociologists and for exploring the topics in this book. However, there is a lot of rubbish on some internet sites, and information should be treated with caution. One of the best search engines to search for topics generally is <www.google.com>. Try this for any research topic – putting 'UK' at the end usually helps e.g. 'poverty uk'. There are some useful websites referred to throughout this book, but you can find more, and other resources, at <www.polity.co.uk/browne>.

CHAPTER 1 Introducing Sociology

Contents

Key issues 3

What is sociology? 3

Sociology and common sense 4

Sociology and naturalistic explanations 5

Some key introductory ideas 6

Socialization, culture and identity 6
Roles, role models and role conflict 6
Values and norms 7
Social control 9
Social class, social mobility and status 10

Sociological perspectives 13

Structuralism 14
Social action or interpretivist theories 19

Structuration: a middle way between structure and action 21
Feminist perspectives 23
New Right perspectives 24
Postmodernism 24

Sociological problems, social problems and social policy 26

Accidents as a social and a sociological problem 27

Chapter summary 28

Key terms 28

CHAPTER

1

Introducing Sociology

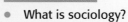

KEY ISSUES

- What is sociology?
- Sociology and common-sense and naturalistic explanations
- Key introductory ideas
- Sociological perspectives
- Sociological problems, social problems and social policy

In this chapter the focus is on introducing sociology and some of the key terms, ideas and sociological approaches which will be referred to throughout this book. It is an important chapter which will help to lay the groundwork for later chapters. It is therefore worth spending some time on learning the main points covered.

Newcomers to sociology often have only quite a vague idea of what the subject is about, though they often have an interest in people. This interest is a good start, because the focus of sociology is on the influences from society which shape the behaviour of people, their experiences and their interpretations of the world around them. To learn sociology is to learn about how human societies are constructed and where our beliefs and daily routines come from; it is to re-examine in a new light many of the taken-for-granted assumptions which we all hold, and which influence the way we think about ourselves and others. Sociology is above all about developing a critical understanding of society. In developing this understanding, sociology can itself contribute to changes in society, for example by highlighting and explaining social problems like divorce, ill-health and poverty. The study of sociology can provide the essential tools for a better understanding of the world we live in, and therefore the means for improving it.

What is sociology?

Sociology is the systematic (or planned and organized) study of human groups and social life in modern societies. It is concerned with the study of social institutions. These are the various organized social arrangements which are found in all societies. For example, the family is an institution which is concerned with arrangements for marriage, such as at what age people can marry, whom they can marry and how many partners they can have, and the upbringing of children. The education system establishes ways of passing on attitudes, knowledge and skills from one generation to the next. Work and the economic system organize the way the production of goods will be carried out, religious institutions are concerned with people's relations with the supernatural, and the law is concerned with controlling and regulating the behaviour of people in society. These social institutions make up a society's social structure – the building blocks of society.

> **Social institutions** are the various organized social arrangements which are found in all societies.

Sociology tries to understand how these various social institutions operate, and how they relate to one another, for example the way in which the family might influence how well children perform in the education system. Sociology is also concerned with describing and explaining the patterns of inequality, deprivation and conflict which are a feature of nearly all societies.

> **Social structure** refers to the social institutions and social relationships that form the 'building blocks' of society.

Sociology and common sense

Sociology is concerned with studying many things which most people already know something about. Everyone will have some knowledge and understanding of family life, the education system, work, the mass media and religion simply by living as a member of society. This leads many people to assume that the topics studied by sociologists and the explanations sociologists produce are really just common sense: what 'everyone knows'.

This is a very mistaken assumption. Sociological research has shown many widely held 'common-sense' ideas and explanations to be false. Ideas such as that there is no real poverty left in modern Britain, that the poor and unemployed are inadequate and lazy, that everyone has equal chances in life, that the rich are rich because they work harder, that men are 'naturally' superior to women, that sickness and disease strike people at random have all been questioned by sociological research. The re-examination of such common-sense views is very much the concern of sociology.

A further problem with common-sense explanations is that they are very much bound up with the beliefs of a particular society at particular periods of time. Different societies have differing common-sense ideas. The Hopi Indians' common-sense view of why it rains is very different from our own – they do a rain dance to encourage the rain gods. Common-sense ideas also change over time in any society. In Britain, we no longer burn witches when the crops fail, or see mental illness as evidence of satanic possession, but seek scientific, medical or psychiatric explanations for such events.

Not all the findings of sociologists undermine common sense, and the work of sociologists has made important contributions to the common-sense understandings of members of society. For example, the knowledge most people have about the changing family in Britain, with rising rates of divorce and growing numbers of lone parents, is largely due to the work of sociologists. However, sociology differs from common sense in three important ways:

- Sociologists use a sociological imagination. This means that, while they study the familiar routines of daily life, sociologists look at them in unfamiliar ways or from a different angle. They ask if things really are as common sense says they are. Sociologists re-examine existing assumptions, by studying how things were in the past, how they've changed, how they differ between societies and how they might change in the future.
- Sociologists look at evidence on issues before making up their minds. The explanations and conclusions of sociologists are based on precise evidence which has been collected through painstaking research using established research procedures.
- Sociologists strive to maintain objectivity and value freedom in their work. These involve keeping an open mind, considering all the evidence, allowing others to scrutinize research findings, and keeping personal beliefs out of the research process.

Objectivity means sociologists should approach their research with an open mind – a willingness to consider *all* the evidence, and to have their work available for scrutiny and criticism by other researchers.

Value freedom means sociologists should try not to let their prejudices and beliefs influence the way they carry out their research and interpret evidence.

Sociology and naturalistic explanations

Naturalistic explanations are those which assume that various kinds of human behaviour are natural or based on innate (inborn) biological characteristics. If this were the case, then one would expect human behaviour to be the same in all societies. In fact, by comparing different societies, sociologists have discovered that there are very wide differences between them in terms of customs, values, beliefs and social behaviour. For example, there are wide differences between societies in the roles of men and women and what is considered appropriate 'masculine' and 'feminine' behaviour. This can only be because people learn to behave in different ways in different societies. Sociological explanations recognize that most human behaviour is learnt by individuals as members of society, rather than something with which they are born. Individuals learn how to behave from a wide range of social institutions right through their lives. Sociologists call this process of learning socialization.

Some key introductory ideas

Socialization, culture and identity

Socialization is the lifelong process by which people learn the culture of the society in which they live. Socialization is carried out by agencies of socialization, such as the family, the education system, religious institutions or the mass media.

Culture is socially transmitted (passed on through socialization) from one generation to the next.

Socialization plays a crucial part in forming our identities. **Identity** is about how we see and define ourselves – our personalities – and how other people see and define us. For example, we might define ourselves as gay, black, a Muslim, Welsh, English, a woman, a student or a mother. Many aspects of our individual identities will be formed through the socialization process, with the family, friends, school, the mass media, the workplace and other agencies of socialization helping to form our individual personalities. Many chapters in this book refer to aspects of this socialization process and the formation of our identities.

However, while lifelong socialization plays a very important part in forming our identities, individuals also have the free will to enable them to 'carve out' their own personal identities and influence how others see them, rather than simply being influenced by them. Individuals are not simply the passive victims of the socialization process. While individual identities are formed by various forces of socialization, the choices individuals and groups make and how they react to these forces can also have an influence. For example, while the mass media might influence our lifestyles, attitudes and values, and how we see ourselves and how others see us, individuals may also react to what they read, see or hear in the media in different ways. A woman from a minority ethnic background may define herself as black or Asian, but she may also see herself mainly as a woman, a mother, a teacher or a Muslim. Similarly, we have some choices in the consumption goods we buy, the clothes we wear, and the leisure activities we choose to follow. Through these choices, we can influence how others see us, and the image of ourselves we project to them. Individuals may also have multiple identities, presenting different aspects of themselves in different ways to different groups of people. People may therefore not adopt the same identity all the time, and different people will see them in different ways.

Roles, role models and role conflict

Roles are very like the roles actors play in a theatre or television series. People in society play many different roles in their lifetimes, such as those of a man

Socialization is the lifelong process of learning the culture of any society.

The term **culture** refers to the language, beliefs, values and norms, customs, dress, diet, roles, knowledge and skills which make up the 'way of life' of any society.

Identity is concerned with how individuals see and define themselves and how other people see and define them.

Roles are the patterns of behaviour which are expected from people in different positions in society.

Activity

1 Suggest *three* ways, with examples, by which individuals learn the culture of society in contemporary Britain.
2 Describe *three* factors that inflence how others define your identity. Explain your answer with examples.
3 Suggest *three* ways that individuals' choices in consumer goods may influence how other people define them.
4 Suggest reasons why people may have difficulty in getting other people to accept whatever identity they wish to project to others.

or a woman, a child and an adult, a student, a parent, a friend, and work roles like factory worker, police officer or teacher. People in these roles are expected to behave in particular ways. The police officer who steals, the teacher who is drunk in the classroom or the parent who neglects his or her children are clearly not following the behaviour expected in these roles, and these examples show how important such expectations of others are.

Roles are often learnt by copying or imitating the behaviour and attitudes of others. Children, for example, will often learn how to behave by copying the behaviour of their parents, teachers or friends. Those whose behaviour we consciously or unconsciously copy are known as role models.

One person plays many roles at the same time. For example, a woman may play the roles of woman, mother, student, worker, sister and wife at the same time. This may lead to role conflict, where the successful perform-ances of two or more roles at the same time may come into conflict with one another.

A woman who tries to balance, and is often torn apart by, the competing demands of being a night-class student, having a full-time job, looking after children and taking care of a dependent elderly mother illustrates this idea of role conflict.

> **Role models** are the patterns of behaviour which others copy and model their own behaviour on.

> **Role conflict** is the conflict between the successful performance of two or more roles at the same time, such as worker, mother and student.

> **Values** are general beliefs about what is right or wrong, and about the important standards which are worth maintaining and achieving in any society or social group.

> **Laws** are official legal rules, formally enforced by the police, courts and prison, involving legal punishment if the rules are broken.

Values and norms

Values provide general guidelines for behaviour. In Britain, values include beliefs about respect for human life, privacy and private property, about the importance of marriage and the importance of money and success. While not everyone will always share the same values, there are often strong pres-sures on people to conform to some of the most important values in any society, which are often written down as laws. These are official legal rules which are often based on matters that many people think are very impor-tant. Laws against murder and theft, for example, enforce the values attached to human life and private property in our society. Laws are formally enforced by the police, courts and prisons, and involve legal punishment if they are broken.

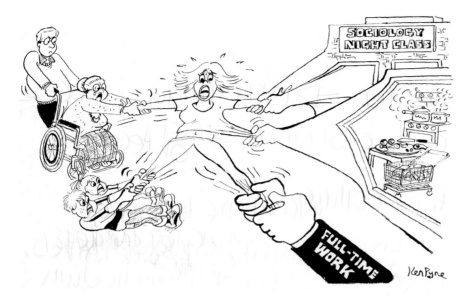

Role conflict for working women

Norms are social rules which define the correct and acceptable behaviour in a society or social group to which people are expected to conform. Norms are much more precise than values: they put values (general guidelines) into practice in particular situations. The norm that someone should not generally enter rooms without knocking reflects the value of privacy, and rules about not drinking and driving reflect the values of respect for human life and consideration for the safety of others. Norms exist in all areas of social life. In Britain, those who are late for work, jump queues in supermarkets, laugh during funerals, walk through the streets naked or never say hello to friends when they are greeted by them are likely to be seen as unreliable, annoying, rude or odd because they are not following the norms of expected behaviour. Norms are mainly informally enforced – by the disapproval of other people, embarrassment or a 'telling off' from parents or others. Customs are norms which have lasted for a long time and have become a part of society's traditions – kissing under the mistletoe at Christmas, buying and giving Easter eggs or lighting candles at Divali are typical customs found in Britain.

Values and norms are part of the culture of a society, and are learned and passed on through socialization. They differ between societies – the values and norms of an African tribe are very different from those of people in modern Britain. They may also change over time and vary between social groups even in the same society. In Britain, living together without being married – a cohabiting relationship – is much more accepted today than it was in the past, and wearing turbans – which is seen as

Norms are social rules which define the correct and acceptable behaviour in a society or social group to which people are expected to conform.

Customs are norms which have lasted for a long time and have become a part of society's traditions.

Norms control behaviour in nearly all aspects of our lives, with positive and negative sanctions to enforce them. Try jumping queues to see the sanctions that follow

normal dress among Sikh men – would be seen as a bit odd among white teenagers.

Social control

Social control is the term given to the various methods used to persuade or force individuals to conform to the dominant social norms and values of a society.

Deviance is the failure to conform to social norms.

Sanctions are the rewards and punishments by which social control is achieved and conformity to norms and values enforced.

Positive sanctions are rewards of various kinds.

Negative sanctions are various types of punishment.

Social control is the term given to the various methods used to persuade or force individuals to conform to the dominant social norms and values of a society, and to prevent **deviance** – a failure to conform to social norms.

Processes of social control may be formal, through institutions like the law or school rules, or they may be informal, through peer group pressure, personal embarrassment at doing something wrong, or the pressure of public opinion.

Sanctions are the rewards and punishments by which social control is achieved and conformity to norms and values enforced. These may be either **positive sanctions**, rewards of various kinds, or **negative sanctions**, various types of punishment. The type of sanction will depend on the seriousness of the norm: positive sanctions may range from gifts of sweets or money from parents to children, to merits and prizes at school, to knighthoods and medals; negative sanctions may range from a feeling of embarrassment, to being ridiculed or gossiped about or regarded as a bit eccentric or 'a bit odd', to being fined or imprisoned.

> **Activity**
>
> 1 Identify three important values in Britain today and three norms relating to these values. Suggest ways in which these norms and values are enforced.
> 2 Identify at least four roles that you play, and describe the norms of behaviour to which you are expected to conform in each case.
> 3 Describe the sanctions you might face if you failed to conform to the norms you have identified.
> 4 Identify how the successful performance of one role might conflict with the successful performance of another.

Social class, social mobility and status

Social class is a term you will read a lot about in sociology, including in this book. Social class is generally associated with inequality in industrial societies. It is often used in a very general and imprecise way, but generally refers to a group of people sharing a similar economic situation, such as occupation, income and ownership of wealth.

Often, occupation, income and ownership of wealth are closely related to each other and to other aspects of individuals' lives, such as how much power and influence they have in society, their level of education, their social status, their type of housing, car ownership, leisure activities and other aspects of their lifestyle.

An individual's social class has a major influence on his or her **life chances**. Life chances include the chances of obtaining things like good quality housing, a long and healthy life, holidays, job security and educational success, and avoiding things like unemployment, ill-health and premature death. **Social mobility** refers to the movement of groups or individuals up or down the social hierarchy, from one social class to another.

To help you to understand the different social classes in modern Britain, the following simplified classification will suffice for the purposes of this book:

- The **working class** is one of the largest social classes, referring to those working in manual jobs – jobs involving physical work and, literally, work with their hands, like factory or labouring work.
- The **middle class** is also a large class, and refers to those in non-manual work – jobs which don't involve heavy physical effort, and which are usually performed in offices and involve paperwork or ICT (information and communication technology) of various kinds. Some argue that those in the lowest levels of non-manual work, such as supermarket check-out operators and those in routine office work, should really be included in the working class, as their pay and working conditions are more like those of manual workers than like those of many sections of the middle class.

A **social class** is a group of people who share a similar economic situation, such as a similar occupational level, income and ownership of wealth.

Life chances are the chances of obtaining those things defined as desirable and of avoiding those things defined as undesirable in any society. **Social mobility** refers to the movement of groups or individuals up or down the social hierarchy, from one social class to another.

The **working class** consists of those working in manual jobs, involving physical work and, literally, work with their hands, such as factory or labouring work. The **middle class** consists of those in non-manual work – jobs that don't require heavy physical work and are usually performed in offices and involve paperwork or computer work.

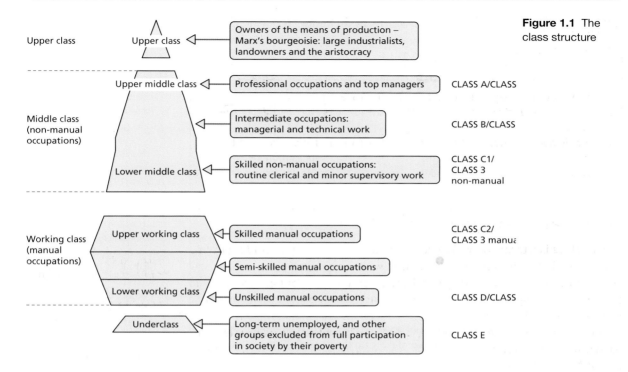

Figure 1.1 The class structure

- The upper class is a small class, and refers to those who are the main owners of society's wealth, including wealthy industrialists, landowners and the traditional aristocracy. Often these people do not work for others, as their assets are so large that work is not necessary to survive.
- The underclass is a small class, and refers to a group of people who are right at the bottom of the class structure, and whose poverty often excludes them from full participation in society. The term 'underclass' is used in different ways, and is a controversial concept. It is discussed more fully in chapter 4 on wealth, poverty and welfare.

Figure 1.1 above illustrates the class structure of modern Britain, and is a useful guide to the use of social class in this book.

The term status is used in sociology in two main ways. It is often used to refer to the role position someone occupies in society, like a father, worker or consumer. It is also sometimes used to refer to the ranking of individuals in society according to the differing amounts of prestige or respect given to different positions by other members of that group or society – people's social standing in the eyes of others. Ascribed status is status given by birth or family background, while achieved status is status that is achieved by an individual's own efforts or talents.

The **upper class** consists of those who are the main owners of society's wealth. It includes wealthy industrialists, landowners and the traditional aristocracy. The **underclass** is the social group right at the bottom of the social class hierarchy, consisting of those who are in some ways cut off from or excluded from the rest of society.

Status sometimes refers to the role position someone occupies in society, but more commonly refers to the amount of prestige or social importance a person has in the eyes of other members of a group or society.

Three other concepts you will come across in sociology, and which are also referred to widely in this book, are those of ethnicity, minority ethnic group, and gender, which are defined in the box in the margin.

Activity

Using the word list below, fill in the blanks in the following passage. Each dash represents one word.

identity	social structure	values
social control	norms	social mobility
status	working class	role conflict
value freedom	ascribed status	status
social class	positive	upper class
achieved status	socialization	objectivity
ethnicity	roles	underclass
minority ethnic group	social institutions	negative sanctions
social classes	deviance	life chances
gender	social classes	

Sociology involves studying the social world, but as sociologists are themselves part of this social world, they need to take care that they look at things in a detached and impartial way. They should approach research in an open-minded way, considering all the evidence before making up their minds. This is known as _____. They should also try not to let their own beliefs and prejudices influence their research. This_____ _____ is important if sociology is to be seen as something more than newspaper journalism.

Society is constructed of a range of _____ _____, like the family, religion, the education system and the law. These make up the _____ _____ – the 'building blocks' of society. Sociologists generally believe that people learn the culture of their society, and this learning process is known as _____. For example, males and females often learn to behave in different ways. This difference is known as _____. The learning process influences the formation of the individual's _____ – how they see and define themselves and how others see and define them. _____ refers to the shared culture of a social group which gives its members a common identity in some ways different from other social groups. If a group has a cultural identity different from the majority population of a society, such as black and Asian groups in Britain, it is known as a _____ _____ _____.

Everyone in society is expected to behave in particular ways in particular situations, and these patterns of expected behaviour are known as _____, but sometimes these come into conflict with each other, causing _____ _____. Every society has sets of guidelines for behaviour. _____ establish the important standards about what is important in a society and what is right or wrong. _____ provide rules about how to behave in particular situations. People are encouraged to conform to these rules by _____ _____, which is carried out by a range of rewards and punishments known as _____ and _____ _____. Non-conformity to social rules is known as _____.

Ascribed status is status given by birth or family background and which, in general, cannot be changed by individuals. Examples of such status include a person's age, ethnic group, sex, or place or family of birth.

Achieved status refers to any social position or position of prestige that has been achieved by an individual's own efforts, such as through education, skill and talent, promotion at work and career success.

Ethnicity refers to the shared culture of a social group which gives its members a common identity in some ways different from other social groups.

A **minority ethnic group** is a social group which shares a cultural identity which is different from that of the majority population of a society, such as African-Caribbean, Indian Asian and Chinese ethnic groups in Britain.

Gender refers to the culturally created differences between men and women which are learnt through socialization, rather than simply **sex** differences, which refer only to the biological differences between the sexes.

A _____ _____ is a group of people who share a similar economic situation, and this can have an important influence on their chances of obtaining the desirable, and avoiding the undesirable, things in life – their _____ _____. The two largest _____ _____ are the _____ _____ and the middle class. The main owners of society's wealth are known as the _____ _____, while the very poorest group which is excluded from full participation in society by poverty is known as the _____. Sometimes people can move up or down between _____ _____, and this is known as _____ _____. Some people and some positions in society are ranked by others in terms of different amounts of prestige or respect, and this is known as _____. If this is given by birth or family background, it is known as _____ _____. However, some people can achieve their _____ through their own individual efforts and talents. This is known as _____ _____

The solution to this activity can be found on the teachers' pages of www.polity.co.uk/browne.

Sociological perspectives

A **perspective** is a way of looking at something. A **sociological perspective** involves a set of theories which influences what is looked at when studying society.

A perspective is simply a way of looking at something. A sociological perspective is a set of theories which provide a way of looking at society. Newcomers to sociology often find the different perspectives in sociology difficult, as there appears to be no 'right answer'.

A useful insight might be gained from the following situation. Imagine there are five people looking at the same busy shopping street – a pickpocket, a police officer, a roadsweeper, a shopper and a shopkeeper (see cartoon overleaf). The pickpocket sees wallets sticking out of pockets or bags, and an opportunity to steal. The police officer sees potential crime and disorder. The roadsweeper sees litter and garbage left by everyone else. The shopper might see windows full of desirable consumer goods to buy, and the shopkeeper sees only potential customers, and possibly shoplifters. All are viewing the same street, but are looking at different aspects of that street. What they see will depend on their 'perspective' – what they're looking for. They might all be seeing different things, but you can't really say any of their views is more correct than another – though you might think some views provide a more truthful, rounded and fuller description of the street than others do.

Sociological perspectives are basically similar, in that they are the different viewpoints from which sociologists examine society. We might say that different sociological perspectives, and the different research methods they lead to, simply emphasize and explain different aspects of society. Often, debates between and criticisms of these different perspectives help us to understand social issues much more clearly.

People may view the same scene from different perspectives

Sociological perspectives are often best understood by looking at particular areas, and this book will illustrate them in various chapters, particularly those on the family and education. However, what follows is an introduction to some of these perspectives.

Sociological perspectives centre on the themes of how much freedom or control the individual has to influence society. To what extent is the individual's identity moulded by social forces outside her or his control? How much control does the individual have over these social forces, and how free are individuals to form their own identities?

There are two main approaches here:

- the sociology of system, often referred to as structuralism
- the sociology of action – social action or interpretivist theories.

Structuralism

Structuralism is concerned with the overall structure of society, and the way social institutions, like the family, the education system, the mass media and work, act as a constraint on, or limit and control, individual behaviour. Structuralist approaches have the following features:

> **Structuralism** is a perspective which is concerned with the overall structure of society, and sees individual behaviour moulded by social institutions like the family, the education system, the mass media and work.

- The behaviour of individual human beings and the formation of their identities are seen as being a result of social forces which are external to the individual – the individual is moulded, shaped and constrained by society through socialization, positive and negative sanctions, and material resources like income and jobs. For example, institutions like the family, the education system, the mass media, the law and the workplace mould us into our identities. According to the structuralist approach, the individual is like a puppet, whose strings are pulled by society. We might see people almost like jelly, poured into a 'social mould' to set.
- The main purpose of sociology is to study the overall structure of society, the social institutions which make up this structure, and the relationships between these social institutions (or the various parts of society) such as the links between the workplace and the economy, the economy and the political system, the family and the education system, and so on. The focus of sociology is on the study of social institutions and the social structure as a whole, not on the individual. This is sometimes referred to as a **macro approach**.

> A **macro approach** focuses on the large-scale structure of society as a whole, rather than on individuals.

There are two main varieties of structuralism: functionalism (consensus structuralism) and Marxism (conflict structuralism).

Activity

1 To what extent is our behaviour moulded by social forces beyond our control? Try to think of all the factors which have contributed to the way you are now, and which prevent you from behaving in any way you like. You might consider factors like the influences of your parents and family background, the mass media, experiences at school, your friendship groups, income and so on.

2 Imagine you were creating an ideal society from scratch. Plan how you would organize it, with particular reference to the following issues:
   - the care and socialization of children
   - the passing on of society's knowledge and skills from one generation to the next
   - the production of food and other goods necessary for survival
   - how you would allocate food and other goods to members of society
   - the establishment and enforcement of rules of behaviour
   - how you would deal with people who didn't conform to social rules
   - how you would coordinate things and resolve disputes between members of society

3 Consider how your ideal society is similar to, or different from, the organization of contemporary Britain. How would you explain these differences?

Functionalism (consensus structuralism)

Functionalism sees society built up and working like the human body, made up of interrelated parts which function for, or contribute to, the maintenance of society as a whole. For example, in order to understand the importance of the heart, lungs and brain in the human body, we need to understand what function or purpose each carries out and how they work together in providing and maintaining the basic needs of human life. Similarly, functionalists argue that any society has certain functional prerequisites (certain basic needs or requirements) that must be met if society is to survive. These include the production of food, the care of the young and the socialization of new generations into the culture of society. Social institutions like the family or education exist to meet these basic needs, in the same way as we have to have a heart and lungs to refresh and pump blood around our bodies.

Just as the various parts of the human body function in relation to one another and contribute to the maintenance of the body as a whole, so, according to functionalist sociology, social institutions meet functional prerequisites, maintaining the social system and order and stability in society. In this view, social institutions like the family, education and work are connected and function in relation to one another for the benefit of society as a whole. Stability in society is based on socialization into norms and values on which most people agree. These shared norms and values are known as a value consensus. It is this value consensus which functionalists believe maintains what they see as a peaceful, harmonious society without much conflict between people and groups.

> **Functionalism** is a sociological perspective which sees society as made up of parts which work together to maintain society as an integrated whole. Society is seen as fundamentally harmonious and stable, because of the agreement on basic values (value consensus) established through socialization.
> **Functional prerequisites** are the basic needs that must be met if society is to survive.

> **Value consensus** is a general agreement around the main values and norms of any society.

Activity

Try to think of all the connections or links you can between the following institutions – for example, how what happens in the family may influence what happens at school and educational achievement:
- the family and the education system
- the family and the workplace
- education and the workplace

Marxism (conflict structuralism)

Marxism comes from the work of Karl Marx, who lived from 1818 to 1883. Marxism sees the overall structure of society as primarily determined (or influenced) by the economic system – the means of production like the land, factories and offices necessary to produce society's goods. These means of production are privately owned, and most people depend on the owners for employment. Marx argued that workers produce more than is needed for employers to pay them their wages – this 'extra' produced by workers is what

> **Marxism** is a structural theory of society which sees society divided by conflict between two main opposing social classes, due to private ownership of the means of production. The **means of production** are the key resources necessary for producing society's goods, such as land, factories and machinery. The private ownership of the means of production enables the owners (employers) to extract surplus value from the workers.

Karl Marx, 1818–1883

Surplus value is the extra value added by workers to the products they produce, after allowing for the payment of their wages, and which goes to the employer in the form of profit.

Marx called surplus value, and provides profit for the employer. For example, in a burger chain, it is the workers who make, cook, package and serve the burgers, but only half the burgers they sell are necessary to cover production costs and pay their wages. The rest of the burgers provide profit for the burger chain owners. This means the workers who produce the burgers do not get the full value of their work, and they are therefore being exploited.

The **bourgeoisie** is the class of owners of the means of production. **Capitalists** are the owners of the means of production in industrial societies, whose primary purpose is to make profits. The **proletariat** is the social class of workers who have to work for wages as they do not own the means of production. **Labour power** refers to people's capacity to work. People sell their labour power to the employer in return for a wage, and the employer buys only their labour power, but not the whole person.

> **Activity**
>
> Do you think those who produce the wealth should get the full share of what they produce? Do you think most goods today are produced because people need them, or because they are persuaded to buy them by advertising? See what other people think about this.

Capitalists and workers   Marx argued that there were two basic social classes in capitalist industrial society: a small wealthy and powerful class of owners of the means of production (which he called the bourgeoisie or capitalists – the owning class) and a much larger, poorer class of non-owners (which he called the proletariat or working class). The proletariat, because they owned no means of production of their own, had no means of living other than to sell their labour, or labour power as Marx called it, to the bourgeoisie in exchange for a wage or salary. The capitalists exploited the working class by making profits out of them by keeping wages as low as possible instead of giving the workers the full payment for the goods they'd produced.

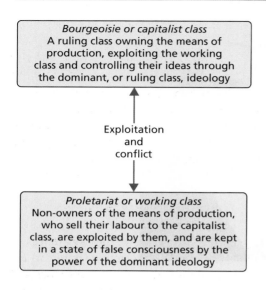

> **Bourgeoisie or capitalist class**
> A ruling class owning the means of production, exploiting the working class and controlling their ideas through the dominant, or ruling class, ideology

Exploitation
and
conflict

> **Proletariat or working class**
> Non-owners of the means of production, who sell their labour to the capitalist class, are exploited by them, and are kept in a state of false consciousness by the power of the dominant ideology

Figure 1.2 A summary of the Marxist view of society

Class conflict is the conflict that arises between different social classes. It is generally used to describe the conflict between the bourgeoisie and proletariat in Marxist views of society.

Class conflict   Marx asserted that this exploitation created major differences in interest between the two classes, and this created conflict. For example, the workers' interests lay in higher wages to achieve a better lifestyle, but these would be at the expense of the bosses' profits. The bosses wanted higher profits to expand their businesses and wealth, but this could only be achieved by keeping wages as low as possible and/or by making the workers produce more by working harder. The interests of these two classes are therefore totally opposed, and this generates conflict between the two social classes (**class conflict**). Marx believed this class conflict would affect all areas of life.

The **ruling class** is the social class of owners of the means of production, whose control over the economy gives them power over all aspects of society, enabling them to rule over society.

The ruling class   Marx argued that the owning class was also a **ruling class**. For example, because they owned the means of production, the bourgeoisie could decide where factories should be located, and whether they should be opened or closed down, and they could control the workforce through hiring or firing. Democratically elected governments could not afford to ignore this power of the bourgeoisie, otherwise they might face rising unemployment or other social problems if the bourgeoisie decided not to invest its money.

Ideology is a set of ideas, values and beliefs that represents the outlook, and justify the interests, of a social group. The **dominant ideology** is the set of ideas and beliefs of the most powerful groups in society, which influences the ideas of the rest of society. **Ruling class ideology** is the set of ideas of the ruling class.

Dominant ideology   Marx believed the ruling or dominant ideas in any society, what he called the **dominant ideology**, were those of the owning class (hence it is sometimes also called **ruling class ideology**) and the major institutions in society reflected those ideas.

For example, the law protected the interests of the owning class more than it did those of the workers; religion acted as the 'opium of the people', persuading the working class to accept their position as just and natural (rather than rebelling against it), by 'drugging' them and giving hallucinations with promises of future rewards in heaven for putting up with their present suffering; the bourgeoisie's ownership of the mass media meant only their ideas were put forward. In this way, the workers were almost brainwashed into accepting their position. They failed to recognize they were being exploited and therefore did not rebel against the bourgeoisie. Marx called this lack of awareness by the working class of their own interests false consciousness.

Revolution and communism   However, Marx thought that one day the circumstances would arise in which the workers did become aware of their exploitation. They would develop class consciousness (an awareness of their real interests and their exploitation) and would join together to act against the bourgeoisie through strikes, demonstrations and other forms of protest. This would eventually lead to a revolution against and overthrow of the bourgeoisie. The means of production would then be put in the hands of the state and run in the interests of everyone, not just of the bourgeoisie. A new type of society – communism – would be created, which would be without exploitation, without classes and without class conflict.

Marx therefore saw society based on the exploitation of one large class by a small group of owners, creating social classes with opposing interests, and inequalities of wealth and power in society. Rather than seeing society functioning harmoniously as the functionalists do, Marxists see society based on conflict between rival social classes (class conflict) with social institutions serving to maintain the interests of a ruling class. However, like functionalists, Marxists see the behaviour of individuals as still largely determined or moulded by social institutions.

> ### Activity
>
> Comparing the views of functionalists and Marxists, which view of society do you think provides the most accurate and useful insights into the way British society is currently organized? Is it mainly based on consensus or conflict? Give reasons for your answer, with examples to illustrate the points you make.

Social action or interpretivist theories

Individual behaviour in everyday social situations is the main focus of social action or interpretivist approaches. These theories are concerned with discovering and thereby understanding the processes by which interactions

---

False consciousness is a failure by members of a social class to recognize their real interests.
Class consciousness is an awareness in members of a social class of their real interests.
Communism refers to an equal society, without social classes or class conflict, in which the means of production are the common property of all.

Social action theories or **interpretivist** approaches are perspectives which emphasize the creative action which people can take, making people not simply the passive victims of social forces outside them. Social action theory suggests it is important to understand the motives and meanings people give to their behaviour, and how this is influenced by the behaviour and interpretations of others. The focus of research is therefore on individuals or small groups rather than on society as a whole.

between individuals or small groups take place, how people come to interpret and see things as they do, how they define their identities, and how the
reactions of others can affect their view of things and the sense of their own
identity.

Social action or interpretivist theories include the following features:

- Society and social structures/institutions are seen as the creation of
  individuals. An emphasis is placed on the free will of people to do things
  and form their identities, rather than the determinism of structuralism.
  Determinism means that the activities and identities of individuals are
  moulded by forces beyond their control, and they have little control or
  choice in how they behave. It almost suggests people are programmed to
  behave the way they do by society.

- An emphasis is placed on the individual and everyday behaviour rather
  than the overall structure of society. The focus of sociology is on the
  individual or small groups of individuals, not on the social structure as a
  whole. Rather than studying general trends and the wider causes of
  crime, for example, interpretivists are more likely to study a juvenile
  gang, to see how they came to be seen and labelled as deviant, and
  how they themselves see the world. This is sometimes referred to as a
  micro approach.

- People's behaviour is viewed as being driven by the meanings they give to
  situations: their definitions of a situation, or the way they see things and
  therefore behave, become very important. For example, a parent might
  interpret a baby crying as a sign of tiredness, hunger, fear or illness. The
  action the parent takes – putting the baby to bed, feeding her, comforting
  her or taking her to the doctor – will depend on how the parent defines
  the situation, and to understand the parent's behaviour we have to
  understand the meaning he or she gives to the baby's crying. In turn, how
  the parent acts in response to the meaning given to the baby's behaviour
  is likely to affect the baby's behaviour – whether it stops crying because it
  is no longer tired, hungry, afraid or ill.

- The main purpose of sociology is to study, uncover and interpret the
  meanings and definitions individuals give to their behaviour.

Determinism is the idea that people's behaviour is moulded by their social surroundings, and that they have little free will, control or choice over how they behave.

A **micro approach** focuses on small groups or individuals, rather than on the structure of society as a whole.

Activity

1 How do the attitudes and interpretations of other people affect your view of
  yourself? Give examples to illustrate the points you make.
2 Imagine you wanted to study the family and the education system. Identify
  three things for each institution you might be interested in if you adopted a
  structuralist approach, and three things for each institution if you adopted an
  interpretivist approach.

What consequences might follow for someone who has been labelled a deviant?

Symbolic interactionism is a sociological perspective which is concerned with understanding human behaviour in face-to-face situations, and how individuals and situations come to be defined in particular ways through their encounters with other people.

Labelling refers to defining a person or group in a certain way – as a particular 'type' of person or group.

Symbolic interactionism

Symbolic interactionism is a social action perspective particularly concerned with understanding human behaviour in face-to-face situations, and how individuals and situations come to be defined or classified in particular ways. This is known as **labelling**. It is also concerned with the consequences for individual behaviour of such definitions, since people will behave according to the way they see situations. For example, the sociologist's task is to understand the point of view and experience of, say, the disillusioned and hostile student who hates school, as well as the teachers and others who label him or her as 'deviant'. Sociologists should try to understand how and why teachers classify some students as deviant, and what happens to the behaviour of those students once they have been classified in that way.

Structuration: a middle way between structure and action

In real life, society is probably best understood using a mixture of both structural *and* action approaches. In other words, constraints from social structures, like the family, work (and the income it does or doesn't produce), the law and education, limit and control the behaviour of individuals or groups, and have important influences on the formation of individual and group identities. However, individuals can, within limits, make choices within those structures and act accordingly. For example, the school is part of the education system – a social structure. Young people are constrained (forced) by law to go to school, and that school continues to exist even after generations of young people have come and gone. It therefore has an existence separate from the individuals who attend that school at any one time. That structure continues only so long as people support the law and agree to attend school – if everyone stopped sending their children to school, the system would either have to be changed or it would collapse. This shows human beings create and reinforce, or can change or destroy, these structures.

If we take a particular school or group of schools, while they are constrained by the demands of the National Curriculum, the laws on education and the income they have, what happens within each individual school is controlled to some degree by the people within it – governors, students, teachers and parents. If attendance is poor, behaviour dreadful, teaching quality inadequate, exam results a catastrophe, and the school has a weak or incompetent headteacher, we may see this as a 'failing' school. It might be inspected by Ofsted (the Office for Standards in Education), and officially classified as a school requiring 'special measures' to put it right. If parents opt to send their children to another school, it may face declining income, making things worse. As a result, it might face closure.

However, the school might be dramatically improved by teachers and others in the school community working harder to try and turn the school around. We might then eventually see it as a 'good' school. The school might be held up as a showpiece of improvement by the government, and used as a model or 'beacon school' for all other schools to follow. This change shows that within social structures like education, human action – human activity – can make differences by changing those structures.

This means that while people operate within the constraints of the social structure, they can also act, make choices, and sometimes change that social structure. It has to be supported by people, and constantly recreated: parents have to send their children to school because it is against the law not to do so, and most parents don't question this. But they do have to agree to this, and there are lots of cases where parents refuse to send their children to school because they believe there is something wrong with the school. If they refuse, especially a lot of them, then there would undoubtedly be a change in the schooling system.

This third or middle way, between structuralism and action theories, recognizes the importance both of the constraints of social structure and of choice: the actions people can take to accept or change those structures. This is Anthony Giddens's highly influential theory of structuration.

The three approaches of structuralism, social action theory and structuration are illustrated in the cartoon.

> **Structuration** is an approach between structuralism and social action theory. It suggests that, while people are constrained by social institutions, they also have choice and can at the same time take action to support or change those institutions.

Structuralism

Social action or interpretivist theories

Structuration

Feminism is a view that examines the world from the point of view of women, coupled with the belief that women are disadvantaged and their interests ignored or devalued in society.

Marxist feminism takes a Marxist approach to the study of women and women's interests, and emphasizes the way in which women are doubly exploited – both as workers and as women.

Radical feminism tends to focus more on the problem of **patriarchy** – the system whereby males dominate in every area of society, such as the family, the workplace and politics. For radical feminists, the main focus is on the problem of men and male-dominated society.

Liberal feminism wants to ensure that women have equal opportunities with men within the present system, through steps such as changes to the law to stop sex discrimination, removing obstacles to women's full participation in society, and better childcare measures so that women can play their full part in paid employment.

Activity

Some argue that living in society is like living in a goldfish bowl – you are constrained by the bowl, even though you can't see the glass walls. In the light of what you have read in this chapter, discuss in a group to what extent you think this is an accurate view of society. Give reasons for your answers.

Feminist perspectives

Feminism examines society particularly from the point of view of women. Feminists argue that a lot of mainstream sociology has been focused on the concerns of men – 'malestream sociology' – and has failed to deal with the concerns of women and the unequal position they have traditionally occupied in society. There are a number of strands within feminist approaches, but three of the main ones are **Marxist feminism**, **radical feminism** and **liberal feminism**. These are explained in the box in the margin. Marxist feminism and radical feminism fundamentally challenge the way society is presently organized and seek major social change, while liberal feminism basically accepts the system as it is but seeks to ensure women have equal opportunities with men within that system.

New Right perspectives

The New Right is more a political philosophy than a sociological perspective, and is associated mainly with the years of the Conservative government in Britain between 1979 and 1997. This approach is, however, found in the work of some sociologists, and is referred to in various parts of this book. This approach has four main features:

- *An emphasis on individual freedom*, and the need to reduce the power of the state to the minimum, and reduce control of the individual by unnecessary state interference.
- *Reduced spending by the state*, by making individuals more self-reliant. An example is cutting welfare benefits and encouraging people into work to make them 'stand on their own two feet', and not expect them to be dependent on the state for support if they are physically and mentally capable of supporting themselves.
- *A defence of the free market*. This means that free competition between individuals, companies, schools and other institutions is encouraged, to give individuals maximum choice between competing products, such as in health care and education. An example might be giving parents a free choice of schools as 'consumers' of education, and the right to reject some schools in favour of others, just as people choose between competing products in a supermarket. The selling off to private companies of state-owned industries like gas, electricity, water, British Airways and British Telecom was seen as a way of introducing competition in these areas, on the assumption that more competition would lead to lower prices and better quality services or products.
- *A stress on the importance of traditional institutions and values*, such as traditional family life, and a condemnation of anything that challenges these values. For example, lone parent families have been viciously attacked by the New Right, and blamed for a whole range of social problems, such as poor discipline and underachievement at school, immorality, crime, a culture of laziness, welfare dependency and the lack of a work ethic, and the existence of poverty.

Postmodernism

Postmodernism is most likely to be considered and examined in the second year of an A-level course, rather than at AS level. However, it is included here since you may come across the term in any wider reading you might do, and it is useful to have a bit of background, especially as some postmodernist ideas influence parts of this book.

Postmodernism stresses the chaos and uncertainty in society, and argues that social structures like the family or social class are breaking down. These

The **New Right** approach stresses individual freedom and self-help and self-reliance, reduction of the power and spending of the state, the free market and free competition between private companies, schools and other institutions, and the importance of traditional institutions and values.

Postmodernism is an approach in sociology, as well as in other subjects, which stresses that society is changing so rapidly and constantly that it is marked by chaos and uncertainty, and social structures are being replaced by a whole range of different and constantly changing social relationships. Societies can no longer be understood through the application of general theories like Marxism or functionalism, which seek to explain society as a whole, as it has become fragmented into many different groups, interests and lifestyles. Society and social structures cease to exist, to be replaced by a mass of individuals making individual choices about their lifestyles.

are replaced by a whole range of different and constantly changing social relationships. Postmodernists argue that it is nonsense to talk of an institution called the family, for example, as people now live in such a wide range of ever-changing personal relationships. Gay and lesbian couples, cohabiting heterosexual couples who do not marry, multiple partners, divorce and remarriage, lone parents, step-parents and stepchildren, dual income families with both partners working, people living alone, people living in shared households with friends, couples who have differing arrangements for organizing household tasks: all mean that any notion of the 'typical family' or 'the family as an institution' is absurd.

Because society is now changing so constantly and so rapidly, societies can no longer be understood through the application of general theories. There can therefore be no 'big' theories (called *meta-narratives*) like Marxism or functionalism, which seek to explain society as a whole, because society has become fragmented into so many different groups, interests and lifestyles that are constantly changing that society is essentially chaotic.

Postmodernists believe there are few of the social constraints on people that structuralist approaches identify, and society and social structures cease to exist – there is only a mass of individuals making individual choices about their lifestyles. In postmodern societies, the emphasis is on individuals as consumers, making their own choices in education, health, their personal relationships and lifestyle. People can now form their own identities – how they see and define themselves and how others see and define them – and they can be whatever they want to be. People are free to make choices about their lifestyles, and the image they want to project to other people. Postmodern society involves a media-saturated consumer culture where individuals are free to 'pick 'n' mix' identities and lifestyles, chosen from a limitless range of constantly changing consumer goods and leisure activities, which are available from across the globe.

Activity

Go through the following statements, and classify them as one of the following:

- functionalist
- Marxist feminist
- liberal feminist
- New Right
- Marxist
- radical feminist
- interpretivist

(a) We will challenge all aspects of society not relevant to women, bring about a complete female takeover, eliminate the male sex and begin to create a female world.

(b) The family is one of the main building blocks in creating the shared values which are such an important part of a stable society.

(c) There are conflicts between the rich and the poor in our society. This is hardly surprising, given that the richest 10 per cent of the population own over half the country's wealth.

(d) To make sure women have equal opportunities with men, there must be more free childcare provided.

(e) Women are exploited both as women and as workers – they get exploited in paid employment, and they get exploited at home, where they do most of the housework and childcare and get nothing for it.

(f) The ruling ideas in society are those of the ruling class.

(g) Some people may see an amber traffic light as a warning to speed up before it turns red. Others may see it as a sign to slow down before stopping. In order to understand such behaviour, you need to understand the meaning people give to events.

(h) The education system is of major importance in preparing a well-trained and qualified labour force so the economy can develop and grow.

(i) The education system prepares an obedient workforce which won't rock the boat and complain about being exploited at work.

(j) If you think people are out to get you, even if they're not, then this is likely to affect the way you behave. To understand behaviour, we have to understand people's point of view.

(k) Women will never achieve equality in society so long as men hold all the positions of power in society.

(l) It is in everyone's interests to pull together at work for the benefit of society as a whole.

(m) Although girls now do better than boys in education, they could do better still. We must make sure that any obstacles to girls' progress in school are removed.

(n) We must make sure women get equal pay for equal work.

(o) Some students are almost bound to fail, because teachers give the impression that they're thick, and this undermines the self-confidence of the students, who then think it isn't worth bothering.

(p) The welfare state has produced an underclass of people who are idle and don't want to work, and are content to scrounge off overgenerous welfare state benefits rather than get a job to support themselves.

The solution to this activity can be found on the teachers' pages of www.polity.co.uk/browne.

Sociological problems, social problems and social policy

Social problems are nearly all sociological problems, but not all sociological problems are social problems. However, very often sociologists have been able to show by research that many social problems are not simply a result of the behaviour of individuals, but are created by wider social factors. A useful example is that of accidents.

A **sociological problem** is any social issue that needs explaining.
A **social problem** is something that is seen as being harmful to society in some way, and needs something doing to sort it out.

Accidents as a social and a sociological problem

Accidents are a social problem, and the accident statistics show a clear social pattern in terms of age, class and gender. For example, young people and old people, the poor and males are more likely to die or be seriously injured because of an accident. Accidents may happen to us individually, and sometimes randomly, but the causes are often socially influenced, by factors such as poor quality housing, inadequate home care for the elderly, low income, dangerous working conditions and a dangerous environment, with busy roads and no safe play areas for children. Accidents provide an often dramatic and tragic but nevertheless excellent example of how seemingly random or individual experiences and events are in fact socially patterned and socially influenced.

The study of accidents shows how clear-sighted C. Wright Mills (1970) was when he wrote about the distinction between 'the personal troubles of milieu' (immediate social surroundings) and 'the public issues of social structure'. Every single accident is a personal experience but the social pattern of these experiences in Britain every year is for all of us a social problem – not least because of the harm they cause and the millions of pounds spent treating them by the National Health Service. This social problem is also a sociological problem – something which needs explaining by sociologists. The pattern of accident statistics illustrates well Mills's distinction between 'personal troubles' and 'public issues' to which we referred above. To paraphrase Mills, when in a nation of 60 million only one person has an accident, then that is his or her personal trouble, and for its solution we look at the circumstances of that person. But when in a nation of 60 million 8 million have accidents, with a clear social pattern, that is a public issue and a social problem, and we cannot hope to find a solution within the personal situations and characteristics of individuals.

Sociological research has often made major contributions to the **social policy** solutions needed to tackle social problems like accidents, ill-health, crime, poverty or educational failure. Social policy refers to the packages of plans and actions taken to solve social problems or achieve other goals that are seen as important. These are usually adopted by national and local government or various voluntary agencies. For example, measures taken to solve the social problem of obesity and achieve the goal of a healthier nation. However, sociologists also try to explain social issues that aren't social problems, like the improved performance of females in the educational system, or why the birth rate is declining and why people are having smaller families.

It is this ability of sociology to explain social events and to contribute to the understanding and solution of social problems, and the social policy solutions adopted, which makes it such a worthwhile, useful and exciting subject.

Social policy refers to the packages of plans and actions adopted by national and local government or various voluntary agencies to solve social problems or achieve other goals that are seen as important.

CHAPTER SUMMARY

After studying this chapter, you should be able to:

- explain what is meant by a 'social institution' and 'social structure'

- explain how sociology is different from common-sense and naturalistic explanations

- define the meaning of socialization, culture, identity, roles, role models, role conflict, values, laws, norms, social control, deviance, and positive and negative sanctions, and explain their importance in understanding human behaviour in human society

- explain what is meant by 'social class' and identify the main social classes in contemporary Britain

- explain what is meant by a sociological perspective, and identify the main features of the structuralist approaches of functionalism and Marxism, and the social action or interpretivist approaches, including symbolic interactionism

- explain what is meant by structuration, and how it provides a middle way between structural and action perspectives

- explain the variety of feminist perspectives, and the features of the New Right approach in sociology

- explain what is meant by, and the differences between, a sociological problem and a social problem, and the contribution of sociology to social policy

KEY TERMS

achieved status
ascribed status
bourgeoisie
capitalists
class conflict
class consciousness
communism
culture
customs
determinism
deviance
dominant ideology
ethnicity
false consciousness
feminism
functional prerequisites
functionalism
gender

identity
ideology
interpretivism
labelling
labour power
laws
liberal feminism
life chances
macro approach
Marxism
Marxist feminism
means of production
micro approach
middle class
minority ethnic group
negative sanctions
New Right
norms
objectivity

patriarchy
perspective
positive sanctions
postmodernism
proletariat
radical feminism
role conflict
role models
roles
ruling class
ruling class ideology
sanctions
sex
social action theory
social class
social control
social institution
social mobility
social policy

social problem
social structure
socialization
sociological perspective
sociological problem
status
structuralism
structuration
surplus value
symbolic interactionism
underclass
upper class
value consensus
value freedom
values
working class

Culture and Identity

Contents

Key issues 31

The meaning and importance of culture 31

Dominant culture 31
Subculture 32
Folk culture 32
High culture 32
Mass, popular or low culture 33
The changing distinction between high culture and mass culture 35
Global culture 36

The concept of identity 38

Different types of identity 41

The socialization process 43

Primary socialization 44
Secondary socialization 44

Socialization and the social construction of self and identity 46

Theoretical approaches to the role of socialization in the formation of culture and identity 46

Structural approaches 47
Social action approaches 47
A third way: structuration 50

Social class and identity 50

Social class 51
Life chances 51
Objective and subjective dimensions of class 52
Social class cultures 53
Is social class of declining importance in forming identities? 59
The continuing importance of social class 60

Gender and identity 61

Sex and gender 61
Gender and biology 62
The significance of gender as a source of identity 63
Gender stereotypes and hegemonic gender identities in Britain 63
The social construction of hegemonic gender identities through socialization 65
Changing gender identities 70

Is there a crisis of masculinity? 74
Is gender still an important source of identity? 74

Sexuality and identity 76

Gender, sexuality and 'normal' sex 76
Changing sexual identities 76
Stigmatized or spoiled sexual identities 77
Gay and lesbian identities 77
A note of caution 78

Ethnicity and identity 79

What is meant by an ethnic identity? 79
Diaspora and globalization 80
Changing ethnic identities: new ethnicities and hybrid ethnic identities 81
Ethnicity as resistance 82
Ethnic identities in Britain 82

Nationality and identity 87

What is nationality? 87
Nationality as a source of identity 88
What is meant by a British identity? 88
Globalization and declining national identities 91
A British identity crisis? 92

Disability and identity 93

The social construction of disability 93
Disability, socialization and stereotyping 94
Disability as a 'master identity' 95
Disability – a stigmatized or spoiled identity: an identity of exclusion 95

Age and identity 96

The social construction of age 96
Age groups and identity 97

Leisure, consumption and identity 100

Postmodernism and identity 100
The creation of identity in a media-saturated society 101
How much free choice is there in choosing identities and lifestyle? 103
Conclusion on leisure, consumption and identity 109

Chapter summary 110

Key terms 111

Exam question 112

Culture and Identity

- The meaning and importance of culture
- The concept of identity
- The socialization process
- Socialization and the social construction of self and identity
- Theoretical approaches to the role of socialization in the formation of culture and identity
- Social class and identity
- Gender and identity
- Sexuality and identity
- Ethnicity and identity
- Nationality and identity
- Disability and identity
- Age and identity
- Leisure, consumption and identity

The meaning and importance of culture

The term 'culture' refers to the language, beliefs, values and norms, customs, dress, diet, roles, knowledge and skills, and all the other things that people learn that make up the 'way of life' of any society. Culture is passed on from one generation to the next through the process of socialization. Although there are many aspects of everyday life which are shared by most members of society, there are different conceptions and definitions of culture within this general approach. These are discussed below.

Dominant culture

The **dominant culture** of a society refers to the main culture in a society, which is shared, or at least accepted without opposition, by the majority of

> The **dominant culture** of a society refers to the main culture in a society, which is shared, or at least accepted without opposition, by the majority of people.

people. For example, it might be argued that the main features of British culture include it being white, patriarchal and unequal, with those who are white and male having things they regard as worthwhile rated as more important than those who are female or from a minority ethnic group. Similarly, those who are rich and powerful (who are mainly also white and male) are in a position to have their views of what is valuable and worthwhile in a culture regarded as more important, and given higher status, than those of others.

Subculture

When societies are very small, such as small villages in traditional societies, then all people may share a common culture or way of life. However, as societies become larger and more complicated, a number of smaller groups may emerge within the larger society, with some differences in their beliefs and way of life. Each group having these differences is referred to as a subculture.

> A **subculture** is a smaller culture held by a group of people within the main culture of a society, in some ways different from the main culture but with many aspects in common. Examples of subcultures include those of some young people, gypsies and travellers, gay people, different social classes and minority ethnic groups.

Folk culture

Folk culture is the culture created by local communities and is rooted in the experiences, customs and beliefs of the everyday life of ordinary people. It is 'authentic' rather than manufactured, as it is actively created by ordinary people themselves. Examples include traditional folk music, folk songs, storytelling and folk dances which are passed on from one generation to the next by socialization and often by direct experience. Folk culture is generally associated with pre-industrial or early industrial societies, though it still lingers on today among enthusiasts in the form of folk music and folk clubs, and the Morris dancing which features in many rural events.

> **Folk culture** is the culture created by local communities and is rooted in the experiences, customs and beliefs of the everyday life of ordinary people.

High culture

High culture is generally seen as being superior to other forms of culture, and refers to aspects of culture that are seen as of lasting artistic or literary value, aimed at small, intellectual elites, predominantly upper-class and middle-class groups, interested in new ideas, critical discussion and analysis and who have what some might regard as 'good taste'.

High culture is seen as something set apart from everyday life, something special to be treated with respect and reverence, involving things of lasting value and part of a heritage which is worth preserving. High culture products are often found in special places, like art galleries, museums, concert halls and theatres. Examples of high culture products include serious news programmes and documentaries, classical music like that of Mozart or

> **High culture** refers to cultural products seen to be of lasting artistic or literary value, which are particularly admired and approved of by elites and the upper middle class.

> An **elite** is a small group holding great power and privilege in society.

Morris dancing is an example of traditional folk culture

Beethoven, the theatre, opera, jazz, foreign language or specialist 'art' films, and what has become established literature, such as the work of Charles Dickens, Jane Austen or Shakespeare, and visual art like that of Monet, Gauguin, Picasso or Van Gogh.

Mass, popular or low culture

Mass culture, sometimes called popular culture or low culture, is generally contrasted with high culture. This refers to everyday culture – simple,

Mass culture, sometimes called **popular culture** or **low culture**, refers to cultural products produced for sale to the mass of ordinary people. These involve mass-produced, standardized, short-lived products of no lasting value, which are seen to demand little critical thought, analysis or discussion.

Video games are an example of popular culture

undemanding, easy-to-understand entertainment, rather than something 'set apart' and 'special'. Mass culture is seen by many as inferior to high culture. Such aspects of culture are a product of industrial societies. They are aimed at the mass of ordinary people, but lack roots in their daily experiences as in folk culture, and are manufactured by businesses for profit rather than created by the community itself reflecting its own experiences of daily life. Popular culture involves mass-produced, standardized and short-lived products, sometimes of trivial content and seen by some as of no lasting 'artistic' value, largely concerned with making money for large corporations, especially the mass media.

Popular culture might include mass circulation magazines, extensive coverage of celebrities, 'red top' tabloid newspapers like the *Sun* or the *Mirror*, television soaps and reality TV shows, dramas and thrillers, rock and pop music, video games, blockbuster feature films for the mass market, and thrillers bought for reading on the beach. Such culture is largely seen as passive and unchallenging, often fairly mindless entertainment, aimed at the largest number of people possible.

Some Marxists argue that mass culture maintains the ideological hegemony (or the dominance of a set of ideas) and the power of the dominant social class in society. This is because the consumers of mass culture are lulled into an uncritical, undemanding passivity, making them less likely to challenge the dominant ideas, groups and interests in society.

The changing distinction between high culture and mass culture

Some now argue that the distinction between high culture and mass culture is weakening. Postmodernist writers, in particular, argue that mass markets and consumption now make the distinction between high and popular culture meaningless. There has been a huge expansion of the creative and cultural industries, such as advertising, television, film, music, and book and magazine publishing. This means there is now a huge range of media and cultural products available to all.

Technology in industrial societies, such as mass communication technology like the internet, music downloads, cable, satellite and digital television, film and radio, printing for both mass production and personal use in the home, the global reach of modern mass media technology, the mass production of goods on a world scale and easier international transportation, make all forms of culture freely available to everyone. Such technology enables original music and art and other cultural products to be consumed by the mass of people in their own homes without visiting specialized institutions like theatres or art galleries. High culture is no longer simply the preserve of cultural elites.

People now have a wider diversity of cultural choices and products available to them than ever before in history, and can 'pick and mix' from either popular or high culture. High culture art galleries, like Tate Modern in London, are now attracting very large numbers of visitors, from very diverse backgrounds. Live opera is now available to the masses, through popular figures like the OperaBabes, or concerts in the park.

Strinati (1995) argues that elements of high culture have now become a part of popular culture, and elements of popular culture have been incorporated into high culture, and that there is therefore no longer any real distinction between high and popular culture, and it is ever more difficult for any one set of ideas of what is worthwhile culture to dominate in society. For example, artist Andy Warhol painted thirty pictures of Leonardo da Vinci's *Mona Lisa* in different colours, arguing that 'thirty was better than one', turning high culture art into popular culture. Although Warhol's work has been marketed to millions through postcards and posters, at the same time it is widely admired by the supporters of high culture. In 2007 there was some controversy in Britain when the Victoria and Albert Museum in London, generally seen as an institution of high culture, held 'Kylie: The Exhibition' – an exhibition of costumes, album covers, accessories, photos and videos from the career of the then 38-year-old pop singer Kylie Minogue. This drew widespread accusations from critics that high culture was being 'dumbed down'.

High culture art forms are themselves increasingly being turned into products for sale in the mass market for consumption by the mass of ordinary people, and there is no longer anything special about art, as it is incorporated into daily life. Technology now means mass audiences can see and study high culture products, such as paintings by artists like Van Gogh, on the internet or TV, and have their own framed print hanging on their sitting-room wall. The originals may still only be on show in art galleries and museums, but copies are available to everyone. High culture art like the *Mona Lisa* or Van Gogh's *Sunflowers* are now reproduced on everything from socks and t-shirts to chocolates and can lids, mugs, mouse mats, tablemats, jigsaws and posters. (Visit <www.studiolo.org/Mona> or <www.megamonalisa.com> for some bizarre images and uses of the *Mona Lisa*.) Classical music is used as a marketing tune by advertisers, and literature is turned into TV series and major mass movies, such as Jane Austen's *Pride and Prejudice*.

Global culture

Global culture refers to the way **globalization** has undermined national and local cultures, with cultural products and ways of life in different countries of the world becoming more alike. The same cultural and consumer products are now sold across the world, inspired by media advertising and a shared mass culture spread through a media-generated culture industry, and they have become part of the ways of life of many different societies. For example, television companies sell their programmes and programme formats like *Big Brother* and *Who Wants to be a Millionaire?* globally. Companies like McDonald's, Coca Cola, Vodaphone, Starbucks, Nescafé, Sony and Nike are now symbols that are recognized across the world, along with the consumer lifestyles and culture associated with them. As Ritzer (2004) shows, using the example of the American food industry, companies and brands now operate on a global scale. For example, McDonald's is a worldwide business, with 26,500 restaurants in more than 119 countries (in 2007), Pizza Hut and Kentucky Fried Chicken operate in 100 countries, and Subway in 72 countries, with Starbucks growing at a colossal speed. It is now possible to buy an identical food product practically anywhere in the world, promoting a global culture and also weakening local cultures, as local food outlets close in the face of competition and local diets change. Combined with global marketing of films, music, computer games, food and clothes, football and other consumer products, these have made cultures across the world increasingly similar, with people watching the same TV programmes and films, eating the same foods, wearing the same designer clothes and labels, and sharing many aspects of their lifestyles and identities.

Global culture refers to the way cultures in different countries of the world have become more alike, sharing increasingly similar consumer products and ways of life. This has arisen as **globalization** has undermined national and local cultures.

Globalization is the growing interdependence of societies across the world, with the spread of the same culture, consumer goods and economic interests across the globe.

The Mona Lisa ...

Leonardo da Vinci's *Mona Lisa*, c. 1503–1507, oil on poplar,
The Louvre, Paris

… now has a spliff to relax and a mobile to keep in touch

Mona Stoner, c. 2006, posted on internet:
<www.megamonalisa.com>

Fine art is now available on cubes to play with

Source: <www.megamonalisa.com>

The *Mona Lisa* is transformed
into a window blind

In what ways do these pictures illustrate the erosion of the distinction between high culture and popular culture?
Try to think of other examples of this

Globalization means that many of the same product brands are now found in many countries of the world.

Activity

1 Refer to the pictures on this page, and explain in what ways they illustrate global culture. Try to think of other consumer products that are also global.
2 In what ways do you think consuming these products also involves lifestyle choices? For example, what's the difference between having a coffee in Starbucks and in the local café (apart from the coffee itself)? Explain what lifestyle you think is identified with your selected products.
3 Identify and explain, with examples, three differences between high culture, mass culture and folk culture.
4 Identify and explain three reasons why the distinction between high culture and popular culture might be weakening.

The concept of identity

Identity is about how individuals or groups see and define themselves, and how other individuals or groups see and define them. Identity is formed through the socialization process and the influence of social institutions like the family, the education system and the mass media.

The concept of identity is an important one, as it is only through establishing our own identities and learning about the identities of other individuals and groups that we come to know what makes us similar to some people and different from others, and therefore form social connections with them. How you see yourself will influence the friends you have, who you will marry or live with, and the communities and groups to which you relate and belong. If people did not have an identity, they would lack the means of identifying with or relating to their peer group, to their neighbours, to the communities in which they lived or to the people they came across in their everyday lives. Identity therefore 'fits' individuals into the society in which they live.

The identity of individuals and groups involves both elements of personal choice and the responses and attitudes of others. Individuals are not free to adopt any identity they like, and factors like their social class, their ethnic group and their sex are likely to influence how others see them. The identity that an individual wants to assert and which they may wish others to see them having may not be the one that others accept or recognize. An Asian woman, for example, may not wish to be identified primarily as an Asian or a woman, but as a senior manager or entertainer. However, if others still

'Look, don't identify me by the size and shape of my body, my social class, my job, my gender, my ethnicity, my sexuality, my nationality, my age, my religion, my education, my friends, my lifestyle, how much money I earn, the clothes I wear, the books I read, where I go shopping, the way I decorate my house, the television programmes and movies I watch, my leisure and sports activities, the car I drive, the music I listen to, the drinks I like, the food I eat, the clubs I go to, where I go on holiday, the way I speak or my accent, the things I say, the things I do, or what I believe in. I'm just me. OK?'

continue to see her primarily in terms of her ethnic and gender characteristics, she may find it difficult to assert her chosen identity. Similarly, the pensioner who sees him or herself as 'young at heart' may still be regarded as an old person by others.

Individuals have multiple identities, asserting different identities in different circumstances. An individual may, for example, define herself primarily as a Muslim in her family or community, as a manager at her work, as a lesbian in her sexual life, or as a designer-drug-user in her peer group. While the example of the Muslim, lesbian, drug-taking manager might seem a somewhat unlikely mix of identities, it does suggest that it is possible for people to assert different identities or impressions of themselves in different social situations.

Identities may also change over time. For example, as people grow older they may begin to see themselves as different from when they were younger, and may well be viewed differently by others, particularly as their status changes as they move into retirement, and are detached from the identities arising from their job in paid employment.

Figure 2.1 shows a wide range of factors which may influence individuals' identity, but some of the main sources of identity include their social class, their gender, their ethnicity, their nationality, their disabilities, their age, their sexuality, their leisure activities and their consumption patterns. These sources of identity will be examined later in this chapter.

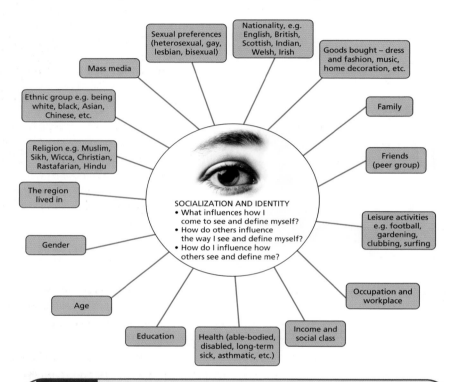

Figure 2.1 Some social influences on the formation of identities

Factors shown around the figure:

Sexual preferences (heterosexual, gay, lesbian, bisexual)

Nationality, e.g. English, British, Scottish, Indian, Welsh, Irish

Mass media

Goods bought – dress and fashion, music, home decoration, etc.

Ethnic group e.g. being white, black, Asian, Chinese, etc.

Family

Religion e.g. Muslim, Sikh, Wicca, Christian, Rastafarian, Hindu

Friends (peer group)

The region lived in

SOCIALIZATION AND IDENTITY
• What influences how I come to see and define myself?
• How do others influence the way I see and define myself?
• How do I influence how others see and define me?

Leisure activities e.g. football, gardening, clubbing, surfing

Gender

Occupation and workplace

Age

Income and social class

Education

Health (able-bodied, disabled, long-term sick, asthmatic, etc.)

Activity

Refer to figure 2.1

1 Suggest *one* example in each case of how the various factors may influence the individual's sense of identity.
2 Suggest *five* ways that individuals can influence how others see them.
3 Describe the *five* most important factors that you think have influenced how you define yourself and how others see you. Explain your answer with examples.
4 Suggest *three* ways you can influence how others see and define you, such as a particular type of person – e.g. 'cool', 'odd', 'sporty' or 'Goth'.
5 Give examples of ways you try to present different identities to different groups of people. How and why do you do this?

Different types of identity

Individual or personal identity

Woodward (2000) suggests that individual identity is concerned with the question 'Who am I?' – how individuals define themselves, what is important and matters to them, how they see themselves as individuals different from other people, and the things that give them their own unique personal or individual characteristics. Their name, their passport, their National Insurance number, their fingerprints, their DNA, their birth certificate and their signature are some obvious examples of these, as well as people's personal histories, friends and relationships and their own understanding of who they really are as individuals: their own self-concept of the 'inner me', or 'I', as Mead referred to it.

Social identity

Social identity offers little choice and defines individuals in relation to the social groups with which they are identified and to which they belong, and how they differ from other social groups and individuals. Such groups might include men and women, ethnic groups, or national groups like the English, Scots or Welsh. The formation of social identities may also arise from the characteristics associated with the social roles that people play. For example, the identities and the related behaviour that might be expected of them when playing their social roles as mothers and fathers, sons and daughters, students or workers, or as members of social groups like students, males or females, Muslims or Sikhs, gays, lesbians or heterosexuals, or Welsh or Scottish.

Collective identity

A collective identity is an identity shared by a social group, and involves elements of both personal and social identities, but differs from both as it involves considerable elements of choice by individuals in that they actively choose to identify with a group and adopt the identity associated with it. For example, while social identities like gender, ethnicity or nationality are largely defined by others and individuals have only limited choice in whether or not to adopt them, being identified as a football or rock music fan, a Goth, a gang member, a Hell's Angel, a feminist, an eco-warrior protecting the environment, an anti-war, animal rights or Labour Party activist is almost completely a matter of personal choice.

Multiple identities

The idea of multiple identities simply means that people have several identities, rather than just one. Individuals may draw on more than one source of identity, such as identities formed around their social class, and/or their ethnicity, their sexuality, their gender, their nationality and/or their age,

To what extent do you think going to festivals like Glastonbury is an important aspect of the identity of young people? What other groups or activities do young people engage with to form their collective identities?

etc., or a combination of all of them. Individuals may assert different 'selves' in different circumstances. For example, at home they may assert the identity of a good son or daughter or a good Muslim, at school or college they may assert their identity as a good student, in their personal relations as gay, in their peer group as a Goth, in their leisure activities as a sporty type or drinker, in their workplace as a good worker, or as primarily having an Asian Muslim identity in Britain, but a British identity while travelling abroad.

Stigmatized or 'spoiled' identities

A **stigma** might be:

- a physical impairment, like being blind, losing the use of lower limbs, or having an illness like AIDS or a sexually-transmitted disease
- a social characteristic, like being mentally ill, a sex offender, a criminal or a child abuser.

Goffman (1990) said a **stigmatized identity** is an identity that is in some way undesirable or demeaning, excluding people from full acceptance in society. The disabled, for example, are often said to have a stigmatized identity in a society which places a high premium on bodily perfection. Those with stigmatized identities can face serious social consequences, with others treating them with contempt, poking fun at them, denying them proper medical treatment (as happens with some older people and the disabled), or refusing them employment (as with former prisoners, the mentally ill or the elderly). Having a stigmatized identity nearly always means that any attempts made

A **stigma** is any undesirable physical or social characteristic that is seen as abnormal or unusual in some way, that is seen as demeaning and stops an individual being fully accepted by society. A **stigmatized identity** is an identity that is in some way undesirable or demeaning, and excludes people from full acceptance in society.

by individuals to present an alternative 'normal' impression of themselves will fail. This alternative 'failed' identity is sometimes called a spoiled identity. As Goffman put it, 'stigma is a process by which the reaction of others spoils normal identity'.

The socialization process

The newborn child is not born with an understanding of culture, and human societies are not based on instinctive behaviour, like that of animals. Children born in Britain will most likely develop into members of society much like any other British child, but if those same children were born in France, India, China or Peru, they would be likely to develop many different ways of behaving because they would learn different cultures.

Learning culture through the socialization process, and the values, norms and roles that are part of this culture, helps to ensure some stability in society, and enables individuals to operate in the societies into which they are born. For example, a common language enables people to communicate with each other, to learn and share meanings and to develop ideas. People need to know what is expected of them in the societies in which they live, and the learning of social roles generally means we know how we are expected to behave when we are, for example, teachers or students, or sons or daughters, and how to behave and what to expect from the people we meet. Socialization therefore makes possible some predictability in social life, and avoids the chaos and confusion in everyday life that would arise if we had to reinvent or guess at social rules every time we met someone or entered a new situation, or if people made up their own rules and meanings as they went along. Socialization therefore gives people enough in common with others to relate to them and know what is expected of them as they share a broadly similar way of life.

Functionalist writers like Durkheim and Parsons see learning culture through socialization as the means by which individuals are integrated or 'stitched' into the societies to which they belong, with socialization acting as a kind of social glue bonding people together. Functionalists tend to see individuals socialized into a value consensus – they all share the same values and it is this that binds them together. Marxists, on the other hand, would argue that there is not a value consensus, but, rather, that people are socialized into the beliefs and values of the dominant social class in society – what is known as the dominant ideology. However, both recognize that it is culture and socialization that form the integrating link between the individual and society. Socialization is carried out by a number of agencies of primary and secondary socialization.

Activity

Feral children

Evidence of the importance of culture and socialization in binding the individual into society is found in the study of feral ('feral' means 'wild' or undomesticated) children. Feral children are children who, for one reason or another, miss out on some important stages of human learning as they have been removed from human contact and the normal processes of human socialization. They remain unaware of human social behaviour and language from a very early age and therefore fail to develop many aspects of behaviour we would regard as 'human'. Feral children are extremely rare, and many studies of so-called feral children need to treated with care. Some of the cases may appear to be feral, but, rather than lacking human socialization, they actually had severe learning or physical disabilities before they were abandoned and were abandoned because of these disabilities. There are many possible examples of feral children at <www.feralchildren.com>. One example is Tissa, the 'Monkey Boy of Sri Lanka', who was found in Sri Lanka in 1973, and who showed more animal than human characteristics. For example, he walked on all fours with a group of monkeys, yelped and snarled at humans, ate his food off the ground and did not smile.

Go to <www.feralchildren.com>
1. Identify *five* case studies in which children are raised differently from normal human children.
2. Identify in each case study the characteristics these children display that children raised in human societies usually don't.
3. Explain carefully the ways these examples might show that human behaviour is learnt rather than based on instinct.

Primary socialization

It is during **primary socialization** that children first begin to learn about the basic values and norms of society, and begin to acquire their sense of who they are as individuals – their individual identities – and significant elements of their social identities such as their gender, ethnicity and sexuality. In most cases, these identities formed during childhood will remain throughout people's lives and are much more difficult to change in adulthood than other identities.

Secondary socialization

Secondary socialization is carried out through agencies of secondary socialization, like those outlined below:

Primary socialization is socialization during the early years of childhood, and is carried out by the family or close community.

Secondary socialization is socialization which takes place beyond the family and close community, such as through the education system, the peer group, the workplace, the mass media and religious institutions.

- *The education system.* It is at school that most children learn a great deal of knowledge about the society in which they live, as well as the values and norms to which they will be expected to conform as adults.

- *The peer group.* The desire for approval and acceptance by peers is a powerful socializing influence, and peer group pressure to conform, and the fear of rejection and ridicule by peers, may exert an enormous influence on an individual's self-identity and behaviour. Such pressure may promote conformity to the wider norms of society, such as acceptance of traditional gender roles.

- *The workplace.* The very fact of finding and keeping a job, and getting along with workmates, involves learning about and conforming to the social rules governing work, like getting there on time, regular attendance and obeying the instructions of managers. The workplace has traditionally been seen as an important source of the individual and social identities of adults, as what people do for a living affects both people's view of themselves, how others define them, and the kind of lives they are able to lead outside work.

- *The mass media* are major sources of information, ideas, norms and values, as well as spreading images of, for example, fashion, music, role models and lifestyles that can influence people's values and behaviour.

- *Religious institutions* spread beliefs which influence people's ideas about right and wrong behaviour, important values and norms, and morality, and these may in turn affect the behaviour of individuals. In some cases,

The **peer group** is a group of people of similar age and status, with whom a person often mixes socially.

In what ways does the peer group influence the individual's socialization and sense of identity?

religious beliefs and institutions are important aspects of both the culture of communities and the identities of individuals, as for example in the case of Islam and Sikhism among the minority ethnic communities in Britain.

Activity

Suggest *two* ways in each case that (a) the mass media (b) peer groups and (c) religion might be a source of identity and meaning for individuals.

Socialization and the social construction of self and identity

Identity is something that is socially constructed. That is, it is something created by the socialization process, and the individual and social interpretations and actions of people. It is not something that is given by biology or nature. For example, being black or white, or male or female, only have significance in society because people attach some importance to these characteristics, and define people in terms of these categories.

There is a close link between culture, identity and socialization. It is the socialization process that transmits both culture and identities from one generation to the next. Jenkins (1996) argues that identities are formed in the socialization process. Through learning their culture, and through their involvement with other individuals, social groups and subcultures, people come to develop ideas about what makes them similar to, or different from, others, and their identities are formed. Learning the culture of a society involves learning the roles, or patterns of behaviour, that are expected from individuals in different positions in society. These roles entail individual and social identities, such as the identities adopted in the roles of mother or father, son or daughter, worker or student, or masculine or feminine gender roles. During the socialization process, and through meeting other people, individuals learn to know what they can expect from others, to have a particular view of themselves, and also learn about how others see and define them. These all contribute to the formation of identities.

Theoretical approaches to the role of socialization in the formation of culture and identity

There are different theoretical approaches to the formation of culture and identity, and these are the structural and action approaches which were

Structural approaches see identities formed by the wider social forces making up the social structure of society.

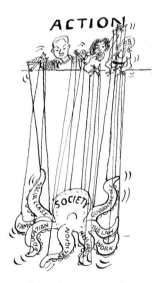

Social action approaches see individuals having control over the formation of their identities, rather than identities simply formed by the social structure.

outlined in the first chapter. If you haven't yet read the relevant section of chapter 1, you should read it now.

Structural approaches

Structuralists, like functionalists and some Marxists, adopt a macro approach, seeing culture and individual identities created by the wider social forces making up the social structure of society. Individuals are seen like puppets or programmed robots, who are socialized and manipulated by social institutions like the agencies of socialization mentioned above. Wider social forces, with culturally defined norms and values, form and limit the identities that are adopted, and individuals have little choice or control over their identity formation. Their identities are handed down to them by the socialization process, based on sources like social class, ethnicity, gender and age, and to which they are compelled to conform by various positive and negative sanctions. It is therefore wider social forces – rather than individual choice – that shapes the identities of individuals.

Criticisms of structural approaches

Criticisms of these approaches are that individuals as seen simply as puppets, what Garfinkel (1984) called 'cultural dopes', simply controlled by the social structure with little input from the individual. Structural approaches don't recognize that individuals have free will, and can take initiatives, make choices, challenge and disobey social rules, and have a role in carving out their own identities in interaction with others.

Social action approaches

Social action or interpretivist theories adopt a micro approach, focusing much more on the individual and everyday behaviour rather than the overall structure of society. This micro approach places much more emphasis on the role of individuals in creating culture and defining their identities, and is concerned with the meanings and interpretations individuals give to situations as they interact with other individuals and groups in the socialization process. Such theories suggest that identity is something individuals can create rather than simply have imposed on them. Norms, values and roles are not orders but guidelines that individuals can interpret, and they provide flexibility for individuals to manoeuvre within – they may alter some rules, ignore others, or can, of course, reject them altogether.

These approaches suggest individual and social identities are produced by the interaction between individuals and the culture and society to which they belong. The way that interaction between individuals can form and change identities is illustrated in works by Goffman, Mead and Cooley.

The 'looking-glass self'

Mead argues that as children grow up, they learn to develop a sense of themselves – their self-concept – and the qualities they have that make them different from others. As they relate to (or *interact* with) other people, they begin to develop ideas about how others see them and, by seeing how people respond to them, they may modify their self-concept and sense of identity and begin to see themselves as others see them. This means the self-concepts and identities of individuals are changing and developing all the time as they go through daily life in society. Cooley used the concept of the 'looking-glass self' to explain this. The 'looking-glass self' is the idea that our image of ourselves is reflected back to us (like a mirror) in the views of others. As we consider the image of ourselves reflected in the reactions of other people to us, we may modify and change our view of ourselves and our behaviour. An individual, for example, might see her or himself as outgoing, friendly and sociable, but if others see them as introverted, unfriendly and stand-offish, then they might adopt a new self-identity in accordance with how others see them, or modify their behaviour and try and change people's views of them. Our self-concept or our individual identity is therefore a social construction, and not a purely individual one.

The looking-glass self

Goffman: the presentation of self and impression management

Goffman (1990) sees society like a stage, with people acting out performances like actors do in a play or TV drama. Good actors are able to persuade audiences or viewers that they really are the characters they are playing. Similarly, in society people try to project particular impressions of themselves – what Goffman calls 'the presentation of self' – by putting on dramatic performances or a 'show' to try to influence or manipulate how others see them. By managing the impressions they give to other people – Goffman calls this **impression management** – individuals try to convince them of the identities they wish to assert. This is often achieved by the use of symbols of various kinds to show off the kind of person they want to be seen as, such as the way they speak, their body language and the words they use (like using a lot of swear or 'cool' words), wearing certain types of clothing and jewellery, having tattoos, following certain leisure activities, buying particular consumer goods, reading particular newspapers or listening to particular types of music. Such symbols try to present a particular impression to others. Everyone is engaged in this process of manipulating others and being manipulated by them to give the best possible impression of themselves. Through adopting social roles, like those of actors in a play who put on costumes and speak from scripts to convince audiences that they really are who they seem to be, and by responding to the reactions of others, individuals therefore develop their individual and social identities.

> **Impression management** is the way individuals try to convince others of the identity they wish to assert by giving particular impressions of themselves to other people.

While the individual may try to present a certain impression to others, there is no certainty that their impression management will always succeed. This is particularly the case for those with stigmatized identities. For example, someone with a physical impairment – like being confined to a wheelchair, for example – may not wish to give the impression that they are primarily a disabled person, but rather a black person, a Muslim, a woman, a news reporter or a doctor, but other people may continue to define them in terms of their impairment. People's failure to establish their chosen identity through such impression management then spoils their preferred identity.

Criticisms of social action approaches

Critics of the social action approach suggest that individuals are seen as having too much control over their identity formation, and not enough emphasis is given to the importance of power inequalities in society and the role of social institutions in limiting and controlling the identities that individuals can adopt. While individuals might be able to choose some aspects of their identity, they are limited in their choices by factors such as the social disapproval that may arise if values and norms are not complied with, by the need to work and earn money to feed themselves or their families, or to purchase the consumer goods necessary to assert an alternative identity. A road sweeper for a local council cannot simply choose to adopt the identity of a council manager, or a horse-riding, fox-hunting, shooting member of the upper class, because he probably lacks the financial means, social background, educational qualifications or skills to do so.

A third way: structuration

Giddens (2006) argues that there is a middle way between these structure and action approaches, which he calls 'structuration'. He accepts that social structures limit how people may act and the identities they may adopt, but they also make it possible for people to act and form identities in the first place. The culture and structure of society provides people with the means of establishing their identities, the tools necessary to make sense of society, and provide some degree of predictability in social life through an understanding of and agreement on basic social norms and values and a common language. Without these, it would be very difficult for individuals to establish their identities. While people can make choices and have opportunities to form and change their identities, they can only make choices within the cultural framework of the society in which they live. Social structure and social action are therefore interdependent.

Structuration sees the social structure and society's culture making it possible for individuals to form their identities. It recognizes that while identities are partly formed by individual choice, that choice is limited by the social structure and the culture in which people live

Activity

1 Explain what Garfinkel meant by a 'cultural dope' and Goffman by 'impression management'.
2 Suggest ways in which you try to manage the impressions of yourself that you give to other people, drawing on things like behaviour, speech, dress, consumer goods, personal appearance and so on. Do you always succeed in giving the impression you want? Explain why or why not you might succeed.
3 With reference to Cooley's idea of the 'looking-glass self', explain, with examples, how the reactions of others might encourage people to change how they view themselves.
4 Write a short essay, about one and a half sides of A4 paper, answering the following question: *Examine different sociological approaches to the formation of identities through socialization.*

Social class and identity

Social class

The identities that people adopt are formed within the cultures and subcultures to which they belong. One of the factors that has traditionally had a major effect on people's identity is their social class, and the class subcultures into which they are socialized.

Social class is a term that refers to a group of people who share a similar economic situation, such as a similar occupational level, similar income and ownership of wealth. Often occupation, income and ownership of wealth are closely related to each other and influence the lives of individuals, for example:

- how much power and influence they have in society
- their level of education
- their social status
- their type of housing
- their car ownership
- their leisure activities
- the consumer goods bought and lifestyle adopted

Occupation – work – is often a central part of how people see themselves – their individual identity – as well as how other people define them – their social identity. It is usually one of the first things we find out about people when we meet them for the first time. The time and money available to participate in social life, enjoy leisure activities and buy the consumer goods and services to support the lifestyles we aspire to, which are also important aspects of our identity, are all linked to some degree to the work we do.

> **Activity**
>
> List all the ways you can think of how a person's occupation might affect their self-identity and how others see them. Think about aspects of his or her life, such as family life, status in society, housing, health, leisure activities, beliefs and values, future planning and so on. Make sure you explain precisely how the effects on identity you mention are linked to a person's job.

Life chances

Social class is an important influence on people's lives, and pretending that it is not significant will not make it go away, any more than not being able to see a plate-glass door will stop you from hurting yourself when you walk into it. An individual's social class has a major influence on his or her life chances – that is, the chances of obtaining those things defined as desirable and of avoiding those things defined as undesirable in any society. There are wide, measurable differences in life chances between social classes:

- Higher social classes have better housing, cars, food, holidays, income and job security.

- Just 5 per cent of the population owned around 40 per cent of the UK's wealth (in 2004), and 10 per cent of the population owned over 53 per cent. The poorest 50 per cent of the population owned only about 7 per cent.
- The top 20 per cent of income earners get over five times the share of the bottom 20 per cent, and Britain has one of the widest gaps between the high-paid and the low-paid in Europe.
- Around one-fifth of the population of Britain lives in relative poverty.
- A man from the top social class on average lives seven years longer than a man from the lowest social class.
- Nearly twice as many babies die at birth or in the first year of life in the bottom social class as in the highest social class.
- Sickness increases as one moves down the social class hierarchy. Lower-working-class people suffer more from almost all diseases than those in the upper middle class.
- Smoking, drug and alcohol abuse and obesity are all more commonly found in the lower social classes.

Given all these class inequalities, it is not perhaps surprising that social class has been an important influence on people's identities.

Objective and subjective dimensions of class

There are two dimensions of social class: the objective and the subjective dimensions. The objective dimension refers to those aspects of social class which exist independently of people's thoughts and ideas – these are the material differences in people's life chances, such as those discussed above. Belonging to a social class is not, however, simply an objective fact.

The subjective dimension of class refers to people's personal perception of the social class they think they belong to – their class identity. While people's income means they don't always have a free choice in adopting the activities of any class they wish, the class they identify with will influence their attitudes, beliefs and values, and cultural choices, such as the music they listen to, the films and TV programmes they watch, the books, magazines and newspapers they read and their tastes in food, fashion and leisure, which are all part of the subculture of the class with which people identify. These subjective dimensions are part of what Bourdieu has called a 'habitus'.

Bourdieu and class 'habitus'

Bourdieu (1971) was a French Marxist, who argued that each social class possesses its own cultural framework or set of ideas, which he called a habitus. Individuals will operate according to the social class habitus they have learned during socialization, and this will influence:

> A **habitus** is the cultural framework and set of ideas possessed by a social class, into which people are socialized, initially by their families, and which influences their cultural tastes and choices.

- the knowledge they have
- the way they use language and their accent
- manners and forms of behaviour
- attitudes and values
- cultural tastes, including choices in cultural preference (high/popular culture), diet and leisure activities, consumer goods, clothing and fashion, and general lifestyles

This cultural framework contains ideas about what counts as 'good' and 'bad' taste, 'good' books, music, food, newspapers, TV programmes and so on. The dominant class has the power to impose its own views on what counts as good taste on the rest of society. The high culture which was discussed earlier reflects the good taste of the habitus of the dominant class, while the working class is more associated with the inferior tastes of popular or mass culture. Those who have access to the habitus of the dominant class possess what Bourdieu called cultural capital.

> **Cultural capital** is the knowledge, education, language, attitudes and values, and lifestyle possessed by the upper and upper middle class.

Social class cultures

Social class influences how people orientate themselves in society, as they are socialized into class identities from quite an early age, through living with and encountering in their communities people in the same social class as themselves, who are like them, who share similar lifestyles, attitudes and values, and with whom they feel comfortable in their everyday lives. The following sections give a brief outline of some of the traditional cultural features of the various social classes in British society, which provide sources of identity for those subjectively identifying with them.

Upper-class culture and identity

The upper class is a small class, and refers to those who are the main owners of society's wealth. The upper class includes three main groups.

1. The traditional upper class. This consists of Royalty and the 'old rich' traditional landowning aristocracy, as well as the titled ranks of dukes, duchesses, lords, ladies, earls and so on.
2. The owners of industry and commerce – the 'corporate rich' of the business world, such as Sir Richard Branson of Virgin.
3. Stars of entertainment, media and sport make up the third group, including people such as Paul McCartney, Mick Jagger, Elton John and Sean Connery, J. K. Rowling (author of the Harry Potter books) and David and Victoria Beckham.

Traditional upper-class culture and identity is largely associated with the first group (the 'old rich'), which has a strong sense of identity created by close family networks established through intermarriage, a shared educational experience and a shared culture. Features of upper class culture include:

- an education based around private boarding schools, particularly the public schools, like Eton and Harrow, followed by Oxford and Cambridge Universities: it is here that an appreciation of high culture is developed, and a sense of leadership and superiority; contacts are established among their peers, forming the 'old boys' network', which provides a self-help network in later life, and the links around which marriages are formed
- military service (in regiments like the Guards or Cavalry)
- the employment of domestic staff, like nannies, butlers, cooks and gardeners
- a taste for high culture, like opera, ballet and classical music
- particular codes of etiquette and manners
- leisure activities like hunting and shooting, tennis at Wimbledon, horse racing at 'Royal' Ascot, and weekends at country houses
- a sense of leadership, self-confidence and superiority over others

The other two groups both make up the 'nouveau riche' (new rich), who have acquired their wealth in their own lifetimes rather than through inheritance, and often come from humble origins. These groups may attempt to achieve acceptance by the traditional upper class by attempting to copy their lifestyles, but they often find acceptance difficult, as the 'old rich' tend to regard the nouveau riche as culturally inferior, lacking cultural capital, with poor taste, and who splash out with their wealth in conspicuous 'flashy', 'in-your-face'

Traditional upper-class culture includes a taste for opera and ballet, military service as commissioned officers and the employment of domestic servants

ways, like expensive sports cars, houses and clothes. They are thought to lack the sophisticated taste, 'breeding' and high culture of the traditional upper class. The nouveau riche more commonly establish their identities independently through their lifestyles and extravagant consumption patterns, which are discussed later in this chapter.

Middle-class culture and identity

The middle class is a large class, and refers to those in non-manual work – jobs which don't involve heavy physical effort, and which are usually performed in offices and involve paperwork or ICT work (Information and Communication Technology) of various kinds.

The middle class has expanded rapidly in recent years, and it consists of such a wide range of different groups, with different occupations, educational qualifications, incomes and lifestyles, that, as writers such as Savage (1995) and Roberts (2001) argue, it is difficult to generalize with any accuracy about a shared middle-class culture and identity. Despite this, some general features that might distinguish the middle class from the working class, and that are found in aspects of the identity of most sections of the middle class and into which children are socialized, include:

- a commitment to education, including private education, and recognition of its importance for career success
- a recognition of the importance of individual effort, personal ambition and self-help for success in life
- a sense of individual and family self-interest
- a concern with *future orientation* (planning for the future) and *deferred gratification* (putting off today's pleasures for future gains)
- a commitment to, or a leaning towards, greater respect for high culture than popular culture
- a concern with their own fitness, health and well-being

Several major groups make up the middle class, and each of them may display variations from the features identified above. The following five groups give some idea of the characteristics of the major groups in the middle class.

1 *The professionals*, such as lawyers, doctors, teachers and social workers, who value education, their independence, high culture products, and possess high levels of what Bourdieu called cultural capital.
2 *Managers* in the private sector of business, and government officials (senior civil servants). These will have upper-range salaries, and their identity is likely to be formed in terms of their consumer spending and the lifestyles and leisure activities their incomes will support. They are

likely to adopt identities associated with more traditional middle-class respectability, like politeness, respect for the law and refined behaviour, including an appreciation of high culture, moderation in behaviour – such as not overindulging in alcohol or drugs – and visiting museums, National Trust properties and so on.

3   *The self-employed small business owners.* These are likely to have a very individualistic identity, as they are forced to stand on their own two feet, and they are likely to be very work-centred.

4   *The financial and creative middle class.* This consists of those involved in finance (stockbrokers, investment managers, etc.) and the media and advertising. These groups tend to be young and very well-off, with high levels of consumer spending. Features include elements of both high and popular culture, clubbing, expensive restaurants, use of designer drugs, with lots of specialized leisure activities and holidays to reveal the affluent identity they wish to project. This group tends to be very individualistic, concerned primarily with its own self-interest, earning a lot of money and consuming things to mould and show off their identities.

5   *The lower-middle-class 'white-collar' workers.* These are employed in routine, non-manual work, like routine clerical and sales staff, with limited promotion prospects, and with lifestyles very similar to those of the new working class (see page 58). People in this group are more likely to have a shared collective identity than other middle-class groups, expressed through membership of trade unions to protect against declining status and pay.

In what ways do business people try to present identities associated with middle-class respectability?

Working-class culture and identity

The working class is one of the largest social classes, and refers to those working in manual jobs – jobs involving physical work and, mainly, work with their hands, like factory or labouring work. There are two broad groups within the working class: the traditional working class and the 'new' working class.

The traditional working class   The traditional working class declined rapidly in the last quarter of the twentieth century, as the industries in which it was found closed down, and it has practically disappeared in Britain today. It was associated mainly with the north of England and Scotland, and was found in traditional (long-established) basic industries, such as mining, docking, iron and steel, fishing and shipbuilding.

Cultural features included:

- A close-knit community and community life: as people knew each other and were in the same boat, they 'looked out' for and protected one another.
- Men were the main breadwinners, and women primarily housewives, looking after their men and their children.
- As Willis (1977) found, hard manual work was central to men's sense of masculinity as 'real men', and was their main source of identity.
- Obtaining a skill and getting a job and money were seen as more important than educational qualifications.
- A strong sense of working-class identity and loyalty to their social class, with class solidarity expressed through a strong commitment to trade unions and the joining together ('collectivism') this involved.
- A strong commitment to the old Labour Party, as it was then seen as the party of the working class.
- A view of society based on a struggle between the social classes, identifying themselves – 'us' – as engaged in a conflict with 'them' – the bosses.
- Enjoyment of and participation in popular culture, and some elements of traditional folk culture (like brass bands in mining communities).
- As Charlesworth (2000) found in his study of a traditional working-class community in Rotherham, language may involve a lot of swearing, and the use of insults (like 'shit fo' brains' or 'daft fucka') as forms of endearment to display friendship.

According to writers such as Hoggart (1969), there were very strong moral values, with clear conceptions of right and wrong, and maintaining respectability in the community was closely linked to 'doing the right thing'. The insecurity of life in the traditional working class, with few chances of promotion at work, ever-present risks of unemployment, industrial injury, ill-health, premature death and poverty led to three particular attitudes:

In what ways might traditional working-class jobs like coal mining create a sense of solidarity and be a source of masculine identity?

- *Immediate gratification*: enjoying pleasures today while the going's good rather than putting them off for later.
- *A present orientation*: a focus on the here and now rather than the future and long-term goals
- *A sense of fatalism*: an acceptance of the situation they found themselves in, as they didn't see much hope of improving or changing their lives. In traditional working-class jobs, educational qualifications were often not very important for work, and children tended to be socialized into traditional working-class identities, with sets of values and attitudes that didn't encourage ambition and educational success.

The 'new' working class   By far the largest section of the working class today is what is commonly called the 'new' working class, though it is actually quite old now and has been growing since the 1960s. The new working class originally emerged in the south of England, but it has now spread to become by far the largest section of the working class.

Cultural features include:

- A privatized, home-centred family lifestyle, with little involvement with neighbours or the wider community.
- An instrumental approach to life and work. Work is more likely to be seen as a means simply of making money, rather than as a means of making friends or as a major source of identity.
- There is little sense of loyalty to others in the same class. Those identifying with this class don't regard social class and power differences

Consumption and lifestyle are likely to be more important than work in forming the identity of the new working class

between classes as very important – the only real difference between people is that some have more money and possessions than others.

- Women are more likely to be in paid employment, though still retaining prime responsibility for the home.
- There are high levels of home-ownership, with home-centred lifestyles and consumption of popular culture.
- There is more emphasis on consumer goods, leisure activities and lifestyle in forming identity, than on work.

Is social class of declining importance in forming identities?

Some writers, like Clarke and Saunders (1991), suggest that social class is of declining importance today as a source of identity, as classes become fragmented into a range of different groups, and are being replaced by a whole range of other influences on identity, including gender, religion, ethnicity and consumer lifestyles. Pakulski and Waters (1996) suggest that class is dead as an important factor in a person's identity, being replaced with the lifestyle and consumptions patterns of different status groups. Lash and Urry (1987) argue that class subcultures have weakened, and people's cultural choices, tastes and lifestyles have become more individualistic and less influenced by their close communities and work situations. Postmodernist writers suggest that identities have become much more fluid and changeable, and people can now choose, 'pick and mix', chop and change any identities they want from a range of different lifestyles presented to them through the mass media, and by the choices they make in their leisure activities and the lifestyles they express through their consumer spending. For postmodernists, consumer culture has replaced class culture as the major influence on people's identity. This is discussed in the last section of this chapter.

Activity

1 Refer to the section above and mark the following statements as more likely to be true or false:

(a) Traditional working-class people are less likely to value education than the middle class.

(b) Members of the new working class are less likely to be involved in community activities than the traditional working class.

(c) The traditional working class is likely to have a lifestyle more like the lower middle class.

(d) People in the new working class are more likely to live in a tight-knit community than the traditional working class.

(e) Traditional working-class people are likely to identify with others in their class.

(f) The middle class is likely to be concerned with planning for the future.

(g) Members of the middle class are more likely to be interested in high culture than the traditional working class.

(h) Members of the traditional working class are likely to see society divided by conflict between opposing social classes.

(i) The traditional upper class is likely to have a sense of its own superiority to others.

(j) The traditional upper class sees itself as having a similar identity to the corporate rich and the stars of sport, entertainment and the media.

2 Identify and briefly explain *two* characteristics of (i) upper-class culture, (ii) middle-class culture, (iii) traditional working-class culture and (iv) the culture of the new working class.

3 Suggest *two* ways in which the experience of education may reinforce class identity.

4 What social class do you think you belong to? Give reasons for your answer.

5 Do you subjectively *identify* yourself as a member of a particular social class? Which one, and explain why.

6 Explain what is meant by the subjective dimension of class, and why this might be important when considering whether class is still a source of identity.

7 Conduct a short survey among people you know to see how they identify social class and what social class they would put themselves in, and why.

The continuing importance of social class

The views discussed above tend to underestimate the importance that social class still has today. Class remains a common social identity, and in surveys many people continue to identify themselves with a social class. For example, the British Social Attitudes Survey published in 2007 found:

• 94 per cent of people identified themselves with a social class, with only 6 per cent saying they did not identify with any class

- 38 per cent of people identified themselves as middle class
- 57 per cent identified themselves as working class

In addition, those who suggest that identity is now formed around people's choices in leisure activities and consumer goods don't take adequate account of the fact that these are not free choices, but are influenced by their income. Sky-diving, swimming with dolphins, up-to-the-minute worn-once fashion clothing, lots of latte coffees, designer kitchens and exotic foreign holidays are not lifestyle options that are available to everyone. Social class is a major limitation on people choosing any identity they may wish.

Social class is still the major influence on people's standard of living and lifestyle, their chances of educational success, their health and life expectancy, their home ownership, their risks of unemployment and poverty, and other life chances. We may no longer be able to assume that social class is the key influence on people's identity. However, whether or not people express their identities in traditional terms of social class is one thing; to escape the influence of social class on identity formation is another thing altogether.

Gender and identity

One of the first questions we ask when someone has a baby is: 'Is it a boy or a girl?', and the sex of a person is one of the first things we notice about someone when we meet them for the first time.

Stratification by sex is a feature found in most societies, with men generally being in a more dominant position in society than women. Our sex has major influences on how we think about ourselves, how others think about us, and the opportunities and life chances open to us. This section will examine how the different gender identities of men and women are constructed by socialization in modern Britain, and how they might be changing.

Sex and gender

Sex refers to the biological differences between men and women, while **gender** refers to the culturally created differences between men and women which are learnt through socialization. A **gender role** is the pattern of behaviour which is expected from individuals of either sex. **Gender identity** refers to how people see themselves, and how others see them, in terms of their gender roles and biological sex.

The term **sex** (whether someone is male or female) refers to the natural or biological differences between men and women, such as differences in genitals, internal reproductive organs and body hair, while **gender** (whether someone is masculine or feminine) refers to the cultural, social and psychological socially constructed differences between the two sexes. It refers to the way a society encourages and teaches the two sexes to behave in different ways through socialization. These different ways of behaving, which society expects from individuals of either sex – how a boy/man or girl/woman should behave in society – are known as **gender roles**. **Gender identity** refers to how people see themselves, and others see them, in terms of their gender roles and biological sex – the meaning that being a man or a woman has to people.

Gender and biology

Our sexual or biological characteristics do not determine or decide gender roles and identities. We know this because although the biological differences between men and women are the same everywhere, the behaviour and identities adopted by men and women differ both within the same society, and between societies. Mead (2001) carried out research on three distinctly different tribes from New Guinea, which led her to believe that many so-called masculine and feminine characteristics are not based on fundamental sex differences, but reflect the cultural conditioning of different societies. She uncovered examples where male and female behaviour was quite different from that most commonly found in modern Britain. For example, in the Tchambuli tribe in New Guinea, the traditional gender roles found in modern Britain were reversed – it was the men who displayed what we might regard as traditional 'feminine' characteristics, such as doing the shopping and putting on make-up and jewellery to make themselves attractive. Women were the more aggressive, practical ones, who made the sexual advances to men and did all the trading.

Even in Britain today, there is a diversity of masculine and feminine behaviour, with both males and females adopting a range of identities. There are, for example, women who present themselves as very traditional feminine figures, while others are tomboyish, or tough as nails in girl gangs, or adopt masculine styles of hard drinking, yobbish 'ladettes'. Similarly, men may be sharing, caring, emotional 'New Men', 'macho' men and so on.

It is evidence like this that has led sociologists to conclude that masculine and feminine gender identities are primarily constructed through socialization,

Male and female babies have the same biological differences across the world, but socialization means there are wide variations in the ways boys and girls behave in different societies

rather than simply a result of the biological differences between men and women.

The significance of gender as a source of identity

Throughout our lives, our gender is an important source of identity. Whether we see ourselves as masculine or feminine, and which aspects of masculinity and femininity we identify ourselves with, influences how we think about ourselves, how we behave towards others, how others see us, the expectations they have of us and the way they treat us.

Having a feminine or masculine identity enables individuals to share things with others (like playing sport or going shopping) and gives people guidelines for identifying and relating to others like themselves, for example through the way they dress, the language they use, the way they sit, their body language, the way they style their hair and the activities they share. The particular gender identity people adopt marks them out as similar to some people and different from others, and they will generally adopt forms of behaviour which 'fit' the identities they construct.

While we may be able to some extent to influence the exact details of our own gender identities – after all, men and women do not display the same masculine and feminine characteristics in a uniform, unchanging way – the options available to us are not unlimited. We are influenced by agencies of socialization such as the family, the school, the peer group and the mass media, which frequently promote socially approved forms of masculine and feminine behaviour.

> ### Activity
>
> 1 List some of the socially approved ways that men and women are expected to behave, and how they should *not* behave, in contemporary Britain.
> 2 Suggest ways in which these expectations might be beginning to change.

A **stereotype** is a generalized, over-simplified view of the features of a social group, allowing for few individual differences among members of the group. The assumption is made that all members of the group share the same features. Examples of stereotypes include views such as 'all women are lousy drivers', 'all young people are vandals and layabouts' or 'the unemployed are all on the fiddle'.

A **hegemonic identity** is one that is so dominant that it makes it difficult for individuals to assert alternative identities.

Gender stereotypes and hegemonic gender identities in Britain

Gender differences are socially constructed by the agencies of socialization, which steer people towards gender stereotypes and encourage them to identify themselves with these stereotypes. A gender **stereotype** is a generalized view of the 'typical' or 'ideal' characteristics of men and women. The gender stereotype of men involves what Connell (1995) called a 'hegemonic masculinity', but we could also consider there to be a 'hegemonic femininity'. Some possible features of these are summarized in table 2.1 overleaf.

Table 2.1

Hegemonic masculine characteristics	Hegemonic feminine characteristics

Heterosexuality	**Heterosexuality**
Sexual dominance	Sexually passive (or a 'slapper' if sexually active)
Repression of emotions/emotional distance (except in sport, when males tend to get very emotional indeed)	Expression of emotions/emotional warmth, caring and sensitive
Physical strength/muscular/tall	Weak, fragile/small
Aggression	Gentleness and non-aggressive
Independence and self-reliance	Dependence (on men)
Competitiveness and ambition	Non-competitive
Lack of domesticity (housework and childcare) – only occasional practical DIY round home	Concerned with and responsible for housework and practical and emotional aspects of childcare
Rational and practical	Emotional and unpredictable
Risk taking	Avoids risk
Task-oriented – focus on 'doing things' like work success, playing sports, making things, DIY in the home or activities to escape from work	People-oriented – focus on forming and maintaining friendships, family, children, and 'customer care' (keeping customers happy)
Lack of concern with or interest in personal appearance, taste in dress or personal health and diet	Major concern with physical appearance (being slim and pretty), health, diet, dress sense, and attractiveness to men

Activity

1 Discuss the suggested features of the hegemonic stereotypes of masculinity and femininity shown in Table 2.1. To what extent do you think they give an accurate impression of gender characteristics in Britain? Back up your view with evidence of both child and adult behaviour.

2 Suggest ways that these stereotypes might be changing in modern Britain, with evidence drawn from areas such as work, education and the mass media to back up your view.

Heterosexuality involves a sexual orientation towards people of the opposite sex.
Sexual orientation refers to the type of people to whom individuals are either physically or romantically attracted, of the same or the opposite sex.

Girls and women who fail to identify themselves with and conform to the feminine stereotype are liable to be seen as 'tomboys', while men and boys who fail to conform to the masculine stereotype are likely to be seen as 'wimps' or 'sissies'. It is still the case that one of the worst taunts a male child can face, which is a challenge to his emerging masculine identity, is to be called 'girl' by his peer group.

Feminist sociologists particularly emphasize the ways the processes of socialization into these hegemonic masculine and feminine identities reproduce and reinforce male dominance (patriarchy), and make it difficult for either men or women to construct gender identities different from the hegemonic stereotypes.

The social construction of hegemonic gender identities through socialization

There is a wide range of primary and secondary agencies of socialization which establish traditional gender roles and mould males and females into the hegemonic gender identities. Examples of this are considered below, and summarized in figure 2.2 on page 70.

Gender stereotyping of the worst kind: this was how Mr Justice Harman responded when someone explained to him the difference between Miss, Mrs and Ms

The role of the family

Parents and relatives tend to hold stereotyped views of the typical or ideal characteristics of boys and girls, and they often try to bring up their children in accordance with their view of what they see as normal masculine or feminine behaviour. Oakley (1985) identifies four processes during primary socialization:

1 *Manipulation*: boys and girls are handled differently – e.g., boys are more likely to be bounced in physical play, with girls treated more gently and more likely to be cuddled.

2 *Canalization*: boys and girls are directed towards different toys and games – e.g., construction kits, cricket bats, footballs, chemistry sets, electronic toys, guns, cars and trucks, aeroplanes, and computer games for boys, developing the technological interest and technical and sporting skills regarded as part of a 'normal' masculine environment; sewing machines, dolls, prams, cookers, teasets, drawing books and playing with domestic technology like microwaves and vacuum cleaners for girls, developing the skills and interests reflected in their mothers' traditional roles in the kitchen and as nurturers. When girls play the role of nurse to their brother's doctor, or play with dolls and make-up and different types of clothing, and wear clothes bought by parents that are generally more colourful and pretty, while the boys get more practical clothing, they are learning adult gender stereotypes by mimicking them.

3 *Verbal appellations*: boys and girls are exposed to different language and praised or rebuked for different things – e.g., parental praise, such as 'you're a good boy or good girl', rewarding behaviour which is seen as appropriate for their gender.

4 *Differential activity exposure*: boys and girls are exposed to and encouraged to do different activities, for example by watching and imitating the role models provided by the usually different activities carried out by their fathers and mothers. Other examples include boys and girls being given different rules to follow, or jobs around the home – e.g., girls are more likely to do indoor housework, generally helping their mothers with domestic jobs, while boys are more likely to do outdoor jobs with their fathers, like cleaning the car, sweeping the paths and being shown how to do repairs and make things.

In what ways are gender identities formed through socialization and play in the early years?

The role of the school

The **hidden curriculum** refers to the attitudes and behaviour which are taught through the school's organization and teachers' attitudes, but which are not part of the formal timetable.

Much of this gender socialization goes on through the school's hidden curriculum. This consists of the hidden teaching of attitudes and behaviour, which are taught at school through the school's organization and teachers' attitudes but which are not part of the formal timetable. Examples of this include:

- Teachers' attitudes, with teachers traditionally encouraging boys more in sciences and computing, placing more emphasis on their progress than that of girls, giving different career advice to boys and girls, and treating disruptive, unruly behaviour by boys and girls differently.
- Subject choice: girls and boys have traditionally been counselled by parents and teachers into taking different subjects. Within the National Curriculum, girls are more likely to study home economics, textiles and food technology, while boys are more likely to choose electronics, woodwork or graphics technology. After the age of 16, other subject divisions still remain, with girls more likely to take arts subjects (like English literature, history and foreign languages) and boys more likely to choose the sciences. This gender division is also found in sport, with rugby and cricket for the boys and hockey and netball for the girls.

The importance of the peer group

Generally, people try to gain acceptance among their peers by conforming to the norms of their peer group, and this frequently involves conformity to stereotyped masculine or feminine identities. A boy, for example, who saw himself as a collector of soft toys would be quite likely to face ridicule from his peer group; a girl who identified herself as a rugby player or a boxer might be seen as a bit of a tomboy. There are also double standards in terms of the sexual aspects of masculine and feminine identities. Among teenage boys (and often adult men too), sexual promiscuity and sexual 'conquest' are encouraged and admired as approved masculine behaviour, and are seen as a means of achieving status in the male peer group. However, males – and other women – will condemn this same promiscuity among women – promiscuous girls and women are most likely to be seen as 'up for it', and have a spoiled identity of slappers, slags or sluts or some other insulting term assigned to them. Willis (1977) confirmed this in his study of a group of working-class 'lads'. The 'lads' constantly chased girls for sex, but then often dropped them, labelling them as 'loose' once they had had sex with the boys who had been after it. Girls and women who have sex outside some steady relationship are likely to find themselves condemned by men and women alike. In short, promiscuous men are seen as 'stags' or 'studs'; promiscuous women are seen as 'slags' or 'sluts'.

This double standard helps to encourage conformity to separate gender identities for men and women, with the stereotyped man as sexual athlete and woman as the passive and faithful lover, wife or girlfriend.

The role of the mass media

The mass media create and reinforce gender stereotypes in a number of ways. Comics, for example, present different images of men and women. Girls are usually presented as pretty, romantic, helpless, easily upset and emotional, and dependent on boys for support and guidance. Boys are presented as strong, independent, unemotional and assertive. Boys and girls are often presented in traditional stereotyped gender roles such as soldiers (boys) or nurses (girls). A similar pattern is shown on children's television, and much TV and other advertising show gender stereotypes. Around 80 per cent of TV advertising voice-overs are male voices – suggesting authority. The media, particularly advertising, often promotes the 'beauty myth' – the idea that women should be assessed primarily in terms of their appearance.

There are often very different types of story and magazine aimed at males and females. Romantic fiction is almost exclusively aimed at a female readership. A glance at the magazine shelves of any large newsagents will reveal different sections for 'women's interests' and 'men's interests', reflecting the different hegemonic masculine and feminine identities which men and women are encouraged to adopt. Women have been traditionally presented in the mass media in a limited number of stereotyped roles, for example:

Women are still primarily portrayed as sex objects in the 'red top' tabloid press and in men's magazines

- As a 'sex object': the image of the slim, sexually seductive, scantily clad figure typically found on page 3 of the *Sun* newspaper is used by the advertising industry to sell everything from peanuts to motorbikes and newspapers. 'Celebrity culture' provides strong role models for the ways girls should dress and behave, and 'supermodels' are the beauty queens of today, at a time when Miss World beauty contests are seen by many as redundant and unacceptable. Such imagery encourages women to believe the key to their happiness lies in how much they appeal to men sexually.
- In their relationships with men, such as bosses, husbands, and lovers.
- As emotional and unpredictable.
- In the housewife/mother role: as the content, capable, and caring housewife and mother, whose constant concern is with the whiteness of clothes, the cleanliness of floors, the evening meal, and as the person who keeps the family together and manages its emotions.

Men are presented in a wider range of roles, and men's magazines reflect interests that are seen as part of the hegemonic masculine identity. These

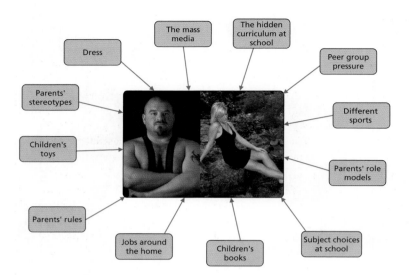

Figure 2.2 The social construction of hegemonic gender identities through socialization

include photography, stereos, computers, DIY and all manner of transport: cars, motorbikes, aircraft, trains and boats. The 'top shelf' soft-porn magazines are aimed exclusively at men.

Changing gender identities

As suggested earlier in this chapter, people are not simply robots or puppets. Both males and females play active roles in the construction of their gender identities and people are beginning to adopt and experiment with alternative gender identities. In recent years, there has been evidence of some change in traditional ideas about masculine and feminine gender identities, and related sexuality. Soap operas give us insights into lesbian and gay relationships, and other images of sexual identities with which we may not be very familiar. People are becoming more tolerant of gays and lesbians, and more accepting of cohabitation.

More males and females are adopting gender identities which combine elements of both genders, and these are constantly changing. We see more unisex hairstyles and clothing, more men wearing what were once seen as women's jewellery or women's clothes, and using a range of cosmetics. Some writers suggest that the old hegemonic conceptions of masculinity and femininity are outdated, and that more people are choosing to ignore the traditional gender stereotypes, and adopt new identities.

Changing female identities

Females are now doing better than males in education, and more positive role models are replacing traditional stereotypes in daily life and in the media.

Activity

1   Refer to figure 2.2, which shows a range of ways that hegemonic gender identities are constructed in modern Britain. Working in groups, take some of the ways and identify examples showing how gender stereotypes are constructed, and how these influence how people come to see themselves, and how others see them.

2   Look at the following list of words, and divide them into *three* groups: those you might use to describe women, those you might use to describe men, and those you might use to describe both men and women.

clever	passive	sulky	thoughtful	bastard
powerful	assertive	gentle	caring	attractive
bimbo	emotional	gossip	elegant	soft
aggressive	pretty	tart	kind	tender
cold	sweet	logical	quiet	competitive
sly	ruthless	delicate	brave	active
muscular	bitchy	weak	clinging	slag
domineering	slim	submissive	frigid	gracious
hideous	hunk	handsome	raving	plain
hysterical	blonde	beautiful	player	stud
cute	babe	fit	mover	dickhead
loose	dog	trophy bird	easy	slut

3   Now compare the two lists of words used to describe men and women. Do they present gender stereotypes? You will probably have found there are some words in both lists that have a similar meaning. Why are some words generally restricted to one gender? Discuss why these words are not used to describe both sexes, and how they show stereotyped assumptions about women and men. Consider generally the way language is used to create gender identities.

Women are becoming more successful than men in many areas of the labour market, such as in the music industry and in business and the professions, like law and medicine. Girls and women often have better 'people' and communication skills than men, and these are the skills that are required for success in the new service economy – dealing with customers, orders, clients and complaints. The traditional stereotype of women as mothers and carers, with prime responsibility for running the home and family, is being replaced by role models of strong, independent and successful women in all spheres of life. With women's growing labour market success, the traditional idea of a single main male family breadwinner is being undermined, and as women's independent income increases, their financial need for marriage reduces. A woman no longer needs a man, through marriage and the family, to achieve status in society. There is now a new and wider range of roles for women, and as traditional stereotypes are eroded, so women can choose from a range of feminine identities: 'being feminine' can increasingly mean a lot of different things.

Some argue that traditional feminine identities are being eroded, and that there is some convergence, or growing similarity, between masculine and feminine identities. For example, there has been the emergence of 'ladettes' – females taking on aspects of lads' masculinity associated with loutishness and loudness, heavy drinking and aggressive sexuality in both dress and behaviour. There has been the emergence of increasingly violent girl gangs, and a 2006 World Health Organization survey found British girls were among the most violent in the world, with nearly one in three Scottish and English adolescents admitting to having been involved in a fight in the past year, and it seemed likely these high levels of violence among adolescent girls were linked to binge drinking and 'ladette' culture.

Changing male identities

The traditional power of men in the family and the labour market, and in society generally, is, some suggest, being challenged by women's growing success and equality. Men used to establish their identities through the public world of work and as family breadwinners, and women through the private realm of family and home. However, women are becoming increasingly assertive and successful in a wide range of areas, and they can now do everything men can do, and they are often doing it more successfully. At the same time, the prospects for young men are diminishing:

- Males are underachieving in education.
- Traditional employment in 'macho' manual work is disappearing, with the closure of traditional heavy industries, such as mining, shipbuilding, and steel.
- Women are increasingly doing better than men in the labour market, particularly in the new service industries.
- Men's dominant position in the family, as main breadwinner and decision-maker, is increasingly under threat with the rise of women's equality and their independent incomes: 70 per cent of divorces are initiated by women, and more women are choosing to remain single and childless; marriage and parenthood are in decline; advances in technology are reducing men's role in reproduction, and women can now have children without the necessity of a male partner.
- Equal opportunities laws and policies, and independent taxation and equality in pensions have all undermined male power.

'New Men' and other male identities   Since the 1980s there has been speculation about the emergence of a so-called 'New Man', who was allegedly more caring, sharing, gentle, emotional, sensitive in his attitudes to women, children and his own emotional needs, and willing to do his fair share of housework. Love, family, personal relations and getting in touch with his own emotions were meant to be more important than achieving career success and power in the family and society. Male bodies are now emerging in advertising as sex objects to sell things, in much the same way women's bodies have always been used. New emerging masculine identities are becoming more concerned with appearance (a traditional feminine concern): 8 per cent of cosmetic surgery is now carried out on men, and the proportion is rising, with the growing use by men of face lifts, 'nose jobs' and 'tummy tucking', and beauty treatments such as facials and waxing to remove body hair. An *Observer* and Nivea for Men survey in 2004 found that 83 per cent of men were fairly or extremely interested in their own physical appearance, and 21 per cent of men had been in the past or were currently on a diet. The male grooming market has grown by 800 per cent since 1998. Recent research shows that males of all ages are now worrying about their appearance. A survey of teenage boys by a teen magazine in 2005 said that they agonized about their physique as much as teenage girls did. The growth of eating disorders, like anorexia, among men, and Men's Health weeks suggest a new concern with men's health and attractiveness.

New and ever-changing male identities are often created by the mass media, and marketing campaigns by big business to sell new products, and these open up the range of identity choices for men. Apart from the New Man, other identities that have made appearances in the mass media include:

- *New Lad* – a reaction against the New Man, and associated with the 'yob culture' of aggressive and promiscuous sex, lager, football and loutishness.
- *New Bloke* – a New Lad who has become a recent father, but who as well as hanging around the pub is also to be found changing nappies.
- *New Dad* – a New Man who discovers the joys of fatherhood.
- *Emo Boy* – a version of the New Man, who reads books, appreciates the arts, watches his diet, isn't afraid to show his emotions, and dresses with more care and style than most girls, usually in tight sweaters and pants.
- *Metrosexuals* – heterosexual men who embrace their feminine side, are in touch with their feelings, use moisturiser and designer cosmetic products, who have refined tastes in clothing, and incorporate elements of the gay lifestyle.

Activity

1 Suggest *two* ways in each case that (a) men and (b) women might use gender representations in the mass media as a source of personal identity and meaning.
2 Try to identify *three* examples of how men are being represented more as sex objects in the contemporary mass media, including advertising.
3 Drawing on your own experiences of the mass media, discuss examples of the ways new masculine and feminine identities might be emerging in contemporary society.

Are more men now 'new Dads' and involved in the care of their children? How does this challenge traditional conceptions of hegemonic masculinity?

The rise of the gay movement and the growth of anti-sexist ideas have further contributed to the undermining of men's traditional role, and opened up the possibility for aspects of masculine identity to merge with aspects of traditional femininity.

Is there a crisis of masculinity?

Though the New Man has turned out to be a very rare specimen, with the New Lad emerging in the 2000s as a reaction against the New Man, men are said to be facing anxiety, uncertainty and confusion about what their role and identity is in today's society. A growing sense of insecurity accompanies the loss of men's sense of purpose in relation to the traditional hegemonic masculine identity of what Gilmore (1991) described as 'the provider, the protector and the impregnator'. Mac an Ghaill (1994) argues that the changes discussed above, summarized in figure 2.3, are creating a 'crisis of masculinity', with men feeling lost and searching for a gender identity that fits in the modern world.

Is gender still an important source of identity?

The material above suggests that gender identities may be changing and becoming much more fluid, with both men and women having a wider choice in the gender identities available to them. Postmodernists, as will be seen later, suggest that people are now free to choose any identity they like, without the constraints of gender identities.

Figure 2.3 A crisis of masculinity?

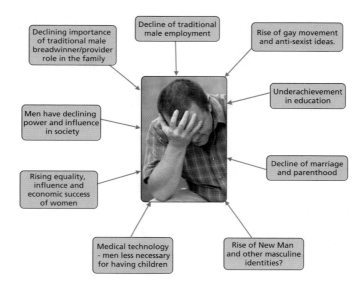

Declining importance of traditional male breadwinner/provider role in the family

Decline of traditional male employment

Rise of gay movement and anti-sexist ideas.

Underachievement in education

Men have declining power and influence in society

Decline of marriage and parenthood

Rising equality, influence and economic success of women

Medical technology - men less necessary for having children

Rise of New Man and other masculine identities?

However, it is easy to exaggerate the extent of the changes. The narrow, stereotyped gender roles of thirty years ago are still held by many of today's children, and many still grow up forming their identities around these stereotypes. People may have more choice today over the elements of masculinity and femininity they adopt, but traditional gender roles have not changed as much as we might like to think. Women still earn less than men, and still do most of the housework, childcare and emotional work in the family. The majority of women still strive to conform to the hegemonic femininity discussed earlier in this chapter, and often have feelings of guilt and inadequacy when their physical appearance and sense of self fail to 'measure up' to this stereotype. Similarly, most men still conform to the fairly typical, 'unreconstructed' hegemonic masculinity. There is still some way to go before people are so freed from the constraints of gender role socialization and social pressures to conform that they can 'pick and mix' their gender identities in any way they wish, or reject it altogether as a source of identity.

Activity

1 Explain what is meant by a 'crisis of masculinity'. To what extent do you think there is such a crisis? Give reasons for your answer.
2 Suggest evidence for the view that there is a new femininity emerging, which is more assertive and less dependent on men.
3 Suggest *three* arguments for, and three against, the view that there is a 'New Man' emerging.
4 Write a short essay, about one side of A4 paper, answering the following question: *Examine the extent to which traditional gender identities are changing.*

Sexuality and identity

Gender, sexuality and 'normal sex'

Like gender identity, sexual behaviour is socially constructed, and what counts as normal sexual behaviour, or 'normal sex', is part of the culture of any society and established through the socialization process. For example, in ancient Greece, homosexuality among men was seen as part of normal everyday sex. In contemporary Britain, the dominant view of normal sexuality is that of heterosexuality, which is a central aspect of the hegemonic masculine and feminine identities discussed in the previous section. In the case of women, this is particularly linked to romance and/or steady and meaningful personal relationships.

Sexuality has always been a central part of the hegemonic feminine identity, as women have been defined, in Britain and other Western countries, by their physical attractiveness and sexual appeal to men. Women have traditionally been regarded as sex objects, subjected to the 'male gaze', particularly in the mass media, like the top-shelf soft-porn magazines, page 3 of the *Sun* newspaper, in advertising, and through media pictures and stories of the exploits of female celebrities. In terms of normal sex, it is worth recalling the point that was made earlier – that there is still a double standard of sexual morality for men and women, with sexually promiscuous females likely to be condemned by both sexes.

Changing sexual identities

In recent years, the physical appearance and 'sex appeal' aspects of sexuality long associated with femininity have become a more important part of masculinity as well. New alternative masculine identities appear to be emerging, with the rise of the gay movement and the growing crisis of masculinity opening up new choices for men. This is reflected in much of the material in the earlier discussion on gender. Men's increasing concerns with things like their appearance and attractiveness, their body size and shape, their diet, their health and their dress sense; their growing use of cosmetics and cosmetic surgery; and the increase in eating disorders among men – all point to men's rising concern with sexual attractiveness.

Men's bodies have also become much more sexualized, with more naked men's bodies appearing in the media and advertising on a greater scale than ever before, with a growing importance attached to men's physical body image, rather than just women's.

An example of this, almost paralleling the traditional obsession with women's breasts, was the media obsession with 'moobies' (men's boobs) in

> **Homosexuality** involves a sexual orientation towards people of the same sex, with lesbian women attracted to other women, and gay men attracted to other men.
> **Sexuality** refers to people's sexual characteristics and their sexual behaviour.

the 2000s. This began with the *Sun* newspaper publishing in 2005 a 'Hall of Shame' series of pictures showing the different shapes and sizes of famous men's breasts, and making disparaging comments about them. Other tabloid newspapers soon followed with criticisms of flabby stomachs – 'holiday podges' – and love handles.

The release of *Casino Royale* in 2006, with actor Daniel Craig appearing as the new James Bond, was met with endless comments about Craig's body, and how he appeared mostly naked more than anyone else in the film, where even 'the hotsy-totsy women kept their kits on', as one reviewer put it, with 'Craig's ripped pecs being the most public symbol of British masculinity'.

The point is that men are beginning to face similar physical scrutiny by both women and other men as women always have. As McRobbie (1994) put it: 'The beauty stakes have gone up for men, and women have taken up the position of active viewers.'

Stigmatized or spoiled sexual identities

Individuals whose view of themselves – their conception of self – is that reflected in the hegemonic gender identities discussed earlier are likely to regard sexuality outside 'normal sex', such as homosexuality, as deviant activities, and those practising them as having stigmatized or spoiled identities. The consequences of this for gay men and lesbians include hostility in pubs, clubs and in the street, bullying at school, mockery in the mass media (anti-gay jokes, for example) and discrimination in employment. Some forms of sexuality, such as paedophilia, sado-masochism, transvestitism, necrophilia and some forms of exhibitionism, can be even more stigmatized. It is for this reason that many forms of sexuality which do not conform with normal sex are concealed, with practitioners using what Goffman called 'impression management' to conceal these aspects of their sexuality from others, to prevent them from becoming part of their public identity, and the stigmatization that would accompany it.

Gay and lesbian identities

In Britain, stigmatization of homosexual identities, particularly of gay men, is reducing, and is much diminished compared to what it once was. There is more fluidity about sexual identity, and new identities are emerging with more TV soaps and dramas featuring gay and lesbian relationships. However, the changes are fairly recent, particularly in relation to the law. While lesbianism has never been specifically against the law in the UK, it was only in 1968 that it became legal for there to be sexual relations between men over the age of 21 in England and Wales, with Scottish men having to wait until 1980. The age of consent for gay men only became the same as for heterosexual adults

Many people are now more tolerant of gay and lesbian relationships, and there is a wider range of sexual identities available today, particularly for men

(age 16) in 2000, and it was as recently as 2005 that gay and lesbian couples were allowed to achieve the same legal status as heterosexual married couples by forming civil partnerships.

The rise of the gay movement, the importance of gay spending (the 'pink pound') and newly emerging forms of masculinity have overcome much of the stigma attached to male homosexuality, as well as weakening the sense of difference and opposition between gay and straight masculine identities. In this sense, masculine sexual identity has become more fluid and changeable, and homosexuality much more widely accepted.

As a result of the gay movement, gay people who 'come out' (openly declare themselves to be gay) and participate in the gay subculture now have a wide range of sexual identities open to them beyond the effeminate 'gay' or 'butch' stereotypes found in the media, such as 'camp' queens, macho men, cross-dressers, gay cowboys, leather boys, etc.

A note of caution

There is some evidence that attitudes to sexuality have become more relaxed, with wider acceptance of homosexuality and bisexuality, and people having more freedom to choose from a range of sexual identities. However, it is important not to exaggerate the extent of these changes. The norms of sexual behaviour, and the sexual identities arising from them, are still constructed by the agencies of socialization, and homosexuality, let alone other sexual practices, is still regarded as deviant by most people. Homophobia, an irrational fear of or aversion to homosexuals, is still very common.

Queer Bashing, a national survey by Stonewall of hate crimes against lesbians and gay men, found that one in three gay men and one in four lesbians had experienced at least one violent attack in the period between 1990 and 1996, and because of fear of becoming the victim of homophobic violence, 65 per cent of respondents always or sometimes avoided telling people they were gay. Of those aged under 18, 90 per cent had experienced verbal abuse,

Bisexuality involves a sexual orientation towards people of both sexes.

Homophobia is an irrational fear of or aversion to homosexuals.

and 48 per cent violence, because of their sexuality. A 2007 survey by Stonewall found that while nine out of ten people supported laws to protect gay people, almost one in six adults in Britain had seen gay or lesbian colleagues being physically or verbally bullied at work as a direct result of their sexuality.

Women are still very much more likely to be seen as sex objects than men, particularly in pornography, with even young boys and girls widely exposed to sexualized images of females. Porn now seems quite deeply embedded, through the internet and mobile phone technology, in the culture of young men. In 2007, the Sex Education Forum found that half of children using the internet were exposed to porn and that almost a third of children receive unwanted sexual comments via email, instant messaging or text. It does then still appear that men have more choice in choosing their sexual identities than women, who remain constrained by traditional stereotypes.

Activity

1 With examples, suggest ways that advertising, the mass media and shop displays show a sexual image of men today.
2 Do you think that men are as concerned with their physical appearance as women?
3 To what extent do you think that young people today have more freedom to express their sexuality?
4 To what extent have you been aware of gay and lesbian relationships in contemporary soap and reality TV shows?
5 Do you think there is now less stigma attached to 'non-normal' sexuality?

Ethnicity and identity

Ethnicity refers to the shared culture of a social group which gives its members a common identity in some ways different from other social groups.

Ethnicity is not the same as race or skin colour, as there are many groups that may appear physically similar, but belong to different ethnic groups. For example, the English and the Scots, or Indian Sikhs and Pakistani Muslims. Everyone has an ethnicity, with the largest ethnic group in Britain being white British, though the concept of ethnicity is generally used in everyday life in connection with minority ethnic groups, such as African Caribbean, Indian Asian, Chinese and Polish ethnic groups in Britain.

A **minority ethnic group** is a social group that shares a cultural identity which is different from that of the majority population of a society.

What is meant by an ethnic identity?

An ethnic identity is one where individuals assert their identity primarily in terms of the ethnic group and culture to which they belong, including values, beliefs, traditions, language, diet, dress and religious ideas. It is this that gives them meaning and a sense of belonging with others like themselves. Ethnicity is just one identity, and individuals can adopt more than one identity depending on the social context in which they find themselves. For example, British Asians may have multiple identities, adopting an Asian identity at home, a 'white mask' identity (adopting the features of white culture and 'acting white') at school or in other situations, and seeing themselves as very fashionable, with designer gear and awesome musical tastes and so on in their leisure and consumption patterns. These multiple identities, sometimes merging into 'hybrid' identities (discussed below) help them to fit into the different communities and social groups in which they find themselves.

Ethnic identity is formed and transmitted from one generation to the next by agencies of socialization, such as the family, religious institutions, and the mass media.

Activity

1 Identify and explain, with examples, *three* ways in each case that (a) the family, (b) religious institutions, (c) the mass media and (d) peer groups might form ethnic identities and pass them on from one generation to the next.
2 Explain what you understand by a 'white mask' identity, and suggest ways that people from minority ethnic groups might adopt such an identity. Why might they do this?

Diaspora and globalization

Diaspora is the dispersal of an ethnic population from its original homeland, and its spreading out across the world, while retaining cultural and emotional ties to its area or nation of origin. Diaspora suggests that a dispersed ethnic population adopts two (or more) ethnic identities: it will retain some links to its original culture and heritage, while also adopting elements of the culture of the host societies in which individuals now live, and manoeuvres between them. An example might be the Sikh community in Britain maintaining close links with family and culture in the Punjab region of India, speaking Punjabi and observing Sikh customs at home, and speaking English and adopting what may be radically different peer group values and norms at school or college.

Globalization, including the impact of the global mass media and popular culture, also means that cultures may be beginning to lose their separate identities. With diaspora and globalization, different cultures interact, and new cultural and ethnic **hybrid identities** emerge, formed from a mix of other identities. For example, the diaspora created by the centuries of slavery, and

Diaspora is the dispersal of an ethnic population from its original homeland, and its spreading out across the world, while retaining cultural and emotional ties to its area or nation of origin.

A **hybrid identity** is a new identity formed from a mix of two or more other identities.

In what-way does this picture suggest a hybrid identity? What other hybrid identities are you aware of?

the mass emigration in the 1950s and '60s from the Caribbean and the Indian subcontinent, means that black and Asian populations are now dispersed around the globe, and in Britain new ethnic identities like British Asian, Brasian, black British and Muslim British have emerged.

Some minority ethnic people may adopt a 'white mask' as part of their hybrid identity. This involves playing down their own ethnicity and culture, and adopting features of white culture in some circumstances. This may be a response to racism, and a means of 'fitting in' in social situations, and gaining acceptance in groups and communities which they might otherwise find difficult to achieve.

Changing ethnic identities: new ethnicities and hybrid ethnic identities

Hall (1992) suggests that ethnic identities are becoming harder to identify, with globalization and diaspora merging cultures and creating 'new ethnicities'. For example, African Caribbean music and dress are now popular among Punjabi and Bengali males, minority ethnic cultures are becoming integrated into mainstream culture, such as in reggae, hip hop and rap music, as well as in dress and diets. Burdsey (2004) found evidence of the consumption of designer clothes, recreational drugs and other leisure activities among young British Asians that was previously associated with young white and black males.

People of all ethnic groups are drawing on a range of cultures to create either new hybrid ethnic identities (this is called 'hybridization'), or multiple identities. Ethnic identity is also becoming more confused by new, predominantly British-born, ethnic minorities, with more children born to parents of inter-ethnic partnerships, involving a fusion of two ethnic groups. Bradford (2006) showed that the mixed ethnic group in the United Kingdom included children of white and black Caribbean parents, white and Asian parents and white and black African parents, as well as a number of other mixed identities. The majority of people who had a mixed ethnic identity had a white parent and were born in Britain. For such groups, it is difficult to establish whether they identify themselves as having a white ethnic identity drawn from one parent, an identity arising from the ethnic minority group of the other parent, or whether they see themselves as having a new hybrid identity drawing on both parental ethnic groups.

Ethnicity as resistance

Ethnicity as an identity has often been asserted as a way of resisting racism and disadvantage, especially among younger south Asian and African Caribbeans. By asserting an ethnic identity and drawing on the strengths of their cultures, they can resist their denial of status and the devaluing of their own culture by racism. They may seek to reclaim their identity through, for example, embracing Islam, or other aspects derived from their cultures of origin.

Ethnic identities in Britain

What follows below are brief profiles of some of the main ethnic identities in Britain today. Britain is a multicultural society, with a wide diversity of ethnic groups, and as Trevor Phillips (2007), Chair of the Commission for Equality and Human Rights, pointed out: 'There are more and more different kinds of people rubbing up against each other than at any time in human history.'

Some minority ethnic groups have fairly distinctive cultures, with relatively clear customs and values to draw on in constructing their ethnic identities, like the Indian Asian community. Others have more hybrid identities drawing on a range of cultures, as discussed above. Minority ethnic groups in Britain are, however, limited in their attempts to establish the identity they might want, as they may face racist stereotypes fuelled by labelling by teachers, an ethnocentric school curriculum, negative reporting by the media, unfair treatment by the police and the refusal of some white British people to regard them as British at all, or to see them *only* in terms of their ethnicity (whether they want to be seen that way or not).

Ethnocentrism is a view of the world in which other cultures are seen through the eyes of one's own culture, with a devaluing of the others.

White identities

The identities of white people in Britain are largely taken-for-granted, as much of British society and the main agencies of socialization promote and favour white people and their culture. White people do not generally need to assert their identities as they have the power in society that minority ethnic groups lack, and do not face the racism, discrimination and devaluing of their culture that minority ethnic groups experience. The assertion of a white identity is also associated with racism, and the sense that white people are superior to other ethnic groups. This is promoted by right-wing groups like the British National Party, which seek aggressively to promote a British and white identity based on a 'pure white Britishness' that has probably never really existed, but which excludes other ethnic identities. It is also worth pointing out that 'white' is not an ethnic group with a shared culture, history and national identity. There are different cultural traditions and different identities amongst the English, Scottish, Irish, Welsh and Polish communities in Britain, for example.

African Caribbean identities

Gilroy (1993, 2002) believes there is no single black identity or black culture, but that the historical experience of slavery affects the perceptions of black people, and black identity and culture have roots in the 'Black Atlantic' – a cultural network and source of support to black people, spanning Africa, the Americas, the Caribbean and Britain, reflecting the diaspora of slavery and its legacy. For second-generation younger African Caribbeans, who were born in Britain, certain styles of dress and tastes in music, like hip hop and reggae, the use of the patois dialect, dreadlocks and a sense of pride in their black skin as a form of resistance to racism all help to establish a distinctive black identity. This may be reinforced by distinctive black subcultures, like Rastafarianism, or the anti-school subculture discussed in research by Fuller (1980) among African Caribbean girls in a London comprehensive school. Fuller saw this black anti-school subculture as a means for the girls to resist and overcome negative stereotyping by teachers.

Asian identities

It is simplistic to talk of an 'Asian identity', as there is a diversity of different Asian groups, with important differences between them. Modood et al. (1994) carried out a study using interviews and group discussions to explore what ethnic identity meant to people of Caribbean or South Asian origin. The authors suggest that the identity of the various Asian groups is defined in terms of their different cultures, languages and religions. In Britain, the largest Asian groups include Indian Asians, Bangladeshis and Pakistanis. Extended families and arranged marriages are common to all these groups, as well as enjoyment of Bollywood films (Bollywood is the name given to the Mumbai-based Hindi-language film industry in India) and Bhangra music and dance. However, there are differences between these groups. They speak different languages (Punjabi, Hindi, Gujarati, Urdu), have different diets (Hindus eat no beef, Muslims eat halal food – food that is permissible according to Islamic law, with no pork or alcohol), have different religions (Hindu, Sikh and Muslim) and religious institutions (mosques and temples), and celebrate different festivals, such as Ramadan by Muslims and Divali for the Hindus, and often have different forms of dress, such as turbans for men and veils for women.

Religion is particularly important in the different Asian groups, and religious institutions frequently provide a focus for community life as well as religious belief. Of particular significance here is the worldwide growth of Islam, and their religion is an important part of the identity of British Muslims. For many young Pakistani Muslims, Islam and its symbols and values have become central features in building a positive identity which they see as otherwise denied to them by a white, racist, **Islamophobic** British culture. This is discussed below.

Those wishing to assert their ethnicity as their main source of identity are likely to emphasize aspects of their minority ethnic cultures in their 'impression management' to others. This is illustrated by Mirza et al. (2007), when they suggested the growing popularity for wearing of the hijab (headscarf) by Muslim girls was not due to family or religious pressure or about preserving a cultural tradition, but mostly influenced by 'peer behaviour or pressure and a sense that the headscarf marks out one's identity as a Muslim. This is a statement of difference, perhaps more than a desire to be religious.' The hijab is essentially a statement of identity: 'This is who I am, these are my values, and this is the group I identify with.'

> **Islamophobia** is an irrational fear and/or hatred of or aversion to Islam, Muslims or Islamic culture.

Mirza et al. suggest that the growing popularity for wearing the hijab (headscarf) by Muslim girls is not driven by religious pressure, but by peer pressure, and is essentially a means of marking out the group they identify with

Changing Asian identities

Among the younger Asian generations, Johal (1998) suggests there is evidence of the emergence of two new ethnic identities – British Asians and 'Brasians'. British Asians have two identities – the Asian one they inherit through socialization from their family and ethnic group, and the British one they learn through the agencies of secondary socialization and living daily life in British society. British Asians adopt whichever identity is appropriate for the context in which they find themselves. 'Brasians' (a term derived from

---

Activity

1 Those wishing to assert their ethnicity as their main source of identity are likely to emphasize aspects of their ethnic cultures in their 'impression management' to others. With reference to the pictures below, identify *five* 'symbols' that people might use to project their ethnic identity to others.
2 Identify *three* cultural features associated with the identities of three different minority ethnic groups in Britain, and *three* with the ethnic majority group (white British).
3 To what extent do you think there are new hybrid ethnic identities emerging in modern Britain? Give examples.

both 'British' and 'Asian') involves a single new hybrid identity drawing on and fusing or blending both British and Asian cultures. This entails elements of both cultures, but with a strong dimension of personal choice, and 'picking and mixing' between them to forge a new identity. For example, the religious beliefs of Brasians might be important to them, but they might expect to marry whomsoever they wish, rather than have an arranged marriage or a partner from the same ethnic or religious group, and they may not necessarily follow traditional customs, such as constraints over diet, drinking alcohol or dress. Butler's (1995) interviews with 18–30-year-old Muslim women in Bradford and Coventry showed that while the family and religion remained important in shaping the identities of young Muslim women, these women were also attempting to mould a new identity with more independence. They were seeking the same opportunities in terms of education and careers and the same legal equality as white British women, and challenging some of the restrictions that traditional Asian Muslim culture imposed on them, while still having some attachment to the values of their culture.

'Muslim' – a stigmatized identity?

Since the later years of the twentieth century, there has been a huge international surge in Islam, particularly Islamic fundamentalism. Islamic fundamentalism has become associated with the removal of Western, particularly American, 'decadent' cultural influences, changes in the position of women (such as the wearing of veils, being banned from driving and going out in public unaccompanied, and being refused access to some education and occupations), and the establishment of Islamic law involving legal punishments which to most Western eyes are barbaric, such as public flogging, beheading or the amputation of the hands of persistent thieves. The atrocities of the Taliban regime in Afghanistan in the 1990s, the worldwide terrorist network of Al-Qaeda, which was responsible for the bombing of the Twin Towers in New York in 2001 and behind the London bombings in July 2005, and the media reporting of the activities of a tiny minority of Muslims in Britain have all formed the basis for the stereotyping in the popular imagination of all Muslims. As a result, the identity 'Muslim' has practically become a stigmatized identity, which brings with it harassment and fear for many Muslims who have little sympathy with Islamic Fundamentalism, much less terrorism of any kind. As Phillips pointed out, the balance of media reporting of Muslims in the 2000s was such 'that the very word "Muslim" is conjuring up images of terrorism and extremist preachers, rather than Mrs Ahmed down the road, who might be the mother of your son's best friend'.

Research among Muslims living in Britain suggests that 'Mrs Ahmed down the road' is in fact far more typical than the media might suggest: according to a 2005 Mori poll conducted for the *Sun* newspaper, 86 per cent felt strongly

Fundamentalism is a return to the literal meaning of religious texts and associated behaviour.

that they belonged to Britain, and felt part of British society. Mirza et al. (2007) found:

- 59 per cent of Muslims preferred to live under British law, compared to 28 per cent who would prefer to live under sharia (Muslim) law
- 59 per cent felt they had as much, if not more, in common with non-Muslims in Britain as with Muslims abroad
- 84 per cent believed they had been treated fairly in British society
- The majority of British Muslims were moderates who accepted the norms of Western democracy.

This research suggests that the stigmatizing stereotyping of Muslims by non-Muslims may be wholly unjustified, and may actually generate resentment among them because of the way in which they and their beliefs are treated.

Activity

1 Explain what is meant by diaspora, and why this might lead to the emergence of hybrid ethnic identities.
2 What tensions do you think there might be for young people from minority ethnic or mixed ethnic backgrounds seeking to establish their identities in a predominantly white culture?
3 Suggest reasons why asserting an ethnic identity might help people from minority ethnic backgrounds resist the effects of racism.
4 Explain what is meant by a 'stigmatized identity'.
5 To what extent do you agree with the suggestion that a Muslim identity may have become a stigmatized identity in contemporary Britain? Give reasons for your answer.

Nationality and identity

What is nationality?

> A **nation** is a particular geographical area with which a group of people identify, and share among themselves a sense of belonging based on a common sense of culture, history and usually language. A **nation-state** is a nation which has its own independent government controlling a geographical area. **Nationality** is having citizenship of a nation-state, including things like voting rights, a passport, and the right of residence.

Hall (1992) suggests that every **nation** has a collection of stories, images and symbols about its shared experiences, which people draw on to construct and express their national identity. Examples might include a flag, a national anthem, festivals, national heroes and stories, national sports teams, national drinks or foods (in Britain, perhaps tea and fish and chips?), national dress or music. A national identity is formed by the agencies of socialization, through which it is passed from one generation to the next. A nation may or may not be a **nation-state**. Most of those living within a nation-state will have citizenship, which gives people their legal **nationality**.

Nationality usually involves the rights and responsibilities attached to being a citizen, with rights such as being able to access government services like health care and education, having a passport and the right of residence, and responsibilities such as obeying the law and paying taxes. Nationality is most commonly based on place of birth or marriage, but can also be achieved by naturalization, where people choose their nationality after meeting legal requirements.

Nationality as a source of identity

Generally, having a particular nationality involves a national identity. National identity usually involves a sense of belonging to a nation-state and sharing things in common with others of the same nationality, and a consciousness of differences with those of other nationalities.

National identity and nationalism are usually linked to nationality and membership of a nation-state, but this is not necessarily the case. For example, the British nation-state includes the nations of England, Scotland, Wales and Northern Ireland, together forming the United Kingdom. Citizens of the British state all have British nationality, but they do not all have this nationality as their main source of national identity. There is a growing sense of nationalism and national identity within the countries making up the British state, and a declining number of people are identifying themselves as 'British', adopting instead distinct English, Scottish or Welsh identities, or regional identity in Northern Ireland. This process has resulted in elected Assemblies for Wales and Northern Ireland, and a Parliament for Scotland. These have further accelerated the growth of nationalism and national identities in these countries. This was shown when the Scottish National Party became the largest party in the Scottish Parliament in 2007, fuelling speculation about growing independence for Scotland, and the Welsh nationalist party, Plaid Cymru, becoming the second largest party in the Welsh Assembly.

> **Nationalism** involves a sense of pride and commitment to a nation, and a very strong sense of national identity.

What is meant by a British identity?

Britain is made up of a wide variety of ethnic groups, including the Welsh, Irish, Scottish, English, Poles, Indian-, Bangladeshi- and Pakistani-Asians and African Caribbeans, so it can sometimes be difficult to identify a specific British identity and a British culture, and a national identity shared by all citizens. What is sometimes suggested as making up 'British culture' or a 'British identity' may just be a reflection of the ability of those with power to impose their view of 'Britishness' on the rest of society.

It is relatively easy to describe some British national symbols, like the Queen, the Union Jack flag and the British passport, and some common cultural bonds like the English language (though British minority ethnic groups, including the Welsh, have their own languages too). However, identifying features of 'Britishness' beyond these becomes quite difficult. The 2004 British

Social Attitudes survey found that most people now define Britishness as speaking English, holding citizenship and respecting the country's laws and institutions.

> **Activity**
>
> 1 Suggest *two* examples, with explanation, of how each of the following helps to form and promote a British identity that is different from other national identities: (a) the family, (b) the education system, (c) the mass media, (d) religious institutions, (e) sport.
> 2 The photos below show the flags of England, Scotland, Wales, the United Kingdom and the European Union. Carry out a small survey and ask people which flag they most closely identify themselves with, and try to draw up some conclusions about people's national identity.

Symbols of national and European identity

Surveys have found that many children from all cultural and class backgrounds have no strong sense of a British identity. In 2007 there were plans for secondary schools in England to be made to teach more British history to help pupils have a better understanding of their own identity. These were to include lessons on the Commonwealth and Empire, the slave trade and conflicts like those in Northern Ireland as part of citizenship education, alongside learning about British heritage and supposedly core British values like tolerance, respect, freedom of speech and justice, and the rule of law.

This idea of 'Britishness' and 'British values' was echoed in 2007 by future Prime Minister Gordon Brown. He commented: 'It is very important to recognise that Britishness and Britain itself is not based on ethnicity and race. It is founded on shared values that we hold in common: a commitment to liberty for all, a commitment to social responsibility shown by all, and a commitment to fairness to all.' However, it is difficult to see these values as being a defining feature of British identity, as they are found in all Western democratic countries. It is equally difficult to identify a history that is shared by all Britons. For example, British history is littered with battles between the English and the Scots and Irish, and the history of the British Empire is not something that black and minority ethnic Britons are likely to want to relate to, with its associations with slavery and exploitation of non-white peoples.

The British Home Office has devised a 'Life in the UK Test' for those wishing to apply for British citizenship, which is meant to identify features of 'British-ness' that immigrants should be familiar with. However, it is doubtful whether even most people who were born and bred in Britain would pass the test. The activity below includes some of the sample questions available on the Home Office website.

Activity

1 Suggest *three* ceremonies and *three* symbols which you think show a *British* national identity.

2 The following questions are samples from the UK government's 'Life in the UK Test'. You can read more about this at <www.lifeintheuktest.gov.uk>. Try to answer the questions, and discuss whether you think they are a fair test of 'Britishness'.

   (a) Where have migrants come from in the past and why?

   (b) Do women have equal rights and has this always been the case?

   (c) Do many children live in single-parent families or step-families? When do children leave home?

   (d) When do children take tests at school? How many go on to higher education?

   (e) What are the minimum ages for buying alcohol and tobacco? What drugs are illegal?

   (f) What is the census and how is census data collected and used?

   (g) How many people belong to an ethnic minority and which are the largest minority groups? Where are there large ethnic communities?

   (h) How many people say they have a religion and how many attend religious services? What are the largest religious groups?

   (i) What is the Church of England and who is its head? What are the main Christian groups?

   (j) Where are Geordie, Cockney and Scouse dialects spoken?

   (k) What and when are the main Christian festivals? What other traditional days are celebrated?

   (l) What are MPs? How often are elections held and who forms the government?

   (m) What is the Queen's official role and what ceremonial duties does she have?

   (n) How are local services managed, governed and paid for?

   (o) What rights do citizens of European Union states have to travel and work?

   (p) What rights and duties do UK citizens have?

   (q) Who has the right to vote and at what age? How and when do you register to vote?

3 Some believe that some members of minority ethnic groups living in the UK and who are British citizens do not mainly identify themselves as British, but identify with the country from which they or their families originally came. The most famous 'test' of this was made by Conservative politician Norman Tebbit in 1990, in what became known as the 'Tebbit test'. Tebbit said: 'A large proportion of Britain's Asian population fail to pass the cricket test. Which side do they cheer for? It's an interesting test. Are you still harking back to where you came from or where you are?' Do you think the Tebbit test is a fair test of British identity?

4 Woodlands Junior School in Kent has an 'A–Z Guide of British Life and Culture'. You can see this at <www.woodlands-junior.kent.sch.uk/customs/topics/index.htm>. Have a look at this and, using this list and also using the material in questions 1 and 2 above if you wish, draw up a questionnaire containing ten questions about Britain which you think might find out whether there is such a thing as a British identity. Explain why you think the questions you have drawn up show a British identity.

Globalization and declining national identities

A **culture of hybridity** is a culture that is a 'mix' of two or more other cultures, creating a new culture (a 'hybrid').

As discussed earlier, globalization is changing national cultures, and blurring national identities. Hall suggests that one possible consequence of globalization is that national cultures may decline, leading to new cultures of hybridity and new hybrid identities. There does seem to be some evidence for this. Decisions and events in one part of the world can now have significant consequences for people across the globe. The mass media now report events across the world almost instantaneously, as well as exposing people to other cultures, including attitudes, values, religious beliefs, fashions and diets. It is difficult any longer, for example, to identify a 'British diet', with lattes, curries, samosas, chicken tikka, pasta and pizza, and Chinese, Thai, Italian and Indian foods all now widely eaten in Britain. People travel abroad much more than they used to, and more British people are buying homes in foreign countries. Britain's membership of the European Union means that some decisions affecting British life are now taken in collaboration with other European countries, and the same currency (the Euro) is now used across much of Europe. Widespread immigration means there are substantial minority ethnic groups in Britain as well as in many other countries. Individual countries appear to be of declining importance, with national identities becoming diluted. Postmodernists see such changes opening up more opportunities for people to choose from a far wider range of cultures and identities than they had in the past. Consequently, nationality and national cultures may be less significant as a source of identity, and people might see a European or global identity, for example, as more significant than a British or English identity.

On the other hand, while globalization may be undermining traditional conceptions of national identity, Hall recognizes that this, as well as the growth of wider political units like the European Union, can also give rise to nationalism and a reassertion of national identity as a means of opposing the trend. In Britain, the appearance in recent years of groups like the British National Party, the UK Independence Party and the English Democrats might all be seen as attempts to reassert national identity. Certainly, in national sporting events, national identities are strongly asserted, with millions of flags of St George sold to English football supporters, and the Welsh and Scottish similarly asserting their national identities.

A British identity crisis?

There does appear to be a growing 'identity crisis' in the UK, and particularly over what is meant by a 'British identity'. This identity is becoming less important to the majority of people, and the survey evidence below suggests that the 'British' identity is fraying, with English, Scottish and Welsh identities replacing it.

- 67 per cent of adults in Wales considered their national identity as wholly or partly Welsh (2001 Labour Force Survey)
- 77 per cent of people in Scotland thought 'Scottish' best described their national identity; 86 per cent thought of themselves as Scottish compared to just 50 per cent who thought of themselves as British (2001 Scottish Social Attitudes survey)

The British Social Attitudes Survey of 2006–7 found:

- 44 per cent of the British public thought 'British' was the best or only way to describe their national identity, and less than half of even those living in England (48 per cent)
- 40 per cent of people living in England identified themselves as primarily or solely English

The only exception to this is among the minority ethnic groups, the majority of whom were more likely to identify themselves as 'British' than any other national identity, according to the Office for National Statistics.

> ### Activity
>
> 1 Suggest reasons why minority ethnic groups living in Britain might be more likely than any other groups to identity themselves as British rather than English, Scottish or Welsh.
> 2 Identify and explain *three* reasons why British national identity appears to be in decline.

Disability and identity

The social construction of disability

> An **impairment** is some abnormal functioning of the body or mind, either that one is born with or which arises from injury or disease.

Impairment is some abnormal functioning of the body, which only becomes a **disability** when it prevents people from carrying out normal day-to-day activities. Impairment is therefore not the same as disability. Shakespeare (1998) suggests that disability should be seen as a social construction – a problem created by the attitudes of society and not by the state of our bodies.

Shakespeare argues that disability is created by societies that don't take into account the needs of those who do not meet with that society's ideas of what is 'normal'. The stereotype in any society of a 'normal' or acceptable body may generate a disabled identity among those with bodies that do not conform to this stereotype, particularly those with a physical impairment, even when the impairment does not cause mobility or other physical difficulties for that person. An example of this might be people of very small stature (dwarfs), or with facial disfigurements that cause an adverse reaction among others.

> **Disability** is a physical or mental impairment which has a substantial and long-term adverse effect on a person's ability to carry out normal day-to-day activities.

Whether someone is disabled or not is then a social product – it is social attitudes which turn an impairment into a disability, as society discriminates against them. For example, people parking on pavements make it difficult for those in wheelchairs or the blind to get by; buildings may make access difficult or impossible for those who have lost the use of their lower limbs and need wheelchairs to aid their mobility. People who are short-sighted only become disabled if they have no access to glasses to correct their sight, or if documents are printed in small type or colours which people with visual impairments find hard to read. Workplaces can be disabling if adjustments to the working environment are not made to enable people with impairments to perform their jobs successfully. People with facial disfigurement only become disabled because of the reactions of other people to this deviation from a 'normal' appearance.

As Shakespeare argues, 'people become disabled, not because they have physical or mental impairments, but because they have physical or mental differences from the majority, which challenge traditional ideas of what counts as "normal". Disability is about the relationship between people with an impairment and a society which discriminates against them'.

Disability, socialization and stereotyping

Most of us learn about disability as part of the socialization process, rather than as a result of personal experience. Popular views of disability, for those without direct experience, are often formed through the mass media. Media images of disability are often linked with socially unacceptable behaviours, or suggest that we have good reasons to fear people with impairments, especially those with mental or behavioural difficulties, or who display violent or inexplicable behaviour.

Stereotypes of disability, particularly those generated by the mass media, include ideas that disabled people are dependent on others, less than human, are monsters or wicked people, or have maladjusted personalities and 'aren't like other people'. Alternatively, they may be seen as people to be made fun of or pitied, or praised for their courage in coping with their disability. Only rarely does the media treat disability as a perfectly normal part of everyday life. Disability therefore becomes an identity marking people out as different from others.

Photo: James O. Jenkins

Disability is often seen by the non-disabled as a stigmatized identity – as something to be hidden or ashamed of. This sculpture in Trafalgar Square in London by Marc Quinn, *Alison Lapper Pregnant*, is of disabled artist Alison Lapper, who was born in 1965 without arms and with shortened legs. As Alison Lapper herself said, 'It is so rare to see disability in everyday life – let alone naked, pregnant and proud. This sculpture makes the ultimate statement about disability – that it can be as beautiful and valid a form of being as any other'

Disability as a 'master identity'

A person has multiple identities, and disabled people may not see their impairment as the defining characteristic of their identity – they may regard themselves, and wish others to see them, for example, mainly as black, and/or working class and/or gay, rather than as 'disabled'.

However, many people with impairments may experience difficulty in asserting their own choice of identity in the face of the 'disabled' identity, based on stereotypes, that others seek to impose on them. They may find it hard to make others see the 'real me' inside the disabled person. The other dimensions of their identity in terms of ethnicity, social class, gender, sexuality or lifestyle, for example, may be ignored once the label of 'disabled person' is applied by others. To borrow and adapt the term 'master status' from the sociology of deviance, disability might be regarded as a 'master identity' – an identity that overrides all other aspects of that person's identity, whether they want it to or not.

Disability – a stigmatized or spoiled identity: an identity of exclusion

The label 'disabled' frequently carries with it a stigma arising from stereotyping, which prevents people with impairments from achieving full social acceptance. An impairment may be seen by others as involving total disablement, rather than as just one aspect, and remaining abilities may not be recognized. A person with no legs, for example, can function and think perfectly normally, and it may only be in activities requiring the use of their lower limbs that they experience difficulties. The stigma attached to disability, leading to what Goffman called a stigmatized or spoiled social identity, means it can also become an identity of exclusion, excluding disabled people from full participation in society, as they face, for instance, unnecessary physical barriers in buildings and streets, discrimination in employment, inadequate medical care, negative portrayals in the media, and mocking, patronizing or dismissive attitudes from others. For example, wheelchair users often find that people will look at and talk to the person pushing a wheelchair, rather than the disabled person, or patronize the disabled person or speak in a loud voice, giving the impression the disabled person is either deaf or stupid, and that the disability is total. Disabled people may fail at what Goffman called 'impression management', because stereotypes of disability spoil their presentation of self, and the identity they wish to project to others through managing the impressions others have of them.

Activity

1 Suggest *three* ways that disability may be a stigmatized social identity.
2 Suggest *two* ways that people with impairments may face difficulties in managing the impressions other people have of them.
3 Explain what is meant by the idea that disability is an 'identity of exclusion'.
4 The six pictures below show people with various impairments. Although you can't know how they identify themselves, try to put them in rank order, 1–6, of those you think most likely to those you think least likely to identify themselves mainly in terms of their disability. Give reasons for your answer, and compare your answers with other people in your class. What does this suggest, if anything, about different views on disability and identity?

(T–B): Disabled marathoner; young woman in a wheelchair; blind man walking; older person being pushed in a wheelchair; older woman with a walking frame; young girl with a hearing aid

Age and identity

The social construction of age

How old you are is not simply, or even most importantly, a matter of biological development. There is also a social dimension to ageing, and there are often different norms, values and expectations of behaviour associated with different ages. Age is a social construction, in the sense that the identity and status allocated to people of different biological ages is created by society and social attitudes, and not simply moulded by biology.

There can be wide biological differences between people of the same age, which may impact on how others see and define them, and attitudes to age vary between cultures. In some societies old people have high status as the 'elders' of a community, while in modern Britain older people generally tend to lack status and authority, though this can vary between ethnic groups. In the Asian community, for example, elderly people are still often held in high esteem.

Social attitudes to people of different ages can change over time. Philippe Ariès (1973) showed that in medieval times childhood did not exist as a separate status. Children often moved straight from infancy, when they required constant care, to working roles in the community. Children were seen as 'little adults'. They did not lead separate lives, and dressed like, and mixed with, adults. 'Childhood' was certainly not the specially protected and privileged time of life we associate with children today, with their legal protection, extended education and freedom from work.

Age groups and identity

The social construction of age means that we tend to think of people in terms of age groups in contemporary British culture, such as 'infancy', 'childhood', 'teenager', 'youth', 'young' and 'mature' adulthood, 'middle age' or 'old age'. The age group to which we belong can have important consequences for identity and status, particularly for the young and the old. For example, our age influences whether we can get employment, or keep employment, go into pubs, clubs and films, and whether it is legally possible to marry or socially acceptable to have sex.

There are often broad cultural stereotypes and assumptions about the lifestyles of some of these age groups, and different norms and expectations of behaviour associated with them, which can help to mould the identities of those in these groups. For example, behaviour considered appropriate for a child might be regarded as very odd in a middle-aged man. These age groups are therefore a form of social identity and may be a source of individual identity as well. In other words, how old you are can have a direct impact on your own sense of identity, how you behave and how others see you. For example, being a 'teenager' involves a frequently difficult period of transition between childhood and adulthood, and the teenage identity may be seen as confusing, troublesome and angst-ridden for the individual, and 'trouble' for others.

In what ways might teenagers be regarded as having a stigmatized identity?

Young people commonly establish their identities through youth subcultures. What youth subcultures are around today, and why do you think people identify with them?

Bradley (1995) sees age as an important aspect of identity for individuals. She recognizes that it tends to be a short-lived and changing identity as people spend only a short period in a particular age group (though this may be changing for the retired elderly, with growing life expectancy).

Bradley suggests that age becomes a particularly significant aspect of identity in two main age groups – the young (teenagers and 20-somethings) and older people who are retired from work.

Youth and identity

Young people in contemporary Britain face an extended period of time between leaving childhood behind and becoming independent adults. Dependency on parents, often living with them well into their 20s, and extended periods in education mean that many young people find difficulty in establishing a clear adult identity. Functionalist writers suggest this leads to status frustration, with youth subcultures emerging as one way of dealing with the extended transition from childhood to adulthood.

Youth subcultures enable young people to carve out an identity for themselves as they make the transition to the establishment of an independent adult identity. Over the last fifty years, a whole range of youth subcultures has emerged. Teddy Boys, mods and rockers, skinheads, punks, Goths and Rastas have all emerged as very distinctive youth identities, with related styles of dress, appearance, behaviour and music.

Older people and identity

With greater life expectancy, retired people may be in the 'older' age group for perhaps longer than in any other age group. Retirement brings with it a loss of identity that arises from work, as well as the income. Older people today are healthier and more affluent than they have ever been, but there is

Status frustration is a sense of frustration arising in individuals or groups because they are denied status in society.

still widespread poverty among the old, particularly among working-class widowed women and/or those without occupational pension schemes. Even relatively well-off pensioners will face a substantial drop in income compared to those who are working, and this makes it harder for some older people, especially the poor, to establish alternative identities through their leisure and consumption patterns (discussed later in this chapter).

In mid-2005 one in three people in Britain were aged 50 or over, and one in six aged 65 or over. The 'grey pound' (older people's spending) is very important to businesses and, increasingly, new businesses are opening up that market to older people and are dedicated to their needs, such as SAGA.

Despite being a significant proportion of the population and a major market for business, older people often suffer prejudice and discrimination, with negative stereotyped assumptions that they are less intelligent, forgetful, 'grumpy' and 'moaning', in poor health, incapable and dependent on others and so on – simply because they are old. Older people, particularly, are likely to encounter ageism.

Ageism is stereotyping, prejudice, and discrimination against individuals or groups on the grounds of their age.

Ageism can have detrimental effects on older people, and they may face being called derogatory names and having negative media images ('dirty old man', 'boring old fart', 'grumpy old woman'), being infantilized (treated like infants/children), being denied a sexual identity, facing barriers to proper medical treatment (such as not being referred to a consultant for being too old) and losing jobs or facing obstacles to getting jobs on the grounds of being too old. Old age might be regarded as an example of a stigmatized identity, which prevents older people from establishing identities other than that of simply being the 'old person' found in negative stereotypes.

Why is old age in Britain often a stigmatized social identity?

Activity

1   Suggest ways that the law enforces age-related identities.
2   Explain what is meant by 'ageism', and suggest three ways that both older people and younger people experience ageism.
3   Suggest *four* reasons why the peer group might be particularly important in establishing the identities of young people.
4   Suggest reasons why both 'old age' and 'teenager' might be regarded as stigmatized identities.

Leisure, consumption and identity

Postmodernism and identity

Much of this chapter has suggested that identities are strongly influenced by social position, with factors such as social class and occupation, gender, ethnicity and age providing the basic sources of identity formation and difference from others.

However, postmodernist writers argue that these social factors are no longer significant in forming identities. Lyotard (1984) argues these all-embracing explanations or 'big theories' (like class, gender or ethnicity) for identity – what he calls metanarratives – no longer explain the identities people adopt and the differences between them, and people no longer relate to these metanarratives in forming their identities.

Postmodernists argue that identities are now much more fluid and subject to constant change. Rojek (1995) and Roberts (1978, 1986) believe that what we choose to do in our leisure time, the products we consume and the lifestyles we follow, are far more significant in forming our identities today. They suggest that most people now have an almost unlimited free choice of leisure activities and lifestyle, and they can adopt any identity or image they wish. Bocock (2004) believes that people's consumer choices – their tastes and the type, image and style of the goods they buy – are important aspects in defining their identities and the image and status they wish to project to others. Through their leisure and consumption choices, people are shopping for lifestyles, and in effect buying and creating identities.

Their identities are established through their consumption of the huge diversity of consumer leisure goods and services now on offer, such as music, household decor, holiday destinations or clubs, the type of shops they buy from, the 'labels' they purchase, the type of food and drinks they buy to display in their homes, and the leisure activities they follow. Holidays, for example, are no longer simply about sun, sea and sand, but about lifestyle identity – showing people how well-off, interesting, successful or imaginative

A **metanarrative** (literally, a 'big story') is a broad, all-embracing 'big theory' or explanation for how societies operate.

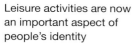

Leisure activities are now an important aspect of people's identity

you are. Going llama trekking in the Andes, wine-tasting in Australia, staying in a villa in Tuscany or having winters in Barbados gives a quite different indication to others of who you are than going clubbing in Ibiza or having a week in Blackpool; shopping from the Oxfam shop projects a different image from that of buying your clothes from Gap; bungee-jumping, surfing, white-water rafting or 'extreme' sports suggest a different identity from knitting or being a 'couch potato' television viewer.

The creation of identity in a media-saturated society

Strinati (1995) emphasizes the importance and power of the mass media and popular culture in shaping consumer choices. Popular culture, like the culture of celebrity, and media images and messages bombard us daily, through books, magazines, newspapers, TV, radio, advertising and computers, and form our sense of reality and increasingly dominate the way we define ourselves. We live in what Baudrillard called a media-saturated society. In this media-saturated society, the mass media create desires and pressures to consume, and individual identity is no longer formed predominantly by factors such as class, ethnicity or gender, but by information and images gained from the media. In a globalized popular culture, the mass media present to us a massive choice of lifestyles, images and identities drawn from across the world. Bradley (1995) argues that new identities are created by globalization, bringing different cultural groups into contact. People now adopt different identities to meet the diversity in their lives – they no longer identify with class alone, but with ethnicity, gender, disability, race, religion, nationality, music, fashion designer labels, dress, sport and other leisure activities – they can 'pick and mix' to create whatever identities they wish.

Shopping for identities – Who do you want to be today?

In today's consumer society, shopping has become a leisure activity in its own right, particularly for women. It is not just about buying products, but about buying into lifestyles, giving meaning to people's lives and establishing identities. Even something as basic as the human body can now be 'bought' to establish an identity, with diet products, fitness clubs and equipment, cosmetic surgery, breast implants, body piercing, tattoos, hair extensions and so on encouraging people to shape their bodies in accordance with the image they wish to project of themselves. Bauman and May (2004) suggest that advertising for consumer products like perfumes, alcoholic drinks, cars and clothing is not simply about selling the products, but that these goods have symbolic significance – the label, the make of trainer, is more important than the product, the trainer, itself. These products come packaged with an associated lifestyle, as shown in the dress, language, pastimes, home decor and physical appearance of people in advertisements. These provide lifestyle models which people are encouraged to buy into, and from which they can choose to shape their personal identities, and establish their individuality and difference from others. Advertising and shopping provide what Bauman and May call 'do-it-yourself identity kits'. The founder of Revlon, Charles Revson, summed it up neatly when he said: 'In the factory we make cosmetics; in the store we sell hope.'

Shopping for identity

Activity

With reference to particular advertisements, referring to both the products and the people appearing in them and the setting of the advertisements:
1 Identify the ways that advertising is used to promote the desirability of particular lifestyles, and the products that are connected to such lifestyles.
2 Work out roughly what buying these items to establish this lifestyle identity might cost, and discuss whether this is available to everyone.

Bauman (1996) argues that life has become a shopping mall, to stroll around consuming whatever you want, trying out and constructing whatever identities you choose, and changing them whenever you want. As Taylor (1999) put it, society is transformed into 'something resembling an endless shopping mall where people now have much greater choice about how they look, what they consume, and what they believe in'. In the postmodern 'pick and mix' consumer society, the influences of class, gender and ethnicity are no longer relevant, and people can become whatever they want to be, adopting lifestyles and identities built around the almost unlimited choice of leisure activities and consumer goods available.

Activity

1 Explain, with examples, what you understand by the 'pick and mix' consumer society.
2 Do you think 'shopping' has become a leisure activity in its own right? Think about your own shopping behaviour and the importance it has, or hasn't, for you.
3 Suggest *three* ways, based on your own knowledge and experiences, in which men and women might experience shopping differently.
4 Devise a short questionnaire, based on your answer to the question above, and carry out a small survey to see if other people's experiences are similar to or different from your own.
5 What are the most important factors influencing how you define and see your own identity, and how others see you? Think about factors like your status as a student or worker, your lifestyle, the consumer goods you buy, your leisure choices, the clothes and labels you buy, the shops you buy from, your musical tastes, the pubs and clubs you go to, and so on.

How much free choice is there in choosing identities and lifestyle?

The postmodernist view that we now have unrestrained choice in our leisure activities, and that we are completely free to adopt any lifestyle and identity we like through our leisure choices and consumer spending, ignores a range of factors which still have important influences, or constraints, on the consumption patterns, leisure activities and lifestyles we can choose, and the identities we can adopt and project onto others. These are considered below.

Occupation and work experience

Work remains an important element in occupying, directing and structuring the individual's time – the demands of working life involve a high degree of discipline if paid jobs are to be kept. It is, for most people, the single biggest

commitment of time in any week, and it is perhaps one of the most important experiences affecting people's entire lives. How money is earned, how much, in what working conditions, the length of working hours and the amount of pension all decide in many ways a person's status and the kind of life they will lead. Work has major effects on the time and money people have to enjoy and spend on the leisure and consumer goods which are an increasingly important source of identity.

The work we do has important effects on our status in society, and on our leisure activities and consumption patterns

Parker (1971, 1976) believes that people's occupations and the way they experience their work, such as the amount of independence and satisfaction they have there, have important influences on their leisure. He suggests that there are three patterns in the link between work and leisure, which he calls the opposition, neutrality and extension patterns. These are shown in table 2.2.

Activity

1 List all the ways you can that our working lives might influence our leisure activities. Explain in each case the influences you identify.
2 To what extent do you think people's work is central in forming their identity – how they see themselves and how others see them? Do you think work is more important than people's leisure activities and lifestyle in forming their identity?
3 Parker suggests work extends into and becomes merged with leisure because people find their work is so satisfying. Suggest examples of occupations where you think this might be the case, giving your reasons.
4 What other reasons, apart from enjoyment of work, might there be for work extending into leisure time?

Criticisms of Parker   Parker's emphasis on the way the experience of work influences leisure patterns has been heavily criticized, particularly for putting too much importance on work experience, and not paying enough attention to factors other than work that might shape leisure patterns.

Table 2.2 Patterns of relationship between work and leisure

Work–leisure pattern	Nature of work	Typical occupations	Nature of leisure
Opposition	Physically hard and dangerous male-dominated occupations, hostility to work.	Mining, deep-sea fishermen, steelworkers.	Opposition to work. Leisure is a central life interest – a sharp contrast in opposition to work, and an opportunity opportunity to escape from the hardships of work.
Neutrality	Boring and routine work, with little job satisfaction, leading to apathy and indifference to work.	Routine clerical workers, assembly-line workers, supermarket staff.	Nothing much to do with work (neutral); leisure for relaxation with home and family, like DIY and going out with the family.
Extension	Work involving high levels of personal commitment, involvement, and job satisfaction.	Professionals and managers – doctors, teachers, social workers, business executives.	Because work is so interesting and demanding, leisure is work-related, and there is a blurring of the distinction between work and leisure. Work extends into leisure time, which may be used to improve work performance. For example, business executives playing golf or eating out with clients, teachers using their own time to run school trips/holidays with students, or preparing lessons or developing computer skills at home.

- *Parker over-emphasizes the importance of work in shaping leisure activities.* In Britain in 2007, only about 60 per cent of the population over the age of 16 were in employment, and one in four of these was working part time. Experiences at work can therefore not explain the leisure activities of substantial sections of the population, including those who are retired, those in full-time education, full-time housewives, others who are economically inactive and the unemployed.

- *Parker over-simplifies the influence of work on leisure,* even for those in full-time paid employment. Roberts (1978, 1986) and Clarke and Critcher (1995) say he doesn't take into account the choices that people can make in leisure activities, and such activities vary among those even in the same occupation.

- *Parker's research is focused primarily on men in full-time paid employment.* Feminist writers like McIntosh (1988) and Deem (1990) say that Parker does not take into account the way gender influences leisure, particularly as many women work only part time and their leisure is far more influenced by the demands of domestic labour (housework and childcare), and control by men, than by paid employment.

Social class

Scraton and Bramham (1995) argue that the postmodernist view that people have a free choice of leisure and create their own identities through participating in leisure-based consumer activities, like shopping, are only available to the most well-off members of society. Bauman and May point out that choice takes place within a society in which resources are unequally distributed. This means that for some the opportunity to choose is more real than for others, and most people simply don't have enough money to make free choices. People's choices will also be influenced by the amount of cultural capital they possess (Bourdieu's concept as discussed earlier in this chapter). Their taste will influence what they choose to buy and the identity they project to others, regardless of how much money they have.

Many leisure activities have become highly commercialized, money-making businesses, and some leisure activities are denied to the working class simply because of the high costs involved. For example, the high membership fees of private golf clubs and the expense of activities such as flying and motor-racing effectively bar such activities to the working class, and much of the middle class. For many people, shopping is not about buying identities, but about seeking out the cheapest bargains to stretch limited incomes to feed and clothe themselves and their children. Those in the poorest social classes, who are unemployed or in low-paid work, have few opportunities to establish their personal identities through buying into consumer products and the associated lifestyles. Freedom of consumer choice is limited by social class and the unequal distribution of wealth and income.

Age

Age continues to influence the choice of leisure activities, and identities established through them. The leisure of young single people tends to be spent outside the home in the company of their peer group. They may gain some economic independence from either a wage packet or benefits obtained on training schemes, but lack the financial commitments and responsibilities of household bills, children and the burden of paying rent or a mortgage. This means that young people are more leisure-centred than perhaps any other age group except the retired. They are therefore more likely to have the opportunity of forming their identities through participation in leisure-based consumer lifestyles, expressed through the purchase of clothes and music, and the clubs, pubs and concerts they go to.

The family life cycle

The family life cycle will also influence leisure activities and opportunities. Young couples who set up households together and have children will face more restrictions on their leisure activities, with household costs, mortgages and the costs of children. As children become less dependent on their parents, and as mortgages get paid off, people will have more disposable income to spend on leisure activities and consumer goods. Ill health as people get older, with reduced income in retirement, may once again limit leisure opportunities.

Gender

Gender has an important influence on the choice of leisure activity. As a result of gender-role socialization, men and women show different leisure interests and some leisure activities are more associated with one sex than the other. Shopping is a good example of this – men tend to view shopping as a chore, a necessary way of obtaining things they need; for women it is more likely to be seen as an enjoyable leisure activity in its own right, concerned with improving their personal appearance and making themselves feel good.

Feminist researchers have shown that women generally have less time and opportunity for leisure activities than men, as they often have responsibility for housework and childcare, and sometimes for dependent elderly relatives or the sick and disabled, on top of paid employment. Women also earn less than men, which further restricts their opportunity to participate in commercial leisure activities.

Research by Deem (1986) in Milton Keynes found that women's leisure activities were often combined with aspects of childcare, such as driving the children to leisure centres and going swimming with them. This does raise questions of how far such activities are really freely chosen and enjoyable leisure activities, rather than aspects of unpaid domestic labour.

Deem's research in Milton Keynes, and Green, Hebron and Woodward's (1990) research in Sheffield, found that patriarchy and patriarchal control (dominance and control by men) restricted women's leisure opportunities to 'approved' activities. Male partners often felt threatened by women's independent participation in leisure activities that might bring them into social contact with other men. Activities like clubbing and pubs in a 'night out with the girls' are often not approved of by men.

Patriarchy also restricts women's independence and choice in leisure activities, through the harassment that women may face in public places, such as getting 'chatted up' if they go into pubs, clubs or leisure centres on their own, or the risks they face in walking home alone at night. It seems then that gender still remains a very important aspect in leisure choices and identity formation.

Ethnicity

Ethnicity has important influences on leisure activities, and people will often make cultural choices of leisure activity in accordance with the ethnic group to which they belong, such as their tastes in food, music and films. Some minority ethnic groups may find their activities restricted by racism.

A night out with the girls – but patriarchal control and the demands of family life often mean that women have more restricted leisure opportunities than their male partners, particularly those independent leisure activities that might bring them into contact with other men

---

Activity

1   Identify and explain two ways that the leisure activities of males and females differ.
2   The evidence suggests women have less leisure time and opportunities than men. What effects do you think this might have on women forming individual identities and lifestyles?

Asian women are more likely to be restricted to home- and family-based activities because of culturally defined roles. Roberts (1983) found many Asian workers will put in long working hours so they can afford, and have time, to visit kinfolk in their countries of origin.

However, as seen earlier, younger British-born people from minority ethnic groups may be adopting less culturally defined leisure choices and lifestyles, and forming identities that are less constrained by the cultural inheritance of their parents' culture. Whether this reflects everyday life for most people is questionable, and may not be true of everyday life for ethnic minorities who value traditional culture.

The pursuit of profit

Marxist writers like Clarke and Critcher (1995) point out that leisure has become a highly organized and commercialized multinational industry, employing millions of people worldwide, and concerned with making profits. Sport, for example, is a huge international and highly profitable business, with merchandising of goods, and global TV and satellite deals worth

Apple's iPod – a 'must have' symbol of identity in the early 2000s, which was still selling in its millions at the time of writing (2007), and reaping huge profits for the Apple Corporation

millions of pounds. Tourism, together with the associated airline and hotel chains, is a major global industry. Clarke and Critcher argue that large corporations shape and manipulate people's choices of leisure activities, consumer goods and shopping habits. Global marketing of consumer goods through advertising in a media-saturated society creates endless demand for new 'must have' products and services. Rather than having free choices of leisure activities and consumer goods, advertising aims to convince people that their sense of self – their very identity – depends on buying into the very latest and ever-changing lifestyle trends, to the benefit of the large businesses making the products required to establish those identities.

Conclusion on leisure, consumption and identity

The preceding section outlines a range of factors which suggest that the postmodernist idea that people can now 'pick and mix' any identity they wish, through free choices of leisure activities and consumer goods, are somewhat exaggerated. Jenkins (1996) believes that identity remains rooted in social experience and membership of social groups, and is not something that can be changed at will. Bradley (1995) argues that social inequalities remain important, though these no longer shape identities as strongly as they once did. She accepts there is more fluidity and choice now, and that people are less likely to have a single identity, like social class, gender or ethnicity, that overarches all others. She suggests that while there is some choice over identity, and people have become more aware of the multiple sources of identity open to them, there are still constraints on this choice.

Activity

Working in a group, discuss answers to the following questions:

1 What are the 'must have' products which you would like to own, and why?
2 To what extent do you think owning these products is important in the way others see you?
3 Explain briefly what is meant by 'leisure has become a commercialized activity'.
4 Do you think you are manipulated by advertising into buying leisure goods and services, and taking part in some leisure activities rather than others?
5 Identify and explain *three* factors that may limit an individual's ability to have a free choice of leisure activity.
6 In about one and a half sides of A4 paper, answer the following essay question: *Examine the view that a person's social position (including, for example, their social class, gender, ethnicity or age) is still the main influence on their leisure patterns and identity.*

CHAPTER SUMMARY

After studying this chapter, you should be able to:

- explain, with examples, the meaning of culture, dominant culture, subculture, folk culture, high culture, mass (or popular) culture, global culture, the differences between them, and suggest ways the distinction between high culture and mass culture might be disappearing

- explain, with examples, what is meant by identity, individual identity, social identity, collective identity, multiple identities, hybrid identities and stigmatized or spoiled identities and how identity is established by the agencies of socialization

- explain the importance of the process of socialization in the formation and transmission between generations of culture and identity, and the structural and social action theoretical approaches to the role of socialization in the formation of culture and identity

- explain what is meant by the 'looking-glass self' and 'impression management'

- explain what is meant by the social construction of identities

- explain the meaning and importance of social class, gender, sexuality, ethnicity, nationality, disability and age as sources of identity

- examine postmodernist approaches to identity, including how identities are formed through consumer, leisure and lifestyle choices, and the extent to which people now have a free choice in the identities they adopt and are less constrained by traditional sources of identity

- explain what is meant by a 'media-saturated society' and how this might affect people's choice of identity

- examine the factors that influence and restrict people's choice of leisure activities, including occupation and work experience, social class, age, family life cycle, gender, ethnicity, and businesses' search for profits

- examine the extent to which people's identities today are formed by their social position, drawing on all the material in this chapter

KEY TERMS

ageism
bisexuality
culture of hybridity
diaspora
dominant culture
folk culture
fundamentalism

gender role
gender identity
global culture
hegemonic identity
heterosexuality
hidden curriculum
homophobia
homosexuality

hybrid identity
impression management
Islamophobia
low culture
metanarrative
nation
nationalism
nationality

nation-state
peer group
sexual orientation
sexuality
status frustration
stigma
stigmatized identity

EXAM QUESTION

SECTION A: CULTURE AND IDENTITY

Time allowed: 1 hour   **Total for this section: 60 marks**

1 Read Items **1A and 1B** below and answer parts (a) to (e) that follow.

Item 1A

Postmodernists suggest that mass markets and consumption now make the distinction between high and popular culture meaningless. There is now a huge range of media and cultural products available to all. Mass communication technology like the internet, music downloads, cable, satellite and digital television, film and radio, printing for both mass production and personal use in the home, the global reach of modern   5
mass media technology, the mass production of goods on a world scale, and easier international transportation, make all forms of culture freely available to everyone.

Item 1B

Identity is socially constructed. This means it is something created by the socialization process, and the individual and social interpretations and actions of people. It is not something that is given by biology or nature. For example, being black or white, or male or female, only have significance in society because people attach some importance to these characteristics, and define people in terms of these cate-   5
gories. Through learning their culture, and through their involvement with other individuals, social groups and subcultures, people come to develop ideas about what makes them similar to, or different from, others, and their identities are formed. The socialization process transmits both culture and identities from one generation to the next.   10

(a) Explain **two** ways in which high culture differs from popular culture (**Item 1A**, line 2).
(4 marks)

(b) Suggest **two** ways in which 'mass markets and consumption now make the distinction between high and popular culture meaningless' (**Item 1A**, lines 1–2)   *(4 marks)*

(c) Suggest **two** ways in which there may be a 'crisis of masculinity' in contemporary Britain.   *(4 marks)*

(d) Examine sociological explanations for the formation of identities.   *(24 marks)*

(e) Using material from **Item 1B** and elsewhere, assess the view that **either** ethnicity **or** gender are no longer significant sources of identity in contemporary Britain.
(24 marks)

Families and Households

Contents

Key issues	115
What is the family?	**115**
What is a household?	**115**
Different forms of the family and marriage	**116**
Is the nuclear family a universal institution?	**116**
The Nayar	116
Communes	116
The kibbutz	119
Lone parent families	119
Gay and lesbian families	119
Foster care and children's homes	120
Sociological perspectives on the family	**121**
The functionalist perspective	121
The traditional Marxist perspective	123
Marxist feminist and radical feminist perspectives	124
Demographic change and the family	**129**
The decline in the death rate and infant mortality rate	129
The ageing population	132
The decline in the birth rate, fertility rate and average family size	135
Other major changes in the family	**139**
Family change 1: has the family lost its functions?	139
Family change 2: the decline of the classic extended family and the emergence of the privatized nuclear family?	142
Family change 3: the emergence of the symmetrical family?	147

Family change 4: the changing position of children	160
Family change 5: the rising divorce rate	169
Family change 6: remarriage and the growth of the reconstituted family	176
Family change 7: the growth of the lone parent family	177
Family change 8: the decline in marriage and the growing incidence and acceptance of cohabitation	180
Family change 9: the growth in 'singlehood' – living alone	181
Family change 10: more births outside marriage	182
Family diversity and the myth of the 'cereal packet' family	**182**
Why is the 'cereal packet' stereotype misleading?	183
The 'darker side' of family life	**189**
The abuse of children	190
Domestic violence	191
Family ideology	**194**
Politics, social policy and the family	**195**
Laws and social policies affecting the family and households	197
Postmodernism and the family	**198**
Is the family a declining social institution?	**199**
Chapter summary	201
Key terms	202
Exam question	204

CHAPTER

3

Families and Households

KEY ISSUES

- What is the family and a household?
- Different forms of the family and marriage
- Is the nuclear family a universal institution?
- Sociological perspectives on the family
- Demographic changes and the family
- Changes in the family in Britain
- Family diversity and the myth of the 'cereal packet' family
- The 'darker side' of family life
- Family ideology
- Politics, social policy and the family
- Is the family a declining social institution?

What is the family?

A **family** is a social institution consisting of a group of people who are related by **kinship** ties: relations of blood, marriage or adoption.

The **family** unit is one of the most important social institutions, found in some form in nearly all known societies. It is a basic unit of social organization, and plays a key role in socializing children into the culture of their society.

What is a household?

A **household** simply means one person living alone or a group of people who live at the same address and share living arrangements.

Most families will live in a **household**, but not all households are families. For example, students sharing a house together make up a household, though they are not a family. Similarly, in pre-industrial Britain, average household sizes were often larger than they are today, but this was generally because they contained domestic servants or other non-family members. Increasingly today, more households are containing people living alone rather than families. In 2005, around one in three households consisted of people living alone.

Different forms of the family and marriage

Even though the family is found in nearly every society, it can take many different forms. Marriage and family life in earlier times in Britain, and today in many other societies, can be organized in quite different ways from family life in modern Britain. Sociologists use a number of different terms to describe the wide varieties of marriage and household type. Table 3.1 overleaf summarizes these varieties.

Is the nuclear family a universal institution?

Functionalist writers like Murdock (1949) suggest that the nuclear family is such an important social institution, playing such vital functions in maintaining society, that it is found in some form in every society. In other words, it is a universal institution. However, although most societies in the world have some established arrangements for the production, rearing and socialization of children, this does not mean that these arrangements always or necessarily involve prime responsibility resting on the family or biological parents. The examples below help to illustrate some alternative arrangements which suggest the family is not always the main way of bringing up children.

The Nayar

Among the Nayar of south-west India before the nineteenth century there was no nuclear family. A woman could have sexual relations with any man she wished (up to a maximum of twelve) and the biological father of children was therefore uncertain. The mother's brother, rather than the biological father, was responsible for looking after the mother and her children. Unlike our society, where in most cases the biological parents marry, live together and are responsible for rearing their children, among the Nayar there was no direct link between having sexual relations, childbearing, childrearing and cohabitation.

Communes

Communes developed in Western Europe, Britain and the United States in the 1960s, among groups of people wanting to develop alternative lifestyles to those of conventional society because of the political or religious beliefs they held.

Communes often try to develop an alternative style of living and a kind of alternative household, with an emphasis on collective living rather than

Communes are self-contained and self-supporting communities.

individual family units. A number of adults and children all aim to live and work together, with children being seen as the responsibility of the group as a whole rather than of natural parents. Many communes tended to be very short-lived, and only a few remain in Britain today.

The kibbutz

In the early kibbutzim, childrearing was separated as much as possible from the marriage relationship, with children kept apart from their natural parents for much of the time and brought up in the children's house by *metapelets*. These were a kind of 'professional parent' combining the roles of nurse, housemother and educator. The role of the natural parents was extremely limited, and they were only allowed to see their children for short periods each day. The children were seen as the 'children of the **kibbutz**' – they were the responsibility of the community as a whole, which met all of their needs. Children would move through a series of children's houses with others of the same age group until they reached adulthood.

In recent years, the more traditional family unit has re-emerged in the kibbutzim, with natural parents and children sharing the same accommodation, but the kibbutz remains one of the most important attempts to find an alternative to conventional family structures.

Lone parent families

The lone parent family is becoming increasingly common in Western societies, and is usually headed by a woman. Lone parents represent a clear alternative to the conventional nuclear family. This is discussed later in this chapter.

Gay and lesbian families

Same sex (or homosexual) couples with children are becoming more common, though they are still relatively rare. Most same sex couples with children tend to be lesbian couples, that is, two women. However, there are more cases emerging of gay (male) couples adopting children or having children through surrogate mothers. In May 1999 the Canadian Supreme Court declared that gay and lesbian couples are no different from heterosexual couples in their ability to share loving relationships, and suffer tragic breakdowns in those relationships like many heterosexual couples. In April 2001 in Amsterdam, Europe's first officially blessed gay and lesbian weddings took place, as Dutch law granted full equality to same sex couples on issues such as adoption, inheritance, pension rights and tax. The Dutch experience paved the way for greater change and acceptance of gay and lesbian marriage and family life in the

Activity

Refer to table 3.1 and:

1 Interview a few people and try to find out what types of family they live in today. Is there any 'typical' family or is there a variety of family types? Write a report or do a presentation on your findings.

2 Fill in the blanks in the following passage. Each dash represents one word.

The ___ ___ means just the parents and children, living together in one household. This is sometimes called the two-generation family, because it contains only the two generations of parents and children. The ___ ___ is a grouping consisting of all kin. The ___ ___ ___ consists of several related nuclear families or family members who live in the same household, street or area and who see one another regularly. The ___ ___ ___ is one where related nuclear families, although they may be living far apart, maintain close relations made possible by modern communications, such as car travel, phone, letters or e-mail. This is probably the most common type of family arrangement in Britain today.

The ___ ___ is a form of the extended family in a pattern which is long and thin, reflecting the fact that people are living longer but are having fewer children.

The ___ ___ ___ is today largely a result of the rise in the divorce rate, although it may also arise from the death of a partner, the breakdown of cohabiting relationships, or a simple lack of desire to get married. Nine out of ten of these families are headed by women. The ___ ___ is one where one or both partners have been married previously, and they bring with them children of a previous marriage.

It remains a popular impression that the most usual kind of family in contemporary Britain is the ___ ___ where both husbands and wives or cohabiting partners are likely to be wage earners, and to share the housework and childcare. However, some argue that men still dominate in the family and make most of the decisions, and it therefore remains ___ .

___ is the only legal form of marriage allowed in Britain. In modern Britain, most of Western Europe and the United States there are high rates of divorce and remarriage, and some people keep marrying and divorcing a series of different partners. The term ___ ___ is sometimes used to describe these marriage patterns. This type of marriage pattern has been described as 'one at a time, one after the other and they don't last long'.

___ ___ are those where parents organize the marriages of their children to try and ensure a good match with partners of a similar background and status. They are typically found among Muslim, Sikh and Hindu minority ethnic groups. However, this custom is coming under pressure in Britain as younger people demand greater freedom to choose their own marriage partner in the same way as in wider society.

While marrying a second partner without divorcing the first is a crime in Britain, in many societies it is perfectly acceptable to have more than one marriage partner at the same time. ___ is a general term used to describe this form of marriage.

The solution to this activity can be found on the teachers' pages of
www.polity.co.uk/browne

Table 3.1 Forms of marriage and household

Forms of:	Description
Marriage	
Monogamy	One husband and one wife
	Found in Europe, the US and most Christian cultures
Serial monogamy	A series of monogamous marriages
	Found in Europe and the US, where there are high rates of divorce and remarriage
Arranged marriage	Marriages arranged by parents to match their children with partners of a similar background and status
	Found in the Indian subcontinent and Muslim, Sikh and Hindu minority ethnic groups in Britain
Polygamy	Marriage to more than one partner at the same time
	Includes polygyny and polyandry
Polygyny	One husband and two or more wives
	Found in Islamic countries like Egypt and Saudi Arabia
Polyandry	One wife and two or more husbands
	Found in Tibet, among the Todas of southern India, and among the Marquesan Islanders
Family and household structure	
Nuclear family	Two generations: parents and children living in the same household
Extended family	All kin including and beyond the nuclear family
Classic extended family	An extended family sharing the same household or living close by
Modified extended family	An extended family living far apart, but keeping in touch by phone, letters, email and frequent visits
'Beanpole' family	A multi-generation extended family in a pattern which is long and thin, with few aunts and uncles, reflecting fewer children being born in each generation, but people living longer
Patriarchal family	Authority held by males
Matriarchal family	Authority held by females
Symmetrical family	Authority and household tasks shared between male and female partners
Reconstituted family or stepfamily	One or both partners previously married, with children of previous marriages
Lone parent family	Lone parent with dependent children, most commonly after divorce or separation (though may also arise from death of a partner or unwillingness to marry or cohabit)
Gay or lesbian family	Same sex couple living together with children
Single person household	An individual living alone

Lesbian wedding party

European Union, and in 2004 the Civil Partnership Act gave gay and lesbian couples in Britain the same legal rights as married couples.

You might argue that gay and lesbian couples are families like any other, but they do offer an alternative to more conventional views of the nuclear family.

Foster care and children's homes

It is worth remembering that a considerable number of children are 'looked after' by local authorities, and brought up by foster parents or in children's homes. This does demonstrate that the link between natural parents and the rearing of children can be, and sometimes is, separated.

Even though the nuclear family is probably one of the main means of bringing up children in the world today, the examples above mean it would be incorrect to assume that the conventional nuclear family is a universal institution. This is particularly the case today, where new forms of relationship are developing, and where the idea of a lifetime relationship is increasingly diminishing as more people have a series of partners during their lifetimes, and abandon traditional styles of family living.

Sociological perspectives on the family

The functionalist perspective

As we saw in the first chapter, functionalism emphasizes integration and harmony between the different parts of society, and the way these parts work together to maintain society. With regard to the family, functionalists see the family as a vital 'organ' in maintaining the 'body' of society, just as the heart is an important organ in maintaining the human body. Functionalists are interested in the contribution the family makes to satisfying the functional prerequisites, or basic needs, which enable society to survive, and how the family 'fits' with other social institutions (like education or work) so that society functions efficiently and harmoniously.

Murdock argues there are four main functions of the family:

- *Sexual* – expressing sexuality in a socially approved context (note the social disapproval attached to, for example, incest, adultery and homosexuality in many societies).
- *Reproduction* – the family providing some stability for the reproduction and rearing of children.
- *Socialization* – the family is an important unit of **primary socialization** of children, where children learn socially acceptable behaviour and the culture of their society. This helps to build the shared ideas and beliefs (value consensus) which functionalists regard as important to maintaining a stable society.
- *Economic* – the family provides food and shelter for family members.

Murdock regards these functions as necessary in any society, and he suggests that the nuclear family was found in every society to carry them out. However, as has already been seen, the nuclear family is not the only form of arrangement possible for carrying out these functions, and other institutions and arrangements can and do take them over.

Parsons is an American functionalist writer who examined family life in the 1950s. He argued that there are two basic functions of the family that are

Primary socialization refers to socialization during the early years of childhood (contrasted with **secondary socialization**, when other social institutions exert an ever increasing influence on individuals, such as the school, the peer group and the mass media).

found in every society. These are the primary socialization of children and the stabilization of human personalities.

The primary socialization of children

Parsons (1951) sees primary socialization as involving the learning and internalization of society's culture, such as the language, history and values of a society. He argues that society would cease to exist if the new generation were not socialized into accepting the basic norms and values of society. In his view, this socialization in the family is so powerful that society's culture actually becomes part of the individual's personality – people are moulded in terms of the central values of the culture and act in certain ways almost without thinking about it. Parsons therefore argues that families are factories producing human personalities, and only the family can provide the emotional warmth and security to achieve this.

The stabilization of human personalities

In industrial societies, the need for work and money, the lack of power and independence combined with boredom at work, the pressure to achieve success and support the family all threaten to destabilize personalities. Parsons suggests the family helps to stabilize personalities by the **sexual division of labour** in the family.

In Parsons's view, women have an **expressive role** in the family, providing warmth, security and emotional support to their children and male partner. The male partner carries out an **instrumental role** as family breadwinner, which leads to stress and anxiety and threatens to destabilize his personality. However, the wife's expressive role relieves this tension by providing love and understanding: the sexual division of labour into 'expressive' and 'instrumental' roles therefore contributes to the stabilization of human personalities.

> The **sexual division of labour** refers to the way jobs are divided into 'men's jobs' and 'women's jobs'.

> The **expressive role** is the nurturing, caring and emotional role.
> The **instrumental role** is the provider/breadwinner role in the family.

Criticisms and evaluation of the functionalist perspective

The criticisms made of the functionalist perspective see it as:

- *Downplaying conflict* Both Murdock and Parsons paint very rosy pictures of family life, presenting it as a harmonious and integrated institution. However, they downplay conflict in the family, particularly the 'darker side' of family life, such as child abuse and violence against women. Children may become emotionally disturbed by conflict between parents, and children may often be used as **scapegoats** by parents.
- *Being out of date* Parsons's view of the 'instrumental' and 'expressive' roles of men and women is very old-fashioned. It may have held some truth in the 1950s when many married women were full-time housewives, and men the breadwinners in most households. However, this is

> **Scapegoats** are individuals or groups who get blamed for things that aren't their fault.

clearly not the case today, when most married women are wage-earning breadwinners. Nowadays, both partners are likely to be playing expressive and instrumental roles at various times, especially if men are taking on greater responsibilities for childcare, as we are sometimes led to believe.

- *Ignoring the exploitation of women*   Functionalists tend to ignore the way women suffer from the sexual division of labour in the family, with their responsibility for housework and childcare undermining their position in paid employment, through restricted working hours because of the need to prepare children's meals, take them to and from school, and look after them when they are ill. Housework also causes stress, leading to mental illness. These concerns are typically raised by feminist writers, discussed below.

- *Ignoring the harmful effects of the family*   Leach (1967) asserts that, in modern industrial society, the nuclear family has become so isolated from kin and the wider community (this is called **privatization**) that it has become an inward-looking institution that leads to emotional stress. Family members expect and demand too much from one another, and this stress generates conflict within the family. He argues that 'Far from being the basis of the good society, the family, with its narrow privacy and tawdry secrets, is the source of all our discontents.' Writers like Laing and Cooper also argue the family can be a destructive and exploitative institution, and Laing sees family life as one of the factors causing the mental illness of schizophrenia among young people. Both writers regard family life as stunting individual development, with the smothering of individuality leading to unquestioning obedience to authority in later life.

> **Privatization** is the process whereby households and families become isolated and separated from the community and from wider kin, with people spending more time together in home-centred activities.

These criticisms of the functionalist approach suggest we need to think more carefully about the way family life is actually experienced by family members, and particularly to take into account the 'darker side' of family life.

Don't forget you can also criticize the functionalist approach by referring to arguments drawn from other perspectives – like the Marxist and feminist approaches discussed below.

The traditional Marxist perspective

Like functionalists, Marxists adopt a *structural perspective* on the family, looking at how the family contributes to the maintenance of society's structure. However, unlike functionalists, Marxists do not regard the nuclear family as a functionally necessary (and therefore universal) institution. Marxists see the family within the framework of a capitalist society, which is based on private property, driven by profit, and is riddled with conflict between social classes with opposing interests. Marxists argue that the nuclear family is concerned with teaching its members to submit to the capitalist class. Marxists emphasize the ways the family reproduces unequal relationships and works to damp down inevitable social conflict.

Early Marxists like Engels (1820–1895) believed that the monogamous nuclear family developed as a means of passing on private property to heirs. The family, coupled with monogamy, was an ideal mechanism as it provided proof of paternity (who the father was) and so property could be passed on to the right people. Women's position in this family was not much different from that of a prostitute in that a financial deal was struck – she provided sex and heirs in return for the economic security her husband offered.

Althusser, a French Marxist writing in 1971, argued that in order for capitalism to survive, the working class must submit to the ruling class or bourgeoisie. He suggested that the family is one of the main means, along with others such as the education system and the mass media, of passing on the ideology (the ideas and beliefs) of the ruling class. Through socialization into this ideology in the family, the ruling class tries to maintain false class consciousness by winning the hearts and minds of the working class.

Criticisms of the traditional Marxist perspective

The traditional Marxist perspective tends to be a bit old-fashioned. The idea that men marry and have children to pass on property ignores other reasons for getting married. Many women now work and have independent incomes, and in many cases they are more successful than men in some areas of the labour market. Women are therefore far less likely to marry for economic security. Marriage is now less of a social necessity. A 2003 report by the Institute of Education, 'Changing Britain, changing lives', found that people are now more likely to marry for love and affection rather than as a social obligation, with a growing emphasis on the emotional aspects of relationships and personal fulfilment both for men and, especially, for women.

Marxist feminist and radical feminist perspectives

In recent years, feminist writers have probably had more influence on the study of the family than any other perspective. Feminist perspectives are often a more critical development of Marxist views of the family, focusing particularly on the role of the family in the continuing oppression of women. They emphasize the harmful effects of family life upon women.

Not all feminist writings use a Marxist perspective. Many radical feminist writers see **patriarchy** as the main obstacle to women's freedom – a system of male power and dominance.

> **Patriarchy** refers to male dominance with men having power and authority.

Feminist approaches have been extremely valuable in introducing new areas into the study of the family, such as housework and its contribution to the economy; domestic violence; the negative effects of family life on women's careers in paid employment; and the continuing inequality between men and women in the family.

Some of the feminist criticisms of the family are covered in more detail in later sections of this chapter on changes in the family. The following represents a brief outline of the key features of feminist approaches to the family.

Themes in feminist analysis of the family

The family, and particularly women's work in the family, contributes to the maintenance of capitalism in the following ways:

The social reproduction of labour power   The social reproduction of labour power simply means the family provides a place where children can be born and raised with a sense of security, and the ruling class is supplied with a readily available and passive labour force for its factories and offices. The family achieves this in three ways:

Domestic labour is unpaid houswork, including cooking, cleaning, childcare and looking after the sick and elderly.

- By providing a place for eating, drinking and relaxing, helping to ensure that members of the workforce are able to go to work each day with their ability to work (their labour power) renewed.
- By producing and maintaining labour which is free of cost to the capitalists through the unpaid housework of women (what is called **domestic labour**), as women are not paid for their labour in rearing children and looking after male partners.
- By socializing children into the dominant ideas in society (the dominant ideology), and preparing them for the necessity and routines of work, such as the need to work for a living, and to be punctual and obedient at work. Through day-to-day relationships in the family, with parents having power and control over their children, and men over women, family members come to accept, often without questioning them, the power inequalities they will face in 'adult' capitalist society. The family therefore lays the groundwork for submission to 'the boss' in later life, and is one of the mechanisms by which capitalism produces and recruits a moulded and obedient workforce.

Social control of the working class   Social control refers to the means of keeping people conforming to the dominant norms and values of society. The expectation that 'good parents' must work to provide material comforts and good life chances for their children helps to keep people in unsatisfying, boring and unrewarding jobs. It is harder for workers to go on strike for higher pay if there is a family to support, because it might mean cuts in the living standards of themselves and their children. This weakens workers' bargaining power at work, and discourages them from taking action that might disrupt the system.

The family can also act as a 'safety valve', providing a release from the tedium, frustration and lack of power and control at work that many workers experience. The family can be a place to escape from the world and relax – a 'sanctuary' into which adults withdraw to recover – and this helps to prevent frustration at work from spilling over into action against the system. This contributes to the stabilization of the capitalist system, to the benefit of the dominant class.

The family as a place of work   Feminist writers were among the first to state that housework is work – as real as waged work outside the home. Housework and childcare in the family, which are mainly performed by women, are unpaid, and not really recognized as work at all. Men are often the ones who gain from this, as it is they who have their meals cooked, their children looked after and their homes kept clean by women's work. Oakley has emphasized that housework is hard, routine and unrewarding (both personally and in a financial sense), and housework remains the primary responsibility of women, though men might sometimes help. This will be examined later in this chapter.

The myth of the 'symmetrical family'   Feminists attack the notion (put forward originally by Young and Willmott in *The Symmetrical Family* (1973)) that there is growing equality between partners in the family. These issues are discussed later in this chapter, but feminists emphasize it is still mainly women who:

Feminists emphasize that housework is unpaid labour. If women ironed clothes, cooked and cleaned for others outside the family they would get paid for it, but in the family they are not

- perform most housework and childcare tasks
- make sacrifices to buy the children clothes, and to make sure other family members are properly fed
- are less likely to make the most important decisions in the family
- are more likely to be dependent on men's earnings, as the average pay of women is only about 83 per cent of that of men
- are more likely to give up paid work, or suffer from lost or restricted job opportunities, to look after children, the old, the sick, and male partners. Many women now work both outside the home in paid employment *and* inside the home doing domestic labour. In effect, they have two jobs to their male partner's one
- are more likely to be the victims of domestic violence by men.

Criticisms of the Marxist feminist and radical feminist perspectives

Criticisms of the Marxist feminist and radical feminist perspectives include the following points:

- Women's roles are not the same in all families. Many families now consist of dual worker couples, with both partners in paid employment.
- These perspectives assume that women are passive victims in the family, and do not have any choices. Some women may choose to become full-time housewives and mothers because they enjoy it and find it fulfilling and rewarding, and they are not forced to do this. Many choose to take paid employment, even though they still have to combine this with the major responsibilities for housework and childcare (see later in this chapter).
- More women are working and have independent incomes, and this means they may have more power in the family than some feminist writers imply. That around 70 per cent of divorces are initiated by women shows that women can, and do, escape from relationships which are oppressive.
- Day-to-day relationships in the family are less likely today to create an unquestioning and obedient workforce. Children have much more status and power in the family than they used to, with families becoming more child-centred (see later), and they are exposed to a much wider range of socializing experiences outside the family, such as the mass media. Women too are much more likely to assert themselves in family life.

Feminist approaches to the family provide a healthy antidote to functionalist accounts, which tend to emphasize the 'functional' aspects of the family and downplay the negative side of family life. For feminists, the family and marriage are major sources of female oppression and gender inequalities in society – whether we examine housework, childcare, power and authority or women's employment outside the home.

Table 3.2 overleaf summarizes functionalist, Marxist feminist and radical feminist perspectives on the family.

Table 3.2 Sociological perspectives on the family

Functionalism	Marxist feminism	Radical feminism
The family meets the needs of society by socializing children into shared norms and values, leading to social harmony and stability	The family meets the needs of capitalism by socializing children into ruling class norms and values (the ruling class ideology), leading to a submissive and obedient workforce, with false consciousness, and stability for capitalism	The family meets the needs of patriarchy by socializing children into traditional gender roles, with men as 'breadwinners' and women having responsibility for housework and childcare
The family is a social institution providing security for the conception, birth and nurture of new members of society	The family is a social institution responsible for the reproduction of labour power for capitalism	The family is a social institution responsible for the reproduction of unequal roles for women and men
The sexual division of labour in the family, with men performing instrumental roles and women performing expressive roles, stabilizes adult personalities and thereby helps to maintain a stable society	The male's instrumental role as wage earner maintains the family, pays for the reproduction of labour power and acts as a strong control on workers' behaviour in the workplace, thereby helping to maintain the stability of an unequal, exploitative capitalist society	The sexual division of labour in the family exploits women, since their responsibilities for domestic labour and childcare are unpaid, undermine their position in paid employment and increase dependency on men. It thereby maintains an unequal patriarchal society
The family is a supportive and generally harmonious and happy social institution	The family is an oppressive institution that stunts the development of human personalities and individuality. There is a 'dark side' to family life that functionalist accounts play down	The family is an oppressive institution that benefits men and oppresses and exploits women. There is a 'dark side' to family life that includes violence and abuse against women and children

Activity

Refer to pages 121–7 and table 3.2 and to the following statements, and classify each one as nearly as possible as functionalist, traditional Marxist, Marxist feminist or radical feminist. Give a brief justification of your reasons in each case.

1 The family is a socially useful and happy institution providing the best context for bringing up children.
2 The family is an important institution because of its contribution to maintaining social stability.
3 The family is a patriarchal and unequal institution controlled by and for men.
4 Children are socialized by the family and other institutions to conform to the dominant ideology.

5 Only the family provides the warmth, security and emotional support necessary to keep society stable.

6 Patterns of obedience laid down in the family form the basis for acceptance of the hierarchy of power and control in capitalist society.

7 Women's role in the family is to do housework, to care for children, the sick, and the elderly, and to flatter, excuse, sympathize and pay attention to men. This often disadvantages women in many aspects of their lives.

8 The family always benefits either men or capitalism.

9 The image of the caring and loving family ignores the violence against women and the sexual crimes, like rape within marriage, which go on there.

10 The family exists primarily to pass on private property from one generation to the next, and to prepare a submissive and obedient workforce.

11 The family is an important institution in maintaining male power.

12 When wives play their traditional role as 'takers of shit', they often absorb their husbands' anger and frustration at their own powerlessness and oppression in the world of work, and stop rebellion in the workplace.

13 Families are factories producing stable human personalities.

14 It is highly unlikely that any society will find an adequate substitute to take over the functions of the nuclear family.

15 Women's unpaid domestic labour reproduces the workforce at no cost to the capitalist.

Demography is the term used for the study of the characteristics of human populations, such as their size and structure and how these change over time.

The **birth rate** is the number of live births per 1,000 of the population each year.

The **fertility rate** is the number of live births per 1,000 women of child-bearing age (15–44) per year.

The **infant mortality rate** is the number of deaths of babies in the first year of life per 1,000 live births per year.

The **death rate** is the number of deaths per 1,000 of the population per year.

Life expectancy is an estimate of how long people can be expected to live from a certain age, usually from birth.

An **ageing population** is one in which the average age is getting higher, with a greater proportion of the population over retirement age, and a smaller proportion of young people.

Demographic change and the family

Demography is the term used for the study of the characteristics of human populations, such as their size and structure and how these change over time. There have been a number of demographic changes in the population of Britain which have had a number of effects on the family. These include declining **birth rates, fertility rates, infant mortality rates, death rates**, and increased **life expectancy**. These changes have had an impact on family size, but also have increased pressures on families and individuals today as a result of an **ageing population**.

The decline in the death rate and infant mortality rate

In 1902 the death rate was 18 per 1,000, and this had declined to around 10 per 1,000 in 2007. The infant mortality rate has also fallen, from around 142 per 1,000 live births in 1902 to around 5 per 1,000 in 2007. Average life expectancy has consequently risen. Today, men can expect to live, on average, to around the age of 77, and women to around 81, though of course many will live beyond these average ages.

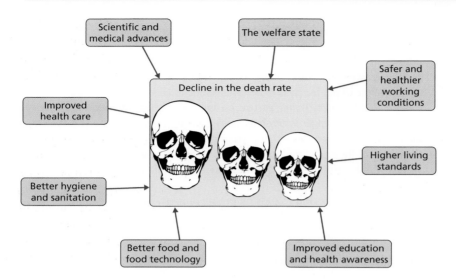

Figure 3.1 Reasons for the decline in the death rate

Explanations for changes in the death rate, infant mortality rate and increased life expectancy

Improved hygiene, sanitation, and medicine   Public hygiene and sanitation have improved enormously since the early nineteenth century, with the construction of public sewer systems and the provision of clean running water. These changes, together with improved public awareness of hygiene and the causes of infection, have contributed to the elimination in Britain of the great epidemic killer diseases of the past, such as cholera, diphtheria and typhoid, which were spread through infected water and food, and these improvements in environmental conditions were more important than medical advances in wiping out these epidemic diseases.

Advances in medicine and science, such as vaccines and the development of penicillin, antibiotics and other life-saving drugs, and advances in surgery and medical technology, such as transplant surgery, have further contributed to the decline in the death rate, and increased life expectancy. More sophisticated medical care means that people now survive illnesses that would have killed them even in the recent past. Before the twentieth century, the highest mortality rates were among babies and young children, but today death rates rise the older you get. The major causes of death today in Britain are from the non-infectious degenerative diseases, such as cancer and heart disease.

Higher living standards   Rising standards of living have further assisted in reducing death rates. Higher wages, better food, more amenities and appliances in the home, and greatly improved housing conditions, with less damp, inside toilets and running hot water, have all assisted in improving the health and life expectancy of the population. Because of improved transportation and food technology, a wider range of more nutritious food is available, with improved storage techniques (such as freezing) making possible the import of a range of foodstuffs, including more affordable fresh fruit and vegetables all the year round.

Public health and welfare   There has been a steep rise in state intervention in public welfare, particularly since the establishment of the welfare state in 1945. The NHS has provided free and comprehensive health care, and there is much better antenatal and postnatal care for mothers and babies. More women have children in hospitals today, and there are health visitors to check on young babies, which helps to explain the decrease in the infant mortality rate. The wide range of welfare benefits available helps to maintain standards of health in times of hardship, and older people in particular are better cared for today, with pensions and a range of services like home helps, social workers and old people's homes.

Health education   Coupled with these changes has been a growing awareness of nutrition and its importance to health. Improved educational standards generally, and particularly in health education, have led to a much better informed public, who demand better hygiene and public health, and welfare legislation and social reforms to improve health. Bodies like NICE (the National Institute for Health and Clinical Excellence) provide national guidance on the promotion of good health and the prevention and treatment of ill health. NICE seeks to improve the health of the public by education, such as emphasizing the benefits of exercise, giving up smoking and eating a balanced diet. Evidence of this growing health awareness include the public outcries in the 1980s and 1990s over risks of food poisoning, such as salmonella in eggs, 'mad cow disease' in beef, listeria in cook-chill foods, the *E. coli* food poisoning outbreak in 1996–7 (which killed twenty people), the public's rejection of genetically modified crops and foods in the early 2000s, and the decline in the numbers of people smoking cigarettes. The Office for National Statistics reported that in the early 1970s around 50 per cent of men and 40 per cent of women smoked, but by 2004/5, this had dropped to 26 per cent of men and 23 per cent of women.

Improved working conditions   Working conditions improved dramatically in the twentieth century. Technology has taken over some of the more arduous, health-damaging tasks, and factory machinery is often safer than it was a hundred years ago. Higher standards of health and safety at work, shorter working hours, more leisure time and earlier retirement ages have all made work physically less demanding and therefore have reduced risks to health.

Britain has an ageing population, with one in six people now over the age of 65, and the proportion is growing

The ageing population

The decline in the death rate and increased life expectancy has meant that more people are living longer. Britain, like most Western industrialized countries, today has an ageing population. This means that the average age of the population is getting higher, with a greater proportion of the population over retirement age, and a smaller proportion of young people.

However, the decline in the birth rate has meant that fewer children are being born as well, and this has changed the overall age structure of the population. For example, in 1901, only about 4 per cent were over age 65, but by 2007, this had risen to about 16 per cent. Figure 3.2 shows this ageing population between 1951 and what it is projected to be in 2031. The changing shape shows that in 1951 there was quite a rapid decline in the proportion of people over the age of 50 in the population as a whole, as they began to die. By 2001 there is more of a 'bulge' in the middle age groups, and by 2031 the older age groups make up a much larger proportion of the population, with most age groups taking up similar proportions of the population. A quick glance at the proportion of over 70s in 1951 compared to 2031 shows this clearly.

Activity

1. Refer to figure 3.2 opposite, and identify three pieces of data that show an ageing population between 1951 and 2031. Explain why they show this.
2. What evidence is there in figure 3.2 that women, in general, live longer than men? Identify data from the figure to back up your view.
3. Identity the largest age group in each of 1951, 2001 and 2031, and suggest two reasons for any differences you identify.

Figure 3.2 Britain's ageing population

Source: Census, Office for National Statistics, Government Actuary's Department

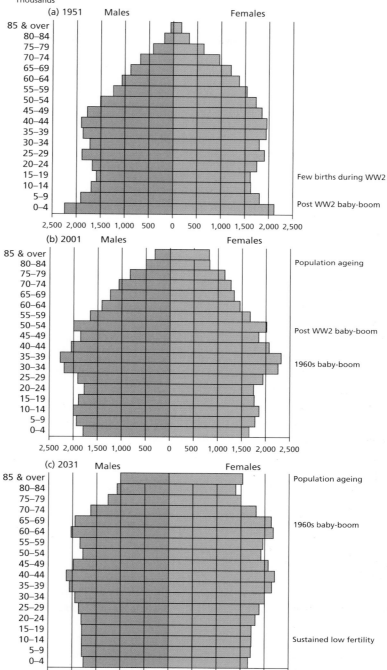

Population: by age and sex, 1951, 2001 and 2031
United Kingdom
Thousands

The growing proportion of elderly people and a relatively smaller proportion of young people, has a number of effects on the family, and individuals:

- There are more lone person households, as partners die.
- Elderly relatives can help with childcare and babysitting, and maybe financially (especially in the middle class).
- If elderly relatives are poor due to inadequate pensions and savings, their family may have to support them. This may lead to financial hardship, as people face having to support not just themselves and their children, but also their parents and possibly grandparents too. This can be made worse if there is a loss of income if one partner has to give up work to care for elderly dependants.
- The growing isolation and loneliness of older people, as friends and partners die and health deteriorates, may lead to growing dependence on their children to visit and support them. This can create problems for planning family holidays and moving for work or promotion.
- There may be emotional strain and overcrowding if an elderly, and possibly infirm, relative moves in with his or her child's family. This might cause conflict between couples, or between children and grandparents, as well as increasing costs to the family.
- There could be a return of the classic extended family. This will be considered later.
- Extra work for women. The practical burdens of caring for the elderly tend to fall mainly on women in the family, even though they already carry most of the burden of housework and childcare in their own homes, as discussed later in this chapter.
- There may well be increased stress and ill health for relatives who have to devote large amounts of time to caring for infirm or disabled elderly relatives. Increasingly, with longer life expectancy, many of these carers are themselves elderly and infirm; for example, 65-year-olds caring for their 90-year-old parents.
- Young people may have difficulty in finding affordable homes of their own, as older people occupy their homes for longer.

Activity

1 If you have, or were to have, an elderly parent, grandparent or great-grandparent living with you, what advantages and problems are or might be created for family life? Discuss these with others if you are in a group.

2 Go to <www.helptheaged.org.uk> (Help the Aged) and/or <www.ageconcern.org.uk> (Age Concern) and identify five issues of concern to older person households, and what these organizations suggest should be done to resolve them.

The decline in the birth rate, fertility rate and average family size

Over the last century, the birth rate has been declining in Britain, from 28 per 1,000 in 1902 to about 11 per 1,000 in 2007. The fertility rate has also been declining. There was an average number of 2.77 children per woman in 1961, but this had reduced to about 1.8 by 2006. This has meant that average family and household size has been dropping, from around 6 children per family in the 1870s to an average of around 1.8 children per family in 2007. The average household size in Britain has also almost halved in the last hundred years, from around 4.6 people to around 2.4 people per household in 2007. The trend towards smaller families, and more people living alone, explains this reduction in average household size.

Figure 3.3 Reasons for the decline in the birth rate, fertility rate and smaller family size

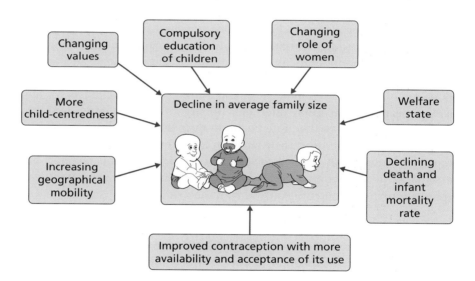

Reasons for the decline in the birth rate and smaller families

Contraception   More effective, safer and cheaper methods of birth control have been developed over the last century, and society's attitudes to the use of contraception have changed from disapproval to acceptance. This is partly because of growing **secularization**, and the declining influence of the church and religion on people's behaviour and morality. The availability of safe and legal abortion since 1967 has also helped in terminating unwanted pregnancies. Family planning is therefore easier.

Secularization is the process whereby religious thinking, practice and institutions lose social significance.

The compulsory education of children   Since children were barred from employment in the nineteenth century, and education became compulsory

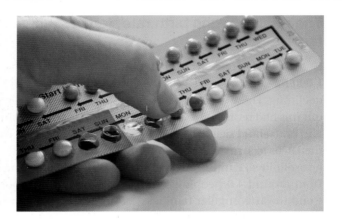

More effective methods of birth control, combined with changing attitudes to the use of contraception, have contributed to the decline in the birth rate

in 1880, they have ceased to be an economic asset that can contribute to family income through working at an early age. Children have therefore become an economic liability and a drain on the resources of parents, because they have to be supported for a long period in compulsory education, and often in post-16 education and training, including university and college years. Parents today often have to support their children well into their 20s. Parents have therefore begun to limit the size of their families to secure for themselves and their children a higher standard of living. The move to a more child-centred society (discussed later in this chapter) has assisted in this restriction of family size, as smaller families mean parents can spend more money and time on and with each child.

The changing position of women   The changing position of women, particularly during the last century, has involved more equal status with men and greater employment opportunities. Women today have less desire to spend long years of their lives bearing and rearing children, and many wish to, and do, pursue their own careers. While most women do eventually have children, there is a growing proportion who are choosing not to do so. For example, around 20 per cent of women born in the early 1960s (aged in their 40s in 2007) were childless in 2007, compared to about 10 per cent of those born in the 1940s by the time they had reached their 40s, and nearly 25 per cent of women born in 1973 are expected to be still childless at age 45. This trend towards childlessness can be expected to continue with women's growing position in paid employment.

The declining infant mortality rate   Until the 1940s, the absence of a welfare state meant that many parents relied on their children to care for them in old age. However, although more babies were beginning to survive

Most women work in paid employment today, and many will combine this with childcare responsibilities. Many wish to pursue careers and will therefore either limit the number of children they have, often putting off having them until their careers are established, or choose to have none at all

infancy, it was still often uncertain whether children would outlive their parents. Parents therefore often had many children as a safeguard against some of them dying. The decline in the infant mortality rate and the death rate has meant that fewer people die before adulthood and old age, so parents no longer have more children as security against only a few surviving. In addition, the range of agencies which exist to help the elderly today means that people are less reliant on care from their children when they reach old age.

A geographically mobile labour force   Contemporary societies generally require a geographically mobile workforce – that is, a workforce that can easily move to other areas for work or promotion. This may have been a factor in encouraging smaller families, because they can more easily pack up and move elsewhere.

Changing values   Parenthood involves greater pressure on couples, a life-long commitment, a loss of freedom and independence, and sacrifices like cuts in money to spend on consumer goods and the loss of time for leisure and pleasure. In the postmodern age, where consumer values dominate and people seek to develop their identities through their consumer spending and leisure choices, couples are becoming more reluctant to have children.

A new baby boom?

In 2007 there was speculation about a new 'baby boom' – a surge in births. While the fertility rate of 1.6 children per woman in Britain was the lowest ever in 2001, between 2001 and 2006 it increased every year. By 2006, it had reached the highest (1.87) it had been for twenty-six years, and there were more babies born than in any year since 1993. While younger British-born women are still choosing to have fewer or no babies, this is being made up for by higher numbers of births among older women. Women are now delaying having children until they are older, as they establish their careers, but also, with high rates of divorce and separation, may be starting new families after forming new partnerships later in life. Younger migrant women who were born outside the UK, many from the Eastern European countries of the European Union, and who tend to have larger families, also explain the rise in fertility. It remains to be seen whether these trends will continue, but it seems highly unlikely ever to return to anywhere near the levels of the last baby boom in the 1960s.

Minority ethnic groups tend to have larger families

Other major changes in the family

The family in Britain is constantly changing over time, and the following pages discuss some of the other major changes that have occurred – or at least that some think have occurred, as the extent of some of these changes has often been exaggerated and misleading conclusions have been drawn. The key changes commonly thought to have occurred are discussed below, and summarized in figure 3.4 below.

Family change 1: has the family lost its functions?

The family in pre-industrial and early industrial Britain and most other societies traditionally had a number of responsibilities placed upon it – these are the functions it performs in society. They are primarily concerned with its role in the preparation of children to fit into adult society.

The case for the view the family has lost its functions

Functionalist writers, like Parsons and Dennis, argue that in contemporary society, many of the functions once performed by the family in pre-industrial society have been removed from the family. These have been transferred to other more specialized institutions, such as the National Health Service and the education and welfare systems. Parsons calls this process **structural differentiation**.

Structural differentiation refers to the way new, more specialized social institutions emerge to take over a range of functions that were once performed by a single institution.

Figure 3.4 Changes in the family

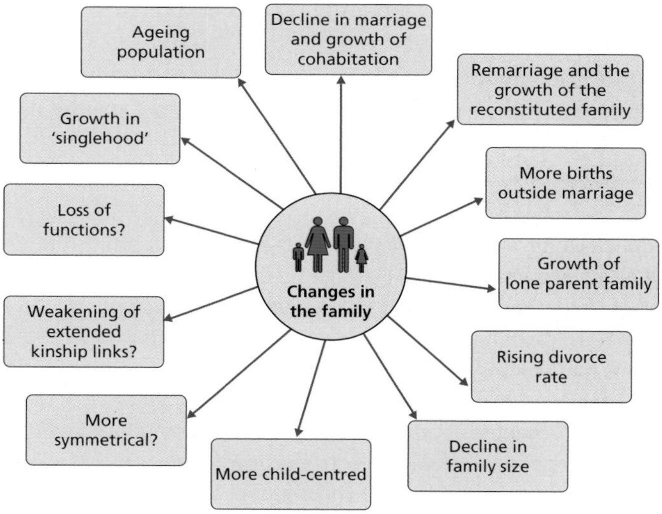

Activity

With reference to figure 3.4, discuss with different generations, such as friends, parents and grandparents or great-grandparents, how the family has changed during the course of the last fifty years. If you are in a group, pool all your findings and discuss the changes you have discovered.

Parsons claims this process of structural differentiation has meant the modern, more specialized family has only two basic functions left: the primary socialization of children and the stabilization of adult personalities.

The case against the view the family has lost its functions

Sociologists like Fletcher (1966) and Shorter deny that the family has lost many of its functions in contemporary society. They suggest that in pre-industrial and early industrial society poverty meant functions such as welfare, education or recreation were often not carried out. Children were frequently neglected, and male peasants often cared more about their animals than their wives. Fletcher argues that the family now has more, not fewer, responsibilities (functions) placed on it. For example, the health and welfare functions of the family have been strengthened by the welfare state, and parents today are more preoccupied with their children's health, and retain responsibility for diagnosis of minor illness and referral to doctors and other welfare state agencies. Social services departments, with their powers to intervene in families if children are neglected or abused, have increased the responsibilities on parents, not reduced them.

Fletcher says that the family plays an important economic role as a unit of consumption. The modern family is particularly concerned with raising the living standards of the family and 'keeping up' with the neighbours through buying a whole host of goods targeted at family consumers, such as washing machines, stereo systems, DVD players, computers and package holidays. Marxists see this pressure to purchase consumer goods as a means of motivating workers in boring, unfulfilling jobs.

Feminist writers see the modern family as a unit of production, since women's unpaid domestic labour (housework and childcare) produces a

Activity

1. To what extent do you consider the family has lost its functions? Examine the arguments in table 3.3 and on pp. 139–41, weigh up the strengths and weaknesses of each argument and reach a conclusion. (This is *evaluation*).
2. Do you think the welfare state has placed more or fewer demands on the family? Give reasons for your answer.
3. Look at TV, newspaper or magazine advertising. Can you find any evidence that the image of family life presented in advertising is used as a way of persuading people to buy consumer goods – for example, by making it appear that buying goods will lead to happier lives, or will make children feel more cared for? If you're in a group, collect or record some adverts and discuss them in your group.
4. Do you have any evidence from your own experience of families buying goods to keep up with the neighbours? If so, why do you think they do this?

Table 3.3 The changing functions of the family

Traditional functions of the family	How they have changed
The reproduction and nurturing of children was often seen as the main reason for marriage, as a means of passing on family property and providing a future workforce	There has been a steady increase in the reproduction of children and sexual relations before, alongside and outside marriage
Before industrialization and the growth of factory production in Britain, the family was a unit of production. This means that the family home was also the workplace, and the family produced most of the goods necessary for its own survival. Children would learn the skills needed for working life from their parents, and the family ascribed the occupational roles and status of adults. In other words, children generally followed in their parents' footsteps	Since the early nineteenth century in Britain, work has moved outside the home to factories and offices (with the exception of housework/domestic labour). Families no longer generally produce the goods they need – they go out to work for wages so they can buy them. The skills required for adult working life are no longer learnt in the family but at the place of work, at colleges or on government-supported job training schemes. Occupational roles and status in society are less likely to be ascribed by the kinship network, but achieved by individual merit
The family traditionally played the major role in caring for dependent children – that is, those children who were still unable to look after themselves. Before the twentieth century in Britain, most children were often poorly looked after because of poverty	The modern nuclear family gets more help and assistance in maintaining and caring for children through a wide range of state welfare services, such as child tax credits, the social services and growing numbers of pre- and after-school clubs, playgroups and nurseries
The family used to have the main responsibility for health and welfare provision for the young, the old, the sick, the disabled, the unemployed and the poor	The welfare state (established in the 1940s) has taken on some of these responsibilities. The National Health Service, social services departments and other agencies of the welfare state, plus a range of welfare benefits, reduce the dependence on kin for money and support when misfortune strikes
The primary and secondary socialization and social control of children, and their education, used to be performed mainly by the family and close community. Before compulsory schooling was provided by the state in Britain from 1880, many children from working-class families had extremely high illiteracy rates	The family still retains important responsibilities for the socialization, social control and education of young children. However, nurseries, playgroups and the state educational system now help the family with these functions, and the mass media also play an important socializing role. Education is now primarily the responsibility of professional teachers rather than parents, although the family still continues to play an important role in supporting children at school. The family still has important influences on how well a child does at school

wide range of goods and services in the family which would prove very expensive if they were provided and paid for outside the family.

The discussion of whether or not the family has lost its functions is outlined in table 3.3.

Family change 2: the decline of the classic extended family and the emergence of the privatized nuclear family?

A second major change in the family to consider is the view that the **privatized nuclear family** has become the most common form of the family in contemporary Britain, and that the classic extended family has largely disappeared.

The privatized nuclear family means that the modern nuclear family is a very private institution, separated and isolated from its extended kin, and often from neighbours and local community life as well. It has become a self-contained, self-reliant and home-centred unit, with free time spent doing jobs around the house, and leisure time mainly spent with the family. In the privatized nuclear family, family members will often know more, and care more, about the lives of media soap stars and computer game heroes than they do about the real people who live in their street. The privatized nuclear family has been called by Parsons the 'structurally isolated' family, since it has also lost many of its functions and links to other social institutions.

In *The Symmetrical Family* (1973), Young and Willmott argue that the main form of the family used to be the classic extended family, but the beginnings of the transition to the privatized symmetrical nuclear family of today began around 1900. They argue that the modern family – what they call the 'symmetrical family' – has strong bonds between married or cohabiting partners, with the relationship becoming more symmetrical, or equal on both sides. Both partners share household chores, childcare and decision-making, and both partners are more likely to be involved in paid employment. Whether the modern family really is 'symmetrical' is discussed later in this chapter.

> The **privatized nuclear family** is a self-contained, self-reliant and home-centred family unit that is separated and isolated from its extended kin, neighbours and local community life.

Is this nuclear family the typical shape of the contemporary family?

Figure 3.5 Reasons for the decline of the classic extended family and the emergence of the privatized nuclear family

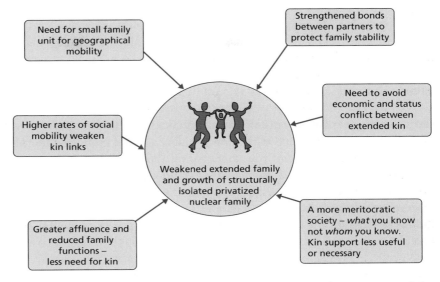

Need for small family unit for geographical mobility

Strengthened bonds between partners to protect family stability

Higher rates of social mobility weaken kin links

Need to avoid economic and status conflict between extended kin

Weakened extended family and growth of structurally isolated privatized nuclear family

Greater affluence and reduced family functions – less need for kin

A more meritocratic society – *what* you know not *whom* you know. Kin support less useful or necessary

Writers like Parsons, Young and Willmott, and Fletcher have suggested that the structurally isolated, privatized nuclear family, or some form of modified extended family, has emerged as the main family form in contemporary British society. According to Parsons, this is because it is well adapted to meet both the needs of industrial society and the needs of individuals.

There are six main reasons why there is thought to have been a decline in extended family life, with the isolated nuclear family 'fitting' contemporary society. These are summarized in figure 3.5.

> The **division of labour** is the division of work or occupations into a large number of specialized jobs or tasks, each of which is carried out by one worker or group of workers.

The need for geographical mobility   Contemporary society has a specialized **division of labour**, with a wide range of different occupations with different incomes and lifestyles. This means that the labour force needs to be geographically mobile – to be able to move around the country to areas where their skills are required, to improve their education or gain promotion. This often involves leaving relatives behind, thus weakening and breaking up traditional extended family life. The isolated nuclear family is ideally suited to this requirement because it is small in size and it is not tied down by responsibilities for extended kin who, in earlier times, might have been living with them.

The higher rate of social mobility in contemporary societies   Social mobility means that people can move up or down the social scale compared to the family they were born into. Higher levels of social mobility mean that different members of the extended family may find themselves in different jobs, with differences in education, income, lifestyle, opportunities, and attitudes and values between kin. These differences weaken relations between kin, as they have less in common.

The growth in people's wealth and income as society has got richer and the welfare state has developed   People are much better off today, and the welfare state has taken over a number of functions previously performed by the family, such as in education, health care and welfare. This has reduced dependence on kin for support in times of distress. This further weakens the extended family.

The growth in meritocracy in contemporary societies   Contemporary societies require more skills and education for jobs, and are more **meritocratic** than in the past – it is *what* you know, rather than *who* you know, that is the most important factor in getting jobs. Extended kin therefore have less to offer family members, such as job opportunities, reducing reliance on kin. However, while this is true for most people, kin links remain very important in the upper class, for the inheritance of wealth and for access to the top 'elite' jobs.

> A **meritocracy** (or a meritocratic society) is a society where occupational status is mainly achieved on the basis of talent, skill and educational qualifications, rather than whom you know or the family you were born into.

The need to avoid the possibility of economic and status differences in an extended family unit causing conflict and family instability   The different occupations, incomes, lifestyles and statuses of extended family members who live together might be a source of family conflict and instability, with conflicts over where to live when different job opportunities arise, and over different incomes and lifestyles in the same family unit. The fact that adult children generally move away from the family home to establish their own independent lives avoids such potential problems.

The need to protect family stability by strengthening the bonds between married or cohabiting partners   There is a lack of support from kin in the isolated nuclear family, and Parsons argues that this helps to cement family relationships by increasing the mutual dependency of partners in a married or cohabiting relationship. This increases the stabilization of adult personalities, which are under particular stress in the face of the impersonal competitive relations of contemporary society as people fight for higher status, more money and promotion at work to support the consumer-led lifestyles of contemporary society. Young and Willmott suggest that rising living standards have made the home a more attractive place to spend time, and family life has become more home-centred. Free time is spent by both partners doing jobs around the home, watching TV and so on, and the family becomes a self-contained and more intimate unit.

Criticisms

While there is some evidence that the isolated nuclear family is more common than the extended family in contemporary Britain, it would be wrong to suggest that extended family life has completely disappeared. Also, families are changing rapidly, and there is no longer a 'typical' family type. There is a wide diversity (or range) of family structures alongside the isolated nuclear family. The issue of family diversity is discussed later in this chapter.

The continued existence of the classic extended family

While the isolated nuclear family may be more common than the classic extended family today, the classic extended family still survives in modern Britain in two types of community:

Traditional working-class communities   These are long-established communities dominated by one industry, like fishing and mining, in the traditional working-class industrial centres of the north of England, and also occurring in inner-city working-class areas. In such communities, there is little geographical or social mobility, and children usually remain in the same area when they get married. People stay in the same community for several generations, and this creates close-knit community life – it is the type of community shown in TV 'soaps' such as *Coronation Street* or *EastEnders*. Members of the extended family live close together and meet frequently, and there is a constant exchange of services between extended family members, such as washing, shopping and childcare between female kin, and shared work and leisure activities between male relatives. Such extended family life declined in the second half of the twentieth century, particularly in the 1990s, as traditional industries closed down and people were forced to move away in search of new employment.

The Asian community   There is evidence that the extended family is still very common among those who came to Britain in the 1960s and 1970s from India, Pakistan and Bangladesh. The extended family usually centres on the male side of the family, with grandfathers, sons, grandsons and their wives, and unmarried daughters. Such family life continues to be an important source of strength and support in such communities.

The modified extended family

While it is true that many families with dependent children in Britain today are nuclear families, we must not assume that just because family members may live apart geographically, all links with kin are severed and destroyed. Kin beyond the nuclear family still play an important part in the lives of many families, particularly in the early years of relationships when homes are purchased or rented and children arrive. Often, in the age of modern communications and easy transportation, the closeness and mutual support between kin typical of classic extended family life are retained through email communication, social networking internet websites like Facebook, Bebo or MySpace, letter writing, telephone and visiting, despite geographical separation. We might therefore conclude that the most common family unit in contemporary society is a modified form of the extended family. This modified extended family is one where related nuclear families, although they may be living far apart geographically, nevertheless maintain regular contact and mutual support made possible by modern communications and easy transportation. This, rather than the isolated nuclear family, is probably the most common type of family arrangement in Britain today.

The 'Beanpole' family: the return of the extended family?

As discussed earlier in this chapter, Britain's ageing population means that a growing number of people are reaching old age, and often living well into their eighties and many into their nineties. At the same time, couples are having fewer children and nuclear families are getting smaller. This means that there is an increase in the number of extended three- and four-generation families. There are declining numbers of children in families, but more of them are growing up in extended families alongside several of their grandparents and even great-grandparents. This new shape of the extended family is sometimes called the 'beanpole' family (Brannen, 2003). This is because the family tree is 'thinner' and less 'bushy': fewer brothers and sisters in one generation leads to fewer aunts and uncles in the next. It is also longer, with several generations of older relatives, as people live longer. This trend

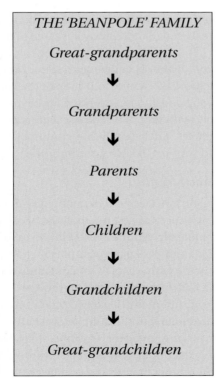

THE 'BEANPOLE' FAMILY

Great-grandparents
↓
Grandparents
↓
Parents
↓
Children
↓
Grandchildren
↓
Great-grandchildren

declining numbers of children in each generation

towards a new emerging 'beanpole' form of the extended family can only be expected to increase with the growing numbers of the elderly, and fewer children being born.

Activity

1 Describe *two* characteristics of the privatized nuclear family.
2 Give *three* reasons for the decline of the classic extended family.
3 Explain what is meant by the 'modified extended family'.
4 Write a short essay of about one and half sides answering the following question: *examine the view that the nuclear family is ideally suited to the needs of contemporary society.*

Family change 3: the emergence of the symmetrical family?

Conjugal roles simply means the roles played by a male and female partner in marriage or in a cohabiting relationship.
Segregated conjugal roles show a clear division and separation between the male and female roles.
Integrated (or joint) **conjugal roles** show few divisions between male and female partners' roles.

Is there more equality between partners in relationships today, or does the family remain a patriarchal, male-dominated unit? There is a common belief that, since the middle of the twentieth century, the relations between male and female partners in the family in Britain have become less patriarchal, or male-dominated, and become much more a 'partnership of equals'. The assumption has been that there has been a change from **segregated conjugal roles** to more **integrated** (or joint) **conjugal roles**. Young and Willmott called this more equally balanced relationship the symmetrical family.

Some of the differences between segregated and integrated conjugal roles are identified in table 3.4.

Table 3.4 Differences between segregated and integrated conjugal roles

Segregated conjugal roles	Integrated conjugal roles
Partners in a married or cohabiting relationship have clearly separated roles.	Partners in a married or cohabiting relationship have interchangeable and flexible roles.
Men take responsibility for bringing in money, major decisions and doing the heavier and more technical jobs around the home, such as repairing household equipment and doing repairs. Women are mainly housewives, with responsibility for housework, shopping, cooking, childcare, etc.; they are unlikely to have full-time paid employment.	Both partners are likely to be either in paid employment or looking for a job. Household chores and childcare are shared, with males taking on traditional female jobs like housework, cooking, shopping, etc., and female partners taking on traditional male jobs, such as household repairs, looking after the car, etc.
Partners are likely to have separate friends and different leisure activities.	Partners share common friends, leisure activities, and decision-making.

This greater equality in marriage or cohabiting relationships is often thought to be shown by women taking on more 'men's work' (especially working outside the home) and men doing 'women's work' (housework, shopping and childcare), with shared leisure and decision-making. This was often combined with discussion, mainly in the mass media, about the emergence of a so-called 'new man', who was more caring, sharing, gentle, emotional and sensitive in his attitudes to women, children and his own emotional needs, and committed to doing his fair share of housework and childcare.

What causes these apparent changes?

The growing equality in family relationships which is thought to be occurring is often explained by several factors:

- Improved living standards in the home, such as central heating, TV, DVDs, computers and the internet, and all the other modern consumer goods, have encouraged husbands and wives, or cohabiting couples, to become more home-centred, building the relationship and the home.
- The decline of the close-knit extended family and greater geographical and social mobility in contemporary society have meant there is less pressure from kin on newly married or cohabiting couples to retain traditional roles – it is therefore easier to adopt new roles in a relationship. There are often no longer the separate male and female networks (of friends and especially kin) for male and female partners to mix with. This increases their dependence upon each other, and may mean men and women who adopt new roles avoid being teased by friends who knew them before they got married or started cohabiting (see Bott's research in the box opposite).
- The improved status and rights of women encourage men to accept women more as equals and not simply as housewives and mothers.
- The increase in the number of women working in paid employment has increased women's independence and authority in the family. Where the female partner has her own income, she is less dependent on her male partner, and she therefore has more power and authority. Decision-making is thus more likely to be shared.
- The importance of the female partner's earnings in maintaining the family's standard of living may have encouraged men to help more with housework – a recognition that the women cannot be expected to do two jobs at once.
- Weaker gender identities. Postmodernists would argue that men and women now have much more choice in how they see themselves and their roles. Couples are free to 'pick 'n' mix' roles and identities based on personal choice, and are therefore less constrained by traditional gender identities. This weakens traditional gender divisions in housework and childcare.

Elizabeth Bott, 'Conjugal roles and social networks' (1957)

Bott tried to explain the apparent changes in conjugal roles. Although her research is old, the theoretical aspects of her work still have some use today.

Bott found that the most important factor influencing whether couples had segregated or integrated conjugal roles was the social network of friends, kin and acquaintances built up by each partner before marriage. Where couples had a tight-knit network, where the members of the network knew each other well and were in regular contact, this helped to reinforce the separation between men's and women's roles. Both husband and wife, or cohabiting partners, had people of their own sex for companionship or help with household tasks, the closeness of the network acted as a form of social control on the couple, and things such as teasing prevented the couple drifting from 'traditional' segregated roles. By contrast, a loose-knit network would make movement towards more role integration easier, because those constraints would be removed.

Using Bott's framework, one would expect that the geographical and social mobility of contemporary societies would lead to looser social networks, more reliance on the partners in the relationship, and therefore more role integration.

Criticisms of the view that modern marriages and cohabiting relationships are really more equal

The view that there is more equality in modern family relationships has been subject to very strong criticism, particularly by feminist writers, and there is not really much evidence that the family is now typically 'symmetrical'. The following summarizes several of these criticisms.

Inequalities in the division of labour in the household   Evidence from a number of surveys, including the British Social Attitudes surveys (see figure 3.6 on pages 152–3), suggests that women still perform the majority of domestic tasks around the home, even when they have paid jobs themselves. This is true even among full-time working women, where one would expect to find the greatest degree of equality. Cooking the evening meal, household cleaning, washing and ironing, and caring for sick children are still mainly performed by women. The Food Standards Agency's 'Consumer Attitudes to Food Standards' survey (2007) found that 77 per cent of women took all or most of the responsibility for household food shopping. Data published in 1997 by the Office for National Statistics showed that women spent on average nearly twice as long as men each day (five hours) cooking, cleaning, shopping, washing and looking after the children. Housework is the second largest cause of domestic rows, after money.

Crude indicators are often used to measure integrated roles. For example, shared friends are often seen as evidence of 'jointness', but shared friends

Have conjugal roles really become move equal?

may mean the male partner's friends, and involve the woman being cut off from *her* friends, resulting in more dependence on her male partner and greater inequality.

Ann Oakley is a feminist sociologist who did much of the pioneering work on housework and roles in the family in *The Sociology of Housework* (1974). Oakley argues that Young and Willmott's evidence for 'jointness' in *The Symmetrical Family* is totally unconvincing. Seventy-two per cent of married men claimed to 'help their partners in the home in some way other than washing up at least once a week'. As Oakley points out, this could mean anything – a quick pass of the vacuum cleaner, tucking children into bed, making breakfast occasionally, going out with the children on Saturday mornings, or even a man ironing his own trousers. This is hardly convincing evidence for symmetry or equality in marriage, and fewer than three-quarters of husbands in Young and Willmott's research did even this much.

Research on families where both partners are working in full-time career jobs, such as Elston's (1980) research on doctors and Rapoport and Rapoport's (1976) study of professional and business couples, suggests that these professional wives are still expected to take major responsibility for dealing with childcare arrangements, sick children and housework. So women who are in full-time demanding career jobs are still treated primarily as housewives/mothers at home, and this is the group Young and Willmott argued would be most likely to display symmetry in marriage.

Three-quarters of households now have dual incomes, but 2005 research by Susan Harkness at the University of Bristol found that women still take responsibility for most of the housework. This research found it is still mainly

Women still do most of the housework and childcare, even when they have full-time jobs in paid employment

How representative is the research on conjugal roles?

The extent to which research on conjugal roles can be applied to the whole population is seriously questionable. For example, Bott's research was based on a small sample of 20 families, research by Oakley on 40 couples, by Boulton on 50 couples, and by Edgell on 38 couples. Much of this research was based in London. These samples are too small and too specific to London to be applied to the whole country. The only survey which can really claim to be representative of everyone is the British Social Attitudes Survey, which uses much larger samples (around 3,000 people) and very careful sampling techniques. These issues are discussed in chapter 5 on sociological methods.

women who take time off to look after sick children, including more than half of women who earn the same as or more than their partners. Working mothers with children put twice as many hours into housework as their partners, and mothers working full-time in dual earner couples faced long working hours, with the burden of unpaid housework and childcare responsibilities increasing the time pressures for many women. These pressures of housework and childcare on top of full-time careers have led to the suggestion by the *Guardian* newspaper that many full-time married career women effectively have the status of 'married lone parents'.

While there is some evidence of more sharing of childcare than household tasks, Mary Boulton argues that many surveys exaggerate how much childcare men really do. As she sees it, while men may help with childcare, it is their

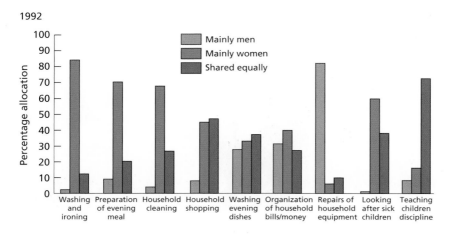

1992

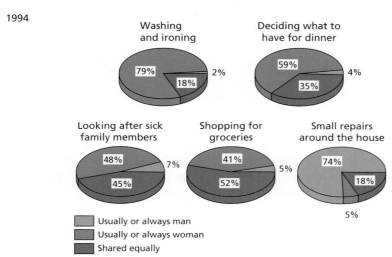

1994

Figure 3.6 Household division of labour among married or cohabiting couples: various years

Source: Based on data from British Social Attitudes surveys (1992, 1994), *Social Trends (1997) and British and European Social Attitudes Report* (1998)

female partners who take the main responsibility for children, often at the expense of other aspects of their lives, like paid employment.

A 2005 report by the Institute for Public Policy Research found that while public attitudes increasingly assume a high degree of gender equality in paid work, this does not apply to home and family life. This research found there was still a widely held belief among the public that women should be responsible for the care of the home and young children. Asked about whether mothers should work, 48 per cent thought they should stay at home while children are under school age, with 34 per cent supporting part-time working. This perception disadvantages mothers with full-time careers, harming their promotion prospects.

It seems that patriarchal ideology still sees housework and childcare as 'women's work', and research over the past 35 years has repeatedly shown

Figure 3.6 (*cont'd*)

1996

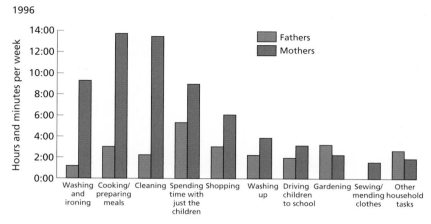

1998

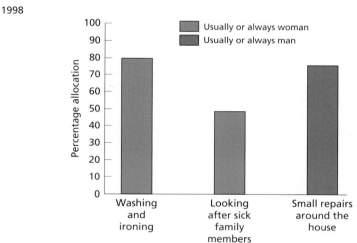

that nothing much has changed since Oakley wrote in *The Sociology of Housework*:

> As long as the blame is laid on the woman's head for an empty larder or a dirty house it is not meaningful to talk about marriage as a 'joint' or 'equal' partnership. The same holds of parenthood. So long as mothers and not fathers are judged by their children's appearance and behaviour . . . symmetry remains a myth.

The unequal distribution of power and authority in marriage and cohabiting relationships   An important issue to consider when assessing whether there is more equality or not in the family is to examine how much control over decision-making each partner has. Research in this area suggests:

- Most decisions which couples think of as 'very important', such as moving house or taking out loans, are finally taken by men alone. While some

Table 3.5 Percentage who never do selected household tasks: United Kingdom, 2001

Activity	Does not do activity	
	Men	Women
Cooking a meal	15	3
DIY repair work	16	46
Gardening	20	22
Non-food shopping	7	3
Food shopping	33	10
Cooking a meal (special occasion)	18	27
Decorating	12	5
Tidying the house	13	4
Helping children with homework	66	60
Washing clothes	39	5
Ironing clothes	42	8

Source: Adapted from UK Time Use Survey, Office for National Statistics

decisions are taken jointly, very few are taken by women alone. Edgell, in *Middle-Class Couples* (1980), found women had sole responsibility for decisions only in relatively unimportant areas like home decoration and furnishing, children's clothes, food and other domestic spending. This was confirmed by a MORI survey conducted for Direct Line Financial Services in June 2000. This found that decisions on major spending (over £1,000) were only made jointly between men and women in 53 per cent of cases. Women made only one in ten of the decisions. In many households, men still hold the purse strings.

- Men are still often the major or sole earners. This puts them in a stronger bargaining position than women, and often puts their female partners in a position of economic dependence.
- There is evidence of widespread male violence in relationships (wife-battering), often resorted to when men are drunk and use their power to try to get women to submit to their wishes. Such violence is all too often not taken seriously by the police or courts, being dismissed as a 'domestic dispute'. This might be interpreted as a view that such violence is almost seen as a 'normal' part of a relationship. Violence in the family is discussed later in this chapter.

Activity

Refer to figure 3.6 and table 3.5. These show the results of surveys which were conducted throughout the 1990s and in 2001. Then answer the following questions:

1 Overall, which household task was the most likely to be performed mainly by women?
2 Overall, which household task was the most likely to be performed mainly by men?
3 Who is most likely to look after sick children or other sick family members?
4 Which household tasks do fathers spend more time on than mothers?
5 Overall, which three households tasks are most likely to be shared equally?
6 When considering whether the time spent on household tasks is fair or not, what other information do you think is required?
7 What percentage of men never iron clothes?
8 What percentage of women never do do-it-yourself repair work?
9 Outline all the evidence in figure 3.6 and table 3.5 which suggests that it is largely a myth that the family is a 'partnership of equals' today?
10 Do a small survey in your own home or in any household where there are children, and find out who performs the various jobs around the home – mainly the man, mainly the woman, or shared equally. You might like to investigate if children do any work.
   (a) *Make a note about whether or not one or both partners are working in paid employment, and whether they do this full-time or part-time. Why might this be important information?*
   (b) *Use the various tasks included in figure 3.6 and table 3.5 to draw up a checklist of jobs. You might also consider some of the following tasks: cleaning floors; cleaning the loo; drawing up the shopping list or working out what's needed when going to the supermarket; changing nappies; bathing the baby; buying children's clothes. You might also consider decision-making in the family, by asking about who finally decides whether to spend a large amount of money (say, over £1,000), buy new furniture, whether and where to go on holiday, whether to buy a new car, deciding on colour schemes when redecorating, deciding what plants to put in the garden, and so on. A further aspect to explore might be who takes responsibility for children, such as making sure they have the right gear for school every day, buying them new shoes, arranging parties and so on.*
   (c) *Examine your results to see if there is any evidence to suggest family roles are becoming more equal. If you are in a group, bring all the results together and discuss what the evidence shows.*

The effects of housework and childcare on women's careers Women's continuing responsibility for housework and childcare often means women's careers suffer. The constraints these pressures put on the energies of working women, particularly mothers, are seen to be holding back their earning power. Surveys suggest many working women are limited in the jobs they can do and the hours they can work because they are still expected to take the main responsibility for housework and childcare, and to be at home when the children leave for and return from school. These family commitments allow little opportunity for working mothers to concentrate on the actions necessary for progressing their careers, and women consequently have less pay, less security of employment and poorer promotion prospects than men, and this reinforces men's economic superiority and greater authority in the family.

More than four out of five part-time workers are women, and about 40 per cent of women in paid employment work only part-time, compared with about 9 per cent of men. The presence of dependent children (under the age of 18) and the age of the youngest child are the most important factors bearing on whether or not women are in paid employment, and whether they work full-time or part-time. Figure 3.7 illustrates the importance of this link between dependent children and part-time status, and provides clear evidence that it is women who retain primary responsibility for childcare.

There is still a lot of male prejudice about women in career jobs and senior positions, and women face a number of disadvantages:

- Women who have children are seen as 'unreliable' by some employers, because of the assumption they will get pregnant again, or be absent to look after sick children.

Youngest dependent child, 0–4 years

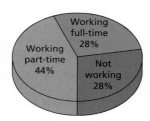

Youngest dependent child, 5–10 years

Youngest dependent child, 11–15 years

Youngest dependent child, 16–18 years

Figure 3.7 Working patterns of women with dependent children: United Kingdom, 2006

Source: Data from Labour Force Survey

Activity

Refer to figure 3.7

1   What percentage of mothers whose youngest child was aged 0–4 years was not working in 2006?
2   Identify *two* trends which occur as the youngest dependent child gets older.
3   What does figure 3.7 suggest might be the main restriction on mothers with dependent children going out to work? Suggest ways this restriction might be overcome.
4   How do you think having young dependent children might affect the working lives of fathers? Give reasons for your answer.

- Employers are sometimes reluctant to invest in expensive training programmes for women, as they may assume women will leave work eventually to produce and raise children.
- Women with promising careers may have temporarily to leave jobs to have children, and therefore miss out greatly on pay and promotion opportunities. Top jobs require a continuous career pattern in the 20–30 age period, yet these are the usual childbearing years for women, so while men continue to work and get promoted, women miss their opportunities. Women with young children may also find difficulties in attending meetings, and this may affect their chances of promotion.
- Highly qualified women who leave jobs to have children, or who take career breaks to spend time with young children, often face 'hidden discrimination' when they return to their jobs. Gatrell (2004) found many of these returning women, labelled 'jelly heads' by hostile employers, had no other option but to accept a downgraded position if they wished even to stay in their chosen professions, particularly if they asked for more flexible working arrangements to cope with their children. Although downgrading like this is illegal, many women don't fight their cases for fear of being labelled as 'awkward' and consequently facing even further career disadvantages.
- It is mainly women who give up paid work (or suffer from lost/restricted job opportunities) to look after children, the elderly or the sick.
- Married or cohabiting women are still more likely to move house and area for their male partner's job promotion rather than the other way round. This means women interrupt their careers and have to start again in a new job, often at a lower level, while the men are getting promoted at the expense of lost opportunities for their partners.

Domestic labour   Domestic labour refers to unpaid housework and childcare, and, as seen above, most of this still falls to women. This is a clear inequality between men and women, and this problem is made worse by some of the features of domestic labour that make it different from a paid job.

These include no pay, no pensions, no holidays, and unlimited working hours. Much of this has been covered in Oakley's work.

These features of domestic labour are illustrated in figure 3.8 below. The Office for National Statistics in 1997 calculated that if the time spent on unpaid work in the home (childcare, washing, ironing, cleaning, shopping and cooking) was valued at the same average pay rates as equivalent jobs in paid employment (for example, if cooking were paid as it is for chefs, or childcare as for nannies and childminders), it would be worth £739 billion a year. The Legal and General insurance company's annual 'Value of a Mum' survey in 2006 valued women's domestic labour and childcare at £470 per week, based on an average 66-hour week around the home, including childcare, cooking, cleaning and housekeeping. This is a very modest £7.12 an hour, and probably too low an hourly rate to purchase all these services outside the home. The same survey found that both men and women severely under-estimated the monetary value of the mother's work at around 58 per cent of its true value, and that mothers put in nearly twice as many hours each week as men on household duties.

There are differing views about who benefits from domestic labour:

- For *radical feminists*, men are seen as the main people who benefit from domestic labour, since it is overwhelmingly women who do it. From this point of view, the inequalities in domestic labour are part of the problem of patriarchy, with the family seen as a patriarchal unit, institutionalizing, reinforcing and reproducing male power.

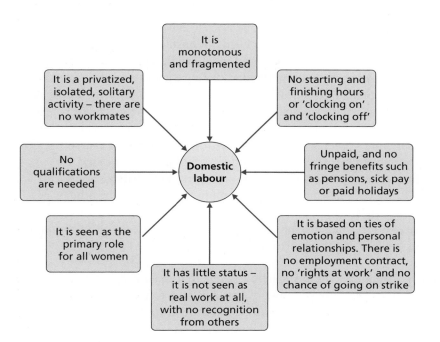

Figure 3.8 How domestic labour differs from paid employment

- *Marxist feminists* see domestic labour as benefiting capitalism by contributing to the reproduction of labour power. Unpaid domestic labour reproduces the labour force at no cost to the capitalist, through the free production and rearing of children, and support for male workers. From this point of view, the family is a 'social factory', producing human labour power. Domestic labour also contributes to the daily reproduction of the labour force by providing for the physical and mental well-being of family members so they are capable of performing labour each day for the capitalist. However, Marxist feminists recognize it is also a problem of patriarchy, as it is women who do most of this unpaid work and it is predominantly men who benefit from it.

The emotional side of family life and women's 'triple shift'   There is evidence that women take the major responsibility for 'managing' the emotional side of family life. Duncombe and Marsden (1995) found that many long-term relationships were held together by women, rather than men, putting in the emotional work necessary to keep their relationships alive. As well as with their partners, women also seem to be more involved in the emotional aspects of childcare, such as talking to, listening to, understanding and supporting children, including older children. This emotional work also involves liaising between family members when there are rows, and acting as the family mediator. This additional work of women is very much in keeping

Activity

Refer to figure 3.8
1 Suggest reasons why domestic labour is often not seen as 'real work'.
2 What might make it difficult for those doing domestic labour to go on strike?
3 Explain what is meant by domestic labour being 'seen as the primary role for all women'.
4 In what ways do you think domestic labour might be (a) more satisfying and (b) less satisfying than work in paid employment?
5 Women who are full-time housewives suffer higher rates of stress, anxiety and depression, and suffer from poorer mental health, than women and men working in paid employment. With reference to figure 3.8, suggest reasons why this might be the case.
6 To what extent do you agree with the view that it is mainly men who benefit from domestic labour?
7 What kind of evidence would you use to judge whether there is 'symmetry' in your own family or relationship, or that of others? Identify the main issues you would want to look at.
8 Do you agree with the view that women are the main managers of family emotions? What evidence from your own or other families can you think of which shows this is or is not the case?

| Paid employment | Housework and childcare | Emotional work |

Women's triple shift

The points discussed in this section mean many female partners now often have three jobs – paid work, domestic labour and childcare, and emotional work – to their male partner's one. This has sometimes been referred to as women's 'triple shift'.

with the functionalist view that Parsons was talking about in the 1950s when he wrote about the expressive role of women. However, this expressive role of women in the emotional side of family life now often comes on top of their 'instrumental' responsibilities in paid employment and domestic labour. This means many female partners often have three jobs (paid work, domestic labour and childcare, and emotional work) to their male partner's one. That women mainly undertake this aspect of family life is perhaps illustrated by the fact that, after separation or divorce, 40 per cent of fathers lose contact with their children within two years.

Family change 4: the changing position of children

Popular views of childhood

In contemporary Britain, and in most Western societies, many people take it for granted that children are fundamentally different from adults. Children are seen as innocent and vulnerable, and who need protecting from the dangers lurking in the adult world. We tend to think of childhood as a clear and separate period of life, with the child's world being a special time of life that is different and separate from the world of adults, with a long period of support and socialization by adults, usually in the family, necessary before they are themselves able to take on the responsibilities of adults. In many ways, childhood today in Britain has become quite a privileged time of life compared to adults. For example, children are protected by laws to discourage them from smoking, drinking alcohol, accessing pornography, viewing unsuitable films, being exploited at work, or being neglected or abused by parents and other adults, and they get cheaper travel, and have special foods,

To what extent do you think childhood in contemporary Britain might be regarded as a privileged time of life?

clothes, toys and leisure activities designed for them. They even have special arrangements made for them by the state, such as schools to educate them, child benefits to help their parents support them and a range of child protection agencies designed to protect their interests. It is often thought that this is a perfectly natural result of children's biological immaturity, which makes them vulnerable and in need of the care and protection of adults. However, sociologists would argue that the identity and status of children, and childhood as a separate phase of life, have been created by society and social attitudes, and are not simply moulded by biological immaturity. In short, they argue that childhood is a **social construction**.

> **Social construction** means that the important characteristics of something, such as statistics, health, childhood, old age or what is regarded as deviance are created and influenced by the attitudes, actions and interpretations of members of society. It only exists because people define it as such.

Evidence for the social construction of childhood

Evidence supporting the idea that childhood is a social construction rather than simply a natural product of biological immaturity is found in three main areas:

- the differing status, responsibilities and treatment of children in different contemporary cultures
- the way the view of the nature of children and of childhood, and the status, responsibilities and treatment of children have changed through history, and continue to change today
- the differences between children's status and responsibilities even in the same society

Cross-cultural differences in childhood

Looking at childhood from a cross-cultural perspective shows there is a wide variety or diversity of childhoods that exist across the world. The freedom from adult responsibilities experienced by many Western children is not found in all societies, especially those of developing countries. In many simpler societies the prolonged period of childhood and adolescence before the transition to adulthood found in contemporary Britain does not exist, and children take on adult roles as soon as they are physically able. In many societies children perform essential work necessary for the economic survival of the family. The International Labour Organization suggests that one in six children in the world work, with 218 million children aged 5–17 involved in child labour. Around 126 million children work in hazardous conditions, with the highest proportion of child labourers in Sub-Saharan Africa, where 26 per cent of children (49 million) are involved in work. A more dramatic and disturbing example of the swift transition to adulthood is found in the case of child soldiers. A 2004 report by the Coalition to Stop the Use of Child Soldiers (www.child-soldiers.org) suggested that between 2001 and 2004 child soldiers were involved in active conflict in twenty-seven countries around the world, with children both being brutalized and killed, and also brutalizing and killing others, as part of adult conflicts. Girls as well as boys are involved, with girl soldiers frequently subjected to rape and other forms of sexual violence as well as being involved in combat and other roles.

Anthropologist Napoleon Chagnon (1996) found how different childhood among the Yanomamö of the Amazonian rainforest is from what we might expect in contemporary Britain. For example, a Yanomamö girl is expected to help her mother from a young age, and by the age of 10 will be running a house, and will probably be married and having children by the age of 12 or 13.

These examples suggest that the nature of childhood is not the same in every society, and in many countries of the world today, small children are expected to take on at an early age what in contemporary Britain might be regarded as adult responsibilities, with many of them being against the law for children.

Historical changes in childhood

The notion of childhood as a distinctive phase of life between infancy and adulthood is a relatively modern development, and didn't develop in Western societies until the sixteenth and seventeenth centuries. Philippe Ariès (1973) showed that, in medieval times, childhood did not exist as a separate status. Children often moved straight from infancy, when they required constant care, to working roles in the community. Children were seen as miniature versions of adults – 'little adults' – and were expected to take on adult roles and responsibilities as soon as they were physically able to do so, and to participate in all aspects of social life alongside their parents. Family portraits of the fifteenth and sixteenth centuries, like the one shown here, often depicted children as these little adults – shrunken versions of their parents, wearing adult clothes.

Sir Thomas Lucy (d.1640) and Alice Spencer, Lady Lucy (d.1648) with seven of their thirteen children, said to be after Cornelius Johnson

Charlecote Park, The Fairfax-Lucy Collection (The National Trust) © NTPL/Derrick E. Witty. Reproduced by kind permission of the National Trust Photo Library

Children did not lead separate lives, and mixed with adults. None of the things we associate with childhood today, such as toys, games, books, music, special clothes, schooling and so on existed. Until the mid-nineteenth century (the 1850s) child labour was commonly practised and accepted. Most children worked, starting around the age of 7. In the early part of the nineteenth century, many factory workers were children under the age of 11. Children worked as long and as hard as adults, and adolescent children often left home for years to work, with boys being taken on as apprentices and girls as servants in richer households. In poor families, parents sometimes forced their children to engage in scavenging and street selling, and occasionally they were used as thieves and prostitutes. Children frequently faced the same legal punishments as adults for criminal activity. The notion that children deserved special protection and treatment did not exist at this time.

In the nineteenth century, the father and husband was the head of the family – it was a patriarchal unit – and fathers often had a great deal of authority over other family members. He would often have little involvement in the care of his children. Children might see relatively little of their parents and, generally, children had low status in the family and were expected to be 'seen and not heard'.

Ariès showed that the social construction of childhood was linked to industrialization. With industrialization, work moved outside the family home. Restrictions on child labour in mines and factories during the nineteenth century isolated most children from the 'real world' of adult work and responsibilities. Children began to be seen as innocent and in need of protection, though they were also seen as weak and vulnerable to temptation.

Strong discipline was applied to teach children appropriate behaviour, and they often experienced severe beatings in the name of discipline which we would regard as child abuse today.

The growing speed of technological change in the nineteenth century meant parents were frequently unable to pass on the knowledge and skills required for working life, and the requirements for a literate and numerate labour force in part led to the development of compulsory education from 1880. These changes made children dependent on parents or other adults. There then emerged a new conception of a phase of 'childhood', with children lacking in power and dependent on, and supported by, adults. This period of dependency is getting ever longer today, as more young people spend time in education and training.

Differences between children in the same society

It is important to recognize that the conception and experience of childhood are not the same even in the same society. In contemporary Britain, inequalities based on social class, ethnicity and gender mean that not all children have the same experiences of growing up. For example, around 29 per cent of children in Britain in 2005–6 were living in officially defined poverty, and girls, particularly Asian girls, will often have a different and more restricted childhood than boys. Some children are forced to take jobs as soon as possible, such as paper rounds or working in shops, in order to supplement any pocket money they may or may not get from their parents, and poorer children are likely to suffer more ill health and disability, and to have fewer educational qualifications than those who are better off.

Children in contemporary Britain

During the course of the twentieth century and in the early twenty-first, families have become more child-centred, with family activities and outings often focused on the interests of the children. The amount of time parents spend with their children has more than doubled since the 1960s, and parents are more likely to take an interest in their children's activities, discussing decisions with them, and treating them more as equals. Often, the children's welfare is seen as the major family priority, frequently involving the parents in considerable financial cost and sacrifice.

The causes of child centredness

- Families have got smaller since the end of the nineteenth century, and this means that more individual care and attention can be devoted to each child.
- In the nineteenth century, the typical working week was between 70 and 80 hours for many working-class people. Today it is more like 44 hours

Figure 3.9 Reasons for a more child-centred society

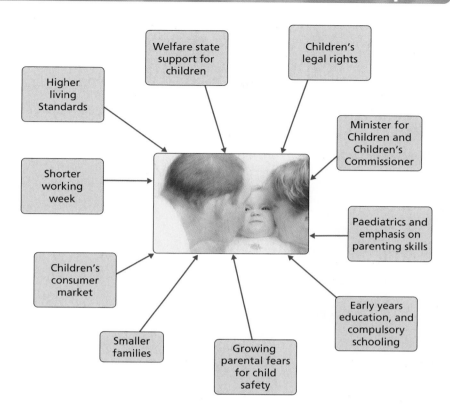

Welfare state support for children

Children's legal rights

Higher living Standards

Minister for Children and Children's Commissioner

Shorter working week

Paediatrics and emphasis on parenting skills

Children's consumer market

Early years education, and compulsory schooling

Smaller families

Growing parental fears for child safety

(including overtime), and is tending to get shorter. This means parents have more time to spend with their children.

- Increasing affluence, with higher wages and a higher standard of living, has benefited children, as more money can be spent on them and their activities.
- The welfare state provides a wide range of benefits designed to help parents care for their children, and has increased demands on parents to look after their children properly. Social workers, for example, have an extensive range of powers to intervene in families on behalf of children, and have the ultimate power to remove children from families if parents fail to look after them properly. The United Nations Convention on the Rights of the Child (1989) and the Children Acts of 1989 and 2004 established children's legal rights, and there is now a Minister for Children and a Children's Commissioner to champion the views of children and protect and promote their interests.
- Paediatrics, or the science of childhood, has developed this century, with a wide range of research and popular books suggesting how parents should bring up their children to encourage their full development. The nurturing, protection and education of children are now seen as a vital

Family life has become more child-centred over the past fifty years

and central part of family life, with parenting skills and early years education now recognized as an important aspect of children's educational and social development. There have been a number of TV programmes, like *Supernanny*, suggesting ways parents can avoid having, or learn to cope with, 'problem children'.

- Compulsory education and more time spent in further education and training have meant that young people are dependent on their parents for longer periods of time. Tuition fees for higher education and the abolition of student grants have recently extended this period of dependency of young people on their parents. In this respect, 'childhood', including the dependency on adults it involves, has itself become extended.

- Children's lives have become more complex, with more educational, medical and leisure services for them. This frequently involves parents in ferrying children to schools, cinemas, friends and so on.

- Growing traffic dangers and parental fears (largely unjustified) of assaults against their children have meant that children now travel more with parents rather than being left to roam about on their own as much as they used to.

- Large businesses have encouraged a specific childhood consumer market. Businesses like Mothercare, Toys "Я" Us, Nike, publishers and the music industry focus on the childhood consumer market, encouraging children to consume and parents to spend to satisfy their children's demands. 'Pester power', where advertisers target children to pester their parents into buying them CDs, clothes, toys and so on, is now an important feature of the advertising business.

Is childhood disappearing?

Despite this growth of child-centredness, we need to be aware of the way children are rapidly becoming exposed to a range of experiences that they share with adults, such as the mass media, especially the internet, television, videos and DVDs. This may be eroding the cultural divisions between childhood and adult status. Postman (1994), first writing in 1982, was concerned with the disappearance of childhood. He argues that the distinction between adults and children is disappearing, and that there is a merging of the taste and style of children and adults, with behaviour, language and attitudes becoming indistinguishable. In the contemporary world, children are increasingly exposed to the same issues, themes and experiences as adults, and are no longer sheltered from adult experiences and knowledge, including sex, pornography, crime, alcohol and drug abuse, and violence. Evidence for this was found in a 2007 report from the Cambridge University-based Primary Review inquiry. This found children of primary school age expressing concern about adult-related themes like climate change, global warming and pollution, the gulf between rich and poor, terrorism, crime and street violence. Cunningham

(2005) argues that parental authority has been undermined by children having pocket money from either parents or part-time work, reducing their dependency and transforming them into consumers, who demand access to the adult world earlier. Adults and children, particularly older children, lead increasingly separate lives. This means parents are no longer able to control or manage the range of information, images, values and other influences their children are exposed to through media influences from film, television, DVDs, video games and the internet, including chat rooms and porn sites, particularly as an increasing number of children have their own rooms with access to their own TV, DVD and computer. This reduces the opportunities for parents to socialize their children, and regulate their behaviour. The Primary Review report mentioned above confirmed this, with parents saying they had little control over such things as mobile phones and the internet, through which children had access to unsuitable or harmful material, and both teaching assistants and parents were concerned about a 'loss of childhood'.

The rapid pace of technological and social change often means that children are more up to date than their parents. Computer technology and use of the internet are good examples of this, as children are often far more adept at using these than their parents. The internet particularly gives young people access to a range of knowledge and imagery of which their parents in many cases have little awareness. This creates the possibility that young people will increasingly develop a culture that parents find goes beyond their comprehension or experience, and is far more in tune with the future than the culture of their parents. This may make parental involvement with their children's activities more difficult, and create a barrier between parents and children.

Has the position of children improved or worsened?

Most people would see the lives of children in contemporary Britain as a major improvement compared to the lives of children in earlier centuries, and as better than the lives of children in many other parts of the world. The status of children in the family has improved substantially, and most children are better cared for, better educated and enjoy healthier and happier lives than ever before in history. Nevertheless, child-centredness doesn't mean that all children are well looked after. Abuse and neglect are all-too-common experiences for some children. This is discussed later in this chapter, in the section on the 'darker side' of family life. An estimated 11 per cent of young people ran away overnight on at least one occasion before their sixteenth birthday, according to a 2005 report from the Children's Society. This suggests that the experience of family life for many children in contemporary Britain may not be a happy one, and their dependency on adults and their inability to obtain legal paid employment means they have few opportunities to escape unhappy family lives. Neither should we assume that children themselves are the innocents they are sometimes made out to be. Figures collected from police forces in England and Wales in 2006 found that almost 3,000 crimes, including criminal damage, arson and sex offences, were reported where the suspects were under the age of 10 – below the age of criminal responsibility, and therefore too young to be prosecuted. Under-age drinking, drug abuse, antisocial behaviour and criminal activity are common complaints by older people about children and young people today. Some may interpret this behaviour as a way for children to assert some independence from the suffocation of child-centredness which maintains their dependency on and regulation by adults, but it does nonetheless suggest that family life is not necessarily as child-centred as some may believe it to be.

Internationally, the position of many children still causes grave concern for many people, with common reports of the sale and trafficking of children, child prostitution, child pornography, children involved in armed conflicts as soldiers and the illegal trafficking of children's organs and tissues.

Activity

1　Explain in your own words what is meant by 'childhood is a social construction'.
2　Suggest *two* reasons why childhood is a relatively modern invention.
3　Identify and explain *three* ways in which the position of children has changed in the past hundred years.
4　Suggest and explain *two* ways that the difference between 'childhood' and 'adulthood' may be changing.
5　Suggest and explain *two* ways that the status of children in contemporary Britain might be improving, and two ways in which it might be getting worse.
6　Write a short essay – about one and a half sides – examining the arguments for and against the view that childhood in contemporary Britain is still a period of protected innocence.

Family change 5: the rising divorce rate

One of the most startling changes in the family in Britain in the last century has been the general and dramatic increase in the number of marriages ending in divorce, with a similar trend found in many Western industrialized countries. The number of divorces rose from 27,000 in 1961 to around 153,000 by 2006; during the 1960s the number doubled, and then doubled again in the 1970s. Britain has one of the highest **divorce rates** in the European Union. About 40 per cent of new marriages today are likely to end in divorce, and, if present rates continue, more than one in four children will experience a parental divorce by the time they are 16.

The **divorce rate** is the number of divorces per 1,000 married people per year.

Divorce and 'broken homes'

Divorce is the legal termination of a marriage, but this is not the only way that marriages and homes can be 'broken'. Homes and marriages may be broken in 'empty shell' marriages, where the marital relationship has broken down but no divorce has taken place. Separation – through either choice or necessity (like working abroad or imprisonment) – may also cause a broken home, as may the death of a partner. So homes may be broken for reasons other than divorce, and divorce itself is often only the end result of a marriage which broke down long before.

Divorce statistics

Divorce statistics are presented in three main ways:

- *the total number of divorce petitions per year* (the number of people applying for a divorce but not necessarily actually getting divorced)
- *the total number of decrees absolute granted per year* (the number of divorces actually granted)
- *the divorce rate* (the number of divorces each year per thousand married people in the population)

Divorce statistics must be treated with considerable caution, and assessed against changing legal, financial and social circumstances, if misleading conclusions about the declining importance of marriage and the family are to be avoided. The increase may simply reflect easier and cheaper divorce procedures enabling the legal termination of already unhappy 'empty shell' marriages rather than a real increase in marriage breakdowns. It could be that people who in previous years could only separate are now divorcing as legal and financial obstacles are removed.

Divorce statistics only show the legal termination of marriages. They do not show:

- the number of people who are separated but not divorced
- the number of people who live in 'empty shell marriages' – many couples may want to split up but are deterred from doing so by their roles as parents
- how many 'unstable' or 'unhappy' marriages existed before divorce was made easier by changes in the law and changing social attitudes to divorce

These points could mean *either* that divorce figures underestimate the extent of family and marriage breakdowns *or* that rising divorce rates only reflect legal changes and do not represent a real increase in marital instability.

There are two broad groups of reasons for the increase in the divorce rate: changes in the law which have gradually made divorce easier and cheaper to get; and changes in society which have made divorce a more practical and socially acceptable way of terminating a broken marriage. These are discussed in the next sections, and figure 3.10 on page 174 summarizes these changes.

Changes in the law as a reason for the rising divorce rate

Changes in the law over the last century have made divorce easier and cheaper to get, and have given men and women equal rights in divorce. This partly accounts for the steep rise in the divorce rate over the last fifty years, particularly in the 1970s and 1980s. These changes in the law are listed in the box overleaf. However, changes in the law reflect changing social attitudes and norms, and there are a number of wider social explanations that must also be considered.

Changes in society as a reason for the rising divorce rate

The changing role of women   This is a very important explanation for the rising divorce rate. Around three-quarters of divorce petitions (requests to a court for a divorce) are initiated by women, and around seven out of ten of all divorces are granted to women. This suggests more women than men are unhappy with the state of their marriages, and are more likely to take the first steps in ending them. This may well be because women's expectations of life and marriage have risen during the course of the last century, and they are less willing to accept a traditional housewife/mother role, with the sacrifices of their own leisure activities, careers and independence this involves.

The employment of married women has increased over the last century. For example, in 1931 only 10 per cent of married women were employed, but this had gradually risen to about 75 per cent by the beginning of this century. This has increased their financial independence, and reduced the extent of dependence on their husbands. There is also a range of welfare state benefits to help divorced women, particularly those with children. Marriage has therefore become less of a financial necessity for women, and this makes it easier for women to escape from unhappy marriages.

Rising expectations of marriage   Functionalist writers like Parsons and Fletcher argue that the divorce rate has risen because couples (especially women) expect and demand more in their relationships today than their parents or grandparents might have settled for. Love, companionship, understanding, sexual compatibility and personal fulfilment are more likely to be the main ingredients of a successful marriage today. The growing privatization and isolation of the nuclear family from extended kin and the community have also meant that couples are more likely to spend more time together. The higher expectations mean couples are more likely to end a relationship which earlier generations might have tolerated.

A brief history of the divorce laws

Before 1857, divorce could only be obtained by the rich, since each divorce needed a private Act of Parliament. As a result, there were very few divorces. Since that time, changes in the law have made it easier to get a divorce, particularly changes over about the past sixty years.

- *The Matrimonial Causes Act of 1857* made divorce procedure easier and cheaper, but it was still beyond the financial means of the lower middle class and working class. Men had more rights in divorce than women, and divorce was only possible if it could be proved in court that a 'matrimonial offence' such as adultery, cruelty or desertion had been committed. Even by 1911, there were only about 600 divorces a year.
- *The Matrimonial Causes Act of 1923* gave women equal rights with men in divorce for the first time, and therefore gave more women the opportunity to terminate unhappy marriages.
- *The Legal Aid and Advice Act of 1949* gave financial assistance with the costs of solicitors' and court fees, which made it far more possible for working-class people to cope with the costs of a divorce action.
- *The Divorce Law Reform Act of 1969*, which came into effect in 1971, was a major change. Before the 1969 Act, a person wanting a divorce had to prove before a court that his or her spouse had committed a 'matrimonial offence', as mentioned above. This frequently led to major public scandals, as all the details of unhappy marriages were aired in a public lawcourt. This may have deterred many people whose marriage had broken down from seeking a divorce. Also, marriages may have broken down – become 'empty shell' marriages – without any matrimonial offence being committed. The 1969 Act changed all this, and made 'irretrievable breakdown' of a marriage the only grounds for divorce. It is now no longer necessary to prove one partner 'guilty' of a matrimonial offence: it simply has to be demonstrated that a marriage has broken down beyond repair. After 1971, one way of demonstrating 'irretrievable breakdown' of a marriage was by two years of separation. This change in the law led to a massive increase in the number of divorces after 1971.
- *The Matrimonial and Family Proceedings Act of 1984* allowed couples to petition for divorce after only one year of marriage, whereas previously couples could normally divorce only after three years of marriage. This led to a record increase in the number of divorces in 1984 and 1985.
- *The Family Law Act of 1996* came into effect in 1999. This increased the amount of time before a divorce could be granted to eighteen months, introduced compulsory marriage counselling for a 'period of reflection', and required children's wishes and financial arrangements for children to be agreed before a divorce was granted. This was an attempt to stem the rising number of divorces by increasing the time for 'cooling off'. These compulsory counselling sessions were later abandoned because it was found they were more likely to encourage people to go through with a divorce, even when they were initially uncertain.

Have rising expectations of marriage made relationships more 'fragile' and therefore more likely to break up?

This functionalist approach suggests that higher divorce rates therefore reflect better quality marriages. This view of the higher expectations of marriage is reflected in the fairly high rate of remarriage among divorced people. In other words, families split up to re-form happier families – a bit like 'old banger' cars failing their M.O.T. test, being taken to the scrapyard and being replaced with a better quality car, thereby improving the general quality of cars on the road.

Growing secularization   Secularization refers to the declining influence of religious beliefs and institutions. Writers such as Goode (1971) and Gibson (1994) argue that this has resulted in marriage becoming less of a sacred, spiritual union and more a personal and practical commitment which can be abandoned if it fails. Evidence for this lies in the fact that more than 65 per cent of marriages today no longer involve a religious ceremony. The church now takes a much less rigid view of divorce, and many people today probably do not attach much religious significance to their marriages.

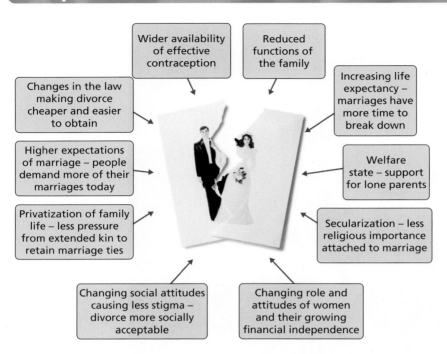

Figure 3.10 Causes of the rising divorce rate

Changing social attitudes   Divorce has become more socially acceptable, and there is less social disapproval and condemnation (stigmatizing) of divorcees. Divorce no longer hinders careers through a public sense of scandal and outrage. As a result, people are less afraid of the consequences of divorce, and are more likely to seek a legal end to an unhappy marriage rather than simply separating or carrying on in an 'empty shell' marriage.

The greater availability of, and more effective, contraception   The greater availability of and more effective contraception has made it safer to have sex outside the marital relationship, and with more than one person during marriage. This weakens traditional constraints on fidelity to a marriage partner, and potentially exposes relationships to greater instability.

The growth of the privatized nuclear family   Functionalists contend that the growing privatization and isolation of the nuclear family from extended kin and the community in contemporary society has meant it is no longer so easy for marriage partners to seek advice from or temporary refuge with relatives. This isolation can increase the demands on and expectations of each partner in a marriage. There is also less social control from extended kin pressuring couples to retain marriage ties. In this sense, there is both more pressure on marriage relationships arising from the points above, and fewer constraints preventing people abandoning marriage, and increasingly the decision whether to divorce or not lies with the married couple alone.

Figure 3.11 Facts proven at divorce and to whom divorce granted: England and Wales, 2005

Source: Data adapted from Office for National Statistics

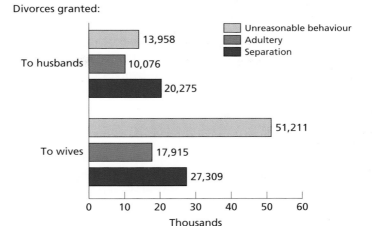

Divorces granted:

Legend:
- Unreasonable behaviour
- Adultery
- Separation

To husbands
- 13,958
- 10,076
- 20,275

To wives
- 51,211
- 17,915
- 27,309

Thousands (0, 10, 20, 30, 40, 50, 60)

Activity

1 Suggest reasons why the following groups might be more 'at risk' of divorce than other groups in the population:
   - teenage marriages
   - childless couples
   - couples where each partner is from a different social class or ethnic background
2 Suggest reasons why women are more likely to apply for divorce than men.
3 Refer to figure 3.11, which shows the different numbers and reasons for divorce by husbands and wives:
   (a) Which reason for divorce shows the largest difference between husbands and wives?
   (b) Approximately how many more divorces were granted to wives than husbands?
   (c) Outline the main differences in the reasons for divorce by husbands and wives, and suggest explanations for them. What conclusions might you draw about the different behaviour of men and women in marriage?

The reduced functions of the family   As we saw earlier in this chapter, some functionalist writers argue that, with industrialization, a number of family functions transferred to other social institutions. This has perhaps meant that marriage has become less of a practical necessity, and there are fewer bonds linking marriage partners. Love and companionship and personal compatibility are the important dimensions of contemporary marriages, and if some or all of these disappear, there may be nothing much left to hold marriages together.

Increasing life expectancy   People live to a greater age today than they did in the early years of the twentieth century, and this means the potential number of years a couple may be together, before one of them dies, has increased, and is continuing to increase as life expectancy lengthens. This gives more time for marriages to go wrong and for divorces to occur. Some suggest that the divorce courts have taken on the role in finishing unhappy marriages once performed by the undertaker.

Variations in divorce rates between social groups

While divorce affects all groups in the population, there are some groups where divorce rates are higher than the average. Teenage marriages are twice as likely to end in divorce than those of couples overall, and there is a high incidence of divorce in the first five to seven years of marriage and after about ten to fourteen years (when the children are older or have left home). The working class, particularly semi-skilled and unskilled, has a higher rate of divorce than the middle class. Childless couples and partners from different social class or religious backgrounds also face a higher risk of divorce, as do couples whose work separates them for long periods. The rising divorce rate therefore does not affect all groups of married people equally, and some face higher risks of divorce than others.

Family change 6: remarriage and the growth of the reconstituted family

While marriage is still the usual form of partnership between men and women, marriages where it is the first time for both partners are declining substantially. The number of these has more than halved since 1970. Just over two-fifths of marriages now involve a remarriage for one or both partners, mainly reflecting the increase in the divorce rate. A lot more divorced men remarry than divorced women, reflecting women's greater dissatisfaction or disillusionment with marriage. This is perhaps not surprising, given the way women often have to balance the triple and competing demands of paid employment, domestic labour and childcare, and emotional 'management' of the family.

These trends have meant that there are more reconstituted families (sometimes called 'stepfamilies') with step-parents, stepchildren, and stepbrothers and stepsisters arising from a previous relationship of one or both partners. Stepfamilies are the fastest growing family type. Stepfathers are more common than stepmothers, since most children remain with the mother after a break-up, and around nine out of ten stepfamilies consist of a couple with at least one child from a previous relationship of the woman. This reflects the fact that it is nearly always women who gain custody of children in the event of a relationship breakdown. One in six men in their thirties are now stepfathers, raising other men's children – nearly double the proportion in the mid-1990s. Official estimates suggest there are around three-quarters of a million stepfamilies with dependent stepchildren in the UK – 10 per cent of all families with dependent children .

Family change 7: the growth of the lone parent family

One of the biggest changes in the family has been the growth of the lone parent family (also known as the single parent or one parent family). The percentage of lone parent families has tripled since 1971, and Britain has one of the highest proportions of lone parent families in Europe. More than one in four of all families with dependent children were lone parent families in 2005 – nine out of ten of them headed by women. Nearly one in four (23 per cent) of dependent children now live in such families, compared to just 7 per cent in 1972.

Why are there more lone parent families?

The rapid growth in the number of lone parent families can be explained by a number of factors, some of which have already been discussed earlier in explaining the rising divorce rate. These include:

- *The greater economic independence of women.* Women have greater economic independence today, both through more job opportunities and through support from the welfare state. This means marriage, and support by a husband, is less of an economic necessity today compared to the past.
- *Improved contraception, changing male attitudes, and fewer 'shotgun weddings'.* With the wider availability and approval of safe and effective contraception, and easier access to safe and legal abortion, men may feel less responsibility to marry women should they become unintentionally pregnant, and women may feel under less pressure to marry the future father. There are therefore fewer 'shotgun weddings' (where reluctant couples are forced into marriage by the father of the pregnant women wielding an imaginary shotgun to ensure that the man marries his daughter).
- *Reproductive technology is available to women,* enabling them to bear children without a male partner, through surrogate motherhood and fertility treatments like IVF (in vitro fertilization).
- *Changing social attitudes.* There is less social stigma (or social disapproval and condemnation) attached to lone parenthood today. Women are therefore less afraid of the social consequences of becoming lone parents.

Those with New Right views particularly blame the generosity of the welfare state for the growth in lone parenthood. Writers such as Charles Murray (1990) argue that generous welfare benefits encourage women to have children they could not otherwise afford to support. This is often linked to the idea of the underclass, which is discussed in chapter 4.

The growth in lone parenthood has been seen by some as one of the major signs of the decline of conventional family life and marriage. Lone parent families – and particularly lone never-married mothers – have been portrayed by some of the media and conservative politicians of the New Right as promiscuous parasites, blamed for everything from rising juvenile crime through to housing shortages, rising drug abuse, educational failure of children and the general breakdown of society. The problems created by lone parenthood, particularly for boys, are usually explained by the lack of a male role model in the home, and consequently inadequate socialization.

Lone parenthood has therefore been presented as a major social problem, and there have been **moral panics** about lone parenthood in the mass media.

In an effort to cut the welfare costs to the state of lone parents, the Child Support Agency was established in 1993. This was designed to encourage absent fathers to take financial responsibility for their children, thereby reducing benefit costs to the state. There have been a number of attempts to encourage lone parents to support themselves through paid employment. For example, since 1997 a new Childcare Tax Credit to help with the costs of childcare has been introduced, along with a national childcare strategy to ensure good quality affordable childcare, the expansion of nursery places for children aged 3 and 4, and more pre- and after-school clubs. These policies arise from the fact that it is the lack of affordable childcare that is the major deterrent to lone parents working. The national minimum wage helps to avoid the exploitation of lone parents, who are mainly women, by unscrupulous employers, and the New Deal for Lone Parents enabled many lone parents to find paid employment. In 2006, about 57 per cent of lone parents were in employment.

> A **moral panic** is a wave of public concern about some exaggerated or imaginary threat to society, stirred up by exaggerated and sensationalized reporting in the mass media.

Nailing the myths

Never-married lone mothers only account for less than half of all lone parents, with lone parenthood mostly arising from divorce, separation or widowhood, as figure 3.12 shows. Even among never-married lone mothers, the vast majority cohabited with the father and have registered his name on the child's birth certificate.

The problems allegedly created by absent fathers have been questioned on the grounds that it is not the presence or absence of a father that is important, but whether fathers actually involve themselves in the children's upbringing. There are probably many fathers in two-parent families as well who fail to involve themselves in the care and discipline of their children, and problems like juvenile delinquency are likely to arise in any household where children are inadequately supervised and disciplined. This problem, often blamed on lone parenthood, is therefore just as likely to occur among two-parent families. A Home Office report has found no difference in the crime rates between youngsters from lone-parent and two-parent families. Even if there were such a link, it is likely to be caused by poverty rather than lone parenthood – because lack

Figure 3.12 Lone mother families with dependent children, by marital status: Great Britain, 2005

Source: Data from General Household Survey

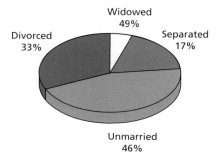

Widowed
49%

Separated
17%

Divorced
33%

Unmarried
46%

Activity

1. Suggest reasons why, in the event of divorce, women are more likely than men to be given custody of the children.
2. Suggest explanations why most lone parent families are headed by women.
3. To what extent do you agree with the following statements, and why?
   - 'A lone mother can bring up her child as well as a married or cohabiting couple'
   - 'People who want children ought to get married'
   - 'To grow up happily, children need a home with both their mother and father'
4. What are the advantages and disadvantages of lone parenthood compared to two-parent families?
5. Suggest reasons why the stereotypes held by professionals (like teachers, police officers and social workers) might mean children from lone parent families are more likely (a) to underachieve in education, and (b) to be overrepresented in the official crime statistics.
6. Try the following websites, and identify five issues that seem to be of particular concern to lone parents. Describe each issue briefly, and outline any solutions that are suggested.

   www.gingerbread.org.uk
   www.lone-parents.org.uk
   www.oneparentfamilies.org.uk

---

of childcare facilities means many lone parents have to depend on inadequate state benefits to live, and lone parents are more likely to live in overcrowded or poor quality housing. This probably explains other factors linked in the popular imagination to lone parenthood, such as lower educational achievement.

A misleading myth is that of lone teenage mothers getting pregnant to jump the queue for social (council and housing association) housing. There is very little evidence for this. A 1999 report from the National Council for One Parent Families pointed out that the average age of a lone parent is 34, and that at any one time, less than 3 per cent of all lone parents are teenagers. In 2001, 74 per cent of lone mothers were 30 or over with just 12 per cent under 25. Research in 1996 commissioned by the Economic and Social Research Council found that only 10 per cent of the small minority of women who were not in a regular relationship with the father when they became mothers were living alone with their child in social (council) housing six months after the birth. Many live with their parents, and many single, never-married parents have been in cohabiting relationships which break down. In effect, this is no different from marriages that break down.

Family change 8: the decline in marriage and the growing incidence and acceptance of cohabitation

The decline of marriage and the growth of living together before or outside marriage were two of the major social changes at the turn of the twenty-first century. Marriage rates are declining in Britain, and there are more and more couples cohabiting rather than seeking official recognition of their relationships through marriage. In 2005, there were 244,710 marriages in England and Wales – 19 per cent fewer than in 1991, and the lowest number ever. Over a quarter of non-married males and females in Britain under age 60 were cohabiting in 2005–6, twice the proportion recorded around 20 years ago. A number of these included people who were separated but not divorced. By the early 2000s, the majority of people in first marriages had lived with their partner beforehand, and cohabitation is now the norm rather than the exception. Seven in every ten couples married in 2000 gave identical addresses, and this 'living in sin' included 56 per cent of those getting married in a religious ceremony. There are well over a million and a half cohabiting couples who have refused to tie the marriage knot – more than one in ten of all couples. Around 11 per cent of dependent children are now being brought up by unmarried, cohabiting couples. Many cohabiting relationships eventually end up in marriage – about 60 per cent of first-time cohabitations turn into marriages.

The reasons for the decline of marriage and growing cohabitation have been considered earlier, including:

- the changing role of women, whose growing economic independence has given them more freedom to choose their relationships
- the growing divorce rate, and the message it is sending out to potential marriage partners
- growing secularization
- changing social attitudes and reduced social stigma: young people are more likely to cohabit than older people, and this may in part reflect the evidence that older people compared to younger people are more likely to think that 'living together outside marriage is always wrong'; this reveals more easygoing attitudes to cohabitation among the young, showing the reduced social stigma attached to cohabitation

Younger people are more likely to cohabit, and have children outside marriage, and the trend is rising

- the greater availability of, and more effective, contraception
- higher expectations of marriage

> **Activity**
>
> Drawing on the points in this section, but explaining them more fully, write a short essay of about one side of A4 paper explaining why marriage is in decline, and why cohabitation is becoming more common and accepted.

Family change 9: the growth in 'singlehood' – living alone

About one in three households today contains only one person, compared to one in twenty in 1901. Around half of these households are over pensionable age (age 60 for women, 65 for men), compared to two-thirds in 1971. This means there is a growth in the number of younger people living alone. This trend can be explained by the decline in marriage, the rise in divorce and separation, and the fact that people are delaying marriage or cohabitation until they are older. There are nearly twice as many men as women living alone in the 25–44 age group, but there are twice as many women as men aged 65 and over, because women tend to live longer than men. Longer lives, particularly for women, explain the increase in the number of pensioner one-person households.

Family change 10: more births outside marriage

Around four in every ten births (44 per cent in 2006 are now outside marriage – about five times more than the proportion in 1971. Despite the record numbers of children being born outside marriage, about 85 per cent of those births in 2006 were registered jointly by the parents. Both parents in two out of three of these cases gave the same address. This suggests the parents were cohabiting, and that children are still being born into a stable couple relationship, even if the partners are not legally married.

The explanations for the increase of births outside marriage are very similar to those for the increase in the divorce rate, the decline in the marriage rate and the increase in cohabitation, which were discussed above.

Family diversity and the myth of the 'cereal packet' family

The popular impression that many people have of the family in Britain at the turn of the twenty-first century has been described as the 'cereal packet family'. This is the **stereotype** often promoted in advertising and other parts of the mass media, with 'family size' breakfast cereals, toothpaste and a wide range of other consumer goods.

This popular happy family image often gives the impression that most people live in a typical family with the following features:

> A **stereotype** is a generalized, oversimplified view of an institution or social group.

- It is a privatized, nuclear family unit consisting of two parents living with one or two of their own natural dependent children.
- These parents are married to one another, and neither of them has been married before.
- The husband is the breadwinner and responsible for family discipline, with the wife staying at home and primarily concerned with housework and childcare (expressing herself through maternal love), or perhaps doing some part-time paid employment to supplement the family income.

The 'cereal packet' family, with a working father in a first marriage to a home-based mother, caring for their own two natural children, makes up only about 5 per cent of all households

This image also often includes ideas that this family is based on romantic love, as well as love of children (particularly maternal love), and that it is a nurturing, caring and loving institution – a safe and harmonious refuge from an uncaring outside world.

It is this 'cereal packet' stereotype of the 'typical family' that is found in **family ideology**. This is discussed later in this chapter.

This stereotype of the 'typical family' is very mistaken, because there are a wide range of households and family types in contemporary Britain. This is known as family diversity.

Family ideology is that dominant set of beliefs, values and images about how families are and how they *ought* to be.

Why is the 'cereal packet' stereotype misleading?

This image of the cereal packet stereotyped conventional or typical family is very misleading because, as discussed earlier in this chapter, there have been and continue to be important changes in family patterns, and there is a wide range of family types and household arrangements in modern Britain. This growing diversity of relationships that people live in shows that traditional family life is being eroded as people constantly develop new forms of relationship and choose to live in different ways. The meaning of 'family' and 'family life' is therefore changing for a substantial number of parents and children.

Households and families

Figure 3.13 overleaf shows the different types of household in Britain in 2006, and what percentages of people were living in them. In 2006, only 22 per cent of households contained a married or cohabiting couple with dependent children, and only 37 per cent of people lived in such a household. Meanwhile, 29 per cent of households consisted of one person living alone, and at least 68 per cent of households had no dependent children in them. Twelve per cent of people lived in lone parent families, and 10 per cent of households were lone parent families. This alone shows that the cereal packet image of the nuclear family does not represent the arrangement in which most people in Britain live.

Families with dependent children

Figure 3.14 examines families with dependent children. This shows that in 2005, about 26 per cent of such families were lone parent families, with nearly nine out of ten of them headed by women. Although a married or cohabiting couple headed 74 per cent of families with dependent children, this doesn't mean that most of these families conformed to the cereal packet image.

- A number of these families involved a cohabiting rather than a married relationship. Twelve per cent of families with dependent children were headed by a cohabiting couple in 2005. Such arrangements do not conform to the cereal packet stereotype.
- A number were reconstituted families, in which one or both partners were previously married. More than two in five marriages currently taking place will end in divorce, and more than 40 per cent of all marriages now involve remarriage for one or both partners. About 10 per cent of all families with dependent children were stepfamilies in the early 2000s.
- Most of these families were dual worker families, where both parents were working. In 2005, about 69 per cent of couples with dependent children were both working. As figure 3.7 (on page 156) showed, large numbers of mothers with dependent children work in paid employment, with the numbers increasing as children get older. In 2005, about 69 per cent of all women with dependent children were working. This often involves complex and costly alternative arrangements for childcare while both parents are working.

The cereal packet happy family stereotype of family ideology, of a working father married to a home-based mother caring for two small children made up in 2005 only about 5 per cent of all households.

Cultural diversity

Cultural diversity refers to differences in family lifestyles between ethnic and religious groups.

South Asian families   Ballard (1982) found extended family relationships are more common in minority ethnic groups originating in South Asia, from Pakistan, Bangladesh and India. Such families are commonly patriarchal in

Figure 3.13 Households and people, by type of household: Great Britain, 2006

Source: Data from Labour Force Survey

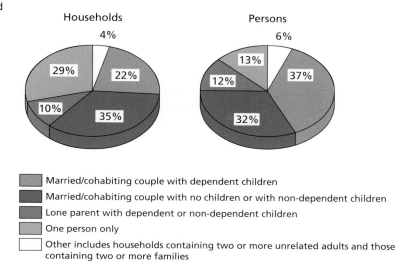

Households

Persons

- Married/cohabiting couple with dependent children
- Married/cohabiting couple with no children or with non-dependent children
- Lone parent with dependent or non-dependent children
- One person only
- Other includes households containing two or more unrelated adults and those containing two or more families

Figure 3.14 Families with dependent children, by family type and, for lone mothers, by marital status: Great Britain, 2005

Source: Data from General Household Survey

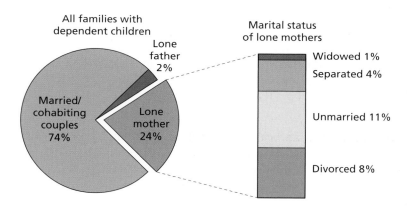

All families with dependent children

Marital status of lone mothers

Lone father 2%

Married/ cohabiting couples 74%

Lone mother 24%

Widowed 1%
Separated 4%
Unmarried 11%
Divorced 8%

Activity

Refer to figures 3.13 and 3.14

1   What percentage of households in 2006 consisted of one person only?
2   What percentage of people in 2006 were living in households consisting of a married or cohabiting couple with no children or with non-dependent children?
3   In 2005, what percentage of all families with dependent children were headed by a lone mother who was widowed?
4   What was the main cause of lone motherhood?
5   Suggest reasons why so many people seem to believe that the 'cereal packet' family is the most common type of family.

structure, with seniority going to the eldest male, and males in general. A report in 2000 from the Institute for Social and Economic Research, *Family Formation in Multicultural Britain,* found the highest rates of marriage were among Pakistani and Bangladeshi women (three-quarters were married by age 25, compared to half of white women), and virtually all South Asians with a partner were in a formal marriage. A majority of Bangladeshi and Pakistani women reported their primary activity to be looking after the house and family. In many ways, the traditional British 'cereal packet' family of a working male married to a home-based female is more likely to be found among Pakistanis and Bangladeshis than any other ethnic group. Divorce rates are low in such families because of strong social disapproval and a wide support network of kin for families under stress. Arranged marriages are still common in such communities.

African-Caribbean families   African-Caribbean families are often centred on the mother, who is in many cases the main breadwinner. Lone parenthood is higher among African-Caribbean mothers than any other ethnic group – over half of African-Caribbean families with children are lone parents, and there are low marriage rates. This partly reflects a cultural tradition, but also high rates of black male unemployment and men's inability and reluctance to support families. African-Caribbean families often belong to a female network of friends and kin to support women with children.

Class diversity

Class diversity refers to differences between middle-class and working-class families. For example, extended families are still found in traditional working-class communities, and the nuclear family may be more common in middle-class families. Differences in income will also lead to differences in lifestyle between such families.

Life cycle diversity

Life cycle diversity refers to the way families may change through life, for example as partners have children, as the children grow older and eventually leave the home, as partners separate and form new relationships, as people grow old and have grandchildren, etc. All these factors mean the family will be constantly changing. For instance, levels of family income will change as children move from dependence to independence, levels of domestic labour and childcare will differ, and levels of participation in paid employment will alter, particularly for women, depending on the absence or presence of children and the children's age. This means there will always be a diversity of family types at different stages of the family life cycle. Figure 3.15 shows an example of a family life cycle.

Figure 3.15 A family life cycle

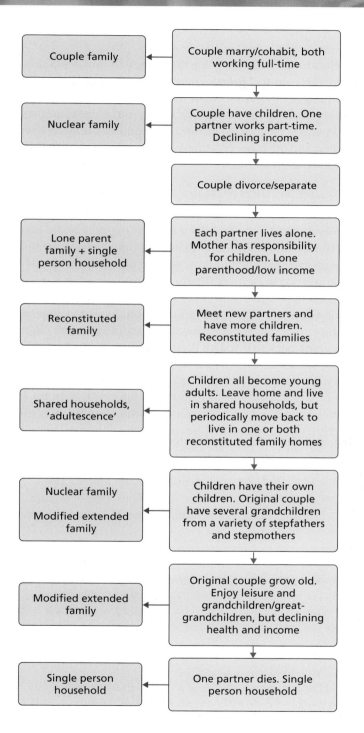

Regional diversity

Regional diversity refers to the way family life differs in different geographical locations around the country. Eversley and Bonnerjea (1982) suggest there are distinctive patterns of family life in different areas of Britain. For example, on the south coast there is a high proportion of elderly couples; older industrial areas and very traditional rural communities tend to have more extended families; and the inner cities have a higher proportion of families in poverty and lone parent families.

Shared households and 'families of choice'

Shared households are becoming much more common, particularly among young people. Sue Heath (2004) has described how young people are now less likely to follow the traditional route of living at home, leaving school, going into a job or higher education, and then 'settling down' into a married or cohabiting couple relationship. Increasingly, they are adopting a wider range of living arrangements before forming couple relationships later in life. This transitional period between youth and adult roles has been described as 'kidulthood' or 'adultescence'. These transitional living arrangements might include living alone, going back to live with their parents, or living in shared households with their peers. There may often be a greater loyalty among young people to their friends than to their family. Such shared households, where people choose to live with and form relationships with a group of people with whom they have closer relations than with their families of birth, have therefore sometimes been called 'families of choice' (although they are not strictly speaking 'families' as they are not based on kinship relations). Such households may involve shared domestic life (cooking, eating and socializing together), and shared leisure, sporting activities and holidays.

Such households are on the increase because of the high costs of buying or renting houses, the growing numbers of young people entering higher

---

Activity

1 Identify all the ways that family life might change during its life cycle.
2 Suggest *three* ways the rising divorce rate contributes to family diversity in contemporary Britain.
3 Suggest differences you might expect to find between working-class and middle-class families.
4 Identify and explain *three* reasons why the conventional nuclear family no longer remains the norm in contemporary Britain.
5 Write an essay of about one and a half sides of A4 paper answering the following question: *Discuss the view that there is no 'typical' family or household in Britain today.*

Figure 3.16 Family and household diversity

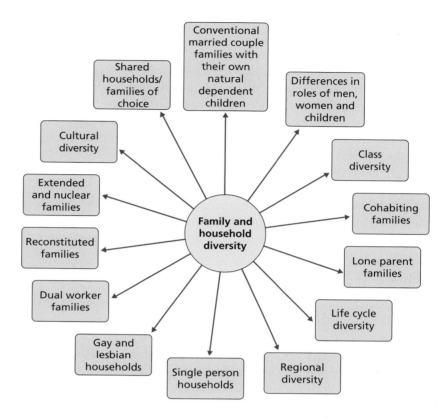

education, and the desire of young people to explore alternative living arrangements rather than simply settling down into a conventional couple household.

Figure 3.16 summarizes the range of family diversity in contemporary Britain.

The 'darker side' of family life

The cereal packet image of the typical family has already been questioned on a number of levels, but the view often put forward by functionalists of the warm and supportive 'happy family' has been questioned on a more fundamental level by many writers, particularly feminists.

While the family may often be a warm and supportive unit for its members, it can also be a hostile and dangerous place. The growing privatization of family life can lead to emotional stress in the family. Family members are thrown together, isolated from and lacking the support of extended kin, neighbours and the wider community. Tempers become easily frayed, emotional temperatures and stress levels rise, and – as in a pressure cooker without a safety valve – explosions occur, resulting in family conflict. This may lead to violence, divorce, and psychological damage to children, perhaps even mental illness and crime.

The breakdown of marriages which leads to divorce is often the end result of long-running and bitter disputes between partners. The intense emotions involved in family life often mean that incidents that would appear trivial in other situations take on the proportion of major confrontations inside the family. The extent of violence in the family is coming increasingly to public attention, with rising reports of sexual and physical abuse of children, emotional neglect of children, the rape of women by their husbands or partners, and wife and baby battering. One in four murders takes place in the family. This is the darker side of family life.

Because of the private nature of the family, accurate evidence on the extent of violence and abuse inside the family is difficult to obtain, and fear or shame means that it is almost certain that many such incidents are covered up.

The abuse of children

There are several different types of abuse of children, as figure 3.17 shows. *Sexual abuse* refers to adults using their power to perform sex acts with children below the age of consent (age 16). *Physical abuse* refers to non-sexual violence. *Emotional abuse* refers to persistent or severe emotional ill-treatment or rejection of children, which has severe effects on their emotional development and behaviour. *Neglect* refers to the failure to protect children from exposure to danger, including cold and starvation, and failing to care for them properly so that their health or development is affected.

A report in 2000 from the NSPCC (the National Society for the Prevention of Cruelty to Children), *Child Maltreatment in the United Kingdom*, found that around 10 per cent of children suffered serious abuse or neglect at home, with most of it committed by natural parents. In 2005, the most comprehensive survey ever of teenagers and domestic abuse, conducted by the teen magazine *Sugar* in association with the NSPCC, found one-fifth of teenage girls were hit by parents – a quarter of them regularly. In 2006, statistics from the Department for Education and Skills (DfES) showed there were 26,400 children and young people under the age of 18 on child protection registers in England because of various forms of abuse. There were 7,700 children registered for physical injury or sexual abuse, 13,700 for neglect, and a further 6,700 for emotional abuse, with some children registered more than once during the year.

This was just for England, and only for abuse which was brought to the attention of social services departments. It is very likely that much abuse goes on that is undiscovered. Some indication of this is shown by statistics from ChildLine, the free confidential counselling service for children, established in 1986. ChildLine has counselled well over a million children and young

Figure 3.17 Children and young people on child protection registers, by category of abuse: England, year ending 31 March 2006

Source: Department for Education and Skills (DfES)

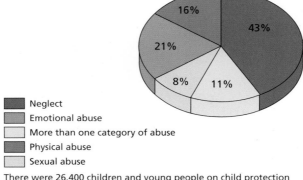

- Neglect
- Emotional abuse
- More than one category of abuse
- Physical abuse
- Sexual abuse

There were 26,400 children and young people on child protection registers in England, year ending 31 March 2006

people, and almost one in five of the calls received has been about sexual and physical abuse.

Domestic violence

There is widespread evidence of violence by men and women against their partners. It is estimated that one in four women, and one in six men, will suffer some form of domestic violence at some point in their relationships. Most of the assaults and physically most violent incidents – 89 per cent – are committed by men against their female partners. Each year about 150 people are killed by a current or former partner, and 80 per cent of them are women. Domestic violence accounts for an estimated 16 per cent of all violent crime, and about 650,000 incidents are recorded by the police each year, with around four out of five of the victims being women. Around 45 per cent of all violent crime experienced by women is domestic, and estimates suggest there may be as many as 6.5 million violent incidents each year. It is women who are most likely to experience domestic violence, to experience repeated violence, and to sustain injuries requiring medical treatment. Female victims of domestic violence will suffer an average of 35–37 assaults for an average period of seven years before informing any agency. Every year in England and Wales, approximately 63,000 women and children spend at least one night in a refuge for battered women. For many women, home is neither a secure nor a safe place to be.

Such violence is often not taken very seriously by the police or courts, being dismissed as a 'domestic dispute' – which seems to suggest violence in the family, and particularly against women, is seen in some quarters as an acceptable and normal part of a relationship. Certainly the type of physical violence carried out in the family, mainly by male partners, would quite probably result in prosecution and imprisonment if it was carried out against a stranger outside the family. Nonetheless, an estimated two-thirds of victims of

Domestic violence is overwhelmingly committed by men against their female partners. Why do you think this is?

domestic violence do not seek help because they are afraid the violence will get worse, are ashamed, or see it as a private matter, and only about a quarter of all domestic violence incidents are reported to the police.

Statistics such as those discussed above reflect the extent and seriousness of the problem of violence in the home, particularly against women, much of which goes unreported and undiscovered.

Despite the high level of violence against women in married and cohabiting relationships, many women do not leave their violent partners. This is often because of fear, shame and embarrassment, financial insecurity, lack of alternative housing and concerns about disruption to their children's lives.

Disturbingly, many young women today still seem to believe that violence and aggression are acceptable parts of relationships. The 2005 survey conducted by *Sugar* magazine, referred to above, found that 16 per cent of teenage girls had been hit by a boyfriend – a quarter of them regularly. Yet over two-thirds of the girls who had been hit then stayed with their boyfriends. Of all the teenage girls who replied to the survey, 43 per cent thought it acceptable for a boyfriend to get aggressive, and 6 per cent thought it was OK for a boy to hit his girlfriend, for reasons such as cheating on him, flirting with someone else or if she was 'dressing outrageously'. Over 40 per cent of all the girls said they would 'consider giving a boy a second chance if he hit them'.

Rape in marriage

Rape is when someone is forced to have sex against her or his will, often accompanied by the actual or threatened use of violence. Estimates suggest more than one in four women has been raped, with most rapes being committed by men on their female partners. Nearly half of these rapes within marriage are accompanied by the actual or threatened use of violence, and one in five women suffer physical injury.

Such sexual violence in the family, then, would appear to be disturbingly common, but it was only as recently as 1991 that rape within marriage was confirmed as a criminal offence by the Court of Appeal. None the less, in 2005, only about 5 per cent of all reported rapes led to a rapist being convicted and rape in marriage or cohabitation relationships are the most difficult cases to prove in court that there was no consent.

Activity

Go to www.womensaid.org.uk (the Women's Aid site), or www.crimereduction.gov.uk (search 'domestic violence') and find out the extent of domestic violence and the policy measures being taken to combat it.

Feminist explanations for domestic violence

Radical feminists explain domestic violence as a result of patriarchy. In a society where men dominate women, violence is often used by men, often when they are drunk, to control and intimidate women, and to keep them in a state of submission. Marxist feminists are likely to emphasize structural factors as well. These include social deprivation (which may, for example, generate stress and disputes about money), a culture of violence – particularly in some parts of the working class – and the generally lower status of women in society. Both radical feminists and Marxist feminists would agree that domestic violence stems from structural inequalities in society, and that only by improving the position of women in society generally, and making housing and employment policies and the legal system more responsive to domestic violence and the needs of women, will domestic violence be tackled at its roots.

Activity

1 Why do you think child abuse and domestic violence statistics are likely to understate the extent of these social problems?
2 Do you think domestic violence by women against men is more or less likely to be reported than domestic violence by men against women? Give reasons for your answer.
3 How would you define child abuse? Do you think ideas about what child abuse is have changed over time? Give reasons for your answer.
4 What difficulties do you think sociologists might face in trying to research the areas of child abuse and domestic violence?
5 What explanations might there be for child abuse?

Family ideology

Family ideology refers to a dominant set of ideas, beliefs and images about family life, family structure and family relationships which suggest what the ideal family is and how family life ought to be lived. At the heart of this ideology is the patriarchal 'cereal packet' family model discussed earlier. This family is seen as the 'normal' family, and a symbol of natural, wholesome goodness, and supporting such a traditional family and parental responsibilities is often seen as crucial to maintaining moral values in society. Family ideology represents a powerful view of how people should lead their lives, even if this ideology does not reflect the reality of how most people do actually live their lives.

As seen earlier, this cereal packet image no longer corresponds to the typical household unit, and does not reflect the reality of everyday experience for the majority of families or people. Writers such as Barrett and McIntosh (1982) have argued that this stereotype found in family ideology is patriarchal, harmful and anti-social:

- *It is patriarchal* because it involves the exploitation of women through the triple burden of domestic and emotional labour in the family, on top of paid employment. This benefits men to the disadvantage of women. Women remain disadvantaged in paid work compared to men because of their assumed or actual responsibilities for housework, childcare and looking after other dependants, like disabled or elderly relatives. This increases women's dependency on men in relationships.
- *It is harmful* because it suggests that those living in other relationships, or living alone, are somehow deviant, are a threat to normal family life and lack any meaningful relationships in their lives. Every time politicians or policy-makers make appeals to 'strengthen the family', they are at the same time condemning those who live outside such a family, such as lone parents, lesbian and gay couples, and those living alone. Lone parents, particularly, have been subject to attack by conservative politicians and the mass media because they are seen as inadequate units for bringing up children, and the source of a range of social problems. Attacks on gays are often justified by the threat they are perceived to present to heterosexual relationships found in family ideology. Yet those living outside conventional families now make up a substantial proportion of the population. The stereotype is also harmful because it pretends there is no darker side of family life, as discussed above, and prevents such issues being treated as seriously as they should be, at great cost to the women and children who are mainly the ones victimized in the family. The stereotyped image of family ideology overlooks the way women become isolated at home with children, or struggle to combine

paid work with childcare, situations which may be very stressful and lead many women towards tranquillizer use and mental illness. Lone parent and other non-conformist household units may face discrimination by social workers, teachers, the police and magistrates, and therefore face higher risks of labelling or stereotyping, with children being branded failures at school, or being taken into care, or arrested and prosecuted because they are seen as 'deviant'.

- *It is anti-social*, because it devalues life outside the family. Much of social life today centres around family activities, and it is often difficult for those outside such conventional arrangements to participate. For example, schools are organized in such a way that it is difficult for lone parent families and dual worker families to combine paid work with childcare. Package holidays are overwhelmingly geared to families, and those who are lone parents or who live alone may often find it difficult to get the same financial deals as family groups. Family ideology separates people from one another – from 'us' in the family and 'them' outside the family, and therefore sets up barriers between people. It devalues life outside the family, and discourages alternative forms of household organization and relationships between people from developing, such as same sex relationships, lone parenthood, communal living or serial monogamy.

Politics, social policy and the family

Debates over family life have become a major feature of politics in Britain. The family ideology and family values discussed above have had important consequences for government social policies on the family. Both Labour and Conservative politicians have expressed similar views on the importance of the family, and both have sought to strengthen the traditional family. Both main parties, and particularly the New Right wing of the Conservative Party, have tended to support family ideology's cereal packet view of the traditional family, to see it as one of society's central and most important institutions, and to encourage support for living in traditional family units. They see the family as being under threat from increasing divorce rates, rising numbers of lone parents and births outside marriage, with the growing diversity of alternative lifestyles undermining the stability of society and generating serious moral decline. Wider social problems, such as teenage pregnancies, sexual promiscuity, educational failure, welfare dependency, poverty, drug abuse, and crime and delinquency, have all at one time or another been blamed on the failure of the family. The blame generally falls on the inadequate socialization and supervision of children by parents, and in some cases the lack of a male role model for boys.

The similarity of Labour and Conservative approaches was made very clear in the 1997 general election manifestos. The Conservative Party manifesto stated: 'The family is the most important institution in our lives. It offers security in a fast-changing world. . . . Conservatives believe that a healthy society encourages people to accept responsibility for their own lives . . . we want families to help themselves.' The Labour Party manifesto made very similar points: 'We will uphold family life as the most secure means of bringing up our children. Families are the core of our society. They should teach right from wrong. They should be the first defence against anti-social behaviour. The breakdown of family life damages the fabric of our society.' Things continued in a similar vein in 2001, with the Labour manifesto saying: 'Strong and stable family life offers the best possible start to children. And marriage provides a strong foundation for stable relationships. The government supports marriage. But it has to do more than that. It must support families, above all families with children.' The 2001 Conservative manifesto similarly headlined that 'common sense means strengthening the family' and 'support for marriage'.

In the 2005 election, the Conservative Party manifesto – at around nineteen pages of text, the shortest in forty years – had little to say about family values, but nonetheless managed to include sixteen references to the family. These included such phrases as 'rewarding families', 'trust families', 'working families', 'help families', 'enabling families' and 'giving more power to . . . families'. The 112-page Labour manifesto of 2005 seemed to signal for the first time a recognition of the growing diversity of family forms, with more emphasis placed on the care, protection and development of children rather than on the social institution in which they are raised. Nonetheless, the manifesto contained around thirty-six references to the family, including references to 'a typical family', 'family doctors', 'family incomes', 'family-friendly government' and 'family prosperity', and made clear statements that 'strong families are the bedrock of a strong society' and 'the financial support we are giving families, along with new rights to flexible working and access to childcare, are all designed to support family life'. Only the Liberal Democrats explicitly recognized that 'in the twenty-first century, the modern British family comes in many different shapes and sizes. We are no longer a nation that has one universal family structure.' But they nonetheless still felt it necessary to produce a special 'Manifesto for families' for the 2005 general election, and still emphasized that their policies were 'all designed to increase support for families and maintain the family's central place in our society'.

So, despite a changing world where a majority of the population no longer live in families, or families with dependent children, family life still seems to be central to the thinking of the major political parties.

Laws and social policies affecting the family and households

Given these political views of the family, and the welfare state, it is perhaps not surprising that there are a huge number of laws and social policies influencing families and households. This chapter, for example, has mentioned a range of laws and social policies affecting the family. These include compulsory education and the welfare state, which have affected family size and divorce, laws protecting children, promoting women's rights, and the right of gays and lesbians to form civil partnerships; the law also defines marriage age and divorce procedures, and establishes monogamy as the only legal form of marriage. Legal changes often reflect changing attitudes, and enable social policies to be carried out. For example, it was changing attitudes to homosexuality that led to the Civil Partnership Act in 2005 which enabled gay people to, in effect, get legally married. The activity below is designed to encourage you to examine and think about how social policies and laws affect families and households.

Activity

1 The column on the left in the table below lists a range of social policies and laws that might be considered to have an effect on families and households. The column on the right is left blank, for you to explain what these effects might be on families and households, and roles and relationships within them. You probably don't need to do them all, but you might explore three or four of them in some detail, or even suggest ones of your own choosing. You can probably find a lot of references to these issues by searching on the Internet, but the following sites might be useful:
   - www.dwp.gov.uk (Department for Work and Pensions)
   - www.familyandparenting.org (the National Family and Parenting Institute)
   - www.crae.org.uk (Children's Rights Alliance for England)
   - www.everychildmatters.gov.uk (Every Child Matters)
   - www.surestart.gov.uk (Sure Start – help for the early years)
   - www.homeoffice.gov.uk (the Home Office – useful for investigating family or child-related crimes)
   - www.ondivorce.co.uk (providing advice and support for those getting divorced)
   - www.childrenscommissioner.org (the Children's Commissioner)
   - www.dfes.gov.uk (Department for Children, Schools and Families)

Law or social policy	Effects on families and households, or roles and relationships within them
Abortion law	
Child benefit	
Child protection policies	

Children Act (2004)
Civil Partnership Act 2005
Compulsory education
Divorce laws (including custody of
    and access to children)
Domestic violence laws/policies
Equality laws to improve the rights
    and position of women
Eradicating child poverty by 2020
Free contraception
Free early years education for all
    three- and four-year olds
Free NHS health care
Laws and policies on adoption
    and fostering of children
Maternity and paternity leave
National Minimum Wage
Support for lone parents, like the
    New Deal for Lone Parents
Sure Start programmes

2 What are the main political parties currently saying about family roles and
   relationships? Go to the websites of the political parties below, and briefly
   outline two policies on the family and family roles and relationships. Identify
   any differences you can between them. Look for a 'policy' heading or button,
   but be prepared to search (try 'policy', 'manifesto' or 'family' first)
   ● www.labour.org.uk (the Labour Party)
   ● www.libdems.org.uk (the Liberal Democrats)
   ● www.conservatives.com (the Conservative Party)

Postmodernism and the family

Postmodernists believe that contemporary society is rapidly changing and
full of uncertainties, with people questioning a whole range of traditionally
accepted values, morals and norms. No longer are individuals constrained by
social structures, like the family, social class or religion, and they are rejecting ideas about the traditional family as a mainstay of social order. Society
has become fragmented into a mass of individuals who are making their own
choices over what they choose to believe in, and how they live their daily lives.
Diversity and consumer choice are two key features of postmodern society,
and this consumer choice is reflected, postmodernists argue, in the disinte-
gration of the traditional family. This is being replaced by a wide diversity of
relationships in which people are choosing to live. They no longer feel bound

by traditional ideas and expectations about marriage, lifelong monogamy, parenthood and family life, or traditional sexual identities. They are adopting new lifestyles and ways of relating to one another suited to their needs, rather than being constrained by traditional norms.

Many of the changes in family life discussed in this chapter – such as the decline in family size and marriage rates, the rising divorce rate, growing lone parenthood and individuals living alone, more shared households and 'families of choice', changing roles in the family and civil partnerships (gay marriage) – are widely regarded by politicians and social policymakers as a threat to the family and something to worry about, as support networks are weakened, and individuals face growing insecurity, uncertainly and anxiety in their lives.

Postmodernists see these changes as simply reflecting individuals making their consumer choices. Individuals pick and choose and 'mix and match' relationships as it suits them, and change these over a period of time – just like buying goods in a supermarket and going to another one if the quality and price isn't right. The rise of alternative family units, cohabitation, multiple partners and more diversity in sexual relationships, with greater tolerance of homosexuality, make the notion of the traditional family as a social institution redundant, as it has been replaced by a huge range of ever-changing personal relationships and household arrangements in which people are choosing to live.

Is the family a declining social institution?

We have seen how complex the question of 'family' has become today. The activity below will help you to decide to what extent the conventional family is the declining social institution that postmodernists suggest.

Activity

Below are fourteen statements. Some provide evidence for, and some against, the view that the conventional family is in decline, and some might be used in a conclusion.

1 First mark each statement 'for decline', 'against decline' or 'conclusion'.
2 Match up the competing arguments for and against which seem most linked to each other.
3 Using the material below, and the 'organizing work' you have just done, and drawing on ideas of your own and what you've read in this chapter, write a short essay (about one and a half to two sides) answering the question: *To what extent is the family in Britain a declining social institution*? Include arguments for and against, and reach a conclusion.

(a) Marriages today are more likely to be based on love and companionship rather than the custom and necessity of the past. Of all divorced people, 75 per cent remarry, a third of them within a year of getting divorced. This shows that what they are rejecting is not the institution of marriage itself but a particular marriage partner – they divorce hoping to turn an unhappy marriage into a new, happier one. The marriages that exist today are therefore probably much stronger and happier than ever, since unhappy relationships are easily ended by divorce.

(b) Postmodernists suggest that the traditional family unit is dead, with people choosing to live in a wide variety of household and family arrangements, which are constantly changing. It therefore no longer makes sense to talk of the family unit as a key institution in contemporary societies.

(c) It doesn't really matter whether or not couples are married or have been married before, or whether there is one parent or two. Though the form of the family will keep on changing, the importance of the family lies in its role as a stable and supportive unit for one or two adults, whether of the opposite or same sex, and their dependent children. In that sense, the ideal of the family perhaps still remains intact.

(d) There are well over a million and a half cohabiting couples who have refused to tie the marriage knot – about one in ten of all couples. This is expected to rise to 1.7 million by 2020, making up around one in seven of all couples. Over a quarter of all non-married males and females in Britain under the age of 60 were cohabiting in 2005–6. Living together before or outside marriage was one of the major social changes of the late twentieth century.

(e) What really seems to be happening is not so much that the family and marriage are in decline but that they are changing. People are choosing to live in a diversity of relationships and household types. There are more lone parent families, more reconstituted families, more gay and lesbian families, more experiments in living together before marriage, and fewer people prepared to marry simply to bring up children. Nevertheless, marriage remains an important social norm, and strong pressures from parents, peer groups and the responsibilities brought about by the birth of children continue to propel most people into marriage.

(f) It is estimated that more than 40 per cent of marriages will end in divorce, with almost one in four children experiencing a parental divorce by their sixteenth birthday.

(g) Many of those who cohabit eventually marry – about 60 per cent of first-time cohabitations turn into marriages – and about 75 per cent of the population have been married by the age of 50. It would appear that marriage remains an important social institution, even in the light of the high divorce rate and previous experience of living together outside marriage.

(h) Despite the record numbers of children being born outside marriage, about 85 per cent of those births in 2006 were registered jointly by the parents, and both parents in two out of three of these cases gave the same address. This suggests that most children are still being born into a stable relationship, and live in family situations with concerned parents who are simply reluctant to tie the legal marriage knot. Most dependent children still live in families headed by a married or cohabiting couple.

(i)   About 45 per cent of births are outside marriage today.

(j)   The failure of the family has been blamed for a wide range of social ills, such as declining moral standards, social disorder, drug abuse, rising crime rates, vandalism, football hooliganism, educational failure and increasing levels of violence in society.

(k)   The Policy Studies Institute has calculated that if these trends continue, by the year 2010 the majority of couples will cohabit before marriage, the majority of marriages will end in divorce followed by remarriage, and nearly all births will be outside marriage.

(l)   The causes of those social problems all too often blamed on the family are many and complex, and those who blame the family are often searching for simple solutions to complex problems.

(m)   Statistics like these have made the state of the family a major battleground for politicians, with the suggestion that the very existence of the family is threatened by rising rates of divorce, cohabitation, lone parenthood and reconstituted families.

(n)   In Britain today, a quarter of families with dependent children have just one parent.

(o)   Although the divorce rate has gone up, the evidence suggests that it is easier divorce laws, the growing economic independence of women, reduced social stigma and more sympathetic public attitudes which have caused this, rather than more marriage breakdowns. In the past, many couples may have been condemned by legal and financial obstacles and social intolerance to suffer unhappy 'empty shell' marriages or to separate without divorcing. If the law were changed to make divorce harder to get, couples would continue to separate without divorcing

CHAPTER SUMMARY

After studying this chapter, you should be able to:

- describe the different forms of marriage, the family and household

- identify arguments about the universality of the nuclear family

- explain and criticize the functionalist, Marxist, Marxist feminist and radical feminist perspectives on the family

- explain how demographic changes like the decline in the birth rate, death rate, infant mortality rate and increased life expectancy have affected the family

- examine the significance of the ageing population for family life

- examine the arguments about whether or not the family has lost its functions

- discuss reasons why the classic extended family is less common today

- critically examine the links between the isolated nuclear family and contemporary society
- examine the view that roles in marriage and cohabiting relationships have become more equal
- examine the ways in which women's responsibilities for housework and childcare undermine their positions in paid employment
- identify the features of domestic labour, and how these differ from paid work
- identify and explain the main changes in the position of children in the family and society
- explain why average family size has decreased, and why women are having fewer, or no, children
- explain the reasons for the rising divorce rate, the emergence of the reconstituted family and the groups most 'at risk' of divorce
- explain why there has been a large increase in the number of lone parent families
- explain why there has been a decline in marriage, the growth of cohabitation and more people living alone
- explain why there are more births outside marriage
- describe and explain why the 'cereal packet' family is a myth, and identify the diversity of family and household forms in Britain
- identify and discuss the darker side of family life
- explain what is meant by family ideology and critically discuss its main features
- discuss political views of the family and social policies and laws affecting families
- examine the arguments and evidence for and against the view that the family and marriage are of declining social importance

KEY TERMS

ageing population
arranged marriage
'beanpole' family
birth rate
classic extended family
commune
conjugal role
death rate
demography
division of labour
divorce rate
domestic labour

expressive role
extended family
family
family ideology
fertility rate
household
infant mortality rate
instrumental role
integrated conjugal role
kibbutz
kinship
life expectancy
meritocracy

modified extended family
monogamy
moral panic
nuclear family
patriarchy
polyandry
polygamy
polygyny
primary socialization
privatization
privatized nuclear family
reconstituted family
scapegoat

secondary socialization
secularization
segregated conjugal role
serial monogamy
sexual division of labour
social construction
stereotype
structural differentiation
symmetrical family

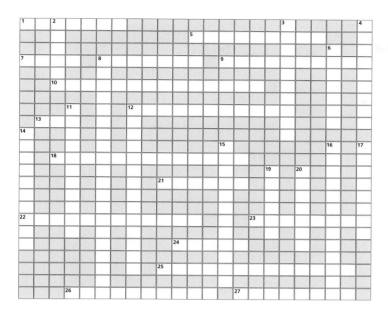

Across

1) Israeli alternative to the nuclear family (7)
5) The term used to describe an individual or group of people living under the same roof and sharing facilities (9)
7) She first identified the importance of social networks in understanding roles in the family (4)
8) An American functionalist writer who thought families were 'factories producing human personalities' (7)
9) The opposite to an instrumental role (10)
10) In marriage, one at a time, one after the other and they don't last long (6, 8)
12) The number of divorces per 1000 married people (7, 4)
13) These families with same sex parents have a happy name (3)
18) A family type involving the remarriage of one or both partners and the children of a previous marriage (13)
21) She was one of the first to study the sociology of housework (6)
22) One of the fastest growing forms of family relationship and unlikely to be regarded as 'sinful' (12)
23) This legal bonding is in decline (8)
24) A writer who argued 'the family . . . is the source of all our discontents' – sounds like a bloodsucker (5)
25) A two-generational family (7, 6)
26) A family form usually arising from death of a partner, divorce or choice (4-6)
27) This approach challenged the male view of the family (8)

Down

2) Around 45 per cent of these take place outside marriage (6)
3) The people we learn from by imitating their behaviour (4, 6)
4) These children are below working age and rely on their families to support them financially (9)
6) Relations of blood, marriage or adoption (7)
8) The process of learning the culture of society within the family (7, 13)
11) A type of family where there are similar roles performed by each partner (11)
12) Technical term for housework (8, 6)
14) Where males are dominant (10)
15) The traditional family stereotype (6, 6)
16) The term used to describe relationships between husband and wife (8, 5)
17) A nuclear family with vertical or horizontal extensions (8)
19) A male partner who takes an active role in housework and childcare (3, 3)
20) The legal termination of a marriage (7)

The solution to this crossword can be found on the teachers' pages of www.polity.co.uk/browne

EXAM QUESTION

SECTION B: FAMILIES AND HOUSEHOLDS

Time allowed: 1 hour   **Total for this section: 60 marks**

2 Read **items 2A and 2B** below and answer parts (a) to (e) that follow.

Item 2A

Functionalist writers suggest that the typical family in contemporary societies is the structurally isolated privatized nuclear family. This is because it is seen as well adapted to the needs of industrial society. For example, this family unit is small and geographically mobile, and is not tied down by obligations to wider kin. Others suggest that there is no 'typical' family unit. Demographic changes, including   5
declining birth rates, infant mortality and death rates, and greater life expectancy, are some of the factors changing families and households, and creating a diversity of arrangements in which people now live.

Item 2B

There have been some major changes in the family in the last 30 or 40 years in Britain. One area of change is the dramatic increase in the number of marriages to end in divorce, with divorce numbers increasing around six times the number in 1961. The number of people who are cohabiting is now at an all-time high, and the number marrying is at an all-time low. One in four families with dependent children   5
is now a lone-parent family, and about four out of every ten children now grow up in either a lone parent or reconstituted family. Around 45 per cent of births are now outside of marriage.

(a)   Explain what is meant by a 'privatized nuclear family' (**Item 2A**, line 2)   *(2 marks)*

(b)   Suggest **two** ways that greater life expectancy has changed families and households (**Item 2A**, lines 6–7)   *(4 marks)*

(c)   Suggest **three** reasons for the decline in the birth rate since 1900.   *(6 marks)*

(d)   Examine the contribution of feminist writers to the study of the family.   *(24 marks)*

(e)   With reference to **Item 2B** and elsewhere, assess the view that the family in Britain is in decline.   *(24 marks)*

CHAPTER
4

Wealth, Poverty and Welfare

Contents

Key issues	**207**
Introduction	**207**
Wealth and income	**208**
The distribution of wealth and income	**208**
Who are the rich?	209
Attempts to redistribute wealth and income	211
Explaining the distribution of wealth and income	212
The welfare state	**215**
What is the welfare state?	215
Who provides welfare?	217
Theoretical approaches to welfare	**220**
The social democratic approach (the welfare model)	220
The New Right or market liberal approach	221
Marxist approaches	221
Feminist approaches	222
The welfare state and social inequality	**223**
The inverse care law	224
Inequalities between ethnic groups	225
Gender inequality	225

The welfare state and poverty	**226**
The Labour government of 1997	226
Poverty	**227**
Changing views of poverty	227
Defining poverty (1): absolute or subsistence poverty	228
Defining poverty (2): relative poverty	230
Who are the poor in the United Kingdom?	240
Explaining poverty: cultural explanations	243
Explaining poverty: material explanations	246
Poverty and value judgements	255
Chapter summary	**257**
Key terms	**258**
Exam question	**259**

Wealth, Poverty and Welfare

KEY ISSUES

- The distribution of wealth and income, and explanations for it
- The welfare state
- Theoretical approaches to welfare
- The welfare state and social inequality
- Defining and measuring poverty
- Explaining poverty
- The debate over the underclass

Introduction

Many believe that large differences in wealth and income and the contrast between the very rich and the very poor have largely disappeared in modern Britain. However, Britain remains one of the most unequal countries in the European Union, with stark contrasts between the expensive lifestyles of the rich minority, and the poverty and hardship of many of those who are unemployed, sick, old or low paid, who are lone parents, or who are homeless or living in decaying housing. This chapter will demonstrate that massive inequalities in wealth and income and widespread poverty remain in modern Britain, despite the existence of the welfare state.

The unequal distribution of wealth and income creates major differences in life chances between people. Life chances are the chances of obtaining those things defined as desirable and of avoiding those things defined as undesirable in any society. Life chances include the chances of obtaining things like good quality housing, good health, holidays, job security and educational success, and avoiding things like ill-health and unemployment. Life chances are about whether or not you have control over your life and are able to participate fully in society.

Wealth and poverty are two sides of the same coin. The causes of poverty cannot be separated from the causes of wealth, and reducing poverty necessarily involves a redistribution of wealth and income, since it is the unequal distribution of wealth and income that creates the extremes of poverty and wealth.

Wealth and income

Wealth refers to property in the form of assets which can be sold and turned into cash for the benefit of the owner. The main forms of wealth are property such as housing and land, factories, bank deposits, shares in companies, and personal possessions.

- **Productive property** is wealth which provides an unearned income for its owner, for example houses which are rented out, factories and land, or company shares which provide dividends.
- **Consumption property** is wealth for use by the owner, such as consumer goods like fridges, cars, or owning your own home, which do not produce any income.

Income refers to the flow of money which people obtain from work, or from their investments.

- *Earned income* is income received from paid employment (wages and salaries).
- *Unearned income* is received from interest on savings and other personal investments, such as rent on buildings and land, interest on savings, and dividends on shares.

The distribution of wealth and income

Figure 4.1 shows that in 2004 the poorest 50 per cent of the population owned only 7 per cent of the wealth, while the richest 5 per cent owned 40 per cent. A quarter of the population possessed around three-quarters of the nation's wealth. The pattern becomes even more unequal when you exclude the value of people's homes, with nearly two-thirds (62 per cent) of wealth owned by just 5 per cent of adults. These figures are official figures from the Inland Revenue (the government's tax collectors), and they therefore underestimate the inequalities of wealth, as the wealthy have an interest in concealing their wealth to avoid taxation.

As figure 4.2 overleaf shows, income is also unequally distributed, with the richest fifth of income earners getting 42 per cent of all income in 2005–6 – more

Wealth is property in the form of assets which can be sold and turned into cash for the benefit of the owner.

Productive property is property that provides an unearned income for its owner, such as factories, land, and stocks and shares.

Consumption property is property for use by the owner which doesn't produce any income, such as owning your own car.

Income is a flow of money which people obtain from work, from their investments, or from the state.

Figure 4.1 Distribution of wealth: United Kingdom, 2004

Source: Inland Revenue, 2007

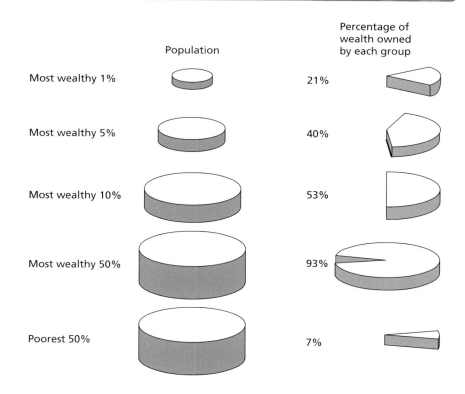

Population

Percentage of wealth owned by each group

Most wealthy 1% — 21%

Most wealthy 5% — 40%

Most wealthy 10% — 53%

Most wealthy 50% — 93%

Poorest 50% — 7%

than twice their 'fair share' if income were equally distributed, and more than the bottom three-fifths of income earners got between them. The poorest fifth got only 8 per cent, less than a half of their 'fair share'.

Who are the rich?

There are three main groups making up the rich:

- *The traditional aristocracy*   They are major landowners, such as the Duke of Westminster, who owns sizeable chunks of London, Cheshire, North Wales and Ireland, forests and shooting estates in Lancashire and Scotland and properties in North America and the Far East. According to the 2007 Rich List published by the *Sunday Times*, the Duke of Westminster's wealth amounts to an estimated £7 billion (£7,000,000,000).
- *The owners of industry and commerce*   These are the 'corporate rich' of the business world. This includes Sir Richard Branson of Virgin, Britain's eleventh richest person in 2007, with estimated assets of £3.1 billion.
- *Stars of entertainment and the media*   These include former Beatle Sir Paul McCartney (£825 million), Sir Mick Jagger (£215 million), Sir Elton

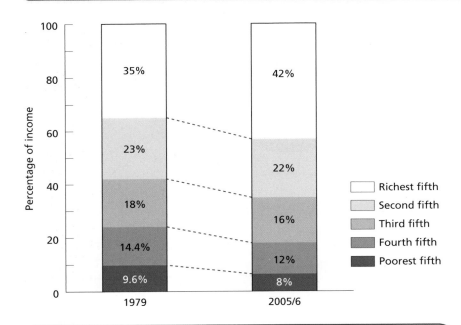

Figure 4.2 Changes in the distribution of income, by fifths of the population: United Kingdom, 1979–2005/6

Source: *Households below Average Income,* Department of Social Security, 1997 and Department for Work and Pensions, 2007

> ### Activity
>
> 1 Describe the changes in the distribution of income between 1979 and 2005/6 shown in figure 4.2.
> 2 What do these changes suggest about the gap between the most and least well-off in the UK?

John (£225 million), and the relatively impoverished David and Victoria Beckham on £112 million, Robbie Williams on £95 million and Sir Sean Connery on £85 million.

Most wealth is inherited, with those inheriting doing nothing to earn their wealth. Most of the rich live on unearned income from investments rather than from employment. The starkness of these inequalities is made clear by the Queen, one of Britain's richest women, with personal assets estimated at £300 million. If she were to pop this into her local building society, she would receive at least £17 in unearned income each minute of every day every year (after tax) – an hourly rate of about 190 times as much as someone on the national minimum wage in 2007, and she'd still have her original £300 million.

High earners and the self-made rich do not necessarily put in more work than those who receive low pay; it is simply that society places different values on people in different positions, and rewards them more or less highly. A senior executive in a large company or a rock star will probably not have to work as hard for his or her high income as an unskilled manual worker working long hours in a low paid job.

The Queen is one of Britain's richest women, though there are other women and men who are *much* richer. She earns in interest on her wealth an hourly income, 24 hours a day, about 190 times greater than someone on the National Minimum Wage. Do you think the rich deserve their high incomes? Explain why or why not

Activity

1 Go to Google (www.google.com) and search on the 'Rich list UK'. Have some fun finding out how rich your favourite celebrities are.
2 Do you agree or disagree with the view that it is wrong that the wealthy should be allowed to live off unearned income, and that large amounts of wealth should be able to be passed from parents to children? Do you think high earners really deserve their high rewards more than people who work in low paid jobs? Give reasons for your answers.

Attempts to redistribute wealth and income

The massive inequalities in wealth and income which have existed over the last century, and the inequalities in life chances these have caused, have provoked various measures by governments to redistribute wealth and income more equally. Some of these measures include:

- *inheritance tax*, which is a tax payable when people give gifts of wealth either before or after death, and is intended to limit the inheritance of vast quantities of wealth from one generation by the next
- *capital gains tax*, which is intended to reduce profits from dealing in property or shares, and is payable whenever these are sold
- *income tax*, which is payable on earned and unearned income; this is generally progressive, as it rises as earnings increase

- *social welfare benefits* from the state, like Income Support and Jobseeker's Allowance, which are generally seen as attempts to divert the resources obtained through taxation to the needy sections of society

Why have attempts to redistribute wealth and income failed?

Despite these measures, attempts to redistribute wealth and income have been largely unsuccessful. Little real redistribution has occurred, and what redistribution has taken place has mainly been between the very rich and the lesser rich, and the gap between the richest and the poorest sections of society has actually grown wider in recent years.

Tax relief   The state allows tax relief, money normally used to pay income tax, on a wide variety of things such as business expenses, school fees and private pensions. These are expenses which only the better off are likely to have. This means that they pay a smaller proportion of their income in tax than a person who is poorer but who does not have these expenses.

Tax avoidance schemes   These are schemes which are perfectly legal, often being thought up by financial advisers and accountants to find loopholes in the tax laws to beat the tax system, thereby saving the rich from paying some tax. Such schemes involve things like living outside Britain for most of the year, investing in pension schemes to avoid income tax, investing in tax-free or low tax areas like the Channel Islands, giving wealth away to kin well before death to avoid inheritance tax, or putting companies or savings in other people's names, such as those of husband/wife, children or other kin.

Tax evasion   This is illegal, and involves people not declaring wealth and income to the Inland Revenue. This is suspected to be a common practice among the rich.

A failure to claim benefits   A final reason for the failure of attempts at wealth and income redistribution is that many people fail to claim the welfare benefits to which they are entitled. Some reasons for this are discussed later in this chapter.

Explaining the distribution of wealth and income

There are three main types of explanation for the unequal patterns of wealth and income distribution.

Functionalist explanations

Functionalist writers like Davis and Moore (1945) argue that inequalities in wealth and income are necessary to maintain society. According to Davis and Moore:

- Some positions in society are more functionally important than others in maintaining society. These require specialized skills that not everyone in society has the talent and ability to acquire.
- Those who do have the ability to do these jobs must be motivated and encouraged to undertake the lengthy training often required for these important positions with the promise of future high rewards in terms of income and wealth. There must therefore be a system of unequal rewards to make sure the most able people get into the most important social positions.

There are three main criticisms of this explanation:

1 There is no way of deciding which positions in society are more important, and this often rests on personal value judgements. There are many poorly rewarded occupations which can still be seen as vital in maintaining society. For example, a rich business executive can only become rich through the work of his or her employees, and a refuse collector is no less important than a doctor in maintaining society's health.
2 Some people have high levels of wealth and income, not because they have talent or occupy a position of 'functional importance', but because they have inherited their wealth. Having rich parents is still one of the major means of becoming wealthy.
3 Material rewards are not, as Davis and Moore suggest, the only means of motivating people to fill important social positions. People may be motivated by the prospect of job satisfaction, or by the attraction of giving service to others, as for example in teaching or nursing.

> **Activity**
>
> Do you think some jobs are more important than others in maintaining society? Do you think some jobs deserve higher rewards than others if people are to be motivated to train for them? Give examples of what you regard as important and unimportant jobs, giving reasons for your answer.

Weberian explanations

Market situation refers to the rewards that people are able to obtain when they sell their skills on the labour market, with the rewards they get dependent on the scarcity of their skills and the power they have to obtain high rewards.

Weberian explanations suggest that inequalities in wealth and income arise from differences in people's **market situation**.

Some people are able to get higher incomes when they sell their abilities and skills in the job market because they have rare skills, talents or qualifications that are in demand, such as doctors and lawyers. This might also happen because society values some skills and talents more highly than others and rewards them accordingly, as might be the case with business executives or company owners, or with football, film and music stars. Some celebrities receive high rewards simply for being famous and in public demand, even though they lack any obvious talents.

The difficulty with the Weberian approach is that it does not easily explain the position of those who inherit their wealth and do not sell their skills on the labour market, as they live on unearned incomes rather than those earned through employment.

Marxist explanations

Marxist explanations suggest that the main reason for inequalities in wealth and income lies in the private ownership of the means of production – the key resources like land, property, factories and businesses which are necessary to produce society's goods. The concentration of ownership of the means of production in the hands of a small upper class is the basis of the inequalities of wealth, and this generates similarly high levels of income inequality through unearned income on investments. The difficulty with this approach is that it does not easily explain the wide inequalities in income that exist between people who do not own the means of production.

Activity

1 Classify each of the following situations as wealth, earned income or unearned income:
   - ownership of a chemical company
   - royalties received from publishing a sociology book
   - a boxer receiving £18 million for a boxing match
   - receiving £435 million for writing Harry Potter books
   - the Queen receiving £7.9 million from the government to support the royal household
   - ownership of the publishing rights to the Beatles songs
   - an actor getting £20 million for making a film
   - rent received from ownership of a string of flats in London
   - dividends on shares held in a computer company
   - £1.4 million received by a footballer for sponsoring football boots
   - having £15 million worth of shares in a computer company
   - profits received from owning a national daily newspaper
   - £150 a week from working in a burger chain

2 Which out of the functionalist, Marxist and Weberian explanations do you find the most convincing in explaining the distribution of wealth and income in our society? Give reasons for your answer.

3 What assumptions and stereotypes do you have of the rich? Draw up your view of the features of rich people, such as their sources of wealth and income and their lifestyle. Where do you think your ideas and assumptions about the rich come from?

4 Do you think large inequalities in wealth and income are justified in society? Give reasons for your answer.

> **Activity**
>
> 1 Explain, with examples, the difference between wealth and income.
> 2 Suggest *three* reasons why some jobs get higher rewards than others.
> 3 Identify *two* policies that might contribute to the redistribution of wealth and income.
> 4 Answer the following essay question, in about one and half sides of A4 paper:
> *Assess sociological explanations for the unequal distribution of wealth and income in contemporary Britain.*

The welfare state

What is the welfare state?

A welfare state is one that is concerned with implementing social policies guaranteeing the 'cradle to grave' well-being of the whole population, and particularly the elimination of poverty, unemployment, ill-health and ignorance. Such policies are generally implemented using resources collected through taxation.

The welfare state in Britain mainly began with the Beveridge Report of 1942. This recommended the development of state-run welfare services (backed up by voluntary organizations) aimed at the destruction of the 'five giants' of want, disease, squalor, ignorance and idleness, and the creation of a society where each individual would have the right to be cared for by the state from 'womb to tomb'. The welfare state as we know it today came into effect on 5 July 1948 – the date of the foundation of the National Health Service.

The welfare state provides a wide range of benefits and services, paid for by taxation. They include:

- A range of welfare benefits through the social security system for many groups such as the unemployed, those injured at work, the sick and disabled, widows, the retired, expectant mothers, lone parents and children.
- A comprehensive and largely free National Health Service, including antenatal and postnatal care, hospitals, local GPs, dentists and opticians (although some charges are payable – for example to dentists and opticians).
- A free and compulsory state education for all to the age of 16 (and subsidies after that age).
- Social services provided by local councils, such as social workers, and facilities for the mentally and physically impaired, the elderly and children. Local councils are also responsible for housing the homeless, and for overseeing the adoption and arranging the fostering of children. The structure and key services of the welfare state (as they were in 2007) are shown in figure 4.3 over the page.

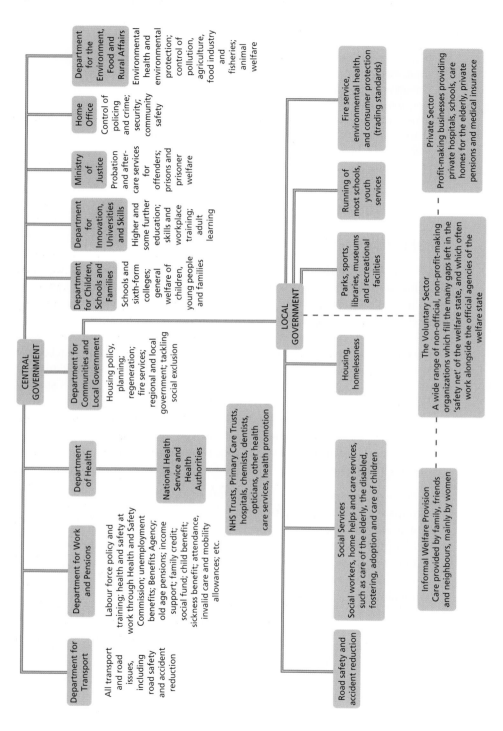

Figure 4.3 'Womb-to-tomb' care: the structure and key services of the welfare state

The Beveridge Report and the development of the welfare state in Britain were based on four main principles and assumptions:

- full employment
- universal welfare – cradle-to-grave provision
- free health care and education
- that women would be primarily housewives and mothers – as the Beveridge Report said, 'women would make marriage their sole occupation'.

Who provides welfare?

Although welfare is generally seen as provided only by the state, it is also provided informally through the family and community, and by a range of voluntary and private agencies as well. There is a suggestion that the population's welfare needs are best met by a number of different kinds of provider. This gives people more choice, enabling them to 'pick and mix' what they most need, with different providers giving different services. Different providers may sometimes compete to provide the same service, offering choice and improving quality, as, for example, with private medicine. However, some argue that not everyone can afford to pay for some care, leading to unequal access to care, with two tiers of services for the rich and the poor. This range of provision is known as **welfare pluralism**.

Welfare pluralism refers to the whole range of welfare provision, including informal provision by the family and community, welfare provided by the government, the voluntary sector and the private sector.

Informal welfare provision

Much welfare provision is provided informally, and free, by family, friends and neighbours. Feminist writers have emphasized that this often means care by women, as it is women who take on the main caring responsibilities in the family for the dependent elderly, the disabled and the sick. The Equal Opportunities Commission (now incorporated into the Equality and Human Rights Commission) has suggested around three times more women than men are involved in this informal care. As seen above, the Beveridge Report included the patriarchal assumption that women would be primarily housewives and mothers, concerned with housework, childcare and looking after the family, with men supporting them through paid employment. This meant it was assumed married women didn't need the same level of social security benefits as men, as these would go to their husbands to support their families in times of need. Much welfare provision today still rests on this assumption, despite the fact that many married women now also work outside the home in paid employment.

The voluntary sector

Voluntary organizations are non-official, non-profit-making organizations, often charities, which are 'voluntary' in the sense that they are neither

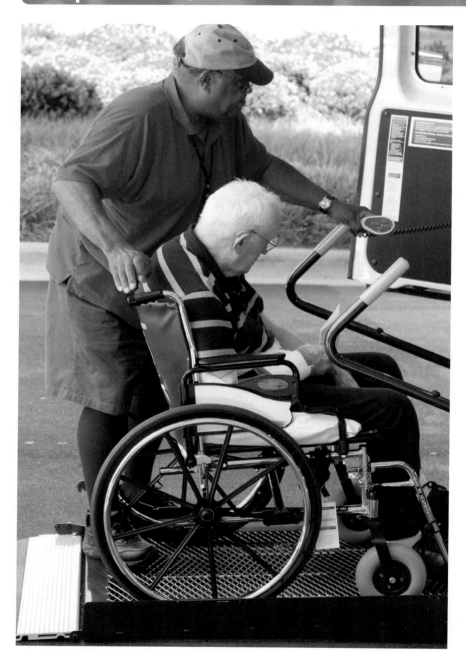

Volunteer helpers play an important role in the voluntary sector of welfare provision

created by, nor controlled by, the government. They are staffed by both salaried employees and voluntary helpers, and are funded by donations from the public and grants from, or sale of services to, central and local government. Voluntary organizations try to fill some of the gaps left by the 'safety net' provided by the state, by providing help and information in areas where state assistance is too little or non-existent.

Voluntary organizations include groups such as the Salvation Army, which provides hostel accommodation and soup kitchens; Shelter, which campaigns for the homeless and helps with finding accommodation; Help the Aged and Age Concern; the Citizens' Advice Bureau (CAB); the NSPCC (the National Society for the Prevention of Cruelty to Children) and the Child Poverty Action Group, which promotes action for the relief of poverty among children and families with children. The churches also provide a range of welfare support, particularly to the elderly.

Voluntary organizations have the advantage of providing cheaper services than those provided by the state or private sectors, combined with high levels of expertise. They can therefore be better able to respond in specialized areas, like domestic violence, homelessness debt, welfare rights or disability, where state provision may be under pressure, inadequate or non-existent. However, voluntary organizations often lack adequate funds to be as effective as they might otherwise be, and they do not exist in all the areas where they are needed.

> **Pressure groups** are organizations which try to put pressure on those with power in society to implement policies which they favour.

Voluntary organizations also play important roles as **pressure groups**. Many voluntary organizations lead public campaigns to improve welfare benefits and services for the poor and socially excluded. (Social exclusion is discussed later in this chapter.) Voluntary organizations play a major role in highlighting the weaknesses of the welfare state, and keeping problems such as poverty, homelessness and the care of the mentally ill in the public eye. They frequently provide expert knowledge and make recommendations to governments for changes to improve social welfare.

The private sector

The private sector consists of profit-making private businesses, from which individuals or local and central government purchase welfare services. This sector provides welfare services such as private hospitals, schools, care homes for the elderly, private pensions and medical insurance. Those with conservative views (see the New Right or market liberal approach, below) often see the private sector as cheaper, providing more choice, and as more efficient and effective than state provision, because it has to compete for customers and provide a decent service if it is to survive in the face of competition. However, the need to make profits may mean cost-cutting takes a higher priority than the quality of services provided. Access to the private sector is only available to those who can afford it, and poor people may therefore not get services at all if the state doesn't provide or pay for them. This can mean that those who are able to afford it can 'queue jump', for example by seeing NHS consultants privately and paying, and then getting put at the top of their list for a free NHS operation. The rich can also buy expensive drugs that the NHS won't provide.

Activity

1 Do you think the state should be the main provider of welfare for all? What are the advantages and disadvantages of welfare provision by the state compared to the voluntary and private sectors?
2 Suggest reasons why informal welfare provision is mainly carried out by women. What consequences do you think this might have for women's lives and careers?

Theoretical approaches to welfare

There are four main approaches to the welfare state, and to the way welfare services should be provided. The main differences are between those who think welfare should be the responsibility of individuals, provided by the private sector and with people buying services themselves, and those who think the state should provide welfare funded through taxation.

The social democratic approach (the welfare model)

Social democratic approaches include the following beliefs:

- *The government should be responsible for social welfare*, and for action to eliminate problems such as unemployment and poverty, providing care for the disabled, children in need, the elderly and other vulnerable and socially excluded groups facing **marginalization**.
- *Social inequality threatens the stability of society*, and wealth and income should be redistributed through progressive taxation (the more you earn, the more tax you pay), with benefits and health care available to all to reduce social inequality and tackle poverty. Only the state has the power and resources to do this, and should provide 'womb to tomb' care.
- *Benefits should be available to all* (universal benefits), because selective, means-tested benefits, which are only payable to those whose income falls below a certain level, create a stigma on those claiming them. This stigma means those in greatest need often fail to claim benefits to which they are entitled. Means testing also discourages people from taking low paid work when it becomes available, catching them in a poverty trap (see table 4.1 overleaf).
- *The need for more social cohesion* – universal provision, like free education, pensions, full employment and free health care, bring economic benefits through an employed, healthy and well-qualified workforce, and help to promote a more cohesive, less divided, society.

> **Marginalization** refers to the process whereby some groups are pushed by poverty, ill-health, lack of education, disability, racism and so on to the margins or edges of society and are unable to take part in the life enjoyed by the majority of citizens.

> **Universal benefits and means testing**
>
> *Universal benefits* are those available to everyone regardless of income, such as the basic state pension, child benefit and free health care and education.
>
> *Means testing* involves people having to pass a test of their income and savings (their 'means') before receiving any benefits: only if these are low enough will they receive any benefits.

The New Right or market liberal approach

The New Right approach mainly developed in Britain in the years of the Conservative government between 1979 and 1997. This is also known as a market liberal approach because it believes that individuals should have the freedom to choose welfare provision from all those competing in the 'welfare market', and should take responsibility themselves for obtaining it, mainly through the private sector. According to this approach:

A **dependency culture** is a set of values and beliefs, and a way of life, centred on dependence on others, particularly benefits from the welfare state.

The **underclass** is a social group right at the bottom of the social hierarchy, whose members are in some ways different from, and cut off or excluded from, the rest of society.

- *The generosity of the 'nanny' welfare state is seen as undermining personal responsibility and self-help*, and people's willingness to work to support themselves. Writers like Murray (1989, 1990) and Marsland (1989) argue that the welfare state has created a **dependency culture** and a work-shy **underclass** which wants to avoid work by living off welfare benefits. The generosity of the welfare state has undermined the importance of support from families, and encourages lone parenthood, as women have children they could not otherwise have supported, knowing they can get help from state benefits.
- *Taxation should be kept to the minimum*, and should not be wasted on providing welfare benefits or health care to those who are able to support themselves.
- *State benefits should be restricted only to the very poor*, and those unable to work through sickness or disability, and should be means tested (see table 4.1 overleaf). The rest of the population should provide their own welfare services by buying them from the private sector, such as private medicine and private pension plans.

The social democratic or welfare model was that which underpinned the welfare state in Britain until 1979. Since then, the market model has become more dominant, with a greater emphasis on tackling the dependency culture, cutting the soaring levels of state spending on welfare provision, on encouraging provision by the voluntary and private sectors, and on more support through the family and community.

Table 4.1 The case for and against means testing of benefits

For (New Right or market liberal approach)	Against (social democratic or welfare model)
Benefits are targeted only at those who really need them. People who are able to work should support themselves. Money is saved on universal benefits which most people don't need and shouldn't have. More money is available to invest in the economy, create jobs and cut taxes	Means-tested benefits, which are received only by the very poor, may lead to some people being worse off if they take a low paid job. They may lose means-tested benefits like housing or council tax benefits, and the extra they earn is not enough to compensate for the lost benefits. This 'poverty trap' discourages people from taking work. Universal benefits avoid this
Means testing stops voluntary unemployment being an option for some people, and fights the welfare dependency culture	Because of the poverty trap, means testing might drive people into a dependency culture and a reluctance to get a job
Families, communities and voluntary organizations are strengthened as alternative sources of support	Families and communities caught in the poverty trap are likely to be weakened by poverty and stress. Some will be encouraged to become 'benefit cheats' to get around means testing. Universal benefits keep everyone's standards up to an acceptable minimum level
Selective means-tested benefits will enable more benefits for the most disadvantaged, by no longer wasting money on those who can afford to support themselves	Often the most deprived do not take up or make full use of even universal benefits, as they're unsure of how to do so. Means-tested benefits attach a stigma to those who claim them, and make it even more unlikely they will claim benefits to which they are entitled

Marxist approaches

Marxist approaches tend to see the welfare state mainly as a way of buying off working-class protest, by reducing the risks to social order and political stability created by extreme poverty. By keeping the labour force healthy and efficient to the benefit of the capitalist class, the welfare state attempts to make a system based on inequality, exploitation and conflict appear caring and just. The welfare state is then a form of social control – an attempt to keep the workforce efficient and trained, and the capitalist system stable, by giving workers a stake in society.

Feminist approaches

Feminist approaches emphasize the way the welfare state supports patriarchy, and the inadequacy of the welfare state in meeting the needs of women. They point to the way the benefit system is frequently based on contributions records built up by full-time workers, who are less likely to be women, and the way the founding principles of the welfare state, discussed earlier, were based on an assumption of women being financially supported by men, with important levels of care of the elderly, children, the sick and disabled being provided free by women.

> ### Activity
>
> Refer to the following statements, and say in each case which model of welfare it most closely matches. Give reasons for your answers.
>
> 1 'Those who are working resent seeing neighbours, apparently as fit as themselves, living on incapacity benefit. It has become known as "bad back" benefit.'
> 2 'If it wasn't for the safety net of the welfare state, there would be widespread discontent and protest by working-class people against the inequalities and exploitation they face.'
> 3 'The welfare state simply doesn't recognize the amount of unpaid work that women do in the home.'
> 4 'If you withdraw benefits, people will be forced to bear the consequences of their behaviour. Gradually a traditional morality will re-emerge, whereby the two-parent family becomes the norm again, and bastards and single parents are stigmatized.'
> 5 'A lot of unemployment is produced by the very policies we are talking about. It is avoidable. You have little boys growing up who literally do not know how to work. They have not been socialized to get up at 7 o'clock and go into work even if they don't feel like it.'
> 6 'Get the poor off our overtaxed backs.'
> 7 'Investment, investment, investment in health, education, pensions and other public services is what this country needs. The government has done a lot, but a lot more needs to be done and this government will do it.'
> 8 'The government should stop squandering money on a spending binge, and invest in the economy to raise the living standards of all.'
> 9 'The state's welfare services should be financed largely from the income of those who can most afford to pay. The state should ensure that resources are redistributed from the rich and top salary earners to those in our society who suffer ill-health, unemployment, poverty and deprivation.'
>
> The solution to this activity can be found on the teachers' pages of www.polity.co.uk/browne

The welfare state and social inequality

Social democratic approaches generally see the welfare state as a device for reducing social inequality through progressive taxation providing benefits for all, but particularly for the disadvantaged, through increased state spending on education, health, social security and other welfare services. In other words, the welfare state is seen as *redistributive* – passing income from the rich to the poor – so society becomes more equal.

Activity

1 Explain what is meant by 'welfare pluralism'.
2 Explain what is meant by the 'voluntary sector', and outline its role in welfare provision.
3 Explain the difference between universal and means-tested benefits.
4 Suggest *two* ways in which private sector welfare provision might create unequal access to welfare services.
5 Identify and explain *two* differences between the New Right (market liberal) and social democratic approaches to the welfare state.
6 Identify *two* feminist criticisms of the welfare state.
7 Write a short essay, of about one and a half sides of A4 paper, answering the following question: *Examine the view that social welfare is likely to be most effective when services are delivered by a range of providers rather than by the state alone.*

However, the welfare state has failed to do this. Means testing of benefits, prescription charges, dental charges, fees for universities and the abolition of student grants have all affected those on lower incomes the most. Some benefits, like the Jobseeker's Allowance (formerly unemployment benefit) and state pensions, are linked to income and previous employment, so those on lower incomes or with an interrupted paid employment record (for example, because they were raising children) get lower benefits.

Both basic and higher rates of income tax have been cut, and there has been an increase in indirect taxes like VAT (value added tax) and those on petrol, alcohol and tobacco. Indirect taxes are payable on people's spending rather than their income, and take up a greater proportion of the income of the poor compared with the better off. In these circumstances, the tax system has become less progressive, and in some ways hits the poor harder than the rich.

The inverse care law

The **inverse care law** suggests that those whose need is greatest get the least spent on them, and those whose need is least get the most spent on them. Julian Le Grand (1982) has argued that this inverse care law is found throughout the whole range of welfare state provision. He argues that most welfare spending consists of either universal benefits going to everyone (like the basic state pension, or free education and health care) or is spent in ways that provide services from which the middle class gains most. For example, people in the more advantaged middle class:

- receive more spending per head on health
- make better use of the health service, as they are more self-confident, effective and assertive in dealing with doctors, and therefore get longer

> The **inverse care law** suggests that those in the greatest need of help from the welfare state get the fewest resources allocated to them, while those whose need is least get the most resources.

consultations, ask more questions, receive more explanations from their doctors and are more likely to be referred for further treatment

- receive more spending per person in education, as their children are more likely to stay in education after school-leaving age, and they have more knowledge and confidence in dealing with educational professionals to get the best deals in education for their children
- benefit more from spending on roads and public transport (particularly rail travel), as they are more likely to be commuters and have cars
- benefit more from tax relief on private pensions and business expenses

Westergaard and Resler (1976) argue that the welfare system is largely concerned with transferring or redistributing resources *within* rather than *between* social classes, for example from one section of the working class to another, such as from those in work to those who are unemployed, and from the healthy to the sick. They see support for the old, the unemployed, the sick and disabled as being largely paid for by other working-class taxpayers, or through their own national insurance payments taken from their wages.

Inequalities between ethnic groups

In chapter 7 on health, there is a discussion of inequalities in health between ethnic groups. The weaknesses in health care discussed there are only part of the general pattern of disadvantage faced by some minority ethnic groups in the welfare state generally. Pakistani, Bangladeshi and African-Caribbean minority ethnic groups are marginalized, and encounter racism and discrimination in welfare provision. Literature is often not translated, and staff are often not trained in their cultural backgrounds. They are more likely to be unemployed, and so lose out on income-related benefits. Pakistani and Bangladeshi people are the poorest social groups in Britain.

Gender inequality

Feminist views have already been mentioned earlier in the context of the patriarchal assumptions of women as primarily wives, mothers and carers which have traditionally underpinned the welfare state. There are a number of other inequalities where women are concerned.

Women are more likely to work part-time rather than full-time, and to interrupt their working lives for childrearing or caring for dependent elderly relatives. A lack of free childcare often makes it difficult for women to take full-time jobs. This means they often lose out on a range of income-related benefits, like the earnings-related state pension and the Jobseeker's Allowance. Poverty is much more a problem for women than men, throughout their lives, but particularly in old age. (The 'feminization of poverty' is discussed later.) Feminists advocate making the welfare state more responsive to the needs of women, such as through the provision of better cancer screening, Well Woman clinics to meet women's health needs, and a recognition of women's unpaid work in the home.

The welfare state and poverty

Despite the welfare state, Abel-Smith and Townsend (1965) showed that in the 1960s poverty was still a major social problem in Britain. It remains so in contemporary Britain.

Until the end of the 1970s, the main thrust of state welfare policy was to tackle the problem of poverty. However, since the 1980s there has been a growing concern with the escalating costs of the welfare state. This was mainly due to rising unemployment in the 1980s, but in the 2000s it is mainly focused on the ageing population (a growing proportion of elderly people in the population). These have meant more benefits and pensions being paid out, with growing pressures on pension and health spending, but with less tax being collected to pay for them.

The Conservative governments of 1979–97 were strongly influenced by the ideas of the New Right. This meant the government wanted to cut back welfare spending, eliminate the dependency culture, and develop the principles of self-help. It preferred to target benefits only on the sick, disabled and the elderly and others unable to help themselves. The rest of the population was encouraged to rely more on their own resources rather than expecting to be supported by the state.

These years were marked by serious cuts in welfare spending and the value of welfare benefits. Income taxes were reduced, more benefits were means tested, and grants to the poor were replaced with loans. Charges were either introduced or increased for eye tests and dentists, and prescription charges were increased. Student grants were replaced with loans, and the Child Support Agency was set up, so that absent fathers rather than the state could carry the financial costs of looking after their children. State education was starved of cash.

By 1997, Britain had the highest levels of poverty in the European Union, and the largest gap between the highest and lowest paid since records began in 1886. Britain was one of the most unequal countries in the Western world.

The Labour government of 1997

A Labour government came to power in 1997, and began a process back towards a more social democratic model of welfare provision, while still retaining some elements of the New Right approach of using a range of private welfare providers and encouraging self-help. A strong emphasis was placed on tackling the problems of those pushed to the margins of society and unable to fully participate in social life because of poverty, lack of education, old age or ill-health.

A large number of policies were implemented to tackle poverty and social exclusion, including:

- an increase in benefit and pension levels, a minimum income guarantee for pensioners, and big increases on spending on health and education
- the introduction of Britain's first National Minimum Wage, to help the poorest paid
- the introduction of a system of tax credits (allowances) to help the most disadvantaged
- the establishment of 'New Deals' to help the young, lone parents, the long-term unemployed and the disabled to move from welfare into work
- an increase in childcare and nursery education, with all 3 and 4 year olds guaranteed five half-days of nursery education a week
- a Neighbourhood Renewal Strategy, to regenerate the most deprived communities, and to help improve the health and education of the most disadvantaged
- a reduction in child poverty, with the aim of eliminating it within a generation

---

Activity

Go to the government's social exclusion website, www.cabinetoffice.gov.uk/social_exclusion_task_force/, and identify two policies designed to help the most disadvantaged in our society. Explain how they might do this and how successful they are.

Poverty

There are four basic issues in studying poverty:

1 defining poverty – what is it?
2 measuring poverty
3 explaining poverty
4 suggesting policy solutions for it

Changing views of poverty

Much of the early sociological research into poverty was a reaction against the idea that poverty was the poor's own fault – that they were simply idlers and scroungers, an 'undeserving' group who were themselves to blame for their own poverty, and therefore nothing should be done to help them.

Two pieces of research showed the poor were in fact decent, hard-working families who were forced into poverty by circumstances beyond their control, such as irregular or low pay, ill-health or disability, unemployment or old age: the 'deserving poor'. These pieces of research were:

- Booth's *Life and Labour of People in London* – a study of poverty in London between 1886 and 1903
- Joseph Rowntree's studies of poverty in York, carried out in 1899, 1936 and 1950

Defining poverty (1): absolute or subsistence poverty

A person in **absolute poverty** lacks the minimum necessary for healthy survival. People in absolute poverty would be poor anywhere at any time – the standard does not vary much over time. The solution to absolute poverty is to raise the living standards of the poor above subsistence level.

> **Absolute poverty** or subsistence poverty refers to a person's biological needs for food, water, clothing and shelter – the basic minimum requirements necessary to subsist and maintain life, health and physical efficiency. A person in absolute poverty lacks the minimum necessary for healthy survival.

Measuring absolute poverty

Various attempts have been made to measure absolute poverty. Rowntree, for example, used medical studies of nutrition to identify the cheapest costs of a standard basic diet needed to maintain life, coupled with minimum housing, heating and clothing costs.

The absolute conception of poverty has some advantages, as it makes it relatively straightforward to make national and international comparisons, since basic physical or subsistence needs seem fairly easy to identify (but see later for some problems). Such a view of poverty is generally the one most people consider when they think of poverty – the kind that is often found in less developed countries, for example in Africa, where famines and starvation occur and people lack the basic subsistence needs for biological survival.

Absolute poverty
Photos: Gordon Browne

> ## Activity
>
> 1 Keep a record of everything you consume in one week – food, drinks, leisure activities, rent if you pay it, an estimate of how much electricity and gas you use, travel expenses and so on.
> 2 Find out how much all these things cost, perhaps by visiting a local supermarket.
> 3 Then try to find out how much you would be entitled to in welfare benefits each week if you were unable to work. You may be able to find out from leaflets at a local Job Centre office or a community centre or from the Citizens' Advice Bureau website www.adviceguide.org.uk/.
> 4 Discuss whether you could or would want to live on these benefit levels.

The weaknesses/disadvantages of the absolute conception of poverty

Difficulty in identifying basic subsistence needs It is difficult to identify objectively what basic subsistence needs are. For example, Rowntree's minimum budget was based on a list of nutritional and other requirements essential for life. He was criticized for relying heavily on the values and opinions of those who drew up the list. In particular, his list involved a no-waste budget, in which everything was fully used and food didn't go off or not get eaten. The list reflected the nutritional, cooking and shopping skills of middle-class researchers rather than the reality of the choice of food and the resources of the poor.

Value judgements Rowntree's views of food, clothing and shelter were those thought customary at the time. Even a basic budget may therefore reflect not simply minimal nutritional requirements, but value judgements of what an appropriate diet consists of.

It ignores the reality of people's lives 'Expert' views of the contents and costs of a minimum diet make assumptions that the poor have the same knowledge of nutrition as the experts, and that the poor can shop around and get the cheapest goods. It doesn't really take into account the knowledge people have, their shopping habits, how they actually spend the money they have, and the social, cultural and psychological factors which may influence this. For example, having a Christmas pudding may not be necessary to maintain health, but most people in Britain, including the poor, would want to have one. Is this wasteful and does it make assumptions that the poor should deny themselves diets that most people would regard as perfectly normal? The poor are often unable to buy at the cheapest prices anyway. (See the box 'Trapped in poverty: the poor pay more' on page 252 later in this chapter.)

There is no clear subsistence minimum There are wide differences between societies, and between groups in the same society, in what forms a subsistence minimum. Minimum diets will differ between men and women, by age, by the type of occupation a person has and so on. For example, an unskilled manual labourer doing heavy physical labour will require more calories each day than an office worker, and minimum nutritional and housing needs will be different between hot and cold climates.

It ignores social needs and cultural expectations It treats people as if they were nothing more than biological machines, and ignores the fact that people are social beings, who live in groups which create needs beyond just physical survival. This involves mixing with people, entertaining them, eating with them, participating in community life and leisure activities, and meeting social obligations, such as buying wedding or birthday presents, or giving children parties. This will also involve expectations of appropriate food – eating cats or rats is not something most of us in Britain would see as acceptable behaviour, even though it might be quite nutritious. Value judgements and cultural expectations of what that minimum is therefore influence even a notion of a subsistence minimum.

These criticisms have led most sociologists and poverty researchers to adopt the idea of relative poverty.

> **Activity**
>
> Do you think poverty should be defined only in absolute terms? What other aspects, if any, of people's lives do you think should be considered in defining poverty?

Defining poverty (2): relative poverty

The relative definition of poverty says that people are poverty-stricken when they lack things that wider society regards as the minimum necessary for a socially acceptable standard of living. Townsend (1979) has provided the classic definition of **relative poverty**:

> Individuals, families and groups in the population can be said to be in poverty when they lack the resources to obtain the types of diets, participate in the activities and have the living conditions and amenities which are customary, or at least widely encouraged or approved, in the societies to which they belong. Their resources are so seriously below those commanded by the average individual or family that they are, in effect, excluded from ordinary living patterns, customs or activities.

This type of poverty is a condition where individuals or families are deprived of the opportunities, comforts and self-respect which the majority of people in

Relative poverty defines poverty in relation to a generally accepted standard of living in a specific society at a specific time. This takes into account social and cultural needs as well as biological needs, so that people can join in with the usual pattern of life in their society.

their society enjoy. Minimum needs are then related to the standard of living in any society at any one time, and will therefore vary over time and between societies, as standards of living change. For example, those living in slum housing in Britain would be regarded as poor in Britain, but their housing would appear as relative luxury to poor peasants in some developing countries. Similarly, running hot water and an indoor bathroom and toilet would have been seen as luxuries 150 years ago in Britain, but today are seen as basic necessities, and those without them would be regarded as poor by most people.

The solution to relative poverty necessarily involves a more equal distribution of wealth and income, so no section of society is deprived in relation to the average standard of living. The debate about poverty necessarily becomes a part of the debate about social inequality.

The relative definition of poverty is closely linked with the idea of **social exclusion**.

> **Social exclusion** involves people being marginalized or excluded from participation in education, work, community life, access to services and other aspects of life seen as part of being a full and participating member of mainstream society. Those who lack the necessary resources are excluded from the opportunity to fully join in with society, and are denied the opportunities most people take for granted. It is about being cut off from what most people would regard as a normal life.

Dimensions of relative poverty apart from income: poverty as social exclusion

The ideas of relative poverty and social exclusion suggest there are wider social, cultural and psychological dimensions of poverty apart from just a low income. Poverty is not simply a matter of how much income people have, but can also involve a combination of other linked problems in their lives such as discrimination, poor skills, poor housing, bad health, family breakdown, social isolation, a poor environment, high crime neighbourhoods and poor quality and availability of public services like transport, hospitals, libraries, schools and play areas for children. These problems are linked, and each one can make the others worse, and create a vicious cycle in people's lives which it is hard for them to escape from. Two people may have the same low income, but one may live in an isolated rural community with few facilities, no shop, no doctor's surgery, no car, irregular public transport, no local school and so on. The other may live in an urban area, with lots of facilities, easy transport or easy walking distances and so on. The poor may therefore live a deprived lifestyle apart from simply being short of money.

Figure 4.4 overleaf illustrates this range of linked dimensions of relative poverty, and how they can combine and overlap to create social exclusion.

Examples of poverty apart from income include the following.

Homelessness In the year to December 2006, 89,510 households were officially accepted as homeless and in priority need by local authorities in England. Breakdown of relationships, and mortgage and rent arrears can lead to loss of homes. This can make getting and holding down a job difficult, leading sometimes to a downward spiral.

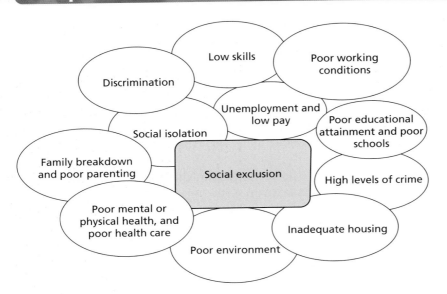

Figure 4.4 Dimensions of relative poverty: poverty as social exclusion

---

Activity

Refer to figure 4.4
1 Suggest *two* ways that high crime areas and poor environments might be linked.
2 Suggest *two* ways that poor schools might be linked to poor parenting.
3 Suggest *two* ways that inadequate housing might be linked to poor health.
4 Suggest *two* reasons why poor health and a low income might contribute to social isolation.
5 Explain what is meant by 'social exclusion', and why relative poverty might be seen as social exclusion.

Poverty in health care   Good health is important to an active life, but:

- There are fewer doctors practising in inner city areas (where many of the poor live), and those who do are often overworked, because the poor have more health problems.
- The poor are less likely to get time off work with pay to visit the doctor.
- The poor face longer hospital waiting lists.
- Many are not fully aware of what health services are available to them, and the poor tend to be less vocal and articulate in demanding proper standards of care from doctors.

Poverty at school   Education can offer a way out of poverty, but:

- Inner city schools often have older buildings and poorer facilities.

Why do you think people become homeless? Why do some become rough sleepers rather than staying in hostels for the homeless?

- There is often a concentration of social problems in these schools, such as drugs and vandalism, and consequently a higher turnover of teachers.
- Parents are less able to help their children with their education, and have less money than better-off parents to enable the school to buy extra resources.

Poverty at work   Poor working conditions include a neglect of health and safety standards and a high accident rate; working at night and long periods of overtime because the pay is so low; lack of trade union organization to protect the workers' interests; lack of entitlement to paid holidays; insecure employment; and no employers' sick pay or pension schemes.

Personal factors linked with poverty   These might include:

- *Poor health*   Examples are respiratory problems like asthma and infectious diseases, as a result of poor diet and damp, overcrowded housing.
- *Social isolation and boredom*   Making friends may be hard because there is no money to get involved in social activities.
- *Stress*   In the face of mounting bills and debts, stress can lead to domestic violence, family breakdown, and mental and physical illness.
- *Low self-esteem*   This can be brought on by dependence on others, the lack of access to the activities and facilities others have, and difficulties in coping with day-to-day life.

Measuring relative poverty

The idea of relative poverty is necessarily based on value judgements as to what constitutes a reasonable standard of living. How do you decide what the minimum standards are in relation to the expectations of a particular society? There have been a number of attempts to come up with various measures of relative poverty, and these are outlined below.

Townsend's deprivation index Townsend measured relative poverty in the UK using a 'deprivation index' of sixty indicators of lifestyle considered to be customary for an acceptable standard of living. He reduced these to twelve which he saw as particularly important indicators of deprivation, clearly linked to low income, and then checked how many households lacked those items. This deprivation index is shown in the box opposite.

Townsend's deprivation index was criticized heavily because:

- It was said to be measuring inequality not poverty.
- The choice of indicators was based on Townsend's own values and had more to do with taste than with poverty.
- It didn't allow for choice – for whether people lacked items because they couldn't afford them or because they simply didn't want them.
- It focused on people's individual behaviour, and ignored indicators of deprivation like the availability of and access to public services, such as public transport, hospitals, clinics and libraries.

The consensual measurement of relative poverty The *Breadline Britain* studies by Mack and Lansley in 1983 and 1990, and *Poverty and Social Exclusion in Britain* by the Joseph Rowntree Foundation (Gordon et al., 2000), were attempts to overcome the criticisms of Townsend's deprivation index, particularly that it simply reflected his own preferences and values, and that it didn't allow for choice.

To avoid this, these surveys asked a representative sample of the public, not experts, to decide what items *they thought* were necessary for a minimum standard of living in Britain. The responses represented a consensus (widespread agreement) on what ordinary people thought made up the minimum standards required for life in Britain at the beginning of the twenty-first century.

The *Poverty and Social Exclusion* survey included only items that 50 per cent or more thought necessities, and then calculated how many people lacked three or more of these items, asking them whether this was because of choice or because they couldn't afford them. This research provided a valuable insight into how the public measures relative poverty. The list is shown in the box overleaf.

Townsend's deprivation index

1   Has not had a week's holiday away from home in the last twelve months.
2   (Adults only). Has not had a relative or friend to the home for a meal or snack in the last four weeks.
3   (Adults only). Has not been out in the last four weeks to a relative or friend for a meal or snack.
4   (Children only – under 15). Has not had a friend to play or to tea in the last four weeks.
5   (Children only). Did not have a party on last birthday.
6   Has not had an afternoon or evening out for entertainment in the last two weeks.
7   Does not have fresh meat (including meals out) as many as four days a week.
8   Has gone through one or more days in the past fortnight without a cooked meal.
9   Has not had a cooked breakfast most days of the week.
10 Household does not have a refrigerator.
11 Household does not usually have a Sunday joint (three in four times).
12 Household does not have sole use of four amenities indoors (flush WC; sink or washbasin and cold water tap; fixed bath or shower; and gas or electric cooker).

Source: P. Townsend, *Poverty in the United Kingdom* (Harmondsworth: Penguin, 1979).

Activity

Study Townsend's deprivation index

1   Do you think the twelve items on Townsend's deprivation index provide useful indicators of poverty? Give reasons for your answers, with reference to each indicator.
2   Do you think such indicators provide an adequate view of poverty? Suggest ways of improving Townsend's index, and suggest five additional or alternative indicators that you think might provide a better guide to poverty in the 2000s.
3   In what ways do you think Townsend's own values might have influenced his choice of indicators? How do you think your own values might have influenced your choice of indicators in the previous question?

> A **poverty line** is a government-agreed dividing point between those who are poor and those who are not.

Income measurements – the 'official' poverty line   The **poverty line** used in Britain in 2007, and by the European Union, was 60 per cent of average income (or strictly speaking, '60 per cent of median income after housing costs'). This line dividing those who are regarded as poor and those who are not was adopted as it was thought that at or below this level of income people would be excluded from a minimum acceptable way of life in the society they were living in. This involves a clear relative conception of poverty, but you

The *Poverty* and *Social Exclusion* survey list

1 Beds and bedding for everyone.
2 Heating to warm living areas of the home.
3 Damp-free home.
4 Visiting friends or family in hospital.
5 Two meals a day.
6 Medicines prescribed by doctor.
7 Refrigerator.
8 Fresh fruit and vegetables daily.
9 Warm, waterproof coat.
10 Replace or repair broken electrical goods.
11 Visits to friends or family.
12 Celebrations on special occasions such as Christmas.
13 Money to keep home in a decent state of decoration.
14 Visits to school, for example on sports day.
15 Attending weddings, funerals.
16 Meat, fish or vegetarian equivalent every other day.
17 Insurance of contents of dwelling.
18 Hobby or leisure activity.
19 Washing machine.
20 Collect children from school.
21 Telephone.
22 Appropriate clothes for job interviews.
23 Deep freezer/fridge freezer.
24 Carpets in living rooms and bedrooms.
25 Regular savings (of £10 per month) for rainy days or retirement.
26 Two pairs of all-weather shoes.
27 Friends or family round for a meal.
28 A small amount of money to spend on self weekly, not on family.
29 Television.
30 Roast joint/vegetarian equivalent once a week.
31 Presents for friends/family once a year.
32 A holiday away from home once a year not with relatives.
33 Replace worn-out furniture.
34 Dictionary.
35 An outfit for social occasions.
36 New, not second-hand, clothes.
37 Attending place of worship.
38 Car.
39 Coach/train fares to visit friends/family quarterly.
40 An evening out once a fortnight.
41 Dressing gown.
42 Having a daily newspaper.
43 A meal in a restaurant/pub monthly.
44 Microwave oven.
45 Tumble dryer.
46 Going to the pub once a fortnight.
47 Video cassette recorder.
48 Holidays abroad once a year.
49 CD player.
50 Home computer.
51 Dishwasher.
52 Mobile phone.
53 Access to the internet.
54 Satellite television.

Source: Adapted from David Gordon et al., *Poverty and Social Exclusion in Britain* (York: Joseph Rowntree Foundation, 2000). Reproduced by permission of the Joseph Rowntree Foundation.

Activity

1 Either alone or through majority agreement in a group, go through the *Poverty and Social Exclusion* survey list shown in the box opposite, ticking those items which you think are necessities, which all adults should be able to afford, and no one should have to go without.

2 Compare your list with that of another person or group. How do your decisions compare with others? Were some items clear-cut and others borderline? Discuss the reasons for any differences of opinion about what count as necessities.

3 The *Poverty and Social Exclusion in Britain* national survey, conducted first in 2000, found that items 1–35 were considered necessities by 50 per cent or more of the population. At least two out of three members of the public classed items 1–25 as necessities which no one should have to go without. How far does your list agree or disagree with these national findings?

4 Do you think if you were in a very poor country you would have the same list of necessities? Give reasons for your answer.

5 What does this exercise tell you about the ways of measuring poverty in modern Britain?

6 Go to www.jrf.org.uk and look up the latest 'Monitoring Poverty and Social Exclusion' survey. Identify the main groups in poverty in Britain today and try to identify in each case two causes of their poverty.

---

should note the limitations discussed above of using income alone as an indicator of poverty.

The strengths/advantages of the relative conception of poverty

The relative conception of poverty:

- Recognizes poverty as a social construction – this means it recognizes that measures of social deprivation are influenced by how other members of society define what is a normal standard of living in any society.
- Recognizes that what constitutes poverty can change between societies and over time in the same society.
- Links poverty to wider issues of social exclusion.

The weaknesses/disadvantages of the relative conception of poverty

On the other hand, there are problems with the relative conception:

- It is not an indicator of poverty, but simply of social inequality. No matter how rich a society becomes, there will always be those who lack things that most people might want and have. Relative poverty will always exist as long as inequality exists.

- It is riddled with value judgements. Relative poverty standards reflect the values of 'experts', as in Townsend's deprivation index, or of the public, as in the *Breadline Britain* and the *Poverty and Social Exclusion* surveys. Lacking three or more necessities was decided by the researchers as a significant indicator of poverty – but why not five, or six or seven or more?
- The 60 per cent of average income poverty line means some people will always be relatively poor, even as society gets richer. The 60 per cent level is fairly arbitrary – why not 50 per cent or 70 per cent?

Activity

1 Go through each of the statements (A–G) below, and explain in each case which definition of poverty is being used. Give reasons for your answer.
2 Explain in your own words what Moore (statement B) meant when he said, 'The poverty lobby would, on their definition, find poverty in Paradise.'
3 With reference to the statements below, identify five aspects of poverty apart from a low income.
4 How do you think those who use a relative definition of poverty might respond to Moore's claim in statement B that 'It is hard to believe that poverty stalks the land when even the poorest fifth of families with children spend nearly a tenth of their income on alcohol and tobacco.'
5 Explain, with examples, the view in statement C that 'The notion of being able to measure what is necessary to live and fully participate in society is fraught with difficulty, as this will to some extent depend on how the person chooses to live and on the researcher's own values.'

Statement A

Poverty curtails freedom of choice. The freedom to eat as you wish, to go where and when you like, to seek the leisure pursuits or political activities which others accept; all are denied to those without the resources . . . poverty is most comprehensively understood as a state of partial citizenship.'
(P. Golding, *Excluding the Poor*, Child Poverty Action Group, 1986)

Statement B

'Poverty in the old absolute sense of hunger and want has been wiped out, and it is simply that some people today are less equal. The lifestyle of the poorest 20 per cent of families represents affluence beyond the wildest dreams of the Victorians, with half having a telephone, car, and central heating and virtually all having a refrigerator and television set. It is hard to believe that poverty stalks the land when even the poorest fifth of families with children spend nearly a tenth of their income on alcohol and tobacco. It is absurd to suggest that a third of the population of Britain is living in or on the margins of poverty. Starving children and squalid slums have disappeared, What the poverty lobby is opposed to is simple inequality, and however rich a society becomes, the poor on their definition would never disappear. The poverty lobby would, on their definition, find poverty in Paradise.'

(Adapted from a speech by John Moore, a former social security minister)

Statement C
'Poverty cannot be defined simply in terms of survival. We need to look at whether individuals have the material resources to fully participate in society – this involves wider social needs (such as money to have a holiday, give children birthday parties, go the cinema, etc.) and goes beyond mere biological or physical survival. The notion of being able to measure what is necessary to live and fully participate in society is fraught with difficulty, as this will to some extent depend on how the person chooses to live and on the researcher's own values.'

Statement D
'They can only be counted as "poor" in relation to contemporary British standards of affluence, but compared to Victorian times they are rich beyond the dreams of avarice. Their condition is only shocking because it is not as comfortable as that of those who are better off. What those who talk of poverty in modern Britain find offensive is not so much the existence of poverty but the existence of inequality.'

(Adapted from Peregrine Worsthorne in the *Daily Telegraph*, 27 Oct. 1979)

Statement E
'Living on the breadline is not simply about doing without things; it is also about experiencing poor health, isolation, stress, stigma and exclusion.'

(Adapted from C. Oppenheim, *Poverty: The Facts*, Child Poverty Action Group, 1988)

Statement F
'To have one bowl of rice in a society where all other people have half a bowl may well be a sign of achievement and intelligence . . . To have five bowls of rice in a society where the majority have a decent, balanced diet is a tragedy.'

(M. Harrington, *The Other America*, London: Macmillan, 1962)

Statement G
'Poverty should be seen in relation to minimum needs established by the standard of living in a particular society, and all members of the population should have the right to an income which allows them to participate fully in society rather than merely exist. Such participation involves having the means to fulfil responsibilities to others – as parents, sons and daughters, neighbours, friends, workers and citizens. Poverty filters into every aspect of life. It is about not having access to material goods and services such as decent housing, adequate heating, nutritious food, public transport, credit and consumer goods.'

(Adapted from C. Oppenheim, *Poverty: The Facts*, Child Poverty Action Group, 1988)

Who are the poor in the United Kingdom?

In 2005–6 in the United Kingdom:

- 12,700,000 people were living in poverty (below 60 per cent of average income) – 22 per cent of the population
- 3,800,000 children (29 per cent of all children) were living in poverty

The identity of the major groups in poverty suggest that poverty is not caused by individual 'inadequacies', but by social circumstances beyond the control of the poor themselves. Poverty is essentially a problem of the working class, because other classes have savings, employers' pensions and sick pay schemes to protect them when adversity strikes or old age arrives. The groups who were living in low income households (on the poverty line – 60 per cent of average income or below) in 2005–6 are shown below:

- *The unemployed* – 10 per cent of those on low incomes were unemployed.
- *The low paid* – 44 per cent were in full-time or part-time work. Many of the poor work long hours in low paid jobs.
- *Pensioners* – 15 per cent were pensioners. Older pensioner couples over the age of 75, and single female pensioners, are the most vulnerable to poverty. Many elderly retired people depend on state pensions for support, and these are inadequate for maintaining other than a very basic standard of living.
- *Lone parents* – 20 per cent were lone parents. Lone parents with young children often face difficulties getting a full-time job because of the lack of affordable childcare facilities, or only work, at best, part-time, which generally gets lower rates of pay. Nine out of ten lone parents are women, who in any case get less pay than men.
- *Children* – 29 per cent of all children lived in poverty. Children living in lone parent families, or with two parents who were unemployed or only working part-time, and in larger families with three or more children were the main groups.
- *Minority ethnic groups* – 63 per cent of households headed by someone of Pakistani or Bangladeshi ethnic origin were living in poverty.
- *Disabled people* – 27 per cent of individuals in families with one or more disabled people not in receipt of disability benefits were more likely to live in poverty than those in families with no disabled person. Disability often brings with it poorer employment opportunities, lower pay and dependence on state benefits.

Figure 4.5 illustrates which groups made up most of those living in poverty in 2005–6 by family type and by economic status. Figure 4.6 overleaf illustrates the risk of poverty facing those in particular social groups. The next section shows why women are more likely to face poverty than men.

Figure 4.5 Who are the poor? Number of individuals living below 60 per cent of average income after housing costs: United Kingdom, 2005/6

Source: Households Below Average Income, Department for Work and Pensions, 2007

By family type

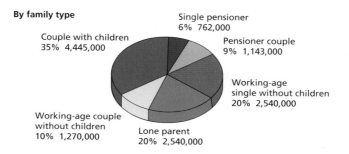

Single pensioner
6% 762,000

Couple with children
35% 4,445,000

Pensioner couple
9% 1,143,000

Working-age
single without children
20% 2,540,000

Working-age couple
without children
10% 1,270,000

Lone parent
20% 2,540,000

By economic status

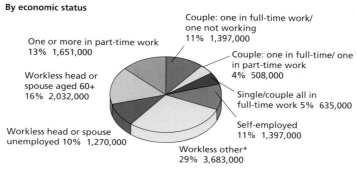

Couple: one in full-time work/
one not working
11% 1,397,000

One or more in part-time work
13% 1,651,000

Couple: one in full-time/ one
in part-time work
4% 508,000

Workless head or
spouse aged 60+
16% 2,032,000

Single/couple all in
full-time work 5% 635,000

Self-employed
11% 1,397,000

Workless head or spouse
unemployed 10% 1,270,000

Workless other*
29% 3,683,000

* Other = all those not included in previous groups, eg. long-term sick, disabled people, and non-working lone parent

Activity

Refer to figure 4.5. In 2005–6:
1. What percentage of individuals in poverty were in pensioner couples?
2. What percentage of individuals in poverty were single without children?
3. How many individuals in poverty were lone parents?
4. How many individuals in poverty were in households with one or more in part-time work?

Refer to figure 4.6 overleaf. In 2005–6:

5. Which family type had the greatest risk of individuals living in poverty?
6. Which family type had the lowest risk of individuals living in poverty?
7. Which group of individuals, by economic status, faced the greatest risk of poverty?
8. Which group of individuals, by economic status, faced the lowest risk of poverty?
9. What evidence is there in figure 4.6 that might be used to show that low pay is a cause of poverty?
10. Suggest how the evidence in figures 4.5 and 4.6 might be used to show that the poor are victims of unfortunate circumstances rather than being themselves to blame for their poverty. Could any of the evidence in the figures be used to support the opposite view?

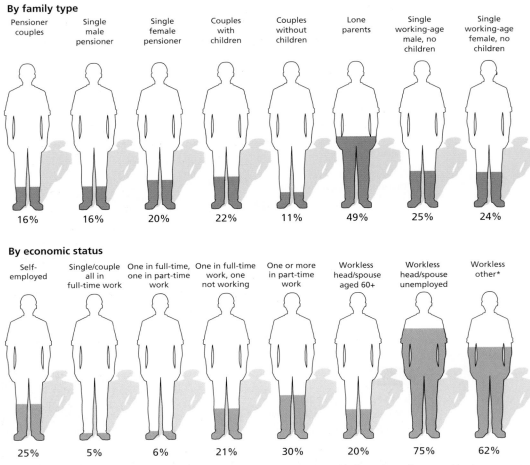

By family type

Pensioner couples	Single male pensioner	Single female pensioner	Couples with children	Couples without children	Lone parents	Single working-age male, no children	Single working-age female, no children
16%	16%	20%	22%	11%	49%	25%	24%

By economic status

Self-employed	Single/couple all in full-time work	One in full-time, one in part-time work	One in full-time work, one not working	One or more in part-time work	Workless head/spouse aged 60+	Workless head/spouse unemployed	Workless other*
25%	5%	6%	21%	30%	20%	75%	62%

* Other = all those not included in previous groups, eg. long-term sick, disabled people, and non-working lone parent

Figure 4.6 The risk of poverty: proportion of individuals in particular groups living in poverty (below 60 per cent of average income after housing costs): United Kingdom, 2005/2006

Source: Households Below Average Income, Department for Work and Pensions, 2007

The feminization of poverty

Women are far more likely than men to experience poverty. This is because:

- *Women are likely to have the major responsibilities for housework and childcare.* This means that many women are forced to combine paid employment with childcare. They are therefore more likely to be in low paid and part-time work, and therefore to miss out on work-related welfare benefits.
- *Women are the majority of homeworkers,* tied to the home by children or others dependent on them (such as the elderly). Many homeworking

jobs are based on piecework (that is, payment for each product or part of a product made), are extremely low paid, and rarely carry such basic employment rights as holidays, pensions, and compensation for industrial accidents.

- *Women are more likely than men to be lone parents* with sole responsibility for children, leading to reduced possibilities for employment, and dependence on state benefits.
- *Women are more likely to sacrifice their own standard of living* to provide food, clothing and extras for the children. In many low income households, it is often mothers rather than fathers who bear the burden of trying to make ends meet.
- *Women live longer than men and retire earlier.* They therefore spend a greater proportion of their lives beyond retirement age. However, because of the time they have taken off work to care for children, combined with low pay throughout their lives, they are less likely than men to have savings for old age, or to be entitled to employers' pensions, and so they are more likely to experience poverty in old age. Only half of women reaching retirement age in the ten years to 2010 will qualify for a full state pension when they retire.

Activity

1 Explain what is meant by 'relative poverty' and identify and explain two criticisms of it.
2 Identify *two* groups of people who are more likely to be in poverty than others in modern Britain, and explain why this is so.
3 Explain what is meant by the 'poverty line'.
4 Identify *three* aspects of poverty *apart from* a low income.
5 In about a side and a half of A4 paper, answer the following essay question: *Critically assess the problems sociologists face in defining and measuring poverty.*

Explaining poverty: cultural explanations

While the welfare state may have removed the worst excesses of absolute poverty, it has failed to solve the real problems of relative poverty. Why is this?

A good way to remember the various explanations of poverty is to think of them as 'blaming theories' – where is the blame placed for poverty? These can be grouped into cultural explanations, looked at here, and material explanations, which we turn to below.

Cultural explanations blame the culture of poverty, and the dependency culture generated by the *generosity* of the welfare state.

The culture of poverty

Early work on the cultural attitudes of the poor was first developed by Oscar Lewis (1961), as a result of his research among the urban poor in Mexico and Puerto Rico in the 1950s. Lewis suggests that the poor have a **culture of poverty** with its own norms and values and way of life. This makes the poor different from the rest of society. He suggests the poor have the following cultural features:

- They are resigned to their situation, seldom taking opportunities when they arise.
- They have a sense of *fatalism* – that nothing can be done to change their situation.
- They are reluctant to work.
- They don't plan for the future.
- They make little effort to change their situation or take the initiative to try to break free of their poverty.
- They are marginalized, and don't see themselves as part of or involved in mainstream society.

> The **culture of poverty** is a set of beliefs and values thought to exist among the poor which prevents them from escaping from poverty.

Children grow up in this culture, which is passed on from generation to generation through socialization. This culture of poverty prevents those exposed to it from taking opportunities to escape from poverty when they arise, and the poor therefore remain poor because of their own values and behaviour. This 'victim blaming' approach was developed further by writers of the New Right.

The dependency culture and the generosity of the welfare state

The New Right sees many of the poor as undeserving – a group of work-shy and lazy inadequates who are not deserving of support from the welfare state. New Right supporter David Marsland (1989) argues that poverty arises from the *generosity* of the welfare state. Marsland claims:

- The generosity of 'handouts' from the 'nanny' welfare state has created a dependency culture. This is where people abandon reliance on work, the family and the local community, and are content to live on welfare state 'handouts', rather than taking responsibility themselves for improving their situation. The more the welfare state provides benefits for people, the less they will do for themselves.
- Universal welfare benefits, which are payable to all regardless of income, such as education, health care and child benefits, take money away from investment in the economy and thus undermine the production of wealth.

- Universal welfare benefits should be withdrawn, and welfare benefits should be more selective and means tested, targeted on groups like the sick and disabled who are in genuine need, rather than given to those who are capable of supporting themselves.

The underclass (New Right version)　Charles Murray (1989), another New Right supporter, goes even further than Marsland. Murray has suggested that the attitudes and behaviour of the poor are responsible for their poverty, and that the poor form an anti-social, deviant underclass. This underclass is marked out by:

- high levels of illegitimacy, lone parenthood and family instability
- drunkenness and 'yob culture'
- crime, fiddling of the benefit system and drug abuse
- exclusion from school and educational failure
- work-shy attitudes leading to dropping out of the labour market and living off benefits

Murray is particularly scathing about lone parenthood, which he says arises from the high level of benefits, which encourage women to have children they could not otherwise afford. Murray argues that the generosity of the welfare state has created, supports and encourages this underclass, and the solution is to cut benefits to encourage self-reliance, or marriage or work.

New Right theories were very influential during the period of the Conservative governments in Britain between 1979 and 1997. There was a strong sense of the poor being punished for their poverty, with cuts in benefits and all welfare state spending, and a growing stress on the need for everyone, including the poor, to take more responsibility for themselves rather than relying on the state to help them out.

Activity

1　Suggest any ways in which you think the attitudes, beliefs and values of poor people might differ from those of the non-poor.
2　How might you carry out research to test whether the ideas of poor people are different from those of the non-poor? Work out a plan for carrying out research in this area.

Criticisms of cultural explanations of poverty

The differences have been exaggerated　The differences between the attitudes of the poor and non-poor have been exaggerated. Kempson, in research conducted for the Joseph Rowntree Foundation in 1996, found that the poor had attitudes to work much like the rest of the population. Robert Walker and colleagues (2000) found there was 'no real indication that a social underclass actually exists', and said the evidence for benefit dependency is 'slight'. He said: 'Life on benefit is mean and harsh. Consequently, people are much more keen to avoid claiming benefits than to choose them as a way of life. Most claimants who are able to work are eager to do so and routinely look for jobs when they can.'

Little evidence that children inherit their parents' attitudes There is little evidence that the cultural attitudes of parents get passed on to their children, and parents often have higher ambitions for their children than they had for themselves. Rutter and Madge (1976) found that 'At least half of children born into a disadvantaged home do not repeat the pattern of disadvantage in the next generation. Over half of all forms of disadvantage arise anew in each generation.'

The poor want the same as everyone else The poor want the same things as the rest of society, but factors like unemployment and social deprivation stop them from achieving them. For example, the poor cannot afford to save for a 'rainy day', planning for the future is difficult when the future is so hopeless or uncertain, and it is hard not to give up and become resigned to being unemployed after endless searching for non-existent jobs. It is the lack of resources that stops participation in society, not the culture of the poor or welfare state generosity. If there is any kind of dependency culture or culture of poverty, it is a *consequence* of poverty, not a *cause* of poverty.

Blaming the victims rather than the causes Cultural explanations of poverty tend to blame the poor for their own poverty, and imply that if only the poor changed their values, then poverty would disappear. If these explanations are accepted, then the problem of poverty will be solved by policies such as cutting welfare benefits to the poor, to make them stand on their own two feet, and job training programmes to get them used to working. However, in most cases it is economic circumstances, not attitudes, which made them poor in the first place. Cultural explanations are convenient ones for those in positions of power, as they put the blame for poverty on the poor themselves. As Westergaard and Resler (1976) put it, 'the blame for inequality falls neatly on its victims.'

Explaining poverty: material explanations

Material explanations blame material constraints, the cycle of deprivation, the *inadequacy* of the welfare state, and the unequal structure of power and wealth in capitalist society.

Unclaimed benefits

Many poor people do not claim the welfare benefits to which they are entitled, particularly those which are means tested. According to the Department for Work and Pensions' own estimates released in 2006, around one in five people were not claiming income-related benefits to which they were entitled in 2004–5 – between 3.25 and nearly 5 million people. This represented between £4.7 and £8 billion left unclaimed.

People may not claim benefits because of:

- the complexity of the benefits and tax system
- inadequate publicity
- the obscure language of leaflets and complex means-testing forms, which mean people often do not know what their rights are or the procedures for claiming benefits.

These bureaucratic hurdles are often so great that many people are deterred from claiming what they are entitled to. This is particularly important as the poor are among the least educated. The mass media periodically run campaigns about welfare 'fraudsters' and 'scroungers' – with headlines like 'Stuff the spongers' – which help to attach a stigma to claiming benefits which may deter some people, particularly the elderly, from doing so. The establishment of the Department for Work and Pensions 'Targeting benefit fraud' website may have further contributed to attaching such a stigma. This has now become 'Targeting benefit thieves' (www.dwp.gov.uk/ campaigns/benefit-thieves/). A number of photos from previous and present campaigns can be seen overleaf.

Activity

Refer to the box 'Unclaimed benefits'. Suggest answers to the questions below, and then discuss them.

1. Do you agree or disagree with the view that the media give the impression that people receiving benefits are 'scroungers'?
2. Do you think most people receiving welfare benefits are deserving?
3. Do welfare benefits discourage people from taking more responsibility for their own lives?
4. Should people be expected to take a job even if they will be worse off than if they received benefits?
5. Go to the 'Targeting benefit thieves' website, www.dwp.gov.uk/campaigns/ benefit-thieves. How much does the government estimate benefit fraud costs each year? Study the advertising campaigns, and discuss whether it might attach a stigma to all people claiming benefit. Do you think such advertising campaigns might stop people claiming benefits, even when they are entitled to them?

but keeping quiet about working a few extra hours doesn't make me a benefit thief.

NO IFS, NO BUTS.

Benefit fraud is a crime, break the law and you face a criminal record.

TARGETING BENEFIT THIEVES

if I make a few quid on the side it doesn't make me a benefit thief.

NO IFS, NO BUTS.

Benefit fraud is a crime, break the law and you face a criminal record.

TARGETING BENEFIT THIEVES

if I keep quiet about coming into some money it doesn't make me a benefit thief.

NO IFS, NO BUTS.

Benefit fraud is a crime, break the law and you face a criminal record.

TARGETING BENEFIT THIEVES

but pretending I live on my own doesn't make me a benefit thief.

NO IFS, NO BUTS.

Benefit fraud is a crime, break the law and you face a criminal record.

TARGETING BENEFIT THIEVES

BENEFIT CHEATS. WATCH YOUR BACK.

WE'RE ON TO YOU
Department for Work and Pensions

TARGETING FRAUD

BENEFIT CHEATS. WHICHEVER WAY YOU TURN, WE'RE ON TO YOU.

Every day hundreds of people are caught by fraud investigators or reported in confidence on the Benefit Fraud Hotline on 0800 854 440 (Textphone 0800 328 0512).

WE'RE ON TO YOU
Department for Work and Pensions

TARGETING FRAUD

BENEFIT FRAUD MAN IS JAILED

BENEFIT CHEAT IS FORCED TO REPAY THOUSANDS

INVESTIGATORS HOME IN ON BENEFITS CHEATS

BENEFIT FRAUDSTERS PROMISED SHORT SHRIFT

COMMUNITY SERVICE FOR FRAUD CHEATS

FRAUDSTERS BEWARE

MAN FINED FOR BENEFIT FRAUD CHARGES

PROBATION FOR BENEFIT FRAUDSTER

THIS HAPPENS EVERY DAY

Every day hundreds of people are caught by fraud investigators or reported in confidence on the Benefit Fraud Hotline on 0800 854 440 (Textphone 0800 328 0512).

WE'RE ON TO YOU
Department for Work and Pensions

TARGETING FRAUD

Material constraints

As seen in the criticisms of cultural explanations above, it is material or situational constraints, the economic and social position of groups like the low paid, unemployed, sick and elderly, that influence the attitudes and behaviour of the poor. The hopelessness of the future undermines their ability and resolve to plan for the future. With a dead-end job or no job at all, and insufficient income to support a family, a person is unable to save and invest in the future or to support a stable family life. Resources are used up simply on week-by-week survival, concentrating the poor's attention on their immediate position. It is these factors that stop the poor from putting the mainstream values they share with everyone else into practice.

Any distinctive cultural features of the poor are therefore more likely to be a response to poverty rather than a cause of it. Once these material constraints are removed, by giving the poor decent housing, well-paid jobs, adequate benefits and some security in their lives, then any apparent culture of poverty or dependency culture will also disappear.

The cycle of deprivation

Coates and Silburn in their early study of the St Ann's area of Nottingham, *Poverty: The Forgotten Englishmen* (1970), emphasized the circumstances in which the poor are trapped, and how these circumstances combine to form a web from which, regardless of attitudes or ability, there is little chance of escape. This has been called the **cycle of deprivation**.

> The theory of the **cycle of deprivation** suggests that poverty is cumulative, in the sense that one aspect of poverty can lead to further poverty. This builds up into a vicious circle of poverty from which the poor find it hard to escape, and it then carries on with their children.

For example, a child born in a poor family may have poor quality housing and diet. This may cause ill-health, and therefore absence from school. This means falling behind and failing exams, which in turn will mean a low paid job or unemployment, and therefore poverty in adult life. It then carries on with their children. Figure 4.7 overleaf illustrates examples of possible cycles of deprivation.

This cycle of deprivation is reinforced by the fact that poor people have to spend money in uneconomical ways – a matter in which they have little choice. The cost of living is higher for the poor than the non-poor, as illustrated in the box 'Trapped in poverty: the poor pay more' on page 252.

The problem with the cycle-of-deprivation explanation is that, while it explains why poverty continues, it does not explain how poverty begins in the first place.

The inadequacy of the welfare state

While the welfare state has provided some important assistance to the poor, and has removed the worst excesses of absolute poverty, widespread deprivation remains and the welfare state has failed to reduce the inequalities between the rich and the poor. Poverty persists, some argue, because benefit

What factors push people into a cycle of deprivation and prevent them escaping from poverty?

levels are too low to lift people out of poverty. From this viewpoint, the welfare state is not generous enough, and the poor get trapped in poverty by an inadequate, means-tested benefit system from which they find it hard to escape. This has led to an alternative view of the underclass to that suggested by Charles Murray.

Figure 4.7 Cycles of deprivation

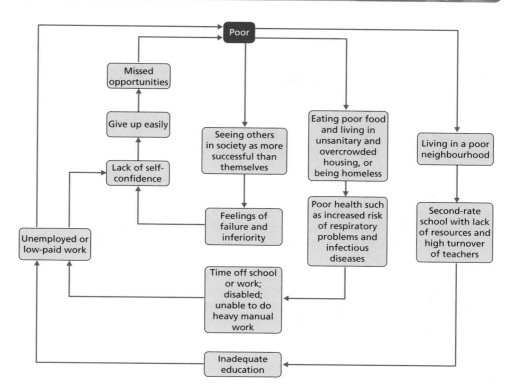

Activity

Refer to figure 4.7:

1 Which of the cycles of deprivation suggested in this figure mainly consist of material factors, and which cultural?
2 Try to make up *two* further examples of such cycles of deprivation – one material, and one cultural.
3 Suggest *five* policies that a government might adopt to overcome these cycles of deprivation.

The underclass (social democratic version) The social democratic view of the underclass is in keeping with the social democratic view of welfare discussed earlier in this chapter. This suggests the underclass consists of disadvantaged groups right at the bottom of the social class hierarchy whose poverty means they are excluded from taking part in society to the same extent as the non-poor.

Sociologists like Frank Field (1989) and Peter Townsend suggest this underclass consists of groups like the elderly retired, lone parents, the long-term

---

Trapped in poverty: the poor pay more

One of the great ironies of poverty is that the cost of living is higher for the poor than the non-poor, and this hinders the poor in their attempts to escape poverty. The poor pay more because:

- They often live in poor quality housing, which is expensive to heat and maintain.
- They live mainly in inner city areas, where rents are high.
- The price of goods and services is higher is poorer areas, due to factors like shoplifting and vandalism.
- They have to buy cheap clothing, which wears out quickly and is therefore more expensive in the long run.
- They have to pay more for food as they can only afford to buy it in small quantities (which is more expensive) and from small expensive corner shops as they haven't cars to travel to supermarkets. They also lack storage facilities like freezers for buying in bulk.
- They pay more for credit, as banks and building societies won't lend them money because they consider them a poor risk. Loans are therefore often obtained from loan sharks at exorbitant rates of interest.
- They suffer more ill-health, and so have to spend more on non-prescription medicines.
- The cost of house and car insurance is higher as a result of more theft and vandalism in poor areas.

---

unemployed, the disabled and the long-term sick. These groups are forced to rely on inadequate state benefits which are too low to give them an acceptable standard of living. More recently, we might include illegal migrant workers and asylum-seekers in this group, who often have to work illegally in very low-paid jobs and are unable to claim benefits. These groups are frequently subject to horrendous exploitation by unscrupulous employers, as they lack the legal protection available to other workers. These groups are all prevented from participating fully in society, and are left vulnerable to the poverty trap.

This view of the underclass differs from that of Charles Murray and the New Right, as it is not the attitudes of poor people which are to blame for their poverty, but the difficulties and misfortune they face which are beyond their control (like unemployment, illness or disability). The poor live depressingly deprived lifestyles, and want many of the things most people in society already have, like secure and decently paid jobs and opportunities. As Frank Field said, 'No one in their right mind believes that [the underclass] has volunteered for membership.'

It is a lack of opportunities and jobs, low pay and inadequate benefits, not their attitudes, which leaves them excluded from full participation in society. This view suggests social policies should tackle unemployment and low pay, improve the living standards of those on benefits (for example, through higher pensions and child benefits), and give incentives to the poor to get off benefits through decently paid jobs, and a more generous national minimum wage. Only in this way will the excluded underclass disappear in our society.

Marxists such as Miliband (1974) and Westergaard and Resler are critical of the view that the poor are an underclass. They see the poor not as a separate, specially disadvantaged group, but simply as the most disadvantaged section of the working class, and argue that all working-class people face the risk of joining the ranks of the poor in circumstances of unemployment, sickness, disability, lone parenthood or old age.

Structural explanations: blaming the unequal structure of society

Structural explanations explain poverty as arising from the inequality of capitalist society, with its unequal distribution of wealth, income and power. Poverty is seen as an aspect of social inequality and not merely an individual problem of poor people. The problem of poverty is the same as the problem of riches, and the reason the poor remain poor is because they are either exploited by the rich (Marxist approach), lack skills and power (Weberian approach) or because they serve a necessary function in maintaining society (functionalist approach).

The Marxist approach   The Marxist approach, such as that adopted by Miliband and Westergaard and Resler, suggests:

- Wealth is concentrated in the hands of the ruling class, and this generates class inequality. Poverty is the inevitable result of capitalism, and low paid workers provide the source of profits which enables the rich to achieve high incomes.
- The privileged position of the wealthy ultimately rests on working-class poverty. The threat of poverty and unemployment motivates workers, and provides a pool of cheap labour for the capitalist class.
- The existence of the non-working poor helps to keep wages down, by providing a pool of reserve labour which threatens the jobs of the non-poor should their wage demands become excessively high.
- Poverty divides the working class, by separating off the poor from the non-poor working class, and preventing the development of working-class unity and a class consciousness that might threaten the stability of the capitalist system.

The Weberian approach   Weberian approaches, such as that adopted by Townsend, suggest inequality arises from the different market position of individuals – the different skills that people have and the different rewards

Activity

Item A

The underclass are a group who have developed a lifestyle and set of attitudes which means they are no longer willing to take jobs. They have developed a dependency culture, which means they are not prepared to help themselves but are prepared to live off the welfare state. Lack of morality, high crime levels, cohabitation and large numbers of lone parents are associated with this view of the underclass. Their 'sponging' attitudes and lack of social responsibility are to blame for their poverty. Most of the poor have only themselves to blame.

Item B

The underclass are a group whose poverty means they are excluded from taking part in society to the same extent as the non-poor, even though they want to. This group consists of people like the disadvantaged elderly retired, lone parent families, the disabled and the long-term sick and unemployed. Their attitudes are the same as the rest of society, but they are forced to rely on inadequate state benefits which are too low to give them an acceptable standard of living. This prevents them from participating fully in society, and gives them little opportunity to fulfil their ambitions and escape the poverty trap.

Item C

'When I use the term "underclass" I am indeed focusing on a certain type of person defined not by his condition e.g. long-term unemployed, but by his deplorable behaviour in response to that condition, e.g. unwilling to take the jobs that are available to him . . . Britain has a growing population of working-aged, healthy people who live in a different world from other Britons, who are raising their children to live in it, and whose values are contaminating the life of entire neighbourhoods . . .'

1 Compare the *three* views of the underclass which are considered above. Identify in each case one researcher who might support that view. Explain your reasons.
2 Using the items and elsewhere, identify *four* features of the 'deplorable behaviour' (Item C) of the underclass.
3 Identify and explain *three* criticisms of Charles Murray's view of the underclass.
4 Outline the evidence that the attitudes of the so-called underclass are no different from those of the rest of society.
5 Identify the arguments and evidence you might use to show that the underclass is not a cause of poverty, but a result of poverty.
6 With reference to the items and elsewhere, identify and explain the solutions you would adopt to solve the problem of the underclass as identified in items A, B and C. Explain in each case how the policy adopted might solve the problem.
7 With reference to the items, discuss which view you think provides the most accurate picture of poor people.

attached to them when they sell their labour in the job market. The poor frequently have a weak position in the labour market. They are marginalized because they lack the education and skills which might bring them higher rewards, and the demand for unskilled and unqualified labour is declining. For many, such as the sick, lone parents, the disabled, the elderly and the unemployed, their circumstances often mean they are excluded from competing in the labour market at all.

Poverty remains because the poor lack the power to change their position. They don't have the financial resources to form powerful groups to change public opinion, and they often lack the means to apply pressure on the rich, through strikes for example, as they are often not working or are in low paid and poorly organized workplaces.

Functionalist approaches   Functionalist writers like Gans (1973) and Davis and Moore argue that the existence of poverty has important functions in contributing to the maintenance and stability of society. This is because:

- The existence of poverty ensures that the most undesirable, dirty, dangerous or menial low paid jobs that most people don't want, but which are important to the smooth running of society, are performed. Poverty means some people have no other choice than to do these jobs.
- Poverty creates jobs in a range of occupations, such as social work, social security staff, the police and so on.
- The threat of poverty provides necessary incentives and motivation for people to work.
- The existence of the poor provides a living example to the non-poor of what not to be – an undesirable, deviant state to be avoided – and reinforces the mainstream values of honesty, hard work, seizing opportunities and planning for the future. As Gans said, 'The defenders of the desirability of hard work, thrift, honesty and monogamy need people who can be accused of being lazy, spendthrift, dishonest and promiscuous to justify these norms.'
- The existence of the low paid keeps some industries and services running. Hospitals, catering, agriculture and the clothing industry all depend on low paid workers.

Poverty and value judgements

Defining and measuring poverty is inevitably a value-laden exercise. The definitions, measurement and explanations of poverty, and the social policies adopted to tackle the problem, rely to some extent on the value judgements of researchers and politicians. For example, if you adopt an absolute definition of poverty, then you will find very little in modern Britain. If you

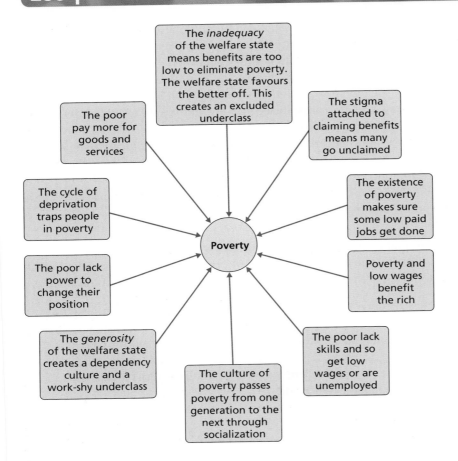

Figure 4.8 Why the poor remain poor

The *inadequacy* of the welfare state means benefits are too low to eliminate poverty. The welfare state favours the better off. This creates an excluded underclass

The poor pay more for goods and services

The stigma attached to claiming benefits means many go unclaimed

The cycle of deprivation traps people in poverty

The existence of poverty makes sure some low paid jobs get done

Poverty

The poor lack power to change their position

Poverty and low wages benefit the rich

The *generosity* of the welfare state creates a dependency culture and a work-shy underclass

The culture of poverty passes poverty from one generation to the next through socialization

The poor lack skills and so get low wages or are unemployed

use the relative definition of 60 per cent of average income, you will find a lot (around 22 per cent of the population).

The solutions to poverty often reflect the political/ideological values of the researchers and their different interpretations of a similar range of evidence. The role of the welfare state in relation to poverty ultimately rests on judgements about what kind of society we should have. For example, New Right or conservative solutions to poverty frequently start with the assumption that the problem of poverty is primarily created by the nature of the poor themselves, and therefore the poor need harsh, punitive policies like cuts in benefits as an incentive for them to change their behaviour.

More liberal or left-wing researchers are less likely to blame individuals for their poverty. They are more likely to focus on the structural constraints on the poor arising from the unequal nature of society. Such researchers are likely to see solutions to poverty in providing opportunities for the poor to escape their poverty, through means like the national minimum wage, better education, better health care, more job opportunities, more childcare support and higher pensions.

These different analyses and policy solutions often rest on a similar base of evidence, but the different values of the researchers lead to different interpretations of that evidence.

Does this mean that poverty research is therefore so value-laden as to be pointless? The answer is no, because the intense sociological, political and media debates about the definition, measurement and solutions to poverty have overcome the value judgements of individual researchers. Poverty research, regardless of values, has certainly exposed the extent to which many people in our society face social exclusion, and are cut off from what most of us take for granted as a normal life. This alone makes it a worthwhile and productive research area.

Activity

1 Explain what is meant by an 'underclass'.
2 Suggest *two* ways that the existence of poverty might be of benefit to society.
3 Explain the difference between cultural and material explanations of poverty.
4 Identify and explain *three* reasons why women are more likely than men to face poverty during their lives.
5 Make a chart in *two* columns. In the left column very briefly summarize the main definitions and the main explanations for poverty discussed in this chapter. In the right column, identify and explain briefly the solution which would be adopted for each definition and explanation.
6 In about one and half sides of A4 paper, answer the following essay question: *Assess the view that the definition and measurement of poverty is inevitably a value-laden exercise.*

CHAPTER SUMMARY

After studying this chapter you should be able to:

- outline the inequalities of wealth and income in contemporary Britain, and suggest different explanations for them

- identify measures to redistribute wealth and income, and why they have not been very successful

- identify and discuss the features of the welfare state, including welfare pluralism

- identify and discuss the social democratic, New Right/market liberal, Marxist and

feminist theoretical approaches to social welfare

- identify the arguments for and against means testing of welfare benefits

- discuss areas of inequality in the welfare state, including the inverse care law

- examine the role of the welfare state in tackling poverty

- identify and discuss the absolute, relative and consensual definitions and measurements of poverty, and the strengths and weaknesses of them

- explain what is meant by social exclusion
- identify a range of aspects of poverty apart from lack of income
- identify the major groups in poverty, and suggest reasons why these groups are in poverty
- explain why women are more likely to suffer poverty than men
- identify and critically discuss a range of cultural and material explanations for the continuation of poverty, including the culture of poverty, the dependency culture, the cycle of deprivation, the generosity or inadequacy of the welfare state, and structural explanations
- discuss different views of the underclass
- identify the links between poverty and the value-judgements of researchers and social policy-makers.

KEY TERMS

absolute poverty
consumption property
culture of poverty
cycle of deprivation

dependency culture
income
inverse care law
marginalization
market situation

poverty line
pressure groups
productive property
relative poverty
social exclusion

underclass
wealth
welfare pluralism

EXAM QUESTION

SECTION C: WEALTH, POVERTY AND WELFARE

Time allowed: 1 hour   **Total for this section: 60 marks**

3 Read **Items 3A and 3B** below and answer parts (a) to (e) that follow.

Item 3A

The welfare state was set up to help those in the greatest need. Tudor-Hart suggested this was not happening, with the middle class – the least in need – benefiting most from welfare services like health care and education, and any universal or means-tested welfare benefits to which they might be entitled. This finding – those in greatest need of help from the welfare state get the fewest   5
resources allocated to them, while those whose need is least get the most resources spent on them – became known as the 'inverse care law'.

Item 3B

In contemporary Britain, poverty remains widespread. Around one-fifth of the population, and 29 per cent of children, were living in officially defined relative poverty in 2006. Some explanations of poverty take a 'victim blaming' approach. This suggests the poor have inadequacies in their own personalities and culture, and are themselves to blame for their poverty. This 'victim blaming' approach has been   5
challenged by others who take a structural or 'system-blaming' approach. They suggest that social inequalities are built into the structure of society, and the poor are kept in poverty by a cycle of deprivation and circumstances beyond their control. They therefore find it hard to escape from poverty.

(a) Explain the difference between a universal and a means-tested benefit (**Item 3A**, lines 3–4). *(4 marks)*

(b) Suggest **two** reasons why the middle class 'benefits most from welfare services like health care and education' (**Item 3A**, lines 2–3). *(4 marks)*

(c) Explain the difference between voluntary sector and informal welfare provision. *(4 marks)*

(d) Examine the reasons given to explain the large inequalities in wealth and income in contemporary Britain. *(24 marks)*

(e) Using material from **Item 3B** and elsewhere, assess the view that 'the poor are kept in poverty by a cycle of deprivation and circumstances beyond their control' (**Item 3B**, lines 7–8). *(24 marks)*

Sociological
Methods

Contents

Key issues   263

Influences on the choice of research method   264

Positivism and research methods   265
Interpretivism and research methods   265
Other influences on the choice of research method   269

Key issues in social research   269

Reliability   271
Validity   271
Ethics   271

Primary and secondary data   272

Qualitative secondary sources   272

The advantages and uses of qualitative secondary sources   272
The disadvantages and limitations of qualitative secondary sources   273
Content analysis   274

Quantitative secondary sources   275

The advantages and uses of official statistics   276
The problems and limitations of official statistics   276

The experimental (laboratory) method of research   281

Problems of using the experimental method in sociology   281
Field experiments   283

The comparative method   283

Surveys and sampling methods   285

Who uses the survey method?   285
Representativeness and sampling   285

The stages of a survey   291
Problems of the social survey   293

Questionnaires   294

The nature and use of questionnaires   294
Questionnaire design: some principles and problems   295
Types of questionnaire   297
The validity of questionnaire research   298

Interviews   301

Structured or formal interviews   301
Unstructured or informal (in-depth) interviews   303
General problems of interviews   306
Concluding remarks on interviews   308

Participant observation   309

The theoretical context of participant observation   309
The stages of participant observation and related problems   310
The strengths and weaknesses of participant observation   313
Reliability and validity in participant observation   315

Non-participant observation   316

Longitudinal studies   318

Case studies and life histories   319

Methodological pluralism and triangulation   321

Chapter summary   323
Key terms   324

CHAPTER

5

Sociological Methods

KEY ISSUES

- Influences on the choice of research method
- Positivism and research methods
- Interpretivism and research methods
- Other influences on the choice of research method
- Key issues in social research: validity, reliability and ethics
- Primary and secondary data
- Qualitative secondary sources
- Quantitative secondary sources
- The experimental or laboratory method of research
- The comparative method
- Surveys and sampling methods
- Questionnaires
- Interviews
- Participant observation
- Non-participant observation
- Longitudinal studies
- Case studies and life histories
- Methodological pluralism and triangulation

Introductory note

This chapter is a very important one. In Unit 2 of the AQA AS Sociology course – the one you are doing now – you are encouraged to use examples drawn from your own experience of small-scale social research. You are also required to answer a free-standing question on research methods, and to show how sociological research methods can be applied to the study of either education or health. This chapter should provide you with all the information you need to deal with these research methods questions, and some exercises on research methods which might provide examples of small-scale research. There are also suggestions on how research methods might be applied in the education and health chapters. It is also worth noting that if you plan to do the second year of the A-level course, then research methods are required there as well. The message should be clear – make sure you know and can apply the ideas and methods in this chapter.

Much of this book concentrates on what sociologists have already found out about society. But how do sociologists go about finding these things out in the first place? Sociological methods are the variety of tools or techniques sociologists use to collect evidence to find out something about an area which remains relatively unexplored, to describe some aspects of social life, or to discover the causes of some social event, such as the causes of crime or ill-health. This chapter will examine the various research methods that sociologists use to collect such evidence. These are summarized in figure 5.1

Influences on the choice of research method

The main research methods flow from two different theoretical approaches to the study of society. These two approaches are known as **positivism** and **interpretivism**. Positivists and interpretivists often use different research methods because they have different assumptions about the nature of society, which influences the type of data they are interested in collecting.

Positivism is an approach in sociology that believes society can be studied using similar scientific techniques to those used in the natural sciences, such as physics, chemistry and biology.

Interpretivism is an approach emphasizing that people have consciousness involving personal beliefs, values and interpretations, and these influence the way they act. They do not simply respond to forces outside them.

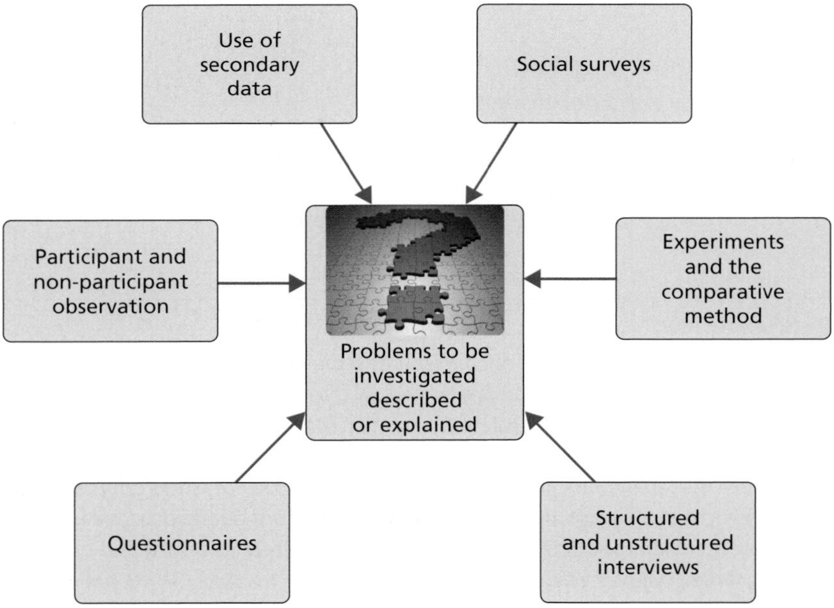

Use of secondary data

Social surveys

Participant and non-participant observation

Problems to be investigated described or explained

Experiments and the comparative method

Questionnaires

Structured and unstructured interviews

Figure 5.1 The range of research methods

Positivism and research methods

Positivists believe that just as there are causes of things in the natural world, so there are external social forces, making up a society's social structure, that cause or mould people's ideas and actions. Durkheim, a positivist, called these external forces **social facts**.

Positivists believe social institutions create expectations of how individuals should behave and limit their choices and options, with social control making individuals behave in socially approved ways.

Durkheim said the aim of sociology should be the study of social facts, which should be considered as things, like objects in the natural world, and could in most cases be observed and measured quantitatively – in number/statistical form. The feelings, emotions and motives of individuals cannot be observed or measured, and should therefore not be studied. These are in any case the result of social facts existing outside the individual, such as the influences of socialization, the law, the mass media, family, the experiences of work and so on.

Examples of positivist approaches might be to look at whether people in some social classes suffer more illness than those in other classes, or are more likely to commit crime, by looking at statistics on health and crime. Similarly, positivist research on relationships in the family might collect statistical data on who does what around the home, the length of time spent by partners on housework and childcare and so on.

Positivists argue that without quantification, sociology will remain at the level of insight, lacking evidence, and it will be impossible to replicate (or repeat) studies to check findings, establish the causes of social events, or make generalizations.

Just as the data of the natural sciences are drawn from direct observation and can be measured and quantified, so positivists use research methods which involve the collection of **quantitative** (statistical) **data** to test their ideas. Such quantitative methods are more likely to involve large-scale or macro research on large numbers of people. These methods include:

- the experiment
- the comparative method
- social surveys
- structured questionnaires
- formal/structured interviews
- non-participant observation

Interpretivism and research methods

Interpretivists believe that, because people's behaviour is influenced by the interpretations and meanings they give to social situations, the researcher's

Social facts are phenomena which exist outside individuals and independently of their minds, but which act upon them in ways which constrain or mould their behaviour. Such phenomena include social institutions like the law, the family, the education system and the workplace.

Quantitative data are anything that can be expressed in statistical or number form or can be measured in some way, such as age, qualifications, income or periods of ill-health. Such data are usually presented in the form of statistical tables, graphs, pie charts and bar charts.

Positivist researchers are more likely to collect quantitative (statistical) data through questionnaires and interviews

task is to gain an understanding of these interpretations and meanings, and how people see and understand the world around them. Sociology should therefore use research methods which provide an understanding from the point of view of individuals and groups. This process is called **verstehen** (pronounced *ver-stay-un*).

Verstehen is the idea of understanding human behaviour by putting yourself in the position of those being studied, and trying to see things from their point of view.

Instead of collecting statistical information, interpretivists suggest there is a need to discuss and get personally involved with people in order to get at how they see the world and understand it. Examples might be to look at whether people in some social classes tolerate or dismiss ill-health more than those in other classes, or are more likely to be arrested because of the way police see them. Similarly, interpretivist research on relationships in the family might carry out in-depth interviews with family members, finding out how they feel about doing jobs around the home, whether they see house-work and childcare as shared out equally or not and whether they'd want them to be.

The methods interpretivists use are therefore those which involve the collection of **qualitative data**. This consists of words giving in-depth description and insight into the attitudes, values and feelings of individuals and groups, and the meanings and interpretations they give to events. Such qualitative methods include:

- participant and (sometimes) non-participant observation
- informal (unstructured/in-depth) interviews
- open-ended questionnaires
- personal accounts like diaries and letters

These are more likely to involve in-depth small-scale or micro research on small numbers of people.

The interpretivists question the value of the research methods used by positivists, such as structured questionnaires and interviews. This is because they impose a framework on research – the sociologist's own view of what is important, rather than what may be important to the individuals being researched.

Figure 5.2 overleaf shows the broad links which exist between the two different theoretical approaches of positivism and interpretivism, other wider theories of society identified with them, and the research methods most likely to be used.

Qualitative data are concerned with people's feelings, meanings and interpretations about some event, and try to get at the way they really see things. Such data are normally in the form of the sociologist's description and interpretation of people's feelings and lifestyles, often using direct quotations from the people studied.

Activity

Imagine you wanted to do a study of how tasks are divided up between men and women in the home. You are interested in:
- housework and other household jobs
- childcare (not just who does it, but who takes responsibility for making sure children have new clothes, shoes, the right gear for school, get food they like and so on)
- decision-making
- dealing with family conflicts and emotions

Suggest ways that positivists and interpretivists might approach these issues differently, and what types of methods they might use to obtain their information.

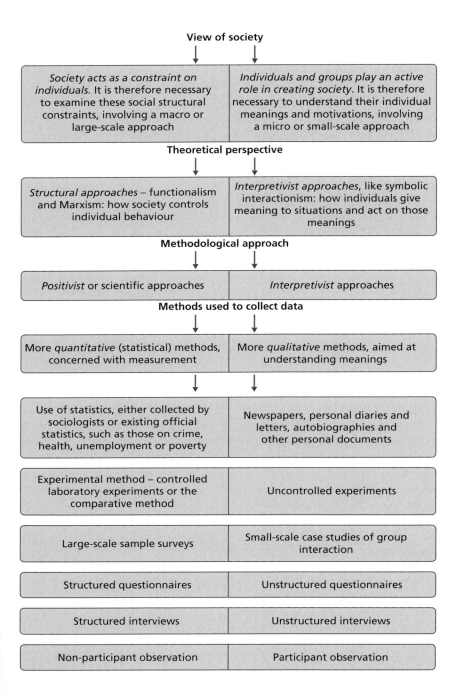

Figure 5.2 The link between sociological theories and research methods: a summary

View of society

Society acts as a constraint on individuals. It is therefore necessary to examine these social structural constraints, involving a macro or large-scale approach	Individuals and groups play an active role in creating society. It is therefore necessary to understand their individual meanings and motivations, involving a micro or small-scale approach

Theoretical perspective

Structural approaches – functionalism and Marxism: how society controls individual behaviour	Interpretivist approaches, like symbolic interactionism: how individuals give meaning to situations and act on those meanings

Methodological approach

Positivist or scientific approaches	Interpretivist approaches

Methods used to collect data

More quantitative (statistical) methods, concerned with measurement	More qualitative methods, aimed at understanding meanings

Use of statistics, either collected by sociologists or existing official statistics, such as those on crime, health, unemployment or poverty	Newspapers, personal diaries and letters, autobiographies and other personal documents
Experimental method – controlled laboratory experiments or the comparative method	Uncontrolled experiments
Large-scale sample surveys	Small-scale case studies of group interaction
Structured questionnaires	Unstructured questionnaires
Structured interviews	Unstructured interviews
Non-participant observation	Participant observation

Other influences on the choice of research method

It is not simply theoretical issues that influence the choice of methods sociologists use. This will also depend on a range of non-theoretical factors:

- *The time and funding that are available* to complete the research will influence the scale of the research and the types of method used. For example, large-scale research is expensive, and beyond the means of most sociologists. Research for military or defence purposes will attract funding more easily than research into help for disabled people. Government-backed research is likely to open more doors to researchers and produce more sponsorship than private individuals or small research departments are able to achieve by themselves. Government-backed research often favours quantitative data gathered through large-scale surveys, such as the British Crime Survey funded by the Home Office.
- *The availability of existing data* on a topic may limit or decide the method.
- *The values and beliefs of the researcher* will inevitably influence whether she or he thinks issues are important or unimportant and therefore worthy of study or not, and what aspects should be investigated and how. Townsend (1979), for example, clearly believed the study of poverty was important, and particularly the investigation of relative poverty, and his values are reflected in his devotion to poverty research – and methods of exploring it – throughout his academic life.
- *Sociologists are professionals with careers and promotion prospects* ahead of them, and they face a constant struggle to get money to fund their research. There is therefore an understandable desire to prove their own hypotheses right. The desire for promotion may influence what topics are seen as useful to do research on and what methods might be most likely to produce speedy results, as will the current state of knowledge and what constitutes a 'trendy' or lucrative research area.
- *The pressure to publish findings* and publishers' deadlines may mean research is not as thorough as it ought to be.

Figure 5.3 overleaf illustrates some of these influences on the choice of research topic and the methods used.

Key issues in social research

There are three key issues that should always be considered when carrying out or assessing research. These are the issues of reliability, validity and the ethics of research.

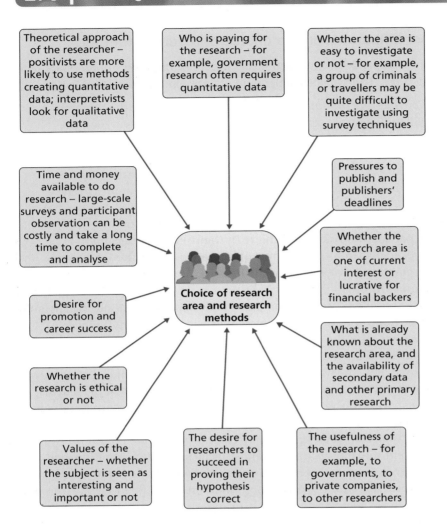

Figure 5.3 Influence on choices of research topic and method

The diagram shows "Choice of research area and research methods" at the centre, with the following influences pointing towards it:

Theoretical approach of the researcher – positivists are more likely to use methods creating quantitative data; interpretivists look for qualitative data

Who is paying for the research – for example, government research often requires quantitative data

Whether the area is easy to investigate or not – for example, a group of criminals or travellers may be quite difficult to investigate using survey techniques

Time and money available to do research – large-scale surveys and participant observation can be costly and take a long time to complete and analyse

Pressures to publish and publishers' deadlines

Whether the research area is one of current interest or lucrative for financial backers

Desire for promotion and career success

Whether the research is ethical or not

What is already known about the research area, and the availability of secondary data and other primary research

Values of the researcher – whether the subject is seen as interesting and important or not

The desire for researchers to succeed in proving their hypothesis correct

The usefulness of the research – for example, to governments, to private companies, to other researchers

Activity

Refer to figure 5.3
1 Suggest *two* ways that sources of funding for research might influence that research.
2 Suggest *two* reasons why investigating some social groups may be much more difficult than others.
3 Answer in about one and a half sides of A4 paper the following essay question: *Examine the view that the main influences on a researcher's choice of research method are practical considerations.*

Reliability

Reliability refers to whether another researcher, if repeating research using the same method for the same research on the same group, would achieve the same results.

Reliability is concerned with *replication*: whether another researcher using the same method for the same research on the same group would achieve the same results. For example, if different researchers use the same question-naire on similar samples of the population, then the results should be more or less the same if the techniques are reliable.

Validity

Validity is concerned with notions of truth: how far the findings of research actually provide a true, genuine or authentic picture of what is being studied.

Validity is concerned with notions of truth: how far the findings of research actually provide a true, genuine or authentic picture of what is being studied. Data can be *reliable* without being valid. For example, official crime statistics may be reliable, in so far as researchers repeating the data collection would get the same results over and over again, but they are not valid if they claim to give us the full picture of the extent of crime. Another example might be people responding untruthfully to questions, therefore not providing valid evidence of what is being investigated.

Ethics

Ethics concerns principles or ideas about what is morally right or wrong.

The **ethics** of research are concerned with morality and standards of behaviour, and when sociologists carry out research they should always consider the following points:

- They should take into account the sensitivities of those helping with their research. For example, it would not be appropriate to ask about attitudes to abortion in a hospital maternity ward where women may be having babies or have suffered miscarriages.
- Findings should be reported accurately and honestly.
- The physical, social and mental well-being of people who help in research should not be harmed by research; for example, by disclosing information given in confidence which might get the person into trouble, or cause them embarrassment.
- The anonymity, privacy and interests of those who participate in your research should be respected. You should not identify them by name, or enable them (or an institution) to be easily identified.
- As far as possible, your research should be based on the freely given consent of those studied. Researchers should make clear what they're doing, why they're doing it, and what they will do with their findings. This is commonly referred to as 'informed consent'.

Primary and secondary data

Primary data is that which is collected by sociologists themselves, usually obtained by carrying out a social survey, using questionnaires and interviews, or by participant observation.

Secondary data is that which already exists and is collected from secondary sources. Figure 5.4 shows a range of these sources that might be used by sociologists in carrying out research.

Both types of data can take either quantitative (statistical) or qualitative (non-statistical) forms.

> **Primary data** is that which is collected by sociologists themselves – it only exists because the sociologist has collected it.

> **Secondary data** is that which the sociologist carrying out the research has not gathered himself or herself, but which already exists.

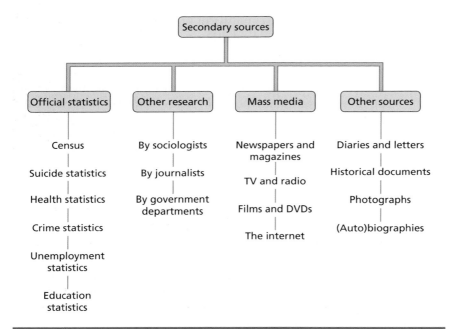

Figure 5.4 Secondary sources of data

Qualitative secondary sources

Qualitative secondary sources include newspapers, novels, literature, art, autobiographies, letters, diaries, radio and TV programmes, parish registers, historical documents, previous sociological studies, school records, social work files, police records, minutes of meetings, and some official government reports.

The advantages and uses of qualitative secondary sources

- Qualitative secondary sources may provide valuable, or the only, sources of information in an area. For example, historical documents are often

Secondary research

the only way of investigating the past, and without them it would be very difficult to find out about history. Much historical work on the family would have been impossible without reference to records going back several centuries.

- They are useful for interpretivists who wish to gain insights into the worldview or ideologies of those who produced them. Some historical documents and autobiographies can be particularly useful for these purposes.

- They may be very useful for assessing people's concerns or worries. For example, the letters pages and agony columns of newspapers and magazines may give valuable insights into the thinking of their readers (or the thinking of the editor on what she or he chooses to print).

The disadvantages and limitations of qualitative secondary sources

Scott, in *A Matter of Record* (1990), suggests four criteria for judging secondary data in general, but his points are very useful in assessing secondary qualitative data:

- *Authenticity*   Is the evidence genuine or a forgery? For example, diaries apparently by Adolf Hitler were purchased for millions of pounds and published in 1983 after being certified authentic by top historians. They were later found to be a complete forgery.
- *Credibility*   Is the evidence believable, sincere and honest? Does it contain biases, distortions and exaggerations by the writers to deceive or mislead readers? Is the evidence reliable? Who was a document written for? Does it simply reflect the values and beliefs of those who produced it? The mass media, for example, are often seen as very biased (one-sided) sources of evidence, and material written for publication may be very different from material meant to be private. For example, auto-biographies and published diaries of politicians should be treated with some scepticism, as they're likely to be very selective in the material included; at the same time, they may show how the politicians' minds worked, which might be useful for interpretivist research.
- *Representativeness*   Is the document typical of those appearing at the time? Is the evidence complete or merely a partial, biased account? Are other documents missing? Many historical documents have been destroyed, and governments often ban the publication of official records for a number of years after the events they relate to. What about those people in the past who couldn't read or write? Does the secondary data available simply reflect the views of the privileged minority in the past who were able to read and write well enough to produce diaries, letters and other documents?
- *Meaning*   What do documents mean? Do they have the same meaning now as they did at the time they were first produced?

Content analysis

Content analysis is a way of trying to analyse the content of documents and other qualitative material by quantifying it. This is done, for example. by sorting out categories, and then going through documents, books, magazines, television programmes and so on systematically, recording the number of times items in each category appear. Examples might include feminist researchers analysing reading books for children and seeking evidence of gender-role stereotyping: they might use categories such as male leader/female led, female works or plays indoors/male outdoors, and so on.

The Glasgow University Media Group has adopted this type of method in analysing television news. They video-recorded all TV news bulletins for a year and then made a content analysis, categorizing reports on industrial unrest and evaluating them. Their research showed statistical evidence of television's biases towards management and against workers, with managers, for example, more often portrayed in calm, peaceful surroundings and workers in noisy conditions against a background of traffic noise. This gave the impression that managers were more rational and calm than workers. This research challenged the mass media's claims of impartiality and balance in news reporting.

Activity

1 Go through the following examples, marking each as primary or secondary *and* quantitative or qualitative data:
   - exam results of schools in your area published in a local newspaper
   - newspaper stories from the 1930s
   - information collected by you showing the proportions of students doing different AS-level subjects
   - teenage magazines
   - statistics produced by the local NHS showing inequalities in health
   - video-recordings of a week's news reports
   - letters in a newspaper complaining about the risks to health of mobile phone masts
   - the published diaries of a former prime minister

2 Explain, with reasons, in what circumstances you might, or might not, consider each of the above pieces of data to be (a) reliable, and (b) valid, as sources of evidence.

3 Outline what ethical problems and problems of validity of the data collected, if any, there might be in each of the following situations:
   - a researcher joining a religious group to study it, concealing their role as a researcher
   - a researcher joining the police force to discover if there was evidence of racism among police officers, and then publishing his or her research
   - standing outside a gay club and noting the car numbers of drivers using the club, then using a friend in the police force to get hold of their addresses for a follow-up questionnaire on what it's like being gay
   - pretending to be ill and going to the doctor to investigate how doctors decide whether someone is ill or not

4 Do you consider there are ever any situations where a researcher might be justified in deceiving people to obtain research data? Explain your answer with examples of particular situations.

Quantitative secondary sources

Quantitative secondary sources include a huge range of statistical data produced by groups like companies, charities and pressure groups. A major source of such data is the mass of official statistics collected by national and local government and other official agencies. These include census data,

Activity

Go to www.statistics.gov.uk, the website of the Office for National Statistics, and identify (a) five government statistical publications, and (b) statistics for the current year (or the most recent year for which data are available) on unemployment, suicide, health, crime, divorce and marriage.

statistics on births, marriages and deaths, and social services, unemployment, education, crime and health statistics.

The advantages and uses of official statistics

- Official statistics are important for planning and evaluating social policy, such as responding to housing needs, transport and education planning and meeting the care needs of the elderly.
- They are frequently the only available source of data in a particular area.
- They are readily available and cheap to use. There is no need to spend time and money collecting data, and some data, such as census data, would be impossible for an individual to collect.
- They are often comprehensive in coverage, and therefore more likely to be representative.
- They often cover a long timespan, and therefore allow the examination of trends over time, such as those on crime, unemployment, health and divorce. They can be used for 'before and after' studies, for example, to judge the effect of government policies on reducing inequalities in health or the extent of poverty.
- They allow intergroup and international comparisons to be made, such as between working-class and middle-class family sizes, or suicide, divorce and crime rates between countries. They can therefore be used for the comparative method in sociology (discussed later in this chapter).

The problems and limitations of official statistics

If official statistics are basically accepted at face value as a true, or valid, record of events (as some researchers do with crime statistics and other official statistics), problems are likely to centre on their presentation, accuracy and completeness. For example, attempts have been made to overcome the inadequacy of the official crime statistics and make them more accurate by using **victim surveys** like the British Crime Survey to discover the 'dark number' of unrecorded crimes.

Many sociologists would argue any statistics, and especially official statistics, can't be taken at face value as they are socially constructed and may be politically biased. For example:

A **victim survey** is one that asks people to say whether they have been a victim of crime, whether they reported it to the police or not.

- Official statistics are collected for administrative purposes rather than for purposes of sociological research – so the definitions and classifications adopted may be unsuitable for sociological research.
- Official statistics are produced by the state. This means they may be 'massaged' to avoid political embarrassment to the government (see, for example, the discussion of unemployment figures below). The political process also affects which statistics are collected and which are not – for example, data on working days lost through strikes rather than industrial injuries; on social security 'scroungers' rather than tax evaders; on house-building rather than homelessness; on the poor but not the rich, and so on.
- Interpretivists argue that statistics are not objective facts but simply social constructions: the product of a process of interpretation and decision-making by those with authority. The following examples illustrate why sociologists should treat official statistics with some caution and pages 170–1 showed the limitations of official statistics on divorce.

Suicide statistics

J. M. Atkinson (1978) and other interpretivists argue that suicide statistics are simply social constructions reflecting the behaviour of coroners, doctors, relatives, etc., and their definitions of suicide. They tell us more about the decision-making processes of the living than the intentions of the dead and the real number of suicides (see the activity on page 280).

Unemployment statistics

Between 1979 and 1997, the method of calculating unemployment statistics was changed about thirty times, with each change creating a statistical drop in unemployment. 'Claimant count' unemployment figures only include those who sign on at job centres, are eligible for jobseeker's allowance, and are immediately available to start work. They therefore exclude many married women, people who have retired early, those reluctantly staying on at school or college because of no jobs, those on government training schemes, and those reluctantly working part-time. They have therefore massively underestimated the real extent of unemployment, to the advantage of the government at the time. The International Labour Organization (ILO) definition of unemployment, which includes all those who are actively seeking work and available to start, whether or not they receive jobseeker's allowance, gives far higher numbers of the unemployed. If the 'economically inactive' are included as well – a category which includes those who want work but are not immediately available to start work or aren't actively seeking it – then the numbers of the unemployed are higher still.

Health statistics

Health statistics can be inaccurate because:

- They depend on people persuading doctors they are ill, and are therefore simply a record of doctors' decision-making.
- Doctors may diagnose illnesses incorrectly, reflecting the state of the doctor's knowledge – and therefore recorded illnesses may not be accurate. Many AIDS deaths may have been recorded as pneumonia or another illness before doctors 'discovered' AIDS. Recent research has suggested that deaths from AIDS may have occurred in the 1950s in Britain, although the disease was not really discovered until the 1980s.
- Not all sick people go to the doctor and not all people who persuade the doctor they're sick are actually so – some may be malingerers or hypochondriacs.
- Private medicine operates to make a profit, and therefore is perhaps more likely to diagnose illness, as patients receiving treatment produce profits.

Crime statistics

Official crime statistics can be inaccurate for a number of reasons, and have to be treated very carefully by sociologists, because they do not show the full extent of crime in society. The following outlines these problems.

They only include crimes known to the police   Only around a quarter of all crimes are reported to the police, and even fewer are recorded by them as offences. There is a 'dark number' of undiscovered, unreported and unrecorded crimes. Victim surveys like the British Crime Survey show that many offences go unreported, such as vandalism, theft from the person, theft from motor vehicles, crimes of domestic violence, rape, and many burglaries.

Low clear-up rates   Only about one in four of all crimes is 'cleared up', with offenders caught. This leaves open the possibility that the other 80 per cent of known offences are committed by very different criminal types from those who come before the courts.

Unreported crime   People may not report offences to the police because:

- They may think that the incident is too trivial to report; for example, where the incident did not involve loss or damage, or the loss was too small.
- They may think there is little point in reporting the incident because they feel the police could not do anything about it, either by recovering their property or by catching the offenders.

- They may fear embarrassment or humiliation at the hands of the police or in court, as happens, for example, in cases of rape and domestic violence.
- They fear they will themselves be in trouble. This may happen, for example, in crimes where there is no obvious victim and both parties benefit, such as the illegal supplying of drugs, or giving and accepting bribes. Illegal drug users who get ripped off by drug dealers are extremely unlikely to report the incident, as they would get themselves into trouble.
- They may fear reprisals if the crime is reported, as in crimes of domestic violence.
- They may feel it is a private matter they would rather deal with themselves, such as assault between friends.
- They may not be aware an offence has been committed against them – people may have had 'lost' property stolen, been robbed by hoax gas meter readers or ripped off by cowboy builders without even realizing it.
- The crime may have no single victim or be seen as legitimate (justified), such as tax evasion, or not paying customs duty.
- They may wish to protect the public reputation of the institution in which the offence occurs. For example, computer fraud in banks may be dealt with unofficially, without involving the police, in case the bank's customers lose confidence that their money is safe in its hands. A similar example might be a student caught with illegal drugs in a school or college, where reporting to the police might give a bad impression to parents and harm the reputation of the institution.

Why might victims of crime not report it to the police?

Activity

1 Go to www.homeoffice.gov.uk/rds, find the latest British Crime Survey, and look for the *five* main reasons included in the latest survey for why the public don't report crime, and the two offences or groups of offences that are most likely to go unreported.

2 Read the following passage and then answer the questions beneath:

'Suicide is, by definition, the death of a person who intended to kill himself or herself. The problem for coroners is they can't ask dead people if they meant to kill themselves, so they can only guess at the truth by looking for "clues" in the circumstances surrounding the death. Atkinson has suggested there are four main factors which coroners take into account when deciding whether a death is a suicide or not:

- *Whether there was a suicide note.*
- *The way the person died, for example by hanging, drowning or a drug overdose. Death in a road accident rarely results in a suicide verdict.*
- *The place the death occurred and the circumstances surrounding it; for example, a drug overdose in a remote wood would be more likely to be seen as a suicide than if it occurred at home in bed. A coroner might also consider circumstances such as whether the person had been drinking alcohol before taking the drugs, and whether the drugs had been hoarded or not.*
- *The life history and mental state of the dead person, such as her or his state of health, and whether the victim was in debt, had just failed exams, lost a job, got divorced and was depressed or not.*

Coroners do not always agree on the way they interpret these clues. For example, Atkinson found one coroner believed a death by drowning was likely to be a suicide if the clothes were left neatly folded on the beach, but another coroner might attach little importance to this.'

(a) How is suicide defined in the passage?

(b) Why do you think coroners attach such importance to suicide notes?

(c) Suggest *two* reasons why the presence or absence of a suicide note might be an unreliable 'clue' to a dead person's intention to die.

(d) Suggest ways, with reasons, in which relatives and friends might try to persuade a coroner that a death was not a suicide but an accident.

(e) On the basis of the evidence in the passage, suggest reasons why (i) some deaths classified as suicides may have been accidental, and (ii) some deaths classified as accidents may in fact have been suicides.

(f) With reference to the evidence in the passage, suggest reasons why sociologists should be very careful about using official statistics on suicide as a record of the real number of suicides in society.

3 In about one and a half sides of A4 paper, answer the following essay question: *Assess the usefulness of official statistics for sociologists in their research.*

The experimental (laboratory) method of research

A **hypothesis** is an idea which the researcher guesses might be true, but which has not yet been tested against the evidence.

The experiment is the main means of conducting research in the natural sciences. In natural science, experiments are used to test a **hypothesis** in laboratory conditions in which all variables or causes are under the control of the researcher. By manipulating variables and studying and measuring the results, the researcher tries to test a hypothesis by isolating the causes of some phenomenon under investigation (such as, why pigs get fat).

The researcher will take two groups that are alike in every way: one is the *control group* and the other is the *experimental group*. The researcher will then alter some factor (the *independent variable*) in the experimental group to see if the variable being investigated (the *dependent variable*) changes compared to the control group (for example, alter heat in pigsties to see if this affects pigs getting fat). If nothing changes in the experimental group, then that variable can be dismissed as a cause of the thing being investigated, and other variables can be tested (for example, type of food). Through this experimental method, the researcher can eventually arrive at an explanation for the issue being investigated that has been tested against evidence, since any difference between the two groups after the experiment can only be because of the experimental variable, as the two groups were otherwise identical before the experiment.

Such laboratory experiments in the natural sciences have the advantage of:

- enabling scientists to test their hypotheses in controlled conditions
- making it easy to isolate and manipulate variables to isolate the causes of events
- being repeatable (replicable) and therefore able to be checked by other researchers
- enabling comparisons to be made with other similar experimental research

Problems of using the experimental method in sociology

- In the social sciences, and sociology in particular, it is often difficult to isolate a single cause of a social issue like crime, or underachievement in school, and it is extremely difficult to isolate variables for testing. For example, crime and low achievement in school are the result of a range of causes.
- Experiments need to treat one group differently from another similar group and compare results. However, this poses ethical problems for sociologists, as it may have negative effects on the experimental group. People may also object to being experimented on.

Why might the laboratory experiment not be a suitable method for studying the behaviour of people in society?

- Experiments are often only possible in small-scale settings with very limited, specific aims, but sociologists are often interested in wider settings like achievement in education and the causes of crime or ill-health, and such small-scale settings may be unrepresentative.

A particular problem is the **Hawthorne effect**.

The Hawthorne effect and the problem of validity

Sociologists want to study people in their 'normal' social context, but the laboratory and experimental conditions are artificial situations. People, unlike chemicals and many animals, can and do know what is going on in an experiment. The knowledge that an experiment is taking place, even if it is not fully understood, may mean people behave differently from their usual, everyday behaviour. They may deliberately sabotage the experiment, or 'play up' for the researcher. The very presence of the observer may become the principal independent variable in social scientific experiments. The classic example of this 'experimental effect' is the Hawthorne effect, which is explained in the box opposite.

Such circumstances throw some doubt on the validity of using the experimental method for sociological research, and it is hardly ever desirable or possible to perform laboratory experiments in sociology. However, some experimental techniques have been used in sociology in the form of field experiments.

The **Hawthorne effect** is where the presence of a researcher, or a group's knowledge that it is the focus of attention, changes the behaviour of a group.

The Hawthorne effect

In 1927, a team of researchers led by Elton Mayo set up an experiment in the Hawthorne plant of the Western Electricity Company of Chicago, to try to find the factors affecting the productivity of workers. Using a control group and an experimental group, they set up a test area involving five workers who knew the experiment was taking place. Working conditions were matched with the rest of the factory, then the researchers varied factors such as room temperature, lighting, work hours, rest breaks, etc. They found output went up *even when conditions were made worse*. It turned out the most important variable affecting production was not environmental factors etc. but the *presence and interest of the researchers themselves*: being the focus of attention increased productivity. This influence of the researchers on research is known as the Hawthorne effect.

Field experiments

Field experiments are those conducted in the real world under normal social conditions, but trying to follow similar procedures to the laboratory experiment. They have mainly been carried out by interpretivists, who are interested in how meanings and labels, like 'bright' or 'mentally ill', get attached to people, and how others then react to them. This is illustrated in the work of Rosenthal and Jacobson and of Rosenhan, described in the box overleaf, 'Examples of field experiments in sociology'.

The comparative method

The comparative method rests on the same principles as the experiment, and is an alternative to it. However, instead of setting up artificial experiments or situations, the researcher collects data about different societies or social groups in the real world, or the same society at different times (this is called the historical method). The researcher then compares one society or group with another in an attempt to identify the conditions that are present in one society but lacking in the other, as a way to explain the causes of some social event.

This approach is most commonly used by positivists concerned with trying to isolate and identify the causes of social events and behaviour.

An example of the use of the comparative method is Durkheim's study of suicide. Durkheim could hardly experiment with people to see what kinds of factors made them commit suicide, and he couldn't control the social situations in societies whose suicide rates he wished to compare. All he could do was to compare official suicide statistics in various societies and examine what seemed to be the most frequent factors linked with high suicide rates. He collected suicide statistics from a number of European countries and, by

Examples of field experiments in sociology

Rosenthal and Jacobson, *Pygmalion in the Classroom* (1968)

In the 1960s, Rosenthal and Jacobson wanted to test the hypothesis that teachers' expectations had important effects on pupils' academic performance. They told teachers that 20 per cent of children had been tested and shown to have high intelligence and were expected to make rapid progress in the next year compared to other students. In fact, the students had been chosen totally at random, and were no different from the other students. Within a year, those students whom the teachers were told were bright made very rapid progress compared to other students. This was seen as evidence that pupil progress was affected by teacher expectation, and teachers' predictions of pupil progress could actually influence the progress they made – a self-fulfilling prophecy. This research posed ethical problems, as it may well have been that teachers' high expectations of the students labelled 'bright' may have been linked with low expectations of those labelled not bright, and had negative consequences on their progress – a self-fulfilling prophecy with negative effects on student progress.

Rosenhan, 'On being sane in insane places' (1973)

Rosenhan was interested in discovering how the staff of mental hospitals made sense of and labelled people as mentally ill. He arranged for perfectly sane 'patients' to fake the symptoms of schizophrenia (hearing voices), and they were admitted to hospital, unknown to staff as fakes. Once admitted to hospital, they behaved normally. All were diagnosed as schizophrenics, even though they were perfectly healthy. Rosenhan reversed the experiment, telling hospital staff they could expect patients who would be faking illness. The staff eventually thought they had identified the fake patients, but all those they identified were actually genuine patients who wanted help.

Activity

1 Identify and explain *three* reasons why the experimental method may not be suitable for sociological research.

2 Refer to the examples of field experiments by Rosenthal and Jacobson, and Rosenhan:
   - What aims did Rosenthal and Jacobson have in carrying out their piece of research?
   - In what ways do you think their research might be useful to others?
   - Do you think there are any ethical difficulties in either piece of research?
   - To what extent do you think it might be possible to generalize these pieces of research to the whole of society? Would you need more information to answer this question?

comparing variables such as religion, marital status and geographical location, he concluded that differences in suicide rates could be partly explained by differences in religious belief between societies.

Surveys and sampling methods

Surveys are a means of collecting primary data from large numbers of people, and are commonly carried out using questionnaires or structured interviews.

Surveys are a means of collecting primary data from large numbers of people, usually in a standardized statistical form.

Who uses the survey method?

Because surveys mainly produce quantitative statistical data, they are the method most favoured by positivists.

Townsend used the survey method to produce a mass of statistical data, with questionnaires carried out by trained interviewers, about the causes and extent of poverty in his classic study *Poverty in the United Kingdom* (1979). Many people use surveys apart from sociologists, for instance the government when it carries out the ten-yearly census, market researchers who want to test people's attitudes to products, and election pollsters trying to find out how people will vote in elections.

A **sample** is a smaller *representative* group drawn from the survey population. The **survey population** is the whole group being studied, and will depend on the hypothesis the researcher wishes to investigate.

Representativeness and sampling

In some cases, it may be possible to interview every member of the population under investigation because it is such a small group, such as a class of college students, or because the organization doing the research has the resources to investigate everyone. For example, the government surveys the entire population of Britain in the census every ten years.

Sociologists rarely have the time or money to question everyone in large-scale and expensive surveys, so they usually collect information from a smaller group called a **sample**.

If it is a **representative sample**, containing all the relevant characteristics of the whole group under investigation (known as the **survey population**), such as age and gender groups, ethnic groups and social class, then the results obtained from the sample can be generalized or applied to the whole survey population.

The representativeness of a sample can be affected by:

A **representative sample** is a smaller group drawn from the survey population which contains a good cross-section of the survey population, such as the right proportions of people of different ethnic origins, ages, social classes and sexes. The information obtained from a representative sample should provide roughly the same results as if the whole survey population had been questioned

- *Sample size*   Too small a sample may mean that it is not representative, and in general the larger the sample taken, the more representative it will be. However, a sample is at its ideal size when making it any larger won't produce much more accurate or representative results than if the entire survey population had been questioned.

Social surveys often use questionnaires on large numbers of people, carried out by post, and completed by those surveyed, or by interviewers, either in person (face-to-face) or over the telephone

- *The sampling frame*   A **sampling frame** is a list of names of all those in the survey population. A commonly used sampling frame is the Register of Electors, which includes the names and addresses of all adults over the age of 18 in Britain who are registered to vote in elections. Another nationwide sampling frame, which is now the most complete one available in Britain,

> A **sampling frame** is a list of names of all those included in the survey population from which the sample is selected.

is the Royal Mail's Postcode Address File, which lists all addresses in the UK. Doctors' lists of patients are also commonly used as sampling frames, as most people are registered with a doctor. It is extremely important that a sampling frame should be complete: no individuals or particular groups of individuals should be missing. Otherwise, the sample drawn from the sampling frame may be unrepresentative of the entire survey population. For example, a telephone directory would be an unreliable sampling frame if the researcher wanted to select a sample which was representative of the entire adult population, as it only contains those who have a land-line, and excludes those who may not be able to afford or want a tele-phone, or who are ex-directory and therefore not included in the phone book, or who only have a mobile phone.

- *The sampling method used*   Careful **sampling methods** mean that often the information provided by the sample can be generalized with great accuracy to the whole survey population. For example, opinion polls on the voting intentions of electors often produce extremely accurate predic-tions of the outcome of general elections from questioning samples of only about 1,500 people, drawn from millions of adult voters.

> **Sampling methods** are the techniques sociologists use to select representative individuals to study from the survey population.

The problem for sociologists is how to obtain as representative a sample as possible, and this is achieved by various sampling methods.

Sampling methods

Figure 5.5 overleaf summarizes the main sampling methods discussed below, with examples.

Random sampling   Random sampling simply means that every individual in the survey population has an equal chance of being picked out for investiga-tion. For example, all names are put in a hat and enough names picked out to make up the sample size required. This is most commonly done by numbering all the names in the sampling frame and then getting a computer to select numbers at random to fill the sample size. However, such a method is subject to the laws of chance, which may result in an unrepresentative sample – there may be too many people of one sex, age group or social class or who live in the same area. For example, a small survey of a school might by chance select only black females, and miss out black males and white males and white females.

Systematic sampling   Systematic sampling is where names are selected from the sampling frame at regular intervals until the size of sample is reached, for example by selecting every tenth name in the sampling frame. This has much the same risk of being unrepresentative as a random sample. For example, every tenth name might, purely by chance, happen to be a white and middle-class person.

Figure 5.5 Examples of sampling methods

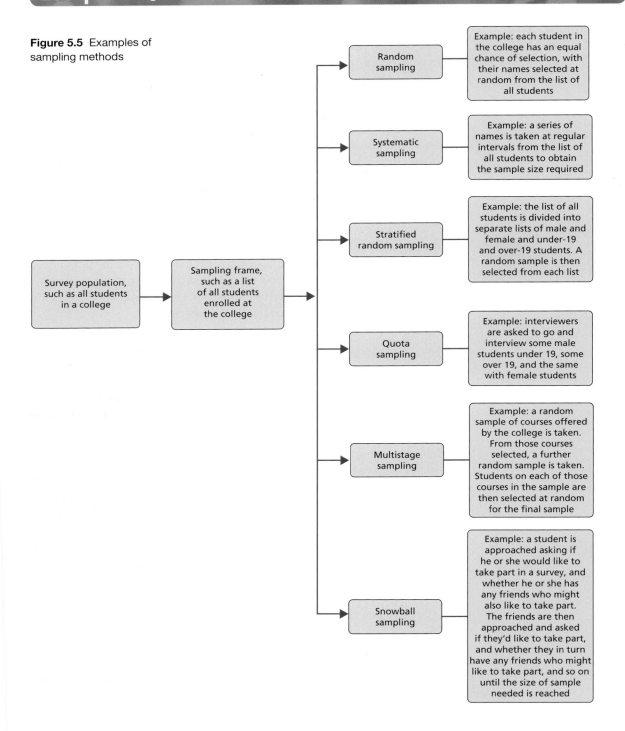

A random sample is a bit like a lottery draw – every person has an equal chance of being selected but, like the lottery, you've got to be in it to win it, or, as in surveys, to be in the sampling frame to have a chance of being selected

Stratified random sampling   Stratified random sampling is a way of attempting to avoid the possible errors caused by simple random sampling. This is achieved by subdividing (stratifying) the sampling frame into a number of smaller sampling frames drawn up on particular bases, such as social class, age, sex, ethnic group or education, according to their proportions in the population under investigation. The criteria used will depend on the factors being investigated. Individuals are then drawn at random from each of these sampling frames. For example, in a survey of doctors, we may know from earlier research that 8 per cent of all doctors are Asian, and so the sociologist must make sure 8 per cent of the sample are Asian. To do this, the sociologist will separate out the Asian doctors from the sampling frame of all doctors, and then take a random sample from this list of Asian doctors to make up 8 per cent of the sample of all doctors in the survey population. In this way, the final sample is more likely to be representative of all doctors in the survey population. Stratified random sampling has the advantage over simple random sampling of being much more representative, because all the characteristics of the survey population are more certain to be represented in the sample. See the box 'Obtaining a stratified random sample' and figure 5.6, which shows an example.

Quota sampling   In quota sampling, interviewers are told to go and select people who fit into certain categories according to their proportion in the survey population as a whole, such as so many men and women over the age of 45. **The** choice of the actual individuals selected is left to the honesty of the interviewer (unlike other sampling methods where actual named individuals are identified). The problem with quota sampling is that it is not

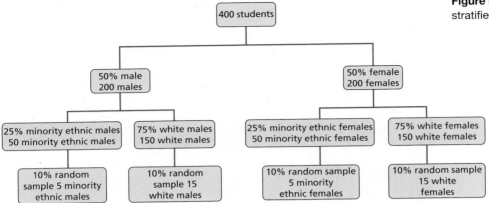

Figure 5.6 An example of stratified random sampling

Obtaining a stratified random sample

Suppose there were 400 students in a school. Of these, 50 per cent are male and 50 per cent are female. In each group, 75 per cent are white and 25 per cent are from minority ethnic groups. You want a 10 per cent representative sample (40 people).

Figure 5.6 shows how you might obtain a stratified random sample by dividing up the sampling frame of 400 names, first into two sampling frames (by sex), and then by subdividing each again into two (by ethnic group). You then take a 10 per cent random sample from each of the final four sampling frames.

This stratified random sample of 40 people (10 per cent of the original 400 students) should be representative of the sex and ethnic characteristics of the entire school population, as these features of the survey population are now certain to be included in the 10 per cent sample.

---

necessarily representative. For example, the quota might be filled by stopping people while shopping during the week, but this would exclude those not shopping or who are at work. The fact that the choice of person rests on the interviewer's discretion means there may be bias in the choices they make. For instance, they may not approach people who don't look very welcoming, even though they fit the category, or they might ignore those who refuse to cooperate and simply find another person who fits the quota. This could well lead to a bias in the sample.

Multistage or cluster sampling   Multistage or cluster sampling involves selecting a sample in various stages, each time selecting a sample from the previous sample until the final sample of people is selected. For example, in a national survey of school students, you might first take a random sample of schools, then take a random sample of students in those sample schools.

Non-representative sampling

In some cases a non-representative sample might be useful in sociological research: for example, selecting a group for a particular purpose which is not representative, but because it has the particular characteristics you want to study. For example, in studying a hypothesis like 'roles in the family are more likely to be equal among younger middle-class couples', it might be useful to study a group that is young and middle class, to test or disprove the hypothesis, or gain insights into those couples.

Snowball sampling   Snowball sampling is used when a sampling frame is difficult to obtain or doesn't exist, or when a sample itself is very difficult to obtain. The researcher may identify one or two people with the characteristics they're interested in, and ask them to introduce them to other people willing to cooperate in the research, and then ask these people to identify others. For example, Laurie Taylor, in *In the Underworld* (1984), used this technique to investigate the lifestyles of criminals. There was no readily available sampling frame of criminals. He happened to know a convicted criminal, who was willing to put him in touch with other criminals who were willing to cooperate in his research. These criminals in turn put him in touch with other criminals, and so his sample gradually built up, just as a snowball gets bigger as you roll it in the snow.

Such samples may be useful, but they are not random or representative. They rely on volunteers recommending other volunteers to the researcher, and the sample is therefore self-selecting, and this may create bias. For example, such volunteers may have particular views for or against a particular issue and that may be why they volunteered.

Figure 5.7 overleaf shows how a major national annual survey, the British Social Attitudes Survey, used a combination of multistage, systematic and random sampling to obtain a final sample of 3,146 individuals drawn from nearly all people over the age of 18 in Britain.

The stages of a survey

Before carrying out a large-scale survey, it is important to carry out a **pilot survey** (sometimes called a pilot study).

The purpose of a pilot survey or a pilot study is to iron out any problems which the researcher might have overlooked, and avoid wasting time and money in the final survey. For example, some of the sample may have moved

A **pilot survey** is a small-scale practice survey carried out before the final survey to check for any possible problems.

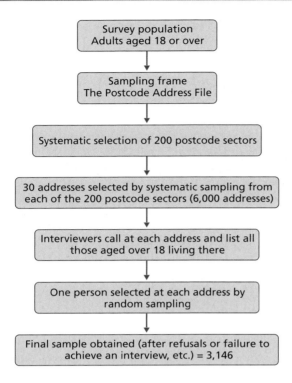

Figure 5.7 Obtaining a sample: the example of the British Social Attitudes Survey

---

Activity

In each of the following cases, suggest both a hypothesis you might wish to test and how you might obtain your sampling frame and your sample:

- the attitudes of family doctors (GPs) to changes in the National Health Service
- the reasons why few female school-leavers in a town go on to computer courses at a local college
- a survey of young mothers
- a survey of old age pensioners
- a survey of football hooligans
- the opinions of adults in your neighbourhood about how they will vote in the next election
- the attitudes of gay men to the police

---

away or died, there may be problems with non-response or non-cooperation by respondents, or some questions may be unclear.

After the pilot survey is completed, the results are reviewed, any necessary changes are made, and the main survey can then proceed. The stages of a survey are shown in figure 5.8.

Figure 5.8 The stages of a survey

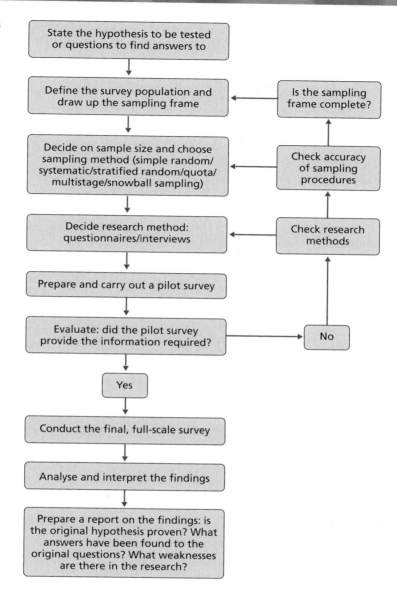

Problems of the social survey

There are three major problems faced by social survey researchers in achieving 'scientific' accuracy:

- *Validity*   Surveys need to be very carefully planned if they are to obtain data which are valid – which really provide a true, genuine or authentic picture of what they claim to represent. The statistical data produced by surveys are questioned by interpretivists, who would argue statistical data lack the depth to describe accurately people's meanings and motives, and that they use categories which are imposed by the sociologists.

- *Generalization*   This is concerned with representativeness: how far the findings of a piece of research can be generalized to other sections of the survey population rather than simply restricted to the sample selected. For example, the sample selected may be too small, or unrepresentative, or people selected may have moved, died, etc., in which case the results may not be able to be generalized.

- *Reliability*   Whatever the survey finds should be found by anyone else conducting the same survey again. This may be a particular problem where face-to-face interviews are used. This issue is discussed below under 'Interviewer bias' on pages 306–8.

Activity

1 Explain what is meant by a representative sample.
2 Suggest *two* reasons why sociologists might use a sample when doing a survey.
3 Suggest *two* reasons why sociologists might undertake a pilot study.
4 Explain what is meant by a quota sample.
5 Identify three factors that may influence the representativeness of a sample.

Questionnaires

The nature and use of questionnaires

Most surveys involve the use of a questionnaire of some kind. A questionnaire is a list of pre-set questions to which the *respondents* (the people answering the questions) are asked to supply answers – either by filling in responses themselves (a self-completion questionnaire) or by giving information to an interviewer, either face to face or over the telephone. When administered by an interviewer, these take the form of interviews.

Researchers using questionnaires see them as a comparatively cheap, fast and efficient method (compared to other methods like unstructured interviews or participant observation) for obtaining large amounts of quantifiable data on relatively large samples of people.

The questionnaire is one of the main tools of measurement in positivist sociology, as data obtained by structured questionnaires are easily quantified and can be analysed more 'scientifically' and objectively than qualitative data.

Questionnaires are very commonly used in survey research to collect quantitative data

Questionnaire design: some principles and problems

Great care is needed in questionnaire design. Because the idea is to present all respondents with the same questions and therefore obtain comparable data, questionnaires can't be changed once a survey has begun. They should be kept as simple and clear as possible, otherwise those being interviewed or filling in the questionnaire themselves will be unlikely to complete it.

A pilot survey is therefore very important to clear up problems and avoid wasting time and money on a poorly designed questionnaire. Pilot studies are used to test questions, make sure their meaning is clear, and to ensure layout and wording are suitable for the intended sample.

The section below identifies some important issues in designing a questionnaire.

Designing a questionnaire

As short as possible, with clear layout and instructions   Completing the questionnaire should be made as easy as possible for the respondent:

- The questionnaire should be clearly laid out and well printed. Instructions for completing it should be easily understood by the respondent, and it should be easy to follow and complete.
- The number of questions should be kept to the minimum required to produce the information. Respondents may be unwilling to answer

long lists of questions, or may stop giving serious thought to their answers.

- Start the questionnaire with the simplest questions and shortest answers first, leaving the more complicated questions or more detailed answers until the end. Otherwise people may be put off right from the beginning.
- There should be just enough alternative answers (including 'don't know') to allow respondents to express their views and to provide the information required.

Clear and neutral language, and the avoidance of 'leading questions' The form of questions needs careful thought:

- Questions should be simple and direct – capable of being answered 'yes' or 'no', by a choice from fixed responses, or with short open-ended answers.
- Questions should be phrased in neutral terms – otherwise respondents might feel they are expected to give a particular answer. Questions which encourage people to give a particular answer are called 'leading questions', and they are likely to produce distorted or invalid (untruthful) results. A question like 'Why do you think sex before marriage is wrong?' is a poor, leading question because it encourages people to accept that sex before marriage is wrong because of the way the question is worded.
- Questions should be clear in meaning and phrased in simple, everyday language, avoiding technical or unfamiliar words which people may not understand. For example, a question like 'Do you have joint conjugal roles in your household' is a bad question because people are unlikely to understand what 'conjugal roles' are. Similarly, a question like 'Do you watch television a lot?' is a poor question, as people might interpret 'a lot' in different ways – it is better to specify actual time periods such as 1-2 hours, 3–4 hours a day and so on.
- Questions should only be asked which the respondents are likely to be able to answer accurately – for example, to give responses or opinions on things they might reasonably be expected to know about, or remember accurately.
- Questions should mean the same thing to all respondents. The researcher can't automatically assume that questions will have the same meaning to the respondent as they do to the researcher.
- Offensive questions should be avoided.

Confidentiality Those being surveyed should be reassured that their answers will be kept confidential or anonymous.

Questionnaires should always be phrased in simple, everyday language

Activity

1 Refer to the section 'Designing a questionnaire' on pages 295-6. Draw up a five-question questionnaire on attitudes to poverty, health or education (or some other sociological topic of interest to you).
2 Test your questionnaire on five people.
3 Identify and explain any difficulties you come across in your questionnaire, and amend your questions as necessary.
4 Suggest as many criticisms as you can of the following questions:
   • 'Do you read newspapers often?'
   • 'Have you been diseased recently?'
   • 'What do you think of help given to the disabled?'
5 In the light of your criticisms, write new questions, and a choice of answers, to overcome the difficulties you have identified.

Types of questionnaire

There are two main types of questions used in questionnaires: pre-coded or structured questions, and open-ended questions. Both types of question may be combined in the same questionnaire.

Pre-coded questionnaires

Pre-coded questionnaires are highly structured, and involve individuals being asked a number of pre-set questions with the choice of a limited number of multiple-choice answers. They are sometimes known as closed, structured or multiple-choice questionnaires. Table 5.1 summarizes their advantages and disadvantages.

Table 5.1 The strengths and weaknesses of pre-coded questionnaires

Advantages and strengths	Disadvantages and problems
<ul><li>They are fairly quick to complete.</li><li>They produce standardized data that is easy to classify and produce in quantitative statistical form.</li><li>They allow data to be collected to produce new theories or to test existing hypotheses.</li><li>They enable comparisons to be made between different groups and populations. Since individuals are answering the same questions, and using the same choices of answers, their answers should show real dfferences between people rather than differences arising because of the way the questions were formulated or asked.</li><li>The statistics produced should be reliable and other researchers can check the findings, and repeat the research if they wish.</li></ul>	<ul><li>The meaning of questions may not be clear to some respondents. Extra questions cannot be asked or added to get the respondents to expand or explain themselves more fully.</li><li>The *imposition problem*. This is the risk that, when asking questions, researchers might be imposing their own views and framework on the people being researched, rather than getting at what they really think. The limited choice of answers imposes strict and artificial limits on what kind of information can be given or collected, as the constraints don't allow the respondent to develop or qualify their answers. The answer the respondent wants to give may simply not be there. This poses problems of *validity*, as the researcher may be imposing a choice of answers which may not really apply to that particular respondent.</li></ul>

Open-ended questionnaires

Open-ended questionnaires are less structured than pre-coded question-naires. Although open-ended questionnaires will still usually have a num-ber of pre-set questions, there is no pre-set choice of answers. This allows individuals to write their own answers or dictate them to an interviewer. They are sometimes known as unstructured questionnaires. Table 5.2 sum-marizes their advantages and disadvantages.

Postal/mail or self-completion questionnaires

This kind of questionnaire is either left with the respondent and picked up later, or sent through the post with a pre-paid addressed envelope for the reply, or posted on an internet site for people to reply to, or it may be sent and returned via e-mail. The respondent will complete the questionnaire himself or herself. The strengths and weaknesses of postal and other self-completion question-naires are shown in table 5.3.

The validity of questionnaire research

Interpretivists question whether questionnaires produce a valid picture of the social world and human behaviour. They make the following major criticisms of questionnaire research.

Table 5.2 The strengths and weaknesses of open-ended questionnaires

Advantages and strengths	Disadvantages and problems
• They produce more valid data, since the respondent is using his or her own words to express what they really mean rather than being given a pre-set choice of answers reflecting what the researcher thinks important. The *imposition problem* is less serious. • They produce more detail and depth than pre-coded questionnaires.	• The range of possible answers often makes it difficult to classify and quantify the results of such questionnaires. For example, the meaning of the answers may be unclear. • Because of the wide variety of answers, it may be difficult to compare results with other similar research.

Table 5.3 The strengths and weaknesses of postal and other self-completion questionnaires

Advantages and strengths	Disadvantages and problems
• They are a relatively cheap method compared to paying interviewers, particularly for collecting data from large numbers of people spread over a wide geographical area. • Results are obtained quickly: most that get returned at all get returned within a couple of weeks. • People can reply at their leisure and not just when an interviewer is present, so more precise answers may be obtained (especially if documents need to be consulted). • Questions on personal, controversial or embarrassing subjects are more likely to get a better response than if an interviewer is present. • There is no problem of interviewer bias (see the later discussion on this).	• There is a major problem of *non-response* in postal and other self-completion questionnaires (a 50 per cent response is very good), and of not getting representative responses in internet surveys. Those replying may be an unrepresentative sample of the survey population, for example in being more educated, or interested in the topic being researched, or having a particular axe to grind. This poses major problems for the *representativeness* and *validity* of the results. • People may not give valid truthful replies, due to forgetfulness or dishonesty, or because of different interpretations or meanings attached to the questions. There is no interviewer present to prompt replies or explain questions. • There is no way of knowing whether the right person completed the questionnaire – they may have let someone else do it.

Imposition

The **imposition problem** refers to the risk that the researcher, when asking questions, might be imposing their own views or framework on the people being researched, rather than getting at what they really think.

Positivist-based questionnaires risk what has been called the **imposition problem**. This is because they have already decided what the important questions are before the research, and questionnaires don't really discover the way respondents see the world. Such researchers are therefore simply imposing their own structure (what they think is important) on what they are investigating, possibly affecting the *validity* of the research (see below). It is therefore difficult to develop hypotheses during research, and respondents cannot provide information they haven't been asked for. It is also impossible for respondents to express feelings and subtle shades of opinion in statistical

The 2003 Children's Dental Health Survey

Postal questionnaires were used in this 2003 Department of Health survey. This was based on a representative sample of 12,698 children aged between 5 and 15 years of age, attending schools in the UK. The sample was first asked to take part in a dental examination at school, and then questionnaires were sent by post to parents to collect background data on their children's oral hygiene and dental care, with a response rate of 61 per cent.

What problems might there be with the validity of parents' answers to questions about their children's oral hygiene and dental care?

form. It is, for example, impossible to measure subjective factors such as the nature and strength of religious belief.

Validity

There is no guarantee people will tell the truth in questionnaires. People may give answers they think are socially acceptable – what they think they ought to say, rather than what they really believe or how they behave in real life. This poses problems about the validity of the research. In 1983, for example, following major public concerns about children viewing unsuitable 'video nasties', questionnaire research was carried out, with results which suggested that 40 per cent of 6-year-old children had seen some of the famous video nasties. This had major repercussions in the press and Parliament, leading to legislation. The research was later repeated by other sociologists on another sample of 11-year-olds. They found 68 per cent claimed to have seen video nasties – but the researchers had named films which didn't even exist. In the 2001 census, 0.7 percent of the population of England and Wales described their religion as 'Jedi' – fictional characters from the Star Wars films.

There may be different meanings attached to the wording of questions, which may influence the results. For example, many people prefer to call themselves 'middle class' when offered the choice of middle class or lower class, but when offered 'working class' more are prepared to put themselves in this category. Researchers need to be aware of how such meanings may differ between classes, ethnic groups, age groups and so on if their questionnaires are to produce valid data.

The scrounging Piresans

TÁRKI, a social research centre in Hungary, carried out a survey in that country in 2007, asking people about their opinion of immigrants from the nation of Piresa. Of those who responded, 68 per cent said that Piresans should not be let into the country under any circumstances. They were seen as scroungers, and most people said those who were already living in Hungary should be sent back immediately to Piresa. The survey was properly conducted, but there was one problem: there was no such place as Piresa, so there was no Piresa to stop immigration from, nor any Piresans to send back.

Researchers had made up the country to test the tolerance of Hungarians. This was a perfectly reasonable research strategy, but it shows in a particularly stark way that questionnaires do not always provide valid data.

Activity

1 Identify and explain *three* reasons why questionnaire research may not produce valid data.
2 Suggest *three* reasons why unstructured questionnaires might produce more valid data than structured questionnaires.
3 Explain what is meant by the 'imposition problem' in questionnaire-based research.
4 In about one and a half sides of A4 paper, answer the following essay question: *Assess the usefulness of unstructured questionnaires in sociological research.*

Interviews

Questionnaires may also form the basis of interviews by social researchers. Interviews are one of the most widely used methods of gathering data in sociology. They may be conducted face-to-face, with either individuals or small groups of people, or via the telephone. There are two main types of interview: structured or formal interviews, and unstructured or in-depth, informal interviews.

Structured or formal interviews

Structured or formal interviews are based on a structured, pre-coded questionnaire (the interview schedule). They are much like postal questionnaires administered by an interviewer. The interviewer asks the questions set in the same order each time, and does not probe beyond the basic answers received: a formal question and answer session. Table 5.4 summarizes the advantages and disadvantages of these interviews.

Table 5.4 The strengths and weaknesses of structured interviews

Advantages and strengths	Disadvantages and problems
• They are generally the most effective way of getting questionnaires completed and the problem of non-response found with postal and other self-completion questionnaires is much rarer. Skilled interviewers can persuade people to answer questions, and problems of illiteracy are overcome.	• The interview schedule/questionnaire may impose limits on what the respondent can say, as the interviewer cannot probe beyond the basic questions asked. This means there is a limited depth of understanding of what the respondent may mean.
• Data so obtained is often seen as more *reliable*, since all respondents will be answering the same questions, so results can be compared with other groups. The research can, if necessary, be replicated by other interviewers to check the findings.	• They are more time-consuming and costly than postal and other self-completion questionnaires – interviews are often slow, and interviewers have to be paid. Many more people can be questioned with a postal or other self-completion questionnaire for the same cost.
• They are useful for obtaining answers to questions about facts like the age, sex and occupation of those being interviewed.	• There is the possibility of interviewer bias (see below on page 306).
• They usually involve pre-coded questions and answers which make them relatively easy to put into quantitative statistical form (note the *positivist* implication here).	
• There is less of a problem with interviewer bias than in unstructured interviews, as there is little involvement of the interviewer with the interviewee beyond basic politeness (see the later discussion on interviewer bias).	

Interviewers may not always get the cooperation they hope for . . . especially if they choose the wrong moment

A group interview

A focus group

Group interviews and focus groups are both forms of in-depth interview. A group interview involves interviewing several people at the same time, with the interviewer controlling the direction the interview takes as he or she is seeking to obtain particular information; usually, responses will be to the interviewer rather than other members of the group. A focus group is a form of group interview, but which focuses on a single topic or group of related topics to discover people's views, such as whether or not they support nuclear power. The researcher's role in a focus group is to get people discussing the issue and to draw out their opinions and ideas.

What are the advantages and disadvantages for sociologists of obtaining information in these ways, and how valid do you think the findings might be?

Unstructured or informal (in-depth) interviews

A **group interview** is an interview in which the researcher interviews several people at the same time, with the researcher controlling the direction of the interview and to whom responses will normally be directed.

A **focus group** is a form of group interview in which the group focuses on a particular topic to explore in depth and people are free to talk to one another as well as the interviewer.

An unstructured interview is like a guided conversation. The interviewer has topics in mind to cover (the 'interview schedule') but few if any pre-set questions. If there is a questionnaire at all, it will be of the open-ended, unstructured variety. The interviewer will seek to put the respondent at ease, in a relaxed, informal situation, and will then ask open-ended questions which may trigger off discussions or further questions. The interviewer aims to obtain further depth or detail than is possible in a postal or other self-completion questionnaire or in a structured interview, and draw out the respondent's feelings, opinions and confidences. This approach was used by Oakley in *From Here to Maternity* (1981), a study of the experience of becoming a mother in British society. Unstructured interviews may also be carried out with a group of people. This can help to trigger off discussions, and gain more detailed and in-depth qualitative information. These **group interviews** sometimes take the form of **focus groups**, when the group interview focuses on a particular topic, and people are free to talk to one another as well as the interviewer. In a group interview, the interviewer's role is to question, whereas in a focus group the researcher's role is to feed in ideas or questions for the participants to discuss and draw out their feelings, experiences and opinions. The researcher also has to make sure the group remains focused on the topic under discussion. Table 5.5 shows the strengths and weaknesses of these interviews.

Developing a hypothesis in unstructured interviews

During the research which led to her theory of conjugal roles (the roles played by each partner in marriage) and social networks, Bott (1957) interviewed twenty couples in London. It was only because the link between social networks and conjugal roles emerged in the course of her interviews that Bott was able to develop her theory. This would have been impossible using questionnaires, since she wouldn't have known what questions to ask, as she hadn't developed a hypothesis on social networks before she began interviewing.

Activity

1 Make up a short five-question structured questionnaire (with a choice of answers) to find out about attitudes to poverty (you might adapt the questionnaire you drew up in the earlier activity on 'Designing a questionnaire').

2 Test this out on five people, using a structured interview, and record your findings.

3 Now, using the same questions as 'prompts', do unstructured interviews with two people. Be prepared to probe further and ask extra questions and enter discussions. Record your findings.

4 Compare the data collected by each type of interview, and the time it took to complete the interviews. Is there any difference between the information collected by these two types of interview, and the time taken to carry them out? Explain why you think this might be the case.

5 Identify and explain *three* reasons why a sociologist might use an unstructured interview rather than a structured interview in sociological research.

6 Identify *two* ways that unstructured interviews might be unreliable as a method of research.

7 Suggest *three* ways in each case in which group interviews or focus groups might
   (a) provide a greater depth of qualitative information than interviews with a single individual
   (b) provide less valid information than interviews with a single individual.

Table 5.5 The strengths and weaknesses of unstructured interviews

Advantages and strengths	Disadvantages and problems
• Their greater flexibility increases the validity of the data obtained compared to structured interviews. This is because they provide more opportunity for the respondent to say what they really think and feel about an issue (note the *interpretivist* implication). For example, Oakley found in *From Here to Maternity* that unstructured interviews enabled her to develop close relationships of trust and openness with the women concerned, and allowed women to speak for themselves openly and personally about motherhood. • There is the possibility of probing much deeper than a structured questionnaire. • Ambiguities in questions and answers can be clarified, and the interviewer can probe for shades of meaning. • The ideas of the sociologist can develop in the course of the interviews. The interviewer can adjust questions and change direction as the interview is taking place if new ideas and insights emerge. It is possible a new hypothesis might emerge during the research. By contrast, structured interviews have already decided the important questions. • Interviewers may be able to assess the honesty and validity of replies during the course of the interview: this may be difficult with structured interviews. • Group interviews or focus groups can spark off discussions and ideas which can yield more in-depth information.	• Unstructured interviews are time-consuming and costly, and this may mean fewer interviews are conducted, raising problems of representativeness. • They may be less reliable than structured interviews as questions may be phrased in a variety of ways and the researchers are more involved with the respondents. Differences between respondents may therefore simply reflect differences in the nature of the interview and the questions asked, rather than real differences between people. • It is difficult to replicate such interviews. The success of an informal interview depends heavily on the personality and personal skills of the interviewer, such as in getting people to answer questions that produce useful information, and in keeping the conversation going. Another researcher repeating the interviews may therefore not get the same results again, so findings from such research may therefore not be comparable with other groups (a criticism *positivists* might make). • It is difficult to compare and measure the responses of different interviewees as they may be expressed in many different ways. Unstructured interviews are therefore more popular with *interpretivists*, who are concerned with increasing their understanding of respondents and obtaining qualitative data. *Positivists* don't often use this method, except for exploratory research to develop a hypothesis for further investigation (using other methods). • Group interviews or focus groups may act as a form of 'peer pressure' and individuals may conceal their true feelings in case others disapprove. They may be reluctant to reveal personal issues in such a group setting. They may also exaggerate or distort their views to impress others.

General problems of interviews

The general problems of interviews centre on two main, and related, issues: the validity of the data obtained, and in particular, the problem of interviewer bias.

Validity

- Interview data are often taken by positivists as revealing the attitudes and behaviour of people in everyday life. However, interpretivists would argue that an interview is a very artificial situation, and what people say in an interview may have little to do with their real or normal behaviour. There is no guarantee people will give a true account in interviews, and they may lie, forget or otherwise mislead the interviewer. This may be particularly true in a group interview, when individuals may be concerned about what others may think, and therefore not tell the truth, or exaggerate or distort things. This poses problems for the validity of the data obtained by interviewing techniques.
- It is unlikely that anyone in an interview situation will give honest answers to questions that involve very personal or embarrassing issues.
- Interviews involve words and phrases, and meanings may vary between social groups. A structured interview, where there is little opportunity to qualify meaning, might not provide comparable data when administered to members of different social groups. For example, words like 'bad' and 'wicked' are used in different ways by younger and older people.
- Members of different social groups may attach different importance to the content of questions. For example, mental illness carries less stigma among Puerto Ricans than among the Jews, the Irish or black people in the United States. This means Puerto Ricans are more willing to admit to the symptoms of mental illness – but this doesn't mean there is necessarily more mental illness among them than among other ethnic groups. This again raises doubts about the validity of some interview data, as it may simply reflect how much people are willing to admit to things to an interviewer, rather than real differences between people.

> **Interviewer bias** refers to the answers given in an interview being influenced or distorted in some way by the presence or behaviour of the interviewer.

Interviewer bias

Interviewer bias refers to the way answers in an interview may be influenced or distorted in some way by the presence or behaviour of the interviewer. Interviews involve face-to-face social interaction between people, and the success of interviews often relies on the personal skills of the interviewer. The results of an interview will also partly depend on the way participants define the situation, and their perceptions of each other. For example, the interviewer's personality, sex, age, ethnic origin, tone of voice, facial expressions, and dress (such as suit or jeans) all impose a particular definition of the situation on the respondent, and this may influence the responses given. Status differences,

Study the two photographs above and suggest possible sources of interviewer bias. In what ways might the interview on the right produce more (or less) valid information than the one on the left?

such as age and ethnicity, between the respondent and the interviewer can lead to bias too. For example, an adult carrying out interviews with school students may not be given honest answers. The interviewer may give the impression, however unwittingly or unintentionally, of wanting to hear a certain answer.

In such circumstances, it is possible that the interviewees might adapt their answers to impress the interviewer by giving answers they think the interviewer wants to hear and would approve of, rather than giving their real opinions. This is perhaps unsurprising, as nearly everyone likes to obtain the approval of the person they're talking to.

There is therefore a danger (particularly with unstructured interviews) that the interviewer and the interview context may unduly influence the interviewee (the person being interviewed). This may mean that differences between interviews reflect differences in the way the interviews were conducted rather than real differences in what the respondents were actually saying. This interaction situation can therefore affect the quality, validity and reliability of the data.

An example of this arose in the course of the 1992 general election in Britain, when all the opinion polls (mainly using face-to-face interviews) predicted a narrow Labour victory, when in fact the Conservatives won. Subsequent research suggested that Conservative voters were more reluctant to admit in face-to-face interviews that they were going to vote Conservative at a time when the Conservative government was very unpopular, and when admitting voting for them appeared to be flying in the face of public opinion.

All the above suggests that in interview research it is very difficult for the researcher to avoid influencing what is obtained as data. It could therefore be argued that the data obtained by interviews are socially constructed – created and influenced by the presence, actions and behaviour of the interviewer, and the context in which the interview is conducted.

Overcoming interviewer bias   To overcome interviewer bias and try to ensure that interviews produce valid data, interviewers are carefully trained to be non-directive. This means not to offer opinions, or show approval or disapproval of answers received. 'Be friendly but restrained', showing a polite indifference to the answers received, is often the advice given to interviewers to reduce the risks of interviewer bias. Another way is to try and match the social characteristics of the interviewer and the people being interviewed. For example, Nazroo's (1997b) research into the health of Britain's ethnic minorities involved translating questionnaires into six Asian languages, and as often as possible respondents were interviewed by someone from their own ethnic group who spoke the same language.

However, Becker (1970) suggests a more aggressive style of interviewing is more likely to squeeze information out of respondents which may not otherwise have been volunteered. This involves 'playing dumb', playing the devil's advocate by taking positions on issues, or 'winding people up' in the hope of prompting the respondent into saying more. Another way of avoiding interviewer bias is to avoid face-to-face interviews altogether, and use telephone interviews instead. This has, since the 1992 general election, been a more common practice among opinion poll researchers.

Concluding remarks on interviews

The more structured the interview, the more easily can results be quantified statistically and comparisons made. However, the tighter the structure, the less the respondent can state and develop what she or he really means. The degree of structure of interviews will vary from highly structured to very unstructured depending on whether the researcher feels the need is for quantification, or for an understanding of meanings. This will depend on the theoretical perspective of the researcher – whether he or she adopts a more positivist or more interpretivist approach to understanding society. However, the other influences identified in figure 5.3 earlier in this chapter (page 270) will also affect the type of interview approach adopted.

Participant observation

Participant observation involves a researcher actually joining the group or community she or he is studying, and participating in its activities over a period of time. The researcher tries to become an accepted part of the group to see the world the way members of the group do.

The theoretical context of participant observation

Participant observation is typically used by interpretivists to develop an understanding of the world from the point of view of the subjects of the research. Interpretivists argue that a sociological understanding of society can only be gained by understanding people's meanings. They suggest the most effective way of doing this is for researchers to put themselves in the same position as those they are studying. The idea is to get 'inside' people's heads to see the world as they do and how they make sense of it. Rather than testing hypotheses against evidence and searching for the causes of social events, *verstehen* (an understanding developed through empathy or close identification) and qualitative research are what sociology should be about.

The problem for interpretivists who choose participant observation is not the positivist concern with scientific detachment, but how to become involved enough to understand what is going on as seen through the eyes of group members, and not letting the researcher's own values and prejudices distort the observations.

The stages of participant observation and related problems

The stages of participant observation can be summed up in terms of *getting in*, *staying in* and *getting out* of the group concerned.

Getting in

Joining a group raises many questions about the researcher's role. The researcher may adopt an **overt role** where the researcher declares his or her true identity to the group and the fact he or she is doing research. Alternatively, the researcher may adopt a **covert role** (concealing his or her role as a researcher), or a 'cover story' (partially declaring his or her role as a researcher, but concealing elements of it). To participate successfully, particularly if adopting a covert role, the researcher would need to share some of the personal characteristics of the group, such as age, gender or ethnicity.

A covert role   A covert role is likely to be adopted where criminal or highly deviant activities are involved, where overt researchers may be seen as a threat and unwelcome, such as the research by Humphreys on homosexuals in *The Tea Room Trade* (1970). The researcher who called himself 'James Patrick' (not his real name) in *A Glasgow Gang Observed* (1973) had to keep even his name secret, as he feared for his personal safety when studying violent gangs in Glasgow. A covert role may also be adopted where there is a risk of people's behaviour changing if they know they are being studied.

If a covert role is to be adopted and maintained, the researcher has little choice but to become a full participant in the group, because there is a risk of the research being ruined if the covert researcher's real identity and purpose are discovered. This may involve participation in illegal or unpleasant activities. It is also difficult to ask questions and take notes without arousing suspicion, and there are also moral and ethical concerns over observing and reporting on people's activities in secret, without obtaining their consent first.

An overt role   Adopting an overt role has the advantage that things might be hidden from a member of a group in a way that they might not be from a trusted and known outsider – since she or he will have nothing to gain in the group. Other advantages are that the researcher may be able to ask questions or interview people, and avoid participation in illegal or immoral behaviour, without arousing suspicion. Ethically and morally, it is right that people should be aware they are being studied.

Adopting an overt role does have problems though. For example, there is always the possibility that the behaviour of those being studied may be affected, raising questions over the validity of the research. As Whyte admitted in *Street Corner Society* (1955), quoting the gang leader 'Doc': 'You've slowed me up plenty since you've been down here. Now when I want to do something,

> An **overt role** is one where the researcher reveals to the group being studied his or her true identity and purpose.

> A **covert role** is one where the researcher conceals from the group being studied his or her true identify as a researcher, to gain access to the group and avoid disrupting its normal behaviour.

I have to think what Bill Whyte would want me to know about it and how I can explain it . . . Before I used to do things by instinct.'

After deciding the nature of the role, the next problem is getting access to the group. The presence of a stranger needs explanation, and researchers need to establish 'bona fide' credentials for getting access to the group. This may involve gaining friendships with key individuals. For example, Whyte was able to do his research because of his contacts with the gang leader 'Doc', and Patrick knew a gang member called 'Tim' who was able to get him into the gang and provide some protection for him. Participant observation in some contexts may require permission from higher authorities. This may mean the researcher is identified with authority, which may affect the behaviour of those being observed. For example, participant observation by an adult of students in a school will require the permission of the headteacher. This may mean the researcher is identified with the staff rather than the students. Paul Willis required permission to carry out his research in a secondary school in Wolverhapton, and on occasion found that the teachers expected him to take responsibility for disciplining the students, undermining his participant observer role.

Staying in

The observer has to develop a role which will involve gaining the trust and cooperation of those observed, to enable continued participation in and observation of the group. Initially this will involve learning, listening and getting a sense of what's going on: 'Initially, keep your eyes and ears open but keep your mouth shut' was Doc's advice to Whyte in *Street Corner Society*.

Problems of 'staying in' involve issues such as the need for extensive note-taking, which may be disruptive of the behaviour of the group, and how far to involve yourself without either losing the trust of the group or the objectivity of a researcher. Maintaining the trust of the group may involve getting involved with acts that the researcher doesn't agree with. Eileen Barker (1984), for example, gave a talk to the Moonies which reinforced the beliefs of one Moonie, despite Barker's protests that she didn't believe a word of what she had said. Staying in might also involve the observer with unpleasant acts or people, and possibly criminal behaviour. For example, Whyte actually did some 'personating' – voting twice in an election – as this was common practice in the group he was studying.

Getting out

'Getting out' of the group involves issues such as leaving the group without damaging relationships, becoming detached enough to write an impartial and accurate account, and making sure members of the group cannot be identified. There may be possible reprisals against the researcher if criminal activities are involved. Patrick faced threats to his personal safety after adopting a covert role in a Glasgow street gang and when his research was finally published in *A Glasgow Gang Observed* (1973).

Four classic studies of participant observation research

William Foote Whyte, *Street Corner Society* (1955)

This is a study of an Italian-American street corner gang in Boston in the United States. Whyte spent three and a half years in the area as a participant observer, including living in an Italian house with the group he was studying and he became a member of the gang.

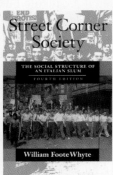

Laud Humphreys, *The Tearoom Trade: Impersonal Sex in Public Places* (1970)

Humphreys wanted to study the gay subculture, and observed the sexual activity of gay men in ninety public toilets (the 'tearooms') in American cities in the 1960s. He initially adopted a covert role as a 'gay voyeur' (someone who liked watching sex between men) and 'watch-queen' – a lookout for other men in case of police interference. Humphreys became an accepted part of the gay scene in Chicago, through visiting gay bars and other parts of the gay scene. Adopting a more overt role, he also interviewed some men. Humphreys noted the car numbers of many gay men who used the 'tearooms' and, through police contacts, was able to get their addresses and background information for interview research a year later as part of a health survey. Humphreys had to disguise his appearance during this survey so he wouldn't be recognized by men he had met.

James Patrick, *A Glasgow Gang Observed* (1973)

James Patrick used a covert role to study a violent and delinquent teenage Glasgow gang over a period of four months between October 1966 and January 1967.

Eileen Barker, *The Making of a Moonie* (1984)

This is a study of members of the Unification Church, a controversial religious sect headed by the Rev. Moon. Barker used overt participant observation over a period of six years, accepting the risk this could mean the people she was studying could be affected by her presence.

The strengths and weaknesses of participant observation

Table 5.6 summarizes participant observation's advantages and disadvantages.

Table 5.6 The strengths and weaknesses of participant observation

Advantages and strengths	Disadvantages and problems
● The sociologist gains first-hand knowledge of the group being studied. By building a relationship of trust, more in-depth, valid data can be obtained than by other research techniques. It is the method least likely to impose the sociologist's own views on the group being studied, therefore providing a more valid understanding of a social group. ● It allows hypotheses and theories to emerge from the research as it goes along. This enables the researcher to discover things she or he may not even have thought about before. As Whyte noted in *Street Corner Society*, 'As I sat and listened, I learned the answers to questions that I would not even have had the sense to ask if I had been	● Positivists argue there are problems with the validity and reliability of participant observation studies. For example, there is no real way of checking the findings, as there is no real evidence apart from the observations and interpretations of the researcher. What one researcher might regard as important may be missed or seen as unimportant by another. Even direct quotations from group members are often written down later, and may be only partially recalled – the researcher may remember what she or he *thought* was said. ● The presence of a researcher, if she or he is known to the group, may in some ways change the group's behaviour simply because they know they are being studied. This 'Hawthorne effect' may lead to problems for the validity of the research. For example, Whyte admits in *Street Corner Society* that knowledge of his presence and intentions may well have changed the behaviour of the gang.

cont . . .

Table 5.6 (continued)

Advantages and strengths	Disadvantages and problems
getting my information solely on an interviewing basis.' • It is the best way to get at the meanings that a social activity has for those involved in it, through seeing the world through the eyes of members of the group. • It may be the only possible method of research. For example, criminal and other deviant activities may be very difficult to investigate using other methods like interviews and questionnaires. • People can be studied in their normal social situation over a period of time, rather than the rather artificial and 'snapshot' context of a questionnaire or interview. • There is less of a chance that the people being studied can mislead the researcher than there is using other methods. This might therefore produce more valid data.	• There is a danger of the researcher becoming so involved with the group, seeing the world only as the group does, and developing such loyalty to it, that she or he may find it difficult to stand back and report findings in a neutral way. 'Going native' – becoming so involved that all detachment is lost – is a possible problem. The researcher may then stop being a participant observer and become a non-observing participant. • It is very time-consuming and expensive compared to other methods, as it involves the researcher being physically present in the group for long periods. • Because only a small group is studied, it may not be representative, so it is difficult to make generalizations. • There may be ethical issues if people do not know they are being observed, and therefore will not have the opportunity to give their consent to the research. • In personal terms, such research may be difficult for the researcher – for example, mixing with people they would rather not be with, getting involved in distasteful or illegal activities (in order to fit in), or even facing personal danger – as James Patrick did in *A Glasgow Gang Observed*. Humphreys was actually arrested during his research on gays.

Activity

'Of course it was known that I was not a Moonie. I never pretended that I was, or that I was likely to become one. I admit that I was sometimes evasive, and I certainly did not always say everything that was on my mind, but I cannot remember any occasion on which I consciously lied to a Moonie. Being known as a non-member had its disadvantages, but by talking to people who had left the movement I was able to check that I was not missing any of the internal information which was available to rank-and-file members. At the same time, being an outsider who was "inside" had enormous advantages. I was allowed (even, on certain occasions, expected) to ask questions that no member would have presumed to ask either his leaders or his peers. Furthermore, several Moonies who felt that their problems were not understood by the leaders, and yet would not have dreamed of being disloyal to the movement by talking to their parents or other outsiders, could confide in me because of the very fact that I was both organisationally and emotionally uninvolved.'

(Eileen Barker, *The Making of a Moonie*, Oxford: Blackwell, 1984)

1 With reference to the passage above, explain in your own words the advantages Barker found in adopting an overt role.

2 What ethical problems are involved in Barker's admission that she was 'sometimes evasive'?

3 Barker says, 'Being known as a non-member had its disadvantages.' What disadvantages do you think she might have come across (either read the research, or think and guess!).

4 Do you consider there are any circumstances in which adopting a covert role in research might be justified? Explain your answer.

5 Humphreys took car numbers of gay men who used public toilets to obtain gay sex and, through police contacts, was able to get their addresses and background information for interview research a year later as part of a health survey. What ethical difficulties do you think this poses?

 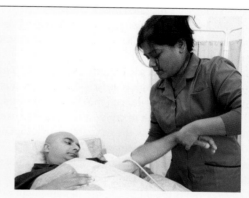

How would you set about a participant observation study of a primary school classroom or a hospital ward? Make a list of the things you would need to consider. For example, what kind of observer role might you adopt (overt or covert)? How would you get in and stay in? What steps would you take to ensure your research was valid? What ethical issues would you need to consider?

Reliability and validity in participant observation

Positivists tend to be critical of participant observation because they argue the data obtained is rarely quantified and is unreliable. Participant observation depends heavily on the sensitivity, skills, personality and personal characteristics of the observer, and this makes it very difficult to replicate a participant observation study in order to check the findings. As Whyte said in *Street Corner Society*: 'To some extent my approach must be unique to myself, to the particular situation, and to the state of knowledge existing when I began research.'

Participant observation is always to some extent selective observation – the researcher's interpretation of the significant and important things happening in a group. What one participant observer reports or interprets as significant may not be seen as such by another. Positivists would ask how interpretivists can prove they have interpreted the attitudes and experiences of others correctly. Participant observers use devices like extensive note-taking to accumulate evidence to help to ensure that their research is reliable as well as valid and can be checked by others. Other sociologists are, though, ultimately left to rely on the memory, observational and interpretive skills of the researcher, and this raises problems for the validity and reliability of the research that are difficult to resolve.

Activity

1 Identify and explain *two* criticisms positivists might make of participant observation as a research method.

2 Identify and explain *two* reasons why interpretivists might argue that participant observation is the most effective method of understanding and explaining social life.

3 Suggest *two* reasons sociologists who employ participant observation might give to claim their work is as 'scientific' as any positivist research.

4 Suggest all the ways you can that the social characteristics of the researcher might make it difficult to conduct participant observation.

5 With examples, explain the advantages of adopting (a) a covert role and (b) an overt role in participant observation.

6 What are the ethical and moral issues which make participant observation difficult, particularly if using a covert role?

7 Explain what is meant by the risk in participant observation that 'the researcher may stop being a participant observer and become a non-observing participant'.

8 Look at the weaknesses and disadvantages of participant observation listed earlier. Suggest ways that a skilled participant observer might be able to overcome the problems identified.

9 Much participant observation research has been done on deviant groups. Suggest reasons why this might be the case.

10 In about one and half sides of A4 paper, answer the following essay question: *Assess the usefulness of participant observation in sociological research.*

Non-participant observation

Some sociological research is carried out by observation alone (without the researcher participating). The main reason for this is to reduce or eliminate the risk that people will be affected by the presence of a researcher or new member of their social group. It may also be used when groups might be unwilling to cooperate in research (though this raises ethical issues). Non-participant observation also allows sociologists to observe people in their normal social situations, and avoid the Hawthorne effect. This can only be achieved fully when the observation is carried out without the knowledge of the observed, for example from a distance, by blending into the background, through one-way glass or using video cameras. If the observer is visibly present, even though not participating, there is still the possibility that his or her presence will influence what is happening.

A problem with this method is that it does not allow the researcher to investigate the meanings people attach to the behaviour that is being observed. The data produced may well reflect simply the assumptions and interpretations of the researcher, raising serious issues over the reliability and validity of the data.

An example of non-participant observation

Flanders (1970) studied interaction in classrooms. He produced a list of ten categories of interaction, and he then observed lessons and ticked the category that best described what was happening at particular times. These categories, with explanations, are listed below. Categories 1–7 are concerned with what the teacher is saying or doing, and categories 8 and 9 with what students are saying or doing.

1 *Accepts feelings* (teacher accepts an attitude or feeling of a student).
2 *Praises or encourages* (teacher praises/encourages student behaviour, including jokes, smiles, nods of the head and similar teacher responses).
3 *Accepts/uses idea of student* (teacher accepts and uses/builds on/develops ideas suggested by a student).
4 *Asks question* (teacher uses own ideas to ask questions of a student, to which an answer is expected).
5 *Lecture* (teacher gives own facts, opinions and explanations – the teacher, not student, makes the first move).
6 *Gives direction* (teacher gives commands or orders to student).
7 *Criticizes or justifies authority* (teacher criticizes student to make student behaviour more acceptable, or justifies teacher's own behaviour/actions).
8 *Student response* (student responds to teacher's questions or ideas).
9 *Student initiated* (student makes the first move to express his or her own ideas/opinions, asks teacher questions or introduces a new topic).
10 *Silence or confusion* (a category to describe times when interaction can't be easily understood or categorized by the observer, such as periods of silence or confusion).

The observer then produces a tally chart to show what type of interaction (1–10) is going on in the classroom in particular time periods, for example every minute of a lesson. This produces a quantitative account of teacher–student interaction during the course of a lesson, which can then be used for comparison with other teachers and lessons.

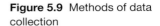

Figure 5.9 Methods of data collection

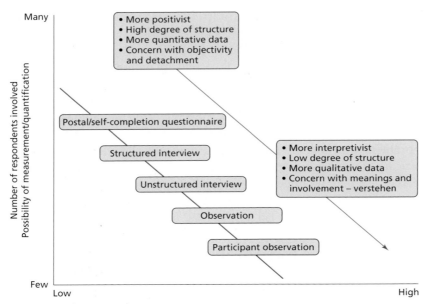

Activity

Refer to figure 5.9

1 According to figure 5.9, which method of data collection involves the largest number of respondents?
2 Which method has the highest level of personal involvement of the researcher with the respondents?
3 Which method, apart from observational methods, provides the most qualitative data?
4 What method is most likely to be used by interpretivists?
5 Identify *four* advantages and *four* problems with research using postal or other self-completion questionnaires involving large numbers of individuals.
6 Identify and explain *four* difficulties that might face researchers who have a high level of personal involvement with those they are researching.

Longitudinal studies

Most sociological researchers study a group of people for a short period of time, producing a 'snapshot' of events. It is therefore difficult to study change over time.

The longitudinal study attempts to overcome this problem by selecting a sample – sometimes called a 'panel' – from whom data are collected at

Table 5.7 The strengths and weaknesses of longitudinal studies

Advantages and strengths	Disadvantages and problems
• They make it possible to study change over time, and provide detail on the changes that occur. • As long as the sample remains the same, it may be possible to discover the causes of changes. By comparing earlier studies with later ones, researchers can be sure that the changes measured do not result from changes in the composition of the sample. • They may provide more valid data in some circumstances. Studies which ask people about past events rely on human memories, and people may also distort or exaggerate past events. Longitudinal studies help to avoid this, as there are previous studies to refer back to.	• It is necessary to select a sample who are available and willing to assist in the research project over a long period. However, it is likely that the original sample size will drop as people die, can't be traced, or become unwilling to cooperate. This may reduce the representativeness of the sample. • Those in the sample are conscious of the fact that they are being studied. This may change their behaviour because they think more carefully about what they do (especially if they know they may be questioned about it in the future). This Hawthorne effect may bring into question the validity of the findings. • There is the problem of cost. Most funding agencies are unwilling to take on a commitment over a long period of time.

Examples of longitudinal studies

• J. W. B. Douglas studied the educational progress of a sample of children through their school careers, studying them at the ages of 8, 11 and 16. The findings of Douglas and his colleagues were published in *The Home and the School* (1964) and *All our Future* (1968).

• The census, carried out every ten years since 1801 (with the exception of 1941), is in effect a longitudinal study of the entire population. This enables researchers to trace broad patterns of social change, and to make comparisons between the social conditions of one period and another.

• Parker et al. (1998) studied illegal drug use among 1,125 young people aged 14 for five years between 1991 and 1996, using a combination of self-completion questionnaires and interviews.

---

regular intervals over a period of years. Table 5.7 summarizes the method's advantages and disadvantages.

Case studies and life histories

A case study involves the intensive study of a single example of whatever it is the sociologist wishes to investigate. A case study can be carried out using

How might a case study or a life history provide insights for sociological researchers?

almost any method of research, though the more interpretivist, qualitative methods are more common, such as in-depth unstructured interviews or participant observation. Life histories are case studies which usually focus on one individual or one small group. Life histories are most commonly obtained through in-depth unstructured interviews and guided conversation, backed up with reference to personal documents such as diaries and letters. Great importance is placed on the person's own interpretations and explanations of her or his behaviour.

Case studies and life histories do not claim to be representative. However, researchers using these approaches do claim that an in-depth account of a single example can make an important contribution to our knowledge about an area. Table 5.8 lists the strengths and weaknesses of these methods.

An example of a case study

Learning to Labour (1977) by Paul Willis was a case study of a group of male students in a single school in Wolverhampton. It stimulated widespread debate about the relationship between schooling and capitalism, how students resist schooling, and the formation of counter-school subcultures, and encouraged the development of theories by other sociologists.

Table 5.8 The strengths and weaknesses of case studies and life histories

Advantages and strengths	Disadvantages and problems
• A particular study can be used to test the usefulness of theories of social life. Willis's study, for example, challenged previous approaches to explaining how working-class young people got working-class jobs through the education system. • They may be useful in generating new hypotheses which can then be tested by further research. • They enable the researcher to see the world from the point of view of the individual or group, and give far more detail and understanding than can be obtained by surveys or quantitative measurements.	• They may not be representative, and it may therefore not be possible to generalize on the basis of their findings. • They may not be reliable or valid. Life histories view the past from the standpoint of the present. This raises questions about the accuracy of recall of facts, and the benefit of hindsight might generate a reinterpretation of the past. This might raise questions about the validity of such research.

Methodological pluralism and triangulation

It is easy to get the impression that sociological research is divided into two opposing camps, with positivists pursuing methods generating quantitative data, and interpretivists using methods generating qualitative data.

In the real world of practical research, most sociologists will use a range of methods to collect a range of different kinds of data, regardless of whether they are quantitative or qualitative. They will use whatever methods seem best suited and most practical for producing the fullest possible data to understand the subject being studied. This use of a variety of methods is known as **methodological pluralism**, and is very useful for increasing sociological understanding of social life.

Sociologists will also often use a variety of methods, and different types of data, to check that the results obtained by a particular method are valid and reliable. For example, participant observation might be used to investigate further, or check the accuracy or validity of statistical (quantitative) evidence collected by questionnaires in a survey, or to observe to check whether people act as they said they did in an interview. This approach of using a range of methods (usually two or three) to check findings is called **triangulation**.

Methodological pluralism and triangulation frequently go hand in hand, because the use of several methods producing different types of data (methodological pluralism) not only gives a fuller picture of what is being explained but, *at the same time*, is a valuable approach for checking the reliability and validity of research findings (triangulation).

Methodological pluralism is the term used to describe the use by sociologists of a variety of methods in a single piece of research.

Triangulation is the use of two or more research methods in a single piece of research to check the reliability and validity of research evidence.

Examples of these two approaches are considered below:

- Humphreys in *The Tearoom Trade* (1970) used a combination of questionnaires, unstructured interviews and participant observation.
- Eileen Barker, in her 1984 study of the Moonies, used participant observation (lasting six years) to gain first-hand insight, living in various Moonie centres in Britain and abroad. Barker supplemented this with in-depth interviews to investigate the background of individual Moonies, and to help form hypotheses to guide her participant observation, and used questionnaires to obtain further information from a larger sample.
- Hobson's (2000) research on teacher training courses used questionnaires to obtain the views of over 300 trainee teachers in four teacher training institutions. He supplemented this with informal interviews with twenty trainee teachers to gain in-depth knowledge of the trainee teachers' views. Participant observation was also used to observe the training process and the trainees' responses to it. As a result, Hobson 'discovered things that I might not have thought to ask or have been told by trainees through the use of other methods'. He was able to check the responses of individual trainees in closed questionnaires with what they said in the interviews and how they acted on the training course. Hobson also used secondary data in his research. In this way, Hobson argues, the use of several methods enabled him to check the validity of his findings and produce a fuller and more accurate picture of teacher training courses.

Figure 5.10 illustrates a range of possible uses of methodological pluralism and triangulation.

Activity

Refer to figure 5.10

1 Imagine you were doing some research on how household tasks were divided up between men, women and children in the home, and what they each thought about it. Suggest at least three different methods you might use to collect the information, saying what information you might expect to collect using each method.

2 Give examples of ways you might apply each of the main uses of methodological pluralism and triangulation suggested in figure 5.10 to the research area in question 1. Write a brief sentence explaining each use, in each case drawing on an example based on the research area in question 1.

3 Explain *two* ways in each case that methodological pluralism and triangulation might help to improve the (a) validity, (b) reliability, and (c) representativeness of a piece of research.

Figure 5.10 The uses of methodological pluralism and triangulation

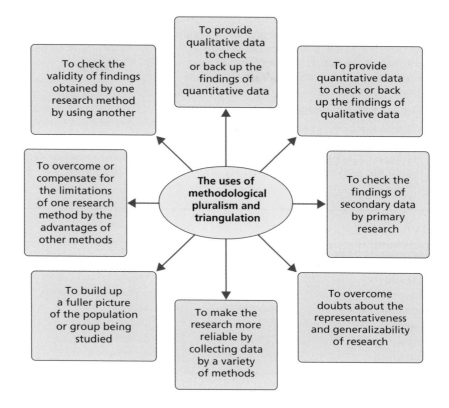

Figure contents:

Central: **The uses of methodological pluralism and triangulation**

- To provide qualitative data to check or back up the findings of quantitative data
- To provide quantitative data to check or back up the findings of qualitative data
- To check the validity of findings obtained by one research method by using another
- To check the findings of secondary data by primary research
- To overcome or compensate for the limitations of one research method by the advantages of other methods
- To overcome doubts about the representativeness and generalizability of research
- To build up a fuller picture of the population or group being studied
- To make the research more reliable by collecting data by a variety of methods

CHAPTER SUMMARY

After studying this chapter, you should be able to:

- discuss a range of theoretical and practical considerations that sociologists consider in conducting research

- explain the difference between positivism and interpretivism, and how these two approaches use different research methods

- distinguish between quantitative and qualitative data, and the advantages and limitations of each

- identify the difference between primary and secondary sources, and the strengths and limitations of the data obtained from each

- explain the problems of reliability and validity of research evidence

- identify the ethical considerations sociologists must consider when carrying out social research

- explain the advantages, uses and limitations of official statistics, with examples

- explain the uses and problems of the experimental method in sociology

- explain how the comparative method might be used as an alternative to the experimental one

- explain the main features and stages of the social survey, and the various sampling methods sociologists use to gain representative samples

- explain the uses, strengths and weaknesses of different types of questionnaires and interviews, including the problems of imposition and the validity and reliability of these methods
- explain fully the problem of interviewer bias
- explain the uses, strengths and weaknesses of participant observation as a research method, including theoretical and practical problems, and the issues of validity and reliability

- discuss the strengths and weaknesses of longitudinal studies, case studies and life histories
- explain what is meant by methodological pluralism and triangulation, and why sociologists might want to use a range of methods in sociological research
- carry out small-scale research of your own drawing on the various methods outlined in this chapter

KEY TERMS

covert role	interviewer bias	quantitative data	social facts
ethics	methodological pluralism	reliability/replication	survey population
Hawthorne effect	overt role	representative sample	surveys
hypothesis	pilot survey	sample	triangulation
imposition problem	positivism	sampling frame	validity
interpretivism	primary data	sampling methods	verstehen
	qualitative data	secondary data	victim survey

6 Education

Contents

Key Issues	327
Education in Britain before the 1970s	327
Comprehensive schools and selection	328
The case against selection: the advantages of comprehensive education	329
The case for selection: criticisms of comprehensive education	331
Education from 1988 onwards: the free market in education	332
The marketization of education	332
The key aims of educational change	335
Vocational education	335
Raising standards	336
Equality of educational opportunity and helping the most disadvantaged groups	339
Criticisms of the free market in education, vocational education and other recent changes	340
The middle class has gained the most	340
Student needs at risk and social divisions increased	340
Specialist schools and selection by ability	341
The unfairness of league tables	341
Difficulties in improving schools and colleges	342
'Dumbing down'	342
Problems with the National Curriculum and testing	342
Inadequate vocational education	343
Sociological perspectives on education	344
The functionalist perspective on education	344
Marxist perspectives on education	348
A comparison of functionalist and Marxist perspectives on education	353
Interactionist perspectives on education	355
Is contemporary Britain a meritocracy?	355
Natural Intelligence or IQ	356
Social class differences in educational achievement	357
Explaining social class differences in educational achievement	359
Gender differences in educational achievement: the underachievement of boys	381
Problems remaining for girls	383
Explaining gender differences in education	383
Some concluding comments on gender and underachievement	390
Ethnicity and educational achievement	393
Explanations for ethnic group differences in education	394
Some words of caution	399
Private education: the independent schools	401
The case for independent schools	402
The case against independent schools	403
Elite education and elite jobs	403
Researching education	406
Collecting information on education	406
Examples of research	409
Chapter summary	413
Key terms	413
Exam question	414

CHAPTER

6 Education

> **KEY ISSUES**
>
> - Education in Britain before the 1970s
> - Education reforms since 1988
> - Vocational education
> - Sociological perspectives on education
> - Is Britain a meritocracy?
> - Social class differences in educational achievement – working-class underachievement
> - Compensatory education and positive discrimination
> - Gender differences in educational achievement – the underachievement of boys
> - Ethnic group differences in educational achievement
> - Private education
> - Researching education

Education is a major social institution, and schools in Britain command a captive audience of virtually all children between the ages of 5 and 16. During this period of compulsory schooling, children spend about half of the time they are awake at school during term time – about 15,000 hours of their lives. School is therefore a major agency of secondary socialization in advanced industrial societies.

Education in Britain before the 1970s

The 1944 Education Act established three types of secondary school – grammar, technical, and secondary modern schools. These three types of secondary school became known as the tripartite system. It was thought that children had three different sorts of ability, which were fixed by the age of 11, were unlikely to change, and could be reliably and accurately measured at age

327

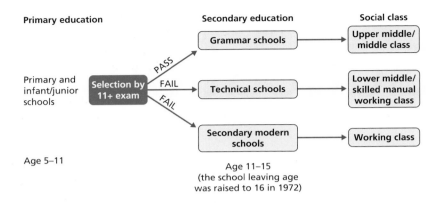

Figure 6.1 The tripartite system after the 1944 Education Act

11 by a special intelligence quotient test (IQ test). This became known as the 11+ exam. Until the 1960s, all children went first to primary schools (as they do now) but then were selected by whether they passed or failed the 11+ examination to go to one of the three types of secondary school. The 15–20 per cent of children with the best 11+ exam results went to grammar schools, with most children going to secondary modern schools. There were hardly any technical schools established.

During the 1960s the tripartite system came under increasing attack. The 11+ exam was seen as an unfair, unreliable and inaccurate selection test, which disadvantaged children from working-class homes and damaged the self-esteem and educational opportunities of children who failed to win a place at a grammar school. Secondary modern schools were seen as inferior, second-rate schools, with grammar schools having higher status and offering better life chances to their pupils. Figure 6.1 shows the tripartite system, and the social classes young people were being prepared for as adults.

Research in the 1950s and 1960s suggested that the talent, ability and potential of many children in the secondary modern schools were being wasted. It was felt that this wasted talent could be better developed in comprehensive schools, which accept pupils of all abilities. As a result, in the 1960s the tripartite system was abolished in most of the country, and by the 1970s most children attended comprehensive schools.

Comprehensive schools and selection

Comprehensive education abolished both selection at age 11 by the 11+ exam and the three types of secondary school. Children in most areas now, regardless of their ability, generally transfer to the same type of school at the age of 11, with no selection by examination. Around nine out of ten young people in the UK in 2007 were attending some form of comprehensive school, with just 233 state grammar schools remaining.

'True' comprehensive schools have no selection by ability at all, and children of all abilities are admitted to the same types of school and taught in mixed ability classes. While most schools are now comprehensive schools in that they do not select the majority of the pupils they admit by ability, there are different types of comprehensive school, and some selection by ability does continue in the education system and, through streaming, in many comprehensive schools as well.

The issue of selection by ability for secondary education, and whether this is necessary to give young people the most suitable form of secondary education, are still hotly disputed matters. In 2005, secondary 'specialist' schools were allowed to select up to 10 per cent of their pupils by ability, and there has been a return to streaming and a move away from mixed ability teaching. Policy-makers of all political parties in the early years of the twenty-first century were increasingly talking of a return to selection for secondary education, based on student attitudes, aptitudes, interests, capabilities and skills.

That the issue of selection is still a very 'live' and controversial issue was shown in 2007 by a huge row in the Conservative Party, traditionally a defender of grammar schools and selection by ability. David Willetts, the Conservative education spokesperson in Parliament, said in a speech that 'selection at age 11 did not work or help social mobility, and disadvantaged poorer parents'. He was supported by the Conservative Party leader David Cameron, who said that selective education was 'unpopular with parents. They don't want children divided into successes and failures at 11.' This caused such a row in the Conservative Party that Willetts was sacked, and Cameron had to backtrack on his comments very quickly.

School and college 'league tables' and the judging of schools and colleges on their results (see later in this chapter) constantly raise the issue of whether students should be selected by ability so some schools get the best, most able students in an area.

The case against selection: the advantages of comprehensive education

Opportunities remain open

In comprehensive schools, the possibility of educational success and obtaining qualifications remains open throughout a child's school career, since moving between streams and classes within one school is easier and more likely to happen than moving between different types of school in a selective system.

Late developers benefit

Late developers, whose intelligence and ability improve later in life, can be catered for better in the comprehensive system, rather than having their opportunities limited at an early age.

Middle-class parents are generally better placed to coach a less bright child, who might therefore have once got a grammar school place at age 11, than parents from a less well-off background with a late-developing bright child, who might have failed to get a grammar school place. Comprehensives cater for both, and disadvantage neither.

More get better qualifications

Fewer students leave school without any qualifications in the comprehensive system, and more obtain higher standards than under selective systems, such as where grammar schools continue to exist or where there are other forms of selection by ability.

More social mixing and fewer social divisions

As all children attend the same type of school, there is more social mixing between students from homes of different social class and ethnic backgrounds, and this helps to overcome divisions between different social groups. Selection by ability in education often benefits the middle class, which dominates selective schools and the top streams in streamed comprehensive schools. The reasons for this are discussed later in this chapter.

Reduced risk of the self-fulfilling prophecy

Children are less likely to be branded as 'failures' at an early age, lowering their self-esteem (how they feel about themselves and their ability) and avoiding the damaging effects of the **self-fulfilling prophecy**. This is discussed later in this chapter.

Benefits of mixed ability teaching

Where all pupils of the same age, regardless of their ability, are taught in the same type of school and in the same classroom (mixed ability teaching) the more intelligent pupils can have a stimulating influence on the less able, and the problems created by the self-fulfilling prophecy are easier to avoid. Recent research has shown that mixed ability teaching has no negative effect on the 'high flyers', improves the performance of the less able, and makes no difference to a school's overall examination performance.

More choice and opportunity

The large size of many comprehensive schools, designed to contain all pupils in an area, means there are more teachers teaching a wider range of subjects

> The **self-fulfilling prophecy** is the process whereby people act in response to predictions of the way they will behave, thereby making the prediction come true. In education, this means that when testing and selection by ability predicts that a student won't do well, the prediction actually comes true, because of the low expectations of teachers, and the consequent poor image students have of their own ability.

to meet the needs of pupils of all abilities, with a great variety of equipment and facilities. This benefits all pupils and gives them greater choices and opportunities to develop their talents, to reach their full potential and gain some educational qualifications.

Benefits for working-class students

Selective schools and streamed comprehensives can be much like the tripartite system, with working-class students less likely to gain places in selective schools, and more likely to be placed in the bottom streams. True comprehensive education avoids this.

The case for selection: criticisms of comprehensive education

'Creaming off'

Where selective (grammar) schools continue to exist alongside comprehensive schools, as happens in some areas, they 'cream off' the most able students, so the so-called comprehensives are not true comprehensives at all, as they lack the brightest students, and are little different from the secondary moderns of the tripartite system.

'High flyers' are held back

Because comprehensive schools contain pupils of all abilities, brighter children are held back by the slower pace of learning of the less able. Critics argue this wouldn't happen with selection, as 'high flyers' are taught in the same school or streams within a school.

Selection by ability can have harmful effects on the self-esteem of students, and create a self-fulfilling prophecy

Overlooked talents and discipline problems

The large size of some comprehensives, containing all students in an area, may make it impossible for staff to know all pupils personally, and this may create discipline problems and the talents of individuals may not be noticed and developed.

Stretching the most able

Selection by ability through streaming or setting (rather than mixed ability teaching) in the same school means brighter students can be 'stretched', rather than being held back by slower learners who take up the teacher's time, and who may be disruptive because they are unable to cope with the work. Many so-called comprehensive schools are not true comprehensives, as they stream or set pupils, and this is really a form of selection in the same school.

Activity

1 Do you think young people should be selected by ability for secondary schools? What arguments would you put forward both for and against the idea of selection by ability?
2 Do some people develop their talents and abilities later in life? Can you think of examples from your own experience of people who seem to have become 'more intelligent' as they grew older?

Education from 1988 onwards: the free market in education

While the comprehensive system has succeeded in improving overall educational standards, the comprehensive system came under increasing criticism in the 1980s and 1990s for not meeting the needs of employers and industry closely enough, for not reaching high enough standards, and for failing to benefit the most disadvantaged, poorest groups in society. As a result, attempts have been made to tie all parts of the education system more closely to the needs of industry and business, to raise standards, and to raise the educational standards of the most disadvantaged groups.

The marketization of education

The 1988 Education Reform Act was the most important piece of educational legislation since the 1944 Education Act. It reduced local control of the education system, for example by teachers and local education authorities. At the same time, it increased control by the central government over some aspects of schools, like the National Curriculum, testing and the inspection of schools, but it also handed over more control to school governors, head-teachers and the consumers of education – parents and students – in the running of schools.

These changes were based on free market principles, in what has become known as the **marketization** of education.

Since 1988, schools and colleges have gained a lot more control over how they run their institutions, and they compete with each other for students. Parents and students now have a wider choice of which schools or colleges to attend, instead of being obliged to go to their local one. It was thought that by increasing parental choice and competition for students, schools and colleges would become more efficient and accountable to parents and students. Giving parents a choice as 'consumers' of education in a free market – rejecting some schools or colleges in favour of others, in the same way that people choose between competing supermarkets or products – was expected to drive up education standards. Poorly performing schools or colleges would risk losing money as student numbers fell, and might face closure, while those that performed well would grow and improve even more. Marketization was originally an idea of the New Right, but the marke-tization of education now appears to be accepted by all the main political parties.

Table 6.1 overleaf illustrates some of the main features and policies linked to the marketization of education since 1988, and a number of these are explained and discussed in the pages that follow.

> **Marketization** is the process whereby services, like education or health, that were previously controlled and run by the state have government or local council control reduced, and become subject to the free market forces of supply and demand, based on competition and consumer choice.

The free market in education has made schooling a bit like supermarket shopping, where parents can 'read the labels' and pick and choose the type and quality of school they want. However, middle-class parents and young people have gained the most benefits from the marketization of education. Why do you think this is?

Table 6.1 The marketization of education

Policy	Aim
National testing (SATs and other exams) and target-setting, with publication of the results	• to drive up standards and show which schools and colleges are performing the best • to give parents and students the information to choose the best schools and colleges • to encourage competition between schools and colleges
National 'league tables' of exam results	• to give parents and students information to choose the best schools and colleges by ranking them by their exam performance
Local Management of Schools (schools mainly run by headteachers and school governors), and independence for further education and sixth-form colleges	• to give schools and colleges more independence to control their own affairs, so they can improve quality and results to compete for students in the education marketplace
Formula funding (money allocated per student enrolled)	• to reward schools and colleges that succeed in attracting customers (students) – those who succeed in the education market will get the most money and be able to expand and improve further. Those who don't will risk going out of business (being closed)
Parental choice and open enrolment: parents have more choice of schools, and schools have to accept students if they have vacancies	• to enable consumers (parents and students) to choose in the education marketplace, and allow the most popular schools to expand and fill every place they have.
Establishment of specialist schools – specializing in up to two out of ten particular areas (arts, business and enterprise, engineering, humanities, languages, mathematics and computing, music, science, sports and technology)	• to improve standards by making schools expert in certain areas, in partnership with private business • to provide parents and students with a choice of schools which serve their children's needs and interests best • to bring in extra funds and private business expertise
Office for Standards in Education (Ofsted), to inspect schools, with published, publicly available Ofsted reports	• to inspect schools and colleges and publicly report on them, making sure they are doing a good job • to encourage improvements, and to close schools of poor quality that don't improve • to enable parents to identify the best schools to choose from
Business sponsorship of schools, and private financing and running of some state schools	• to bring in more money for successful schools • to use private business expertise to help schools compete in the education market, and improve standards

There has been a rapid and bewildering number of changes in education since 1988. The following sections examine some of the main changes, and some will be referred to during the course of this chapter.

The key aims of educational change

The move to comprehensive schooling, and more recent changes in the education system, have been driven by four main aims:

- Economic efficiency: developing the talents of young people to improve the skills of the labour force so Britain maintains a successful position in the world economy.
- Making the education system meet the needs of industry and employers through more emphasis on vocational education.
- Raising educational standards.
- Creating **equality of educational opportunity** in a **meritocratic society**, and establishing a fairer society by opening up opportunities for secondary and further/higher education to the working class and other disadvantaged groups.

Vocational education

The emphasis on making education meet the needs of industry, and preparing young people for work, is known as vocational education. A key feature of this has been on improving the quality of the basic skills of the workforce, with a particular focus on the 14–18 age group. The aim has been to develop the talents of young people to improve the skills of the labour force so Britain maintains a successful position in the world economy, and to produce a more flexible labour force, fitting education more to the needs of employers. Measures to achieve this have included:

- Work experience programmes for pupils in school years 10 and 11 to ease the transition from school to work, and help/encourage them to get jobs successfully and carry them out well, with a better understanding of work and the economy.
- More educational courses, and government training schemes for those leaving school, which are more closely related to the world of work, and concerned more with learning work-related skills. For example, work-based NVQs (National Vocational Qualifications) and school/college-based GNVQs (General National Vocational Qualifications) were developed to provide nationally approved and recognized qualifications for vocational courses. Vocational GCSEs and Applied GCEs (vocational 'A' levels) were intended as vocational alternatives to academic GCSEs and A levels.

Equality of educational opportunity is the idea that every child, regardless of his or her social class background, ability to pay school fees, ethnic background, gender or disability, should have an equal chance of doing as well as his or her ability will allow.

A **meritocracy** (or meritocratic society) is a society where occupational positions (jobs) and pay are allocated on the basis purely of people's individual talents, abilities, qualifications and skills – their individual merits. In Britain today, this nearly always means educational qualifications.

- An expansion of post-16 education and training, with coordination and funding through business-dominated Learning and Skills Councils.
- A stronger emphasis on key skills in the use and application of number, and in communication and information technology. These are the skills that most employers find that school leavers lack, with poor communication skills mentioned by almost two-thirds of employers in 2004 as one of the most frequent problems they face in recruiting staff.

All these changes were designed to produce a more flexible labour force, fitting education to the needs of employers.

Raising standards

More money for schools, more nursery education, and smaller primary school classes

The Labour government, first elected in 1997, established a national maximum class size of thirty for all 5, 6 and 7 year olds, and allocated huge amounts of extra money to schools to enable them to provide the staff, materials, buildings and facilities to enable them to provide a high quality learning environment for children, and thereby improve standards. All children aged 3 and 4 now get a guarantee of five half-days of nursery education a week.

Activity-based learning

Teaching has become more student centred and activity based, with the aim of developing students' skills and understanding. GCSE, AS and A levels, GNVQ and applied GCEs have become more activity- and skills-based exams. This has led to much better exam results among 16–18 year olds. Modular exams (which students can take in parts) aim to ensure that all students can obtain some qualifications by allowing them to resit parts of a course. AS levels aim to encourage 16–18 year-olds to study a broader range of subjects, and make them more flexible and less specialized. In 2008, coursework was dropped from most AS & A level courses, as it was thought there was too much assessment and that the courses were not demanding enough, or stretching the most able students.

The National Curriculum, national testing, target-setting and the literacy and numeracy hours

To improve standards across the country, and ensure all students had access to the same high quality curriculum, the 1988 Education Reform Act set up the National Curriculum, a range of subjects and set programmes of study that must be followed by all school students. There are attainment targets (goals

National testing through SATs, even for young children, has been one method used to improve and check on the quality and standards of education

which all teachers are expected to enable students to reach), with testing (the Standard Assessment Tests or SATs) at ages 7, 11 and 14 (Key Stages 1, 2 and 3) to ensure these targets are met. In addition, all primary schools (Key Stages 1 and 2) must have a literacy hour and a numeracy hour each week, to improve basic skills in these areas.

National 'league tables'

Schools and colleges are now required to publish tables of testing (SATs) and exam results (GCSE, AS level, A level, applied GCE and GNVQ). These have become known as 'league tables' and are designed to give parents and students an idea of how well schools and colleges are doing so they can choose the best. By encouraging competition for students between schools and colleges, these league tables aim to raise overall standards.

Local management of schools (LMS)

Local management of schools (LMS) gives schools (rather than the local education authority – county and city councils in most areas) much greater control of their budgets, and of a wide range of other aspects of the school.

Further education and sixth form colleges have also become completely independent of the local education authority. This is designed to make schools and colleges more responsive to local needs and the wishes of parents. These changes aimed to encourage schools and colleges to run on market principles, where they compete with one another for students and therefore funds.

Formula funding

Schools and colleges are funded by a formula which is largely based on the number of students they attract. It was thought this would drive up standards by rewarding successful schools and colleges that attracted students (and hence money), giving less successful schools and colleges the incentive to improve.

Open enrolment and parental preference

Parents are now allowed to express a preference for the school of their choice, and a school cannot refuse a pupil a place if it has vacancies. This was designed to raise the quality of teaching and exam results by encouraging competition between schools. Unpopular schools run the risk of losing pupils and therefore money, and the government has taken steps to close what it sees as 'failing' schools which are unpopular with parents and where exam and test results, and standards of behaviour, are poor. In most cases, parents don't really have much choice of school, as places are usually filled up by those living in the school's 'priority area' (the area from which children are admitted first).

More information for parents

To help parents to choose the best schools and encourage schools to improve their standards and performance, schools now have to provide, by law, a wide range of information for parents, including the standards achieved, examination and National Curriculum test results, details of the school budget, the amount of authorized and unauthorized absence, including truancy, and what school leavers do after they leave school.

Specialist schools and selection by ability

Since the early 2000s there has been a huge growth in the number of 'specialist schools', those with the highest status being the city academies. These schools have a special focus on their chosen subject area, such as technology, languages, business and enterprise, or music. These are an attempt to move away from what were called 'bog standard' comprehensives. These schools have to raise money from private business, but they then get extra money from the government and are allowed to select up to 10 per cent of their pupils by 'aptitude' (ability) in the specialist subject. It is thought that by specializing these schools will raise standards in their specialist subjects, and that selection by ability will raise standards, not just in the specialist subjects, but across the whole school curriculum.

The Office for Standards in Education (Ofsted)

The Office for Standards in Education (Ofsted) was established to conduct inspections of all state schools, further education colleges and local education authorities at least once every six years. This aimed to ensure schools, colleges and local education authorities were doing a good job, by publishing their inspection reports and requiring action to be taken on any weaknesses identified.

Equality of educational opportunity and helping the most disadvantaged groups

The Labour government, first elected in 1997, emphasized the need to create equality of educational opportunity for all, particularly focusing on the most deprived and most disadvantaged areas where educational results were poor. This was carried out through a number of measures, including schemes such as SureStart to ensure children in disadvantaged areas had the best start in life, and more money and better-paid teachers were provided for schools in the poorest areas through schemes such as Excellence in Cities and Education Action Zones. According to a 2003 Ofsted report, these schemes had only mixed success, and seemed more successful in improving standards among primary, rather than secondary school students. These measures are considered a little more later in this chapter.

Activity

1. Identify and explain *four* ways in which the educational reforms from the late 1980s to the 2000s have introduced market forces into the education system.
2. Is competition between schools and colleges a good thing? Identify and explain its advantages and disadvantages.
3. Do you think the recent changes in education will succeed in raising standards? Go through each of the changes since the 1980s, and explain why they might or might not improve standards.
4. Do you think schools alone can be held responsible for exam results and truancy rates? What other factors might influence how good a school's exam results are, and whether pupils play truant or not?
5. What should the aims of schooling be? Do you think schools and colleges should be mainly concerned with meeting the needs of business and industry, and fitting people into the job market? Or should they be concerned mainly with the development of individuals' talents and interests? Give reasons for your answer.

Criticisms of the free market in education, vocational education and other recent changes

While the changes in education may have given individual schools more control of their affairs, and made them more responsive to parents, this has been at the expense of greater central government control, such as through the National Curriculum, and cooperation between schools has been replaced with competition. The development of the free market in education, increased intervention by central government, the attempt to raise standards and the more vocational emphasis in education have been very controversial, and these changes have been criticized in a number of ways. The main criticisms are outlined below.

The middle class has gained the most

Middle-class parents have been able to make the greatest use of parental choice and open enrolment, and it is they who are better placed to make the most effective use of the education system and exploit the new system to their children's advantage. The educational system remains socially selective, and the higher the social class of the parents, the better are the schools to which they send their children. Because of their own higher levels of income and education, and higher levels of social and cultural capital (discussed later in this chapter), they are better placed than many working-class parents to:

- shop around and find the best schools
- understand and compare schools in the league tables
- know more about how to assess school Ofsted inspection reports and what constitutes a 'good school'
- afford more easily to move into the priority areas of the 'best' schools
- afford higher transport costs, giving their children a wider choice of schools
- make more effective use of appeals procedures should they be refused a place at their chosen school

This means that those who have already benefited from education the most will gain more, while those who are more disadvantaged may become further disadvantaged.

Student needs at risk and social divisions increased

As Whitty et al. (1998) have pointed out, in a free market: 'the advantaged schools and the advantaged parents gravitate toward each other and the disadvantaged families are left in schools with falling enrollment, falling funding, and, as a result, more difficulty in climbing out of the spiral of decline'.

The free market has therefore opened up further the gap between the educational achievements of working-class and middle-class young people. The traditional pursuit of equality of educational opportunity, so all do as well as they are able, has been replaced with the need to demonstrate high results to keep up the image of the school or college to parents and achieve high positions in the league tables of results. Weaker students, who are more likely to come from working-class backgrounds (as is explained later in this chapter), may find their needs are neglected because of the risk of them getting poorer results and therefore undermining the position of the school/college in the league tables.

Because of the competitive climate, brighter students, or those, for example, on the C/D grade borderline at GCSE, are likely to get more resources spent on them, disadvantaging weaker students who are less likely to deliver the prestige results.

As a result, social divisions between the middle class and the working class are widened.

Specialist schools and selection by ability

As seen earlier, and later in this chapter, selection by ability can lead to a lowering of the self-esteem of those not selected, and may lead to lower expectations by teachers and the self-fulfilling prophecy. Specialist schools are often seen as being 'better' schools, and therefore given higher status by parents and pupils than other schools, and are given extra resources. As pupils compete for places, specialist schools may increasingly select their pupils by aptitude/ability (up to 10 per cent of their intake). This will create unfair competition between schools, and increase inequality between them. Middle-class parents are likely to gain most from this, and the working class to lose out, adding further to social divisions between social classes.

The unfairness of league tables

League tables of test and exam results don't really reveal how well a school or college is doing. This is because, as later parts of this chapter show, the social class, ethnic and gender backgrounds of students can affect how well they perform in education. Schools and colleges in more deprived working-class areas may produce results which are not as good as those in middle-class areas, yet their students have actually made much more progress than middle-class students compared to what they started school with. For example, a sixth form or college where students enter with four GCSEs grade

C cannot normally be expected to get results at AS and A level as good as one where students enter with seven GCSEs grades *A, A and B. The latter sixth form or college might get better results and a higher league table position than the first one, but the scale of achievement of the students in the first one might in reality have been greater.

League tables therefore do not show how much value has been added by the educational institution (the 'value-added' approach). They may conceal underperforming schools or colleges in advantaged middle-class areas, where results should be much better given their social class intake, and successful schools and colleges in more deprived working-class areas.

Difficulties in improving schools and colleges

Competition between schools and colleges for students, and therefore for money, the emphasis on exam results, and presenting a good image to parents in the free market may make it harder for poorer schools and colleges to improve, as students go elsewhere. Such schools and colleges may therefore lack the resources to improve their performance – the opposite of what was intended by the reforms.

'Dumbing down'

As school students, and particularly post-16 further education and sixth form students, now have a choice of institutions, this may lead to a 'dumbing down' of teaching and subject content. The need for schools and colleges to retain students – and the money they bring with them – means that if students have too much work to do or find the work difficult, they may go to another course or educational institution where things seem easier and less demanding. Retaining (keeping) students may mean not pushing students too hard for fear of losing them.

Problems with the National Curriculum and testing

The National Curriculum has been criticized for not giving teachers enough opportunity to respond to the needs of their pupils, as teachers are told what they have to teach and when they have to teach it. Testing (the SATs) has been criticized, particularly at Key Stage 1 (age 7), for putting too much pressure on young children, and possibly giving them a sense of failure early in their schooling. More generally, teaching may become too focused on the content of the tests as a way to get the good test results needed for a high position in the league tables, at the expense of the wider school curriculum.

Inadequate vocational education

Work experience is often seen by school students as boring and repetitive, involving little development of their skills and little to do with their future ambitions. Post-school training schemes are often similarly criticized for providing little development of skills, for being used as a source of cheap labour by employers, and for not leading to 'proper' jobs at the end of the training. Such schemes are sometimes seen as having more to do with reducing politically embarrassing unemployment statistics, reducing the proportion of NEET 16–18-year-olds (NEET means 'not in education, employment or training) and thereby keeping young people away from crime and other forms of deviance, rather than producing a skilled labour force. Vocational education and qualifications, like NVQs and vocational GCSEs and Applied GCEs (vocational A levels), are often seen as having lower status than more traditional academic subjects and courses. Vocational qualifications are, in general, less likely to lead to university entry, and are more likely to lead to lower status, lower paid jobs as adults. University qualifications generally lead to better paid jobs and higher social class positions. Parents, teachers and students themselves therefore often see vocational qualifications as 'inferior' or a second-rate option compared to more traditional academic subjects and courses. Those from working-class backgrounds are more likely to find themselves taking vocational subjects and courses, reinforcing divisions between social classes.

A university education generally leads to better-paid jobs and higher social class positions. Young people from middle-class homes are more likely to get to university than those from the working class. How might sociologists explain this?

> **Activity**
>
> 1 Think back over your school work experience programmes. Were they very useful to you? Give reasons for your answer.
> 2 Do you think AS and A levels have the same status as vocational qualifications, such as NVQs, GNVQs and applied GCEs?
> 3 Do you think there is any evidence of 'dumbing down' in standards, or do you think standards are going up? Ask a few of your teachers or lecturers what they think.
> 4 Is offering the option of vocational GCSEs at age 14 a sensible idea? How might this affect the future career prospects of young people compared to those doing traditional academic GCSEs? Do you think this might have any effect on equal opportunities for all in education?

> **Activity**
>
> 1 Explain what is meant by a meritocracy.
> 2 Suggest *three* educational policies that have attempted to improve standards in education in the last twenty years.
> 3 Identify and explain *two* reasons why league tables of test and exam results may not give a fair impression of how effective a school or college is.
> 4 Explain what is meant by the self-fulfilling prophecy.
> 5 Explain why middle-class parents might be more effective in achieving better schooling for their children than those from working-class backgrounds.
> 6 Suggest *two* reasons why selection by ability in education may have harmful effects on some children.
> 7 On about a side and a half of A4 paper, answer the following question: *Examine the view that recent reforms in education have not benefited all children equally.*

Sociological perspectives on education

This section is concerned with the different explanations of the role of the education system in society. The focus here is on two structural or 'macro' approaches, functionalism and Marxism, which try to understand the role of education in relation to other social institutions, such as the economy (the world of work and production).

The functionalist perspective on education

The functionalist perspective on education follows the same principles as all functionalist approaches to the study of society. It is concerned with the functions or role of education for society as a whole, in particular its contribution to maintaining social stability through the development of value consensus, social harmony and cohesion. It examines the links between education and other social institutions, such as the family and the workplace. The two most important writers on education from a functionalist perspective have been Émile Durkheim (1858–1917) and the American functionalist Talcott Parsons. They identified four basic functions of education:

1 Passing on society's culture and building social solidarity

Education meets a key **functional prerequisite** by passing on to new generations the central or core values and culture of a society. This is achieved by both the '**hidden curriculum**' and the actual subjects learnt at school (the curriculum), for example through subjects like Citizenship and Personal, Social and Health Education (PSHE). This unites or 'glues' people together and builds **social solidarity** by giving them shared values (a value consensus) and a shared culture.

2 Providing a bridge between the particularistic values and ascribed status of the family and the universalistic values and achieved status of industrial society

Durkheim argued that schools are a 'society in miniature' – a small-scale version of society as a whole that prepares young people for life in the wider adult society.

Parsons sees schools as important units of secondary socialization, increasingly taking over from the family as children grow older. He argues schools provide a bridge between the 'particularistic' values and ascribed status of the family, and the 'universalistic', meritocratic values and achieved status of contemporary industrial societies.

Children's status in the family is ascribed and they are judged in terms of **particularistic values**. For example, their status is ascribed as a child and not an adult, or as a younger rather than an older brother or sister, and they are treated as special individuals and judged differently from everyone else outside the family. However, wider adult industrial society is meritocratic. People have to earn their status positions according to their individual achievements, such as talent, skill, or educational qualifications.

In this situation of achieved status, the same **universalistic values** or rules apply to everyone, regardless of who they are. For example, a teacher marking student essays might reasonably be expected to mark every essay by the same criteria (universalistic values), not give different marks depending on whether they liked the student or not (particularistic values), and those same students might be expected to achieve a place at university because of their exam grades, not because they knew someone who worked there.

Functional prerequisites refer to the basic needs that must be met if society is to survive.

The **curriculum** of a school or college is the formal content of subject lessons and examinations. The **hidden curriculum** concerns not so much the content of lessons as the way teaching and learning are organized. This includes the general routines of school life which influence and mould the attitudes and behaviour of students, such as the school rules, dress codes, obeying the authority of teachers, and so on.

Social solidarity refers to the integration of people into society through shared values, a common culture, shared understandings and social ties that bing them together.

Particularistic values are rules and values that give a priority to personal relationships.

Universalistic values are rules and values that apply equally to all members of society, regardless of who they are.

> **Activity**
>
> 1 Identify those features which make school life like a 'society in miniature', preparing people for wider society.
> 2 Parsons suggests that schooling provides a bridge between the family and wider adult society. Think about your own schooling, and the way that, as you moved from infant school through to the end of secondary schooling, teacher attitudes and the experience of schooling changed. Can you identify any evidence of a move from particularism to universalism?
> 3 Identify all the features of both the formal curriculum and the hidden curriculum, with examples, which transmit values and culture from one generation to the next. To what extent do you think those things learnt in school actually unite people in society?

3 Providing a trained and qualified labour force

Functionalists see the expansion of schooling and higher education as necessary to provide a properly trained, qualified and flexible labour force to undertake the wide range of different jobs which arise from the specialized **division of labour** in a modern economy. They argue the education system prepares this labour force, and makes sure the best and most qualified people end up in the jobs requiring the greatest skills and responsibilities.

4 Selecting and allocating people to roles in a meritocratic society, and legitimizing social inequality

For functionalists, like Davis and Moore (1945), the education system is a means of selecting or sifting people for different levels of the job market, and ensuring the most talented and qualified individuals are allocated to the most important jobs. By grading people through streaming and test and exam results, the education system is a major method of role allocation – fitting the most suitable people into the hierarchy of unequal positions in society.

In a meritocratic society, access to jobs, and the inequalities of wealth, status and power, depend mainly on educational qualifications and other skills and talents. Davis and Moore suggest that in this educational race for success there is equality of educational opportunity, and everyone who has the ability and talent and puts in the effort has an equal chance of coming out ahead. Inequalities in society are therefore legitimized – made to seem fair and just. Those who succeed deserve their success, and those who fail have only themselves to blame.

Table 6.2 summarizes some criticisms of the functionalist view of education.

> The **division of labour** is the division of work or occupations into a large number of specialized tasks, each of which is carried out by one worker or a group of workers.

> **Activity**
>
> To what extent do you think the school work you are doing, or did, and the qualifications you obtain(ed) at school might be preparing, or did prepare you, for doing a job? Identify, with examples, the links between your school subjects and exams and earning a living.

Table 6.2 Criticisms of the functionalist view of education

Functionalist view	Criticism
Education passes on society's culture from one generation to the next, including shared norms and values. These provide the 'social glue' which creates social solidarity and social cohesion.	*Marxists* would argue that this view ignores the inequalities in power in society. There is no value consensus, and the culture and values passed on by the school are those of the dominant or ruling class. *Feminists* might argue the school passes on patriarchal values, and disadvantages girls and women.
Education provides a bridge between the particularistic values and ascribed status of the family and the universalistic values and achieved status of wider industrial society.	There is some doubt about how far contemporary industrial society is really based on universalistic values and achieved status. Many in the upper class inherit wealth, and there are many elite jobs where ascribed status characteristics such as social class, gender and ethnic background still have a very important influence.
Education provides a trained and qualified labour force.	The link between educational qualifications and pay and job status is a weak one, and certainly much weaker than functionalists assume. The content of what people learn in schools often has very little to do directly with what they actually do in their jobs. Collins (1972) argues most occupational skills are learned 'on the job' or through firms' own training schemes. The demand for educational qualifications for many occupations is simply an attempt to raise the status of the occupation, rather than providing the knowledge and skill requirements necessary for performing the job.
Effective role selection and allocation. Education selects the 'right' people for the most suitable jobs in a meritocratic society.	The education system does not act as a neutral 'sieve', simply grading and selecting students according to their ability. Social class, ethnicity and gender seem to be the major factors influencing success or failure in education. There is no equality of opportunity in education – everyone does not start at the same point, and not everyone has the same chance of success in education, even when they have the same ability.
Education legitimizes social inequality.	Bowles and Gintis (1976) (discussed later) argue that the education system simply disguises the fact that there is no equality of opportunity in education, and that it is social class, ethnicity and gender that are the main influences on educational success.

Marxist perspectives on education

Marxist perspectives on education emphasize the way the education system reproduces *existing* social class inequalities, and passes them on from one generation to the next. At the same time, it does this by giving the impression that those who fail in education do so because of their lack of ability and effort, and have only themselves to blame. In this way, people are encouraged to accept the positions they find themselves in after schooling, even though it is disadvantages arising from social class background that create inequalities in educational success.

The work of Althusser: education as an ideological state apparatus

The French Marxist Althusser (1971) saw the main role of education in a capitalist society as the reproduction of an efficient and obedient labour force. This involves two aspects:

- the reproduction of the necessary technical skills
- the reproduction of ruling class ideology (the dominant beliefs and values) and the socialization of workers into accepting this dominant ideology (this is known as false consciousness).

Althusser argues that to prevent the working class from rebelling against their exploitation, the ruling class must try to win their hearts and minds by persuading them to accept ruling class ideology. This process of persuasion is carried out by a number of **ideological state apparatuses**, such as the family, the mass media, the law, religion and the education system. Althusser argues that in contemporary Western societies the main ideological state apparatus is the education system. The education system:

- passes on ruling class ideology justifying the capitalist system
- selects people for the different social classes as adults, with the right attitudes and behaviour; for example, workers are persuaded to accept and submit to exploitation, and managers and administrators to rule.

> **Ideological state apparatuses** are agencies which serve to spread the dominant ideology and justify the power of the dominant social class.

> ### Activity
>
> 1 Refer to figure 6.2. Suggest the attitudes and values that might be required by those leaving the education system at different stages for different levels of employment.
> 2 Can you think of values or ideas that are passed on through the education system which might be in the interests of the dominant groups in society rather than in the interests of all?

Figure 6.2 Education and the class structure

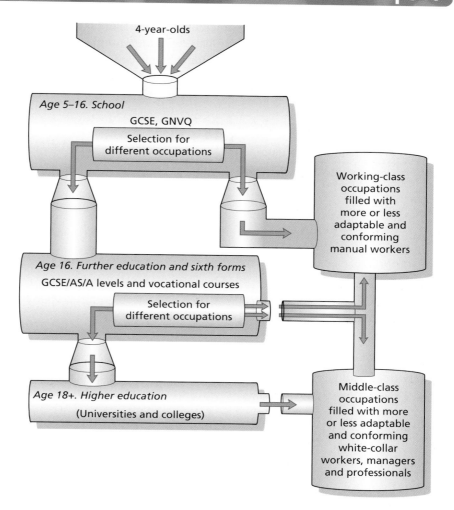

Bowles and Gintis: schooling and the 'long shadow of work'

In *Schooling in Capitalist America,* Bowles and Gintis argue, like Althusser, that the major role of education in capitalist societies is the reproduction of labour power – a hard-working, and disciplined workforce. Bowles and Gintis argue that such a workforce is reproduced in two main ways:

1 Through the hidden curriculum of schooling and the correspondence, or very close similarity, between the social relationships at school and at work – in particular, the way schooling operates in the 'long shadow of work'.
2 Through the role of the education system in legitimizing or justifying inequality.

Schooling and the 'long shadow of work'   Bowles and Gintis argue that the world of work influences the organization of education. They suggest this is like work casting a long shadow over education, with the hidden curriculum in schools corresponding closely to many features of the workplace. Table 6.3 illustrates some elements of this correspondence between the hidden curriculum at school and its links with relations at the workplace.

Table 6.3 The hidden curriculum

Features of the hidden curriculum	What is being taught
Privileges and responsibilities given to sixth formers	Respect for elders and superiors/managers
School rules, detentions and exclusions, rewards like merit badges, prizes, good marks, etc.	Conformity to society's rules and laws, whether you agree with them or not
School assemblies	Respect for religious beliefs and the dominant moral values
Males and females often playing different sports, having different dress rules, and being counselled into different subjects, further education courses, and careers; many teachers having different expectations of boys and girls	Males and females being encouraged to conform to gender stereotypes and work in different jobs; for example, women being encouraged into taking primary responsibility for housework and childcare
Competitive sports and competition against each other in class rather than cooperating together; students being tested individually – being encouraged to rely on themselves rather than others	Workers having to compete for jobs and wages, and individuals having to stand on their own two feet – not joining with other workers to take action
Respecting authority of teachers regardless of what they say or do; pupils always having to justify where they're going and why, and do as they're told	Respect for those in authority, such as bosses at work and the police
Punctuality/being on time – time belonging to the school, not the pupil	Good time-keeping at work – the employer pays for the worker's time, so it belongs to the firm, not the worker
Concentrating on schoolwork, whether or not it's boring and whether or not you want to do it	Workers having to accept boring, menial and repetitive jobs
Value being placed on hard work and getting on	Everyone being able to make it to the top if she or he tries hard enough
Grading by ability, and exam success/failure	The differences in pay and status between social classes being natural and justified – those higher up are more intelligent and better qualified
Rewarding (by high grades) qualities of dependability, punctuality and acceptance of authority	Workers' duty to be dependable, be punctual and accept bosses' authority
Different streams and bands	Getting used to accepting the different levels of the job market, such as professional, managerial, skilled, semi-skilled and unskilled manual occupations, which are seen to be based on ability

Table 6.3 (continued)

Features of the hidden curriculum	What is being taught
Pupils lack power and control about the subjects taught or how the school is run or the school day organized	Workers' lack of power and control at work
The authority hierarchy of the school, involving pupils fitting into a complex organization of heads, deputies, heads of department, year heads, etc.	Messages about being placed in the hierarchies of power and control in society and accepting it – for example, in the authority hierarchy at work
The school curriculum being broken up into separate subjects which are clearly separated from one another	Work is divided into many separate jobs (the division of labour) which keeps the workforce from having knowledge of the whole process
Schools aim to motivate pupils by marks, grades and qualifications	Working for pay in unfulfilling and powerless jobs

Activity

1 Describe in detail five features of the hidden curriculum found in your school, or the one you once attended, which reflect the expectations of employers and the demands of the workplace after school.
2 Drawing on your own experiences at school, what features of your education do you think prepared/will prepare you most for life after school? Think of particular subjects studied and activities undertaken, and the features of the hidden curriculum in table 6.3 which were/are found in your school.
3 Using examples from your own school life, to what extent do you agree with Bowles and Gintis that 'schooling operates in the long shadow of work'?
4 The features of the hidden curriculum shown in table 6.3 are mainly influenced by Bowles and Gintis's Marxist approach. The functionalists also see the hidden curriculum as an important means of students being taught the culture and values of society so that a value consensus can be built and society can be kept stable and harmonious. Suggest ways that functionalist writers might alter the second column above ('What is being taught') to give it more of a functionalist than a Marxist 'flavour'.

The legitimation of inequality Bowles and Gintis argue that the educational system:

- helps to maintain, justify and explain (legitimate or legitimize) the system of social inequality of capitalist society
- helps people to come to terms with their own position in it
- and therefore helps to reduce discontent and opposition to inequality

Bowles and Gintis reject the functionalist view that social class inequalities in capitalist society arise from fair competition in education, in which everyone stands an equal chance. In contrast, they argue that social class background, ethnicity and sex are the main factors related to success or failure in education and the job market. People from upper and upper middle-class backgrounds (and who are white and male) tend to obtain higher qualifications and jobs than working-class children of similar ability. Bowles and Gintis see both equality of opportunity and meritocracy as myths that promote the idea that failure in education arises from lack of ability or hard work, when in most cases it arises because of social class and family background. Education is therefore seen as a kind of 'con trick' that hides the fact that it maintains and reproduces the existing pattern of social class inequalities between generations, and in most cases simply confirms individuals' class of origin (the one they were born into) as their class of destination (the one they end up in as adults).

Criticisms of Althusser and Bowles and Gintis

Althusser and Bowles and Gintis have been criticized on two main fronts:

- There is a lack of detailed research into schools. Althusser and Bowles and Gintis assume the hidden curriculum is actually influencing pupils, but pupils are often not passive recipients of education, and often have little regard for teachers' authority and school rules and discipline (as Willis's research below shows).
- Bowles and Gintis ignore the influence of the formal curriculum. This does not seem designed to promote the ideal employee for capitalism, and develop uncritical, passive behaviour. The humanities and subjects like sociology produce critical thinkers, while work-related courses remain of relatively low status. Employers often complain that the education system does not produce well-qualified workers with suitable skills.

The work of Willis

Paul Willis's work, *Learning to Labour: How Working Class Kids Get Working Class Jobs* (1977), helps to overcome some of the weaknesses of more traditional Marxist approaches like those of Althusser and Bowles and Gintis. Willis adopts a Marxist approach, but also draws on the interactionist perspective.

Willis recognizes that schools do not produce a willing and obedient workforce – a quick glance at almost any secondary school provides evidence that students do not always obey teachers, that they can be disruptive and challenge the school. Willis says it is easy to understand why middle-class young people willingly go into secure and well-paid middle-class career jobs, but what is more difficult to explain is why working-class young people go so willingly into dead-end, low paid and boring manual working-class jobs.

Paul Willis sought to explain why working-class lads went so willingly into dead-end, low-paid and boring manual working-class jobs

An **anti-school** or **counter-school subculture** is a group organized around a set of values, attitudes and behaviour in opposition to the main aims of a school.

Willis studied a group of twelve working-class male pupils he referred to as 'the lads' in a school on a working-class housing estate in Wolverhampton in the 1970s. The 'lads' developed an **anti-school** or **counter-school subculture** opposed both to the main aims of the school, and to the 'ear 'oles' – conformist pupils who generally conformed to school values. 'The lads' attached little value to the aims of the school, such as gaining qualifications, and their main priority was to free themselves from control by the school, to avoid or disrupt lessons, to have a 'laff' and to get into the world of work as soon as possible.

Rejecting schooling and wanting to leave school as soon as they could and escape from the 'pen-pushing' of the 'ear 'oles', the 'lads' did not see school as relevant to them. Their priorities were to get their hands on money, to impress their mates, to keep up with older drinkers in the pub, to impress the girls, and to show they could 'graft' in male manual jobs as well as the next man.

In this context, school was boring, pointless and irrelevant to their lives, and stopped them smoking, drinking, going out at night, getting a job and cash, and involving themselves in the 'real' world of male, manual work.

Willis found a similarity between the counter-school culture and the workplace culture of male lower working-class jobs, such as **sexism**, a lack of respect for authority and an emphasis on 'having a laff' to escape the boring and oppressive nature of both school and work.

Sexism refers to prejudice or discrimination against people, especially women, because of their sex.

Willis's research suggests that schools are not directly preparing the sort of obedient and docile labour force required by capitalism which Althusser and Bowles and Gintis suggest. Young, working-class males are not forced or persuaded by the school to leave and look for manual jobs, but actively *reject* school through the counter-school culture and willingly enter male semi-skilled and unskilled work the minute they leave school.

> **Activity**
>
> 1 To what extent do you think Willis's research might be true of all schools? Do you think there are any reasons why there might be uncertainty about this given the size of Willis's study?
> 2 What evidence is/was there at your own school of an anti-school or counter-school subculture like that of 'the lads'? Give examples of the types of behaviour displayed by such students, and suggest reasons for it.

A comparison of functionalist and Marxist perspectives on education

Similarities and differences

The functionalist and Marxist views of education have a number of similarities:

- Both see schools playing a role in legitimizing (justifying and explaining) social inequality.
- Both are 'macro' (large-scale) theories concerned with the structural relationship between education and other parts of the social system, such as the economy and social inequality.
- Both see education as serving the 'needs' of industrial and/or capitalist society.
- Both see the education system as a powerful influence on students, ensuring they conform to existing social values and norms.

But they have differences too, summarized in table 6.4.

Table 6.4 Differences between the functionalist and Marxist perspectives on education

Functionalism	Marxism
Education serves the needs of an *industrial* society with an advanced division of labour	Education serves the needs of a capitalist society divided into social classes
Education serves the needs of the social system by socializing new generations into society's culture and shared norms and values, leading to social harmony, stability and social integration	Education serves the 'needs' of capitalism by socializing children into the dominant ideology (ruling class norms and values), leading to an obedient workforce and the stability of capitalism
The hidden curriculum helps to prepare society's future citizens for participation in a society based on value consensus	The hidden curriculum helps to persuade society's future citizens to accept the dominant ideology and their position in a society based on inequality, exploitation and conflict
Education provides a means for upward social mobility for those who have the ability	With the exception of a few individuals, education confirms individuals' class of origin (the one they were born into) as their class of destination (the one they end up in as adults). Education therefore contributes to the reproduction of present class inequalities between generations, and does not provide a means of upward social mobility for most people
Education justifies and explains (legitimizes) social inequality, as roles are allocated according to meritocratic criteria such as educational qualifications, in a society in which all have equality of opportunity	Education legitimizes social class inequality by persuading working-class individuals to accept that their lack of power and control at work and in society generally is due to their lack of academic ability, effort and achievement, when in fact they do not have the same opportunities as those who are more advantaged

Criticisms of both perspectives

- They both give too much emphasis to the role of education in forming students' identity, and they pay too little attention to the influences of other agencies of socialization, such as the family, the mass media and work.

- They don't fully consider the way students react to schooling in ways that aren't necessarily 'functional' for the social system or capitalism. For example, pupils disrupt schools, play truant and don't learn, and workers go on strike. (However, note the exception of Willis's work here.)
- They both see too tight a link between education and the economy, and exaggerate the extent to which schools provide a ready, willing and qualified labour force. The new emphasis on vocational education and pressure to drive up school standards is a direct response to employers who criticized schools for *not* providing a suitably disciplined and qualified labour force.

Interactionist perspectives on education

Interactionist perspectives study small-scale activities and focus more on what actually happens within schools and classrooms, using qualitative research methods like unstructured interviews or participant observation. They are interested in how students come to be defined in particular ways, for example as 'good' or 'bad' students, and the consequences that arise from these definitions. These approaches will be discussed later in this chapter, but it is worth noting that these micro or small-scale detailed studies are a contrast to the macro or large-scale structuralist approaches of functionalism and Marxism.

Activity

1 Suggest *three* ways in which schooling prepares young people for the world of work.
2 Explain what is meant by the legitimization of social class inequality, and suggest *two* ways in which schooling might do this.
3 Identify and explain *two* ways in which the educational system contributes to the economy.
4 Explain what is meant by the 'hidden curriculum', and suggest *two* ways this might prepare children for adult life.
5 In about a side and a half of A4 paper, answer the following question: *Assess the view that the main role of education is the reproduction of social class inequalities from one generation to the next.*

Is contemporary Britain a meritocracy?

Functionalist writers like Parsons have suggested the education system and society as a whole are based on the principles of meritocracy and equality of opportunity.

In a meritocracy, educational achievements and qualifications should be based only on the ability, skills and hard work of individuals, and everyone should have an equal opportunity to develop whatever skills and talents she or he may have. Factors like social class background, ethnicity, gender or disability should present no obstacle to an individual in developing to the full whatever talents they have.

There is evidence, however, that Britain is not meritocratic, and that social inequality is not based simply on different levels of educational achievement. For example, people with the same educational qualifications often earn vastly different amounts, and the link between educational qualifications and pay levels is relatively weak. Marxists like Bowles and Gintis and many non-Marxists argue that there is no real equality of opportunity in education, and that what the education system really does is to maintain and reproduce existing social class, ethnic and gender inequalities from one generation to the next.

The evidence for this lack of equality of opportunity in education is that, even for students of the same ability, there are wide differences in educational achievement which are closely linked to the social class origins of students, and their gender and ethnic characteristics.

The following sections look at the evidence for these inequalities in educational opportunity and achievement, and seek explanations for them.

Natural intelligence or IQ

Some argue that some people are simply born more 'intelligent' than others – they have more innate (inborn) natural intelligence and this explains the different levels of performance in education of some social groups.

However, sociologists have generally been very critical of the notion of innate intelligence and the accuracy of the IQ (intelligence quotient) tests used to measure this. This is because there is a social pattern of **underachievement** along the lines of social class, ethnicity and gender, and a far more random pattern would be expected if intelligence was simply a product of biological differences. Biological explanations underestimate the importance of material and cultural factors both in forming intelligence and in the patterns of educational achievement. Table 6.5 summarizes the arguments for and against the notion that inborn intelligence explains differences in educational achievement.

Underachievement is the failure of people to fulfil their potential – they do not do as well in education (or other areas) as their talents and abilities suggest they should.

Table 6.5 Arguments for and against the view that natural intelligence explains differences in educational achievement

For	Against
Intelligence is inborn, and is inherited from parents	It is impossible to separate inborn intelligence from environmental factors, and the intellectual development of even very young children will be affected by the stimuli they are exposed to, such as space to play, diet, toys, family income, housing, and interaction with parents, which will influence the way intelligence develops
Intelligence can be measured by IQ tests	IQ tests are bound to be affected by the culture in which people grow up – for example, whether they are used to working individually, or under timed test conditions. Performance in IQ tests can be affected by factors other than intelligence, such as how people react in a test situation, whether they care or not, how they're feeling at the time, their state of health, whether they've had practice or not, and so on. IQ tests are simply testing how good people are at doing them, and this is influenced by early learning and socialization
Intelligence is fixed and can't be changed	IQ tests tell us nothing about people's potential. A stimulating environment, early years education in a playgroup or nursery, and formal education, or a lack of it, can improve or diminish intelligence. There are many instances where people with a low early IQ score go on to achieve educational success, and where people with a high IQ score do not achieve success
High measured intelligence leads to high levels of educational achievement and occupational success	People with similar IQ scores from different backgrounds do not show similar levels of educational and occupational success. Material and cultural factors, and the ways teachers treat pupils with a high IQ score differently from those with a low score, explain these differences, not innate ability

Social class differences in educational achievement

Social class is the key factor influencing whether a child does well or badly at school. There are major differences between the levels of achievement of the working class and middle class and, in general, the higher the social class of the parents, the more successful a child will be in education. Results from a UK-wide longitudinal study published in 2007 by the Centre for Longitudinal Studies, found many children from disadvantaged backgrounds were already up to a year behind more privileged children educationally by the age of 3 – before many had even started school. The degree of social class inequality in education begins in the primary school and becomes greater as children move upward through the education system, with the higher levels of the education system dominated by middle-class and upper-class students.

A comparison of social class differences in educational achievement

When students from the lower working class have been compared to middle-class children of the same ability, it has been found that:

- They are more likely to start school unable to read.
- They do less well in tests like the National Curriculum SATs.
- They are less likely to get places in the best state schools. In 2005, only 3 per cent of those attending state schools which were in the top 200 for performance received free school meals – the standard poverty indicator used in schools – compared to 17 per cent nationally.
- They are more likely to be placed in lower streams.
- They generally get poorer exam results. For example, around three-quarters of young people from upper middle-class backgrounds get five or more GCSEs *A–C, compared to less than a third from lower working-class backgrounds.
- They are more likely to leave school at the minimum leaving age of 16, many of them with few or no qualifications of any kind. Only about half of young people from unskilled manual families stay on in post-16 full-time education, compared to about nine in every ten from managerial and professional families.
- They are more likely to undertake vocational or training courses if they stay in education after 16, rather than the more academic AS- and A-level courses, which are more likely to be taken by middle-class students.
- They are less likely to go into higher education. In 2006 at least 60 per cent of those accepted for higher education came from middle-class backgrounds, even though only about half of the population was middle class. Young people from unskilled backgrounds made up only around 5 per cent of those accepted.

Many children from disadvantaged backgrounds are already up to a year behind more privileged youngsters educationally by the age of 3, according to 2007 research by the Centre for Longitudinal Studies at the London University Institute of Education

Explaining social class differences in educational achievement

There is a range of factors that sociologists have identified in explaining the pattern of differences in educational achievement (figure 6.3). These can be grouped into three main categories:

- material explanations, which put the emphasis on social and economic conditions
- cultural explanations, which focus on values, attitudes and lifestyles
- factors within the school itself

The following sections mainly focus on social class differences, though some of these differences will also be referred to later in discussing gender and ethnic group differences.

Figure 6.3 Social class and educational achievement

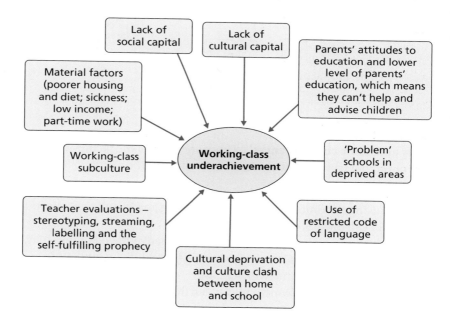

Material explanations

Although schooling and further education are free to the age of 19 (though there are fees for higher education), material factors like poverty and low wages, diet, health and housing can all have important direct effects on how well individuals do at school. Indicators of social deprivation like these make an important contribution to explaining the pattern of working-class under-achievement in education.

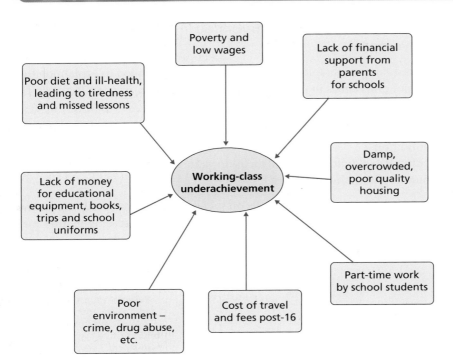

Figure 6.4 Material factors explaining class differences in educational achievement

Poverty and home circumstances   These are some of the factors in a child's background that can affect their chances in education:

- Douglas found in early research in *The Home and the School* (1964) that poor housing conditions such as overcrowding and insufficient space and quiet can make study at home difficult.
- Poorer diets and higher levels of sickness in disadvantaged homes may mean tiredness at school, making learning more difficult, and more absence and falling behind with lessons.
- Low income or unemployment may mean that educational books and toys are not bought, and computers are not available in the home. This may affect a child's educational progress before or during her or his time at school. There may also be a lack of money for out-of-school trips, sports equipment, calculators and other 'hidden costs' of free state education.
- It may be financially difficult for parents on a low income to support students in education after school-leaving age. This is particularly the case in further education, where grants are low (a maximum of £30 a week for the poorest families in 2008) and there may be travel costs involved. In higher education, student grants have been replaced by student loans, and tuition fees are payable, and these are likely to be a source of anxiety to those from poorer backgrounds, deterring them from going to university.

- Poorer parents are less likely to have access to pre-school or nursery facilities, which may affect their children's development compared to those who have such access.
- Young people from poorer families are more likely to have part-time jobs, such as paper rounds, babysitting or shop work. This becomes more pronounced after the age of 16, when students may be combining part- or full-time work with school or college work. This may create a conflict between the competing demands of study and paid work.
- Schools themselves in poorer areas may suffer disadvantages compared to those in more affluent middle-class areas. For example, many schools today rely on support from parents to finance extra resources for the school, and parents in poorer areas are less likely to be able to raise as much as those in more middle-class areas. This will mean schools in poorer areas will have less to spend on pupil activities.

The effects of these material factors tend to be cumulative, in the sense that one aspect of social deprivation can lead to others. For example, poverty may mean overcrowding at home *and* ill-health *and* having to find part-time work, making all the problems worse. The cartoon illustrates this.

> ### Activity
> Explain in your own words how the cartoon shows the effects of social deprivation on educational achievement are cumulative.

The catchment area Catchment areas (or priority areas) are the areas from which primary and secondary schools draw their pupils. In deprived areas, where there may be a range of social problems such as high unemployment, poverty, juvenile delinquency, crime, and drug abuse, there are often poor role models for young people to imitate. The accumulated effects of the environment on children's behaviour mean schools in such areas are more likely to have discipline problems that prevent students from learning, and a higher turnover of teachers. This may mean children from the most disadvantaged backgrounds have the worst schools. In contrast, schools in middle-class neighbourhoods will probably have stronger and more conformist role models for young people, have fewer discipline problems and therefore offer a better learning environment.

Material explanations therefore have a major impact in explaining the underachievement of many children from poorer backgrounds. This was confirmed by research by Gibson and Asthana (1999), which found that the greater the level of family disadvantage, measured in terms of lack of parents' qualifications, unemployment, and not owning a car or house, the smaller the percentage of students gaining five or more GCSEs at grades *A to C.

Cultural explanations – cultural deprivation

Cultural explanations of underachievement in education suggest that the values, attitudes, language, and other aspects of the life of some social groups is deficient or deprived in various ways in relation to the white, middle-class culture of the education system. This is known as **cultural deprivation**, and places the blame for educational underachievement on young people's socialization in the family and community, and on the cultural values with which they are raised.

Cultural deprivation is the idea that some young people fail in education because of supposed deficiencies in their home and family background, such as inadequate socialization, failings in pre-school learning, inadequate language skills and inappropriate attitudes and values.

Parents' attitudes to education   Douglas found the single most important factor explaining educational success and failure was the degree of parental interest and encouragement in their children's education. He found that middle-class parents, compared to working-class parents, on the whole:

- took more interest in their children's progress at school, as indicated by more frequent visits to the school to discuss their children's progress
- became relatively more interested and encouraging as the children grew older, when exam options are selected and career choices loom
- were more likely to want their children to stay at school beyond the minimum leaving age and to encourage them to do so

Parents' level of education   Because they are generally themselves better educated, middle-class parents tend to understand the school system better than working-class parents. Lower working-class parents may feel less confident in dealing with teachers at parents' evenings, and in dealing with subject options and exam choices. Middle-class parents know more about schools, the examination system and careers and so are more able to advise and counsel their children on getting into the most appropriate subjects and courses. They can 'hold their own' more in disagreements with teachers (who are also middle

Figure 6.5 Cultural factors explaining class differences in educational achievement

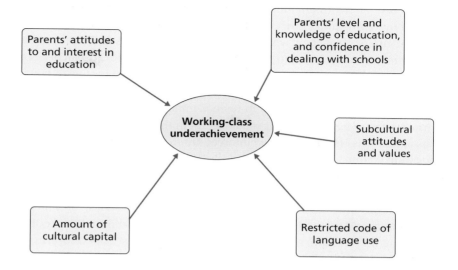

Parents' attitudes to and interest in education

Parents' level and knowledge of education, and confidence in dealing with schools

Working-class underachievement

Subcultural attitudes and values

Amount of cultural capital

Restricted code of language use

In what ways might parents influence success or failure in their children's education?

class) about the treatment and educational progress of their child; they know more about complaints procedures, and fighting sex discrimination against their daughters; they know which educational toys, games and books to buy, or 'cultural' events to go to, to stimulate their children's educational development both before and during schooling (and they have the money to pay for them); and they can help their children with school work generally. As a consequence, even before they get to school middle-class children may have learned more as a result of their socialization in the family. These advantages of a middle-class home may be reinforced throughout a child's career in the education system.

Subcultural explanations   These explanations suggest that different social classes have some different values, attitudes and lifestyles, or different **subcultures**, and that these affect the performance of children in the educational system. Two main researchers have developed these subcultural explanations: the British sociologist Sugarman (1970) and the American H. H. Hyman (1967). Table 6.6, based on the work of Hyman and Sugarman, shows how the different values and attitudes of the middle class and working class might influence children's progress in school.

> A **subculture** is a smaller culture held by a group or class of people within the main culture of a society, in some ways different from the main culture, but with many aspects in common.

Activity

1   Identify some subcultures in contemporary Britain, and describe the ways you think their values, attitudes and lifestyles might differ from 'mainstream' culture. An example of such a subculture might be that of travellers (but think of your own examples too).
2   Do you think working-class people and middle-class people have different subcultures? Suggest ways in which the attitudes and values of these two social classes might differ.

Language use and educational achievement: Bernstein and the restricted and elaborated codes   Success in education depends very heavily on language – for reading, writing, speaking and understanding. The ability to read and understand books, to write clearly, and to be able to explain yourself fully in both speech and writing are key language skills required for success in education. If these skills are not developed through discussion, negotiation and explanation in the family, then such children will be disadvantaged in education.

Bernstein (1971) has argued that there are two types of language use, which he calls the 'elaborated code' and the 'restricted code'. It is middle-class young people's familiarity with the elaborated code that gives them a better chance of success in education.

Table 6.6 Class subcultures and educational achievement

Class	Subculture	Effects on educational achievement
Middle class	In middle-class jobs, the promise of career progress through individual effort and educational qualifications leads to a *future orientation* (planning for the future) and *deferred gratification* (putting off today's pleasures for future gains). *Individual effort* and intelligence are seen as the key to success	Children are socialized into values and attitudes which encourage ambition and educational success. A *future orientation* and *deferred gratification* creates a recognition of the need for individual hard work, staying in and doing homework, and staying on in further/higher education in order to get the qualifications needed for career success. *Individual effort* is seen as providing the key to educational success
Working class	In working-class jobs, educational qualifications are often not very important for work. The lack of promotion opportunities leads to a *present-time orientation* (a lack of emphasis on long-term goals and future planning), *immediate gratification* (getting pleasures now, rather than putting them off for the future), and *fatalism* (an acceptance of the situation rather than attempts to improve it). Working together (*collectivism* through trade unions) provides more gains than individual effort	Children are socialized into general sets of values and attitudes which don't encourage ambition and educational success. Immediate gratification, a present-time orientation and fatalism discourage effort for future rewards, such as exam success. Leaving school and obtaining a skill/getting a job and money are seen as more important than educational qualifications. Loyalty to the group (collectivism) discourages the individual effort and achievement which success at school demands

> The **restricted code** is the informal, simple, everyday language, sometimes ungrammatical and with limited explanations and vocabulary, which is used between friends or family members.

> The **elaborated code** is the sort of formal language used by strangers and individuals in some formal contexts where explanation and detail are required, and uses a much wider vocabulary than the restricted code.

- The **restricted code** is the sort of language which is used between friends or family members – informal, simple, everyday language (such as slang), sometimes ungrammatical and with limited explanation and vocabulary. The restricted code is quite adequate for everyday use with family or friends because they generally know what the speaker is referring to – the context is understood by both speakers and so detailed explanation is not required. The restricted code is used by both middle-class and working-class people, but Bernstein argues lower working-class people are mainly limited to this form of language use.

- The **elaborated code** is the sort of language which is used by strangers and individuals in some formal context, where explanation and detail are required, such as that used by teachers in the classroom when they are explaining things, or in an interview for a job, writing a business letter, writing an essay or an examination answer, or in a school lesson or textbook. It has a much wider vocabulary than the restricted code. According to Bernstein, the elaborated code is used mainly by middle-class people.

Activity

1 With reference to the cartoon above, explain the difference between the elaborated and restricted codes of language use;
2 Explain *two* ways that having access to the elaborated code might provide advantages in education.

Bernstein argues that the language used in schools is the elaborated code of the middle class. It is this that gives the middle-class student an advantage at school over working-class students, since understanding textbooks, writing essays and examination questions, and class discussions require the detail and explanation which is found mainly in the formal language of the elaborated code. Middle-class young people who are used to using the elaborated code at home will therefore find school work easier and learn more than those working-class students whose language experience is limited only to the restricted code. The cartoon illustrates these two different types of language use.

Bernstein's work has been subject to a number of criticisms:

- Bernstein tends to put all the middle class together as having equal use of the elaborated code, but there are wide differences between the higher and lower sections of the middle class. A similar point can be made about higher and lower sections of the working class and the use of the restricted code. It is difficult to generalize about all working-class and middle-class families, and there is likely to be a diversity of arrangements in the way language is used in the family.

- Rosen argues that Bernstein gives few examples to back up his claims of the existence of restricted and elaborated codes. He accuses Bernstein of creating a myth of the superiority of middle-class speech.

- Labov (1973) is very critical of the notion that working-class speech is in any way inferior to that of the middle class. Based on his research in Harlem, in New York, Labov claims they are simply different.

Bourdieu's theory of cultural capital   Bourdieu (1971) was a French Marxist, who saw the culture of the school as giving an inbuilt advantage to middle-class children. He argues that each social class possesses its own cultural framework or set of ideas, which he calls a **habitus**.

> A **habitus** is the cultural framework and set of ideas possessed by a social class, into which people are socialized and which influences their cultural tastes and choices.

This cultural framework contains ideas about what counts as 'good' and 'bad' taste, 'good' books, newspapers, TV programmes and so on. This habitus is picked up through socialization in the family. The dominant class has the power to impose its own habitus in the education system, so what counts as educational knowledge is not the 'culture of society as a whole', but that of the dominant social class.

Those who come from better-off middle- and upper-class backgrounds have more access to the culture of the dominant class. Bourdieu calls this advantage **cultural capital**.

Possession of cultural capital gives greatly improved chances of success in education, and can be turned into educational capital (educational qualifications), which can in turn lead to possession of economic capital (material advantages like a high income).

> **Cultural capital** is the knowledge, language, manners and forms of behaviour, attitudes and values, taste and lifestyle which gives middle-class and upper-class students who possess them an in-built advantage in a middle-class controlled education system.

Upper- and middle-class children are more successful in education because they possess more cultural capital and consequently feel more comfortable in the education system and are more familiar with what they have to do at school. Those from the working class are more likely to fail exams, to be pushed into lower-status educational streams or courses, or to drop out or be pushed out of the educational system, because they lack cultural capital.

Bourdieu therefore suggests that, while the schooling process appears to be 'neutral' and fair, since schools measure all pupils against the same culture and knowledge, it is not really neutral at all because the culture of the educational system is that of the dominant class, which middle-class children already possess – and working-class children lack – through socialization in the family.

Bourdieu also refers to **social capital**, which is linked to cultural, economic and educational capital.

> **Social capital** refers to the social networks of influence and support that people have.

Social capital refers to the social networks of influence and support that people have, such as knowing the 'right people', who to talk to, who to get advice from, who is in a position to help them (or their children) in times of difficulty or need and influence others in their favour. Possession of social capital is highest in the middle and upper classes, and can provide a network of support to help their children's education. Examples of this might include knowing people who can provide extra help to their children with specialist subjects, knowing teachers who can give them inside information about the best schools – and which to avoid – or knowing teachers or university admission tutors who can brief them on what their children should say at interviews.

It is the possession of economic, educational, cultural and social capital by middle-class parents that gives their children in-built advantages in the education system.

Cultural and social capital in action

Criticisms of cultural explanations

Cultural explanations place the blame for educational underachievement on the home and family background, with the culture of the lower working class

The culture clash

Cultural explanations suggest that schools are mainly middle-class institutions, and they stress the value of many features of the middle-class way of life, such as the importance of hard work and study, making sacrifices now for future rewards (deferred gratification), the elaborated code of language, 'good' books, good TV programmes, 'quality' newspapers and so on. School for the middle-class child often represents an extension of earlier home experiences, while for the working-class child there may be a clash between home and school. Middle-class children therefore arrive at school with the cultural capital enabling them to be more 'tuned in' to the demands of schooling, such as the subjects that will be explored there, seeking good marks, doing homework, showing good behaviour and a cooperative attitude to teachers, and other features of middle-class culture. Consequently, they may appear to teachers as 'more intelligent' and more sophisticated, promising students. By contrast, working-class children may face a difference and conflict between the values of the home and those of school. This is known as the **culture clash.**

seen as deficient or deprived in various ways compared to that of the middle class. For example, the working class lacks the attitudes and values, the necessary language skills or the cultural capital which are important for educational success. However, there have been a number of criticisms of these cultural explanations of working-class underachievement:

Exaggeration   They tend to exaggerate the differences and downplay the similarities between the attitudes and beliefs of the different social classes.

Overlooking practical difficulties and lack of self-confidence   Many working-class parents are very concerned and ambitious for their children's success in education. Douglas, for example, used measures of 'parental interest' based on teachers' comments about parents' attitudes, and the number of times parents visited schools. However, manual workers work longer hours, have less flexibility and choice in their working hours, do more shift work, get less time off with pay, and are less educated than teachers and many other members of the middle class. Not visiting a school may not be evidence of a lack of interest or encouragement by working-class parents, but of the material constraints of their jobs, and a lack of confidence arising from their own lack of education, which prevent them turning parental interest into *practical* support in the way middle-class parents can.

Ignoring the role played by schools themselves Schools do not simply 'process' children whose attitudes and ambitions are pre-formed in the family, but play an active part in forming those attitudes and ambitions. Middle-class students may perform better because they receive more praise and encouragement from teachers, as they are more 'in tune' with teachers. Blaming the family and social class background can lead to low expectations by teachers and may encourage some teachers and schools to label lower working-class children as 'born to fail', and therefore to neglect their needs. This 'not worth bothering' approach and the resulting self-fulfilling prophecy, rather than so-called cultural deprivation, may lead to the poor performance of some children in school. These issues are discussed shortly.

The need for schools to change If there is a culture clash for working-class children going to school, then rather than blaming their family and social class background, schools should be pressed to improve the situation. Keddie in *Tinker, Tailor . . . the Myth of Cultural Deprivation* (1973) argues that there is no cultural deprivation, but merely a cultural difference. She suggests that the idea of cultural deprivation fails to recognize the cultural strengths of those said to be deprived. The problem arises because education is based on white middle-class culture, which disadvantages those from other backgrounds. It is not that the working class is in some ways deficient, but that the school is failing to meet the needs of working-class children and to recognize their culture as worthwhile. Explanations for class differences in educational achievement should therefore focus more on the nature of what happens inside the school, and the cultural values it promotes.

Compensatory education and positive discrimination

Cultural deprivation theories suggest that for all young people to have an equal chance in the educational system, those from culturally deprived backgrounds need extra help and resources to help them compete on equal terms with other children. This idea of extra help is known as **compensatory education**, and involves **positive discrimination**.

Schools in disadvantaged areas, where home and social class background are seen as obstacles to success in education, are singled out for extra favourable treatment, such as more, and better-paid teachers and more money to spend on buildings and equipment, to help the most disadvantaged succeed in education.

The idea of positive discrimination is based on the idea of equality of educational opportunity. In this view, children from disadvantaged backgrounds and poor homes can only get an opportunity in education equal to those who come from non-disadvantaged backgrounds if they get unequal and more generous treatment to compensate.

> **Compensatory education** is extra educational help for those coming from disadvantaged groups to help them overcome the disadvantages they face in the education system and the wider society.
> **Positive discrimination** involves giving disadvantaged groups more favourable treatment than others to make up for the disadvantages they face.

Education Action Zones and Excellence in Cities   In Britain, a recent attempt at compensatory education was the setting up in the late 1990s of **Education Action Zones** in socially disadvantaged areas. Schools in these areas were given extra money to help them improve the educational performance of the most disadvantaged young people.

An Ofsted report in 2003 found that Education Action Zone schools were succeeding in improving standards in disadvantaged areas, with better attendance and fewer exclusions, and rising levels of educational achievement. There were more opportunities for young people, who had higher aspirations, confidence and self-esteem. However, improvements in educational achievement were much greater in primary schools, and Ofsted said educational achievements in some Education Action Zone secondary schools 'often remain very low and give cause for continuing concern'.

Education Action Zones became Excellence in Cities Action Zones (EiCAZs) in 2005.

There are many attempts being made to overcome the disadvantages that young people from deprived communities face in achieving success in education. Material and cultural disadvantages have many complex causes, and solutions are likely to take a number of years, and involve a wide range of social policies to reduce the poverty, low income and ill-health that underlie much educational failure. It still remains to be seen how successful these programmes of compensatory education will be, but previous experience would suggest that schools alone cannot compensate for inequalities of educational opportunity arising from inequalities in society as a whole.

> **Education Action Zones** are disadvantaged areas where unemployment, poverty, poor housing and overcrowding, and ill-health contributed to poor educational performance. Schools in these areas are given extra money and teachers, especially directed at the pre-school and primary years. In 2005, Education Action Zones became Excellence in Cities Action Zones (EiCAZs).

Activity

1   Go to the following websites, www.standards.dfes.gov.uk/sie/eic and www.standards.dfes.gov.uk and identify *three* policies which are currently being followed to improve educational opportunities in the most disadvantaged communities. Explain in each case how these might improve educational opportunities.

2   Suggest *three material* factors in pupils' home and family background that may affect how successful they are in education.

3   Explain what is meant by 'immediate gratification' and 'fatalism', and how these might affect working-class pupils' educational achievements.

4   Explain, with examples, what is meant by a 'culture clash' between the home and the school.

5   Identify *three cultural* factors that may affect pupils' educational achievements.

6   Identify *two* ways in which a school's catchment area might influence the education of pupils from the area.

7   Suggest *three* criticisms of cultural explanations for underachievement in education.

Factors inside the school – the interactionist perspective

The explanations of working-class underachievement discussed so far have centred largely on the structural material and cultural factors outside the school that shape children before and during schooling. It is almost as if those from upper- and middle-class backgrounds are born to succeed in education, while those from the most disadvantaged, poor backgrounds are born to fail.

However, many would argue that schools can make a difference to the life chances of students whatever their backgrounds, as for example Rutter's work has suggested (see the box on 'Do schools make a difference?').

Much research has suggested that social patterns of underachievement in education are affected by what goes on in school classrooms, and how the meanings constructed there – how teachers and students come to see each other – affect student progress. For example, it is possible that sociological evidence demonstrating a link between working-class origin and

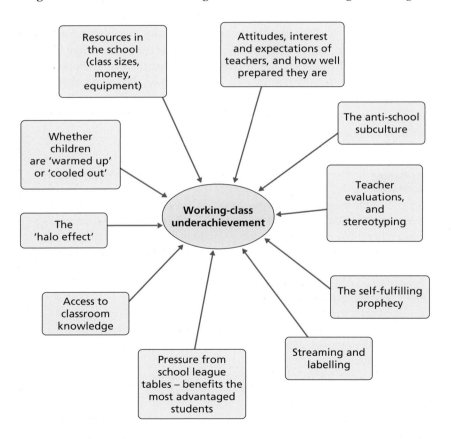

Figure 6.6 Factors inside the school explaining class differences in educational achievement

Do schools make a difference?

Michael Rutter and his colleagues in *Fifteen Thousand Hours: Secondary Schools and their Effects on Children* (1979) reported research that showed, in the face of much previous research suggesting the opposite, that 'good' schools can make a difference to the life chances of all pupils. Rutter suggested that it is features of the school's organization which make this difference. These positive features are summarized below:

- Teachers are well prepared for lessons.
- Teachers have high expectations of pupils' academic performance, and set and mark classwork and homework regularly.
- Teachers set examples of behaviour; for example, they are on time and they use only officially approved forms of discipline.
- Teachers place more emphasis on praise and reward than on blame and punishment.
- Teachers treat pupils as responsible people, for example by giving them positions of responsibility looking after school books and property.
- Teachers show an interest in the pupils and encourage them to do well.
- There is an atmosphere or ethos in the school which reflects the above points, with all teachers sharing a commitment to the aims and values of the school.
- There is a mixture of abilities in the school, as the presence of high-ability pupils benefits the academic performance and behaviour of pupils of all abilities.

Activity

Refer to the box above.
1 Explain how you think each of the features of a 'good' school which Rutter and his colleagues describe might or might not help pupils of all backgrounds and abilities to make more progress.
2 Do you agree or disagree with Rutter's features of a 'good' school? Are there any other features that you would expect to find in a 'good' school or college? Give reasons for your answer.
3 List at least *six* characteristics, based on your own opinions and reading, of a 'good teacher'.
4 How important do you think the role of the school and teachers is in the educational progress of pupils compared to the material and cultural factors discussed earlier in this chapter?

underachievement may have led teachers to expect working-class pupils to perform poorly, and these low expectations may actually be an important factor contributing to their failure.

Much of the research in this area is based on the Interactionist perspective. From this perspective, pupils are not seen simply as passive 'victims' of structural material or cultural forces outside the school which cause underachievement. On the contrary, the emphasis is on the way, through interaction with others, teachers or pupils come to interpret and define situations, and develop meanings which influence the way they behave.

Teacher evaluations, stereotyping, labelling and the self-fulfilling prophecy
Teachers are constantly involved in judging and classifying pupils in various ways, such as 'bright' or 'slow', as 'troublemakers' or ideal pupils, or as hard-working or lazy. This process of classification or *labelling* by teachers has been shown to affect the performance of students. The stereotype held by the teacher (good/bad or thick/bright student and so on) can produce a **halo effect**.

Writers such as Hargreaves (1976), Cicourel and Kitsuse (1971), Becker (1971) and Keddie (1971) found teachers initially evaluate pupils in relation to their stereotypes of the 'ideal pupil'. A whole range of non-academic factors such as speech, dress, personality (how cooperative, polite and so on), enthusiasm for work, conduct and appearance make up this stereotype of the 'ideal pupil', and influence teachers' assessments of students' ability. The social class of the student has an important influence on this evaluation. Students from working-class homes are often seen as being poorly motivated and lacking support from the home, and showing disruptive behaviour in the classroom. This may mean they are perceived by teachers as lacking ability, even if they are very able. By contrast, those from middle-class backgrounds

A **halo effect** is when pupils become stereotyped, either favourably, or unfavourably on the basis of earlier impressions, and these impressions colour future teacher–student relations.

In what ways might attitudes and behaviour of teachers affect a atudent's progress?

most closely fit the teacher's 'ideal pupil' stereotype, and teachers may assume that children who enter school already confident, fluent and familiar with learning, who are more likely to be from middle-class homes, have greater potential and will push them to achieve accordingly.

The way teachers assess and evaluate students affects achievement levels, as pupils may gradually bring their own self-image in line with the one the teacher holds of them ('what's the point in trying – the teacher thinks I'm thick'). Those labelled as 'bright' and likely to be successful in education are more likely to perform in line with the teachers' expectations and predictions, while those labelled as 'slow', 'difficult' or of 'low ability' and unlikely to succeed are persuaded not to bother. In both cases, the teachers' predictions may come true. This suggests the difference between 'bright' and 'slow' or 'good' and 'bad' students, and the progress they make in school, are created by the processes of typing and labelling. This is the self-fulfilling prophecy, which is illustrated in figure 6.7 overleaf.

Research by Rosenthal and Jacobson (1968) in California provided useful evidence of the self-fulfilling prophecy. They found that a randomly chosen group of students whom teachers were told were bright and could be expected to make good progress, even though they were no different from other students in terms of ability, did in fact make greater progress than students not so labelled.

Banding is where either schools try to ensure their intakes have a spread of pupils drawn from all bands of ability, or, more commonly, it is used as an alternative word for **streaming**. Streaming is where in schools students are divided into groups of similar ability (bands or streams) in which they stay for all subjects. **Setting** is where students are divided into groups (sets) of the same ability in particular subjects.

Banding, **streaming** and **setting** are ways of grouping students according to their actual or predicted ability. Banding is used in two ways. It is sometimes used to describe the situation where comprehensive schools try to ensure their intakes have a spread of pupils drawn from all bands of ability. More commonly, it is used as an alternative word for streaming. Streaming is where students are divided into groups of similar ability (bands or streams) in which they stay for all subjects. Setting is where school students are divided into groups (sets) of the same ability in particular subjects. For example, a student might be in a top Maths set, with the most able Maths students, but in a bottom set for English.

Being placed in a low stream or set may undermine pupils' confidence and discourage them from trying, and teachers may be less ambitious and give less knowledge to lower-stream children than they would with others. This was confirmed by Ball's research in *Beachside Comprehensive* (1981). Ball found that top-stream students were 'warmed up' by encouragement to achieve highly and to follow academic courses of study. On the other hand, lower-stream students were 'cooled out' and encouraged to follow lower status vocational and practical courses, and consequently achieved lower levels of academic success, frequently leaving school at the earliest opportunity.

Since streaming, or banding, is often linked to social class – the higher a pupil's social class, the greater the chance of being allocated to a top stream – it contributes to the underachievement of working-class pupils. This is illustrated in figure 6.8 over the page.

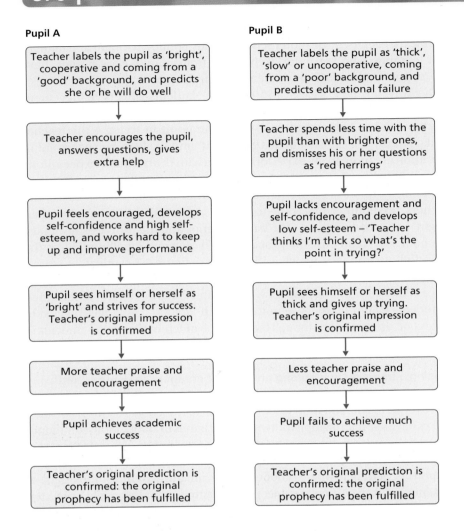

Figure 6.7 The self-fulfilling prophecy: two examples

Pupil A

Teacher labels the pupil as 'bright', cooperative and coming from a 'good' background, and predicts she or he will do well

↓

Teacher encourages the pupil, answers questions, gives extra help

↓

Pupil feels encouraged, develops self-confidence and high self-esteem, and works hard to keep up and improve performance

↓

Pupil sees himself or herself as 'bright' and strives for success. Teacher's original impression is confirmed

↓

More teacher praise and encouragement

↓

Pupil achieves academic success

↓

Teacher's original prediction is confirmed: the original prophecy has been fulfilled

Pupil B

Teacher labels the pupil as 'thick', 'slow' or uncooperative, coming from a 'poor' background, and predicts educational failure

↓

Teacher spends less time with the pupil than with brighter ones, and dismisses his or her questions as 'red herrings'

↓

Pupil lacks encouragement and self-confidence, and develops low self-esteem – 'Teacher thinks I'm thick so what's the point in trying?'

↓

Pupil sees himself or herself as thick and gives up trying. Teacher's original impression is confirmed

↓

Less teacher praise and encouragement

↓

Pupil fails to achieve much success

↓

Teacher's original prediction is confirmed: the original prophecy has been fulfilled

Unequal access to classroom knowledge Keddie found that teachers taught those in higher-stream classes differently from those in lower streams. Pupils were expected to behave better and do more work, and teachers gave them more, and different types of, educational knowledge, which gave them greater opportunities for educational success. Lower-stream working-class pupils might therefore underachieve in education partly because they have not been given access to the knowledge required for educational success.

The anti-school (counter-school) subculture Most schools generally place a high value on things such as hard work, good behaviour and exam success. One of the effects of streaming and labelling is to divide students into those in the top streams who achieve highly, who more or less conform to these aims

Figure 6.8 Social class divisions and streaming/banding

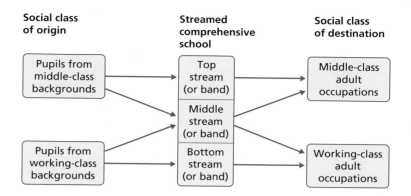

and therefore achieve high status in the school, and those in the bottom streams who are labelled as 'failures' by the school and are therefore deprived of status. In response to this, as studies by Hargreaves in *Social Relations in a Secondary School* and Ball in *Beachside Comprehensive* have shown, bottom-stream pupils often rebel against the school and develop an alternative set of values, attitudes and behaviour in opposition to the academic aims of the school. This is the anti-school or counter-school subculture, as Willis found among 'the lads' discussed earlier in this chapter.

The anti-school subculture provides a means for bottom-stream pupils to improve their own self-esteem, by giving them status in the eyes of their peer

The anti-school, or counter-school, subculture

group which has been denied them by the school. In this subculture, truancy, playing up teachers, messing about, breaking the school rules, copying work (or not doing any) and generally disrupting the smooth running of the school become a way of getting back at the system and resisting a schooling which has labelled them as failures and denied them status. These are responses to the labels which have been placed on pupils by the school, and as bottom-stream pupils are more likely to be from working-class backgrounds, this contributes further to poor educational performance.

Activity

1 List all the reasons you can think of to explain why pupils from lower working-class homes are more likely to be placed in lower streams than those from middle-class backgrounds.
2 Have you had any experience of the self-fulfilling prophecy in your own schooling? How do teachers communicate impressions of whether they think you are 'bright' or not, and how do you think this might have affected your progress?
3 In what ways do you think students in lower streams are treated differently and given different knowledge from those in higher streams? Give examples to illustrate your answer.
4 How do you think schools and teachers 'warm up' or 'cool out' students?
5 Is there any evidence of an anti-school subculture in your own school, or the school you once attended? What do you think membership of an anti-school subculture might mean to those who belong to it? Draw on examples from your own schooling.

An evaluation of interactionist approaches to education

Interactionist approaches recognize the importance of what happens inside schools Interactionists emphasize the importance of what happens in schools and classrooms, rather than putting the whole blame for educational failure on deficiencies in the pupil, their family, their cultural values and attitudes, or material circumstances arising from their social class background.

They are too deterministic Interactionist theories can be too deterministic, in the sense that they suggest that once a negative label is applied, it will always have a negative effect, with the self-fulfilling prophecy coming into effect. In fact, a negative label like 'thick' or 'waster' may have the opposite effect, and encourage those so labelled to prove the label wrong via hard work and academic success.

They do not pay enough attention to the distribution of power in society
Interactionist theories do not explain why so many teachers seem to hold similar views on what counts as an 'ideal pupil', what constitutes 'proper' educational knowledge and ability, and why these appear to be related to social class. They therefore do not take enough account of the distribution of power in society, which means some definitions of knowledge, culture and ability are given more importance than others (as Bourdieu's theory of cultural capital and habitus suggests).

They do not pay enough attention to factors outside the school   Interactionists do not take enough account of the structural, material and cultural factors outside the school, discussed earlier, which influence what happens inside the school. Teachers and schools cannot be held solely responsible for what happens in schools, and they certainly cannot be blamed for problems which have their roots outside the school in the structure of inequality in the wider society.

They do not pay enough attention to other factors inside the school   Interactionists do not take sufficient account of other factors inside the school, apart from the labelling process, which have an influence on the achievement levels of students, and are often beyond the control of teachers themselves. These include:

- class sizes
- the financial resources given to education
- the demand to publish 'league tables' of exam results (which may influence who gets entered, and whether pupils – and therefore money – are attracted to the school or not)
- teacher morale (partly arising from pay and conditions issues, and how much upheaval they are expected to deal with as a result of government changes in schools)
- the need for teachers, regardless of their philosophy or beliefs, to classify/stratify pupils at an early age for different exams and occupational routes

They do not provide full explanations   The interactionist approach is very helpful in drawing attention to the factors inside schools which explain working-class underachievement. However, a full explanation of underachievement in education needs to take account of factors both outside the school and inside the school, both material and cultural factors and interaction in the classroom. In other words, a full account of working-class underachievement needs to look at both structural *and* interactionist explanations.

The double test for working-class students

Taken together, the factors in the home, social class background and the school discussed above help to explain why working-class young people do less well at school than their middle-class peers of the same ability. Schools test all pupils when doing subjects like mathematics, English or science. However, for the working-class student there is a double test. At the same time as coping with the academic difficulties of school work which all pupils face, working-class students must also cope with a wide range of other disadvantages and difficulties.

These problems, on top of the demands of academic work, explain working-class underachievement in schools. These disadvantages start in the primary school and become more and more emphasized as young people grow older, as they fall further and further behind and become more disillusioned with school. In this context, it is perhaps not surprising that a large majority of those who leave school at age 16 every year, with few or no qualifications, come from lower working-class backgrounds.

Activity

Complete the following summary of explanations for social class differences in educational achievement, filling in the gaps from the word list below. Each dash represents one word.

'cooled out'	ability	Bourdieu
meritocratic	dominant class	deprivation
anti-school	poverty	functionalist
streaming	Marxist	legitimize
material circumstances	deficient	interactionist
'warmed up'	self-fulfilling prophecy	evaluations
compensatory	social class stereotypes	restricted
intelligence		educational qualifications

___ theories argue that education selects and allocates the most talented people to the most functionally important roles according to ___ criteria like ability, talents and skills as shown by ___ ___ and achievement. Achievement reflects ___, and middle-class young people are more intelligent and harder working than working-class young people.

___ theories argue that schools ___ social class inequality by making it *appear* that working-class students fail because of their lack of ___ , when in fact it is a consequence of their home and social class background, and the culture and ideology of the school.

___ explains working-class underachievement as a consequence of the lack of cultural capital, and the fact that the culture of the school is the culture of the ___ ___.

___ ___ of the home affect educational achievement, with factors such as ___ and low wages, poor housing and overcrowding, poorer health and more sickness all contributing to the underachievement of working-class pupils.

Cultural ___ theories suggest that the culture of the lower working class is ___ or deprived. Their different values and attitudes, the lack of parental interest and encouragement, their use of the ___ code of language and their lack of cultural capital undermine their chances of success in education, though positive discrimination and ___ education might help.

___ theories emphasize the importance of what goes on inside schools and classrooms. Teachers' ___ through typing, labelling, banding and ___ generate the ___-___ ___. Middle-class pupils are ___ ___ to succeed, and working-class pupils are ___ ___ to fail. Teachers give different knowledge to, and make different demands on, pupils depending on the stream the students are in. Streaming often reflects ___ ___ ___. These factors can lead to the formation of ___-___ subcultures with opposition to and rejection of educational success.

The solution to this activity can be found on the teacher's pages of www.polity.co.uk/browne.

Activity

1   Identify and explain *three* factors inside schools which may explain the underachievement of pupils from disadvantaged backgrounds.
2   Explain what is meant by 'labelling', and how it might influence the educational achievements of pupils.
3   Answer the following essay question, in about one and a half sides of A4 paper: *Evaluate the arguments and evidence for the view that poverty and material circumstances are the most important reasons for educational underachievement.*

(Hint: remember there is a range of explanations apart from poverty and material circumstances.)

Gender differences in educational achievement: the underachievement of boys

While the educational achievements of both males and females have improved in recent years, there are still big differences between them. Until the 1980s, the major concern was with the underachievement of girls. This was because, while girls used to perform better than boys in the earlier stages of their education, up to GCSE, after this they tended to fall behind, being less likely than boys to get the three A levels required for university entry, and less likely to go into higher education. However, in the early 1990s girls began to outperform boys, particularly working-class boys, in all areas and at all levels of the education system. The main problem today is with the underachievement of boys,

Girls are generally much more successful in education than boys

---

Facts on gender differences in educational achievement

- Girls do better than boys at every stage in National Curriculum SAT (Standard Assessment Test) results in English, maths and science.
- Girls are now more successful than boys at every level in GCSE, outperforming boys in every major subject (including traditional boys' subjects like design, technology, maths and chemistry) except physics. In English at GCSE, the gender gap is huge, with more than two-thirds of girls getting grades *A–C, compared to about half of boys.
- A higher proportion of females stays on in post-16 sixth-form and further education, and post-18 higher education.
- Female school leavers are now more likely than males to get three or more A-level passes.
- More women than men get accepted for university. In 2006, women made up about 56 per cent of top-graded entrants (with the best A-level scores). Over half (54 per cent) of those accepted on degree courses were female, and women now make up a larger proportion of graduates with upper-second and first-class university degrees.

---

although there are still concerns about the different subjects studied by boys and girls. There are also concerns that girls could do even better if teachers spent as much time with girls as they are obliged to do with boys.

Figure 6.9 Some male and female differences in educational achievement: United Kingdom, 2006

Source: Data from DfES and UCAS

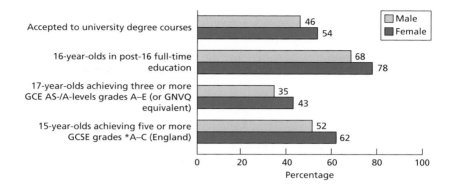

Problems remaining for girls

Despite the general pattern of girls outperforming boys, problems do still remain for girls. The attention given to girls outperforming boys and the underachievement of boys can draw attention away from the fact that large numbers of girls are also low attainers and are underachieving. Girls still tend to do different subjects from boys, which influences future career choices. Broadly, arts subjects are 'female', science and technology subjects 'male'. This exists at GCSE, but becomes even more pronounced at A level and above. Girls are therefore less likely to participate after 16 in subjects leading to careers in science, engineering and technology.

Girls tend to slip back between GCSE and A level, with girls achieving fewer high-grade A levels than boys with the same GCSE results. There is little evidence that the generally better results of girls at 16 and above lead to improved post-school opportunities in terms of training and employment. Women are still less likely than men with similar qualifications to achieve similar levels of success in paid employment and men still hold the majority of the positions of power in society. Among people in the 16–59 age group in the population as a whole who are in employment or unemployed, men tend to be better qualified than women. However, this gap has decreased among younger age groups, and can be expected to disappear if females keep on outperforming males in education.

Explaining gender differences in education

What follows are some suggested hypotheses and explanations, based on further research, including updated research by Eirene Mitsos and Ken Browne (1998), for the huge improvement in the performance of girls, the underperformance of boys and the subject choices that continue to separate males and females. The explanations are summarized in figure 6.10.

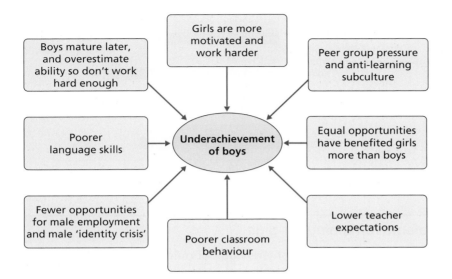

Figure 6.10 Gender and educational underachievement

Diagram boxes:
- Girls are more motivated and work harder
- Boys mature later, and overestimate ability so don't work hard enough
- Peer group pressure and anti-learning subculture
- Poorer language skills
- **Underachievement of boys**
- Equal opportunities have benefited girls more than boys
- Fewer opportunities for male employment and male 'identity crisis'
- Poorer classroom behaviour
- Lower teacher expectations

Why do females now do better than males?

The women's movement and feminism The women's movement and feminism have achieved considerable success in improving the rights and raising the expectations and self-esteem of women. They have challenged the traditional stereotype of women's roles as housewives and mothers, and this means many women now look beyond being a housewife/mother as their main role in life.

Equal opportunities The work of sociologists in highlighting the educational underperformance of girls in the past led to a greater emphasis in schools on equal opportunities, in order to enable girls to fulfil their potential more easily. These policies included, among others, monitoring teaching and teaching materials for gender bias to help schools to meet the needs of girls better, encouraging 'girl-friendliness' not only in male-dominated subjects but across the whole range of the experience of girls in schools. Teachers are now much more sensitive about avoiding gender stereotyping in the classroom, and this may have overcome many of the former academic problems which girls faced in schools.

Growing ambition, more positive role models and more employment opportunities for women The number of 'male' jobs, particularly in semi- and unskilled manual work, has declined in recent years, while there are growing employment opportunities for women in the service sector. As a consequence, girls have become more ambitious, and they are less likely to see having a home and family as their main role in life. Many girls growing up today have mothers working in paid employment, who provide positive role models for them. Many girls now recognize that the future involves paid employment, often combined with family responsibilities. Sue Sharpe found in *Just Like a Girl* in 1976 that girls' priorities were 'love, marriage, husbands, children, jobs, and careers, more or less in that order'. When she repeated her research in 1994, she found these priorities had changed to 'job, career and being able to support themselves'. Becky Francis (2000) carried out research involving observation of twelve classes of 14–16 year olds and interviews with students in three London secondary schools in 1998–9. Her interviews with girls confirmed Sharpe's findings, and she found many girls were very ambitious, aiming for higher professional occupations like doctors and solicitors, rather than the traditional female occupations like clerical work, hairdressing or beauty therapy. These factors may all have provided more incentives for girls to gain qualifications.

Girls work harder and are better motivated   There is mounting evidence that girls work harder, are more conscientious and are better motivated than boys. Girls put more effort into their work, and spend more time on doing their homework properly. They take more care with the way their work is presented, and they concentrate more in class (some research has shown the typical 14-year-old girl concentrating for about three to four times as long as her fellow male students). Girls are generally better organized: they are more likely to bring the right equipment to school and meet deadlines for handing in work. These factors may have helped girls to take more advantage of the increased use of coursework in GCSE, and AS-/A-level and vocational courses. Such work often requires good organization and sustained application, and girls do better than boys in these respects. It remains to be seen whether the abolition of coursework in most AS and A levels from 2008 onwards will have a greater negative impact on girls' than on boys' achievement levels.

Girls mature earlier   By the age of 16, girls are estimated to be more mature than boys by up to two years. Put simply, this means girls are more likely to view exams in a far more responsible way, and recognize their seriousness and the importance of the academic and career choices that lie ahead of them.

Why do boys underachieve?

Many of the reasons given above also suggest why boys may be underachieving. However, there are some additional explanations.

Lower expectations   There is some evidence that staff are not as strict with boys as with girls. They are more likely to extend deadlines for work, to have lower expectations of boys, to be more tolerant of disruptive, unruly behaviour from boys in the classroom and to accept more poorly presented work. This will mean boys perform less well than they otherwise might.

Boys are more disruptive   Boys are generally more disruptive in classrooms than girls. They may lose classroom learning time because they are sent out of the room or sent home. Four out of every five permanent exclusions and three out of four fixed-term exclusions from schools are of boys; most of these are for disobedience of various kinds, and usually come at the end of a series of incidents.

The anti-learning subculture   Boys, especially working-class boys, appear to gain 'street cred' and peer group status by not working, and some develop almost an anti-education, anti-learning subculture, where schoolwork is seen as 'girly' and 'unmacho'. This was shown by Epstein et al. (1998), who found that working-class boys faced harassment, bullying and being labelled as 'gay' if they appeared to be hard-working at school. This may explain why they are less conscientious and lack the persistence and application required for exam success. This anti-learning subculture is like that adopted by 'the lads' in Paul Willis's *Learning to Labour*, discussed earlier in this chapter. This was rediscovered by Stephen Byers, a former schools minister, in January 1998 when he said, 'We must challenge the laddish, anti-learning culture which has been allowed to develop over recent years and should not simply accept with a shrug of the shoulders that boys will be boys.' Francis's research referred to above confirmed this view that boys achieved more peer group 'macho' status by resisting teachers and schools, through 'laddish' behaviour like messing about in class and not getting on with their work, contributing to their underachievement.

Teaching is often seen as a mainly female profession, and there is a lack of positive male role models, especially in primary schools. This may be a further reason why learning comes to be seen by some boys, from an early age, as a 'feminine' and 'girly' activity. This may further contribute to a negative attitude to schools and schooling.

Declining male employment opportunities and the male 'identity crisis'
The decline in traditional male jobs is also a factor in explaining why many boys are underperforming in education. They may lack motivation and ambition because they may feel that they have only limited prospects, and getting qualifications won't get them anywhere anyway, so what's the point in bothering? These changing employment patterns have resulted in a number of (predominantly white and working-class) boys and men having lowered expectations, a low self-image and a lack of self-esteem, and have brought about an identity crisis for men, who feel unsure about their role and position. This insecurity is reflected in schools, where boys don't see the point in working hard and trying to achieve. The future looks bleak to them and without clear purpose. This leads boys to attempt to construct a positive self-image away from achievement and towards 'laddish behaviour' and aggressive macho posturing in attempts to draw attention to themselves.

Feeling and behaving differently   Boys and girls feel differently about their own ability, with most boys overestimating their ability, and girls underestimating theirs. Research by Michael Barber (1996) at Keele University's Centre for Successful Schools showed 'that more boys than girls think that they are able or very able, and fewer boys than girls think they are "below average"'. Yet GCSE results show these perceptions to be the reverse of the truth. Boys feel that they are bright and capable but at the same time they say they don't like school and they don't work hard enough to get the results they think they're capable of. This was confirmed by Francis's research in three London secondary schools in 1998–9 , which found that some boys thought it would be easy to do well in exams without having to put in much effort. When they do fail, boys tend to blame either the teachers or their own lack of effort – not their ability. Girls on the other hand lack confidence in and underestimate their ability, and feel undervalued, as researchers such as Licht and Dweck (1987) and Michelle Stanworth (1983) found.

Different leisure – doing not talking   More research is coming to the conclusion that the differences in the achievement of girls and boys is due to the differing ways in which the genders behave and spend their leisure time. To simplify and generalize: while boys run around kicking footballs,

Girls relate to one another by *talking*, while boys are more likely to relate to each other by *doing* things. Do you think this is true in your own experience?

playing sports or computer games, and engaging in other aspects of 'laddish' behaviour, girls are more likely to read or to stand around talking. Girls relate to one another by *talking*, while boys often relate to their peers by *doing*. The value of talking, even if it is about the heartthrob of Year 11, is that it tends to develop the linguistic and reasoning skills needed at school and in many non-manual service sector jobs. Peter Douglas argues that 'school is essentially a linguistic experience and most subjects require good levels of comprehension and writing skills'. Further research is revealing an emerging picture of boys viewing the crucial reading and linguistic skills as 'sissy'.

Boys don't like reading   Girls like reading while boys don't: boys see reading as a predominantly feminine activity, which is boring, not real work, a waste of time and to be avoided at all costs. Reading is 'feminized' in our culture: women are not only the main consumers of reading in our society, but they are also the ones who read, talk about and 'spread the word' about books, and they are more likely to be the ones who read to their children (and they are more likely to read to their daughters than to their sons). Girls are therefore more likely to have positive role models of their own sex than boys. Research has shown that boys tend to stop being interested in reading at about 8 years old.

Girls and boys also tend to read different things: girls read fiction while boys read for information. Schools tend to reproduce this gendered divide: fiction tends to be the main means of learning to read in the primary school years and this puts girls at an early advantage in education.

Activity

Drawing on your own experience, and giving examples, do you think:
- Boys overestimate their ability, while girls underestimate theirs?
- Boys and girls behave differently in school, particularly in relation to how they behave with their peer group?
- Boys don't read as much as girls, and when they do, read different things?
- Boys are more likely to show an anti-education, anti-learning subculture than girls?
- Girls work harder than boys?

Why do males and females still tend to study different subjects?

There is still a difference between the subjects that males and females do at GCSE and above, as figure 6.11 on page 391 shows.

Females are still more likely to take arts and humanities subjects, like English literature, foreign languages and sociology, and males are more likely to take scientific and technological subjects – particularly at A level and above (even though girls generally get better results when they do take them).

This is despite the National Curriculum, which makes maths, English and science compulsory for all students. However, even within the National Curriculum, there are gender differences in option choices. For example, girls are more likely to take home economics, textiles and food technology, while boys are more likely to opt for electronics, woodwork or graphics. How can we explain these differences?

Gender socialization   From an early age boys and girls are encouraged to play with different toys and do different activities at home, and they very often grow up seeing their parents playing different roles around the house. Research in 1974 by Lobban found evidence of gender stereotyping in children's books, with women more clearly linked to traditional domestic roles. Research by Best in 1993 found that little had changed since Lobban conducted her research. Such socialization may encourage boys to develop more interest in technical and scientific subjects, and discourage girls from taking them. In giving subject and career advice, teachers may be reflecting their own socialization and expectations, and reinforcing the different experiences of boys and girls by counselling them into different subject options, according to their own gender stereotypes of 'suitable subjects'.

Science and the science classroom are still seen as mainly 'masculine'   As Kelly (1987) found, boys tend to dominate science classrooms – grabbing apparatus first, answering questions aimed at girls and so on, which all undermine girls' confidence and intimidate them from taking up these subjects. Gender stereotyping is still found in science, with the 'invisibility' of females particularly obvious in maths and science textbooks, where examples are often more relevant to the experience of males than females. This reinforces the view that these are 'male' subjects. Research by Colley (1998) suggested that the gender perceptions of different subjects are important influences on subject choice, with the arts and humanities seen by students as feminine, and science and technology as masculine. Colley suggested that the changing content of the curriculum of some subjects can change its gender identity. For example, she found that music, which has traditionally been seen as a feminine subject, is becoming more popular with boys. This is borne out by recent figures. For example, in 2001, boys made up 42 per cent of GCSE music entries, 47 per cent of AS entries, and 43 per cent of A-level entries. By 2006, this had increased to 49 per cent at GCSE, 58 per cent at AS, and 54 per cent at A level. The entry of boys for music GCSE increased in this period by 38 per cent (compared to 13 per cent for girls), by 84 per cent for AS (36 per cent for girls) and by 61 per cent for A-level music, compared to 21 per cent for girls. Colley's research suggested that this change may largely be because the subject has become more computer and electronics based. This application of technology to music production has contributed to the

Activity

Refer to figure 6.11

1 In which three A-level subjects was the gap between the percentages of male and female entries the greatest?
2 In which three GCSE subjects was the gap between the percentages of male and female entries the greatest?
3 In which A-level subjects were there more male than female entries in 2006?
4 Which subject showed the greatest gap between the percentages of male and female entries at both GCSE and A level?
5 Which subject had more male entries at GCSE, but more female entries at A level?
6 Why do you think the gap in subject entries between males and females tends, in general, to be smaller at GCSE than at A level?
7 Drawing on the data in figure 6.11, outline the main gender differences in subject choices at GCSE and A level, and suggest reasons for them, with reference to specific subjects.

Activity

Applying the research methods studies in the previous chapter:

1 Observe classroom activities and try to see if boys and girls behave differently in class or are treated differently by teachers. For example, do they sit separately? Are boys or girls asked more questions? Are boys more disruptive? Does this vary between different subject classes and between male and female teachers? (If you plan to do classroom observation, applying Flanders Interaction Analysis might be useful – see page 317 in chapter 5.)
2 Interview a sample of male and female students, asking them about what influenced them in making subject and exam choices.

'masculinization' of the subject's content, making it more appealing as a subject option for boys.

Some concluding comments on gender and underachievement

Educational research, such as that of Spender (1982), has shown that teachers' time is spent mostly on the troublesome boys, rather than on the girls who are keen to learn and to get on with their schooling. Stanworth found students themselves thought boys got more than twice the amount of attention from teachers than girls, in terms of getting help, being asked questions and being encouraged to get involved in class discussions. Francis's research in 1998–9 found classrooms were still dominated by boys, and girls were

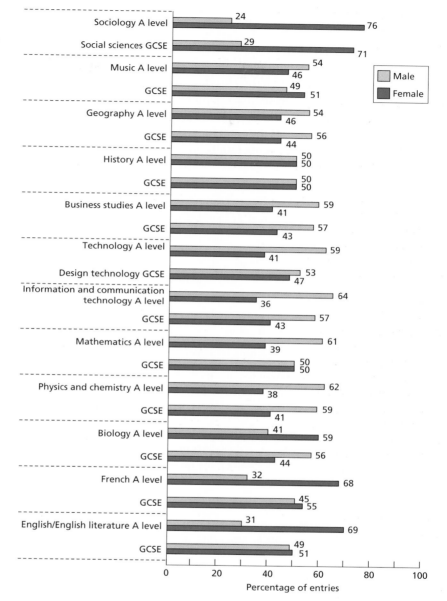

Figure 6.11 Percentages of male compared to female students entering for different subjects at GCSE and A level: United Kingdom, 2006

Source: Joint Council for Qualifications, 2007

getting less attention. Girls therefore see teachers spending more time with the boys than with them.

In the face of girls' marked disadvantages, such as underrating themselves and a lack of confidence in their ability, getting less of teachers' time, and having to tolerate the dominance of boys in the classroom, it is perhaps surprising that they tend to do much better at school than boys. This suggests that girls may still be underachieving, even if they are not doing so in relation to the boys.

It is still men who hold most of the highly paid, powerful positions in society – it is still mainly men who pull the strings and run our society. Women go out to work more than they used to, and they now make up about half the workforce. However, as seen in chapter 2, research has shown that in the home gender roles have not changed that much: women now not only go out to paid work a lot more, but they still have the majority of the burden of housework, childcare and managing family emotions.

Activity

The following comments are from Year 11 boys talking about doing English and science:

'I hate it! I don't want to read books.'

'Science is straightforward. You don't have to think about it. There are definite answers. There are no shades to it.'

'In science, everything is set out as a formula, and you have the facts. All you have to do is apply them to the situation.'

'When you read a book, it's like delving into people's lives. It's being nosey.'

'English is about understanding, interpreting . . . you have to think more. There's no definite answer . . . the answer depends on your view of things.'

'I don't like having discussions – I feel wrong . . . I think that people will jump down my throat.'

'That's why girls do English, because they don't mind getting something wrong. They're more open about issues, they're more understanding . . . they find it easier to comprehend other people's views and feelings.'

'You feel safe in science.'

(Adapted from Eirene Mitsos, 'Boys and English: classroom voices', *English and Media Magazine*, nos 33 and 34 (1995 and 1996))

1 What points are being made above about why females are more likely to choose to study English than males?
2 Identify all the ways you can think of that gender differences in subject choices might be linked to gender role socialization in society as a whole.
3 Go through the reasons suggested in the sections above for why girls outperform boys in education. List the explanations in what you think is their order of importance, and explain/justify your reasons.
4 Using your answer to question 3, suggest measures that might be taken to improve the educational performance of boys.
5 Drawing on your own experience of schooling, can you identify ways in which

boys and girls are treated differently by teachers? Do boys behave differently in class to girls? Are they more disruptive in the classroom? Do boys have a different attitude to school work and to different subjects? Were/are there some subjects in your school which attracted more of one sex than another? Why do you think this might be?

6   Do you think girls, even though they are doing better than boys, are still underachieving in education?

7   Go to the following website, www.standards.dfes.gov.uk/genderandachievement, and identify and explain three policies which are currently being followed to try to improve the educational performance of boys.

Activity

1   Identify and explain *three* reasons why girls outperform boys in education.
2   Explain what is meant by an 'anti-learning subculture'.
3   Explain how equal opportunity policies may have contributed to the improved educational performance of girls in recent years.
4   Identify and explain *two* reasons why girls and boys often choose to study different subjects.
5   On about one and a half sides of A4 paper, answer the following question: *Examine sociological explanations for the difference in the performance of boys and girls in the education system.*

Ethnicity and educational achievement

While individuals from all ethnic minorities may do outstandingly well, there is concern about the performance of some groups taken overall (see box overleaf). The key research in Britain on the underachievement of some ethnic minorities comes from the Swann Report of 1985, two Ofsted (Office for Standards in Education) reports, *Recent Research on the Achievements of Ethnic Minority Pupils* (Gillborn and Gipps, 1996) and *Mapping Race, Class and Gender* (Gillborn and Mirza, 2000), and three DfES (Department for Education and Skills, now the Department for Children, Schools and Families – DCSF) reports, *Minority Ethnic Attainment and Participation in Education and Training: The Evidence* (2004) and *Ethnicity and Education: The Evidence on Minority Ethnic Pupils* (2005), and the latter's update in 2006.

Overall, minority ethnic groups tend to do less well than other members of the population, although there are important differences between minority ethnic groups, and the overall statistics disguise wide variations between

Achievement and underachievement among ethnic groups

Many children from minority ethnic groups tend to do as well as, and often better than, many white children. For example, Indian Asians are more likely to get better GCSE and A-level results, to stay in education after the age of 16, and to enter university than white students. However, those of Pakistani and Bangladeshi origin, and particularly males from African-Caribbean backgrounds, tend to do less well than they should given their ability:

- Taken overall, they appear to have below average reading skills.
- African-Caribbean, Pakistani and Bangladeshi pupils consistently have lower levels of attainment than other ethnic groups across all National Curriculum key stages and are less likely to attain higher grade (*A–C) GCSE results than children of white or Indian origin.
- African-Caribbeans are overrepresented (there are more than there should be given their numbers in the population as a whole) in special schools for those with learning difficulties. They are one and a half times as likely to be categorized as having emotional, behavioural or social difficulties as white British students.
- The performance of African-Caribbean pupils worsens as they go through the schooling system, deteriorating between Key Stage 1 and Key Stage 4.
- Despite rising standards of achievement for all ethnic groups, the gap between African-Caribbean and Pakistani pupils and their white peers is now larger than it was ten years ago.
- African-Caribbean school students are between three and six times more likely to be permanently excluded from schools than white students of the same sex, and to be excluded for longer periods than white students for the same offences.
- Where schools are streamed by ability, they are overrepresented in the lower streams. Evidence suggests they are placed in lower streams even when they get better results than some students placed in higher streams.
- They are more likely than other groups to leave school without any qualifications.
- They are less likely to stay on in education post-16, and when they do, they are more likely to follow vocational courses rather than the higher status academic courses, like AS and A levels.

individuals – some minority ethnic group children are very successful in the education system.

Explanations for ethnic group differences in education

There is no single factor that explains the differences between ethnic groups – a range of factors work together to produce the lower levels of achievement of some minority ethnic groups.

Social class, gender and ethnicity

It is important to remember that social class and gender differences in education can also contribute to explaining differential achievement in terms of ethnicity. The variety of explanations already considered in relation to class and gender should always be born in mind when attempting to explain differences between minority ethnic groups. For example, one explanation for the high attainment of children from Indian Asian minority backgrounds is that they come from a relatively middle-class group, with the underachievement of African-Caribbeans, Pakistanis and Bangladeshis explained by reference to their predominantly working-class backgrounds. All the explanations discussed above surrounding material deprivation, language differences, cultural deprivation, lack of cultural capital, teacher attitudes, teacher expectations/labelling and the self-fulfilling prophecy may then contribute to explaining the differences between ethnic groups.

However, while these factors have an impact, social class differences alone cannot explain differences in achievement between ethnic groups. Gillborn and Mirza (2000) noted: 'Social class factors do not override the influence of ethnic inequality: when comparing pupils with similar class backgrounds there are still marked inequalities of attainment between different ethnic groups.' In other words, black pupils from middle-class backgrounds are little better placed to succeed in education than white pupils from working-class backgrounds.

Social class and material factors

Disadvantaged backgrounds   Minority ethnic children are more likely to live in low income households, and to be in the poorer sections of the working class. Around two-thirds of Pakistani and Bangladeshi households are living below the poverty line. African-Caribbean and Pakistani and Bangladeshi people are around three times more likely to be unemployed as white people. In 2006, 20 per cent of white households were low income households, compared with around 41 per cent of African-Caribbean households, and 62 per cent of Pakistani or Bangladeshi households. In 2005, around 70 per cent of Bangladeshi pupils, 60 per cent of Pakistani pupils and around 50 per cent of African-Caribbean pupils lived in the 20 per cent most deprived postcode areas. This means many face problems like poor quality housing, overcrowding, higher levels of unemployment (partly due to racism) and general material disadvantage which may affect achievement levels in school.

Advantaged backgrounds   Indian and African-Asian children are more likely to come from business and professional middle-class family backgrounds, thereby gaining all the benefits that being middle-class confers in education. This variation in background may mean that some of the differences between ethnic groups in terms of educational achievement may have less to do with ethnicity as such, and more to do with social and economic disadvantage. However, this is not in itself adequate to explain all the differences between ethnic groups, as there are differences between ethnic groups from the same social class backgrounds.

While all the main ethnic groups are achieving more than ever before, the achievements of white and Indian Asian people have improved far more than those of Pakistani and Bangladeshi pupils, and the gap between them has actually widened. Social class differences cannot explain this, as Indian Asian students are doing better, and African-Caribbean and Pakistani and Bangladeshi students doing worse, than white students from the same social class background.

Language

In some Asian households, English is not the main language used, and in some black (African-Caribbean) households Caribbean English is used. The 2006 DfES report found that pupils for whom English was an additional language had lower attainment than pupils whose first language was English.

Language differences may cause difficulties in doing some schoolwork and communicating with the teacher, and white, middle-class teachers may mistake language difficulties for lack of ability in general, and therefore have lower expectations of some of their pupils.

Because Caribbean English is a different form of English, it may be unconsciously penalized in the classroom, because most teachers are white and middle class. The active discouragement of children from using their 'mother' tongue in school, and negative labelling, may provide obstacles to learning and motivation in school, as the self-fulfilling prophecy takes effect. However, the Swann Report found that while language factors might hold back some children, for the majority they were of little importance, and the 2005 report referred to above found the lower attainment of pupils for whom English was an additional language, compared to those for whom English was their first language, was narrower at Key Stage 4 than Key Stage 1, and therefore diminishes as children get older.

Family Life

African-Caribbean communities have a high level of lone parenthood, and this may pose financial and practical problems in supporting their children's education, no matter how much concern they may have about their children's progress. For African-Caribbean girls, who display higher levels of achievement than African-Caribbean boys, the fact that women are often the primary breadwinners in many African-Caribbean families may provide positive role models for girls and encourage higher levels of achievement – a recognition that they themselves will in future be major breadwinners.

Asian family life has been characterized by close-knit extended families, which provide high levels of support for education, combined with cultural values encouraging higher levels of achievement.

The Swann Report (1985) and Pilkington (1997) suggested that some minority ethnic groups enjoy greater parental support than others. However, the 2005 DfES report found parental involvement with their children's education was greater in minority ethnic groups than in the population as a whole, and a higher proportion saw their children's education as mainly the parents' responsibility rather than the school's, and this was particularly true of African-Caribbean and Bangladeshi parents. A very high proportion (82 per cent) went to parents' evenings whenever there was an opportunity, although Pakistani and Bangladeshi parents were less confident about helping their children with homework.

Racism

Racism is believing or acting as though an individual or group is superior or inferior on the grounds of their racial or ethnic origins.

A 'culture of resistance'   There are suggestions that **racism** in society as a whole may lead to low self-esteem among black pupils, and a hostility to schooling and the low-paid unskilled work it prepares them for. Stuart Hall, from a Marxist point of view, has discussed a 'culture of resistance' among African-Caribbean youth, leading to a rejection of schooling and to conflict within it when they are compelled to attend. It may well be that higher unemployment rates for African-Caribbeans contribute to a lack of motivation in school.

Teacher stereotyping, labelling and conflict in the classroom   Teachers often hold stereotypes of particular groups of students. Teachers have more positive expectations of Asians, particularly of Asian girls, generally seeing them as relatively quiet, well behaved and highly motivated. In contrast, 1992 classroom research by Wright (1992) conducted over three years in four inner city primary schools found African-Caribbean pupils were often expected to be and labelled as troublemakers by teachers and this may mean teachers take swift action against them. Research in primary and secondary schools has found an unusually high degree of conflict between white teachers and African-Caribbean students, and African-Caribbean children, unlike whites and Asians, are often punished not for any particular offence but because they have the 'wrong attitude'. A London Development Agency Education Commission report in 2004 said that relationships between African-Caribbean students and white teachers were characterized by 'conflict and fear'. An African-Caribbean student in this report pinpointed teacher stereotyping when he said: 'When it is white boys it is a group, but when it is black boys, it is a gang.' African-Caribbean (especially male) pupils are more likely to fight racism at school, and form anti-school subcultures. This may reflect the 'culture of resistance' mentioned above by Stuart Hall. These factors might explain the high level of exclusions among African-Caribbean students, since most permanent exclusions are for disobedience of various kinds, such as refusing to comply with school rules, verbal abuse, or insolence to teachers.

The Swann Report found only a small minority of teachers was consciously racist, but there is evidence of a good deal of unintentional racism, which can affect progress at school. Green, in an appendix to the Swann Report, found that some teachers with racist attitudes favoured and gave more time, individual attention and praise and encouragement to white pupils than to African-Caribbean boys and girls.

Bhatti (1999), carried out a study of Bangladeshi, Pakistani and Indian students in a comprehensive school in the south of England which she called 'Cherrydale' (not its real name). Bhatti used multiple research methods including interviews, questionnaires, and participant observation in classrooms. This research identified examples of pupils' own views of racist behaviour by teachers, which included being ignored and not being given the chance to answer questions in class, not being helped, not being given responsibility, and being unfairly picked on for punishment or a telling-off.

If teachers hold negative stereotypes, with consequent negative labelling, and have low expectations of black pupils ('slow learners'/'lack concentration'/'difficult to control'), this may lead to the development of low self-esteem among such pupils, and the labelling process may itself lead to the self-fulfilling prophecy, reinforced by the hostility to schooling among black students that such attitudes are likely to generate. This view was reinforced by the Ofsted and DfES reports of 2000 and 2005 which showed that the inequalities of attainment for African-Caribbean pupils become progressively greater as they move through the school system, deteriorating between Key Stage 1 and Key Stage 4. It would appear that the education system actively disadvantages black children.

The ethnocentric school curriculum

Many schools have strong equal opportunities policies to tackle racism, and many schools have **multicultural education**, and try to include minority ethnic group cultures within the school curriculum. Despite attempts at multicultural education, many aspects of school life and the school curriculum remain **ethnocentric**.

In education, this involves school subjects and the hidden curriculum concentrating on white British society and culture, rather than recognizing and taking into account the cultures of other ethnic groups. For example, role models are frequently white; 'white' is good and 'black' is evil (as in the white

Multicultural education involves a recognition of the diversity of cultures in society, and teaching about the culture of other ethnic groups besides that of the majority culture.
Ethnocentrism is a view of the world in which other cultures are seen through the eyes of one's own culture, with a devaluing of the others.

knight versus the black knight); history is white and European; history and other textbooks still frequently carry degrading stereotypes of people from non-white races – portrayed often in subservient or 'primitive' roles; positive role models from the history, music, art and culture of black and other minority ethnic groups are frequently absent from the curriculum.

It has been suggested that this, along with the other factors discussed above, contributes to the low self-esteem of some minority ethnic children, and it means the school curriculum may be more attractive and culturally acceptable to some ethnic groups than others. Combining all the factors above may mean there is a culture clash between some minority ethnic groups and the white middle-class culture of the school. To apply Bourdieu's theory of cultural capital, while it might *appear* that all have an equal opportunity in education since they are assessed against the same culture and knowledge, the education system is not really neutral at all because its culture is predominantly white culture. These factors would contribute to explaining patterns of underachievement in education between ethnic groups.

Some words of caution

Explaining the underachievement of some minority ethnic groups is no easy task. It is likely to be a *combination* of the factors outlined above, with the different factors having different significance in particular circumstances. However, all the explanations need to be treated with caution. For example, while some teachers may hold racist beliefs, this does not necessarily mean they behave in a racist way in the classroom, and they may not allow the negative stereotypes of ethnic minorities they may hold to disadvantage children from minority ethnic groups. It should not be assumed all teachers are racist, and many make great and successful efforts to overcome any feelings of **racial prejudice** they hold and do all they can for all students. Racism is not as widespread in teaching as in some professions, like the police and legal professions, and teachers and schools have often been among the first to tackle racism and promote equal opportunities for all. More teachers from minority ethnic backgrounds act as positive role models for professional career success for black and minority ethnic students.

Negative labelling of ethnic minorities by teachers and others in the education system does not necessarily lead to the negative effects that the self-fulfilling prophecy suggests. The negative labels attached to some students from minority ethnic groups might not be accepted by those labelled. Research by Fuller (1980) among African-Caribbean girls in a London comprehensive school suggested that those labelled may reject the label and the low expectations of teachers, and combine a subculture of resistance to schooling with the hard work needed to overcome the obstacles placed

> **Racial prejudice** involves a set of assumptions about a racial or ethnic group which people are reluctant to change even when they receive information which undermines those assumptions.

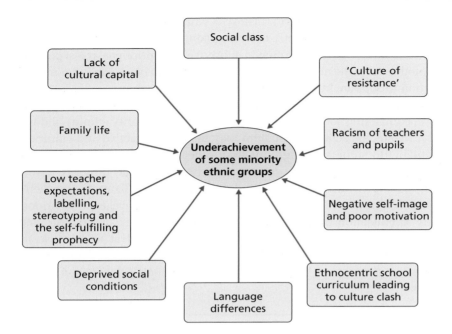

Figure 6.12 Ethnicity and educational achievement

Activity

1 Go through the reasons suggested in these sections for the underachievement of some minority ethnic groups, and refer to figure 6.12 above. List the explanations in what you think is their order of importance. Explain and justify your reasons, and then suggest steps that might be taken in each case to overcome the obstacles you have listed.

2 Drawing carefully on what you have learnt in this chapter, try to draw up a 'league table' of achievement in education, drawing on both social class, gender and ethnicity. For example, middle-class Indian-Asian girls are likely to come at the top, with working-class African-Caribbean males at the bottom. Try to fill in the rest, using categories of middle and working class, male and female, and white, Indian Asian, African-Caribbean, Pakistani and Bangladeshi ethnic groups.

3 Drawing on your own experience of schooling, can you identify any ways in which black and white students were/are treated differently by teachers or by other students? Is/was there any evidence of racism in your own school or college?

4 How ethnocentric is/was the curriculum in your school or college? Was there any evidence of knowledge of other cultures being taught in your school, appearing in textbooks and so on?

5 Go to the DCSF standards website at www.standards.dfes.gov.uk/ethnicminorities and identify three policies that are currently being pursued to improve the educational achievements of minority ethnic groups. Explain how each policy might make such improvements.

before them and to achieve educational success. This partly arose because black girls recognized their future roles as key breadwinners in black families. This demonstrates both that negative labels do not always have negative effects, and also explains why African-Caribbean females in general do better than their male counterparts in education. For example, around 55 per cent of black African-Caribbean girls achieved five or more *A–C GCSEs in 2006 compared to 41 per cent of African-Caribbean boys.

Activity

1 Identify and explain *three* factors that may contribute to a culture clash between the culture of some minority ethnic groups and that of the school.
2 Identify and explain *three material* factors and *three cultural* factors that may contribute to the underachievement in education of some minority ethnic groups.
3 Answer the following essay question, in about one and half sides of A4 paper: *Examine the view that the underachievement of some minority ethnic groups is mainly a result of family and social class background.*

Private education: the independent schools

Around 7 per cent of the school population have chosen to opt out of the free, state-run comprehensive system and attend the fee-paying private sector of education – the independent schools. As Walford (2003) points out, there is a wide diversity of schools in the independent sector, some of which are so small that they are almost 'better thought of as parents home schooling their children'. As Walford says, there are 'schools that practise Transcendental Meditation and Buddhism; others that serve Seventh Day Adventists (a religious sect), Sikhs or Jews. There are more than 60 evangelical Christian schools and more than 50 Muslim schools.' Many of these schools arise because of parents expressing their choice of school, and while such schools may meet parental wishes, they do not necessarily lead to the **elite** careers associated with some of the most prestigious independent schools, which are the focus of attention here.

An **elite** is a small group holding great power and privilege in society.

Most research and discussion of the private sector of education has been about what are known as the 'public schools', which, despite their name, are not in fact 'public' at all, but very expensive private schools. The reason for this attention is because, as Walford says, 'Entry to such schools has been seen as a passport to academic success, to high-status universities and to prosperous and influential careers.' The public schools are a small group of independent schools belonging to what is called the 'Headmasters' and Headmistresses' Conference' (HMC). Pupils at these schools are largely the children of wealthier

Eton College, one of Britain's most famous public schools, with fees of £26,450 a year plus extras in 2007–8, counts among its former students nineteen British prime ministers, numerous princes, kings, archbishops, judges, generals, admirals and other members of Britain's elite

upper- and upper-middle-class parents. These are long-established private schools, many dating back hundreds of years, which charge fees running into thousands of pounds a year. For secondary age students, annual fees for day students typically varied from £7,000 to £13,500 per year, and for boarders from £14,000 to more than £27,000 in 2007–8. The two most famous boys' public schools are probably Eton and Harrow (boarding fees about £25,000–£27,000 a year, plus extras, in 2007–8) and many of the 'top people' in this country have attended these or other public schools. A public school education means parents can almost guarantee their children will have well-paid future careers bringing them power and status in society.

The case for independent schools

The defenders of private education point to the smaller class sizes and better facilities of the public schools than those found in the state comprehensive system, which means children have a much better chance of getting into university. Many defend private education on the grounds that parents should have the right to spend their money as they wish, and improving their children's life chances through a free choice of schools is a sensible way of doing so.

The case against independent schools

Many remain opposed to private education, arguing that most people do not have the money to purchase a private education for their children, and it is wrong that the children of the well-off should be given more advantages in education than the poor. Despite many of the schools catering only for the well-off, they have traditionally had the same tax subsidies and benefits through charitable status as charities helping those in poverty or need. This charitable status has been estimated to be worth about 5–10 per cent on the average school fee (Palfreyman, 2003), or up to about £2,000 per pupil each year – an amount so generous that the government was suggesting in 2005 that these schools should use the full value of these tax subsidies to pay for the education of poor pupils in order to continue to qualify as charities. The tax-payer also pays the cost of training the teachers in these schools, since they attend state-run universities and colleges.

The quality of teaching in independent schools is often no better than in state-run comprehensives, and an Edinburgh University study found there is little difference in exam pass rates between middle-class pupils at state comprehensive schools and those in the independent sector. However, classes tend to be smaller than in comprehensives, allowing more individual attention, and the schools often have better resources and facilities. Eton College in 2003 had assets estimated at £162 million, with the added advantage of charitable status. These investments and fee income allow Eton to spend more than £20,000 per year on each student, compared to the sum of around £4,500 spending planned on the average state school student in 2007–8. The opponents of private education argue more money should be spent on improving the state system so everyone has an equal chance in education.

Research has shown that even when children who go to private schools, especially the public schools, get worse examination results than children who go to comprehensive schools, they still get better jobs in the end. This suggests that the fact of attending a public school is itself enough to secure them good jobs, even if their qualifications are not quite as good as those of students from comprehensives.

Elite education and elite jobs

A public school education remains a prime qualification for the elite jobs in society – that small number of jobs in the country which involve holding a great deal of power and privilege. Although only about 7 per cent of the population have attended independent schools (and public schools are only a proportion of those schools), many of the top positions in the civil service, medicine, the law, the media, the Church of England, and industry, banking and commerce are held by ex-public school students, as shown in table 6.7.

Table 6.7 Some UK elites educated at private schools (percentages)

All pupils attending private schools (2007)	7
Top barristers[1] (2004)	68
Top judges[2] (2007)	70
Top solicitors[3] (2004)	55
Top 100 media personnel (2006)[4]	54
Top doctors[5] (2007)	51
All Members of Parliament (2005)	32
Conservative MPs	59
Labour MPs	18
Liberal Democrat MPs	39
MPs holding government office or shadow ministers (2007)	38
All members of House of Lords (2005)	62
Conservative members	79
Labour members	34
Liberal Democrat members	54
Bishops in House of Lords	60
Leaders of FTSE 100 top companies (2007)	54

[1] Barristers at eight leading corporate and commercial chambers
[2] Law Lords and Appeal and High Court Judges
[3] Partners at the City's five 'magic circle' law firms
[4] Newspaper editors, newspaper columnists, broadcast presenters and editors who have the power to decide the stories that are given most prominence, and how they are presented to the public through newspapers, magazines, radio and TV
[5] Doctors with positions on the Councils of the medical royal colleges or other national representative bodies

Source: Sutton Trust

In many cases, even well-qualified candidates from comprehensive schools will stand a poor chance of getting such jobs if competing with public school pupils. The route into the elite jobs is basically through a public school and Oxford and Cambridge universities (where about 50 per cent of students come from public schools). This establishes the 'old boys' network', where those in positions of power recruit others who come from the same social class background and who have been to the same public schools and universities as themselves (this is shown in figure 6.13). This shows one aspect of the clear relationship which exists between wealth and power in modern Britain, and how being able to afford a public school education can lead to a position of power and influence in society.

Figure 6.13 The old boys' network

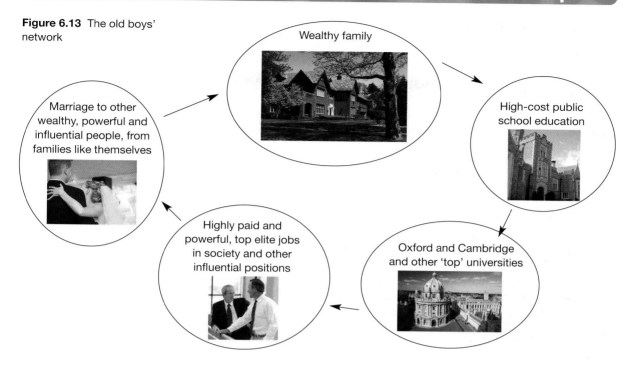

A public school education therefore means well-off parents can almost guarantee their children will have well-paid future careers bringing them similar levels of power and status in society to their parents. This undermines the principle of equality of educational opportunity, and any idea that Britain might be a meritocracy. This is because social class background and the ability to pay fees, rather than simply academic ability, become the

Activity

1 Go to www.etoncollege.com, the website of Eton College, or www.harrowschool.org.uk (Harrow School) and explore how the educational facilities and lifestyle at these schools differ from those of the school you go/went to (unless you went to one of these schools!).

2 Write a brief essay, about one side of A4, on the following: *Examine the arguments for and against the following view:*
'The existence of private schools undermines the principle of equality of educational opportunity, because social class background rather than simply ability becomes the key to success in education. They only exist to help the wealthy and powerful pass on their wealth and power from one generation to the next. Private education should therefore be abolished.'

key to success in education. Not all children of the same ability have the same chance of paying for this route to educational and career success. This would seem to demonstrate in a particularly stark way Bowles and Gintis's Marxist idea that the education system simply confirms and legitimizes social class of origin as social class of destination.

Researching Education

> **Note to students**
>
> This section assumes that chapter 5 has already been studied. If you haven't yet covered chapter 5, you are advised to return to this section once you have done so.

The aim of this section is to get you to apply your knowledge and understanding of sociological research methods to the study of particular issues in education. Many of the research methods and types of data discussed in chapter 5 have been used in researching the field of education. What follows aims to get you thinking about some of these, and some of the theoretical, practical and ethical difficulties in using them to research education.

Collecting information on education

This chapter has already referred to a range of quantitative data used to analyse education, like statistics on examination results, subject choices, those staying on in education post-16, and acceptances to university. These form part of an enormous amount of data collected from sources such as:

- the examination results of schools, colleges and universities
- applications by students to higher education, and their gender, ethnicity and social class
- the number of school leavers entering education, training or employment
- the School Census, which is conducted up to three times a year and collects a wide range of information from all schools
- pupil absence rates
- pupils' characteristics, such as gender, ethnicity, eligibility for free school meals, special educational needs and English as an additional language, linked to test and examination results
- surveys on education, either very large-scale surveys like the School Census, which covers all schools, or smaller surveys that cover more specialized areas, such as the Further Education (FE) Learners Longitudinal Survey (2007) which looked at the experiences of around 7,000 further education students over two years

- government surveys like the General Household Survey and the Labour Force Survey collect data on a range of issues, including educational qualifications
- *longitudinal* surveys: most of the significant quantitative data on education is collected at least every year; as such data is collected on a regular basis, it is possible to carry out longitudinal studies and build up a picture of changes in education over time.

As discussed in chapter 5, there are always questions to be raised about the *reliability*, *validity* and *representativeness* of quantitative data derived from surveys. While data derived from very large surveys like the School Census might provide comprehensive and representative data, smaller surveys may not necessarily do so.

Activity

1 Suggest *two* reasons in each case why the following statistics might or might not provide completely valid and representative information about what is happening in education in the UK:
   (a) pupil sickness absence statistics
   (b) the reasons for pupils being excluded from schools
   (c) the number of times parents attend parents' evenings
   (d) the number of post-16 students who are in education, training, employment or unemployed/not working
2 In the light of your answers to the activity above, in *each* case above suggest *one* step social researchers might take to improve the validity of the statistics, explaining carefully why the steps you suggest might achieve this.

Surveys are the main means of collecting education data, and much of this is collected by the government, which has the resources and legal powers to carry out large-scale, national research into schools and colleges, either with large and representative samples, or complete coverage of schools like the School Census. Depending on whether the aim is to collect quantitative or more qualitative data, these surveys use various forms of questionnaire and interview, and a range of different ways of collecting the data – such as group discussions, structured, semi-structured and unstructured face-to-face or telephone interviews, and postal or internet-based questionnaires.

Qualitative research methods like participant observation are less commonly used in government-funded research, but have been used to great effect by education researchers wishing to adopt a more interpretivist approach. This enables them to gain insights which are not achievable by quantitative methods. The different pieces of research by Willis, Wright and

Bhatti, referred to earlier in this chapter, used such techniques. Willis's research used participant observation in a Wolverhampton school to gain insights into how young working-class lads experienced school and the transition to work. Wright's classroom research, undertaken over three years in four inner-city primary schools, used a range of methods, including participant observation and unstructured interviews, to explore the relationships between black children, their white peers, and teachers and school staff, during the earlier years of schooling. Wright examined the classroom setting and teacher–pupil interaction, interactions in the playground between children, and children and auxiliary staff, home–school relations, and the academic performance of the different groups of children. Using such methods, she gained insights into black and Asian students' experience of schooling that would not have been uncovered by more quantitative methods. Bhatti's study of Bangladeshi, Pakistani and Indian students used participant observation in classrooms at 'Cherrydale' school to gain similar insights.

Ethical issues are always of great concern in education-related research, especially with younger children. Children are vulnerable, and details of individual student progress at any age is a private matter between students, their families and their teachers. It is important, for example, to avoid any possible labelling of students which might have negative effects on their progress and self-esteem. Like most sociological research, care and sensitivity are needed.

Activity

A good way to understand how research methods apply to education issues is to carry out your own small piece of research, perhaps on no more than five or six people.

1 Form a hypothesis or a question you wish to find answers to.
2 Devise a suitable sample and a research method appropriate to your aim or hypothesis.
3 Draw up a short questionnaire, interview schedule or whatever else is needed.
4 Carry out your research.
5 Do a careful analysis of the strengths and weaknesses of your research, including your findings. If you are in a group, you could criticize one another's surveys. Topics could be anything related to education, such as:

  ● Identify a range of factors that might make up what Bourdieu calls 'cultural capital' and ask a sample of students whether they have the cultural factors you have identified.
  ● Observe classroom activities and try to see if boys and girls behave differently in class and are treated differently by teachers. (If you plan to do classroom observation, applying Flanders's interaction analysis might be useful – see the box on page 317 in chapter 5.)

> • Interview a sample of male and female students, asking them about what influenced them in making subject and exam choices.
> • Interview some students who identify with an anti-school or college subculture, and find out about what they get out of it.
> • Do research among a group of students to find out how they feel about the lessons in your school or college.
>
> 6 Suggest a suitable method for studying each of the following topics, and explain in each case why it might be suitable:
>   (a) The relationship between people's educational qualifications and the employment they get.
>   (b) Whether different styles of teaching influence student exam results.
>   (c) What students' ideas are about the 'perfect teacher'.
>   (d) Whether ethnic minority students feel they are treated unfairly in schools.
>   (e) Which ICT-based resources are most frequently used in your school or college.

The following examples of research and research methods, and the activities relating to them, aim to get you thinking about how research methods are applied in some actual education research.

Examples of research

National Child Development Study (Centre for Longitudinal Studies, 2007)

The National Child Development Study (NCDS) examines the factors affecting people throughout their lives. It is a continuing longitudinal study of a cohort of all 17,000 children who were born in one particular week in March 1958, and living in Britain. By 2007, there had been seven 'sweeps' to collect data on the physical, educational, social and economic development of this birth cohort. The first sweep was carried out in 1965, when respondents were aged 7, then in 1969 (aged 11), in 1974 (aged 16), in 1981 (aged 23), in 1991 (aged 33), in 1999–2000 (aged 41–2), with the seventh sweep carried out in 2004–5, when the respondents were aged 46–7. The seventh sweep used telephone interviews and asked questions about a range of topics, including housing, family income, employment status/employment history, academic education, vocational training and other courses, access to and use of computers, basic skills and health. In common with all longitudinal studies, the number of people participating in the NCDS has declined as the cohort grows older. For example, the seventh sweep managed to conduct telephone interviews with 9,534 people. This was about 56 per cent of the original 17,000 cohort, compared to about 97 per cent in the first sweep in 1965.

Activity

1 Identify the research method used in the seventh sweep of the National Child Development Study (see page 409).

2 Explain *two advantages* and *two disadvantages* of this method of investigating the lives of the birth cohort.

3 Suggest *three* reasons why the number of people who participated in the seventh sweep was so much less than the first sweep in 1965.

4 Do you think the findings from the seventh sweep in the NCDS survey could be generalized to represent the lives of people across the country? Explain your answer.

5 Identify and explain *four* pieces of information that the NCDS might produce that might help sociologists understand the factors influencing educational achievement.

6 Suggest *two* methods *other than* that used in the seventh sweep of the NCDS that sociologists might use in a future sweep to collect qualitative information about the birth cohort's experience of their own and their children's schooling.

Perspectives of One-to-One Laptop Access (**Research by Danny Doyle, presented to the National Teacher Research Panel**)

The details below are derived from the summary presented to the Teacher Research Conference, 2004.

Dr Danny Doyle carried out a case study of Les Landes Primary School in Jersey, where all Year 5 and Year 6 children had one-to-one access to a laptop computer. This qualitative insider research sought to explore the children's

How might sociologists research children's experiences of using laptops at school?

knowledge, views, understandings, interpretations and experiences of using laptop computers one-to-one and to gauge the effectiveness of the laptop use for the children's learning. The study explored the perceptions of twenty-three Year 6 children during the 2001–2 school year. Interviews and participant observation were the main methods used for this interpretive research, which included forty-five participant observations, fifteen taped interviews of children in pairs, twelve focus group interviews with five or six children, twenty-five non-participant observations, and seventy-three informal interviews. The analysis of the taped interview data became a starting point for the participant and non-participant observations and informal interviews. One of the research findings was that the children felt that they were more independent, more organized and produced better work because of their one-to-one access to a laptop computer.

Activity

1 Suggest *two* reasons why Doyle's research may have provided a more valid picture of children's attitudes to using laptops at school than a large-scale national questionnaire.
2 Identify *two* methods that were used in the case study above to gain insights into children's experiences of using laptops and their effectiveness in children's learning.
3 Suggest *two* difficulties that Danny Doyle may have faced in carrying out participant observations in a primary school.
4 Suggest *two* reasons why interviewing children in pairs might produce less valid information than informal interviews with children on their own.
5 Suggest *three* reasons why the twelve focus group interviews with five or six children may have produced a greater depth of understanding of children's experiences with laptops in schools than interviews conducted with children either singly or in pairs.
6 Suggest *two* ways in which the analysis of the taped interviews may have provided an essential starting point for the participant and non-participant observations and informal interviews.
7 Suggest *two* reasons why sociologists should be careful before applying the findings of the Laptop study to all schools in Britain.

Longitudinal Study of Young People in England (**LSYPE**) (**DfES; renamed the Department for Children, Schools and Families (DCSF) in 2007**)

This longitudinal study uses annual interviews with the same group of young people and their parents to explore a wide range of factors influencing young people's education. The study began in spring 2004, with interviews completed with 15,770 households from an original sample of just over 21,000 young people in Year 9 (aged 13–14). The first four waves (2004–7) used structured face-to-face interviews with both parents and the young people. In the first wave in 2004, the interviewers asked most of the questions, which they read from a laptop computer on which they recorded their answers. The interviewer had to record who else, if anyone, was present in the room during the interviews, apart from the person being interviewed.

There were some questions which the respondents themselves had to complete. In such cases, the computer was turned to the parent or young person, and they were asked to fill in their own answers on the screen, with help from the interviewer if needed. These self-completion sections involved questions about things like arguments between parents and young people, prolonged absences from school, such as through illness, exclusions and truancy, bullying (including violence and theft), police involvement because of the young person's behaviour, and the young person's experiences of their truancy, smoking, alcohol, illegal drug use and doing graffiti.

Activity

1 Identify *two* research methods that are used in the survey of young people above.
2 Suggest *three* reasons why some questions about the experiences of young people were recorded via a self-completion questionnaire on a laptop rather than by the interviewer.
3 Suggest *two* reasons why it might have been important for the interviewer 'to record who else, if anyone, was present in the room during the interviews, apart from the person being interviewed'.
4 Suggest *three* possible problems with the validity of young people's responses to questions about their truancy, smoking, alcohol, illegal drug use and doing graffiti.
5 Identify all the people who might have to give their consent for this research to be carried out.
6 Identity *two* ethical issues that researchers should be aware of when conducting research like that above.
7 Suggest at least *three* pieces of information you would need to know in order to evaluate whether the survey above was representative.
8 Suggest *two* factors, apart from those given in your answer to question 4 above, that may influence the validity of the findings of the research above.

CHAPTER SUMMARY

After studying this chapter, you should be able to:

- explain what is meant by equality of educational opportunity

- describe and explain the strengths and weaknesses of the tripartite and comprehensive systems of education, and selection by ability in education

- identify the main changes in education since 1988, and discuss the aims, consequences and criticisms of these reforms

- explain what is meant by and criticize the marketization of education

- critically discuss the main purposes of education, as identified by the functionalist and Marxist perspectives

- explain what is meant by the 'hidden curriculum', and how it reflects and reinforces values and ideology outside schools

- explain what is meant by a meritocracy, and why Britain is not a meritocracy

- describe the facts about, and discuss a range of explanations for, social class, gender and ethnic group differences in educational achievement

- discuss the arguments for and against private education

- apply research methods to the study of education

KEY TERMS

anti-school subculture
banding
compensatory education
counter-school
   subculture
cultural capital
cultural deprivation
culture clash
division of labour
Education Action Zones

elaborated code
elite
equality of educational
   opportunity
ethnocentrism
habitus
halo effect
hidden curriculum
ideological state
   apparatuses
labelling

marketization
meritocracy
multicultural education
particularistic values
positive discrimination
racial prejudice
racism
restricted code
self-fulfilling prophecy
setting
sexism

social capital
social solidarity
streaming
subculture
underachievement
universalistic values

EXAM QUESTION

Answer **all** the questions from this Section

SECTION A: EDUCATION WITH RESEARCH METHODS

You are advised to spend approximately 50 minutes on Question 1
You are advised to spend approximately 25 minutes on Question 2
You are advised to spend approximately 40 minutes on Question 3

Time allowed: 2 hours   **Total for this section: 90 marks**

1 Read **Item A** below and answer parts (a) to (d) that follow.

Item A

Recent changes have tried to create a free market in education. Parents now have some choice in their children's school, with Ofsted reports and school and college league tables to help them find the best schools. Schools have much more control of their own affairs, and some schools, further education and sixth-form colleges and universities are completely independent and entirely manage their own affairs. In the educational marketplace, they compete with each other to raise income by attracting students. The government thought this would make educational institutions more responsive to parents and students' needs, and raise standards of teaching and learning. Like supermarkets competing for customers, educational institutions producing good results would be popular with parents and students, and thrive. Institutions that were failing to produce good quality 'products' would lose students and money, and would either improve or be closed.

(a) Explain what is meant by the term 'cultural capital'   *(2 marks)*

(b) Suggest **three** reasons why some minority ethnic groups underachieve in education.
                                                                    (6 marks)

(c) Outline some of the reasons why there is sometimes said to be a 'culture clash' between the home and the school for those from working-class backgrounds.   *(12 marks)*

(d) Using material from **Item A** and elsewhere, assess the view that the 'marketization' of education has mainly benefited middle-class parents and students.   *(20 marks)*

2 This question requires you to apply your knowledge and understanding of sociological research methods to the study of this particular issue in education.

Read **Item B** below and answer the question that follows.

Item B

Investigating teacher attitudes and ethnic minority achievement

Gillborn was interested in exploring how teacher attitudes and expectations influenced the opportunity for ethnic minority pupils to achieve success at school. He did this by observing interaction between teachers and pupils. His study of an inner city comprehensive school in the Midlands described how teachers perceived a threat to their authority in their daily interactions with African-Caribbean pupils. When teachers acted on this perception, it created conflict with African-Caribbean pupils. African-Caribbean pupils responded by asserting their ethnic identity as young black people, which teachers interpreted as a threatening attitude. Such research suggests there is a considerable gap between policies promoting equal opportunities in schools and the daily experiences of many black pupils.

Using material from **Item B** and elsewhere, assess the strengths and limitations of **one** of the following methods for the study of teacher attitudes and ethnic minority achievement:

(i) participant observation
(ii) structured interviews   *(20 marks)*

3 This question permits you to draw examples from **any areas** of sociology with which you are familiar.

(a) Explain what is meant by the term 'sample'. *(2 marks)*

(b) Suggest two sampling methods that sociologists might use, **apart from** random sampling.   *(4 marks)*

(c) Suggest two reasons why sociologists might use official statistics.   *(4 marks)*

(d) Examine the problems sociologists may find when using postal questionnaires in their research.   *(20 marks)*

Contents

Key issues	419
The social construction of the body, health, illness and disease	**420**
The social construction of the body	420
The social construction of health, illness and disease	422
Disability	**423**
The medical and social models of health	**424**
The medical (biomedical) model of health	424
The social model of health	429
Marxist approaches to health and medicine	**431**
How society influences health	**431**
Improvements in health in the nineteenth and early twentieth centuries	432
The new disease burden	**433**
What are the causes of these new diseases?	434
Becoming a health statistic	**436**
Medicine and social control: the sick role	**438**
Features of the sick role	438
Criticisms of Parsons and the sick role	440
The power of the medical profession	**440**
Protecting the patient?	441
Criticisms of the medical profession	442

The erosion of medical power and other contemporary changes in health and health care	**443**
The erosion of medical power in favour of the patient?	443
A shift from the medical to social model of health?	444
Consumer choice	444
Inequalities in health	**446**
Social class inequalities in health	446
Gender differences in health	461
Ethnic inequalities in health	466
Other inequalities in health	**467**
Access to health care	467
Regional and international inequalities in health	471
Mental illness	**477**
What is mental illness?	478
Care in the community	478
The biomedical approach to mental illness	478
The social construction of mental illness	480
Researching Health	**486**
Collecting information on health	487
Examples of research	490
Chapter summary	494
Key terms	494
Exam question	495

7 Health

- The social construction of the body, health, illness and disease
- The medical and social models of health
- Becoming a health statistic
- Medicine, social control and the power of the medical profession
- How society influences health
- The new disease burden
- Social class, gender and ethnic inequalities in health
- Inequalities of access to health care
- Mental illness
- Researching health

Activity

1 Think of some people you know whom you consider to be very healthy. Explain carefully what makes you think of them as healthy. For example, is it because they never appear to be ill, because they seem to be physically fit and have strong bodies, because they seem healthy for their age, because they have no disease or anything 'wrong' with them, or because they have healthy habits and lifestyles? Consider these factors and others of your own.

2 Now write your own definitions, with examples, of 'health', 'illness' and 'disease'. Discuss, with examples, what your definitions might mean for promoting health and eliminating disease.

3 What factors do you consider when deciding whether you are ill? How do you decide when you are ill enough to seek out medical attention from a doctor? Discuss your reasons with others if you are in a group, and see if there are any differences between you.

4 How do you think your definitions of health and illness might differ between different countries, between different age groups, and between rich and poor people?

The social construction of the body, health, illness and disease

When sociologists talk of the **social construction** of something, they mean it only becomes real because it is created and influenced by the attitudes, actions and interpretations of members of society. As will be seen in this chapter, even apparently natural or biological events or categories like disease and the human body are the results of social influences and activity, and the interpretations of people.

> **Social construction** means that the important characteristics of something, such as statistics, health, illness, disability or crime, are created and influenced by the attitudes, actions and interpretations of members of society.

The social construction of the body

The human body may appear to be a wholly natural phenomenon, which exists in a more or less unchanging form everywhere, regardless of social circumstances and the society in which people live. However, this would be an incorrect assumption, as the human body is very much subject to social influences and is very much a social construction as well as a biological category. For example, there are wide differences between societies in ideas about the most desirable size, shape and appearance of bodies, and these differ between what is seen as appropriate for men and women. Societies have always been involved in constructing bodies, and people try actively to control and mould their bodies to create their sense of identity in the society to which they belong. For example, artificially elongating necks, binding feet and waists, extending lower lips, scarring, body-piercing, body-building, cosmetic surgery, dentistry, tanning, dieting, sex-change operations and hormone treatment have all been used at different times to form bodies in their social context.

In contemporary British society, which postmodernists argue is a consumer-led culture, the human body and health are often design projects for people to work on in forming their identities. People often go to great lengths to construct or shape their bodies in accordance with the identity they wish to project, through consuming goods around their bodily images such as health foods and diet products, fitness clubs and equipment, cosmetics and cosmetic surgery, breast implants and reduction, tattoos, hair extensions and tanning salons. Even apparently natural phenomena like pregnancy and childbirth are socially constructed. For example, new reproductive technologies, such as contraception, fertility drugs, artificial insemination and the storage of embryos for future use, mean that women can now choose whether and when to have children, the sex of their baby and whether to have it independently of sexual relations with a man. The same technology has meant that it has become much more difficult to decide when human life begins, as human foetuses can now survive from just a few weeks. The social construction of the

body is also increasingly tied up with health in contemporary Britain. The commercial and advertising pressures which promote and sell fitness products of all kinds are wrapped up in the message that people should take control of their bodies and their health, and that adopting a healthy lifestyle means good-looking bodies, feeling good and being healthy.

Activity

1 With reference to the pictures above, explain what is meant by 'the social construction of the body'.
2 Suggest *three* ways in contemporary Britain that the human body is used as a way for individuals to present particular images or identities to people they meet.
3 Suggest *three* ways that people's attitudes to their bodies might influence how they define good health.

The social construction of health, illness and disease

The definitions of **health**, **illness** and **disease** are not simple matters. What counts as health and illness varies between individuals, between different social groups within a single society, such as between men and women, and between societies. Views of acceptable standards of health are likely to differ widely between the people of a poor African country and Britain. Even in the same society, views of health change over time. At one time in Britain, mental illness was seen as a sign of satanic possession or witchcraft – a matter best dealt with by the church rather than by doctors. Similarly, what were once seen as personal problems have quite recently become seen as medical problems, such as obesity, alcoholism and smoking.

There is no simple definition of illness, because for pain or discomfort to count as a disease it is necessary for someone to diagnose or label it as such. There are also subjective influences on health: some of us can put up with or ignore pain more than others; some feel no pain; and many of us will have different notions of what counts as 'feeling unwell'. Individuals will define and respond to health in different ways. For example, older people may define good health as not having too many aches and pains, and having energy levels that enable them to go about their daily tasks, or being well enough to run their own homes. Younger people may define good health as being well enough to go clubbing or take part in sport. We can also change our views of the state of our health depending on our choices and situations. For example, we might be too ill to go to school or college, but well enough to go clubbing.

Health is probably easiest to define as 'being able to function normally within a usual everyday routine'.

Illness refers to the subjective feeling of being unwell or in ill-health – a person's own recognition of lack of well-being. It is possible both to have a disease and to not feel ill, and to feel ill and not have any disease.

Disease generally refers to a biological or mental condition, such as high blood pressure, a faulty heart or chemical imbalances in the body, which usually involves medically diagnosed symptoms.

Activity

The United Nations World Health Organization defines health as 'a state of complete physical, mental, and social well-being, and not merely the absence of disease or infirmity'. Some have argued that this definition goes far beyond a realistic definition of health, as it implies not simply the absence of disease, but also a personally fulfilling life.

1 Discuss how the World Health Organization's definition of health might apply to the health of the long-term unemployed in Britain.

2 Using the World Health Organization's definition, how might the definition of 'good health' differ between:
   (a) people who live in a poor African country and those who live in modern Britain?
   (b) people in Britain who live in an isolated village in the country and those who live in a town?

3 How do you think the society we live in influences people's ideas of what counts as health and illness?

4 Discuss the view that 'good health is simply a state of mind'.

This means health is a relative concept, which will vary according to the age, lifestyle, personal circumstances, culture and environment in which people live. There are strong subjective (personal) influences on health, and whether a person sees himself or herself as healthy or not will depend on how well they are able to function within their own everyday routines.

So what counts as health and illness can be considered as a social construction – a result of individual, social and cultural interpretations and perceptions.

Disability

Disability is defined by the Disability Discrimination Act 1995 as 'a physical or mental impairment which has a substantial and long-term adverse effect on [your] ability to carry out normal day-to-day activities'.

An **impairment** is some abnormal functioning of the body or mind, arising from birth or from injury or disease.

Disability is often linked with illness, helplessness and weakness. Most of us learn about disability as part of the socialization process, rather than as a result of personal experience. Media images of disability are often linked with socially unacceptable behaviours, or suggest we have good reasons to fear people with disabilities, especially those with mental or behavioural difficulties, or who display violent or inexplicable behaviour. For example, the Glasgow Media Group found in *Message Received* (Philo, 1999) that media reporting portrayed a high level of violence as associated with mental illness, especially schizophrenia.

There are clearly some physical or mental **impairments**, such as loss of use of limbs or sight, or brain damage, that will mean some people will find more difficulty in carrying out everyday tasks than others.

However, impairment is not the same as disability. Tom Shakespeare (1998) suggests that disability should be seen as a social construction – a problem created by the attitudes of society and not by the state of our bodies. Shakespeare argues that disability is created by societies that don't take into account the needs of those who do not meet with that society's ideas of what is 'normal'. Whether someone is disabled or not is then a social product – it is social attitudes which turn an impairment into a disability, because society discriminates against those with some impairments. For example, people parking on pavements makes it difficult for those in wheelchairs or the blind to get by; buildings may make access difficult or impossible for those who have lost the use of their lower limbs and need wheelchairs to aid their mobility. People who are short-sighted only become disabled if they have no access to glasses to correct their sight, or if documents are printed in small type or colours which people with visual impairments find hard to read. Workplaces can be disabling if adjustments to the working environment are not made to enable people with impairments to perform their jobs successfully. With the ageing population (a growing proportion of elderly people in the population), all of us will, if we live long enough, eventually become disabled unless social attitudes change and society adapts to the needs of those with physical or mental impairments.

'People become disabled, not because they have physical or mental impairments, but because they have physical or mental differences from the majority, which challenges traditional ideas of what counts as "normal". Disability is about the relationship between people with impairment and a society which discriminates against them. People are disabled by society, not by their bodies. Disability is about discrimination and prejudice . . . Understanding disability is about flexing the sociological imagination – turning personal troubles into public issues.'

(Adapted from an unpublished paper by Tom Shakespeare, 26 Jan. 2001)

1 Do you agree with the view that people are disabled by society and the attitudes of others rather than by the state of their minds or bodies? What evidence can you think of for and against this view?

2 Explain in your own words what you think Shakespeare means when he says: 'Understanding disability is about . . . turning personal troubles into public issues.'

3 What kinds of impairments in our society create disadvantages for those who have them? What steps might be taken to remove these disadvantages facing people with some impairments?

The medical and social models of health

As seen above, there are different meanings attached to 'health'. There are two main approaches to health arising from different views of what the causes of ill-health are, and the policies needed to solve it. These two competing models of health are often referred to as the medical (or biomedical) and social models of health.

The medical (biomedical) model of health

This is the model of health which has underlined the development of Western medicine, and is the main approach found in the National Health Service. This model sees health in terms of the absence of disease, with ill-health arising from identifiable biological or physical causes. The main aim of medicine, and modern health care systems like the NHS, is therefore to diagnose and tackle these physical symptoms.

Main features of the medical model

- Disease is seen as mainly caused by biological factors, together with the recent emphasis on personal factors such as smoking and diet. Health is defined as the absence of disease or disability.

The medical model of health views the human body as working like a machine that occasionally breaks down, with doctors like mechanics, fixing it in 'body shops' like surgeries and hospitals

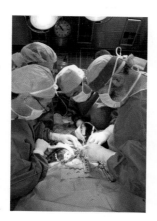

- The human body is seen as working like a machine which occasionally breaks down. In the same way as a car that has broken down, 'body mechanics' (doctors) apply their expert medical knowledge to diagnose the biological or chemical processes that have caused the sickness. Doctors are then able to treat and cure the disease they have identified, through medical or surgical treatments in 'body shops' – clinical situations like doctors' surgeries and hospitals.
- The causes of ill-health are seen as arising either from the moral failings of the individual (such as smoking too much, not eating the right food, or not getting enough exercise) or from random attacks of disease. This is a bit like blaming car breakdowns on poor maintenance and lack of proper servicing, or because of faulty parts and bad luck.
- Scientific medicine is seen as the way to solve health problems. This means good health depends on the availability of trained medical personnel, medical technology, operating theatres, drugs and so on. Medicine is seen as in itself a good thing, and the more of it there is, the better people's health will be.

Activity

1 Suggest *five* ways those adopting the medical model might tackle the issue of improving a society's health.
2 Do you think there are any problems with an approach to improving health which concentrates only on the medical treatment of individuals? What other factors might also be important in influencing the state of our health?

Criticisms of the medical model

- It suggests that health can be defined objectively, as the absence of disease. However, what counts as good health is, as shown above,

The medical model of health tends to concentrate on rescuing sick individuals, rather than looking at health education, preventive measures and the social causes which make people sick in the first place

socially constructed – a product of social influences and not simply biological ones.

- The focus on treating the symptoms of disease in the body by the application of medical knowledge, drugs and surgery ignores the wider social conditions that may have created these symptoms in the first place. These might include factors such as hazardous work environments, poor quality food, poverty or environmental pollution.

- It serves the interests of doctors, and gives them a great deal of power. Doctors have a legal monopoly over treatment, and other alternative approaches, like acupuncture or homeopathy, have traditionally been downgraded and dismissed as ineffective. However, the British Medical Association in 2001 finally conceded that complementary medicines can be integrated into conventional patient care, and called for greater cooperation between practitioners of orthodox and complementary medicine.

- It suggests resources are best channelled into medical science, new drugs and medical technology, and state of the art high-tech hospitals. Health education and preventative medicine are therefore not given the resources needed. This is like standing by a river bank and constantly hauling people out of the water, without asking who is throwing them into the river in the first place.

- It suggests the medical and nursing professions are generally doing a good job. However, writers like Illich (1976) have argued that medicine

The identification of health care with medical care has led to a pill for every ill, with health problems that have social causes being treated medically.

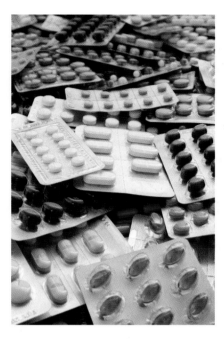

Iatrogenesis is any harmful mental or physical condition induced in a patient through the effects of treatment by a doctor or surgeon.

sometimes does more harm than good. Illich calls this **iatrogenesis**, which suggests that medical intervention, surgery and drugs can actually have more harmful effects than the condition they are meant to be curing. Some tranquillizers, for example, are addictive, and feminists have been particularly critical of mastectomy (the surgical removal of breasts) as a treatment for breast cancer. In 2001, there were major public concerns (largely unjustified) about the safety of the MMR (mumps, measles and rubella) vaccination. The development of antibiotics – the 'wonder drug' of the 1940s – has led to the emergence of antibiotic-resistant organisms, like MRSA.

- The identification of health care with medical care has led to a 'pill for every ill' syndrome. There is a growing trend towards the medicalization of health care. The drug industry, for example, produces medication for all sorts of ailments. Every condition is given a medical label, and new diseases are constantly being invented which may be primarily social rather than biological in character. Examples might include stress, anxiety and depression arising from difficulties at work or unemployment, eating disorders like bulimia or anorexia, and the way some 'naughty children' are now labelled as suffering from emotional and behavioural difficulties (EBD) or attention deficit disorder (ADD) or hyperactivity disorder.

- Illness and disease do not strike at random, out of the blue. They follow consistent social patterns. Ill-health is not simply a matter of fate or bad

Iatrogenesis in Britain

The harmful effects of medical treatment are reported widely in the media, with horror stories of people having the wrong legs amputated or healthy kidneys removed, patients dying because of HIV/AIDS or septicaemia occurring as a result of transfusions of contaminated blood, GPs failing to identify tumours, children dying after incompetent heart surgery, brain damage arising from overdoses of prescribed medicines, wrongly administered injections causing death and disability, and people dying from general anaesthetics in dental surgeries. A Department of Health report in 2000, *An Organisation with a Memory*, admitted that every year:

- More than 400 people die or are seriously injured in 'adverse' events involving medical devices.
- Nearly 10,000 people experience serious adverse reactions to drugs. At least thirteen patients have died or been paralysed since 1985 because a drug was wrongly administered by spinal injection.
- Hospital-acquired infections (HAI) cost the NHS around £1 billion a year. The House of Commons Public Accounts Committee in 2000 reported that MRSA – the 'superbug' immune to antibiotics – and other HAIs affect up to 100,000 hospital patients every year, and that 5,000 of them die in England alone.
- Around 1,150 people who have been in recent contact with mental health services commit suicide.
- Medical negligence claims cost the National Health Service around £400 million.
- Adverse events, in which patients are harmed, occur in more than 10 per cent of admissions to NHS hospitals – 850,000 each year. The estimated cost of this was put at £2 billion, at least, in additional days spent in hospital. Half of these adverse events were preventable.
- 8 per cent of adverse events may result in death, and 6 per cent in permanent disability – amounting to over 34,000 preventable deaths and 25,000 preventable permanent disabilities every year.

The report recognized that these figures underestimated the true scale of the problems. To tackle the high level of negligence claims against the NHS, the National Patient Safety Agency was set up in 2001, modelled on the Air Accidents Investigation Branch. In 2007, this estimated that there were around 850,000 incidents and errors in the NHS every year.

luck, but very much a product of the society and social circumstances in which a person lives.

- The model suggests disease is abnormal, has a clearly identifiable biological cause, and that measures can be taken to treat and cure it. However, Steve Taylor has shown that this model of health is inadequate and increasingly under attack because:

(a) Infectious diseases like smallpox, typhoid and cholera have been replaced by degenerative diseases such as cancer and heart disease as the main killers of people in the twentieth and twenty-first centuries. Modern medicine has often proved unable to provide cures for these new diseases. Medicine is almost completely ineffective in curing some new diseases like AIDS (Acquired Immune Deficiency Syndrome) or vCJD (variant Creutzfeldt–Jakob disease), though there is a constant pursuit of cures, such as the use of combination drugs for AIDS. There is still no cure for the common cold or flu.

(b) Researchers like McKeown (1976) have shown that doctors are not (solely) responsible for improving **life expectancy** and health. Improvements in social conditions, such as public sewers and clean water are far more important.

Life expectancy is an estimate of how long people can be expected to live from a certain age.

> **Activity**
>
> Do you believe you are safe in the hands of doctors and other medical professionals? Do you have any personal experience of medicine being of little help to you or harming you in some way? Are there currently any stories of medical negligence around that you are aware of? Collect together information, and discuss it in your group.

The social model of health

The social model of health highlights the way that social factors are involved in both defining health and the causes of ill-health. This model is the main alternative to the medical model, and recognizes there are important social influences on health which the medical model ignores. The Acheson Report (1998) made a powerful case that many of the factors causing ill-health are rooted in social inequality, and therefore recognized the importance of the social dimensions of health.

Features of the social model of health

- Health and illness are not seen simply as medical or scientific facts. Health is a relative condition. What is defined as health depends on what is regarded as 'normal' in a particular society, and this will vary over time and between cultures, and between individuals in the same culture.
- A choice exists whether someone sees himself or herself as ill or not. Those with power can choose whether or not to classify someone as ill. In most cases, 'those with power' means doctors and other medical experts. What counts as health and sickness is as much about the power of medical professionals as it is about biology.

- Medical science is not the detached objective science the medical model implies. It is influenced by wider social and economic considerations, rather than simply the treatment of biological disease. Drug companies and medical technology manufacturers are likely to have important influences on the way doctors go about their work.

- A strong emphasis is placed on the social causes of health and ill-health, and on how society influences health. Patterns of health and illness cannot simply be explained and treated individually, but should be understood within the social and economic environment in which they occur. It is not just chance individuals who become sick through bad luck, but whole groups of people who are more at risk of ill-health. There is a pattern of social class, gender and ethnic inequalities in health. This suggests that it is social and environmental factors that make some groups of people more vulnerable to disease than others, and not simply lightning bolts from the blue hurled out by nature at unfortunate and randomly chosen individuals.

Activity

1 List *six* social and environmental factors you think influence health, and identify in each case how they affect health.
2 How would you set out to improve society's health if you were particularly concerned with tackling the social and environmental causes of ill-health?
3 Go to www.dh.gov.uk (the website for the Department of Health) and search for three policies being followed by the government to improve the health of Britain. Explain how each of the policies you identify might improve health.

Limitations of the social model

It is important to recognize the social dimensions of health, and the ways conceptions of health and illness are socially constructed. However, there is a danger of overemphasizing these social aspects at the expense of the medical approach. Medicine has contributed to improvements in health, even if not as much as some doctors might claim. Childhood immunization against diseases such as tuberculosis, polio, smallpox, measles, mumps and rubella (German measles) have contributed to reducing these diseases, and in some cases wiped them out in modern Britain. Antibiotics have proved very effective in treating many infections, and medicine has effective treatments for broken bones. Most of us therefore derive some benefit from cures, and knowledge through health education about preventing disease, which come from scientific medicine.

Marxist approaches to health and medicine

Marxists like Navarro (1976) adopt a social model of health, and are very critical of the biomedical model. Marxists argue:

- The medical model of health suggests ill-health is caused by either random attacks of disease or the failure of individuals to follow a healthy lifestyle. This puts the blame on individuals when ill-health is really caused by social influences in an unequal society, such as low pay, unemployment and poverty, unhealthy food, environmental pollution and hazardous workplaces. The state doesn't tackle the real social causes of ill-health, and allows companies to continue making profits out of health-damaging products, like tobacco, alcohol and junk food.
- The National Health Service helps to keep the workforce fit, and this caring face of capitalism conceals the exploitation of the working class by the owning class.
- Doctors are agents of social control – gate-keepers who control access to the sick role and therefore keep the workforce at work in the interests of capitalists.
- The definition of health and the provision of health care are concerned with protecting the interests of the dominant class in an unequal capitalist society. Medicine is mainly concerned with providing capitalists with a healthy workforce.
- The focus on medical treatment, rather than the prevention of ill-health, supports big business in the form of drug and medical technology companies. These companies are mainly concerned with making profits out of ill-health, not reducing it.

How society influences health

That health is the product of society rather than simply of biology or medicine is shown by historical evidence that patterns of disease change over time. While the message has been that medicine can cure us, all the major advances in health have occurred before medical intervention. In Britain, the elimination or substantial reduction of the killer infectious diseases of the past, such as tuberculosis (TB), pneumonia, cholera, typhoid and diphtheria, all took place before the development of modern medicine. It was social changes such as better diet, clean water supplies, sewage disposal, improved housing and general knowledge about health and hygiene that improved health, rather than medical improvements like antibiotics and vaccines. This

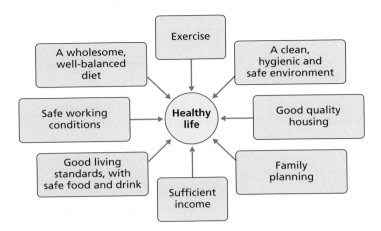

Figure 7.1 Some key social influences on health

> **Activity**
>
> Make a list of as many environmental, political, social and economic factors affecting health as you can think of, such as unemployment, pollution or poor housing. Explain in each case how the factors you identify might influence health. Refer to figure 7.1 to help you in this.

is shown especially in the less developed countries today, where the major advances in health have come about as a result of simple preventive measures such as clean water and sewage control, where vaccines have been less effective because of malnutrition, and where medicines are often not affordable because of the high prices charged by international drug companies. Doctors and medical treatment have therefore not had the impact on health they often claim, and it is incorrect to assume that medicine has been largely responsible for the most significant improvements and promotion of health. Improvements in health are due to wider social, economic and environmental factors, and not simply medical ones.

Changes which occurred during the nineteenth century and the first half of the twentieth century illustrate this well.

Improvements in health in the nineteenth and early twentieth centuries

In the nineteenth century, adult and child mortality (death rates) started to fall, and this was accompanied by a large and rapid population increase. For a long time this was thought to be due to the development of medicine. However, McKeown (1976) showed that the role of medicine in reducing morbidity and mortality rates in the nineteenth and twentieth centuries had been massively exaggerated. It is now agreed that these changes were due to a number of social and economic changes and the general improvement in living standards. These included:

- *Public hygiene*   The movement for sanitary reform and public hygiene in the nineteenth century helped to develop a clean and safe environment and higher standards of public hygiene. Pure drinking water, efficient sanitation and sewage disposal, paved streets and highways all helped to reduce deaths from infectious diseases.
- *Better diet*   Being well fed is the most effective form of disease prevention, as is shown in less developed countries today where vaccination programmes are not as successful as they should be because children are poorly nourished. The high death rates of the past were mainly due to hunger or malnutrition, which led to poorer resistance to infection. The nineteenth and early twentieth centuries saw improved communications, technology and hygiene enabling the production, transportation and import of more and cheaper food. Wages improved, and higher standards of living meant better food and better health.
- *Safer and more effective contraception*   This led to smaller families, enabling a better diet and health care for children. It also improved the health of women, who spent less time childbearing.
- *Housing legislation*   This increased public control over standards of rented housing, which helped to reduce overcrowding and the spread of infectious diseases between family members and in the close community.
- *The war effort*   During the First World War (1914–18) unemployment was virtually eliminated. As part of the war effort, rents were controlled, food rationing was introduced and minimum wages were established in agriculture. The resulting decline in poverty cut childhood deaths, especially among the families of unskilled workers in urban areas.
- *General improvements in living standards*   Higher wages, better food, clothing and housing, laws improving health and safety at work, reduced working hours, and better hygiene regulations in the production and sale of food and drink all improved health.

All the above suggest that good health is more the result of government policy decisions and of economic development than simply of individual initiative or medical intervention.

The new disease burden

The infective diseases of the nineteenth century were often called the 'diseases of poverty' since most victims were malnourished and poor. These have

Adult obesity rates have almost quadrupled in the last twenty-five years, and the number of obese children has tripled in twenty years. Around one in five people in the United Kingdom were officially classified as obese in 2007, and more than 30,000 deaths a year are caused by obesity in England alone. By 2010, an estimated one in three adults will be obese if present trends continue. The World Health Organization predicts that almost 50 per cent of children could be obese by 2025 through a combination of junk food and lack of exercise.

Obesity is much more common among the most deprived sections of society. How might sociologists explain this?

been replaced by 'diseases of affluence' – a result of eating too much poor quality food, a lack of exercise, and smoking and drinking too much.

A well-balanced diet is necessary for good health, and the lack of one makes people more vulnerable to disease. Despite the wealth of contemporary developed Western societies, there is a problem of malnutrition, in the form not of too little food, as you find in less developed countries, but too much of the wrong sort. As a result, advanced industrial societies experience health problems rarely found in simpler rural societies. The new disease burden includes obesity and degenerative (worsening) diseases like cirrhosis of the liver, certain cancers, heart disease, respiratory diseases and diabetes. These kill or disable more people than they did in the past, and many more people are becoming chronically ill for longer periods in their lives than they did in the past.

What are the causes of these new diseases?

It is generally accepted that the causes of these new diseases of affluence are mainly social and environmental, and therefore preventable. Public concerns over the food supply have been rising. There were major scares over BSE ('Mad cow disease') in beef in the 1990s, and the linked human equivalent vCJD (variant Creutzfeldt–Jakob disease) had killed 162 people in Britain up to November 2007. *E. coli* food poisoning outbreaks in 1996–7 killed twenty people, and many worry about GM (genetically modified) crops and foods, while the effects on health of the use of growth-promoting drugs in chickens was of continuing concern in the early 2000s. Between 1989 and 1999, cases of food poisoning serious enough to be reported to a doctor nearly doubled, and the Food Standards Agency estimates there are 5.5 million cases of food poisoning in Britain each year. Some doctors have linked the rise of asthma to poor diet, with insufficient fruit and vegetables. The rise in heart disease has been blamed on factors such as smoking, stress, an inactive life style and a diet

To what extent does the food we eat and drink pose a threat to our health? Is the food we eat a result of individual lifestyle choices or of social pressures?

high in sugar, salt and fats but low in fibre. The *Lancet* medical journal reported in 2003 that women eating too much food high in fat, such as butter, milk, meat, burgers, crisps, biscuits and cakes, were more likely to get breast cancer than others whose fat intake was low. A *Lancet* report in 2005 said that one-third of cancer deaths worldwide were caused by diet, lifestyle factors like smoking and alcohol, and physical inactivity and environmental pollution. This was confirmed by one of the most comprehensive studies of cancer ever. The World Cancer Research Fund's 2007 report, *Food, Nutrition, Physical Activity, and the Prevention of Cancer: A Global Perspective*, said that a third of cancers were caused by diet and lack of exercise, and could be prevented by people taking exercise, staying slim and abstaining from too much fast food, alcohol, red meat and preserved meats like ham, bacon and salami.

The British are now eating a more highly processed diet than at any time in history. We consume a whole range of factory-produced food, which is often low in nutritional value and may well be harmful to health because of additives making up chemical cocktails of flavourings, colourings, preservatives and various drugs. In 2007, the *Independent on Sunday* reported research suggesting that a common food preservative (E211 – Sodium Benzoate), found in a range of fizzy soft drinks like Fanta and Pepsi, had the ability to 'switch off' vital parts of DNA, risking cirrhosis of the liver and other degenerative diseases such as Parkinson's and Alzheimer's. A 2007 Food Standards Agency study on 300 randomly selected children found that hyperactivity rose after a drink containing additive combinations. This may explain why between 5 and 10 per cent of school-age children suffer some degree of ADHD (attention deficit hyperactivity disorder), with symptoms such as impulsiveness, inability to concentrate and excessive activity. Revelations that large food-processing companies were 'bulking up' chicken destined for schools, hospitals and restaurants with poultry skin, beef bits and pig waste were of major concern in 2003. Highly processed junk food reinforces the trend towards a high-sugar, high-salt and high-fat diet which is low in vitamins, minerals, protein and fibre. Research in 2003 suggested that high doses of fat and sugar in fast and processed foods could be as addictive as nicotine and even hard drugs, causing hormonal changes creating a need for even more high-fat foods and generating obesity as a growing health problem.

Becoming a health statistic

The main ways used to measure the extent of health and illness are **morbidity** (the extent of disease) and **mortality** (death) statistics. Major concerns have been raised over the *validity* (or truthfulness) of these statistics. Morbidity statistics are collected from sources such as the number of consultations with GPs, absence from work and self-reported illness surveys. Self-reported illness and absence from work statistics rely on the honesty of those claiming to be ill or absent from work due to illness, and the types of disease recorded based on GP consultations will depend partly on how patients describe their symptoms and on the diagnostic skills of doctors, since their decisions will affect how the symptoms are classified (e.g. as pneumonia or AIDS). Statistics on the causes of death are derived from death certificates. What cause is put on these certificates will depend on the doctor's interpretation of what the cause of death is, and analysis of these statistics will depend on the level of explanation provided.

Health statistics must therefore be treated with considerable care, and

> **Morbidity** refers to the extent of disease in a population, including either the total number of cases or the number of new cases of a disease in a particular population at a particular time.
> **Mortality** refers to the number of deaths in a population, usually measured as a rate per thousand of a population group, such as the number of deaths per thousand of the population each year.

The social construction of health statistics

- Health statistics depend on people persuading doctors they are ill, and are therefore simply a record of doctors' judgements and decision-making.
- Doctors may diagnose illnesses incorrectly, reflecting how patients describe their symtpoms and the state of the doctor's knowledge. Records of illnesses may not be accurate. For example, there may have been many AIDS deaths recorded as pneumonia or other diseases before AIDS was discovered in the 1980s.
- Not all sick people go to the doctor, and not all people who persuade doctors they are ill are really sick.
- Private medicine operates to make a profit, and therefore is perhaps more likely to diagnose symptoms as a disease.

many sociologists argue health statistics are simply social constructions, rather than being valid in providing a true picture of the pattern of health.

Official health statistics have been described as a 'clinical iceberg', as it is estimated that only about 10 per cent of illness is reported to doctors, with most concealed beneath the surface.

The process of becoming ill is not as simple and straightforward as it might seem. People often have choices over whether to report themselves sick or not. People may respond to the same symptoms in different ways. While some may seek medical help, others may choose to ignore their symptoms. They may look for alternative non-medical or less serious explanations for them: bronchitis may become simply a 'smoker's cough', and possible brain tumours may be dismissed as 'headaches'.

Often, whether an individual goes to the doctor or not will depend on the responses of other people, such as whether they can put up with a person's moaning any longer, or whether the individual's friends can continue to play sport with them or not. It may be difficulties experienced with looking after children while feeling unwell, pressures from friends and family, or health scare stories in the media, the costs of taking time off work and so on which finally persuade people to go to the doctor. These examples suggest it may be difficulties in coping with an illness, rather than the illness itself, which bring people to seek medical attention.

For people to be labelled as 'sick' – and to be recorded as a health statistic – there are at least four stages involved:

Stage 1: Individuals must first recognize they have a problem.

Stage 2: They must then define their problem as serious enough to take to a doctor.

Stage 3: They must then actually go to the doctor.

Stage 4: The doctor must then be persuaded that they have a medical or mental condition capable of being labelled as an illness requiring treatment.

Activity

1 List all the factors you can which might influence each of the four stages involved in labelling someone 'sick', and which lead some people to visit the doctor and others not to. For example, in stage 1, you might consider a person's ability to continue his or her responsibilities to friends and family, pressure from relatives, friends and employers, etc. Draw on your own experiences of what makes you decide whether you are ill, and whether or not to go to see the doctor.

2 Devise a short questionnaire, and interview a sample of people, about what they consider to be the most important things influencing whether they go to the doctor or not.

Medicine and social control: the sick role

Social control is concerned with maintaining order and stability in society. Parsons, writing from a functionalist perspective, argues that sickness is really a form of deviance, which threatens the stability of society. This is because those who are classified as sick are able to avoid their normal social responsibilities, like going to work, school or college, or looking after the family. If too many people did this, then society would collapse – imagine a school or factory where the teachers, students, managers or workers were always off ill. Ill-health is therefore something that needs to be kept within careful limits to avoid undermining social order and the smooth functioning of society. Parsons sees the **sick role** as fulfilling this purpose.

The sick role provides an escape route for individuals from everyday responsibilities. This is because, when people are sick, they can reasonably abandon normal everyday activities, and often others will take over their responsibilities so that they are able to recover.

> The **sick role** refers to the pattern of behaviour which is expected from someone who is ill.

Features of the sick role

Parsons suggests the sick role involves both rights and obligations for those who are sick.

Rights

- Depending on the illness, individuals are excused normal social activities, such as going to school or work. This requires approval by others such as teachers, employers and family members. The doctor often plays a key role in this process, by diagnosing the person as 'really ill', and issuing sick notes.
- Individuals are not seen as personally to blame for their illness, nor are they expected to be solely responsible for their recovery by a sheer act of will. There is a recognition they will need help to recover. Relatives, friends and doctors are often very critical of those they see as responsible for their own illness, and those who drink too much or overdose on drugs often don't get much sympathy from the medical profession.

Obligations

- The sick person must see his or her sickness as an undesirable state, and individuals have an obligation to want to get well, and ensure their sickness state is only a temporary one.
- When necessary, sick people are expected to seek and accept medical help and cooperate in their treatment to get well. In other words, sick people are expected to do what the doctor orders, and they cannot

expect sympathy and support if they don't try to get well. Those refusing medical treatment are unlikely to have their illnesses recognized as genuine sickness or get much sympathy if they are suffering. Even if people don't want to call in the doctor because they don't see their illness as serious enough to do so, they are still expected to stay in bed, take non-prescription medicines, or take it easy in an effort to recover.

Parsons argues these obligations are necessary to stop people getting into a subculture of sickness, where sickness, dependence on others and apathy are seen as a normal and desirable state. Such a subculture would disrupt the smooth running of society. People must therefore be obliged to get well and resume their everyday responsibilities as quickly as possible.

Doctors as gate-keepers

Doctors and other medical professionals play a key role in the social control of the sick by acting as **gate-keepers** of entry to the sick role – doctors are the ones who legitimize (justify) sickness by officially classifying it as such. For example, doctors can stop people taking more than a few days off work on the grounds of illness by refusing to issue sick notes. The doctor's role is to cure the sick and get them back to normal, and sort out those who are really sick

> **Gate-keeping** is the power of some people, groups or organizations to limit access to something valuable or useful. For example, doctors act as gate-keepers as they have the power to allow or refuse entry to the sick role.

Doctors play an important part in social control of the sick and access to the sick role

from hypochondriacs, malingerers and skivers who try to evade their responsibilities by faking illness.

Criticisms of Parsons and the sick role

- Not everyone who feels ill adopts the sick role, perhaps because they don't like or are afraid of doctors or cannot afford to have time off work. Lone parents, for example, may not be able to afford the luxury of adopting the sick role as they have to continue looking after their children.
- Not everyone who is ill gets the sympathy of others and avoids the personal blame implied in the rights of the sick role. For example, AIDS, heart disease brought on by smoking, drug abuse and alcohol poisoning often bring little sympathy from others as they are seen as self-inflicted.
- Some diseases, like mental illness and AIDS, involve high degrees of stigma (social disapproval, rejection and inferior status), and sufferers may wish to conceal public knowledge of their illness. They may therefore wish to avoid adopting the sick role because of the consequences of doing so.
- Some illnesses or disorders are not curable, and it may be better for both the individual and society to avoid the sick role and try to carry on with normal life as much as possible. This might well apply to those with terminal illnesses, various forms of impairment, such as blindness or loss of limb functions, or conditions like heart disease or diabetes.
- The sick don't always act as the well-behaved, passive and obedient patients implied by the sick role. They may well refuse to cooperate with doctors, challenge diagnoses and the doctor's authority, and ask for second opinions. The relationship between doctors and patients is changing, and patients now have access to much more information about medical treatments through the internet, and services such as NHS Direct. This means doctors no longer have the monopoly of medical knowledge they once enjoyed.

The power of the medical profession

Doctors play a key role in controlling the sick and legitimizing (justifying) sickness by their gate-keeping function in relation to the sick role. It is doctors who have the power to confirm or deny that people have a genuine illness, and who put them on an approved programme of treatment. Doctors also have an apparently ever-expanding expertise about matters that were not previously regarded as the concern of medicine, such as childbirth, alcohol consumption, childhood behaviour and even the ageing process.

Doctors often have a great deal of power and authority over patients. What factors might contribute to this unequal relationship?

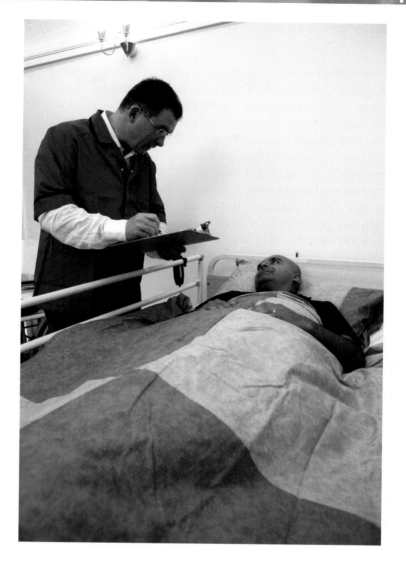

This gives doctors a great deal of power and authority over patients. Patients themselves are very vulnerable when they are sick, and they are often liable to face intimate medical examinations. Functionalist writers like Parsons therefore argue that there is a high level of trust involved in the doctor–patient relationship, and the patient's interests must be protected.

Protecting the patient?

Parsons and other functionalist writers suggest that the following features of the medical profession protect the interests of patients, such as by protecting the confidentiality of their consultations and maintaining high standards of treatment:

- Doctors have a long period of training, giving them the specialized and expert knowledge (biomedical science) and the wide range of diagnostic skills necessary to treat their patients effectively.
- Doctors need legal permission to practise medicine. This monopoly protects the patient from unqualified 'cowboy' doctors.
- Doctors are mainly concerned with patient care, rather than personal gain.
- Doctors are bound by a code of professional ethics, which puts the interests of the patient first and leaves doctors open to disciplinary action if they fail in their duty to patients. The General Medical Council does occasionally 'strike doctors off' the medical register in cases of medical incompetence or breaches of appropriate professional behaviour.

Because of these features of the medical profession, doctors are given high status in society, with high salaries to match. They are also trusted with high levels of independence to get on with their work of curing people.

These functionalist views have not gone unchallenged.

Criticisms of the medical profession

- Because of their long training, and specialized knowledge and skills, doctors have high levels of independence in their work. This means there is little control by others over what they do and often incompetent doctors remain undiscovered and unchallenged. Dr Harold Shipman achieved notoriety as Britain's worst serial killer, killing 215 patients between 1975 and 1998. While Shipman was something of an exception in the medical profession, the Shipman public inquiry was told the independence given to doctors undermined safeguards for patients against an incompetent doctor or, as in this case, a determined killer.
- The professional code of ethics means doctors are forbidden to criticize the work of other doctors publicly. This makes it very difficult for patients to complain about and expose medical incompetence.
- Because doctors have a monopoly over medical treatment, practitioners of alternative medicine of which the British Medical Association does not approve are seen as giving inferior treatments, even though these might benefit patients. This same monopoly of treatment ensures doctors can maintain their high salaries.
- As seen earlier when discussing iatrogenesis, doctors and nurses don't always do a good job, and may actually do more harm than good to patients' health. Feminist writers have been particularly critical of the medical profession, and the way childbirth and pregnancy have come to be defined as medical problems, to be dealt with as an illness and treated

clinically at the doctor's convenience. This takes control over childbirth away from women, and turns what should be a natural process into a medical procedure.

- Most doctors work within the framework of publicly funded health care, like the National Health Service or GP's surgeries. Concern over the costs of treatment may mean doctors do not always provide the best care or prescribe the most effective drugs, but may go for cheaper, less effective treatments.

The erosion of medical power and other contemporary changes in health and health care

The erosion of medical power in favour of the patient?

In contemporary Britain, the power of the medical profession is being eroded to some degree, with more power shifting in favour of the patient. This is because many of the new diseases in contemporary society are degenerative diseases for which there are no medical cures. In such circumstances, doctors are of less use to patients. Many people have growing doubts about the alleged superiority of conventional medical treatment, with more of them turning to alternative therapies, medicines and treatments, such as acupuncture and homeopathy. The rise of these alternatives was given extra force when the House of Lords recognized in 2000 that there was scientific evidence that some, such as acupuncture and herbal medicine, could be effective, and the British Medical Association has now accepted the usefulness of certain alternative treatments.

Public confidence in the medical profession is being eroded by medical scandals of various kinds. An example of this was the wave of public revulsion and distrust arising from the scandal at Alder Hey hospital in Liverpool in 2001, when the organs of dead children were routinely removed during post-mortem examinations and stored for research purposes, without the prior consent of the parents.

Further lack of confidence in medicine arises from the return of diseases which were once thought to be nearly extinct in Britain. For example, tuberculosis has returned as a significant disease. In 2001 there was the worst outbreak of tuberculosis in Britain for twenty years in a secondary school in Leicester, with a further outbreak among children at a school in Newport, South Wales. TB in England has increased by 25 per cent over the last decade or so, and around 350 people in England now die each year from the disease.

Patients are demanding much more from their doctors and nurses, and have growing knowledge of which medical treatments are effective and what they should be entitled to. More patients are questioning the competence of doctors, and losing confidence in them. This is reflected in rising numbers of complaints against medical professionals, with complaints about doctors to the General Medical Council reaching an all-time high in 2000; there are currently around 400 or more complaints against doctors every month. Patients now have the right to see their medical records, and doctors are facing growing threats of legal action when care is inadequate or when mistakes are made.

By 2007, public confidence in the medical profession had reached such an all-time low that the government proposed taking away from doctors their privilege of self-regulation (setting and enforcing their own rules) and to having complaints heard by an independent tribunal rather than by the doctors' own General Medical Council. There were also proposals to introduce five-yearly checks, like 'MOT' tests for cars, on doctors' record-keeping and clinical ability. These proposals aimed to shore up public confidence in the medical profession.

In the National Health Service, managers and administrators, rather than doctors, often make the major decisions about the types and costs of medical care provided. These factors are changing the balance of power between patients and doctors in the patient's favour, giving patients more rights through complaints procedures, and undermining the status of doctors.

Reforms in the National Health Service in the 2000s aimed to provide more personalized health services for individuals, with the health care system fitting the needs of individuals rather than the other way round, giving patients more control over their medical treatment.

A shift from the medical to social model of health?

There is a growing recognition among health professionals that poor health is a result of a combination of individual and structural social and cultural factors, as well as the biological causes which form the core explanation of the medical model. Following the lead of the Department of Health and the growing weight of sociological evidence, many now recognize that lifestyle choices, such as what foods you eat and drink (and how much) the amount of exercise and relaxation people get, as well as structural factors like low pay, poverty, poor housing and unhealthy environments, all influence health. There have, in other words, been some moves away from the medical model to a more social model of health, though the medical model is still a powerful influence among health professionals.

Consumer choice

In postmodern society, there is a growing emphasis on the consumer lifestyle and on meeting the demands and choices of consumers. People are more likely to take control of their health and fitness, consume health and fitness

There's a growing emphasis on patient choice in the National Health Service

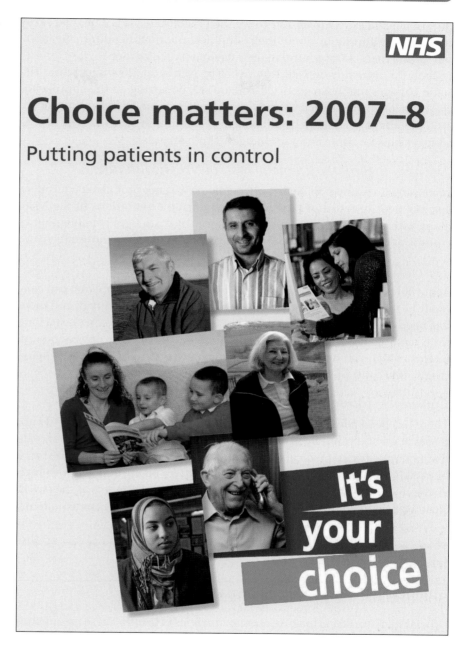

NHS

Choice matters: 2007–8

Putting patients in control

It's your choice

products, and to see their health and fitness as important parts of their identities. Consequently, people now expect more choice – for example, which hospital or GP to go to, whether to be treated in hospital or at the GPs surgery, when the treatment should take place as opposed to being held up on waiting lists. They expect more information about their treatment, are more likely to question it and expect to be able to see their medical records. They can easily now obtain information about their condition and treatment from the internet, giving them more control in their dealings with doctors.

Table 7.1, which is derived from work by Nettleton (2006), identifies the main changes that have occurred and are still occurring, in the approaches to health and health care. Many of these changes formed a central part of the 1997 Labour government's health policies. Nettleton suggests a range of possible reasons for some of these changes. These include:

The need to limit the financial costs of NHS health care

Increasing investment in 'high-tech' medicine was not producing equivalent success rates in terms of patients treated. Rising expectations of the NHS, along with a growing elderly population, meant costs were spiralling out of control, and demand needed to be limited, and money spent more effectively.

The changing disease burden

Acute illness (diseases with an abrupt onset, a short course and that can generally be treated and cured), like infectious diseases, has declined, and there has been an increase in chronic diseases. These are diseases that last a long time, with many modern diseases caused by social and environmental factors, which can be prevented, but which are often not capable of being cured, only controlled.

Consumer culture and postmodern society

There has been a loss of faith in the ability of science and medicine to cure diseases, an undermining of the role of medical professional 'experts', and the distinction between medical experts and ordinary people has become more blurred. Postmodern societies involve consumers taking control, with high elements of consumer choice in picking and mixing treatments as they wish. No longer can medical experts alone simply decide what happens to patients.

Inequalities in health

Social class inequalities in health

Official statistics reveal massive class inequalities in health. These inequalities are often referred to as the 'health divide'. Nearly every kind of illness and disease has a class aspect. Poverty is the major driver of ill-health, and poorer people tend to get sick more often, to suffer more years in poor health and to die younger than richer people. Those who die youngest are people who live on benefits or low wages in poor quality housing and who eat cheap, unhealthy food. Lifestyle choices related to poor health, like smoking, alcohol

Table 7.1 Changing approaches to health and health care

Traditional health care   ⟶   New approaches

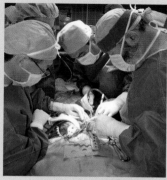

Medical model of health ⟶	*Social model of health*
Disease ⟶	*Health*
Emphasis on treating acute life-threatening and infectious diseases.	Emphasis on preventing ill-health. Health promotion campaigns.
Hospital ⟶	*Community*
Care is provided in hospitals, which are seen as centres of medical or psychiatric expertise and treatment.	Care is provided in the community, such as by nurses and GPs, 'halfway' houses for the mentally ill, and home care for older people.
Intervention and cure ⟶	*Monitoring, prevention and care*
The focus is on medical intervention to protect health, and treating and curing acute illnesses where possible.	The focus is on individuals, either alone or working with their doctors, monitoring their own health and fitness, preventing them developing chronic illnesses, and caring for those with chronic illnesses for which there is no cure.
Patient ⟶	*Person*
The individual is seen as a 'patient' – a malfunctioning biological object requiring treatment, which is directed by medical professionals ('experts') in terms of location and type of treatment. Medical records are secret, and there is hardly any patient choice.	The individual is seen as a combination of biological, social and psychological characteristics. In a consumer-oriented society, medical professionals need to respond to the needs of patients, who have more choice, information and control over where, when and what type of treatment, they receive, and have means of complaining if they don't get it.

misuse, obesity, poor diets and lack of exercise, are all more common among the most deprived sections of society.

A 1995 Department of Health report noted that if everyone was as healthy as the middle class, there would have been 1,500 fewer deaths a year among children under the age of one, and 17,000 fewer deaths among men aged 20–64. In 2005, the Office for National Statistics reported that people in the most prosperous neighbourhoods of England enjoyed seventeen more years of fit and active life than those in the poorest.

The Black Report *(1980) and* The Health Divide *(1987)*

Social class inequalities in health were first most clearly revealed in a British government report in 1980, *Inequalities in Health: Report of a Research Working Group*. This working group was chaired by Sir Douglas Black, and the report therefore became known as *The Black Report*. This report was so contentious and carried such a strong condemnation of health inequalities that the government tried to suppress it, and prevent its conclusions from becoming public. Only 260 duplicated copies were made available, and it was released just before August Bank Holiday weekend – when it was guaranteed to get the absolute minimum of publicity. *The Black Report* was followed up in 1987 by *The Health Divide*, which confirmed yet again the pattern of social inequalities in health. As with *The Black Report*, there was strong evidence of official connivance in suppressing the findings of *The Health Divide*; as Townsend and his colleagues noted (1990), there was 'an attempted cover-up of unpalatable information about the nation's health'.

The Health of the Nation *(1992)*

The Health of the Nation, published by the Department of Health in 1992, set out the main strategy for improving the health of people in England until 1997. The strategy identified five key areas of ill-health: coronary heart disease and stroke; cancer; mental illness; HIV/AIDS and sexual health; and accidents – all major causes of premature death or avoidable ill-health and offering significant scope for improvement in health. It set targets in these areas, and monitored progress towards them.

The Acheson Report *(1998)*

Both *The Black Report* and *The Health Divide* were based on the social model of health, and *The Acheson Report* followed in their footsteps in recommending more help for the poor as a means of improving health. *The Acheson Report* confirmed earlier findings of wide social class inequalities in health, and helped to establish the framework for future health policies. These policies were unveiled in the 1998 Department of Health paper *Our Healthier Nation*, and *Saving Lives* a year later.

Our Healthier Nation *(1998)* and Saving Lives *(1999)*

Although overall trends show an improvement in health since the 1970s, with life expectancy increasing and infant mortality falling, these overall trends mask the fact that the health of the poor has failed to keep up with the improvements of the most prosperous sections of society. In fact, the health gap between those at the top and those at the bottom of the social scale has actually been widening since the last quarter of the twentieth century. The Labour government, in its 1998 paper *Our Healthier Nation*, and *Saving Lives* a year later, finally officially recognized these social class inequalities in health, and the social, environmental and economic causes of ill-health. These documents laid the basis for government health policy for the years ahead.

Our Healthier Nation pointed out that:

> the poorest in our society are hit harder than the well off by most of the major causes of death. Poor people are ill more often and die sooner. The life expectancy of those higher up the social scale (in professional and managerial jobs) has improved more than those lower down (in manual and unskilled jobs). This inequality has widened since the early 1980s.

Figure 7.2 and the box opposite show some of these social class inequalities, which provide strong evidence that it is society and the way it is organized that influences health, rather than simply our biological make-up.

Explanations for social class inequalities in health

The causes of ill-health are complex, and there are clearly some influences on health which go beyond social factors. The ageing process and our genetic inheritance do have important influences on our health, though health education awareness, access to health, leisure and social services and a range of other social factors have an impact on how effectively we cope with them.

There are four main types of explanation for social class inequalities in heath: artefact, natural or social selection, cultural or behavioural, and material or structural explanations.

Activity

Study figure 7.2
1 Which disease shows the greatest difference in deaths between social classes 4 and 5 and social class 1 and 2?
2 Which disease shows the smallest difference in deaths between social class 1 and 2 and social class 4 and 5?
3 Which social classes show the lowest deaths from lung cancer?
4 Identify *two* patterns shown in figure 7.2.
5 Suggest *two* possible social explanations for the social class differences in heart diseases shown in figure 7.2.

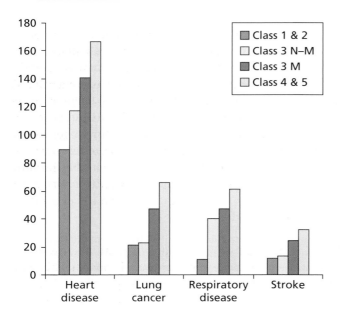

Figure 7.2 Mortality of men in England and Wales aged 35–64, by selected causes of death and by social class, 1997–99 (rates per 100,000 persons years)

Source: Health Statistics Quarterly, Office for National Statistics, 2003

The extent of social class inequalities in health in contemporary Britain

- The death rate in class 5 (unskilled manual workers) is about twice that of class 1. A person born into social class 1 (professional) lives, on average, about seven years longer than someone in social class 5.
- In the first year of life, for every five children who die in class 1, eight die among unskilled workers. The risk of dying before the age of 5 is twice as great for a child born into social class 5 than for social class 1, and children from poorer backgrounds are five times more likely to die as a result of an accident than children from better-off families.
- Men and women in class 5 have twice the chance of dying before reaching retirement age than people in class 1. About 90 per cent of the major causes of death are more common in social classes 4 and 5 than in other social classes.
- Lung cancer and stomach cancer occur twice as often among men in manual jobs as among men in professional jobs, and death rates from heart disease and lung cancer – the two biggest causes of premature death – are about twice as high for those from manual backgrounds. Four times as many women die of cervical cancer in social class 5 as in social class 1.
- Working-class people, especially the unskilled, go to see doctors far more often and for a wider range of health problems than do people in professional jobs.
- Semi-skilled and unskilled workers are more likely to be absent from work through sickness than those in professional and managerial jobs. Long-standing illness is around 50 per cent higher among unskilled manual workers than for class 1 professionals.
- All of the above are worse for the long-term unemployed and other groups in poverty.

The artefact explanation   This suggests that health inequalities between social classes are artificial rather than real – a manufactured explanation arising only because of distortion and bias in the way statistics are used, and the way the link between social class and health is measured. The apparent link between poor health and social class is simply because the number of lower working-class occupations is getting smaller, and those left in these occupations tend to be older than those in other social classes, with younger people going into new skilled or non-manual occupations. It is therefore only to be expected that those in such occupations will suffer poorer health, because the people left are older. This explanation is rejected by sociologists, since social class inequalities in health remain even after using a number of different methods of measurement.

The natural or social selection explanation   This explanation suggests that people in lower social classes are there because of their poor health, with their lack of physical strength, vigour and fitness stopping them getting into, and hanging on to, higher social class jobs. Poor health acts as a 'filter', with

poor health causing their low social class, rather than their social class causing their ill-health. Society is seen as based on 'survival of the fittest', with the
most unhealthy people inevitably ending up in the lowest social classes,
while those in good health succeed in society and achieve the highest
rewards. This explanation is rejected by sociologists, because most adult
health problems seem to arise among those coming from already deprived
backgrounds, and there is significant evidence to show that poor health is a
result of deprived circumstances rather than a cause of them. There are also
some people in higher social classes who suffer poor health, and people in
lower social classes who enjoy good health, so good or poor health cannot by
itself explain a person's social class position.

The following two types of explanation for social class inequalities in
health are those firmly rooted in society itself.

Cultural or behavioural explanations – blaming the victims   Cultural
explanations suggest that those suffering from poorer health have different
attitudes, values and lifestyles which mean they don't look after themselves
properly. Health inequalities are rooted in the unhealthy behaviour and
lifestyles of individuals, and individuals can and should tackle them themselves by making voluntary efforts to change. Examples might include smoking too much, consuming too much alcohol, using too much salt or sugar,
eating junk food and not enough fresh fruit and vegetables, or not bothering
to take any exercise.

These types of factors are linked to a variety of conditions, including heart
disease, cancer, strokes, bronchitis and asthma. *Our Healthier Nation* estimates that alcohol abuse, for example, leads to around 40,000 deaths a year,
and that a third of all cancers are the result of a poor diet.

Cultural explanations for social class inequalities in health tend to place the blame for ill-health on the victims
themselves for having unhealthy lifestyles. To what extent do you think people are themselves responsible for their
poor health? Or do unhealthy lifestyles arise from the material circumstances of people's lives, like social
deprivation?

Cultural explanations essentially place the blame on individuals themselves, in what are called 'victim blaming' theories. However, as Townsend and his colleagues (1990) pointed out:

> While some of the links between deprivation and ill-health are still very poorly understood, life style is clearly far from being the whole answer . . . some people have more freedom than others by virtue of their individual situation and circumstances to choose a healthy lifestyle, the unlucky ones being restrained from adopting a healthier life, even when they would wish to do so, by income, housing, work and other social constraints.

The way material factors can influence lifestyles and health choices was well illustrated in *Our Healthier Nation*:

> low income, deprivation and social exclusion all influence smoking levels. It's harder to stop smoking when you're worrying about making ends meet . . . If the nearest supermarket is miles away or the bus doesn't go there when you can, it can be difficult to buy food which is cheap and healthy; if the street outside your home is busy with traffic or there are drug dealers in the park then it's safer to keep the kids in front of the TV than let them out to play.

The Black Report and *The Health Divide* both pointed out that class differences in health remained even when lifestyle factors were taken into account, and many class differences were not related to factors such as smoking, drinking and other lifestyle choices. It is for all these reasons that sociologists have generally given more emphasis to material, social and economic explanations rather than cultural explanations for social class inequalities in health.

Activity

1 To what extent do you think health and illness are the responsibility of individuals and the lifestyle choices they make?
2 What problems might there be for an approach to improving a society's health which focused only on the behaviour and choices of individuals?

Material or structural explanations – blaming social conditions Material or structural explanations – about the means available to those individuals and the structure of society – suggest that those suffering poorer health do so because of the inequalities of wealth and income in Britain. Those who suffer the poorest health are those who are the most materially disadvantaged and lack enough money to eat a healthy diet, have poor housing, dangerous or unhealthy working conditions, live in an unhealthy local environment and so on.

The Black Report concluded that 'while genetic and cultural or behavioural explanations played their part, the predominant or governing explanation for inequalities in health lay in material deprivation'. *Our Healthier Nation* recognized this link between poverty and ill-health:

it is clear that people's chances of a long and healthy life are basically influenced by how well off they are . . . This means tackling inequality which stems from poverty, poor housing, pollution, low educational standards, joblessness and low pay. Tackling inequalities generally is the best means of tackling health inequalities in particular.

Figure 7.3 on page 456 identifies a range of possible factors which might explain health inequalities.

The Black Report, The Health Divide, The Acheson Report, Our Healthier Nation and *Saving Lives* provided so much evidence of the link between social class and the 'health divide' in Britain that it is doubtful whether any rational person could seriously deny it. As Dr John Collee said in the *Observer* newspaper in 1992:

> Forget everything else I have written on the subject. There is one piece of health advice which is more effective than all the others. One guaranteed way to live longer, grow taller, avoid chronic illness, have healthier children, increase your quality of life and minimize your risk of premature death. The secret is: *be rich.*

What other material or structural factors create social class inequalities in health, apart from living in poor housing or areas with high levels of environmental pollution?

Inequality kills

The importance of the social causes of ill-health is illustrated well by Richard Wilkinson (1996). Wilkinson recognizes the importance of social deprivation, but has argued that health differences cannot be explained simply by material deprivation, such as poverty, but that social cohesion is itself a significant factor. Social cohesion means the extent to which people stick together and identify with each other in a sense of community. Wilkinson suggests that large income differences between social groups divide people from one another, and lead to a lack of social cohesion. Social inequalities, and the social divisions they create, can in themselves have poor effects on health, even among those who are not especially poor in income terms. He concludes that 'societies with narrower income differences are likely to be more socially cohesive and consequently more healthy'. In other words, the more equal a society is, the healthier it is, and a sense of community and social cohesion can in themselves improve health.

The inverse care law

Tudor-Hart first identified the **inverse care law** in 1971. This suggests that health care resources tend to be distributed in inverse proportion to need. This means that those whose need is least get the most resources, while those in greatest need get the least. Social class differences in health are therefore made worse through inequalities in the National Health Service. Why is this?

● Poorer areas have fewer GP practices – so there are fewer doctors for those who are most likely to get ill.
● Poorer people are more likely to be dependent on public transport, and so spend greater time travelling to hospitals and GPs, but they are also more likely to lose pay if they have to take time off work.

In contrast, those in the middle class:

● have more knowledge of illness and how to prevent it
● know more about the health services available and therefore get better service
● are more likely to fight against inadequate medical services
● are more self-confident, effective and assertive in dealing with doctors, and therefore get longer consultations, ask more questions, receive more explanations from their doctors and are more likely to be referred for further treatment
● have more money, so they are better able to jump NHS waiting lists by using private medicine

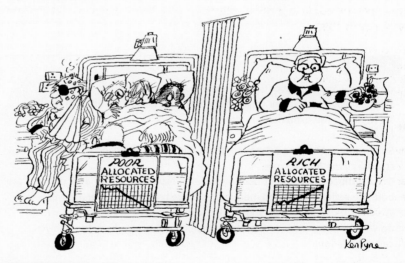

The inverse care law

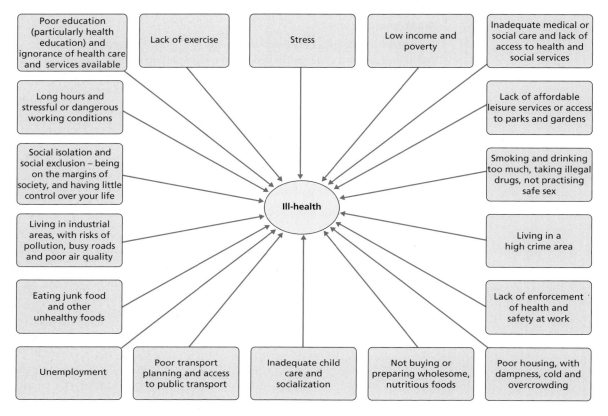

Figure 7.3 Cultural and material influences on health

Activity

Study figure 7.3 and answer the following questions:
1   Suggest ways each factor might explain social class inequalities in health.
2   Try to divide the explanations into 'cultural' and 'structural/material' explanations.
3   Suggest ways the cultural explanations might be influenced by structural/material factors.
4   Do you think cultural or structural/material explanations (or a bit of both) are better in explaining health inequalities? Give reasons for your answer.
5   Which of these factors do you think society can help to tackle, and which do you think are individual problems which only individuals themselves can solve?

Tackling social class inequalities in health

The Acheson Report, Our Healthier Nation and *Saving Lives* laid the basis for government health policy for the years ahead. Their proposals marked a significant change in the focus of health policy away from curative to pre-ventative medicine – from the medical to a social model of health.

There is now recognition by government of the important influence of social deprivation on health, and that social class inequalities in health are very much products of society rather than of simply biological factors, with social and economic life having major influences on the patterns of illness and death. As *Our Healthier Nation* concluded, 'the link between poverty and ill-health is clear. In nearly every case the highest incidence of illness is experienced by the worst off social classes.'

The social, economic and environmental causes of ill-health are complex, and often involve a range of factors, such as poor housing and education, poverty, unemployment or low pay, fear of crime, and social exclusion. The government has recognized that tackling health inequalities involves a range of linked policies, including measures to improve employment opportunities, together with action on crime, poverty, housing and education, as well as on health itself. These policies include, for example, the New Deal for Communities, Neighbourhood Renewal, and the SureStart programme for children's early years.

At the beginning of the twenty-first century, the government set itself a range of targets to tackle inequalities in health, and there have been many new policies developed. An NHS Plan was developed to tackle inequalities through more effective prevention and improved care for disadvantaged populations. Two key Department of Health 'action' documents were produced: *Tackling Health Inequalities: A Programme for Action* (2003) and *Choosing Health* (2004).

These policies and targets had three main aims:

- to improve the health of the population as a whole by increasing the length of people's lives and the number of years people spend free from illness
- to prevent inequalities in health worsening by improving the health of the poorest fastest
- to narrow the health gap between the richest and the poorest

Two particular targets were set to help achieve these:

- by 2010, to reduce by at least 10 per cent the gap in infant mortality between routine non-manual and manual groups and the population as a whole
- by 2010, to reduce by at least 10 per cent the gap between the fifth of areas where people have the lowest life expectancy at birth and the population as a whole

Four national priority areas for health improvement were established:

- heart disease and stroke
- accidents
- mental health
- cancer

The government recognized that to achieve these targets, a wide range of public and private agencies would need to work together, such as GPs, clinics and NHS hospitals, government departments, community and leisure centres, schools and workplaces, and the food industry. To address the underlying causes of ill-health, and to improve the health of the poorest 30–40 per cent of the population where the greatest burden of disease exists, a wide range of policies has been adopted. The table in the activity shows some of these policies.

All the measures identified in the activity to create a healthier nation and reduce inequalities in health depend on resources, commitment and cooperation between the official providers of health care and the public. Tackling health inequalities only through the health service is unlikely to work. It may be the job of the National Health Service to resuscitate people once they have been rescued from drowning, but it is the job of everyone else to prevent them from drowning in the first place. If people don't want to get healthy – as actress Anna Friel once said, 'I smoke because I'm still young enough to feel immortal'– it is hard to see what any government can do. However, health policy at the beginning of the twenty-first century has finally recognized that so long as inequalities of wealth, income, education, occupation, opportunity and social privilege continue, so will inequalities in health. As the government recognized in *Our Healthier Nation*, 'tackling inequalities generally is the best means of tackling health inequalities in particular.'

Activity

Go through the list of policies below. Explain in each case how the policy might help to reduce social class inequalities in health. Three are already done for you, as examples.

Go to www.dh.gov.uk and find out how much progress has been made on three of these policies and how successful they have been. Try searching on 'inequalities' or 'health improvement' to start. Words in *italics* refer to specific programmes or policies that can be searched for.

Policy	How it might help to reduce social class inequalities in health
1 Halve the number of children in poverty by 2010, and eradicate child poverty by 2020.	Poverty is a major cause of ill-health. Tackling child poverty is likely to improve the health of the most disadvantaged children, making them healthier as adults and giving them more opportunities to be successful in society.
2 Improve sexual health, by promoting safe sex and contraception.	These are likely to reduce sexually transmitted infections, such as HIV/AIDS, and unplanned pregnancies. The least educated are more likely to lack awareness of these issues.
3 Develop *Healthy Living Centres* (more than 350 in 2007) across the UK in areas of greatest deprivation.	This would improve health and fitness by making gyms and fitness centres accessible to those people who may find existing facilities too expensive, off-putting or difficult to get to. These are often the most disadvantaged. This would rectify the current situation, where – in keeping with the inverse care law – middle-class customers dominate health and leisure centres.
4 Develop a national *Healthy Schools* programme, to encourage schools to raise awareness of health issues, and promote better health through healthy eating and lifestyles.	
5 Reduce smoking.	
6 Reduce teenage pregnancy, through the *Teenage Pregnancy Strategy*, in particular through action in neighbourhoods with high teenage conception rates.	

conts . . .

Activity (continued)

Policy	How it might help to reduce social class inequalities in health
7 Improve access to, and the quality of, antenatal care, and early years support for children and families in disadvantaged areas, through programmes such as *SureStart*.	
8 Improve the physical activity of the population.	
9 Improve environmental health and reduce the risk of accidents in the home and on the road.	
10 Improve the quality and energy efficiency of housing, particularly in social (council and housing association) housing in the most disadvantaged areas, through programmes such as *Neighbourhood Renewal* (see figure 7.4) and the *UK Fuel Poverty Strategy*.	
11 Tackle alcohol misuse.	
12 Improve mental health and mental well-being.	
13 Provide more information about the health risks of obesity, poor diet and lack of exercise, and action that people can take themselves to improve their health.	
14 Develop better labelling on the nutrition content of packaged food, showing which foods can make a positive contribution to a healthy diet (and which don't).	
15 Reduce crime, the fear of crime, and drug misuse.	
16 Improve educational attainment and skills among disadvantaged groups.	
17 Reduce unemployment, and improve the income of the most disadvantaged groups.	

Figure 7.4 What's involved in Neighbourhood Renewal? Areas of multiple disadvantage and the 'cycle of disadvantage'

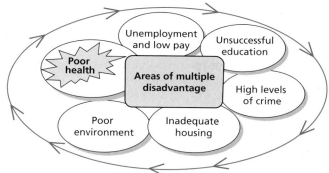

In areas experiencing mutiple disadvantage, each of these six issues impacts on and feeds the others – tackling one by itself will be most unlikely to succeed

If multiple disadvantage isn't tackled then a 'cycle of disadvantage' can start, making breaking out of it very difficult indeed

---

Activity

Refer to figure 7.4 and:

1 Explain how each of the six issues identified 'impacts on and feeds the others'.
2 Explain why 'tackling one by itself will be most unlikely to succeed'.
3 Explain why a 'cycle of disadvantage' can start if all the issues are not tackled, and why 'breaking out' of it can then become very difficult.
4 Identify and explain *three* cultural factors that may affect a person's health.
5 Identify and explain *three* material explanations for social class inequalities in health.
6 Explain what is meant by the 'inverse care law'.
7 In about one and a half sides of A4 paper, answer the following essay question: *Assess sociological explanations for social class differences in health and illness.*

Gender differences in health

As well as a pattern of social class differences in health, there is also a big difference between the health of men and women. At all ages, women's death rates are much lower than men's. Men's death rates are almost double those of women in every class and on average women lived around four and a half years longer than men in 2005. Almost two-thirds of deaths before the age of 65 are male, and about 58 percent of people aged over 65 are women.

Are women healthier than men?

The answer to whether women are healthier than men is 'yes' if we use only the indicators of death rates and life expectancy. However, statistics show

Why do women live longer than men?

- Evidence suggests that boys are the weaker sex at birth, with a higher infant mortality rate – male babies are more likely to die in the first year of life. Women seem to have a better genetic resistance to heart disease than men.
- The process of gender role socialization means men are more likely to be brought up to shrug off illnesses, they are more likely to drink and smoke (with all the consequences for health), are more aggressive and take more risks, and are less careful in what they eat. Men are not socialized to show their emotions as much as women, are more likely to be socially isolated and have fewer support networks, and so have fewer outlets for stress.
- Women are more involved in family health, as they are more likely to be involved in nurturing and caring roles in the family, and sensitive to illness. Women are the biggest users of the health service, both for themselves and because it is generally women who organize the rest of the family going to the doctor's.
- Women are socialized to take care of themselves more than men, and they are more likely to visit doctors, which may mean they receive better health care. Sometimes working fewer hours means women have more opportunity to visit doctors.
- Men generally live more hazardous lives than women. The more dangerous occupations are more likely to be done by men, such as construction work, and therefore men are more at risk of industrial accidents and diseases. In the home, men are more likely to do the dangerous and risky jobs, such as jobs using ladders and climbing on the roof. Men also make up the majority of lorry and car drivers and motor-cyclists, and are therefore more at risk of death through road accidents.
- Men are more likely to work full-time and to work longer and more unsociable hours, such as overtime working and shift work, which can be harmful to health.
- Men retire later than women (age 65 compared to 60). Evidence suggests that the later retirement age of men could be an important factor in reducing their life expectancy (note: women's retirement age is planned to increase to 65 in the period between 2010 and 2020).

Activity

Refer to the box above

1. Which of the reasons given for women living longer than men do you think is most important? Put them in order of importance, giving your reasons.
2. Do you think men's 'macho' behaviour is an important factor in shortening their lives? Suggest evidence for or against this from your own experiences.
3. 'The growing equality of women with men is a threat to women's health.' Explain this statement. Do you agree? How might this situation be avoided (apart from stopping women becoming more equal!)?

that men, who in general die younger, don't seem to experience as much ill-health during their lives as women who live longer. Women are the major users of health care services and apparently get sick more often than men, and are more likely than men to spend more years in poor health or with a disability.

Compared to men, women:

- go to the doctor about 50 per cent more often between the ages of 15 and 64 – though, as Nettleton points out, this may be more for health reasons, such as infertility or pregnancy, than because of illness
- report more head and stomach aches, high blood pressure and weight problems
- consume more prescription and non-prescription drugs
- are admitted to hospital more often and have more operations
- go to see doctors about conditions like insomnia, tension headache and anxiety and depression (which are often labelled as 'mental illness') about twice as often
- receive far more prescriptions for tranquillizers, sleeping pills and anti-depressants
- are off work with reported sickness more often and spend more days in bed
- were twice as likely as men in the same 65–74 age group in 2004–5 to have rheumatism and arthritis

Why do women apparently suffer more sickness?

There are particular features in women's lives compared to men's that may make them more vulnerable to sickness.

Stress   Many women suffer a triple burden of being low-paid workers, carrying responsibilities for housework and childcare, and managing family emotions. In many cases this involves having to manage limited household budgets with pressure to make ends meet, and working long days with little time to relax.

Poverty   Women are more likely to experience poverty than men, because they are more likely to be lone parents, and because they live longer than men while being less likely to have employers' pensions or savings for old age. As Kempson and Bryson (1994) found in a study of seventy-four low-income families, it is usually women who go without to ensure other family members get enough to eat. Nettleton (2002: 191) showed that women also 'spend more of their income on household goods – especially food – than do men, and are more likely to be responsible, in Graham's words, for "maintaining the material and psychological environment of the home and well-being of those who live there".' Women are therefore likely to suffer the effects of poverty more directly than men.

Domestic labour   Domestic labour (housework) is rarely fulfilling (for further discussion on this, see chapter 3 on the family and households). Depression may be linked to the unpaid, repetitive, unrewarding and low status nature of housework in a society where only paid employment is really respected. The high accident rates at home might be influenced by the isolated nature of housework.

Socialization   Women are socialized to express their feelings and talk about their problems more than men. Since women are generally the ones who 'manage' family health matters, they are often more aware of health and health care matters. Women may therefore be more willing than men to report physical and mental health problems. The higher rates of recorded illnesses among women could then be due, not necessarily to greater health problems than men, but to women's greater willingness to admit to them and to take them to doctors. While women go to doctors for prescribed drugs like tranquillizers, men opt for non-prescribed drugs like alcohol. Men's higher death rates may simply be because they bottle everything up until it is too late.

Different diagnoses   Due to gender roles, it may be that women are more willing to report symptoms of mental illness. Doctors are more likely to see symptoms reported by women as mainly mental, while men's are seen as

> **Activity**
>
> 1 Refer to the list of four stages and the activity on page 437 and suggest reasons why women might be more likely to end up as a health statistic than men.
> 2 Discuss the explanations suggested above for women apparently suffering more sickness than men. Do you think women really do suffer more ill-health, or do you think they are simply more open and honest about it than men?

physical. Women are therefore more likely to be diagnosed as depressed or suffering from anxiety than men. Until recently, women had a much higher chance than men of being institutionalized in mental hospitals.

Feminist approaches to health

Feminist writers, like Ann Oakley (1984), Nicky Hart (1985) and Hilary Graham (1993) have been very critical of the biomedical approach to health and the patriarchal nature of the medical profession – what has been called 'malestream' science and medicine. They are particularly critical of the way pregnancy and childbirth have come to be seen as medical problems (this is sometimes called the 'medicalization of childbirth') and the way they have been dealt with as an illness and 'treated' with medical technology, rather than as a natural process, and treated clinically at times suited to doctors. Childbirth has quite literally been taken out of women's own control. For example, births may be induced and babies delivered by caesarean operations at times to suit the working hours of hospitals and doctors rather than the needs of the mother and baby. A survey for *Mother and Baby* magazine in 2005 found that just 43 per cent of the 96 per cent of expectant mothers giving birth in hospital had the same midwife throughout their labour, and half described their postnatal care as 'not kind or compassionate'.

Feminist writers point to patriarchy in the medical profession and the drug and medical technology industry, with women marginalized in many aspects of health care. For example, midwives (nearly all women) are supervised by mainly male obstetricians and gynaecologists, around 70 per cent of whom were men in 2006. Nurses, around 90 per cent of whom are women, have lower status than doctors – around 65 per cent of whom are men – and there is a large body of research evidence which suggests that men have greater career success in the nursing profession than women. Women dominate in the lower levels of every aspect of the National Health Service. Feminists also point out, for example, that contraception is mainly aimed at women rather than men. What male contraception there is has few side-effects. In contrast to this, contraception for women does have harmful effects, with worries, for example, that certain contraceptive pills might be linked to higher risks of cancer, and IUDs (intrauterine devices) and caps leave women vulnerable to infections. Is this because men dominate the development of contraceptive technologies?

Feminist writers are also, of course, concerned with the general issues of women's health discussed above. Marxist feminists focus more closely on the particular impact of social inequality in general on the health of the lives of women in the working class and minority ethnic groups.

Ethnic inequalities in health

Social class and gender are not the only important social inequalities in health; there are also some differences between ethnic groups. As with social class, social and economic factors, rather than culture and biology, are the main factors explaining the poorer health of minority ethnic groups in Britain. There is little evidence that the biology of different ethnic groups explains their poorer health in Britain; rather, it is the social and economic contexts in which they live their lives.

Explanations

Three main kinds of explanations have been given for the health disadvantages of minority ethnic groups.

Language and culture   Asian women are less likely to visit ante- and post-natal clinics, which helps explain their higher levels of infant mortality. Many older Asian women speak poor English, possibly creating difficulties in taking up screening services for things like breast cancer or cervical cancer, and in obtaining treatment, advice and guidance from health workers. This is made worse by the lack of translation services in the NHS. Despite big improvements, there is still a lack of information available in minority ethnic group languages.

Asian women often prefer to see female doctors, and many find it difficult talking to male and white doctors. However, the number of female GPs is lowest in those areas with the largest concentrations of Asian households.

Health professionals are often not familiar enough with the religious, cultural and dietary practices of different ethnic groups, hence their concerns may not be understood, nor their needs met.

Racism, poverty and deprivation   Many of the health problems of some minority ethnic groups arise for the same reasons as social class inequalities, because they are likely to be among the poorest groups in society. Racism in society means some minority ethnic groups are more likely than white people to find themselves living in the worst housing, and to be unemployed or working for long hours and doing shift work in low paid manual jobs, in hazardous and unhealthy environments. Nettleton showed that racism – both the experience and the fear of racist harrassment – affects health adversely. Such conditions create stressful, unhealthy lives. Racism and poverty are the twin planks of ill-health in minority ethnic groups.

Diet   Rickets (which can lead to difficulties in walking) is found more commonly in the Asian community. This is probably due to vitamin D deficiency and there has been much discussion about how to intervene in the diet of Asian children to remedy this. Higher levels of heart disease may arise from aspects of the high-fat Asian diet, which also generates higher levels of obesity – itself a cause of heart disease.

Some findings on minority ethnic group inequalities

Compared to the white majority ethnic group:
- People from African-Caribbean, Indian, Pakistani and Bangladeshi backgrounds are all more likely to suffer and die from TB, liver cancer or diabetes.
- Africans and African-Caribbeans are more likely to suffer from strokes and hypertension (high blood pressure).
- Asians (Indians and Pakistanis) suffer more heart disease and are more likely to die from it.
- Indians and African-Caribbeans are more likely to be compulsorily admitted to hospital for mental illnesses, and once there receive less sympathetic and harsher forms of treatment. African-Caribbeans are more likely to be diagnosed as schizophrenics and compulsorily committed to mental hospitals for this.
- Most ethnic minorities show higher rates of stillbirths, perinatal deaths (dying at birth or within the first week of life), neo-natal deaths (within a month) and infant mortality (within a year of birth).
- Most minority ethnic groups have higher rates of mortality.
- African-Caribbeans, Pakistanis and Bangladeshis are between 30 and 50 per cent more likely to suffer ill-health.

Other inequalities in health

Access to health care

The National Health Service is the main source of formal, clinical health care for most people. However, this does not mean everyone has equal access to health services, and services do vary in the quality of care provided.

There are five major areas of inequality.

Funding

Despite the shift in health policy away from the curative medicine of the medical model towards a greater emphasis on preventative medicine based on the social model of health, the 'acute' sector (hospitals) still gets the most attention and funding. This is often at the expense of other services, such as chiropody and mental illness, and services geared towards the particular needs of groups like adults with learning difficulties and minority ethnic groups. Standards of care are therefore not as good, nor as responsive as they should be.

Geography

Modern 'high-tech' hospitals, with more medical technology and the highest numbers of GPs, are concentrated in urban areas, disadvantaging people living in the countryside. Specialist hospitals and units, such as heart and cancer units, are not spread equally across the country. Health care provision is better in the more affluent south of England than the disadvantaged areas of the north, producing a north–south divide in access to health care. For example, the House of Commons Public Accounts Committee reported in 2005 that people in the cities of northern England were almost twice as likely to die of cancer as those in affluent areas of the south, in what has been called a 'postcode lottery'. The industrial areas of northern England and Wales have fewer and older hospitals, fewer and less adequate specialized facilities, such as for cancer or kidney treatments, fewer hospital beds per head of popula-tion, and higher patient/doctor ratios. Those in the south get faster access to diagnostic tests, scans, anti-cancer drugs and chemotherapy.

 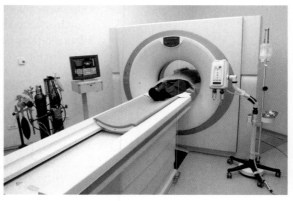

Access to health care is not spread equally across the country. For example, there are more modern 'high-tech' hospitals, with more medical technology, in the affluent south of England than in the more disadvantaged areas of the north

These differences could be because of social class factors rather than simply geography, as these areas contain a higher proportion of people from lower social classes.

Social class

There are differences in health care provision for different social classes, and the evidence suggests that this inequality has not been significantly reduced since the introduction of the National Health Service. For the majority of cancers, there is a five-year gap in the survival rates between the best and worst off. Working-class children, even though they suffer more illnesses and accidents, are less likely to be taken to the doctor than those from the middle class, or for dental checks and treatment. Health services in working-class areas are often less accessible and of poorer quality. There are fewer GPs per head of population in working-class areas, despite higher levels of sickness, and middle-class patients are likely to demand, and get, more time with their doctors. This means working-class people may not get the same quality of consultation and treatment as the middle class. The discussion earlier in this chapter on social class inequalities in health, and the inverse care law, explains many of the reasons why those from the poorest social groups have less opportunity to access the health services. They also don't have the luxury of being able to afford private health care when the NHS or social services let them down.

Disability

'A disability can make you invisible to the health service and normal medical care.' This is what Peter Cardy, chief executive of the MS (Multiple Sclerosis) Society, said to the *Guardian* newspaper in November 2000 to describe the way many disabled people do not have adequate access to medical treatment or equipment. The same article reported a survey by the disability organization SCOPE in 2000 that found 47 per cent of people who cannot use speech were being denied access to electronic communication aids. People with MS have been denied drugs, such as beta-interferon, that might reduce their suffering. Women with MS are often not given routine gynaecological checks. Disabled people are also regularly excluded from routine treatment because of difficulties in travelling to a health centre or dentist.

The Royal College of Physicians has recommended that people with learning disabilities have annual health checks, but in many cases this is not happening, even though such people are more vulnerable to hearing problems, heart disease and epilepsy. *Treat Me Right!*, a 2004 report by Mencap, a charity supporting those with learning disabilities, found that people with a learning disability often die younger than other people, and suggested part of the reason for this was because many of them get poorer health services than other people. In a survey by Mencap, 90 per cent of GPs said they found it harder to diagnose people with a learning disability, and 75 per cent said they had received no training in treating such patients. Seventy per cent of GP surgeries had no information that those with learning disabilities could easily understand. Some GPs do not understand their needs, and think that all the health problems people with a learning disability have are a result of their disability, and so they do not take their health problems as seriously as they would if they were presented by someone without such a disability. The report called for better training in learning disability for all health care staff in order to cut the number of premature deaths.

Age

Older people, particularly the most socially disadvantaged, tend not to get the same access to health care as do younger people, even though they generally have greater need for it. This may be due partly to cultural reasons, with older people simply not wishing to bother the doctor, or playing down their illnesses and not seeking treatment for what they dismiss as symptoms of old age. However, charities dealing with ageing, like Help the Aged and Age Concern, report **ageism** – stereotyping, prejudice and discrimination – in regard to the health and social care of older people.

> **Ageism** is stereotyping, prejudice and discrimination against individuals or groups on the grounds of their age.

For example, geriatric medicine, which specializes in the treatment and care of older people, generally has low status in the medical profession. It has poorer funding and staffing levels, in relation to the rising numbers and needs of older people, than other areas. It therefore doesn't get the allocation of staff expertise and other resources that are needed to give the best care to older people. Age Concern and Help the Aged report that older people:

- feel they have had second-class treatment and care simply because of their age
- are sometimes not referred by doctors to a consultant because of their age
- face inappropriate comments about their age and patronizing attitudes while in hospital
- lack transport to access health care services
- lack NHS specialized services, such as help with podiatry (foot care), leaving them in pain, housebound and at increased risk of falls
- have little help with the difficulties they may face in interpreting and understanding instructions on medication and other aspects of their treatment, perhaps because of confusion or depression, or their visual or hearing impairments

Older people often don't get the help and support they may need in taking medication and understanding their treatment

Regional and international inequalities in health

Regional inequalities in health

Within the United Kingdom, there are wide differences in the health of people living in different parts of the country, and there is a clear north–south divide in health. For example, table 7.2 overleaf shows that women in the east, south-east and south-west of England can expect to live around two and a half years longer than women in the north-east and north-west of England and in Scotland, and these regional inequalities persist across a range of other health indicators, such as infant mortality and cancer deaths. It is difficult to be certain about what causes these differences, and it may be they can be explained by differences in the social class, age, gender or ethnic make-up of different areas of the UK, or different industries in different areas, rather than something about the places themselves. Nettleton suggests that the differences cannot be explained by different levels of health spending or health care facilities. What is clear, though, is that the areas where social deprivation is highest also have the poorest health.

International inequalities in health

Internationally, inequalities in health are huge – with different amounts of money spent on health care as a proportion of national income, and huge differences in the causes, type and extent of disease and death between

Table 7.2 Some regional inequalities in health in the United Kingdom, 2003–5

Region	Life expectancy 2005		Still births[1] (rate per 1,000 live births and still births) 2005	Perinatal mortality[1] (rate per 1,000 live and still births) 2005	Infant mortality[2] (rate per 1,000 live births) 2005	Prescription items dispensed per person 2004	Deaths from circulatory diseases (heart disease and strokes) (rate per 100,000 people) 2003	Deaths from cancer (rate per 100,000 of the population) 2003	Deaths from all causes (rate per 100,000 of the population) 2003
	Males	Females							
England	76.9	81.2	5.4	8.0	5.0	13.8	348	247	926
North-east	75.4	79.8	5.7	7.8	4.5	16.1	390	277	1,041
North-west	75.4	79.9	5.5	8.2	5.8	16.5	394	259	1,025
Yorkshire and the Humber	76.2	80.6	6.2	9.4	6.1	15.7	360	254	960
East Midlands	76.9	80.9	5.0	7.6	4.7	13.9	352	242	944
West Midlands	76.2	80.8	5.9	9.9	6.4	14.1	366	245	965
East	78.0	81.8	4.3	6.4	4.0	13.4	321	229	865
London	76.9	81.4	6.0	8.5	5.1	10.5	339	237	918
South-east	78.1	82.0	4.8	6.9	3.9	12.2	321	226	852
South-west	78.1	82.2	4.3	6.8	4.5	14.0	323	227	849
Wales	76.4	80.7	5.3	7.4	4.3	18.4	384	241	979
Scotland	74.2	79.3	5.3	7.7	5.2	14.8	410	282	1,089
Northern Ireland	76.5	80.8	4.0	8.1	6.1	16.0	357	245	943
United Kingdom	**76.6**	**81**		**8.0**	**5.1**	**....[3]**	**328**	**246**	**945**

1 Still births and deaths of infants under one week of age
2 Deaths of infants under one year of age
3 Data not applicable or not available

Source: Government Actuary's Department; Regional Trends; Office for National Statistics

the richest and poorest countries. Table 7.3 overleaf illustrates some international inequalities in health and health care spending. The highest spending nations spend on average around 150 times more per head than the poorest nations, even though their immediate health care needs are far less. The highest-spending United States spends nearly 400 times more per head than Burundi, and men and women in the USA can on average expect to live around 33 years longer than their equivalents in Burundi. Overall, life expectancy in the poorest countries is about half of that in the richest countries. It is worth noting that the lowest spenders are the poorest countries, and, except for Afghanistan, they are all in Africa – the poorest continent on the planet. While there is a broad general link between the amount of money spent on health and the health of the population, with the richest and poorest countries respectively having the best and poorest health in general, there is not a direct link. For example, the United States has the largest spending per head among the richest nations, but ranks the lowest among the richest countries in terms of most of the indicators of health shown in table 7.3.

Death and disease often have different causes in poorer countries. The diseases of poverty – infectious diseases like typhoid, cholera, malaria and TB – are more common than the diseases of affluence found in the more developed countries – degenerative diseases such as heart disease, strokes, cancer and diabetes.

The explanations for these international inequalities are generally related to the issues that have been considered throughout this chapter, such as poverty, poor hygiene, lack of proper sanitation and safe waste disposal, poor diet/malnutrition and lack of safe drinking water, polluting and dangerous industries, lack of health care facilities and health education, and other social, cultural and environmental factors. These are added to by exploitation of the poorest countries by the richest, most developed countries. For example, there are huge inequalities in trade between the more developed and least developed countries, and the poorest countries are burdened with debts. Interest repayments on loans from the most developed

This is the way many people in the world get water every day, and poor health often arises from a lack of such basic facilities as clean running water, and safe waste disposal and sanitation

Table 7.3 Some international inequalities in health, 2000–4

The ten most advantaged and ten least advantaged countries, ranked on health spending per head (international dollar rate[1]). The United Kingdom is included for comparison.

Country	Total health expenditure per head (international dollar rate[1])	Life expectancy at birth (years)		Probability of dying per 1,000 population between 15 and 60 years (adult mortality rate)		Probability of dying in first 12 months of life per 1,000 live births (infant mortality rate)	Probability of dying in first five years of life per 1,000 live births under 5 years (under-5 mortality rate)	Probability of mothers dying per 100,000 live births (maternal mortality rate)
	2003	Males 2004	Females 2004	Males 2004	Females 2004	Both sexes 2004	Both sexes 2004	Females 2000
10 highest spending countries per head								
United States of America	5,711	75	80	137	81	6	8	14
Monaco	4,487	78	85	105	45	3	4	....[2]
Norway	3,809	77	82	93	57	3	4	10
Switzerland	3,776	78	83	87	49	4	5	7
Luxembourg	3,680	76	81	118	59	5	6	28
Iceland	3,110	79	83	79	52	2	3	0
Germany	3,001	76	82	112	58	4	5	9
Canada	2,989	78	83	91	57	5	6	5
Netherlands	2,987	77	81	89	63	4	5	16
France	2,902	76	83	132	60	4	5	17
UNITED KINGDOM	2,389	76	81	102	63	5	6	11

10 lowest spending countries per head

Sierra Leone	34	37	40	579	497	165	283	2,000
Rwanda	32	44	47	518	435	118	203	1,400
Niger	30	42	41	506	478	152	259	1,600
United Republic of Tanzania	29	47	49	551	524	78	126	1,500
Afghanistan	26	42	42	509	448	165	257	1,900
Madagascar	24	55	59	338	270	76	123	550
Congo	23	53	55	442	390	79	108	510
Ethiopia	20	49	51	451	389	110	166	850
Somalia	18	43	45	524	428	133	225	1,100
Burundi	15	42	47	593	457	114	190	1,000

[1] The international dollar rate measures in US dollars how much what is spent in local currency will actually purchase. This minimizes the consequences of differences in price levels between countries. For example, a dollar spent in Sierra Leone will buy around five times more health care than a dollar spent in the UK. The international dollar measure recognizes this, making comparisons between countries more accurate.

[2] Data not applicable or not available.

Source: Adapted from World Health Report, 2006; World Health Organization

Activity

Refer to Tables 7.2 and 7.3 on regional and international inequalities in health.

1   What evidence, if any, is there in table 7.3 of a direct link between health spending per head and the health of the population?

2   Suggest *three* ways in which the causes of the difference in the life expectancy of males and females in every country of the world might change between the richest countries and the poorest countries.

3   There are growing concerns among some people in the richest countries about the size and shape of their bodies and about the ageing process. Consequently, some seek to define their own bodies and view of health through non-essential surgery and other medical treatments. Suggest three additional demands that might be placed on medical professionals and health services by this concern with body image and identity.

4   Suggest *three* ways that the demands on health care services in the activity immediately above might differ from those in the poorest countries.

5   Either individually or in a group, imagine yourself as a nuclear family – mum, dad, and two twin children, one boy and one girl, aged 3, with a baby on the way. You should take on the role of the mum and dad (or, if you're working in a group, you could adopt the roles of mum, dad, boy and girl – and the unborn baby, of your chosen sex – in which case the 3-year-olds and the baby can represent their own interests). Because of changing circumstances, you've got to move from the area, and even have the option of moving to another country. You're all completely obsessed with having a healthy and long life, and your mum and dad both want as long and as healthy a life as possible for all of you. With reference to tables 7.2 and 7.3, and considering all the evidence and indicators of health inequalities, work out the following and decide which option is the 'healthiest fit' best suiting all your family members:

    (a) which region of the United Kingdom you would be most likely to move to, and which one would you most want to avoid. Clearly explain your reasons.

    (b) which country of the world you would be most likely to move to, and which one would you most want to avoid. Clearly explain your reasons.

6   Suggest *four* other factors apart from those given in tables 7.2 and 7.3 which might also influence your choice of where to live for a healthy long life.

7   Suggest *three* reasons in each case for inequalities in health and health care (a) between different regions of the United Kingdom, and (b) between different countries of the world.

8   Write a short essay, about one side of A4, answering the following question: *Examine the reasons given to explain the wide inequalities in health and health care between different parts of the United Kingdom.*

countries far exceed the amounts the poorest countries receive in aid each year.

Poorer countries cannot afford to provide the health infrastructure necessary to deliver a healthy population. This infrastructure would include things like facilities to train doctors, nurses, midwives and other health professionals, hospitals and clinics, medical technology and affordable drugs, and resources for health education and health promotion campaigns. This runs alongside the problems created by the social, cultural, material and environmental dimensions of health and health care which have been discussed throughout this chapter.

Mental illness

An estimated one in six people of working age suffers some form of mental illness, ranging from depression, through disabling anxiety disorders, to schizophrenia and, for a tiny minority, dangerous and severe personality disorder (DSPD – these are popularly known as 'psychopaths'). According to the *Observer* newspaper (8 April 2007), GPs say that there is a mental health component to at least half of all the cases they see, and one in four of us uses specialist mental health services at any one time. Yet, despite being relatively common, mental illnesses are often seen and treated quite differently from physical ones. The mentally ill often face discrimination at every level of society, because mental illness is among the most stigmatized and misunderstood of illnesses. This is because it involves behaviour we find very hard to understand, and because it does not have any obvious physical symptoms. Treatments for mental illness are also associated in the pubic imagination with horrific treatments that appear more as punishment and control than as care and treatment, as shown in films like *One Flew Over the Cuckoo's Nest* (1975). Research by the Mental Health Foundation charity in April 2001, *Is Anybody There? A Survey of Friendship and Mental Health,* found that four in ten people with mental health problems were worried about telling friends about their problems, and one in three felt friendships had become strained, or lost, because of their mental illness. They felt their friends would not understand, or were likely to react negatively, because of the continuing stigma attached to mental illness. The 2006 British Social Attitudes survey revealed widespread prejudice against people with a mental illness, with fewer than one in five British adults saying they would be happy for a close relative to marry someone with schizophrenia.

People are likely to see mental illness as less 'real' than physical illness. There is, as a consequence, frequently a greater reluctance by other people to accept the legitimacy of the sick role, even though some mental illness, like some kinds of depression, does have a biological basis.

What is mental illness?

Mental illness has been defined as 'a state of mind which affects the person's thinking, perceiving, emotion or judgement to the extent that she or he requires care or medical treatment in her or his interests or in the interests of other persons'.

Mental illness might therefore be seen as any mental disorder affecting the behaviour and personality of an individual so as to prevent him or her functioning adequately within their society. Mental illnesses can range from anxiety and mild depression, through behavioural and emotional problems like eating disorders, to personality disorders and severe neurotic and psychotic disorders.

Care in the community

In the past, the seriously mentally ill were treated in large long-stay psychiatric hospitals, but now, except for the most serious cases, they are more likely to be cared for in the community. Community care involves those who are mentally ill living as much as possible within a 'normal' community, alongside members of the public who are not mentally ill. They are generally cared for and supported in smaller community-based units, or cared for by the family or through GPs. The move to care in the community was prompted by the desire to reduce spending on large-scale hospital care, and the desire to avoid the negative effects that long-stay psychiatric hospitals had on the patients, and the often quite frightening situations that patients faced in them from other mentally ill patients. The underfunding of community care led to a series of scandals arising from inadequate care and supervision by welfare agencies, and a lack of liaison between local authorities and health authorities. However, care in the community provides an important means for people with mental health problems to receive support and treatment in conditions as near normal as possible, and to help them cope with the difficulties they face in a safe context – for both themselves and the public at large.

The biomedical approach to mental illness

In the past, mental illness was often explained as being the result of possession by evil spirits, the Devil, or the work of witches. However, it is now seen as a medical problem, to be treated using the biomedical approach. This involves the use of drugs or other medical or surgical treatments, in clinical environments (psychiatric hospitals), to attempt to cure or control the illness.

An estimated one in six people suffers from some form of mental illness. World Health Organization research in 2007, reported in *The Lancet* medical journal, found that those suffering from depression had the worst health, with a more disabling condition than angina, arthritis, asthma or diabetes

The challenge to the biomedical approach: the social pattern of mental illness

There is, as in other aspects of health, a social pattern to mental illness. This challenges the biomedical model, since it would appear that mental illness affects social groups differently, and is linked to social conditions. It therefore cannot stem simply from biological factors, where a more random pattern would be expected. For example:

- The working class is diagnosed as suffering more mental illness than the middle class, and working-class mothers report more depression than middle-class mothers. This may reflect higher levels of poverty and family stress. Class differences in the treatment given, such as admittance to NHS psychiatric hospitals (where they will become a health statistic) rather than unrecorded private psychotherapy or psychiatric treatments at home or in private clinics, may also explain this difference in the pattern shown in statistics on mental illness.
- More women than men suffer, or at least report, mental illness.
- People of African-Caribbean origin are more likely to be diagnosed as schizophrenic and compulsorily committed to psychiatric hospitals.
- Suicide and depression are more common among young unemployed males.
- African-Caribbeans and some Asian groups suffer higher levels of mental illness, possibly explained by racism, combined with social deprivation.

These social patterns of mental illness have led some researchers to suggest that not only is mental illness caused by social factors, like racism, stress, unemployment and poverty, but that the definition of mental illness itself is created by society – a social construction.

The social construction of mental illness

The decision about whether someone is mentally ill or not involves other people, such as partners, family, friends, workmates and doctors, making judgements about whether someone's behaviour is so outside the boundaries of normal behaviour, so strange, unusual, bizarre or frightening, that it presents a problem for either the individual concerned or other people.

The definition of mental illness therefore rests on what people see as normal and socially acceptable behaviour, and on those people then defining some forms of behaviour as unacceptable deviance. This obviously prompts the question of how the notions of normal and abnormal behaviour are established, and therefore what is and isn't classed as mental illness. This is no easy matter, since what is regarded as abnormal or 'mad' in one society or group may be seen as perfectly normal in another, and notions of normality and deviance change over time. For example, agoraphobia (fear of open spaces) is only seen as a mental illness because other people don't regard staying indoors all the time as normal behaviour.

Certainly the label of 'mental illness' has been used to condemn deviant (non-conformist) behaviour. For example, some young women were once put in mental hospitals simply because they were unmarried mothers, and opponents of the former Communist regime in the Soviet Union (now Russia and its neighbouring countries) were once seen as 'mad' to oppose the government and put in mental hospitals for 'treatment'. Even today in Britain we find an increasing medicalization of odd behaviour so that, for example, badly behaved children are often labelled as suffering from Emotional and Behavioural Difficulties or Attention Deficit Disorder. How often do many of us dismiss people whom we think of as strange, with odd views or bizarre behaviour, as 'crazy'?

The work of Scheff

These issues have led researchers, such as Scheff and Szasz, to claim that what we call mental illness is a social construction – simply a label applied by others, and particularly those with power such as doctors, politicians and the mass media, to those whose behaviour they cannot make sense of, or dislike, or of which they disapprove. It is a label applied to those who display unacceptable forms of deviance which go against the dominant norms in any society.

Thomas Scheff (1966) sees what is called mental illness as a label to explain away, and justify treatment of, bizarre behaviour that cannot be explained or made sense of in any other way. The label mental illness is applied to rule-breaking and odd behaviour which takes place in unapproved contexts, and which might pose a threat to the smooth running of society.

Scheff argues that most people at some time go through stages of stress, anxiety or depression, or show signs of odd or bizarre behaviour. In the majority of cases other people do not label this as evidence of mental illness, and it is dealt with through the normal sick role. A few days off work, a change in social circumstances or a holiday is often enough to deal with these problems. It is only when others label this behaviour as evidence of mental illness that it begins to have important consequences for individuals.

Scheff argues that once others begin to see behaviour as so bizarre, frightening or intolerable that it is seen as a sign of mental illness, then stereotypes of mental illness we have all learnt since childhood – like the 'nutter' or the 'loony' – come into play. The patient then acts according to the stereotype she or he has learnt to expect of the mentally ill. Others react in terms of the same stereotyped expectations. Psychiatrists confirm the 'insane' label, psychiatric treatment begins, and the deviant label of mentally ill is firmly established. People labelled in such a way are thus thrown into the 'insanity role'. Those labelled as mentally ill often have little choice but to accept the label, as refusal of it and of the treatment ('there's nothing wrong with me') is interpreted by others as yet further confirmation of their illness.

The work of Szasz

Szasz (1972), like Scheff, argues that mental illness is not really an illness at all, but a label used by powerful or influential people to control those who are seen as socially disruptive or who challenge existing society or the dominant ideas in some way. Szasz says that it is the views and reactions of others that lead to the mental illness label being applied, and not the abnormal behaviour itself that makes us 'mad'. What we define as mental illness or 'madness' cannot therefore be treated or cured, as the problem lies with the attitudes of other people, not with the behaviour itself.

The work of Goffman

Goffman, in *Asylums* (1961), is concerned with the consequences that follow for those individuals whose behaviour has been labelled as a mental illness. Goffman suggests that once a person is labelled as mentally ill and chooses or is forced to enter a psychiatric hospital as a patient, then the insanity role is confirmed and the career of the psychiatric patient begins.

Goffman argues that psychiatric hospitals develop their own subculture, where people don't get cured but learn to 'act mad' according to the label that has been attached to them. This reduces their chances of release and makes

With permission of Peter Moulder

Researchers like Scheff and Szasz suggest that what we call 'mental illness' is simply a label applied by others to those whose behaviour they simply cannot make sense of, because it is so bizarre or odd. The 'Hatman', pictured above, stands harmlessly every day for long periods of time on a busy main road wearing a range of bizarre headgear, wigs and masks. Why is such behaviour sometimes seen simply as an expression of individuality, personal eccentricity or oddness, and why is it sometimes labelled as a sign of mental illness needing treatment?

it difficult for them to re-enter 'normal' society successfully. He therefore suggests that hospitals for the treatment of mental illness are more likely to create the behaviour they are supposed to be curing, making release and a return to normality even more difficult.

Entering a mental hospital – mortification Entering a mental hospital involves what Goffman calls a process of **mortification**, where the patient's own identity is replaced by one defined by the institution. This is to encourage the patient to conform to the hospital regime. It involves things like removing personal clothing and possessions, lack of privacy, making the patient follow hospital routines, obeying staff and so on.

In these circumstances, Goffman suggests, patients may respond to the institution and the label applied to them in various ways:

- *Withdrawal* Patients keep themselves to themselves – behaviour which is interpreted as part of the illness, confirming the label.

> **Mortification** is a process whereby a person's own identity is replaced by one defined by an institution, such as a psychiatric hospital or prison.

- *Rebellion*   Patients challenge the institution – which is interpreted as part of the illness, but suggests more treatment is needed.
- *Institutionalization*   Patients accept they are mentally ill, feel more secure in hospital and scared of the outside world, and want to remain in hospital.
- *Conversion*   Patients accept their new roles and rules, and creep to staff as a 'model patient'.
- *Playing it cool*   Patients keep their heads down and don't break rules so they can hang on to what's left of their own identity.

Goffman argues that the label of 'mentally ill' carries with it a stigma – a sign of social disapproval, rejection and inferiority – that has severe consequences for people so labelled, even when they have been cured. For example, some employers are reluctant to employ people who have a history of mental illness. This means that, even if patients are released, they are likely to face the social stigma attached to being a former mental patient. Figure 7.5 overleaf illustrates this 'career' of a mental patient.

The work of Rosenhan

Rosenhan's research 'On being sane in insane places' (1973) showed how unreliable diagnoses of mental illness were. This research confirmed the views of Scheff, Szasz and Goffman that mental illness is basically a label placed on behaviour by others.

Rosenhan in 1972 was interested in discovering how the staff of mental hospitals in the United States made sense of perfectly sane 'patients' who, unknown to staff, faked the symptoms of schizophrenia by claiming to hear a voice saying 'thud'. Nine people (including Rosenhan himself) prepared themselves by not washing, shaving or cleaning their teeth for five days before going to the hospitals. All were diagnosed as schizophrenics and admitted to hospital. Once admitted, they behaved normally, and said the voice wasn't bothering them any more. All the pseudopatients were perfectly healthy, but were nonetheless kept in hospital for many days, and aspects of their perfectly normal lives before being admitted to hospital were reinterpreted as signs of their apparent illness. Rosenhan took many notes while in hospital, and this was also interpreted by staff as part of his illness, labelled as 'writing behaviour'.

Rosenhan then reversed the experiment, telling hospital staff they could expect an undisclosed number of patients who would be faking illness. The staff eventually thought they had identified forty-one fake patients, but all those they identified were actually genuine patients who wanted help, and Rosenhan had in fact not sent any fake patients at all. Rosenhan's work illustrated very clearly that the attachment of the label 'mentally ill' is a fairly arbitrary and inaccurate process. This is a matter of concern given the stigma that is attached to mental illness, and the consequences that may flow once the label is applied.

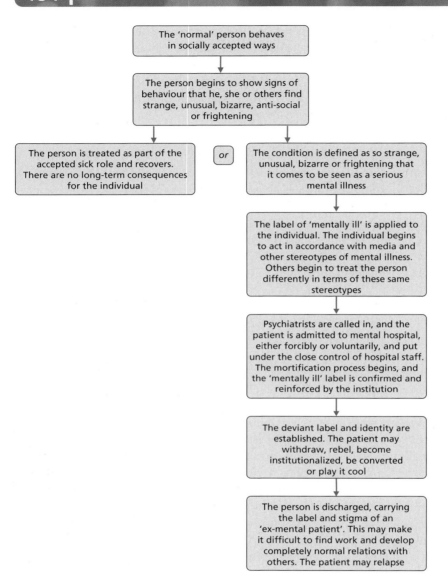

Figure 7.5 The career of a mental patient

Criticisms of the social construction approach to mental illness

The work of writers like Scheff, Szasz, Goffman and Rosenhan has been criticized for the small scale of their studies, which may therefore not be representative of all institutions involved with mental health.

The view that mental illness is simply a social construction – a response to the interpretations of other people – ignores the fact that for many people it is a real illness, often causing a great deal of distress both for individuals and their families and friends. In such circumstances, psychiatric help and medical

Rosenhan revisited

Rosenhan's experiment (see page 483) hit the world of psychiatry like a bombshell, and resulted in changes in the way diagnoses of mental illness were made. Contemporary psychiatrists are convinced that what happened with Rosenhan and his fellow pseudopatients could not happen in the twenty-first century. However, in 2002, the experiment was repeated by the psychologist Lauren Slater. She followed the same procedures as Rosenhan, not washing and so on for five days before going to the hospital, and claimed, like Rosenhan, that 'I'm here because I'm hearing a voice and it's saying "thud".' Like Rosenhan's pseudopatients, Slater had no other symptoms of mental illness or physical ill-health. She was initially diagnosed as having post-traumatic stress disorder, and then as suffering psychosis and depression. She visited eight hospitals, and while she was not admitted, she was prescribed a total of twenty-five antipsychotic and sixty antidepressant drugs. Like Rosenhan thirty years earlier, her non-existent condition was misdiagnosed and mislabelled.

For further information, see 'Into the cuckoo's nest', *Guardian*, 31 Jan. 2004, an edited extract from *Opening Skinner's Box: Great Psychological Experiments of the Twentieth Century* by Lauren Slater (London: Bloomsbury 2004).

Primary deviance is deviant behaviour which is not publicly labelled as deviant.

Secondary deviance is deviant behaviour which is labelled as such by others.

Activity

1   To what extent do you agree with the view that mental illness is simply a social construction? List the arguments for and against.
2   Do you think the media present negative stereotypes of those with mental illness? Try to find evidence from recent media reporting.
3   **Primary deviance** is the type of deviant behaviour we might all display from time to time with few, if any, social consequences, because other people either don't know about it or don't see it as very important. **Secondary deviance** is when that behaviour is seen by others, and labelled as deviant or unacceptable behaviour with a need for action to be taken. Suggest how the concepts of primary and secondary deviance might be applied to the cases of those displaying symptoms of mental illness.
4   Identify and explain *four* reasons why people might try to conceal their mental illness from others.
5   Suggest *three* ways in which the label of 'mentally ill' might affect the identity of a person so labelled.

treatment can sometimes be effective. Nonetheless, the views of writers like Scheff, Szasz, Goffman and Rosenhan do raise serious questions about the way we think about, define and label mental illness. The study of mental illness shows yet again that there are significant social aspects to health which are as important as biological or physical causes.

Activity

1 Conduct a small survey in your school or college, exploring attitudes to mental illness. Ask about things that interest you, but you might consider some of the following issues:
   - whether the welfare state should provide the best possible care for people with mental illness
   - whether the people in your survey think the mass media give unfair treatment to those with mental illnesses
   - whether they believe anyone can become mentally ill
   - what they think the causes of mental illness are
   - whether anyone with a history of mental health problems should be excluded from taking up some jobs
   - whether care units for people with psychiatric problems should be located in residential neighbourhoods
   - whether people with mental illness should live as part of a normal community
2 Analyse and discuss your findings. What do these show about public attitudes to mental illness?
3 In about one and a half sides of A4 paper, answer the following essay question: *Examine the view that mental illness is primarily a social construction*.

Researching Health

Note to students

This section assumes that chapter 5 has already been studied. If you haven't yet done so, you are advised to return to this section once you have.

The aim of this section is to get you to apply your knowledge and understanding of sociological research methods to the study of particular issues in health. Many of the research methods and types of data discussed in chapter 5 have been used in researching the areas of health and illness. What follows aims to get you thinking about some of these, and some of the theoretical, practical and ethical difficulties in using them to research health.

Collecting information on health

This chapter has already referred to a range of quantitative data used to analyse health, for instance *morbidity* statistics, such as those on the extent of heart disease, and *mortality* (death) statistics, like the infant mortality rate or deaths from cancer. These are collected from sources such as:

- the number of consultations with GPs
- hospital admissions
- sickness absence from work
- death certificates (which also record causes of death)
- national surveys on health, such as the Health Survey for England, the GP Patient Survey, and other national surveys that include health-related questions, like the General Household Survey and the ten-yearly census
- longitudinal surveys, like those mentioned above, which are repeated on a regular basis to build up a picture of how health and related issues are changing over time.

The limitations of health statistics have been discussed earlier in this chapter. These raise questions about the *reliability*, *validity* and *representativeness* of

---

Activity

1 Suggest *two* reasons in each case why the following statistics might not provide completely valid information about the health of a country:
   (a) the number of times people consult their GPs
   (b) the number of cases of self-reported illness
   (c) the number of deaths from heart disease (or other causes)
   (d) the number of days lost at work due to sickness
   (e) the number of incidents of food poisoning in different areas
   (f) the number of people suffering from a mental illness
2 In the light of your answers to the above activity, in each case suggest *two* steps that social researchers might take to improve the validity of the statistics, explaining carefully why the steps you suggest might achieve this.

---

some quantitative data derived from surveys in providing a true picture of the health of the population.

Surveys are the main means of collecting health data, and much of this is gathered by the government, which has the resources and legal powers to carry out wide-scale, national research, with large and representative samples. Depending on whether the aim is to collect quantitative or more qualitative data, these surveys use various forms of questionnaires and interviews, and a range of different ways of collecting the data – such as group discussions, structured, semi-structured and unstructured face-to-face or telephone interviews, and postal or internet-based questionnaires.

Person 2 - continued

13 Do you have any long-term illness, health problem or disability which limits your daily activities or the work you can do?
- Include problems which are due to old age.

☐ Yes ☐ No

14 What was your usual address one year ago?
- If you were a child at boarding school or a student one year ago, give the address at which you were living during the school/college/university term.
- For a child born after 29 April 2000, ✓ 'No usual address one year ago'.

☐ The address shown on the front of the form

☐ No usual address one year ago ☐ Same as Person 1

☐ Elsewhere, *please write in below*

Postcode

15 If you are aged 16 to 74 ➤ Go to **16**
If you are aged 15 and under, or 75 and over ➤ Go to **36**

16 Which of these qualifications do you have?
- ✓ all the qualifications that apply or, if not specified, the nearest equivalent.

☐ 1+ O levels/CSEs/GCSEs (any grades)   ☐ NVQ Level 1, Foundation GNVQ

☐ 5+ O levels, 5+ CSEs (grade 1), 5+ GCSEs (grade A-C), School Certificate   ☐ NVQ Level 2, Intermediate GNVQ

19 Were you actively looking for any kind of paid work during the last 4 weeks?

☐ Yes ☐ No

20 If a job had been available last week, could you have started it within 2 weeks?

☐ Yes ☐ No

21 Last week, were you waiting to start a job already obtained?

☐ Yes ☐ No

22 Last week, were you any of the following?
- ✓ all the boxes that apply.

☐ Retired

☐ Student

☐ Looking after home/family

☐ Permanently sick/disabled

☐ None of the above

23 Have you ever worked?

☐ Yes, *please write in the year you last worked*

➤ Go to **24**

☐ No, have never worked ➤ Go to **36**

national **STATISTICS**

Health Survey for

200

The health of older people

Summary of key fi

A survey carried out on behalf of The Information Cer
Edited by Rachel Craig and Jennifer Mindell

Joint Health Surveys Unit

NatCen
National Centre for Social Research

UCL
Department of Epidemiology and Public Health at the
Royal Free and University College Medical School

FOR HEALTH AND SOCIAL CARE

PATIENT SURVEY

Doctor
erience

OUR SAY

In January, some patients registered with this practice will receive a short questionnaire about how easy it is to see or speak to a Doctor here. This will help the NHS and the Department of Health find out what patients think about GP practices across the country.

The questionnaire will be sent by the independent research organisation Ipsos MORI. Your views will help improve the service you and other patients receive. If you are asked to take part please return it as soon as possible. We really want to know what you think.

Want to know more? Visit www.gp-patient.co.uk

People who are selected to take part in the survey will also be able to use a telephone helpline to get more information.

NHS

Some sources of quantitative data on health: extract from 2001 Census form;
Health Survey for England, 2005; *GP Patient Survey*

Participant observation is rarely used in government-funded research, but has been used to great effect by health researchers wishing to adopt a more interpretivist approach. Rosenhan's research, discussed on pages 483 and 485, used participant observation in psychiatric hospitals to gain insights into how medical professionals labelled and responded to symptoms of mental illness. This was also a form of field experiment, as it involved patients faking their symptoms.

Ethical issues are always of great concern in health-related research, as the state of people's health is often a very personal and private matter. Unhealthy people are often quite vulnerable and may find that questions about their own or their family's health cause them anxiety, or they may find such research intrusive or personally threatening. So care and sensitivity is needed in such research.

Activity

A good way to understand how research methods apply to health issues is to carry out your own small piece of research, perhaps on no more than five or six people.

1 Form a hypothesis or a question you wish to find answers to.
2 Devise a suitable sample and a research method appropriate to your aim or hypothesis.
3 Draw up a short questionnaire, interview schedule or whatever else is needed.
4 Carry out your research.
5 Do a careful analysis of the strengths and weaknesses of your research, including your findings. If you are in a group, you could criticize one another's surveys. Topics could be anything health-related, such as:
   - whether there are any differences between men and women in how they experience health and illness (or you could do differences between social class, ethnic or age groups)
   - whether there are differences in the health of people from richer and poorer areas of your town or city
   - how social class, gender, lifestyle, people's occupations, poverty, ethnicity, or other material and cultural factors affect health
   - people's attitudes to mental illness
6 Suggest a suitable method for studying each of the following topics, and explain in each case why it might be suitable.
   - the relationship between people's work and their state of health
   - the effects of 'healthy food' labelling on people's choice of food
   - what people expect from their GP
   - whether government health promotion campaigns, like '5-a-Day Healthy Eating', 10,000 steps and other physical fitness campaigns, Alcohol Awareness and Stop Smoking, are effective in improving the health of the nation (see overleaf)

1 medium apple

2 broccoli florets

2 halves of canned peaches

1 handful of grapes

1 medium banana

3 heaped tablespoons of peas

1 medium glass of orange juice

7 strawberries

3 whole dried apricots

5 A DAY

Just Eat More
(fruit & veg)

www.doh.gov.uk/fiveaday

3 heaped tablespoons of cooked kidney beans

16 okra

NHS

No Smoking day

Wednesday
14 March 2007

Make a fresh start

Free local help on 0800 169 0 169
www.nosmokingday.org.uk

How might researchers find out whether health promotion campaign like these are effective?

Examples of research

The following examples of research and research methods, and the activities relating to them, aim to get you thinking about how research methods are applied in some actual health research.

Food Scares and Food Safety, 2005 (Food Standards Agency)

This research explored changing consumer attitudes and perceptions towards food, food risks, and food scares, whom consumers would trust to provide reliable information and advice on food and food scares, and other food-related matters.

Eight group discussions and twenty short qualitative open-ended interviews were conducted among members of the public who had sole or joint responsibility for buying food. The discussions were held in Birmingham, London and Leeds, with groups made up from different social class, age and ethnic groups, and both single and mixed-sex groups. The interviews were held in Luton with seven men and thirteen women, from different age groups, social class and ethnic backgrounds.

> ### Activity
>
> 1 Identify *two* research methods used in the Food Standards Agency survey above.
> 2 Explain in each case why they might be suitable methods to investigate consumer perceptions and attitudes to food.
> 3 Suggest *two* ways that the researchers sought to ensure any insights they gained came from a representative group of people.
> 4 Do you think the findings from this research could be applied to consumers across the whole country? Explain your answer.
> 5 Identify and explain *two* other methods sociologists might use to study consumer attitudes to food safety.

The Health Survey for England, 2005 (Department of Health and The Information Centre)

The Health Survey for England, 2005 is one of a series of annual surveys that began in 1991. It aims to provide regular information on various aspects of the nation's health. All surveys have covered the adult population aged 16 and over living in private households in England. Children were first included in 1995. The survey covers a complete cross-section of the whole population, including people of different ages and states of health, living in different areas and from differing backgrounds.

Clinical measurements, like blood pressure and blood samples, are taken by specially trained nurses from selected people who have given their consent, and they also ask additional questions. In 2005, individual face-to-face interviews were held with 7,630 adults aged over 16, with a further 2,673 adults aged over 65, and 2,994 children aged 2–15 (parents of those under 11 were asked about their children's health, with the children present so they could comment if they wished).

Questions were asked on a range of topics, such as general health, alcohol consumption, smoking, fruit and vegetable consumption, use of complementary and alternative medicine. All those over the age of 8 were also asked to fill in a booklet (a questionnaire) on health issues related to their age group.

The Mental Health of Children and Young People in Great Britain, 2004 (Department of Health and the Scottish Executive)

This survey explored the type and extent of mental illness among 5–16-year-olds in Britain. There were 7,977 interviews conducted, covering 76 per cent of the children contacted. Teachers nominated by the parents were contacted via a postal questionnaire, with 83 per cent returning them. Face-to-face structured interviews with parents were used, but these were supplemented by open-ended questions to parents when symptoms of mental illness in

Activity

1 Why might the Health Survey have provided a more valid picture of England's health since 1995?
2 Identify *two* methods that were used in the survey above to collect data to measure people's health.
3 Suggest *three* reasons why questions on topics such as general health, alcohol consumption, smoking, and fruit and vegetable consumption might not produce valid answers.
4 Suggest *two* steps not mentioned in the summary of the survey above that might have been taken to ensure the sample selected was representative of the entire population.

children had been identified in the structured questions. This enabled parents to describe the problem in their own words. Additional information was collected by a five-minute self-completion questionnaire. Parents, mostly mothers, were interviewed first, and then, if they and their children gave their permission, their 11–16 year old children were interviewed face-to-face. Questions about the young people's smoking, drinking and drug-taking experiences were recorded via a self-completion questionnaire on a laptop. It was thought by the researchers to be very important for children and parents to be interviewed separately and alone.

Activity

1 Identify *three* research methods that are used in the mental health survey above.
2 Suggest *two* reasons why questions about the young people's smoking, drinking and drug-taking experiences were recorded via a self-completion questionnaire on a laptop rather than by the interviewer.
3 Suggest *two* reasons why the researchers thought 'it was . . . very important for children and parents to be interviewed separately and alone'.
4 Suggest *three* possible problems with the use of postal questionnaires sent to teachers to find out about the mental health of their pupils.
5 Identify all the people who might have to give their consent for this research to be carried out.
6 Identity *two* steps taken that show the researchers were aware of ethical issues in conducting this research.
7 Suggest at least *two* further pieces of information you would need to evaluate whether the survey above was representative.
8 Suggest *two* factors that may influence the validity of the findings of the research above.

Being Sane in Insane Places (Rosenhan, 1972)

Rosenhan in 1972 was interested in discovering how the staff of twelve mental hospitals in the United States made sense of perfectly sane 'patients' who, unknown to staff, faked the symptoms of the mental illness schizophrenia. Eight sane people prepared themselves by not washing, shaving or cleaning their teeth for five days before going to the hospitals. All were diagnosed as schizophrenics and admitted to hospital. None of the pseudo-patients really believed that they would be admitted so easily. Once there, they behaved normally, for instance speaking to patients and staff as they would ordinarily, and doing what they were told and taking (though secretly not swallowing) prescribed medicines. They told the staff they were feeling absolutely fine whenever they were asked, and that they experienced no symptoms. All the pseudo-patients were perfectly healthy, and their main worry was over whether they would be embarrassed at being exposed as frauds. They were nonetheless kept in hospital for many days.

Activity

1 What research method does Rosenhan use?
2 Suggest *two* ethical concerns that might be raised by this research.
3 To what extent is it possible to generalize from this research about how the medical profession understands and labels mental illness?
4 Suggest and explain *two* ways that Rosenhan's research might provide insights into the social construction of mental illness.
5 Identify another research method appropriate for exploring doctors' attitudes to mental illness. Explain all the ways your chosen method is appropriate for this particular aim.

CHAPTER SUMMARY

After studying this chapter, you should be able to:

- explain what is meant by 'the human body is a social construction'

- explain what is meant by health, illness, disease and disability, and how they are socially constructed

- identify and explain the difference between the medical and social models of health, and criticize both

- outline Marxist and feminist contributions to the study of health and health care

- identify and explain a range of social factors which influence health and disease

- identify some problems with health statistics

- suggest the reasons why some people may seek medical or psychiatric help while others may not

- explain what is meant by the 'sick role', and identify its rights and obligations

- identify and criticize the role of doctors in social control

- outline the ways the approach to health and health care is moving away from the biomedical model towards a more consumer-centred and social model

- explain social class, gender and ethnic inequalities and differences in health

- identify inequalities in access to health care, including those related to funding, geographical regions, social class, disability and age

- identify and explain some regional and international inequalities in health

- identify some policies to tackle health inequalities

- explain different sociological approaches to the study of mental illness, including the view that it might be seen as a social construction

- apply research methods to the study of health

KEY TERMS

ageism	health	life expectancy	secondary deviance
disability	iatrogenesis	morbidity	sick role
disease	illness	mortality	social construction
gate-keeping	impairment	mortification	
	inverse care law	primary deviance	

EXAM QUESTION

Answer **all** the questions from this Section

SECTION B: HEALTH WITH RESEARCH METHODS

You are advised to spend approximately 50 minutes on Question 4
You are advised to spend approximately 25 minutes on Question 5
You are advised to spend approximately 40 minutes on Question 6

Time allowed: 2 hours   **Total for this section: 90 marks**

4 Read **Item A** below and answer parts (a) to (d) that follow.

Item A

The medical model of health sees good health as the absence of disease. Ill-health is seen as individuals having random attacks of disease with identifiable biological or physical causes. Doctors apply their expert medical knowledge and technology to diagnose the disease, and treat and cure it through medical or surgical treatments. The main aim of medical professionals and health care systems, like the National Health Service, is therefore to diagnose and tackle these physical symptoms. Scientific medicine is seen as the way to solve health problems, with intervention by trained medical personnel, medical technology, operating theatres, drugs and so on. Medicine is seen as in itself a 'good thing', and the more of it there is, the better people's health will be. Some criticize the medical model for not recognising that social factors are involved in both defining health and the causes of ill-health.

(a) Explain what is meant by the term 'life expectancy'. *(2 marks)*

(b) Identify **three** reasons why health statistics may not provide a true picture of a country's health. *(6 marks)*

(c) Outline some of the reasons why not all sections of society have equal access to health care in the UK. *(12 marks)*

(d) Using material from **Item A** and elsewhere, assess the approach of the medical model to improving a country's health. *(20 marks)*

TURN OVER

5 This question requires you to **apply** your knowledge and understanding of sociological research methods to the study of this **particular** issue in health.

Read **Item B** below and answer the question that follows.

Item B
Investigating what patients want from their GPs

The Department of Health's GP Patient Survey in 2007 surveyed about five million patients. Those surveyed were selected at random from a list of all patients who had had a consultation with a GP between July and October 2006.

The survey used a postal questionnaire, and asked about patients' experience of access to GPs at their practices and practice opening hours, how often they attended their GP practice, and patients' age, gender and ethnicity. Although the GP Patient Survey questions provided detailed information, the questions were not comprehensive and some had a yes/no-style format. This meant that the results did not provide GP practices with all the information they may have needed to know about patient preferences or needs.

Using material from **Item B** and elsewhere, assess the strengths and limitations of **one** of the following methods for investigating what patients want from their GPs

(i) postal questionnaires

(ii) unstructured interviews   *(20 marks)*

6 This question permits you to draw examples from **any areas** of sociology with which you are familiar

(a) Explain what is meant by the term 'primary data'.   *(2 marks)*

(b) Suggest **two** sampling methods that sociologists might use, **apart from** random sampling.   *(4 marks)*

(c) Suggest **two** reasons why sociologists might use official statistics.   *(4 marks)*

(d) Examine the problems sociologists may find when using face-to-face structured interviews in their research.   *(20 marks)*

Glossary

Words in blue within entries refer to terms found elsewhere in the glossary.

absolute poverty Poverty defined as lacking the minimum requirements necessary to maintain human health. *See also* relative poverty.

achieved status Status which is achieved through an individual's own efforts. *See also* ascribed status.

ageing population A population in which the average age is getting higher, with a greater proportion of the population over retirement age, and a smaller proportion of young people.

ageism Stereotyping, prejudice, and discrimination against individuals or groups on the grounds of their age.

anti-school subculture A group organized around a set of values, attitudes and behaviour in opposition to the main aims of a school.

arranged marriage A marriage which is arranged by the parents of the marriage partners, with a view to compatibility of background and status. More a union between two families than between two people, and romantic love between the marriage partners is not necessarily present.

ascribed status Status which is given to an individual at birth and usually can't be changed. *See also* achieved status.

banding Sometimes used to describe how schools try to ensure that their intakes have a spread of pupils drawn from all ability bands. It is more commonly used as an alternative word for streaming in schools, where students are divided into groups of similar ability (bands or streams) in which they stay for all subjects. *See also* streaming.

'beanpole' family A multi-generation extended family, in a pattern which is long and thin, with few aunts and uncles, reflecting fewer children being born in each generation, but people living longer.

birth rate The number of live births per 1,000 of the population per year.

bisexuality A sexual orientation or sexual attraction towards people of both sexes.

bourgeoisie In Marxist theory (*see* Marxism), the class of owners of the means of production.

capitalists   The social class of owners of the means of production in industrial societies, whose primary purpose is to make profits.

class conflict   The conflict that arises between different social classes. It is generally used to describe the conflict between the bourgeoisie and proletariat in Marxist views of society (*see* Marxism).

class consciousness   An awareness in members of a social class of their real interests. *See also* false consciousness.

classic extended family   A family where several related nuclear families or family members live in the same house, street or area. It may be horizontally extended, where it contains aunts, uncles, cousins, etc., or vertically extended, where it contains more than two generations. *See also* modified extended family.

communes   Self-contained and self-supporting communities, where all members of the community share property, childcare, household tasks and living accommodation.

communism   An equal society, without social classes or class conflict, in which the means of production are the common property of all.

compensatory education   Extra educational help for those coming from disadvantaged groups to help them overcome the disadvantages they face in the education system and the wider society.

conjugal roles   The roles played by a male and female partner in marriage or in a cohabiting couple.

consumption property   Property for use by the owner which doesn't produce any income, such as owning your own car. *See also* productive property.

counter-school subculture   A group organized around a set of values, attitudes and behaviour in opposition to the main aims of a school.

covert role   Where the researcher in a participant observation study keeps her or his identity as a researcher concealed from the group being studied. *See also* overt role.

cultural capital   The knowledge, language, attitudes and values, and lifestyle which give middle-class and upper-class students who possess them an in-built advantage in a middle-class controlled education system. Associated with the French Marxist Bourdieu (*see* Marxism). *See also* habitus.

cultural deprivation   The idea that some young people fail in education because of supposed deficiencies in their home and family background, such as inadequate socialization, failings in pre-school learning, inadequate language skills and inappropriate attitudes and values.

culture   The language, beliefs, values and norms, customs, roles, knowledge and skills which combine to make up the way of life of any society.

culture clash   A difference and conflict between the cultural values of the home and those of educational institutions. *See also* culture.

culture of hybridity   A culture that is a 'mix' of two or more other cultures, creating a new culture (a 'hybrid').

culture of poverty   A set of beliefs and values thought to exist among the poor which prevents them escaping from poverty.

customs   Norms which have existed for a long time.

cycle of deprivation   An explanation of how one aspect of poverty, such as poor housing, can lead to further poverty, such as poor health, building up into a cycle which makes it difficult for the poor to escape from poverty.

death rate   The number of deaths per 1,000 of the population per year.

demography   The study of the characteristics of human populations, such as their size and structure and how these change over time.

dependency culture   A set of values and beliefs, and a way of life, centred on dependence on others. Normally used by New Right writers in the context of those who depend on welfare state benefits.

determinism   The idea that people's behaviour is moulded by their social surroundings, and that they have little free will, control or choice over how they behave.

deviance   Failure to conform to social norms.

diaspora   The dispersal of an ethnic population from its original homeland, and its spreading out across the world, while retaining cultural and emotional ties to its area or nation of origin.

disability   A physical or mental impairment which has a substantial and long-term adverse effect on a person's ability to carry out normal day-to-day activities.

disease   A biological or mental condition, which usually involves medically diagnosed symptoms.

division of labour   The division of work or occupations into a large number of specialized tasks, each of which is carried out by one worker or group of workers.

divorce rate   The number of divorces per 1,000 married people per year.

domestic labour   Unpaid housework, including cooking, cleaning, child-care and looking after the sick and elderly.

dominant culture   The main culture in a society, which is shared, or at least accepted without opposition, by the majority of people.

dominant ideology   The set of ideas and beliefs of the most powerful groups in society, which influence the ideas of the rest of society. Usually associated with Marxist ideas (*see* Marxism) of the ruling class and how the ruling class can impose its own ideas on the rest of society.

Education Action Zones   Areas which face a range of social problems, such as poverty and unemployment, in which schools are given extra money and teachers to help children overcome difficulties at school arising from their home backgrounds. In 2005, they became Excellence in Cities Action Zones (EiCAZs).

elaborated code   A form of language use involving careful explanation and detail. The language used by strangers and individuals in some formal context, like a job interview, writing a business letter, or a school lesson or textbook. Associated with the work of Bernstein. *See also* restricted code.

elite   A small group holding great power and privilege in society.

equality of educational opportunity   The principle that every child, regardless of her or his social class background, ability to pay school fees, ethnic background (*see* ethnicity), gender or disability, should have an equal chance of doing as well in education as her or his ability will allow.

ethics   Principles or ideas about what is morally right and wrong.

ethnicity   The shared culture of a social group which gives its members a common identity in some ways different from other groups.

ethnocentrism   A view of the world in which other cultures are seen through the eyes of one's own culture, with a devaluing of the others. For example, school subjects may concentrate on white British society and culture rather than recognizing and taking into account the cultures of different ethnic communities (*see* ethnicity).

expressive role   The nurturing, caring and emotional role, often linked by functionalists (see functionalism) to women's biology and seen as women's 'natural' role in the family. *See also* instrumental role.

extended family   A family grouping including all kin (*see* kinship). There are two main types of extended family: the classic extended family and the modified extended family. *See also* 'beanpole' family, nuclear family.

false consciousness   A failure by members of a social class to recognize their real interests. *See also* class consciousness.

family   A social institution consisting of a group of people related by kinship – ties of blood, marriage or adoption.

family ideology   A set of dominant beliefs and values about what the family and family life should be like.

feminism   The view that examines the world from the point of view of women, coupled with the belief that women are disadvantaged and their interests ignored or devalued in society. *See also* liberal feminism, Marxist feminism, radical feminism.

fertility rate   The number of live births per 1000 women of child-bearing age (15–44) per year.

focus group   A form of group interview in which the group focuses on a particular topic to explore in depth and people are free to talk to one another as well as the interviewer.

folk culture   The culture created by local communities that is rooted in the experiences, customs and beliefs of the everyday life of ordinary people.

functional prerequisites   The basic needs that must be met if society is to survive.

functionalism   A sociological perspective which sees society as made up of parts which work together to maintain society as an integrated whole. Society is seen as fundamentally harmonious and stable, due to the value consensus established through socialization. *See also* Marxism, structuralism.

fundamentalism   A return to the literal meaning of religious texts and associated behaviour.

gate-keeping   The power of some people, groups or organizations to limit access to something valuable or useful. For example, doctors act as gate-keepers as they have the power to allow or refuse entry to the sick role.

gender   The culturally created differences between men and women which are learnt through socialization.

gender identity   How people see themselves, and how others see them, in terms of their gender roles and biological sex.

gender role   The pattern of behaviour which is expected from individuals of either sex.

global culture   The similarity of cultures in different countries of the world, sharing increasingly similar consumer products and ways of life. This has arisen as globalization has undermined national and local cultures.

globalization   The growing interdependence of societies across the world, with the spread of the same culture, consumer goods and economic interests across the globe.

group interview   An interview in which the researcher interviews several people at the same time, with the researcher controlling the direction of the interview and to whom responses will normally be directed.

habitus   The cultural framework (*see* culture) and set of ideas possessed by each social class, into which people are socialized (*see* socialization) and which influences their tastes in music, newspapers, films and so on. Bourdieu, a French Marxist (*see* Marxism), argued the dominant class has the power to impose its own habitus in the education system, giving those from upper-class and middle-class backgrounds an inbuilt advantage over those from working-class backgrounds.

halo effect   When pupils become favourably or unfavourably stereotyped (*see* stereotype) on the basis of earlier impressions by the teacher, and are rewarded and favoured or penalized in future teacher–student encounters.

Hawthorne effect   When the presence of the researcher, or a group's knowledge that it has been specially selected for research, changes the behaviour of the group, raising problems of the validity of social research.

health   Being able to function normally within a usual everyday routine.

hegemony   The acceptance of the dominant ideology by the working class, as a result of the power of the ruling class to persuade others to accept and consent to its ideas.

hegemonic identity   An identity that is so dominant that it makes it difficult for individuals to assert alternative identities.

heterosexuality   A sexual orientation towards people of the opposite sex.

hidden curriculum   Attitudes and behaviour which are taught through the school's organization and teachers' attitudes but which are not part of the formal timetable.

high culture   Cultural products (*see* culture), mainly media based, seen as of lasting artistic or literary value, aimed at small, intellectual, predominantly upper-class and middle-class audiences, interested in new ideas, critical discussion and analysis. *See also* low culture, mass culture.

homophobia   An irrational fear of or aversion to homosexuals (*see* homosexuality).

homosexuality   A sexual orientation towards people of the same sex, with lesbian women attracted to other women, and gay men attracted to other men.

household   An individual or group living at the same address and sharing facilities.

hybrid identity   An identity formed from a mix of two or more other identities.

hypothesis   An idea which a researcher guesses might be true, but which has not yet been tested against the evidence.

iatrogenesis   Any harmful mental or physical condition induced in a patient through the effects of treatment by a doctor or surgeon.

identity   How individuals see and define themselves and how other people see and define them.

ideological state apparatuses   Agencies which serve to spread the dominant ideology and justify the power of the dominant social class.

ideology   A set of ideas, values and beliefs that represent the outlook, and justify the interests, of a social group.

illness   The subjective feeling of being unwell or unhealthy (*see* health) – a person's own recognition and definition of a lack of well-being.

impairment   Some abnormal functioning of the body or mind, either that one is born with or arising from injury or disease.

imposition problem   When asking questions in interviews or self-completion questionnaires, the risk that the researcher might be imposing their own views or framework on the people being researched, rather than getting at what they really think.

impression management   The way individuals try to convince others of the identity they wish to assert by giving particular impressions of themselves to other people.

income   A flow of money which people obtain from work, from their invest-ments, or from the state. *See also* wealth.

infant mortality rate   The number of deaths of babies in the first year of life per 1,000 live births per year.

instrumental role   The provider/breadwinner role in the family, often asso-ciated by functionalists (*see* functionalism) with men's role in family life. *See also* expressive role.

integrated conjugal roles   Roles in marriage or in a cohabiting couple where male and female partners share domestic tasks, childcare, decision-making and income earning.

interpretivism   A sociological perspective that suggests that to understand society it is necessary to understand the meanings people give to their behaviour, and how this is influenced by the behaviour and interpretations of others. The focus of research is therefore on individuals or small groups rather than on society as a whole. *See also* positivism, social action theory.

interviewer bias   The answers given in an interview being influenced or distorted in some way by the presence or behaviour of the interviewer.

inverse care law   In relation to the welfare state and health care, the sugges-tion that those whose need is least get the most resources, while those in the greatest need get the fewest resources.

Islamophobia   An irrational fear and/or hatred of or aversion to Islam, Muslims or Islamic culture

kibbutz   A community established in Israel, with the emphasis on equality, collective ownership of property, and collective childrearing.

kinship   Relations of blood, marriage or adoption.

labelling   Defining a person or group in a certain way – as a particular 'type' of person or group.

labour power   People's capacity to work. In Marxist theory (*see* Marxism), people sell their labour power to the employer in return for a wage, and the employer buys only their labour power, not the whole person.

laws   Official legal rules, formally enforced by the police, courts and prison, involving legal punishment if the rules are broken.

liberal feminism   A feminist approach (*see* feminism) which seeks to research the inequalities facing women, and enable women to achieve equal opportunities with men, without challenging the system as a whole. *See also* Marxist feminism, radical feminism.

life chances   The chances of obtaining those things defined as desirable and of avoiding those things defined as undesirable in a society.

life expectancy   An estimate of how long people can be expected to live from a certain age.

low culture   *see* mass culture

macro approach   A focus on the large-scale structure of society as a whole, rather than on individuals.

marginalization   The process whereby some people are pushed to the margins or edges of society by poverty, lack of education, disability, racism and so on. *See also* social exclusion.

marketization   The process whereby services, like education or health, that were previously controlled and run by the state, have government or local council control reduced, and become subject to the free market forces of supply and demand, based on competition and consumer choice.

market situation   The rewards that people are able to obtain when they sell their skills in the labour market, depending on the scarcity of the skills they have and the power they have to obtain high rewards.

Marxism   A structural theory of society which sees society divided by conflict between two main opposing social classes, due to the private ownership of the means of production and the exploitation of the non-owners by the owners.

Marxist feminism   A Marxist approach (*see* Marxism) to the study of women, emphasizing the way they are exploited both as workers and as women. *See also* feminism, liberal feminism, radical feminism.

mass culture (popular or low culture)   Cultural products (*see* culture), mainly media based, produced as entertainment for sale to the mass of ordinary people. These involve mass-produced, standardized, short-lived products of no lasting value, which are seen to demand little critical thought, analysis or discussion. *See also* high culture.

means of production   The key resources necessary for producing society's goods, such as factories and land.

meritocracy   A society where social positions are achieved by individual merit, such as educational qualifications, talent and skill.

metanarrative   A broad all-embracing 'big theory' or explanation for how societies operate.

methodological pluralism   The use of a variety of methods in a single piece of research.

micro approach   A focus on small groups or individuals, rather than on the structure of society as a whole.

middle class   Those in non-manual work – jobs which don't involve heavy physical effort, are usually performed in offices and involve paperwork or computer work of various kinds. *See also* social class, upper class, working class.

minority ethnic group   A social group which shares a cultural identity (*see* culture) which is different in some respects from that of the majority population of a society.

modified extended family   A family type where related nuclear families, although living apart geographically, nevertheless maintain regular contact and mutual support through visiting, the phone, e-mail and letters. *See also* classic extended family.

monogamy   A form of marriage in which a person can only be legally married to one partner at a time. *See also* polyandry, polygamy, polygyny, serial monogamy.

moral panic   A wave of public concern about some exaggerated or imaginary threat to society, stirred up by exaggerated and sensationalized reporting in the mass media.

morbidity   The extent of disease in a population, including either the total number of cases or the number of new cases of a disease in a particular population at a particular time.

mortality   The number of deaths in a population, usually measured as a rate per 1000 of a population group, such as the number of deaths per thousand of the population each year. *See also* death rate, infant mortality rate

mortification   A process whereby a person's own identity is replaced by one defined by an institution, such as a hospital or prison.

multicultural education   Education which involves teaching about the culture of other ethnic groups (*see* ethnicity) besides that of the majority culture.

nation   A particular geographical area with which a group of people identify, and share among themselves a sense of belonging based on a common sense of culture, history and usually language.

nationalism   A sense of pride and commitment to a nation, and a very strong sense of national identity.

nationality   Having citizenship of a nation-state, including things like voting rights, a passport, and the right of residence.

nation-state   A nation which has its own independent government controlling a geographical area.

negative sanctions   Punishments of various kinds imposed on those who fail to conform to social norms. *See also* positive sanctions, sanction.

New Right   A political philosophy found in the work of some sociologists, but mainly associated with the years of Conservative government in Britain between 1979 and 1997. This approach stresses individual freedom, self-help and self-reliance, reduction of the power and spending of the state, the free market and free competition between private companies, schools and other institutions, and the importance of traditional institutions and values.

norms   Social rules which define correct and approved behaviour in a society or group.

nuclear family   A family with two generations, of parents and children, living together in one household. *See also* extended family.

objectivity   Approaching topics with an open mind, avoiding bias, and being prepared to submit research evidence to scrutiny by other researchers.

overt role   Where the researcher in a participant observation study reveals her or his identity as a researcher to the group being studied. *See also* covert role.

particularistic values   Rules and values that give a priority to personal relationships. *See also* universalistic values.

patriarchy   Power and authority held by males.

peer group   A group of people of similar age and status, with whom a person often mixes socially.

perspective   A way of looking at something. A sociological perspective involves a set of theories which influences what is looked at when studying society.

pilot survey   A small-scale practice survey carried out before the final survey to check for any possible problems.

polyandry   A form of marriage in which a woman may have two or more husbands at the same time. *See also* monogamy, serial monogamy.

polygamy   A form of marriage in which a member of one sex can be married to two or more members of the opposite sex at the same time. *See also* monogamy, serial monogamy.

polygyny   A form of marriage in which a man may have two or more wives at the same time. *See also* monogamy, serial monogamy.

popular culture   *See* mass culture.

positive discrimination   Giving disadvantaged groups more favourable treatment than others to make up for the disadvantages they face.

positive sanctions   Rewards of various kinds to encourage people to conform to social norms. *See also* negative sanctions, sanction.

positivism   An approach in sociology that believes society can be studied using similar scientific techniques to those used in the natural sciences, such as physics, chemistry and biology. *See also* interpretivism.

postmodernism   The belief that society is changing so rapidly and constantly that it is marked by chaos and uncertainty, and social structures are being replaced by a whole range of different and constantly changing social relationships. Societies can no longer be understood through the application of general theories like Marxism or functionalism, which seek to explain society as a whole, as it has become fragmented into many different groups, interests and lifestyles. Society and social structures cease to exist, to be replaced by a mass of individuals who are transformed into consumers making individual choices about their lifestyles.

poverty line   The dividing point between those who are poor and those who are not. The poverty line used in Britain today, and by the European Union, is 60 per cent of average income.

pressure groups   Organizations which try to put pressure on those with power in society to implement policies they favour.

primary data   Information which sociologists have collected themselves. *See also* secondary data.

primary deviance   Deviant behaviour which is not publicly labelled (see labelling) as deviant. *See also* secondary deviance.

primary socialization   The early forms of socialization in the family and close community. *See also* secondary socialization.

privatization   The process whereby households and families become isolated and separated from the community and from wider kin (*see* kinship), with people spending more time together in home-centred activities.

privatized nuclear family   A self-contained, self-reliant and home-centred family unit that is separated and isolated from its extended kin, neighbours and local community life.

productive property   Property which provides an unearned income for its owner, such as factories, land and stocks and shares. *See also* consumption property.

proletariat   The social class of workers who have to work for wages as they do not own the means of production.

qualitative data   Information concerned with the meanings and interpretations people have about some issue or event.

quantitative data   Information that can be expressed in statistical or number form.

racial prejudice   A set of assumptions about an ethnic group (*see* ethnicity) which people are reluctant to change even when they receive information which undermines those assumptions.

racism   Believing or acting as though an individual or group is superior or inferior on the grounds of their racial or ethnic (*see* ethnicity) origins.

radical feminism   A feminist approach (*see* feminism) which focuses on the problem of patriarchy. For radical feminists, the main focus of research is on the problem of men and male-dominated society. *See also* Marxist feminism, liberal feminism.

reconstituted family   A family where one or both partners have been previously married, and bring with them children of the previous marriage. Also known as a stepfamily.

relative poverty   Poverty defined in relation to a generally accepted standard of living in a specific society at a particular time. *See also* absolute poverty.

reliability   Whether another researcher, if repeating or replicating research using the same method for the same research on the same group, would achieve the same results.

replication   *see* reliability.

representative sample   A smaller group drawn from the survey population, of which it contains a good cross-section. The information obtained from a representative sample should provide roughly the same results as if the whole survey population had been surveyed.

restricted code   A form of language use which takes for granted shared understandings between people. Colloquial, everyday language used between friends, with limited explanation and use of vocabulary. *See also* elaborated code.

role conflict   The conflict between the successful performances of two or more roles at the same time, such as worker, student and mother.

role models   Patterns of behaviour which others copy and model their own behaviour on.

roles   The patterns of behaviour which are expected from individuals in society.

ruling class   The social class of owners of the means of production, whose control over the economy gives them power over all aspects of society, enabling them to rule over society.

ruling class ideology   The set of ideas and beliefs of the ruling class.

sample   A small representative group drawn from the survey population for questioning or interviewing.

sampling frame   A list of names of all those in the survey population from which a representative sample is selected.

sampling methods   The techniques sociologists use to select representative individuals to study from the survey population.

sanction   A reward or punishment to encourage social conformity. *See also* negative sanctions, positive sanctions.

scapegoats   Individuals or groups blamed for something which is not their fault.

secondary data   Data which already exist and which the researcher hasn't collected herself or himself. *See also* primary data.

secondary deviance   Deviant behaviour which is labelled (*see* labelling) as such by others. *See also* primary deviance.

secondary socialization   Socialization which takes place beyond the family and close community, such as through the education system, the mass media and the workplace. *See also* primary socialization.

secularization   The process whereby religious thinking, practice and institutions lose social significance.

segregated conjugal role   A clear division and separation between the roles of male and female partners in a marriage or in a cohabiting couple.

self-fulfilling prophecy   People acting in response to predictions of their behaviour, thereby making the prediction come true. Often applied to the effects of streaming in schools.

serial monogamy   A form of marriage where a person keeps marrying and divorcing a series of different partners, but is only married to one person at a time. *See also* monogamy, polyandry, polygamy, polygyny.

setting   A system of dividing school students into groups (or sets) of the same ability in particular subjects

sex   The biological differences between men and women.

sexism   Prejudice or discrimination against people (especially women) because of their sex.

sexual division of labour   The division of work into 'men's jobs' and 'women's jobs'.

sexual orientation   The type of people that individuals are either physically or romantically attracted to, such as those of the same or opposite sex.

sexuality   People's sexual characteristics and their sexual behaviour.

sick role   The pattern of behaviour which is expected from someone who is classified as ill.

social action theory   A perspective which emphasizes the creative action which people can take, and that people are not simply the passive victims of social forces outside them. Social action theory suggests it is important to understand the motives and meanings people give to their behaviour. *See also* interpretivism, structuralism.

social capital   The social networks of influence and support that people have.

social class   A broad group of people who share a similar economic situation, such as occupation, income and ownership of wealth. *See also* middle class, upper class, working class.

social construction   The way something is created through the individual, social and cultural (*see* culture) interpretations, perceptions and actions of people. Official statistics, notions of health and illness, deviance and suicide are all examples of social phenomena that only exist because people have constructed them and given these phenomena particular labels.

social control   The process of persuading or forcing individuals to conform to values and norms.

social exclusion   The situation where people are marginalized (*see* marginalization) or excluded from full participation in education, work, community life and access to services and other aspects of life seen as part of being a full and participating member of mainstream society. Those who lack the necessary resources are excluded from the opportunity to fully participate in society, and are denied the opportunities most people take for granted.

social facts   Social phenomena which exist outside individuals but act upon them in ways which constrain or mould their behaviour. Such phenomena include social institutions such as the family, the law, the education system and the workplace.

social institutions   The organized social arrangements which are found in all societies, such as the family and the education systems.

social mobility   Movement of groups or individuals up or down the social hierarchy.

social policy   The packages of plans and actions adopted by national and local government or various voluntary agencies to solve social problems or achieve other goals that are seen as important.

social problem   Something that is seen as harmful to society in some way, and needs something doing to sort it out.

social solidarity   The integration of people into society through shared values, a common culture, shared understandings, and social ties that bind them together.

social structure   The network of social institutions and social relationships that form the 'building blocks' of society.

socialization   The process of learning the culture of any society. *See also* primary socialization, secondary socialization.

sociological perspective   A set of theories which influence what is looked at when studying society.

sociological problem   Any social issue that needs explaining.

status   The amount of prestige or social importance a person has in the eyes of other members of a group or society. *See also* achieved status, ascribed status.

status frustration   A sense of frustration arising in individuals or groups because they are denied status in society.

stereotype   A generalized, oversimplified view of the features of a social group, allowing for few individual differences between members of the group.

stigma   Any undesirable physical or social characteristic that is seen as abnormal or unusual in some way, that is seen as demeaning, and stops an individual being fully accepted by society.

stigmatized identity   An identity that is in some way undesirable or demeaning, and stops an individual being fully accepted by society.

streaming   A system of dividing school students into groups of similar ability (streams or bands) in which they stay for all subjects. *See also* banding.

structural differentiation   The way new, more specialized social institutions emerge to take over functions that were once performed by a single institution. An example is the way some functions of the family have been transferred to the education system and the welfare state.

structuralism   A perspective which is concerned with the overall structure of society, and sees individual behaviour moulded by social institutions like the family, the education system, the mass media and work. *See also* functionalism, Marxism.

structuration   A perspective between structuralism and social action theory which suggests that, while people are constrained by social institutions, they can at the same time take action to support or change those institutions.

subculture   A smaller culture held by a group of people within the main culture of a society, in some ways different from the main culture, but with many aspects in common.

surplus value   The extra value added by workers to the products they produce, after allowing for the payment of their wages, and which goes to the employer in the form of profit.

survey   A means of collecting primary data from large numbers of people, usually in a standardized statistical form.

survey population   The section of the population which is of interest in a survey.

symbolic interactionism   A sociological perspective which is concerned with understanding human behaviour in face-to-face situations, and how individuals and situations come to be defined in particular ways through their encounters with other people.

symmetrical family   A family where the roles of husband and wife or cohabiting partners have become more alike (symmetrical) and equal.

triangulation   The use of two, or usually more, research methods in a single piece of research to check the reliability and validity of research evidence.

underachievement   The failure of individuals or groups to fulfil their potential – they do not do as well in education (or other areas) as their talents and abilities suggest they should.

underclass   A social group right at the bottom of the social class hierarchy, who are in some ways cut off or excluded from the rest of society.

universalistic values   Rules and values that apply equally to all members of society, regardless of who they are. *See also* particularistic values.

upper class   A small social class who are the main owners of society's wealth. It includes wealthy industrialists, landowners and the traditional aristocracy. *See also* middle class, working class.

validity   This is concerned with notions of truth – how far the findings of research actually provide a true, genuine or authentic picture of what is being studied.

value consensus   A general agreement around the main values of society.

value freedom   The idea that the beliefs and prejudices of the sociologist should not be allowed to influence the way research is carried out and evidence interpreted.

values   General beliefs about what is right or wrong, and about the important standards which are worth maintaining and achieving in any society.

verstehen   The idea of understanding human behaviour by putting yourself in the position of those being studied, and trying to see things from their point of view.

victim survey   A survey which asks people if they have been victims of crime, whether or not they reported it to the police.

wealth   Property in the form of assets which can be sold and turned into cash for the benefit of the owner. *See also* income.

welfare pluralism   The range of welfare provision, including informal provision by the family and community, the welfare state, the voluntary sector and the private sector.

working class   Those working in manual jobs – jobs involving physical work and, literally, work with their hands, like factory or labouring work. *See also* middle class, social class, upper class.

Bibliography

Abel-Smith, B. and Townsend, P. (1965) *The Poor and the Poorest*. London: G. Bell & Son.

Acheson Report (1998) *Independent Inquiry into Inequalities in Health*. London: Stationery Office.

Althusser, L. (1971) *Lenin and Philosophy and Other Essays*. London: New Left Books.

Ariès, P. (1973) *Centuries of Childhood*. Harmondsworth: Penguin.

Atkinson, J. M. (1978) *Discovering Suicide*. Basingstoke: Macmillan.

Ball, S. J. (1981) *Beachside Comprehensive: A Case-Study of Secondary Schooling*. Cambridge: Cambridge University Press.

Ballard, R. (1982) 'South Asian families', in Rapoport et al. (1982).

Barber, M. (1996) *The Learning Game*. London: Victor Gollancz.

Barker, E. (1984) *The Making of a Moonie*. Oxford: Blackwell.

Barrett, M. and McIntosh, M. (1982) *The Anti-Social Family*. London: Verso.

Bauman, Z. (1996) 'From pilgrim to tourist – or a short history of identity', in S. Hall and P. du Gay (eds), *Questions of Cultural Identity*. London: Sage Publications.

Bauman, Z. and May, T. (2004) 'Identity, consumerism and inequality', *Sociology Review*, February.

Becker, H. S. (1970) *Sociological Work*. Chicago: University of Chicago Press.

Becker, H. S. (1971) 'Social class variations in the teacher–pupil relationship', in School and Society Course Team, Open University (ed.), *School and Society*. London: Routledge & Kegan Paul.

Bernstein, B. (1971) 'Education cannot compensate for society', in School and Society Course Team, Open University (ed.), *School and Society*, London: Routledge & Kegan Paul.

Best, L. (1993) 'Dragons, dinner ladies and ferrets: sex roles in children's books', *Sociology Review* 3/3.

Bhatti, G. (1999) *Asian Children at Home and at School: An Ethnographic Study*. London: Routledge.

Bocock, R. (2004) *Consumption*. London: Routledge.

Bott, E. (1957/1978) 'Conjugal roles and social networks', in P. Worsley (ed.), *Modern Sociology* (2nd edn). Harmondsworth: Penguin.

Boulton, M. G. (1983) *On Being a Mother*. London: Tavistock.

Bourdieu, P. (1971) 'Systems of education and systems of thought' and 'Intellectual field and creative project', in M. F. D. Young (ed.), *Knowledge and Control*. London: Collier-Macmillan.

Bowles, S. and Gintis, H. (1976) *Schooling in Capitalist America*. London: Routledge & Kegan Paul.

Bradford, B. (2006) *Who are the 'Mixed' ethnic group?* London: Office for National Statistics.

Bradley, H. (1995) *Fractured Identities: Changing Patterns of Inequality*. Cambridge: Polity.

Brannen, J. (2003) 'The age of beanpole families', *Sociology Review* 13/1.

Browne, K. and Bottrill, I. (1999) 'Our unequal, unhealthy nation: class inequality, health and illness', *Sociology Review* 9/2.

Burdsey, D. (2004) 'One of the lads? Dual ethnicity and assimilated ethnicities in the careers of British Asian professional footballers', *Ethnic and Racial Studies* 27/5.

Butler, C. (1995) 'Religion and gender: young Muslim women in Britain', *Sociology Review*, February.

Chagnon, N. A. (1996) *Yanomamö: The Fierce People* (Case Studies in Cultural Anthropology). London: Thomson Learning.

Charlesworth, S. (2000) *A Phenomenology of Working-Class Experience*. Cambridge: Cambridge University Press.

Cicourel, A. V. and Kitsuse, J. I. (1971) 'The social organisation of the high school and deviant adolescent careers', in School and Society Course Team, Open University (ed.), *School and Society*. London: Routledge & Kegan Paul.

Clarke, J. and Critcher, C. (1995) *The Devil Makes Work: Leisure in Capitalist Britain*. Basingstoke: Palgrave Macmillan.

Clarke, J. and Saunders, C. (1991) 'Who are you and so what?', *Sociology Review*, September.

Coard, B. (1971) *How the West Indian Child is Made Educationally Subnormal in the British School System*. London: New Beacon Books.

Coates, K. and Silburn, R. (1970) *Poverty: The Forgotten Englishmen*. Harmondsworth: Penguin.

Colley, A. (1998) 'Gender and subject choice in secondary education', in J. Radford (ed.), *Gender and Choice in Education and Occupation*. London: Routledge & Kegan Paul.

Collins, R. (1972) 'Functional and conflict theories of stratification', in B. R. Cosin (ed.), *Education, Structure and Society*. Harmondsworth: Penguin.

Connell, R. W. (1995) *Masculinities*. Cambridge: Polity.

Cooley, C. H. (1998) *On Self and Social Organization*, ed. H.-J. Schubert. London: University of Chicago Press.

Cooper, D. (1972) *The Death of the Family*. Harmondsworth: Penguin.

Critcher, C., Bramham, P. and Tomlinson, A. (1995) *The Sociology of Leisure*. London: Chapman & Hall.

Cunningham, H. (2005) *Children and Childhood in Western Society Since 1500*. London: Longman.

Davis, K. and Moore, W. E. (1945/1967) 'Some principles of stratification', in R. Bendix and S. M. Lipset (eds), *Class, Status and Power* (2nd edn). London: Routledge & Kegan Paul.

Deem, R. (1986) *All Work and No Play*. Milton Keynes: Open University Press.

Deem, R. (1990) 'Women and leisure – all work and no play', *Social Studies Review* 5/4.

Department of Health (1992) *The Health of the Nation*. London: HMSO.

Department of Health (1998) *Our Healthier Nation*. London: Stationery Office.

Douglas, J. W. B. (1964) *The Home and the School*. London: MacGibbon & Kee.

Douglas, J. W. B., Ross, J. and Simpson, H. (1968) *All our Future*. London: Peter Davies.

Duncombe, J. and Marsden, D. (1995) 'Women's "triple shift": paid employment, domestic labour and "emotion work"', *Sociology Review* 4/4.

Edgell, S. (1980) *Middle-Class Couples*. London: Allen & Unwin.

Elston, M. (1980) 'Medicine: half our future doctors', in R. Silverstone and A. Warde (eds), *Careers of Professional Women*. London: Croom Helm.

Epstein, D., Elwood J., Hey, V. and Maw, J. (1998) *Failing Boys? Issues in Gender and Achievement*, Buckingham: Open University Press.

Eversley, D. and Bonnerjea, L. (1982) 'Social change and indications of diversity', in Rapoport et al. (1982).

Field, F. (1989) *Losing Out: The Emergence of Britain's Underclass*. Oxford: Blackwell.

Finn, D. (1984) 'Leaving school and growing up', in I. Bates et al. (eds), *Schooling for the Dole*. Basingstoke: Macmillan.

Finn, D. (1987) *Training without Jobs*. Basingstoke: Macmillan.

Flanders, N. A. (1970) *Analysing Teaching Behaviour*. New York: Addison Wesley.

Fletcher, R. (1966) *The Family and Marriage in Britain*. Harmondsworth: Penguin.

Francis, B. (2000) *Boys, Girls and Achievement: Addressing the Classroom Issues*. London: Routledge/Farmer.

Fuller, M. (1980) 'Black girls in a London comprehensive school', in R. Deem (ed.), *Schooling for Women's Work*. London: Routledge & Kegan Paul.

Gans, H. J. (1973) *More Equality*. New York: Pantheon.

Garfinkel, H. (1984) *Studies in Ethnomethodology*. Cambridge: Polity.

Gatrell, C. J. (2004) *Hard Labour: The Sociology of Parenthood, Family Life and Career*, Maidenhead: Open University Press.

Gibson, A. and Asthana, S. (1999) 'Schools, markets and equity: access to secondary education in England and Wales', presentation to American Educational Research Association Annual Conference, Montreal, reported in the *Guardian*, 6 July.

Gibson, C. (1994) *Dissolving Wedlock*. London: Routledge.

Giddens, A. (2006) *Sociology* (5th edn). Cambridge: Polity.

Gillborn, D. and Gipps, C. (1996) *Recent Research on the Achievements of Ethnic Minority Pupils*. London: Office for Standards in Education.

Gillborn, D. and Mirza, H. S. (2000) *Mapping Race, Class and Gender: A Synthesis of Research Evidence*. London: Office for Standards in Education.

Gilmore, D. (1991) *Manhood in the Making: Cultural Concepts of Masculinity*. London: Yale University Press.

Gilroy, P. (1993) *The Black Atlantic: Modernity and Double Consciousness*. London: Verso Books.

Gilroy, P. (2002) *There Ain't no Black in the Union Jack*. London: Routledge.

Goffman, E. (1990) *The Presentation of Self in Everyday Life*. Harmondsworth: Penguin.

Goffman, E. (1990) *Stigma: Notes on the Management of Spoiled Identity*. Harmondsworth: Penguin.

Goffman, E. (1991) *Asylums*. Harmondsworth: Penguin.

Goode, W. J. (1963) *World Revolution and Family Patterns*. New York: Free Press.

Goode, W. J. (1971) 'A sociological perspective on marital dissolution', in M. Anderson (ed.), *Sociology of the Family*. Harmondsworth: Penguin.

Gordon, D. et al. (2000) *Poverty and Social Exclusion in Britain*. York: Joseph Rowntree Foundation.

Graham, H. (1985) *Health and Welfare*. Basingstoke: Macmillan.

Graham, H. (1993) *Hardship and Health in Women's Lives*. Hemel Hempstead: Harvester Wheatsheaf.

Graham, H. (2002) 'Socio-economic change and inequalities in men and women's health in the UK', in S. Nettleton and U. Gustaffson (eds), *The Sociology of Health and Illness Reader*. Cambridge: Polity.

Green, E., Hebron, S. and Woodward, D. (1990) *Women's Leisure, What Leisure?* Basingstoke: Macmillan.

Hall, S. (1992) 'The question of cultural identity', in S. Hall, D. Held and T. McGrew (eds), *Modernity and Its Futures*. Cambridge: Polity.

Hargreaves, D. (1967) *Social Relations in a Secondary School*. London: Routledge & Kegan Paul.

Hargreaves, D. (1976) 'Reactions to labelling', in M. Hammersley and P. Woods (eds), *The Process of Schooling*. London: Routledge & Kegan Paul.

Hart, N. (1985) *The Sociology of Health and Medicine*. Ormskirk: Causeway Press.

Heath, S. (2004) 'Transforming friendship – are housemates the new family?', *Sociology Review*, September.

Hobson, A. (2000) 'Multiple methods in social research', *Sociology Review* 10/2.

Hoggart, R. (1969) *The Uses of Literacy*. Harmondsworth: Penguin.

Humphreys, L. (1970) *The Tearoom Trade: A Study of Homosexual Encounters in Public Places*. London: Duckworth.

Hyman, H. H. (1967) 'The value systems of different classes', in R. Bendix and S. M. Lipset (eds), *Class, Status and Power* (2nd edn). London: Routledge & Kegan Paul.

Illich, I. (1976) *Limits to Medicine*. London: Marion Boyars.

Jenkins, R. (1996) *Social Identity*. London: Routledge.

Johal, S. (1998) 'Brimful of Brasia', *Sociology Review*, November.

Keddie, N. (1971) 'Classroom knowledge', in M. F. D. Young (ed.), *Knowledge and Control*. London: Collier-Macmillan.

Keddie, N. (ed.) (1973) *Tinker, Tailor . . . the Myth of Cultural Deprivation*. Harmondsworth: Penguin.

Kelly, A. (1987) *Science for Girls*. Milton Keynes: Open University Press.

Kempson, E. (1996) *Life on a Low Income*. York: Joseph Rowntree Foundation.

Kempson, E. and Bryson, A. (1994) *Hard Times: How Poor Families Make Ends Meet*. London: Policy Studies Institute.

Labov, W. (1973) 'The logic of nonstandard English', in Keddie (ed.) (1973).

Laing, R. D. and Esterson, A. (1970) *Sanity, Madness and the Family*. Harmondsworth: Penguin.

Lash, S. and Urry, J. (1987) *The End of Organized Capitalism*. Cambridge: Polity.

Le Grand, J. (1982) *The Strategy of Equality*. London: Allen & Unwin.

Leach, E. R. (1967) *A Runaway World?* London: BBC Publications.

Lewis, O. (1961) *The Children of Sanchez*. New York: Random House.

Licht, B. G. and Dweck, C. S. (1987) 'Some differences in achievement orientations', in M. Arnot and G. Weiner (eds), *Gender under Scrutiny*. London: Hutchinson.

Lobban, G. (1974) *Data Report on British Reading Schemes*. London: Times Educational Supplement.

Lyotard, J.-F. (1984) *The Postmodern Condition: A Report on Knowledge*. Manchester: Manchester University Press.

Mac an Ghaill, M. (1994) *The Making of Men: Masculinities, Sexualities and Schooling*. Buckingham: Open University Press

Mack, J. and Lansley, S. (1985) *Poor Britain*. London: Allen & Unwin.

Mack, J., Lansley, S. and Frayman, H. (1992) *Breadline Britain 1990s. The Findings of the Television Series*. London: London Weekend Television.

Marsland, D. (1989) 'Universal welfare provision creates a dependent population. The case for', *Social Studies Review* 5/2.

McIntosh, S. (1988) 'A feminist critique of Stanley Parker's theory of work and leisure', in M. O'Donnell (ed.), *New Introductory Reader in Sociology* (2nd edn). Walton-on-Thames: Nelson.

McKeown, T. (1976) *The Modern Rise of Population*. London: Edward Arnold.

McKeown, T. (1979) *The Role of Medicine*. Oxford: Blackwell.

McRobbie, A. (1994) *Postmodernism and Popular Culture*. London: Routledge.

Mead, M. (2001) *Sex and Temperament: In Three Primitive Societies*. London: HarperCollins.

Miliband, R. (1974) 'Politics and poverty', in D. Wedderburn (ed.), *Poverty, Inequality and Class Structure*, Cambridge: Cambridge University Press.

Mills, C. W. (1970) *The Sociological Imagination*, Harmondsworth: Penguin.

Mirza, M., Senthilkumaran, A., and Ja'far, Z. (2007) *Living Apart Together: British Muslims and the Paradox of Multiculturalism*. London: Policy Exchange.

Mitchell, R., Shaw, M. and Dorling, D. (2000) *Inequalities in Life and Death: What if Britain Became More Equal?* Bristol: Policy Press.

Mitsos, E. (1995–6) 'Boys and English – classroom voices', *English and Media Magazine* 33 & 34.

Mitsos, E. and Browne, K. (1998) 'Gender differences in education – the underachievement of boys', *Sociology Review* 8/1.

Modood, T., Beishon, S. and Virdee, S. (1994) *Changing Ethnic Identities*. London: Policy Studies Institute.

Murdock, G. P. (1949) *Social Structure*. New York: Macmillan.

Murray, C. (1989) 'Underclass', *Sunday Times Magazine*, 26 November.

Murray, C. (1990) *The Emerging British Underclass*. London: Institute of Economic Affairs.

Navarro, V. (1976) *Medicine under Capitalism*. New York: Prodist.

Nazroo, J. (1997a) *Ethnicity and Mental Health*. London: Policy Studies Institute.

Nazroo, J. (1997b) *The Health of Britain's Ethnic Minorities: Fourth National Survey of Ethnic Minorities*. London: Policy Studies Institute.

Nettleton, S. (2006) *The Sociology of Health and Illness* (2nd edn). Cambridge: Polity.

Nettleton. S. and Gustaffson, U. (2002) (eds), *The Sociology of Health and Illness Reader*. Cambridge: Polity.

Newburn, T. and Hagell, A. (1995) 'Violence on screen – just child's play?', *Sociology Review* 4/3.

Nichols, T. and Beynon, R. (1977) *Living with Capitalism*. London: Routledge & Kegan Paul.

Oakley, A. (1974) *The Sociology of Housework*. Oxford: Martin Robertson.

Oakley, A. (1980) *Women Confined*. Oxford: Martin Robertson.

Oakley, A. (1981) *From Here to Maternity*. Harmondsworth: Penguin.

Oakley, A. (1984) *The Captured Womb: A History of the Medical Care of Pregnant Women*. Oxford: Blackwell.

Oakley, A. (1985) *Subject Women*. London: Fontana.

Oppenheim, C. (1980) *Poverty: The Facts*. London: Child Poverty Action Group.

Oppenheim, C. and Harker, L. (1996) *Poverty: The Facts* (3rd edn). London: Child Poverty Action Group.

Pakulski, J. and Waters, M. (1996) *The Death of Class*. London: Sage Publications.

Palfreyman, D. (2003) 'Independent schools and charitable status: legal meaning, taxation advantages, and potential removal', in G. Walford (ed.), *British Private Schools. Research on Policy and Practice*. London: Woburn Press.

Parker, H., Aldridge, J. and Measham, F. (1998) *Illegal Leisure: The Normalisation of Adolescent Drug Use*. London: Routledge.

Parker, S. (1971) *The Future of Work and Leisure*. London: MacGibbon & Kee.

Parker, S. (1976) 'Work and leisure', in E. Butterworth and D. Weir (eds), *The Sociology of Work and Leisure*. London: Allen & Unwin.

Parsons, T. (1951) *The Social System*. London: Routledge & Kegan Paul.

Patrick, J. (1973) *A Glasgow Gang Observed*. London: Eyre Methuen.

Phillips, T. (2007) Interview in the *Guardian* newspaper, 31 January.

Philo, G. (ed.) (1999) *Message Received: Glasgow Media Group Research, 1993–1998*. London: Longman.

Pilkington, A. (1997) 'Ethnicity and education', in M. Haralambos (ed.), *Developments in Sociology*, vol. 13. Ormskirk: Causeway Press.

Postman, N. (1994) *The Disappearance of Childhood*. New York: Vintage Books.

Rapoport, R. and Rapoport, R. N. (1971) *Dual Career Families*. Harmondsworth: Penguin.

Rapoport, R. and Rapoport, R. N. (1976) *Dual Career Families Re-examined*. Oxford: Martin Robertson.

Rapoport, R. N., Fogarty, M. P. and Rapoport, R. (eds) (1982) *Families in Britain*. London: Routledge & Kegan Paul.

Ritzer, G. (2004) *The McDonaldization of Society*. London: Sage Publications.

Roberts, K. (1978) *Contemporary Society and the Growth of Leisure*. London: Longman.

Roberts, K. (1981) *Leisure* (2nd edn). London: Longman.

Roberts, K. (1983) *Youth and Leisure*. London: George Allen & Unwin.

Roberts, K. (1986) 'Leisure', in M. Haralambos (ed.), *Developments in Sociology*, vol. 2. Ormskirk: Causeway Press.

Roberts, K. (2001) *Class in Modern Britain*. Basingstoke: Palgrave MacMillan.

Rojek, C. (1985) *Capitalism and Leisure Theory*. London: Tavistock.

Rojek, C. (1995) *Decentring Leisure: Rethinking Leisure Theory*. London: Sage.

Rosenhan, D. L. (1973) 'On being sane in insane places', *Science* 179.

Rosenthal, R. and Jacobson, L. (1968) *Pygmalion in the Classroom*. London: Holt, Rinehart & Winston.

Rutter, M. and Madge, N. (1976) *Cycles of Disadvantage: A Review of Research*. London: Heinemann.

Rutter, M., Maughan, B., Mortimore, P., Ouston, J. and Smith, A. (1979) *Fifteen Thousand Hours: Secondary Schools and their Effects on Children*. Shepton Mallet: Open Books.

Savage, M. (1995) 'The middle classes in modern Britain', *Sociology Review* 5/2.

Scheff, T. J. (1966) *Being Mentally Ill*. Chicago: Aldine.

Scott, J. (1990) *A Matter of Record: Documentary Sources in Social Research*. Cambridge: Polity.

Scraton, S. and Bramham, P. (1995) 'Leisure and postmodernity', in M. Haralambos (ed.), *Developments in Sociology*, vol. 11. Ormskirk: Causeway Press.

Shakespeare, T. (1998) *The Disability Reader: Social Science Perspectives*. London: Cassell.

Sharpe, S. (1976) *Just Like a Girl*. Harmondsworth: Penguin.

Sharpe, S. (1994) *Just Like a Girl* (2nd edn). Harmondsworth: Penguin.

Spender, D. (1982) *Invisible Women: The Schooling Scandal*. London: Writers and Readers.

Stanworth, M. (1983) *Gender and Schooling*. London: Hutchinson.

Strinati, D. (1995) *An Introduction to Theories of Popular Culture*. London: Routledge.

Sugarman, B. (1970) 'Social class, values and behaviour in schools', in M. Craft (ed.), *Family, Class and Education*. London: Longman.

Swann Committee (1985) *Education for All: Report of the Committee of Inquiry into the Education of Children from Ethnic Minority Groups*. London: HMSO.

Szasz, T. (1972) *The Myth of Mental Illness*. London: Paladin.

Taylor, L. (1984) *In the Underworld*. London: Unwin.

Taylor, S. (1999) 'Postmodernism: A challenge to Sociology', *'S' magazine*.

Townsend, P. (1979) *Poverty in the United Kingdom*. Harmondsworth: Penguin.

Townsend, P., Davidson, N. and Whitehead, M. (1990) *Inequalities in Health: The Black Report and The Health Divide*. Harmondsworth: Penguin.

Tudor-Hart, J. (1971) 'The inverse care law', *The Lancet* 1.

Walford, G. (ed.) (2003) *British Private Schools: Research on Policy and Practice*. London: Woburn Press.

Walker, R., Howard, M., Maguire, S. and Youngs, R. (2000) *The Making of a Welfare Class?* Bristol: Policy Press.

Westergaard, J. and Resler, H. (1976) *Class in a Capitalist Society*. Harmondsworth: Penguin.

Whitty, G., Power S. and Halpin D. (1998) *Devolution and Choice in Education: The School, the State and the Market*. Buckingham, Open University Press.

Whyte, W. F. (1955) *Street Corner Society* (2nd edn). Chicago: University of Chicago Press.

Wilkinson, R. G. (1996) *Unhealthy Societies.* London: Routledge.

Willis, P. (1977) *Learning to Labour: How Working Class Kids Get Working Class Jobs.* Farnborough: Saxon House.

Woodward, K. (2000) 'Questions of Identity', in Woodward, K. (ed.) *Questioning Identity: Gender, Class, Nation.* London: Routledge.

Wright, C. (1992) *Race Relations in the Primary School.* London: David Fulton.

Young, M. and Willmott, P. (1973) *The Symmetrical Family.* Harmondsworth: Penguin.

Index

Using the index

If you are looking for general topics, it is best to refer first to the contents pages at the beginning of this book, or those at the beginning of each chapter. If you can't find what you want there, or want to find a particular item of information, look it up in this index. If you can't find the item, think of other headings it might be given under: the same references are often included several times under different headings. This index includes only the largest or most significant references found in this book, rather than every single occurrence of the theme. It is sensible always to check the largest references first, such as pages 239–44, before 125, 283, and 332. The chances are that what you're looking for will be in the largest entry, and this will save you time wading through a lot of smaller references. Numbers in blue refer to entries in the glossary.

A
absolute poverty, 228–30, 497
abuse of children, 122, 168, 190–1
access to health care, 467–70, 471–3
achieved status, 11–12, 345, 497
'adultescence', 188
African-Caribbeans, 82, 83, 186, 225,
    393–401, 466, 479
age
    age groups, 97–9, 106
    ageing population, 129, 132–4, 146–7,
        226, 423, 497
    ageism, 99, 470, 497
    and identity, 96–8
    social construction of, 96–7
anti-school subculture, 83, 320, 353, 376–8,
    398, 497
arranged marriage, 83, 86, 117, 186, 497
ascribed status, 11–12, 345, 497

B
banding, 375, 497
Bangladeshis, 83–4, 145, 186, 225, 240, 394,
    395, 396, 397, 466
beanpole family, 146–7, 497
Beveridge Report (1942), 215, 217
biomedical model *see* health, medical
    model of
birth rate, 129, 135–8, 497

births outside marriage, 182, 195
bisexuality, 78, 497
Black Report, 448–9, 453–4
bodies
    social construction of, 73, 76–7, 102, 420–1
bourgeoisie, 17–19, 124, 497
Brasians, 85–6
British identity, 88–93

C
case studies, 319–21
census, 285, 300, 319
'cereal packet' family, 182–4
child abuse, 122, 168, 190–1
child centredness, 136, 167–9
Child Support Agency, 178, 197, 226
childcare, 107, 126, 142, 147, 150–1, 155–7,
    159–60, 225, 227, 463
childhood, 96–7, 160–9
    disappearance of, 167–8
    social construction of, 97–8, 161–4
children, 44, 65–6, 96–7, 160–9
    abuse of, 122, 168, 190–1
    changing status of, 160–9
    and the family, 44, 65–6, 122, 125, 135–8,
        140, 141, 150–1, 155–7, 164–8, 190–1,
        345, 360–1, 396, 397
    feral, 44
    and poverty, 240, 246, 360–1, 396, 460

class, 10–11, 16–19
  see also social class
class conflict, 18–19, 498
class consciousness, 19, 253, 498
class structure in Britain, 10–11
  see also social class
classic extended family, 117, 142–7, 498
cluster (or multistage) sampling, 288, 290–1
cohabitation, 180–1
collective identity, 41
communes, 116, 119, 498
communism, 19, 498
comparative method, 283
compensatory education, 370–1, 498
comprehensive schools, 328–32
conjugal roles, 147–60, 304, 498
consensual measurement (of poverty), 234
consumer choice, 100–3, 106, 198–9, 333, 444–6
consumption property, 208, 498
content analysis, 274–5
contraception, 135, 174, 177, 181, 420, 433, 465
counter-school subculture, 320, 353, 376–8, 498
covert role, 310, 311, 312, 498
crime, 78, 169, 191–3, 276, 278–9
crime statistics, 276, 278–9
crisis of masculinity, 74, 75, 386
cultural capital, 52–3, 367–8, 369, 379, 399, 498
cultural deprivation, 362–70, 498
cultural dopes, 47
culture, 6, 31–8, 43, 53–9, 82–6, 91, 498
  of dependency (dependency culture), 221, 244–6, 249, 499
  different conceptions of, 31–4
  dominant, 31–2, 499
  folk, 32, 57, 500
  global, 36–8, 501
  and globalization, 36–8, 80–1, 91–2, 501
  high, 32–3, 35–6, 502
  of hybridity, 91, 498
  mass, 33–6, 504
  of poverty, 243–4, 246, 499
  and social class, 53–9, 364–5
  subculture, 32, 83, 98, 320, 352–3, 364, 365, 376–8, 386, 398, 439, 511
culture clash, 369, 399, 498
culture of hybridity, 91, 498
customs, 8, 499
cycle of deprivation, 249, 251, 499

D
death rate, 129–31, 432–3, 461, 499
demography, 129–38, 499
dependency culture, 221, 244–6, 249, 499
determinism, 20, 378, 499
deviance, 9, 161, 438, 480, 485, 499
  sanctions, 9, 508
  and the sick role, 438–40, 509
diaspora, 80–1, 83, 499
disability, 93–6, 240, 423–4, 469–70, 499
  and access to health care, 469–70
  and identity, 93–6
  social construction of, 93–4, 423–4
disease, 130, 421–2, 424–5, 428, 429, 430, 431–6, 443, 446, 473, 499
  see also health
division of labour, 143, 346, 351, 354, 499
  in the home, 122, 123, 128, 149–53
  sexual, 122, 123, 128, 509
divorce, 169–76
divorce laws, 171, 172
divorce rate, 170, 499
domestic labour, 125–6, 127, 140, 157–60, 242, 463, 464, 499
domestic violence, 125, 191–3, 233
dominant culture, 31–2, 499
dominant ideology, 18, 43, 125, 348, 354, 499

E
education, 322–413
  compensatory, 370–1, 498
  comprehensive schools, 328–32
  and cultural capital, 340, 367–8, 369, 379, 399, 498
  and cultural deprivation, 362–70, 498
  and culture clash, 369, 399, 498
  equality of educational opportunity, 335, 339, 341, 346, 370–1, 405, 500
  and ethnicity, 393–401
  and the family, 345, 360–1, 362, 364, 367–8, 369–70, 396, 397, 405
  functionalist perspective on, 344–7, 353–5
  and gender, 381–93, 395
  grammar schools, 328–9, 330, 331
  and the hidden curriculum, 67, 345, 349, 350–1, 352, 354, 399, 502
  independent schools, 401–5
  interactionist perspective on, 355, 372–9
  and IQ, 356–7
  and labelling, 374–8, 397, 398–9, 400, 503
  and language use, 364–7

education (*cont.*)
  league tables, 329, 334, 337, 340, 341–2,
    379
  marketization of, 332–4, 340–2, 504
  Marxist perspective on, 348–55, 356
  and meritocracy, 335, 346, 352, 355–6,
    405, 504
  and the middle class, 330, 340–2, 357–8,
    361–77, 396, 401–5
  multicultural, 399, 505
  national curriculum, 333, 336–7, 338,
    340, 342, 389
  and positive discrimination, 370–1, 506
  private schools, 54, 401–5
  public schools, 54, 401–5
  and research methods, 317, 355, 406–12
  and social class, 328, 330, 331, 340–2,
    343, 348–53, 357–80, 395, 396, 401–5
  secondary modern schools, 327–8, 331
  selection in, 328–32, 338–9, 341
  and social solidarity, 345, 347, 510
  specialist schools, 329, 334, 338–9, 341
  and streaming, 329, 332, 346, 375–8, 510
  and the self-fulfilling prophecy, 284, 330,
    374–6, 378, 397, 398–9, 400, 509
  tripartite system, 327–8, 331
  underachievement in, 356–401, 511
  vocational education, 335–6, 343, 355
  and the working class, 328, 331, 340–2,
    343, 348–53, 357–80, 386, 395, 396
Education Action Zones, 339, 371, 499
elaborated code, 364–7, 369, 500
elites, 32, 144, 347, 401–5, 500
empty shell marriages, 170, 172, 174
equality of educational opportunity, 335,
  339, 341, 346, 370–1, 405, 500
ethics (in research), 271, 281, 310, 314, 317,
  408, 489, 500
ethnic group, 12, 79–87, 88, 107–8, 184,
  186, 225, 393–401, 466–7
ethnic identity, 79–87
ethnicity, 12, 79–87, 88, 107–8, 184, 186,
  225, 393–401, 466–7, 500
  and education, 393–401
  and the family, 117, 184, 186
  and health, 466–7
  and identity, 79–87
  and leisure, 107–8
ethnocentrism, 399, 500
experimental method, 281–4, 483, 485
expressive role, 122–3, 128, 160, 500
extended family, 47, 117, 142–7, 148, 184,
  500

classic, 117, 142–7, 498
modified, 117, 143, 145–6, 505

F
false consciousness, 19, 124, 128, 348, 500
families of choice, 188–9, 199
family, 115–202, 500
  alternatives to, 116, 119–21
  and ageing population, 129, 134, 497
  'cereal packet', 182–4
  changes in, 129–82
  changing functions of, 139–41
  and child abuse, 122, 128, 168, 190–1
  and childcare, 126, 142, 147, 150–1,
    155–7, 159–60
  and childhood, 160–9
  and children, 44, 65–6, 122, 125, 135–8,
    140, 141, 150–1, 155–7, 164–8, 190–1,
    345, 360–1, 396, 397
  classic extended, 117, 142–7, 498
  conjugal roles, 147–60, 304, 498
  darker side of, 189–93
  decline of, 178, 199–201
  and demographic change, 129–38
  diversity of, 182–9
  and divorce, 169–76
  and domestic labour, 125–6, 127, 140,
    157–60, 242, 463, 464, 499
  and domestic violence, 125, 191–3
  and education, 345, 360–1, 362, 364,
    367–8, 369–70, 396, 397, 405
  emotional side of, 159–60
  feminist views on, 123, 124–8, 140–1,
    149–50, 158–9, 189, 193
  functionalist perspective, 121–3, 128
  functions of, 121–3, 139–41
  ideology of, 183, 184, 194–5, 500
  integrated conjugal roles, 147–60, 503
  lone parent, 24, 117, 119, 177–80, 184,
    185, 186, 194–5, 221, 240, 243, 245, 396
  Marxist perspective, 124–8, 159, 193
  modified extended, 117, 143, 145–6, 505
  and the 'New Man', 72, 147
  and postmodernism, 137, 198–9
  power and authority in, 127, 147–8,
    153–4, 158
  privatized nuclear, 142–4, 174, 507
  radical feminist perspective, 124–8, 158,
    193, 507
  reconstituted, 117, 176–7, 184, 507
  segregated conjugal roles, 147–60, 509
  and social network, 149, 368
  and social policy, 195–8, 510

size of, 135–8
stepfamilies, 117, 176–7, 184
and structural differentiation, 139–40, 510
symmetrical, 117, 126–7, 142, 147–60, 511
types of, 117, 182–9
universality of, 116–21
violence in, 125, 191–3
women's 'triple shift' 159–60
family size, 135–8
femininity, 61–72, 74, 75, 382, 389
    hegemonic, 63–70, 75
    and identity, 61–72, 74, 75
feminism, 23, 123, 124–8, 140–1, 149–50, 158–9, 189, 193, 222–3, 384, 465–6, 500
    liberal, 23, 503
    Marxist, 23, 124–8, 159, 193, 504
    radical, 23, 124–8, 158, 193, 507
feminization (of poverty), 225, 242–3
feral children, 44
fertility, 129, 135–8, 177, 420, 500
field experiments, 283, 284
focus group, 303, 305, 500
folk culture, 32, 57, 500
Food Standards Agency, 434, 435, 490
functional prerequisites, 16, 121, 345, 500
functionalism, 15–16, 121–3, 128, 344–7, 353–5, 501
    and education, 344–7, 353–5
    and the family, 121–3, 128,
    and value consensus, 16, 43, 121, 345, 354, 511
functions of the family, 121–3, 139–41
fundamentalism, 86, 501

G
gate-keeping, 431, 439–40, 501
gays and lesbians, 70, 74, 76, 77–9, 117, 119–20, 194, 197, 199, 312
gender, 12, 61–79, 105, 107, 148, 225–6, 381–93, 395, 461–6, 501
    crisis of masculinity, 74, 75, 386
    and education, 381–93, 395
    and health, 461–6
    hegemonic identities, 63–77
    and identity, 61–75, 148
    and the mass media, 68–70, 73, 76–7
    and poverty, 225, 242–3
    and sex, 12, 61–3, 509
    and sexuality, 64, 67–8, 76–9, 509
    and socialization, 61–70, 389, 462, 464
    stereotyping, 63–71, 75, 274, 350

gender identity, 61–75, 148
gender roles, 61–75, 107, 464–5, 501
generalization, 294
    see also representative sample
global culture, 36–8, 501
globalization, 36, 80–1, 91–2, 501
grammar schools, 328–9, 330, 331
group interviews, 303, 306, 501

H
habitus, 52–3, 367, 501
halo effect, 374, 501
Hawthorne effect, 282–3, 313, 317, 319, 501
health, 131, 224–5, 232, 419–94, 501
    access to health care, 467–70, 471–3
    and deviance, 438–40
    and disability, 469–70
    and ethnicity, 466–7
    and gender, 461–6
    iatrogenesis, 427–8, 442, 502
    inequalities in, 446–77
    international differences, 471–7
    and the inverse care law, 224–5, 455, 469, 503
    Marxist approaches to, 431
    medical model of, 424–9, 431, 444–6, 447, 478–80
    and medicine, 130, 424–9, 430, 431, 432, 443
    mental illness, 306, 422, 463, 464, 465, 477–85, 492, 493
    and poverty, 224–5, 232, 233, 446, 448–57, 463–4, 467, 471–7
    regional inequalities, 468–9, 471
    and research methods, 486–93
    and the sick role, 438–40, 509
    social class inequalities, 446–61, 467, 469
    social construction of, 421–3, 480–5
    social influences on, 429–30, 431–6, 452–4, 456
    social model, 429–31, 444, 447, 449, 454
    statistics, 278, 436–7, 487
health care
    access to, 467–70, 471–3
    contemporary changes in, 443–7
health statistics, 278, 436–7, 487
hegemonic identity, 63, 502
    and gender, 63–77
heterosexuality, 64, 65, 76, 502
hidden curriculum, 67, 345, 349, 350–1, 352, 354, 399, 502
high culture, 32–3, 35–6, 502
    see also mass culture

hijab, 84
homelessness, 231
homophobia, 78–9, 502
homosexuality, 76–9, 119–20, 197, 310, 312, 502
households, 115, 117, 135, 150, 181–2, 183–4, 185, 188–9, 197–8, 199, 396, 502
housework *see* domestic labour
hybrid identity, 80–2, 86, 502
hypothesis, 281, 285, 291, 304, 305, 502

I
iatrogenesis, 427–8, 442, 502
identity, 6, 14, 20, 31–109, 386, 420, 482, 502
    and age, 96–8
    collective, 41
    and consumption, 100–9
    crisis of masculinity, 74, 75, 386
    and diaspora, 80–1, 83, 499
    and disability, 93–6, 499
    and ethnicity, 79–87, 500
    and femininity, 61–72, 74, 75
    and gender, 61–75, 148, 501
    hegemonic, 63–77, 502
    hybrid, 80–2, 86, 502
    and impression management, 49, 77, 84, 95, 502
    individual (or personal), 6, 41, 44, 47–9, 51, 97, 100–2, 106
    and leisure, 54, 56, 59, 61, 81,100–9
    and masculinity, 57, 61–75, 76–8, 386
    multiple, 6, 39, 41–2, 80, 81, 95
    and nationality, 87–93, 505
    personal (or individual), 6, 41, 44, 47–9, 51, 97, 100–2, 106
    and postmodernism, 25, 91, 100–3, 106, 109, 148, 506
    and sexuality, 76–9, 502
    social, 41, 44, 45, 47–9, 51, 60, 97
    and social class, 50–61, 509
    and socialization, 6, 38–9, 46–50, 61–75, 76, 94, 510
    spoiled, 42–3, 67, 77, 95
    stigmatized, 42–3, 49, 77, 86–7, 94–5, 99, 510
    and work, 45, 51, 57, 103–5
ideological state apparatus, 348, 502
ideology, 18, 43, 124, 152, 183, 194, 195, 502
    dominant, 18, 43, 125, 348, 354, 499
    family, 183, 184, 194–5, 500
    ruling class, 18, 124, 128, 348, 508

illness, 421–3, 502
    see also health
impairment, 42, 49, 93–4, 95, 423, 440, 502
    see also disability
imposition problem, 298, 299–300, 502
impression management, 49, 77, 84, 95, 502
income, 207–14, 502
independent schools, 401–5
Indian Asians, 80–1, 82, 83–6, 184, 186, 394, 395, 396, 398, 466
individual (or personal) identity, 6, 41, 44, 47–9, 51, 97, 100–2, 106
inequalities in health, 446–77
    and ethnicity, 466–7
    and gender, 461–6
    and social class, 446–61, 467, 469
infant mortality, 129–31, 136–7, 458, 462, 466, 467, 471, 503
informed consent, 271
instrumental role, 122–3, 128, 160, 503
integrated conjugal roles, 147–60, 503
interactionism, 21, 47–8, 355, 372–9, 511
interpretivism, 14, 19–20, 23, 47–8, 264, 265–7, 268, 277, 309, 503
interviewer bias, 294, 299, 302, 306–8, 503
interviews, 301–8
    validity of, 306–8
inverse care law, 224–5, 455, 469, 503
IQ, 356–7
Islamophobia, 84, 86–7, 503

J
Jedi, 300

K
kibbutz, 117, 503
kinship, 115, 503
    see also family; marriage

L
labelling, 21, 283, 284, 374–8, 397, 398–9, 400–1, 480–5, 503
    in education, 374–8, 397, 398–9, 400, 503
    and mental illness, 480–5
laboratory (experimental) method, 281–3
labour power, 17, 125, 128, 159, 349, 503
language
    and education, 364–7, 396
    in questionnaires, 296
language use
    elaborated code, 364–7, 369, 500
    restricted code, 364–7, 508

leading questions, 296
league tables (in education), 329, 334, 337, 340, 341–2, 379
leisure, 103–9
    and ethnicity, 107–8
    and identity, 54, 56, 59, 61, 81, 100–9
    and work, 103–5
lesbians and gays, 70, 74, 76, 77–9, 117, 119–20, 194, 197, 199, 312
liberal feminism, 23, 503
life chances, 10, 51–2, 207, 211, 328, 372, 373, 402, 503
life expectancy, 61, 98, 129–34, 176, 429, 449, 462, 463, 472–3, 474–5, 503
life histories, 319–21
lone parent families, 24, 117, 119, 177–80, 184, 185, 186, 194–5, 221, 240, 243, 245, 396
longitudinal studies, 318–19, 357, 406–7, 409, 411–12, 487
'looking-glass self', 48
low culture see mass culture

M
macro approach, 15, 47, 265, 268, 344, 354, 504
marginalization, 220, 225, 231, 244, 255, 465, 504
market liberal approach (to welfare), 219, 221, 222
market situation, 213–14, 504
marketization (of education), 332–4, 340–2, 504
marriage, 53–4, 117, 180–1, 182, 186, 192–3, 217, 385
    decline of, 180–1
    forms of, 116, 117
    inequalities in, 126–7, 147–60
Marxism, 16–19, 23, 34, 43, 123–8, 159, 193, 214, 221–3, 253, 348–55, 431, 504
    bourgeoisie, 17–19, 124, 497
    class conflict, 18–19, 498
    class consciousness, 19, 124, 253, 498
    dominant ideology, 18, 43, 125, 348, 354, 499
    false consciousness, 19, 348, 500
    labour power, 17, 125, 128, 159, 349, 503
    Marxist feminism, 23, 124–8, 159, 193, 504
    means of production, 16–19, 214, 504
    proletariat, 17, 507
    ruling class, 18–19, 124, 253, 348, 508
    surplus value, 16–17, 511

masculinity, 57, 61–75, 76–8, 386
    and identity, 57, 61–75, 76–8, 386
    crisis of, 74, 75, 386
    hegemonic, 63–70, 75
mass culture, 33–6, 504
    see also high culture
mass media, 6, 25, 34, 35, 36, 45, 68–70, 73, 76–7, 86, 94, 101–2, 168, 178, 274–5
    and gender, 68–70, 73, 76–7
    and global culture, 36
    and mass culture, 34, 35
    and poverty, 247
media-saturated society, 25, 101, 109
means of production, 16–18, 214, 504
means-testing, 220, 221, 222, 224, 226, 245, 247, 250
media-saturated society, 25, 101, 109
medical model (of health), 424–9, 431, 444–6, 447, 478–80
medical profession, 426–7, 439–46, 447, 465, 467, 470
    power of, 426, 429, 439–46, 447
mental illness, 306, 422, 463, 464, 465, 477–85, 492, 493
    social construction of, 480–5
meritocracy, 144, 335, 346, 352, 355–6, 405, 504
metanarratives, 100, 504
methodological pluralism, 321–3, 504
micro approach, 20, 47, 267, 268, 355, 504
middle class, 10–11, 55–6, 224–5, 340, 357–8, 361–77, 446–50, 455, 504
    culture and identity of, 52–3, 55–6
    and education, 330, 340–2, 357–8, 361–77, 396, 401–5
    and health, 224–5, 446–54, 455, 469
    and the welfare state, 224–5, 455, 469
minority ethnic groups, 12, 79–87, 107–8, 184, 186, 225, 240, 393–401, 466–7, 504
    and education, 393–401
    and the family, 117, 184, 186
    and health, 466–7
    and identity, 79–87
    and leisure, 107–8
    and poverty, 225, 240, 396
modified extended family, 117, 143, 145–6, 505
monogamy, 117, 124, 197, 255, 505
moral panics, 178, 505
morbidity, 432, 436, 487, 505
mortality, 129–31, 136–7, 432, 436, 462, 466, 467, 471, 472–5, 487, 505
mortification, 482, 484, 505

multicultural education, 399, 505
multiple identities, 6, 39, 41–2, 80, 81, 95
multistage (or cluster) sampling, 288, 290–1
Muslims, 84, 86–7

N
nation, 87, 505
nation-state, 87, 505
national curriculum, 333, 336–7, 338, 340, 342, 389
nationalism, 88, 92, 505
nationality, 87–93, 505
   and identity, 87–93
natural sciences, 264, 265, 281
Nayar, the, 116
negative sanctions, 9, 15, 47, 505
new diseases, 429, 434–6, 443
'New Man', 72–3, 74, 147
New Right, 24, 177–8, 195, 221, 222, 226, 244–5, 252, 256, 505
non-participant observation, 316–17
norms, 7–9, 505
nuclear family, 116, 117, 121, 123–4, 142–4, 174, 506

O
objectivity, 5, 311, 318, 506
observation, 282, 308–18, 407–8, 489
Office for Standards in Education (Ofsted), 334, 339, 340
official statistics, 272, 275–7
   on crime, 276, 278–9
   on divorce, 170
   on health, 278, 436–7, 487
   on suicide, 277, 280
   on unemployment, 277
'old boys' network', 54, 404–5
older people, 98–9, 132–4, 182, 240, 422, 470
one parent families
   see lone parent families
overt role, 310, 311, 312, 506

P
Pakistanis, 83–4, 145, 186, 225, 240, 394, 395, 396, 397, 466
participant observation, 308–16
   covert role, 310, 311, 312, 498
   overt role, 310, 311, 312, 506
   validity and reliability of, 315–16
particularistic values, 345, 347, 506
patriarchy, 23, 107, 117, 124, 147, 158–9, 186, 193, 194, 222, 465, 506

peer group, 38, 45, 65, 67–8, 84, 106, 377–8, 386, 506
personal (or individual) identity, 6, 41, 44, 47–9, 51, 97, 100–2, 106
perspective, 13–14, 506
   see also sociological perspectives
pilot study see pilot survey
pilot survey (or pilot study), 291–2, 293, 295, 506
Piresans, 301
polyandry, 117, 506
polygamy, 117, 506
polygyny, 117, 506
popular culture see mass culture
positive discrimination, 370–1, 506
positive sanctions, 9, 15, 47, 506
positivism, 264, 265, 506
postal (and self-completion) questionnaires, 298–301
postmodernism, 24–5, 35, 59, 100–3, 109, 148, 198–9, 446, 506
   and identity, 25, 91, 100–3, 106, 109, 148
   and the family, 137, 198–9
poverty, 98, 207–8, 215, 222, 226–57, 463–4, 467, 473
   absolute, 228–30, 497
   and children, 240, 246, 360–1, 396
   consensual measurement of, 234
   cultural explanations, 243–6
   culture of, 243–4, 246, 499
   cycle of deprivation, 249, 251, 499
   definitions of, 228–33
   and dependency culture, 221, 244–6, 249, 499
   extent of, 240–2
   feminization of, 225, 242–3
   groups in, 240–1
   and health, 224–5, 232, 233, 446, 448–57, 463–4, 467, 471–7
   in health care, 232
   and the mass media, 247
   material (and structural) explanations, 246–55
   measurement of, 228–30, 234–7
   poverty line, 235, 507
   relative, 230–8, 507
   at school, 232–3
   and social exclusion, 231–3, 453, 456, 509
   and the underclass, 11, 177, 221, 245–6, 250–3, 511
   and value judgements, 229–30, 234, 238, 255–7

and the welfare state, 215, 221, 222, 223–7, 455, 469
    at work, 233
poverty line, 235, 507
pressure groups, 219, 507
primary data, 272, 507
primary socialization, 66, 121, 122, 140, 507
private education, 54, 401–5
privatized nuclear family, 142, 143, 174, 507
productive property, 498, 507
proletariat 17, 498, 507
    see also Marxism
public schools, 54, 401–5

Q
qualitative data, 267, 272–5, 321, 507
quantitative data, 265, 275–9, 285, 298, 321, 507
questionnaires, 294–301
    validity of, 298–301
quota sampling, 288, 289–90

R
racial prejudice, 400, 507
racism, 81, 82, 83, 225, 397–8, 399–400, 467, 507
radical feminism, 23, 124–8, 158, 193, 507
random sampling, 287, 288
rape, 162, 192–3, 278, 279
reconstituted family, 117, 176–7, 184, 507
relative poverty, 230–8, 507
reliability (in social research), 271, 294, 307, 315–16, 321, 508
religion, 19, 83–4, 86–7, 135, 300
remarriage, 173, 176–7, 184
representative sample, 285–91, 292, 508
    non-representative sample, 291
research methods, 263–323
    and education, 355, 406–12
    and health, 486–93
    influences on choice of, 264–71
restricted code, 364–7, 508
role conflict, 7, 508
role models, 7, 66, 69, 178, 384–5, 388, 397, 399, 508
roles, 6–7, 46, 49, 122, 508
    conjugal, 147–60, 304, 498
    gender, 61–75, 107, 464–5, 501
    sick, 438–40, 509
ruling class, 18–19, 124, 253, 348, 508

S
sample (representative), 285–91, 292, 508
    non-representative sample, 291
sampling frame, 286–7, 508
sampling methods, 287–91, 508
sanctions, 9, 15, 47, 508
    negative, 9, 15, 47, 505
    positive, 9, 15, 47, 506
scapegoats, 122, 508
schools see education
secondary data, 272–9, 508
secondary modern schools, 327–8
secondary socialization, 44–6, 327, 345, 508
secularization, 135, 173, 180, 508
segregated conjugal roles, 147–60, 509
self-completion questionnaires, 298–301
self-fulfilling prophecy, 284, 330, 374–6, 378, 397, 398–9, 400, 509
serial monogamy, 117, 195, 509
sex, 12, 61–3, 509
    and gender, 12, 61–3, 501
sexism, 353, 509
sexual division of labour, 122, 123, 128, 509
sexual orientation, 65, 76–9, 509
sexuality, 64, 72, 76–9, 509
    and identity, 76–9
sick role, 438–40, 509
single parents see lone parent families
singlehood, 181–2
snowball sampling, 288, 291
social action theory, 19–21, 23, 47–50, 509
social capital, 367–8, 509
social class, 10–11, 16–19, 509
    bourgeoisie, 17–18, 124, 497
    class conflict, 18–19, 498
    class consciousness, 19, 253, 498
    class structure in Britain, 10–11
    and culture, 53–9, 364–5
    and education, 328, 330, 331, 340–2, 343, 348–53, 357–80, 395, 396, 401–5
    false consciousness, 19, 124, 128, 348, 500
    and health, 446–61, 467, 469
    and identity, 50–61
    and life chances, 10, 51–2, 61, 207, 211, 402, 503
    Marxist theory of, 16–19
    middle class, 10–11, 55–6, 224–5, 340, 357–8, 361–77, 446–50, 455, 504
    new working class, 58–9
    objective and subjective dimensions of, 52–3
    proletariat, 17, 507

social class (*cont.*)
 ruling, 18–19, 124, 253, 348, 508
 social mobility, 10, 143, 145, 148, 354, 510
 traditional working class, 57–8, 145
 underclass, 11, 177, 221, 245–6, 251–2, 253, 511
 upper class, 11, 53–5, 144, 209–11, 214, 367–8, 401–5, 511
 working class, 10–11, 17–19, 57–9, 145, 253, 348–53, 357–80, 446–61, 467, 469, 512
social construction
 of age, 96–7
 of the body, 73, 76–7, 102, 420–1
 of childhood, 97–8, 161–4
 of disability, 93–4, 423–4
 of health and illness, 421–3, 480–5
 of health statistics, 436–7
social control, 9, 125–6, 221–2, 431, 438–40, 509
 and the sick role, 438–40
social democratic approach (to the welfare state), 220
social exclusion, 231–3, 453, 456, 509
social facts, 265, 510
social identity, 41, 44, 45, 47–9, 51, 60, 97
social institution, 3–4, 5, 14–15, 16, 19, 510
social mobility, 10, 143, 145, 148, 354, 510
social model (of health), 429–31, 444, 447, 449, 454
social network, 149, 368
social policy, 26–7, 510
social problem, 26–7, 510
social research methods, 263–323
 and education, 355, 406–12
 and health, 486–93
 influences on choice of, 264–71
social solidarity, 345, 347, 510
social structure, 4, 15, 20, 21–3, 47, 50, 198, 265, 510
social surveys, 285–94
socialization, 6, 510
 and gender, 61–70, 389, 462, 464
 and identity, 6, 38–9, 46–50, 61–75, 76, 94
 primary, 66, 121, 122, 140, 507
 secondary, 44–6, 327, 345, 508
 theoretical approaches to, 14–23, 46–50
sociological methods, 263–323
 and education, 355, 406–12
 and health, 486–93
 influences on choice of, 264–71
sociological perspectives, 13–26, 510
 feminism, 23, 123, 124–8, 140–1, 149–50, 158–9, 189, 193, 222–3, 384, 465–6, 500

 functionalism, 15–16, 121–3, 128, 344–7, 353–5, 501
 interactionism, 21, 47–8, 355, 372–9, 511
 interpretivism, 14, 19–20, 23, 47–8, 264, 265–7, 268, 277, 309, 503
 liberal feminism, 23, 503
 Marxism, 16–19, 23, 34, 43, 123–8, 159, 193, 214, 221–3, 253, 348–55, 431, 504
 Marxist feminism, 23, 124–8, 159, 193, 504
 New Right, 24, 177–8, 195, 221, 222, 226, 244–5, 252, 256, 505
 postmodernism, 24–5, 35, 59, 100–3, 109, 148, 198–9, 446, 506
 radical feminism, 23, 124–8, 158, 193, 507
 social action theory, 19–21, 23, 47–50, 509
 structuralism, 14–19, 23, 47, 268, 355, 510–11
 structuration, 21–3, 50, 511
 symbolic interactionism, 21, 47–8, 355, 372–9, 511
sociological problem, 26–7, 510
sociology, 3–4
 and common sense, 4–5
 and naturalistic explanations, 5
specialist schools, 329, 334, 338–9, 341
spoiled identity, 42–3, 67, 77, 95
statistics, 275–7
 on crime, 276, 278–9
 on divorce, 170
 on health, 278, 436–7, 487
 on suicide, 277, 280
 on unemployment, 277
status, 11–12, 144, 345, 347, 510
 achieved, 11–12, 345, 347, 497
 ascribed, 11–12, 345, 347, 497
 status frustration, 98, 510
stepfamilies, 117, 176–7, 184
stereotypes, 63–5, 68–70, 86, 93, 94, 99, 182–3, 194, 374–5, 389, 398–9, 470, 481, 510
stigma, 42–3, 95, 477, 483, 510
 see also stigmatized identity
stigmatized identity, 42–3, 49, 77, 86–7, 94–5, 99, 510
stratified random sampling, 288, 289, 290
streaming, 329, 332, 346, 375–8, 510
structural differentiation, 139–40, 510
structuralism, 14–19, 23, 47, 268, 355, 510–11
structuration, 21–3, 50, 511
structured interviews, 301–2

subculture, 32, 83, 98, 352–3, 364, 365, 376–8, 386, 398, 439, 511
subsistence poverty *see* absolute poverty
suicide statistics, 277, 280
surplus value, 16–17, 511
survey population, 285, 287, 511
surveys, 272, 282–94, 511
   pilot (pilot study), 291–2, 293, 295, 506
   problems of, 293–4
   stages of a survey, 293
symbolic interactionism, 21, 47–8, 355, 372–9, 511
symmetrical family, 117, 126–7, 142, 147–60, 511
systematic sampling, 287, 288

T
taxation, 72, 208, 211–12, 215, 220, 221, 224, 225, 403
trade unions, 56, 57, 233, 365
triangulation, 321–3, 511
tripartite system, 327–8, 331

U
underachievement (in education), 356–401, 511
   and ethnicity, 393–401
   and gender, 381–93, 395
   and social class, 357–80
underclass, 11, 177, 221, 245–6, 250–3, 511
   New Right version, 221, 245
   social democratic version, 251–3
unemployment statistics, 277
universal benefits, 220, 221, 222, 224, 244–5,
universalistic values, 345, 347, 511
unstructured interviews, 303–4, 305
upper class, 11, 53–5, 144, 209–11, 214, 367–8, 401–5, 511

V
validity (in social research), 271, 282–3, 293–4, 298–301, 306–8, 315–16, 436, 511
value consensus, 16, 43, 121, 345, 354, 511
value freedom, 5, 511
values, 7–8, 16, 512
   value consensus, 16, 43, 121, 345, 354, 511
   value freedom, 5, 511
   value judgements, 213, 229, 230, 234, 238, 255–7
verstehen, 266, 309, 512

victim surveys, 276, 278, 512
violence
   against women, 122, 191–3
   and the family, 125, 191–3
vocational education, 335–6, 343, 355
voluntary organizations, 27, 217–19

W
wealth, 51, 207–14, 512
   distribution of, 208–9
welfare benefits, 24, 131, 215, 221, 222, 226, 244–6
welfare pluralism, 217, 512
welfare state, 131, 140, 144, 165, 197, 215–27, 244–5, 249–53
   and the dependency culture, 221, 244–6, 249, 499
   feminist perspectives on, 217, 222–3, 225–6
   generosity of, 177, 221, 244–6
   inadequacy of, 249–53
   and the inverse care law, 224–5, 455
   Marxist perspective on, 222
   New Right perspectives on, 221, 244–6
   and poverty, 221, 226–7, 244–6, 247, 249–53
   social democratic perspectives on, 220, 251–3
   and social inequality, 220, 223–6, 455
   and the underclass, 221, 245–6, 250–3, 511
   and welfare pluralism, 217, 512
   and women, 217, 222, 225–6
'white mask', 80, 81
work
   and education, 335–6, 343, 346–51, 352–3, 355
   and identity, 45, 51, 57, 103–5
   and leisure, 103–5
   domestic labour, 125–6, 127, 140, 157–60, 242, 463, 464, 499
   poverty at, 233
   preparation for, 335–6, 343, 346–51, 352–3, 355
working class, 10–11, 17–19, 512
   culture and identity of, 57–9
   and education, 328, 331, 340–2, 343, 348–53, 357–80, 386, 395, 396
   and health, 446–61, 467, 469
   new, 58–9
   traditional, 57–8, 145

Y
youth, 97–8, 106, 188